To P.J.
Best wishes
from
Kevin & Pat
Christmas 2007

The Who's Who of
PRESTON NORTH END

The Who's Who of
PRESTON
NORTH END

Dean Hayes

breedon **books**
PUBLISHING

First published in Great Britain in 2006 by
The Breedon Books Publishing Company Limited
Breedon House, 3 The Parker Centre,
Derby, DE21 4SZ.

A catalogue record for this book is available from the
British Library.

ISBN 1 85983 516 3

Printed and bound by Cromwell Press,
Trowbridge, Wiltshire.

Contents

Dedication

From 1997 to 2001, I played cricket for Whittle-le-Woods in the Chorley League and many of the players were huge North End fans. So this book is a thank you to the likes of John Cowley, Eddie Morton, Martin Gray, Edward O'Donnell (and Margaret) and Dean McIver.

Let's hope 2006–07 is the season North End finally make it into the Premiership!

Acknowledgements

The author wishes to thank the following organisations for their assistance in compiling the *Complete Who's Who of Preston North End*:

Preston North End Football Club; The Association of Football Statisticians; The Football League; The British Newspaper Library; The Preston Central Library; The Harris Library and the *Lancashire Evening Post* who have kindly provided the majority of the photographs in this book. Thanks also to Breedon Books, especially Steve Caron, Susan Last and Michelle Grainger, for their continued support in this series of *Who's Who* books.

Preface

The *Complete Who's Who of Preston North End* covers a biographical history of every player to have represented North End in a Football League match.

This book features not only the well-known names in North End's past but also those less famous players to have appeared for the club, researched down to every last man, whether they played four or 400 matches.

Piecing together information from numerous sources and slowly identifying a career from birth to death (where applicable) is in many ways like a huge jigsaw. Gathering information on North End's past and present stars is a lifetime's work: players will come and go, and facts will continue to be unearthed in an attempt to obtain a comprehensive biography.

In a text with such a huge amount of data, I have tried hard to eradicate mistakes. Football writing in the past has been prone to error; many have been carried through the years from volume to volume. While every care has been taken, it is maybe inevitable in a work containing so much material that errors have slipped through the net.

This book is a text that will give nostalgic pleasure, reviving memories. It is also, though, a historical research document for present and future generations – a history of the men who made the North End.

Dean P. Hayes
Pembrokeshire
May 2006

ABBOTT, Pawel Tadeusz

Striker

Born: York, 2 December 1981.
Career: LKS Lodz (Poland), 1999.
PRESTON NORTH END, 2001. Bury,
2002 (loan). Bury, 2003 (loan).
Huddersfield Town, 2004.

■ Pawel Abbott signed from Polish club LKS Lodz in February 2001. The young striker began the 2002–03 season on loan at Bury, where he forged a useful partnership up front with Jon Newby. He found the net on a number of occasions before being recalled to Deepdale to cover for an injury crisis. He featured as a substitute against Reading before scoring within 10 minutes of his full

debut in a 5–3 home defeat at the hands of Wimbledon. He had a second loan spell at Gigg Lane, although he was restricted to just 15 days, which took him up to the maximum 93 days allowed under the Football League regulations. Struggling to gain a regular place with North End, despite playing for the Polish Under-21 side, he joined Huddersfield on loan before the move was made permanent. In 2004–05, his first full season with the club, he netted a hat-trick in an away win at Port Vale and ended the season as the club's leading scorer with 27 goals.

AGYEMANG, Patrick

Striker

Born: Walthamstow, 29 September 1980.
Career: Wimbledon, 1999. Brentford, 1999
(loan). Gillingham, 2004. PRESTON
NORTH END, 2004.

■ Patrick Agyemang was unable to break into the Wimbledon side, so he spent three months on loan at Brentford at the start of the 1999–2000 season to further his development. A striker whose style makes it difficult for the opposition – he is more than 6ft tall and weighs more than 13st – he eventually broke into the Dons' side. In 2000–01, as well as becoming a cult figure with the fans, he was voted Wimbledon's Young Player of the Year. Proving to be at his most dangerous playing out wide, he then lost out to David Connolly and Neil Shipperley. In January 2004, he joined Gillingham for £200,000. He not only featured as the leading scorer for both clubs, but scored the winner for the Dons at Gillingham and the winner for the Gills at Wimbledon! Following the signings of Darren Byfield and Iwan Roberts, Agyemang found himself on the bench, so in November 2004 he moved to Preston North End for £350,000. He made an immediate impact with the Deepdale club, but only scored 2 goals in 13 starts before reverting to the bench. He was, however, brought on regularly

by manager Billy Davies to run at tiring defences. In this capacity he netted the clinching goal in a 2–1 win over West Ham United at Upton Park. The burly striker, who netted six goals in 2005–06, was used mainly off the bench, but he was the player to end the club's goal drought when after 500 minutes without the club scoring a goal he netted the equaliser in the 1–1 draw with Southampton.

AINSWORTH, Gareth

Midfield

Born: Blackburn, 10 May 1973.
Career: Northwich Victoria. PRESTON
NORTH END, 1992. Cambridge United,
1992. PRESTON NORTH END, 1992.
Lincoln City, 1995. Port Vale, 1997.
Wimbledon, 1998. PRESTON NORTH
END, 2002 (loan). Walsall, 2002 (loan).
Cardiff City, 2003. Queen's Park Rangers,
2003.

■ Gareth Ainsworth was a fast and skilful winger who endeared himself to the North End faithful during three spells at Deepdale. He first joined the club from Northwich Victoria in January 1992 after completing a YTS contract with his home-town club Blackburn Rovers. He made his North End debut in a 2–0 defeat at Shrewsbury but after a handful of appearances he was allowed to join Cambridge United. After a short stay at the Abbey Stadium, he rejoined North End on a free transfer. On the last day of the club's 1992–93 relegation season, when North End lost 1–0 at Bolton, Ainsworth broke down sobbing after relegation had been confirmed. The following season, Ainsworth was outstanding, scoring 11 goals as North End reached the Play-off Final at Wembley. In October 1995, having scored 14 goals in 106 League and Cup games for North End, he left Deepdale a second time, joining Lincoln City for a fee of £25,000. Ending his first season at Sincil Bank as the Imps' leading scorer, he was voted Lincoln's Player of the Year. He repeated both achievements the following season and won selection for the PFA Division Three team before Port Vale paid a club record £500,000 for his services. A player who never knows when to give up, he was the Valiants' Player of the Year in 1997–98 and not surprisingly attracted offers from the top-flight clubs. After Vale had turned down a bid of £1.5 million from Leeds United, Ainsworth joined Wimbledon for £2 million in November 1998. Dogged by a groin injury, he rarely got the chance to prove his worth in the Premiership and after the Dons were relegated, he again missed matches due to a broken wrist. Having appeared for just 32 minutes of football in 2001–02, he was loaned out to North End in March 2002 where he impressed with some strong wing play. After

coming to the end of his Wimbledon contract, he went on loan to Walsall before joining Cardiff City in a short-term deal to boost their challenge for the Play-offs. He later moved to Queen's Park Rangers, where he scored within five minutes of his debut, but again his progress was hampered by injuries. It was a similar story in 2004–05 and he will just be hoping that his luck changes.

AITKEN, William John

Outside-right, inside-right

Born: Peterhead, 2 February 1894.
Career: Kirkintilloch. Queen's Park. Glasgow Rangers. Port Vale, 1919 (loan). Newcastle United, 1920. PRESTON NORTH END, 1924. Chorley. Norwich City, 1926. Bideford Town, 1927. Juventus (Italy), 1929. Cannes (France), 1930. Reims (France), 1933.

■ William Aitken was a typical winger of his day and good enough to appear in the Anglo Scots v Home Scots fixtures.

He scored plenty of goals north of the border for both Queen's Park and Glasgow Rangers. After a loan spell with Port Vale, Aitken joined Newcastle United. He had his best season with the Magpies in 1920–21 as they finished fifth in Division One. The Scot lost his place in United's side during the first half of the 1924 FA Cup-winning season and soon after the trophy arrived on Tyneside, he joined Preston North End. Aitken made his Preston debut on the opening day of the 1924–25 season as North End went down 1–0 at West Ham United. Though North End were relegated, Aitken, who missed just one game through injury, performed admirably. He was still the club's first-choice right-winger the following season, but midway through the campaign he left to play for Chorley before signing for Norwich City. In 1929 he won the Morpeth sprint and also took part in the Powderhall Run. He spent many years on the continent, where he won honours with Juventus, Cannes and Reims before taking up the role of representative at a wine and spirit merchant in the North East.

AKERS, George

Outside-left

Born: Clitheroe.
Career: PRESTON NORTH END, 1932.

■ Clitheroe-born outside-left George Akers had impressed in a number of reserve-team games before being given his first-team debut in a Second Division game at Millwall in April 1933. Though it was Akers who provided the cross from which Ted Harper slotted home the equaliser in a 1–1 draw, it proved to be his only Football League appearance and he drifted into the local non-League scene.

ALEXANDER, Graham

Right-back

Born: Coventry, 10 October 1971.
Career: Scunthorpe United, 1990. Luton Town, 1995. PRESTON NORTH END, 1999.

■ After beginning his career with Scunthorpe United as a right-sided midfield player and impressing with his

turn of speed and explosive shooting, Graham Alexander attracted enquiries from a number of bigger clubs. In the summer of 1995 he left the Irons to join Luton Town, where he soon established himself as a first-team regular. His best season at Kenilworth Road was 1997–98 when, despite being asked to play at full-back to cover for injuries, he was the Hatters' leading scorer. Alexander joined North End during the transfer deadline weeks in March 1999 and made an impressive debut against Northampton Town. He was ever present during the club's Second Division Championship-winning season of 1999–2000 and was well worth his place in the PFA award-winning side for his outstanding work in both defence and attack. Scoring eight times from the penalty spot, he ended the campaign as North End's second-top scorer with 10 goals. Over the course of the following season, Alexander coped admirably with the higher grade of football and, though he suffered a punctured lung, his positive overlapping, powerful free-kicks and sound defensive play were a feature of the club's run-in to the Play-offs. In April 2002, Alexander became North End's first full Scottish international for over 40 years when he came on as a substitute against Nigeria and was also selected for the PFA Division One team. He continued to be a regular in the Scottish side in 2002–03, while at club level he netted 11 times, all but two from the penalty spot as he benefited from the return from injury of Lee Cartwright. The highlights of the 2003–04 season were his 600th senior appearance against his home-town club Coventry City and scoring with a penalty in his 200th League game for North End. The following season Alexander, who has won 16 caps for Scotland, had a renaissance under Billy Davies, his form again winning him selection for the PFA Championship team of the season. Sadly, he missed the Play-off semi-finals through injury and only made a late substitute appearance at the Millennium Stadium. The long-serving defender had another consistent season in 2005–06. One of the club's best buys in recent seasons, he has now appeared in well over 300 League and Cup games for North End.

ALLAN, Richard

Outside-right

Born: Preston.
Career: PRESTON NORTH END 1894.
Chorley. Dundee. Newcastle United, 1897.
Bristol St George.

■ Richard Allan scored on his North End debut as the Lilywhites went down 3–1 at Sheffield Wednesday. However, he made just one more appearance for the Deepdale club against Sheffield United – a match North End won 2–1 – before moving to play non-League football for Chorley. He then went to play in Scotland for Dundee before signing for Newcastle United. He was a regular in the Magpies' successful promotion-winning side of 1897–98 when, along with Willie Wardrope, he was one of the chief providers for centre-forward Jock Peddie. In spite of this, he was discarded for Newcastle's debut in the First Division and moved on to Bristol St George, where he ended his career.

ALLARDYCE, Craig Samuel

Central defender

Born: Bolton, 9 June 1975.
Career: PRESTON NORTH END, 1993.
Macclesfield Town. Northwich Victoria.
Blackpool, 1994. Chorley. Chesterfield,
1998. Peterborough United, 1998. Welling
United. Mansfield Town, 1998. Boston
United.

■ The son of Bolton manager Sam Allardyce, who was actually North End's caretaker-boss, Craig's only appearance for the Deepdale club was as a substitute for Simon Burton in a 2–2 draw at Port Vale. Unable to force his way into the team on a regular basis, he moved into non-League football, first with Macclesfield Town and then Northwich Victoria. Given the chance to resurrect his League career with Blackpool, he waited 15 months for his chance in the Seasiders' first team but was then released and again moved into non-League circles with Chorley. In March 1998, Chesterfield signed him on a non-contract basis but again he made just one substitute appearance. He arrived at Peterborough United prior to the start of the 1998–99 season and made three starts before departing for non-League

Welling United. He came back into the League with Mansfield Town but was overlooked for much of his time at Field Mill, eventually being allowed to join Boston United where he ended his career.

ALLARDYCE, Samuel

Central defender

Born: Dudley, 19 October 1954.
Career: Bolton Wanderers, 1971.
Sunderland, 1980. Millwall, 1981. Tampa
Bay (United States). Coventry City, 1983.
Huddersfield Town, 1984. Bolton
Wanderers, 1985. PRESTON NORTH
END, 1986. West Bromwich Albion, 1989.
PRESTON NORTH END, 1992.

■ Dudley-born defender Sam Allardyce began his playing career with Bolton Wanderers, making his Football League debut against Notts County in November 1973. Following the departure of Don McAllister to Tottenham Hotspur, Allardyce won a regular place at the heart of the Bolton defence. During his time at Burnden Park, Allardyce scored a number of spectacular goals, perhaps none more so than the fearsome header from fully 18 yards against Second Division promotion rivals Sunderland in December 1975. Impressive in the air, he helped Bolton win the Second Division Championship in 1977–78 but after relegation two

seasons later, Allardyce left to join Sunderland for a fee of £150,000. After just one season at Roker Park, he moved to Millwall followed by brief spells at both Coventry and Huddersfield before he rejoined the Wanderers. Sadly he was hampered by injuries and after appearing in 231 games in which he scored 24 goals, he joined Preston North End. Making his debut in a 1–1 draw at Tranmere on the opening day of the 1986–87 season, he went on to play in 37 League games as the club won promotion from the Fourth Division as runners-up to Northampton Town. He continued to be an important member of the North End side in 1987–88 before leaving to play for West Bromwich Albion, where curiously he made just one appearance as a substitute. Big Sam eventually returned to Deepdale as youth team coach and took over as caretaker boss after the departure of Les Chapman. Though things began to pick up under his leadership, John Beck was appointed the club's new manager and Allardyce took over the reins at Blackpool. Surprisingly sacked after leading the Seasiders to the Play-offs, he took charge of Notts County and led the Meadow Lane club to the Third Division Championship in 1997–98. Appointed Bolton manager in October 1999, his first season at the Reebok saw the club reach the semi-finals of both the FA and League Cup. In 2000–01 he led the Wanderers back into the Premiership with a 3–0 defeat of North End at the Millennium Stadium and has kept the club in the top flight, taking them to the Final of the Carling Cup and into Europe.

ALLATT, Vernon

Forward

Born: Cannock, 28 May 1959.
Career: Hednesford Town. Halifax Town,
1979. Rochdale, 1983. Crewe Alexandra,
1984. PRESTON NORTH END, 1985.
Stockport County, 1986. Hednesford
Town. Crewe Alexandra, 1987.

■ Much-travelled forward Vernon Allatt began his career with non-League Hednesford Town where his goalscoring feats alerted a number of League clubs. In November 1979 he joined Halifax Town and in three seasons at The Shay, he scored 14 goals in 98 League games

before joining Rochdale. After a season at Spotland, he moved to Crewe Alexandra before joining Preston North End in November 1985. After making his debut in a 2–0 defeat at Leyton Orient, he was a member of the North End side that suffered a disastrous 7–3 defeat at the hands of Walsall in a first-round FA Cup tie. Allatt kept his place in the side for much of what was the worst season in the club's history. Making just one League Cup appearance as a substitute at West Ham in the early part of the following season, Allatt left Deepdale to play for Stockport County. Though he scored at a ratio of a goal every other game for the Hatters, including a hat-trick in a 3–1 defeat of Peterborough United, he was allowed to rejoin Hednesford Town before ending his playing days with a second spell at Crewe.

ALLPRESS, Timothy John

Central defender

Born: Hitchin, 27 January 1971.
Career: Luton Town, 1989. PRESTON NORTH END, 1991 (loan). Bayer Uerdingen (Germany). Colchester United, 1993. Hitchin Town.

■ Central defender Tim Allpress appeared in just one game for Luton Town before signing on loan for North End in October 1991. His first appearance for the club came in a 3–2 defeat at Chester before he helped the side to three consecutive victories. Impressing alongside Mike Flynn at the heart of the North End defence, the last of his nine appearances came in a 4–1 home defeat at the hands of Hartlepool United, when Matt Lambert replaced him. Returning to Kenilworth Road, he was unable to force his way into the Luton side and left to try his luck in German football with Bayer Uerdingen. Within a matter of months, he had joined Colchester United and spent two seasons at Layer Road before moving into non-League football with his home-town club Hitchin Town.

ALSTEAD, Anthony

Left-back

Born: Preston, 15 July 1893.
Died: 1973.
Career: Bamber Bridge Corinthians. PRESTON NORTH END, 1914. Lancaster Town.

■ Left-back Anthony Alstead was spotted playing local football for Bamber Bridge Corinthians and joined the Deepdale club prior to the start of the 1914–15 season. An injury to Walter Holbem gave Alstead his chance and he appeared in three games at the turn of the year. Making his debut in a goalless draw at Bury, he was never on the losing side as North End went on to win promotion to Division One. When League football resumed after World War One, Alstead appeared in a further 11 games but after losing out to Fred Broadhurst, who moved from right-back to left-back to accommodate Bill Greatorex, he moved into non-League football with Lancaster Town.

ALSTON, Alexander George

Forward

Born: Preston, 26 February 1937.
Career: Netherfield. PRESTON NORTH END, 1955. Bury, 1963. Barrow, 1965.

■ Signed from non-League Nether-field, Alex Alston was given his League debut midway through the 1957–58 season as a replacement for the injured Tom Finney in a goalless draw at Sunderland. On his second appearance a fortnight later, he was on target in a 3–2 win at Leeds United. Those were his only appearances that season as North End finished the campaign as runners-up to Wolves in the First Division. Over the next couple of seasons, Alston found himself in and out of the Preston side and it was not until 1960–61 that he won a regular place. However, at the end of that campaign, North End were relegated. Alston continued to hold down a first-team place until March 1963 when, after scoring 30 goals in 117 games, he was transferred to Bury. The Shakers had reached that season's League Cup semi-finals but Alston was Cup-tied and therefore was not eligible. He spent three seasons at Gigg Lane before moving to Barrow in September 1965, where he ended his career.

ANDERS, Harry

Outside-right

Born: St Helens, 28 November 1926.
Died: October 1994.
Career: St Helens Town. PRESTON NORTH END, 1945. Manchester City, 1953. Port Vale, 1956. Accrington Stanley, 1957. Workington, 1960.

■ Harry Anders was a diminutive winger who joined North End with his younger brother Jimmy in 1945, having played his early football for his home-town team, St Helens Town. Making his North End debut in a 3–1 defeat at Sheffield United, most of his appearances came when he deputised for the

great Tom Finney. Though he was a good player in his own right, the crowd, who often only came to see Finney, would boo loudly if Harry Anders' name was announced! Anders stayed at Deepdale for six seasons and appeared in 73 games. On leaving Deepdale, he joined Manchester City and made 32 appearances before signing for Port Vale in the summer of 1956. Unable to win a regular spot in the Valiants side, he moved on to Accrington Stanley a year later, where he linked up once more with his brother. There he hit 18 goals in 114 games before completing his career with Workington in the 1960–61 season.

ANDERSON, David Robert

Left-half, centre-forward, inside-right

Born: Shettleston, 1881.
Career: Heart of Midlothian. Bonnyrigg Rose. PRESTON NORTH END, 1910. Queen's Park Rangers. Swansea Town. Halifax Town, 1921.

■ David Anderson was a versatile player who began his career with Hearts before having a brief spell with Bonnyrigg Rose. In 1910 he decided to try his luck south of the border with Preston North End. He made a goalscoring debut on the final day of the 1910–11 season as North End beat Bradford City 2–0. Midway through the following season, in what was his penultimate game for the club, he netted both North End's goals in a 4–2 defeat at Sheffield United. On leaving Deepdale, he had a brief spell with Queen's Park Rangers and later Swansea Town, who were both then members of the Southern League. Shortly after football resumed following the Great War, Anderson played for Halifax Town and was in his 40th year when he hung up his boots.

ANDERSON, Iain

Winger

Born: Glasgow, 23 July 1977.
Career: Dundee, 1994. Toulouse (France), 1999. PRESTON NORTH END, 2000. Tranmere Rovers, 2003 (loan). Grimsby Town, 2003. Dundee.

■ A Scottish Under-21 international, winger Iain Anderson began his career

with Dundee. He spent five seasons with the Dens Park club before he joined French club Toulouse in the summer of 1999 after he had scored 19 goals in 150 games. Unable to hold down a regular place, he joined North End, initially on loan in February 2000 as cover for Lee Cartwright. He became an instant hit with the Preston fans and earned a Second Division Championship medal. The nippy ball-player could have scored a hat-trick at Burnley before coming up with the winner in successive home games against Luton and Wrexham. Signed on a permanent basis, much of his 2000–01 season was spent on the treatment table. When he received both head and hamstring injuries in the same incident against Fulham, it was typical of his bad luck. Able to play as a wide attacker on either side, he began to capture some consistent form for Preston in 2001–02 but the following season, under new manager Craig Brown, he disappeared almost entirely from the first-team scene. He joined Tranmere Rovers on loan on transfer deadline day and scored on his debut against Chester-field. However, despite impressing during his stay at Prenton Park, he returned to Deepdale at the end of the season prior to joining Grimsby Town on a free transfer. After an impressive start, he was laid low by injuries and after one

season at Blundell Park he returned to Scottish League action with his first club, Dundee.

ANDERSON, John Christopher Patrick

Defender

Born: Dublin, 7 November 1959.
Career: West Bromwich Albion, 1977. PRESTON NORTH END, 1979. Newcastle United 1982.

■ After beginning his career with West Bromwich Albion, John Anderson was not considered good enough for the Baggies first team and in August 1979 he was transferred to newly promoted Preston North End for a fee of £40,000. After making his Football League debut in a 3–2 win over Fulham in January 1980, Anderson struggled to hold down a regular place in the North End side. Indeed, it was the 1981–82 season before he became a first-team regular, but at the end of that campaign, in which he took his total of appearances to 54, he was let go on a free transfer and joined Newcastle United. It was a costly error by North End manager Gordon Lee as he went on to become a huge terrace favourite at St James' Park. Whilst with North End, Anderson had won the first of 16 caps for the Republic of Ireland, his only goal coming in his second appearance against the United States. At Newcastle, Anderson soon claimed the right-back berth and in 1983–84, his second season there, he helped the Magpies win promotion to Division One after a six-year absence. Playing in all four defensive positions and in midfield, he spent nine seasons in the North East before an ankle injury forced his retirement in March 1992. He had scored 14 goals in 299 League appearances for the Magpies. Later that summer he was appointed manager of Berwick Rangers but resigned after just eight weeks in the job. He later returned to the North East to work in local radio and assist the New-castle Kestrels women's football club.

ANDERTON, Steven David

Midfield

Born: Lancaster, 2 October 1969.
Career: PRESTON NORTH END, 1988.

■ Midfielder Steven Anderton's only Football League experience came in the game against Mansfield Town on 10 April 1990, when he replaced the injured Sammy McIlroy. However, though North End ran out easy 4–0 winners and Anderton had a hand in Warren Joyce's second goal, the Northern Ireland international was fit to resume his place in the North End side for the next game at home to Bristol City.

ANGELL Brett Ashley Mark

Forward

Born: Marlborough, 20 August 1968.
Career: Portsmouth, 1986. Cheltenham Town. Derby County, 1988. Stockport County, 1988. Southend United, 1990. Everton, 1994. Sunderland, 1995. Sheffield United, 1996 (loan). West Bromwich Albion, 1996 (loan). Stockport County, 1996. Notts County, 1999 (loan). PRESTON NORTH END, 2000 (loan). Walsall, 2000. Rushden and Diamonds, 2002. Port Vale, 2002. Queen's Park Rangers 2002.

■ Much-travelled striker Brett Angell started out as a non-contract player with Portsmouth before moving to Cheltenham Town and then Derby County. He did not make a League appearance for the Rams before Stockport County manager Asa Hartford paid a club record fee of £30,000 for his services. In his first full season at Edgeley Park, Angell scored 23 goals, a major contribution to County finishing in fourth place, thereby winning a Play-off position. Angell had the priceless ability to be in the right place at the right time,

scoring 33 goals in 84 games for the Hatters before opting to join Southend United. Despite lengthy periods of absence through injury, he helped the Shrimps win promotion to Division Two before he was transferred to Everton in 1994 in a deal worth £500,000. Things did not work out at Goodison Park and he moved to Sunderland. After a good start, he found himself out of favour and had loan spells with Sheffield United and West Bromwich Albion before making a triumphant return to Stockport. He scored vital goals in the club's amazing Coca-Cola Cup run and his 20th strike of the season clinched promotion to the First Division in the penultimate match at Chesterfield. In 1997–98 he topped County's scoring charts for a second successive season and repeated the feat the following season before he began to be hampered by injuries. A loan spell at Notts County followed before in February 2000 he joined North End in a similar capacity. He made his first three appearances for the club from the substitutes' bench, scoring twice in the home defeat by Colchester. He claimed the winner on his full debut at Bournemouth and followed this up with two on his home debut against Oxford United. He contributed a total of eight goals to North End's Second Division Championship effort and was rewarded with a winners' medal. However, during the close season he moved on to Walsall and ended his first campaign at the Bescot Stadium with a hat-trick in the final game at Northampton. Midway through the 2001–02 season, he joined Rushden and Diamonds but, despite helping them reach the Play-offs, he was not offered a long-term contract. He had a spell with Port Vale before winding down his career with Queen's Park Rangers.

ANYINSAH Joseph Greene

Winger

Born: Bristol, 8 October 1984

Career: Bristol City 2001; Hereford United (loan); PRESTON NORTH END 2005; Bury (loan) 2006.

■ Joe Anyinsah is an exciting wing man with all the skills to make a real impact in the game. A product of Bristol

City's youth policy, he made his debut for the Ashton Gate club from the bench on the opening day of the 2004–05 season. Though he made a couple of starts, most of his appearances were as a substitute. Anyinsah, who also had a brief loan spell with Conference club Hereford United, joined North End in the summer of 2005. Unable to make much headway at Deepdale – all of his first-team appearances were from the bench – he joined Bury on loan in February 2006, but after three games for the Shakers, being injured at Shrewsbury on his last outing, he returned to Deepdale where hopes are high that he can force his way into the first team on a regular basis.

APPLETON, Michael Anthony

Midfield

Born: Salford, 4 December 1975.
Career: Manchester United, 1994. Lincoln City, 1995 (loan). Grimsby Town, 1997 (loan). PRESTON NORTH END, 1997. West Bromwich Albion, 2001.

■ Midfielder Michael Appleton was unable to break into the Manchester United side as a teenager. He joined

Lincoln City on loan but had little chance to shine in a struggling Imps side. On his return to Old Trafford he made his first-team bow in the Coca-Cola Cup game against Swindon Town, giving a good account of himself alongside Roy Keane. He also played in the next round of the competition against Leicester City, but the lack of first-team opportunities limited his progress and he went on loan to Grimsby Town. After impressing for the Mariners, a price was agreed between the two clubs to make the move permanent, but Appleton preferred to return to Manchester with a view to eventually breaking into the senior squad. However, on the eve of the season,

he became Preston's record signing when North End paid £500,000 for his services. He took some time to adjust to the demands of Second Division football, though being asked to play out of position did not help his situation. Given his favourite central-midfield role by new manager David Moyes, the aggressive ball-winner really began to blossom. However, his 1998–99 season was blighted by injuries after scoring the club's first goal of the season against York, and after recovering from a foot injury – he had special insoles made for his boots – he found he was used mainly as a substitute. He had another in-and-out season in 1999–2000 but chipped in

with four goals as North End won the Second Division Championship. Appleton scored North End's first goal of the following season and then in the games against Sheffield United and Wimbledon before scoring the goal that inflicted Fulham's first defeat of the season. He had scored 15 goals in 140 games when, in January 2001, he was surprisingly transferred to fellow Play-off hopefuls West Bromwich Albion for a fee of £750,000. In the end, though both North End and Albion reached the Play-offs, neither was successful in their hopes of a Premiership spot. In 2001–02, Appleton tore his posterior cruciate ligament and was out of action for the whole of the following season before being forced into premature retirement.

ARNOLD, James Alexander

Goalkeeper

Born: Stafford, 6 August 1950.
Career: Stafford Rangers. Blackburn Rovers, 1979. Everton, 1981. PRESTON NORTH END, 1982 (loan). Port Vale, 1985.

■ Goalkeeper Jim Arnold was an England semi-professional international

who joined Blackburn Rovers from his home-town club Stafford Rangers in June 1979. The following season he established a club record at Ewood Park when he kept 19 clean sheets as the Rovers won promotion from the Third Division. After two seasons he joined Everton and turned in some impressive performances for the Goodison club as they challenged for the First Division title. After losing his place to Neville Southall, he joined North End on loan in October 1982 and made his debut in a goalless draw at home to Huddersfield Town. Arnold kept another clean sheet three days later as Preston were again held to a goalless draw at Deepdale, this time by Newport County. Arnold's remaining four appearances all ended in defeat and he returned to Goodison before joining Port Vale for the start of the 1985–86 season. In keeping 18 clean sheets he helped Vale win promotion to the Third Division and was voted the club's Player of the Year. At the end of that season he decided to retire and work for the Staffordshire Police but returned to Vale Park later in the season following a goalkeeping crisis. He appeared in a further 12 games before making way for new signing Alex Williams.

ARTHURS, Charles Henry

Wing-half

Born: Kilnhurst.
Career: Gainsborough Trinity, 1907. New Brompton. PRESTON NORTH END, 1909. New Brompton.

■ Wing-half Charlie Arthurs began his career with Gainsborough Trinity in 1907 and made 27 appearances for the Lincolnshire club before leaving to play for New Brompton. His impressive displays for the Southern League club led to interest from a number of League clubs and in the summer of 1909, he joined Preston North End. Arthurs, who also appeared occasionally on the wing, made the first of his eight appearances in a 1–1 draw at Manchester United in September 1909, while his only goal for the club came in a 3–1 reversal against local rivals Bolton Wanderers at Burnden Park. Unable to win a regular place in the North End side, he rejoined New Brompton at the end of the season.

ASHCROFT, Lee

Winger

Born: Preston, 7 September 1972.
Career: PRESTON NORTH END, 1991. West Bromwich Albion, 1993. Notts County, 1996 (loan). PRESTON NORTH END, 1996. Grimsby Town, 1998. Wigan Athletic, 2000. Port Vale, 2002 (loan). Huddersfield Town, 2002 (loan). Southport.

■ Lee Ashcroft was a fast and tricky winger who preferred to play wide on the left but could also figure on the opposite flank. He worked his way up through the ranks at Deepdale before making his debut as a substitute during a 2–1 defeat at Wigan Athletic in November 1991. After establishing himself as a regular member of the North End side, he went on to win representative honours for England at Under-21 level, but in the summer of 1993 he left Preston to join

West Bromwich Albion for a fee of £250,000. In his early days at the Hawthorns, he was unable to hold down a regular place and was loaned out to Notts County. He returned to score some vital goals for the Baggies but in September 1996 he left Albion to rejoin Preston North End. His speed on the right-wing finally restored the balance that the club had been missing during Lee Cartwright's long absence through injury. Described as 'a scorer of great goals rather than a great goalscorer', he still ended the 1997–98 season as the club's leading scorer, netting a hat-trick in a 3–1 win over Fulham. Towards the end of that season, Ashcroft rejected a move to Wigan and celebrated by scoring his 50th senior goal against the Latics at the end of the transfer deadline week. On leaving Deepdale a second time during the close season, he became Grimsby Town's record £500,000 signing. After injuries hampered his progress during his first season at Blundell Park, he formed an attacking partnership with Jack Lester that caused problems for many First Division defences. In the summer of 2001, Ashcroft left the Mariners to join Wigan Athletic for £350,000 but again suffered with injuries. His inconsistency saw him struggle to keep his place and he had loan spells with Port Vale and Huddersfield Town before leaving the JJB Stadium to become player-coach of Southport.

ASHTON, Herbert

Winger

Born: Blackburn, 1887.
Career: PRESTON NORTH END, 1905. Accrington Stanley. West Ham United.

■ This Blackburn-born winger made his North End debut in a 3–0 home win over Bolton Wanderers in the penultimate game of the 1905–06 season, a campaign in which the Deepdale club finished runners-up in the First Division to Liverpool. With Dickie Bond still injured, he kept his place in the side for the final game of the season against Newcastle United, a match that ended goalless. With Bond restored to full fitness and Danson and Lockett sharing the number-11 shirt, Ashton was restricted to just two

appearances towards the end of the following season, after which he left Deepdale to play for Accrington Stanley. His impressive displays led to a number of inquiries from other clubs and he later played for West Ham United, where he ended his career.

ASHWORTH, Alec

Inside-forward

Born: Southport, 1 October 1939.
Died: 1995.
Career: Everton, 1957. Luton Town, 1960. Northampton Town, 1962. PRESTON NORTH END, 1963.

■ Inside-forward Alec Ashworth began his career with Everton, making his Football League debut against Sheffield Wednesday in April 1958. Though he spent three seasons at

Goodison Park, he was unable to hold down a regular first-team place. In October 1960, he moved to Luton Town in a player exchange deal that took Billy Bingham to Merseyside. Ashworth's two seasons at Kenilworth Road saw him playing in a slightly deeper role than normal but he still managed a goal every three games. In the summer of 1962, he joined Northampton Town and his 25 goals in 30 League games helped the Cobblers to win that season's Third Division Championship. Ashworth signed for North End in the close season, making his debut in a 2–2 draw at Leyton Orient on the opening day of the 1963–64 season. Forming a good strike partnership with Alex Dawson – the pair of them netted 44 League goals – he scored a hat-trick in a 3–0 home win over Bury. That season, North End just missed out on promotion to the First Division and also reached the FA Cup Final, where they lost 3–2 to West Ham United. After that though, injury problems began to mount up for Ashworth and over the next two seasons he managed just 12 League appearances. Knee ligament damage was the main cause of his problems and after appearing in the game against Derby County at the Baseball Ground in April 1966 – a match North End lost 1–0 – he was forced to hang up his boots.

ATHERTON, James

Outside-right

Born: Preston.
Career: PRESTON NORTH END, 1899.

■ Local-born winger James Atherton joined North End in November 1899 following the club's disappointing showing the previous season when they just avoided relegation to Division Two. Atherton made his Preston debut in a goalless draw at Newcastle United and, though it was another difficult season for the Lilywhites as they finished just above the two relegation places, they did enjoy some success with Atherton in the side. North End beat high-flying Wolves 3–0 at Molineux and enjoyed 3–0 home victories over Nottingham Forest and Stoke, while fellow strugglers West Bromwich Albion were beaten 5–2. Surprisingly, Atherton, who had lost his place to Patrick Murray, was allowed to leave Deepdale at the end of the season.

ATHERTON, John James

Inside-forward

Born: Preston, 1917.
Career: PRESTON NORTH END, 1936. Brighton and Hove Albion, 1938.

■ Inside-forward Jack Atherton played the first of his four games on New Year's Day 1937 as North End drew 2–2 at Everton. Retaining his place in the side for the following day's game at home to Sunderland, Atherton scored North End's opening goal in a 2–0 win over the Wearsiders. He lost his place after North End were beaten 5–0 by Wolves before later playing his final game for the club against the eventual First Division runners-up, Charlton Athletic, a match Preston lost 3–1. Released at the end of the season, he joined Brighton and Hove Albion where, in his only season at the Goldstone Ground, he found the net twice in nine first-team outings.

ATKINS, Robert Gary

Central defender

Born: Leicester, 16 October 1962.
Career: Enderby Town. Sheffield United, 1982. PRESTON NORTH END, 1985.

■ Versatile defender Bob Atkins began his first-class career with Sheffield United, making his debut against Gillingham in October 1982. In his second season at Bramall Lane, Atkins scored 3 goals in 16 appearances, helping the Blades to win promotion to the Second Division. One of his goals was a fine last-minute winner in the Yorkshire derby at Millmoor against Rotherham United. However, during the following season, he found himself in and out of the United side and in February 1985 he joined Preston North End, initially on loan. After playing in a Freight Rover Trophy defeat against Rochdale, Atkins made his League debut for the Deepdale club in the local derby against Burnley, a match North End lost 2–0. After joining the club on a permanent basis, Atkins was a regular in the side for the next five seasons, helping the Lilywhites win promotion from the Fourth Division as runners-up to Northampton Town. During that season, Atkins played in 41 games with his only goal salvaging a point in a 2–2 draw at Crewe Alexandra. The Leicester-born player's career was brought to a premature end through injury after he played the last of his 242 League and Cup games against Shrewsbury Town on the final day of the 1989–90 season.

ATKINSON, Graeme

Winger

Born: Hull, 1 November 1971.
Career: Hull City, 1990. PRESTON NORTH END, 1994. Rochdale, 1997 (loan). Brighton and Hove Albion, 1998. Scunthorpe United, 1998. Scarborough 1999. Rochdale 1999.

■ Hull-born Graeme Atkinson began his career with his home-town club and was equally at home on either flank, and in attack or defence. He spent four years at Boothferry Park, scoring 26 goals in 172 games for the Tigers before joining North End in October 1994. He scored on his Preston debut in a 3–1 reversal at Hartlepool but, though he became a valuable squad member, in his early days with the club he did not show his best form from a regular position. In 1995–96, early season injuries meant a move to central midfield for Atkinson, where he blossomed. His strong running in support of the attack and defence, combined with accurate passing, dangerous dead-ball kicks and powerful shooting, made him a vital part of the team that won the Third Division Championship. However, he spent the 1996–97 season in and out of the North End side. The following season he failed to make the most of his limited first-team opportunities, despite performing well in the reserves. Following a loan spell with Rochdale, he joined Brighton and Hove Albion in March 1998, having appeared in 93 first-team games for North End. Released by Brian Horton in the close season, Atkinson then re-signed for the Seagulls and played in a further eight games before being released on a free transfer for a second time. After a brief spell as a non-contract player with Scunthorpe United, he finished the season with Scarborough before again being released. Atkinson then joined Rochdale and made an immediate impact in his second spell, scoring on his debut and netting four times in the first 10 games. He was a key player in Rochdale's tremendous start to the 1999–2000 season, but damaged knee ligaments in the match at Peterborough forced him to quit the first-class scene.

BAILEY, John Anthony Kenneth

Winger

Born: Manchester, 2 July 1984.
Career: PRESTON NORTH END, 2001.
Hamilton Academicals, 2003 (loan).

■ England Youth international winger John Bailey was a huge success in North End's successful reserve side of 2002–03. He sat on the bench on three occasions

before being called upon to make his Football League debut. He replaced Pawel Abbott in Preston's 2–0 defeat against Wimbledon at Selhurst Park in April 2003. Although he showed an eagerness to take on his man, he did at times overdo the trickery. Possessing the pace and the skills to trouble most defenders, he went back into the club's reserves before joining Hamilton Academicals on loan.

BAINBRIDGE, Simpson

Winger

Born: Silksworth, 3 April 1895.
Career: Seaton Delaval. Leeds City, 1912. PRESTON NORTH END, 1919. South Shields, 1920. Aberdeen. Wheatley Hill Alliance. Shildon Athletic.

■ Winger Simpson Bainbridge played

his early football for Seaton Delaval before joining Leeds City in December 1912. A regular in the Yorkshire club's side for the next three seasons, he also appeared in a number of wartime games. However, when League football resumed in 1919–20, Bainbridge joined Preston North End and made his debut in the number-11 shirt in a 3–2 home defeat at the hands of Newcastle United. North End struggled that season and only just retained their top-flight status. Simpson Bainbridge, who netted the winner in a 2–1 defeat of Liverpool at Anfield, lost his place midway through the season. Though not appearing in the club's first team, he remained at Deepdale until the following season, when he joined South Shields. Bainbridge later had a spell playing for Scottish League side Aberdeen, but on leaving Pittodrie, he ended his playing days with brief spells back in the North East with Wheatley Hill Alliance and Shildon Athletic.

BAIRD, Samuel

Inside-forward

Born: Denny, 13 May 1930.
Career: Clyde, 1949. PRESTON NORTH END, 1954. Glasgow Rangers, 1955. Hibernian, 1960. Third Lanark, 1962. Stirling Albion, 1963.

■ Sammy Baird, who scored on his international debut for Scotland in a 2–0 defeat of Yugoslavia, began his career with Clyde, helping the Shawfield club to win the 'B' Division Championship in 1951–52. His impressive form, which had earned him selection for the Scottish League XI, attracted the attention of some of England's leading clubs and, in June 1954, Preston North End manager Scot Symon paid £12,000 to take him to Deepdale. After making his debut in a 3–1 home win over Arsenal, he kept his place for the game against Sheffield United but failed to get on the score sheet in a 5–0 win. Though he scored against Sunderland and Blackpool, he found it hard to settle in the First Division and when Symon returned to Rangers as manager, he bought Baird once more for £10,000. Using his physique to good effect, Baird soon made a name for himself in the Rangers side as an intimidating player. Very much

a type of inside-forward long identified with Rangers – big, industrious and strong in finishing – he helped the Ibrox club win two League Championships and the 1960 Scottish Cup final when they beat Kilmarnock 2–0. He had scored 52 goals in 179 games by the time he left to have spells with Hibernian and Third Lanark. He ended his involvement with the game following a period as player-manager of Stirling Albion.

BAKER, George

Full-back

Born: Sandiford.
Career: New Tupton Ivanhoe, 1903. Chesterfield, 1905. PRESTON NORTH END, 1909.

■ Full-back George Baker was a first-team regular for Chesterfield for four seasons. In a Second Division side struggling to avoid re-election, he was one of the Spireites' better players. However, Chesterfield lost their League status at the end of the 1908–09 season and he opted to join Preston North End on a free transfer. Signed primarily as cover, he had to wait until the penultimate game of the 1909–10 season before he made his debut in a 3–1 win at Woolwich Arsenal. The following season, he played in eight consecutive games after Rodway sustained a knee injury but, though he gave a good account of himself, he returned to the reserves after Rodway had recovered. During the club's relegation season of 1911–12, Baker appeared in both full-back positions but after just one appearance in the following campaign, he parted company with the club, having made just 24 League and Cup appearances in his four years at Deepdale.

BALL, Aloysius

Left-half

Born: Preston.
Career: PRESTON NORTH END, 1893.

■ After finishing as runners-up to Sunderland in the First Division in 1892–93, North End struggled the following season, a campaign in which left-half Aloysius Ball played in five games. After making his debut in a goalless draw at Wolverhampton Wanderers, Ball played in four consecutive games, which included a 2–0 win over bottom club Newton Heath. Recalled to the side for the visit to Champions-elect Aston Villa, he made both of North End's goals in a 5–2 defeat before drifting into the local non-League scene.

BAMBER, Lee

Goalkeeper

Born: Burnley, 31 October 1968.
Career: Leyland Motors. PRESTON NORTH END, 1993.

■ Leyland Motors' goalkeeper Lee Bamber joined North End as a non-contract player during the course of the 1993–94 season. His League debut came under controversial circumstances as he replaced the sent off Kelham O'Hanlon in the 2–2 draw at Mansfield after the regular North End 'keeper had fouled an opponent 40 yards from his goal-line! That was the only time Bamber appeared in the North End side, although he appeared on the bench a further 18 times over the remaining weeks of the campaign.

BANKS, Richard

Inside-right

Born: Preston.
Career: PRESTON NORTH END, 1899.

■ Versatile forward Richard Banks made four League appearances for North End during the 1899–1900 season, a campaign in which the club just avoided relegation to Division Two, finishing a point ahead of Burnley. Banks made his North End debut wearing the number-nine shirt in a 1–0 defeat at West Bromwich Albion and, though he retained his place for the club's next two games, he was switched to inside-right. Replaced by Matthew Brunton, he returned to the side for the game against Liverpool at Anfield but North End went down 1–0. Unable to command a regular place in the Preston side, he left the club in the close season.

BANNISTER, James

Inside-right

Born: Leyland, 1881.
Career: Chorley, 1900. Manchester City, 1902. Manchester United, 1906. PRESTON NORTH END, 1909.

■ After some impressive displays for Chorley, inside-forward Jimmy Bannister joined Manchester City where he was a regular in the then Hyde Road club's side for three seasons. He scored almost a goal every other game – 21 in 45 – City were never out of the top five. In the summer of 1906, he moved across the city to join Manchester United. In his second season with the club, he helped the Reds win the First Division Championship but then fell out of favour with the management and in October 1909 he moved to Preston North End. Bannister made his debut for the Lilywhites in a 1–0 home win over Middlesbrough, after which he did not miss a game as the club finished the 1909–10 season in mid-table. In the 4–0 home win over Newcastle United, Bannister scored two of North End's goals and in the dying moments struck a post to be denied a hat-trick. The following season, while the club again finished mid-table, they struggled to score goals – just 40 in 38 games. Bannister with seven was joint-top scorer with David McLean. Following the emergence of Ben Green, Bannister lost his place in the North End side and he decided to retire at the end of the 1911–12 season.

BARBER, David Eric

Wing-half

Born: Wombwell, 6 December 1939.
Career: Barnsley, 1958. PRESTON NORTH END, 1961.

■ Wombwell-born wing-half Dave Barber, an England Youth international, began his career with his local club, Barnsley. A virtual ever present in his three seasons at Oakwell, his consistency alerted North End manager Jimmy Milne who persuaded him to join the Deepdale club in the summer of 1961. The highly-rated Yorkshireman made his debut on the opening day of the 1961–62 season as North End crashed 4–1 at Luton Town. In fact, North End made a disastrous start, winning just one of the opening eight games. Barber was injured in a 1–0 home defeat at the hands of Newcastle United and did not return to first-team action until a similar injury to Jimmy Smith ruled him out of the side. After that, Barber found himself in and out of the side, although he did score his first goal for the club on the final day of the season in a 2–0 win over Charlton Athletic. Barber remained at Deepdale for a further couple of seasons, but could never rediscover the form he had shown at Barnsley and left the club in the summer of 1964.

BARBOUR, John

Inside-right

Born: Preston.
Career: PRESTON NORTH END, 1914.

■ Inside-forward John Barbour sadly lost his life during the early stages of World War One. He had played in 13 games during North End's Second Division promotion-winning season of 1914–15, scoring goals in the 2–2 home draw against Clapton Orient and the 1–0 defeat of local rivals Blackpool. Finding himself sharing the number-eight shirt with John Morley, the local-born player would have been hoping to establish himself further, as in his first season his promptings created a number of Fred Osborn's 17 League goals.

BARGH, George Wolfenden

Inside-forward

Born: Bilsborrow, 27 May 1910.
Career: Garstang, 1927. PRESTON

NORTH END, 1928. Sheffield Wednesday, 1935. Bury, 1936. Chesterfield, 1939. Bury, 1946.

■ Modelling his style on the inside-forward play of Alex James, this Bilsborrow-born youngster made his North End debut in place of the great man in a 1–1 draw against West Bromwich Albion in November 1928. After a couple of seasons in and out of the side, Bargh won a regular place in 1930–31 and ended the season as the club's leading scorer. His total of 14 goals included a hat-trick in a 7–0 home win over Cardiff City. One of Bargh's best games for the club came the following season in an FA Cup third-round replay against Bolton Wanderers. Held to a goalless draw at Deepdale, North End travelled to Burnden Park with little hope against the First Division club. However, a Bargh-inspired North End won 5–2 with the inside-forward scoring one of the goals, setting-up others for Crawford and Harper and forcing Griffiths and Wagstaffe to put through their own goal. Though injuries hampered his progress during North End's promotion-winning season of 1933–34, he did net four goals in his nine appearances including another hat-trick in a 4–2 home defeat of Millwall. Bargh was also outstanding in the club's final game of the season at Southampton, which North End had to win, and did 1–0. In April 1935, he left the club after playing the last of his 150 League and Cup games, scoring 43 goals. He had a brief spell with Sheffield Wednesday before joining Bury. He spent three successful seasons with the Shakers before playing in a couple of games for Chesterfield prior to the outbreak of World War Two. He made one further appearance for Bury after the hostilities, before later becoming North End's chief coach. He was responsible for the development of Alan Spavin, George Ross, Peter Thompson and Dave Wilson and was in charge when North End reached the 1960 FA Youth Cup Final and won the Five Nations Tournament at Geneva.

BARLOW, George Herbert
Outside-left
Born: Wigan, 1885.

Career: PRESTON NORTH END, 1906. Everton, 1908. PRESTON NORTH END, 1912.

■ Wigan-born winger George Barlow scored on his North End debut in a 3–1 home win over Liverpool in March 1907. It was his only appearance that season but the following campaign Barlow, who figured more frequently in the North End side, represented England in their amateur international against Holland at Darlington. Despite little more than a handful of games, Barlow had obviously done enough to impress Everton, who signed him in the summer of 1908. In his first season at Goodison Park, he helped the Blues to the runners'-up spot in the First Division, seven points behind League Champions Newcastle United. Though he spent a further two seasons on Merseyside, his first-team appearances were limited and in the 1912 close season he rejoined Preston North End. He had an outstanding 1912–13 season as the Lilywhites won the Second Division Championship and though he only scored one goal, it was good enough for North End to take the points against Fulham. Although North End were relegated again the following season, Barlow played in 34 games and was one of the few players to hold his own in the top flight. In 1914–15, North End won promotion to the First Division as runners-up to Derby County, with Barlow finding the net in the local derby victory at Blackpool. Though he continued to appear for the club in wartime fixtures, he did not reappear when League football returned in 1919–20.

BARNES, Horace
Inside-left
Born: Wadsley Bridge, 3 January 1890.
Career: Wadsley Bridge, 1907. Derby County, 1908. Manchester City, 1914. PRESTON NORTH END, 1924. Oldham Athletic, 1925. Ashton National, 1927.

■ Horace Barnes' first League club were Derby County, for whom he scored 74 goals in 153 League games. It was this goals per game ratio that persuaded Manchester City manager Ernest Mangnall to pay £2,500 for his services in 1914. However, shortly after putting pen to paper, World War One broke out.

His career in wartime football saw him score 56 goals in 57 games for City and incur a fine from the Manchester magistrates when he absented himself from working in a munitions factory to play against Stockport County in 1915. Barnes forged a fine scoring partnership with Tommy Browell and had the distinction of scoring City's first goal at Maine Road against Sheffield United in August 1923. Barnes played for England against Wales in a Victory International in 1919 and appeared twice for the Football League in 1921–22. He had a fierce left-foot shot and scored 108 goals in 192 League games for City after the hostilities. Two of them came against Liverpool in March 1920 in front of King George V, while another brace helped put an end to Burnley's record-breaking run of 30 games without defeat. In November 1924, Barnes joined Preston North End and scored on his debut in a 3–1 defeat of Nottingham Forest. In fact, Barnes scored in each of his first 3 games and netted six times in his first 10 outings but, despite these goals, North End were relegated. Barnes started the 1925–26 season in fine style, netting twice in each game as Portsmouth (3–2) and Swansea (4–2) were beaten at Deepdale. Surprisingly allowed to leave

Deepdale midway through that campaign, he ended his career with Oldham Athletic. However, in the twilight of his career, he proved that he had not lost his goalscoring touch as he scored six goals in the first 30 minutes when playing for the Rest of Cheshire against Port Vale.

BARR, Robert

Inside-right, centre-forward

Born: Kilmarnock, 1865.
Career: Hurlford. Stoke, 1888. Abercorn, 1890. PRESTON NORTH END, 1894. Bury, 1895.

■ Scottish inside-forward Bob Barr played his early football for Stoke but was unable to command a regular place in the Potters' side, so he joined Abercorn. After almost four seasons he returned to Football League action with Preston North End, making his Lilywhites debut on the opening day of the 1894–95 season when he scored in a 3–1 win at Wolverhampton Wanderers. During the early part of that campaign, Barr scored in five successive games and ended it with eight goals in 28 matches as North End finished fourth in Division One. Surprisingly, after playing in the opening game of the following season, he was allowed to join Bury but, midway through the campaign, injuries forced his retirement.

BARRICK, Dean

Left-back

Born: Hemsworth, 30 September 1969.
Career: Sheffield Wednesday, 1988. Rotherham United, 1991. Cambridge United, 1993. PRESTON NORTH END, 1995. Bury, 1998. Ayr United, 1999 (loan). Doncaster Rovers, 2001.

■ Dean Barrick was a left-sided player who featured mainly as an attacking full-back. He began his career with Sheffield Wednesday before a £50,000 move took him to Rotherham United. In a little over two seasons at Millmoor, Barrick played in 118 games before a similar fee saw him join Cambridge United. A key member of the U's defence, it was a complete surprise when he arrived at Deepdale in September 1995 in a straight swap for Paul Raynor. Making his North End

debut in a 2–2 home draw against Scunthorpe United, his ability to make telling crosses in support of the attack was one of the main features of his game as North End went on to win the Third Division Championship. The following season a back injury cost him his place in the side, while in 1997–98 he did not figure as often when the team adopted a wing-back formation. However, he did break his duck for Preston in the early part of the campaign with a long range shot at Chesterfield. He immediately followed this up with the only goal of the match against Blackburn in the second leg of the Coca-Cola Cup-tie. Released during the summer of 1998, he joined Bury and was an automatic choice for the Shakers in the opening three months of the 1998–99 season before he was publicly named as being responsible for the only goal conceded in a 1–0 defeat at Wolves. Barrick was transfer-listed and was allowed to join Ayr United on an extended loan deal. On his return to Gigg Lane, he forced his way back into the Bury side but then suffered a particularly nasty injury against Chesterfield – fracturing his eye socket in two places and breaking his nose. After recovering, he could not force his way into the side on a regular basis and after moving to Doncaster Rovers on loan, he joined the Belle Vue club permanently.

BARRY-MURPHY, Brian

Midfield

Born: Cork, 27 July 1978.
Career: Cork City. PRESTON NORTH

END, 1999. Southend United, 2002 (loan). Hartlepool United, 2002 (loan). Sheffield Wednesday, 2003. Bury, 2004.

■ Brian Barry-Murphy was a strong-running left-sided midfielder who joined North End from Cork City shortly before the start of the 1999–2000 season. He made his Preston North End debut as a substitute at Wrexham in the Worthington Cup but after appearing for the Republic of Ireland at Under-21 level against Yugoslavia and Malta, he was sidelined by a cartilage operation. When fully recovered, he made unwanted history on his full debut. Wrexham were again the opponents in the Auto Windscreens Shield as he became the first player sent off under the experimental '10–yard' rule, having earlier been booked. A second cartilage operation meant that he had to wait until the final game of the season for his first

taste of League action, appearing as a late substitute in the match against Bristol City. Midway through the following season he began to appear regularly from the substitutes' bench, demonstrating a powerful shot and confidence and accuracy when distributing the ball. In 2001–02 he captained North End's title-winning reserve side and was loaned to Southend United to gain more first-team experience, where he scored his first League goal on his final appearance against Leyton Orient. In the early part of the following season, he had a loan spell with Hartlepool United before being recalled to Deepdale after an injury crisis. Soon afterwards he joined Sheffield Wednesday on a free transfer, linking up again with Chris Turner, the former Hartlepool boss, who had just taken charge of the Owls. Though he was a near ever present in his first full season at Hillsborough, he was one of 13 players released in the summer of 2004 and joined Bury, where he had an outstanding first season.

BARTON, John

Outside-right

Born: Preston.
Career: Lytham. PRESTON NORTH END, 1893.

■ Jack Barton was North End's trainer in the late 19th century. At this time, team trainers had to carry out the groundsman's duties and ensure that the team were fit. Barton was extremely popular with the North End crowd and, though his knowledge of first aid left a lot to be desired, he devised a means of restoring players to consciousness after injury that earned him the nickname 'Pinchy'! During the 1893–94 season, injuries stretched the club's playing resources to breaking point and Barton was called up to play on the wing against League Champions-elect Aston Villa, a match North End lost 2–0. He had previously played with Lytham and was a contemporary of Moses Sanders at the Black Knights. Later in the season, Barton was recalled to the side for the visit of Reading in an FA Cup first-round tie. North End won 18–0 and the trainer scored a hat-trick! Retained for the crucial four-pointer against fellow

strugglers Darwen, Barton found their defence a different proposition and though he had a couple of early chances to score, it was not to be. At the end of the season, the North End directors hired a groundsman and let Barton concentrate on his training duties.

BARTON, John Birchall

Goalkeeper

Born: Wigan, 27 April 1942.
Career: PRESTON NORTH END, 1959. Blackburn Rovers, 1966.

■ Very few players have made the impact that 16-year-old goalkeeper John Barton made on his League debut. The youngster was drafted into the North End side at Highbury in the game just before Christmas 1958 against Arsenal. In front of his proud parents, Barton had an outstanding game in a 2–1 win and made the national headlines the next day. Though he continued in place of the injured Fred Else and his deputy Alan Kelly for the games against Blackpool on Christmas Day and Boxing Day, he was not as successful as the Seasiders won 4–2 at Bloomfield Road and 3–0 at Deepdale. Barton did not appear in the North End side again until January 1962 when Preston beat Middlesbrough 4–3. Over the next couple of seasons, he made just a handful of appearances before

winning a regular place in 1964–65 following an injury to Alan Kelly. Following the Republic of Ireland goalkeeper's return to the side, Barton left Deepdale to join Blackburn Rovers, where he made 68 League appearances in a little over five seasons at Ewood Park.

BASHAM, Steven Brian

Striker

Born: Southampton, 2 December 1977.
Career: Southampton, 1996. Wrexham, 1998 (loan). PRESTON NORTH END, 1999. Oxford United 2002.

■ Steven Basham was a regular goalscorer in the Southampton reserve team. However, the form of Egil Ostenstad, David Hirst and Kevin Davies meant that most of his first-team appearances for the south-coast club were from the bench. Loaned out to Wrexham, he then joined North End on a similar basis in February 1999, having been pursued by the Deepdale club for several months. He was an instant hit, scoring twice on his debut in a 2–1 defeat of Wycombe Wanderers and netting 10 in 17 games in his three-month stay at the club. Strong, quick and possessing powerful heading ability, he was extremely popular with the North End fans. Unavailable for the Play-offs, Basham refused Preston's initial approach for the move to become permanent as he needed time to consider

Southampton's new terms during the summer. He eventually opted to leave the Saints and joined North End in a £200,000 deal. A groin injury meant that he was not fully fit for the start of the 1999–2000 season but, although he later turned his ankle, he managed to appear in enough games to win a Second Division Championship medal. After waiting exactly a year for a goal, Basham marked his 50th appearance for North End with the winner against Portsmouth in September 2000. Sadly he then suffered a double fracture of the right leg against Tranmere after netting what again proved to be the deciding goal. Out of first-team action for 10 months, he was brought back into the side earlier than expected but spent much of the campaign on the bench. Basham had scored 16 goals in 78 games when, after rejecting the offer of a new contract, he joined Oxford United, where he was again hampered by injuries before being the club's top scorer with 16 goals in 2003–04. The following season he was tried in midfield but made much more impact when restored to his more familiar role as a striker.

BATEY, John Clarke

Left-half, full-back

Born: Carlisle, 1909.
Career: Carlisle United, 1934. PRESTON NORTH END, 1936. Carlisle United, 1937.

■ Versatile defender John Batey began his Football League career with Carlisle United, his home-town team, but after struggling to win a regular place in the Cumbrian club's side, he left Brunton Park to join Preston North End. Able to play in both full-back positions as well as left-half, he wore the number-two shirt when he made his debut in a 2–1 win at Notts County. His other eight appearances in the Preston side that season were at left-back when he replaced the injured Harry Lowe. He was only on the beaten side once, until his last appearance in a North End shirt saw the side go down 5–2 at home to Manchester City. Released after just one season, he returned to his first club, Carlisle United, but made just a couple of appearances before drifting into non-League football.

BATEY, Robert

Wing-half

Born: Greenhead, 18 October 1912.
Career: South Tyne Rangers. Carlisle United, 1932. PRESTON NORTH END, 1934. Leeds United, 1946. Southport, 1947. Annfield Plain, 1948. Leyland Motors, 1949. Chorley, 1950.

■ After playing his early football for Gateshead South Tyne Rangers, Bob Batey signed amateur forms for Carlisle United in September 1931 and turned professional the following year. After three seasons at Brunton Park, he moved to Preston North End in March 1934 and played his first game in a 2–1 reversal at Sheffield Wednesday. Though he was an industrious wing-half, his first few games for North End were as deputy for the injured Bill Tremelling at the heart of the Preston defence. In his early days at Deepdale, he was unable to oust North End's wing-halves Bill Shankly and Jimmy Milne. When Preston won the FA Cup in 1938, Bob Batey wore the number-six shirt, replacing the unlucky Milne, who had fractured his collarbone against Arsenal the week before the Final. He ended this campaign – in which North End finished third in Division

One – with 14 League appearances. In 1938–39, Bob Batey was a virtual ever present and played in the first three games of the aborted 1939–40 season, though he still did not manage to get on the score sheet. He 'guested' for Leeds United in wartime games and joined them full time in April 1946. Making his debut for the Yorkshire club against North End at Deepdale, he was on the losing side as Preston won 3–2. A free transfer took him to Southport in June 1947 and in the following close season he

was appointed player-coach of North Eastern League side Annfield Plain. After a spell playing for Leyland Motors, he ended his involvement with the game as player-coach of Chorley.

BAXTER, James Cunningham

Inside-forward

Born: Dunfermline, 8 November 1925.
Career: Dunfermline Athletic. Barnsley, 1945. PRESTON NORTH END, 1952. Barnsley, 1959.

■ A talented inside-forward, Jimmy Baxter joined Barnsley from Dunfermline Athletic for £3,000 in 1945 and went on to make 222 League appearances for the Tykes, scoring 54 goals. When North End needing a replacement for Bobby Beattie, who was on the verge of retiring from the game, they turned to Baxter and he signed for the Deepdale club in the summer of 1952. He made his debut in a 1–0 home win over Spurs in October 1952 and went on to score seven goals in 33 games as North End ended the season as runners-up to Arsenal in the First Division. Baxter's style of football suited North End and he quickly forged a tremendous attacking partnership with Tom Finney and Charlie Wayman. He was an ever present in 1953–54 and scored 20 League and Cup goals, including a hat-trick in a 6–0 home defeat of Sheffield Wednesday. He was a member of the Preston side that lost 3–2 to West Bromwich Albion in the 1954 FA Cup Final. He had another excellent season in 1954–55, ending the campaign as the club's leading scorer with 17 goals. He was then switched into a deeper midfield role following the emergence of Thompson and Finney as a strike force, but he showed only glimpses of his earlier play. After scoring 71 goals in 267 League and Cup games, he was allowed to rejoin his former club Barnsley in the summer of 1959, where he took his tally of League goals to 57 in 248 games. Jimmy Baxter was the cousin of Preston legend Willie Cunningham.

BAXTER, Michael John

Centre-half

Born: Birmingham, 30 December 1956.
Died: 1989.
Career: PRESTON NORTH END, 1974. Middlesbrough, 1981. Portsmouth, 1984.

■ Mick Baxter joined the staff of Preston North End shortly after his older brother Stuart, also a central defender, had made his debut for the Deepdale club. After signing professional forms on his 18th birthday, he made his League debut against Grimsby Town in April 1975 and, early the following season, he replaced his brother as the club's regular centre-half. A powerful central defender, he also liked joining the attack. He netted the first of 17 goals for the club during the 1975–76 season in a 4–3 defeat against Hereford United. Mick Baxter eventually made 227 League and Cup appearances for North End, with the club's Third Division promotion-winning campaign of 1977–78 probably being his best season. In the summer of

1981, Baxter joined Middlesbrough for a fee of £350,000 but was unable to prevent the Teesside club's relegation from the First Division. He missed very few games in his three seasons with the club before opting for a move to Portsmouth. Unfortunately he never played for Pompey due to an illness that ended his playing career. He returned to Deepdale as the club's Community Development Officer but sadly died in 1989, aged just 32.

BAXTER, Stuart William

Centre-half

Born: Wolverhampton, 16 August 1953.
Career: PRESTON NORTH END, 1971. Dundee, 1975. Stockport County, 1976.

■ Central-defender Stuart Baxter worked his way up through the ranks at Deepdale before being given his first-team debut as a substitute for Davie Wilson in a 2–1 defeat at Bristol City in April 1973. He kept his place in the side for the remaining two games of a season which saw North End just avoid relegation to the Third Division. Under new manager Bobby Charlton, Baxter found himself sharing the central defensive duties with Sadler and Hawkins and, though the campaign was a disappointing one with Preston losing their Second Division status, Baxter did net his first goal for the club in a 2–1 home win over Portsmouth. Injuries hampered his progress in 1974–75 and it was only towards the end of the season that he returned to first-team action. Though he started the following season as the club's first-choice centre-half, he soon lost his place and opted for a move to Dundee. His stay at Dens Park was brief and he returned to the Football League to see out his first-class career with Stockport County.

BEATTIE, Andrew

Full-back

Born: Aberdeen, 11 August 1913.
Career: Inverurie Loco. PRESTON NORTH END, 1935.

■ Andy Beattie enjoyed a rapid rise to fame as a cultured full-back with Preston North End – his only professional club – whom he joined from his local junior

outfit, Inverurie Loco Works, for £150 in March 1935. Wearing the number-one shirt, he made his North End debut in a goalless draw at West Bromwich Albion on the final day of the 1934–35 season. After failing to make a first-team appearance the following season, he appeared on a regular basis in 1936–37 and played in the 3–1 FA Cup Final defeat by Sunderland. Beattie, who missed just one game in 1937–38, won an FA Cup-winners' medal as a George Mutch penalty helped North End to a 1–0 win over Huddersfield Town. By this time he had become the club's regular penalty-taker but on 11 March 1939 he scored his first goal from open play in a 4–1 home win over Derby County. The war ended a flourishing international career which had seen him represent Scotland on seven occasions, although he was awarded a further five unofficial caps in wartime internationals. Despite spending some of his military service abroad, he was able to help North End to the North Regional League title in 1941,

as well as victory in the Wartime League Cup Final against Arsenal – only seven days after helping the Gunners to a London Cup 'B' success against Millwall. He 'guested' for more than half a dozen clubs and in July 1942 he received the £650 maximum benefit for his service at Deepdale. Though he returned to the League side for the 1946–47 season, he left shortly afterwards on a nomadic management career when he accepted the secretary-manager's job at Barrow. He moved to Stockport County in a similar capacity before taking over the reins at Huddersfield Town. Although he arrived too late to stave off relegation, he helped the Terriers win promotion to the top flight at the first attempt. On parting company with the Yorkshire club, he became sub-postmaster in Penwortham, but football was in his blood and he later managed Carlisle United, Nottingham Forest, Plymouth Argyle and Wolverhampton Wanderers. This was followed by becoming general manager of Notts County and John Harris' assistant at Sheffield United before scouting for both Walsall and Liverpool. Beattie was also Scotland's first manager but it proved to be something of a fiasco, for he resigned midway through the 1954 World Cup tournament, although in March 1959 he was back in charge of the national side, albeit briefly.

BEATTIE, Robert

Inside-forward

Born: Stevenston, 24 January 1916.
Career: Kilmarnock. PRESTON NORTH END, 1937. Wigan Athletic.

■ A ball-juggling inside-forward with a football brain, Bobby Beattie began his career with Kilmarnock before joining North End in October 1937 for a fee of £2,250. When he made his Preston debut in a 2–1 win over Stoke that month, he was one of nine Scottish-born players in the North End side. A superb passer of the ball, he set up numerous scoring chances for his striking partners, yet he could also score his fair share of goals. At the end of his first season at Deepdale he scored 11 goals in 37 games. He also found himself playing in the FA Cup Final at Wembley and came home with a winners' medal as North End beat

Huddersfield Town 1–0. In September 1938, freak weather hit the capital as North End played Arsenal in the Charity Shield at Highbury. Ted Drake scored twice in the opening five minutes before Bobby Beattie pulled a goal back. In the dying moments, the Scot hit the bar with the Arsenal goalkeeper beaten. One of four ever-presents in the North End side in 1938–39, his consistency led to him winning full international honours for Scotland in a 3–2 defeat of Wales. During the war years, Beattie was a member of the North End side that won the Football League War Cup. After drawing 1–1 with Arsenal at Wembley, the replay was held at Ewood Park three weeks later. Bobby Beattie put North End ahead but, with just a few minutes remaining, Frank Gallimore put through his own goal to gift the Gunners an equaliser. However, North End snatched the winner within 30 seconds when Beattie scored again. When League football resumed in 1946–47, Beattie was one of four players in the starting line up for the first game against Leeds United that had played for the club before the war. He continued to

be a regular for the next seven seasons. In September 1948, he netted his first Football League hat-trick in a 6–1 rout of Middlesbrough. He played his last game for the club against local rivals Blackpool in November 1953 before joining Wigan Athletic. His stay at Springfield Park was brief though and he returned to live in his native Scotland.

BEAUMONT, Sidney

Outside-left, right-half

Born: Wrestlingworth, 8 October 1884.
Career: Colchester Town. Lincoln City, 1904. Watford, 1907. PRESTON NORTH END, 1911. Merthyr Town. Troedyrhiw.

■ After spells with Colchester and Lincoln City, where he turned professional, Sid Beaumont played in Chelsea's pre-season matches in 1907, shortly after applying unsuccessfully for reinstatement as an amateur. He then signed for Watford and scored twice on his debut in the Southern Charity Cup. However, he found himself in and out of the side for the next two seasons as a wing-half or forward and in July 1911 he moved to Preston. His only appearance for North End came in January 1912 when he wore the number-four shirt in a 1–0 defeat at Oldham Athletic. After brief spells with a couple of Welsh clubs he spent eight years as manager of Barry before taking charge of Llanelli and Aberdare Athletic. In June 1927, Beaumont was appointed manager of Blackpool but his reign was brief. The following spring, with the Seasiders languishing in the bottom three of the First Division, he parted company with the club. He became assistant-trainer at Chester, a post he held until his death in 1939.

BEAVER, John

Outside-left, right-half

Born: Preston.
Career: PRESTON NORTH END, 1900. Wellingborough.

■ Able to play in a variety of positions, John Beaver made his Preston debut as a replacement for the injured George Smith in a 2–1 defeat at Bury during the club's relegation season of 1900–01. The following season he filled in at right-half following an injury to Rabbi Howell before playing all his games from outside-left in 1902–03. Despite scoring in a 5–0 rout of Doncaster Rovers and netting the only goal of the game against Manchester United at Old Trafford, Beaver was released at the end of the season and moved into non-League football with Wellingborough.

BECKFORD, Darren Richard Lorenzo

Forward

Born: Manchester, 12 May 1967.
Career: Manchester City, 1984. Bury, 1985 (loan). Port Vale, 1987. Norwich City, 1991. Oldham Athletic, 1993. Heart of Midlothian, 1996. PRESTON NORTH END, 1997. Fulham, 1997. Walsall, 1997.

■ An England Schoolboy and Youth international, Darren Beckford started his career with Manchester City, making his League debut against Middlesbrough in 1984. After almost seven years at Maine Road in which first-team opportunities were limited, Beckford joined Port Vale for a fee of £15,000 in the summer of 1987. He had loan spells with Bury and the Valiants before his

move was made permanent. He became the club's top goalscorer for the next four seasons. A hat-trick against North End in the 1988–89 Play-off semi-finals featured in his total of 84 goals in 214 games. In the summer of 1991, Beckford joined Norwich City for a then club record fee of £925,000, but for much of his time at Carrow Road he struggled with injuries and loss of form. In March 1993 he signed for Oldham Athletic but again suffered with injuries. Although the Latics offered him a new contract, he turned it down and joined Scottish Premier League club, Hearts. Unable to settle in Scotland, he joined North End on loan. Appearing in just three games, the first as substitute for Gary Bennett, he later appeared for Fulham and Walsall.

BECKHAM, David Robert

Midfield

Born: Leytonstone, 2 May 1975.
Career: Manchester United, 1993. PRESTON NORTH END, 1995 (loan). Real Madrid, 2003.

■ Though England captain David Beckham made just five appearances while on loan in the Deepdale first team, his great enthusiasm endeared himself to the North End faithful. A member of the famed Manchester United class of 1992, Beckham made his Preston debut at home to Doncaster Rovers and scored North End's second goal in a 2–2 draw direct from a corner. He also found the net in Preston's 3–2 home defeat of Fulham, helping the club reach that season's Play-offs. On his return to Old Trafford, his first full season in the United side brought him both Championship and FA Cup-winners' medals. The following season he scored the goal of the campaign in a match against Wimbledon when he chipped the goalkeeper from the halfway line. Promoted to the full England side, he went from strength to strength, especially as a regular scorer of outstanding goals, and ended the season as the PFA's Young Player of the Year. Though every aspect of his life began to dominate the headlines – notably his engagement to Victoria Adams (Posh Spice) – his form continued to earn rave

notices. Thought by many to be a player who would grace the World Cup stage in France in 1998, he was sent off against Argentina, effectively limiting England's chances of victory. He returned to England a marked man. However, he demonstrated that he had the necessary character to rise above adversity: he was ever present as United lifted the Premier League title, FA Cup and European Cup. However, after his marriage to Victoria Adams, the back pages of the newspapers continued to portray him as either hero or villain. Taking the runner-up spot behind Rivaldo in the 2000 European Footballer of the Year, Beckham continued to juggle his showbusiness lifestyle and career as a professional footballer with great dexterity. His performances as England skipper were high class and he was instrumental in the country qualifying for the Euro 2004 finals, where unfortunately he missed penalties against France and in the shoot-out against Portugal. Awarded an OBE in the 2003 Queen's Birthday Honours List, he signed for Real Madrid that summer. David Beckham is without doubt one of the most outstanding English footballers of his generation.

BECTON, Francis

Inside-left, centre-forward

Born: Preston 1873.
Died: 1909
Career: Fishwick Ramblers. PRESTON NORTH END, 1891. Liverpool, 1894. Sheffield United, 1898. Bedminster. PRESTON NORTH END, 1900. Swindon Town. Nelson. Ashton Town. New Brighton Tower.

■ Frank Becton made his North End debut in a 2–1 win at West Bromwich Albion in November 1891 and ended the following season as the club's leading scorer with 25 League and Cup goals. This total included four against Notts County and hat-tricks in the wins over Burton Swifts (9–2), Middlesbrough Ironopolis (7–0) and Wolverhampton Wanderers (4–0). Though not as prolific the following season, he netted another four goals in the 18–0 defeat of Reading in a first-round FA Cup tie and a treble in January 1895 in a 5–4 win at West Bromwich Albion. His performances for North End led to him winning full international honours for England, when he scored twice in a 9–0 victory over Ireland. Shortly after making his international debut he demanded a large increase in his basic wage. The Preston directors were staggered, but Becton told them that Bolton Wanderers were fully prepared to meet his demands, while Aston Villa and Manchester City were also willing to pay a transfer fee of £250. In the end he was sold to Liverpool for £100. He helped the Reds to win the 1895–96 Second Division Championship, scoring 17 goals in 24 games and continued to find the net on a regular basis before moving to Sheffield United in 1898. He returned to Deepdale for the 1900–01 season but could not prevent the club's relegation from the top flight. In his two spells for North End he scored 63 goals in 129 games. He later played for Swindon Town and New Brighton Tower. Sadly, ill health caught up with him and in 1909 he died of tuberculosis.

BECTON, Martin

Outside-right

Born: Preston, 1883.
Died: Fulwood, 18 April 1965.
Career: Lytham. PRESTON NORTH END, 1906. Nelson, 1908. Watford, 1909.

■ Right-winger Martin Becton, the younger brother of Frank Becton, began his career with Lytham, whom he helped win the Lancashire Amateur Cup. He joined Preston North End in the summer of 1906 but had to wait until New Year's Day 1907 before he made his first-team debut in a 1–1 draw at Blackburn Rovers. Four days later, on his home debut, he scored North End's goal in another 1–1 draw against Everton. However, he was unable to hold down a regular first-team place and, after a season playing for Nelson, moved south to end his career with Watford. Martin Becton was married to England international Dickie Bond's sister.

BECTON, Thomas

Inside-left, outside-left

Born: Preston 1878.
Career: PRESTON NORTH END, 1897. New Brighton Tower, 1898. Sunderland, 1899. Kettering. Bristol Rovers. Kettering. Oswaldtwistle Rovers. Colne. Rossendale United.

■ Predominantly left-footed, Tommy Becton began his career with North End, playing the first of just four League games in a 1–0 defeat at Bolton Wanderers in September 1897. Unable to oust Lawrence Halsall from the number-11 shirt, he moved on to New Brighton Tower, where he spent the 1898–99 season before joining Sunderland. He was a regular in the Wearsiders' team for the first half of the following campaign, netting a goal every other game in his 14 appearances. On leaving Roker Park, he played for Kettering and Bristol Rovers before returning to the North West where he played for a number of non-League teams including Oswaldtwistle Rovers, Colne and Rossendale United.

BEESLEY, Mark Anthony

Forward

Born: Ormskirk, 5 December 1980.
Career: PRESTON NORTH END, 1999. Chester City, 2000.

■ Mark Beesley formed an effective strike force with Mark Wright in North End's reserves and youth sides. His first involvement with the club's first team came when he sat on the bench twice in

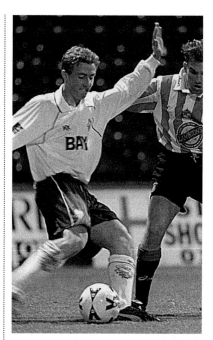

September 1999. He eventually made his North End debut as a late substitute against Hartlepool United in the Auto Windscreens Shield. Beesley's Football League debut came later that season when he was again introduced as a late substitute for Jon Macken in a 4–0 win at Oxford United. Though there were hopes he and Mark Wright would form a successful first-team partnership, it was not to be as Beesley was released during the close season, joining Chester City.

BELL, Graham Thomas

Midfield

Born: Middleton, 30 March 1955.
Career: Chadderton. Oldham Athletic, 1973. PRESTON NORTH END, 1979. Huddersfield Town, 1981 (loan). Carlisle United, 1983. Bolton Wanderers, 1984. Tranmere Rovers, 1986. Hyde United. Mossley.

■ Midfielder Graham Bell began his League career with Oldham Athletic, having been born in Middleton just down the road. Oldham had spotted him playing for Chadderton. While at Boundary Park he won England Youth honours. The then England boss, Don Revie, was so impressed by his midfield artistry that he put him on standby for the full national squad. Bell went on to make 170 League appearances for Oldham before joining North End for a fee of £80,000 in March 1979. Bell made his Preston debut in a 1–0 win at rivals Blackburn Rovers and quickly settled into the North End side. Though he contributed a great deal to the North End cause, he could not prevent their relegation to the Third Division at the end of the 1980–81 season. He spent another couple of seasons with the club until a brief loan spell with Huddersfield Town was following by him joining Carlisle United on a free transfer. He failed to settle in Cumbria and was soon on his way to Bolton Wanderers. The midfield general of a young side, his last game for the Trotters was probably his most memorable, when he appeared as a substitute in the 1986 Freight Rover Trophy Final against Bristol City at Wembley. He joined Tranmere Rovers before drifting into non-League football, first with Hyde United and then as player-manager of Mossley.

BELL, John

Outside-right, inside-right

Born: Dumbarton, 6 October 1869.
Career: Dumbarton Union. Dumbarton. Everton, 1892. Glasgow Celtic, 1898. New Brighton Tower, 1900. Everton, 1901. PRESTON NORTH END, 1903.

■ The sight of John Bell wriggling his way down the right flank was a familiar one around the turn of the century. He was a masterful dribbler who often played as though he had the ball glued to the inside of his right foot. Bell began his career with Dumbarton and was a member of their Scottish League Championship-winning side of 1891–92. The Scottish international left shortly afterwards to continue his career with Everton. Regarded as one of the most inventive forwards of his day, Bell was undoubtedly a footballing craftsman who spent the best part of a decade thrilling the crowds at Goodison Park. He played in the 1897 FA Cup Final and, although Everton were beaten 3–2 by Aston Villa, it was Bell who won the plaudits. On leaving Everton, he served Glasgow Celtic before returning to Goodison via New Brighton Tower. Bell had scored 70 goals in 199 League and Cup games when he left Everton a second time to sign for Preston North

End. Making his debut in a 5–1 win at Stockport County on the opening day of the 1903–04 season, Bell went on to score 10 goals in 32 games as North End won the Second Division Championship. After injuries disrupted his progress the following season, he was back to his best in 1905–06, helping the Lilywhites finish runners-up in the First Division, four points behind Champions Liverpool. In one First Division game that season, he was alleged to have saved the life of a fellow player when he repositioned his dislocated neck with one firm wrench of his massive hands! He became chairman at the first attempt at a Players' Union and was later North End's coach before leaving to take up a similar position in Canada.

BELL, John G.

Inside-left

Born: Hamilton.
Career: Beith. Queen of the South. PRESTON NORTH END, 1933. Queen of the South.

■ Another Scot, inside-left John Bell had played for both Beith and Queen of the South before he arrived at Deepdale.

in December 1933. He made a goalscoring debut in a Boxing Day 3–2 win at home to Brentford and early in the New Year he netted against Grimsby Town. However, shortly after putting the ball in the net, he broke his collarbone and the Mariners scored twice to inflict North End's first home defeat of the season. Though North End ended the season as runners-up to Grimsby and returned to the top flight, Bell continued to suffer from injuries. In 1934–35 he had to have a cartilage operation on his left knee. At the end of that season, he returned home to Scotland and rejoined Queen of the South.

BENNETT, Gary Michael

Forward

Born: Liverpool, 20 September 1963.
Career: Kirkby Town. Wigan Athletic, 1984. Chester City, 1985. Southend United, 1988. Chester City, 1990. Wrexham, 1992. Tranmere Rovers, 1995. PRESTON NORTH END, 1996. Wrexham, 1997. Chester City, 1997.

■ Gary Bennett, or 'Psycho' as he was affectionately known at all his clubs, joined Wigan Athletic from Kirkby Town in October 1984. Although he could not win a regular first-team place, he was a member of the Latics side that beat Brentford 3–1 at Wembley in the Final of the Freight Rover Trophy in 1985. At the end of that season, he joined Chester City and scored 47 goals in 155 games for the Sealand Road club before joining Southend United. He did not really settle at Roots Hall and rejoined Chester after just over a year. After taking his tally of goals to 66 in 253 appearances he joined Wrexham, where he topped the divisional scoring charts with 39 goals in his second season with the Robins. He was even more prolific the following campaign with 47 goals and this prompted Tranmere Rovers to pay £300,000 to take him to Prenton Park. Despite averaging a goal every three games, it did not really work out for him on the Wirral and a £200,000 switch took him to Preston. As the Deepdale club's record signing, his deadly finishing and creative play were soon in evidence when he scored on his debut in a 2–1 win at Scarborough. North End won the Third

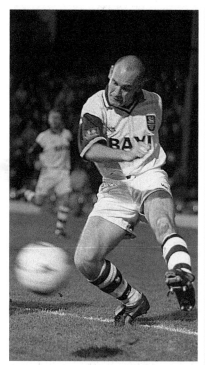

Wanderers as part of an economy drive after Bolton were relegated to the Third Division at the end of the 1982–83 season. He played six times in Wolves' struggling First Division side before joining Cambridge United in January 1984. They too were fighting a relegation battle and he was in the side that fell from the Second Division to the Fourth Division re-election zone in successive seasons. In April 1986, his contract was cancelled and he returned to the North West with Preston North End. Bennett

Division championship but a shin fracture in the pre-season friendlies kept Bennett out of the Second Division action until October. However, it was clear that he was not fully fit and, though he came off the bench to score twice in the 3–0 home win over Blackpool, he was transferred to his former club Wrexham in February 1997. He took his tally of goals for the Welsh club to 103 in 170 games before joining Chester for a third time. Though injuries hampered his performances, he took his total of goals for the Cestrians to 78 before hanging up his boots.

BENNETT, Michael

Left-back

Born: Bolton, 24 December 1962.
Career: Bolton Wanderers, 1980. Wolverhampton Wanderers, 1983. Cambridge United, 1984. PRESTON NORTH END, 1986. Carlisle United, 1990.

■ Michael Bennett was a product of the Bolton Wanderers youth policy and gained recognition while he was in the club's youth team, captaining the England Youth side and forcing his way into the Trotters' first team when only 17. He appeared in 73 games for the Burnden Park club but left the

made his debut in a 1–1 draw at Lincoln City and went on to play in 42 games as North End won promotion to the Third Division as runners-up to Northampton Town. His only goal for the club came in a 2–1 win at fellow promotion contenders Southend United. Though he was a regular in the North End side in 1987–88, he did not appear at all the following season due to a broken leg. At the end of the 1989–90 campaign he moved on to Carlisle United where he ended his first-class career.

BERESFORD, David

Outside-right

Born: Middleton, 11 November 1978.
Career: Oldham Athletic, 1994. Swansea City, 1995 (loan). Huddersfield Town,

1997. PRESTON NORTH END, 1999 (loan). Port Vale, 2000 (loan). Hull City, 2001. Plymouth Argyle, 2002. Macclesfield, 2003 (loan). Tranmere Rovers, 2003.

■ David Beresford came through the FA School of Excellence to make his Football League debut for Oldham Athletic. Known affectionately as 'the Flying Midget', he spent a brief loan spell with Swansea before resuming his career at Boundary Park. Described by Graham Taylor, the former England manager, as faster than a cruise missile, he went on to appear in 74 games for Oldham before Huddersfield Town paid £350,000 for his services in March 1997. Always looking to create chances for others with his excellent crossing ability, his first season with the Terriers was disrupted by a spate of injuries, including the need for a hernia operation. However, on his return to full fitness, his lightning pace caused problems for most opposition defenders. In December 1999 he was surprisingly allowed to join Preston North End on loan. Signed as cover for Lee Cartwright, he made his debut against Blackpool but unfortunately had to be substituted at half-time because of a hamstring injury. He made only one more start for

Preston, although he was also used as an occasional substitute, before he returned to the McAlpine Stadium without having had much chance to impress. The following season saw him join Port Vale on loan but in the four games in which he appeared, all were lost and he returned to Huddersfield. In the summer of 2001 he joined Hull City on a free transfer and went on to play a key part in the Tigers' revolution prior to a move to Plymouth Argyle. Another loan spell with Macclesfield was followed by a return to the North West when he later signed for Tranmere Rovers.

BERESFORD, Frank E.

Inside-forward

Born: Chesterfield, 8 October 1910.
Career: Ouston Park. Doncaster Rovers, 1931. PRESTON NORTH END, 1933. Luton Town, 1935. Crystal Palace, 1936. Carlisle United, 1937. Bradford City, 1939.

■ Inside-forward Frank Beresford played his early football for Doncaster Rovers. His impressive performances for the Belle Vue club prompted North End's committee to secure his services. Signed to strengthen the club's push for promotion to the First Division, he made his debut in a 3–2 home win over Manchester United and held his place in

the side for the final 14 games of the campaign. It was a season in which North End finished runners-up to Grimsby Town and won promotion to the top flight. North End's first game back in the First Division saw them entertain Grimsby, but the team that pipped them to the Second Division title were beaten 1–0. After a promising start, with four wins in their first five matches, North End fell away. After losing his place, Beresford moved on to Luton Town. He later had a brief spell with Crystal Palace before joining Carlisle United. He had a successful time with the Cumbrian club before bringing his career to an end with a single appearance for Bradford City prior to the outbreak of World War Two.

BERESFORD, Joseph

Inside-right

Born: Chesterfield, 26 February 1906.
Career: Mexborough. Mansfield Town. Aston Villa, 1927. PRESTON NORTH END, 1935. Swansea Town, 1937. Stourbridge.

■ England international Joe Beresford joined Aston Villa from Mansfield Town in 1927 and was one of the most popular players ever to pull on a Villans shirt. Playing at inside-forward or centre-forward, the stocky Beresford possessed a powerful shot. He netted a hat-trick in a 7–2 defeat of Portsmouth in only his second game for the club. When Villa scored a record-breaking 128 goals in 1930–31, Beresford scored 14 of them, including another treble, this time against Leicester City. His form during the early 1930s was such that he won an England cap against Czechoslovakia in 1934 yet when Jimmy McMullan, Villa's first-ever manager, arrived Beresford was allowed to leave after scoring 73 goals in 251 games. Beresford joined Preston North End and he profited from a new lease of life. Never was £1,750 better spent on a short-term basis for the Deepdale club needed an old head in attack. Making his debut in a 2–2 home draw against Everton, Beresford missed very few games. Although his scoring touch had vanished with the passing of the years, he did find the net against runaway League Champions Sunderland.

The following season he netted twice in the 5–2 defeat of high-flying Derby County and he appeared for North End in the 1937 FA Cup Final, which Sunderland won 3–1. In December that year, Beresford left Deepdale to play Second Division football for Swansea and he later enjoyed a spell in non-League football with Stourbridge.

BERRY, George Frederick

Centre-half

Born: Rostrup, West Germany, 19 November 1957.
Career: Wolverhampton Wanderers, 1975. Stoke City, 1982. Doncaster Rovers, 1984 (loan). Peterborough United, 1990. PRESTON NORTH END, 1991.

■ Despite being born in Rostrup in Germany, George Berry went on to play for Wales at full international level, winning five caps between May 1979 and February 1983. He made his Football League debut for Wolves in a vital promotion clash against Chelsea at Molineux in May 1977, though it was 1978–79 before he established himself as a first-team regular. Over the next four seasons he went on to take his total of

League and Cup games to 160, including an appearance in the 1980 League Cup Final when Wolves beat Nottingham Forest 1–0. In the summer of 1982, Berry joined Stoke City and had been made captain within a short period of time. He stayed at the Victoria Ground for eight seasons and, despite loan spells at Doncaster Rovers and a brief sojourn into Portuguese football, Berry amassed a total of 269 first-team appearances for the Potters. He then joined Peterborough United and, in his only season, captained the club to promotion from the Fourth Division. This was followed by a move to North End, where he made his debut on the opening day of the 1991–92 season – a 1–0 defeat at his former club Peterborough. He appeared in five first-team games before leaving the club as his legs could not stand the pressure of playing home games on plastic!

BEST, Harry O.

Centre-forward

Born: Poolstock, Wigan.
Career: PRESTON NORTH END, 1910.

■ After impressing in local football, centre-forward Harry Best was given a chance to make a name for himself in the Football League with Preston North End. Replacing the prolific David McLean, who had joined Sheffield Wednesday, he made his debut in a 1–1 home draw against Oldham Athletic in February 1911. Best played in four games that season, including a 5–0 defeat at eventual League Champions Manchester United, but at the end of the campaign he returned to the non-League scene.

BIGGS, Alfred George

Centre-forward

Born: Bristol, 8 February 1936.
Career: Bristol Rovers, 1953. PRESTON NORTH END, 1961. Bristol Rovers, 1962. Walsall, 1968. Swansea City, 1968.

■ Only lack of ambition kept Alfie Biggs from playing for England – and that is not just the blue-and-white-tinted view of Bristol Rovers fans, for whom Biggs scored 197 goals in 463 games in his two spells with the club. Jimmy Milne, the Preston boss who took him to Deepdale and then sent him back to

Eastville after 15 months because he was pining for the West Country, described Biggs as the best player he ever bought. Biggs almost started his career with Bristol City but, when he went to sign, he was kept waiting and took a bus to Eastville. He went on to forge lethal partnerships, first with Geoff Bradford and then Ian Hamilton, netting a Rovers record of 37 goals in 1963–64. Prior to that, he had spent a little over a season playing for North End, topping the club's scoring charts in 1961–62 with 22 goals. On his debut, Biggs had two goals disallowed while, at the other end, future North End forward Alec Ashworth scored twice in the Hatters' 4–1 win. Biggs' tally of 22 goals included hat-tricks in the 4–1 defeat of Scunthorpe United and the 3–1 victory over Brighton. When he left Rovers for a second time, Biggs had brief spells with Walsall and Swansea Town.

BIRCH, Paul

Midfield

Born: West Bromwich, 20 November 1962.
Career: Aston Villa, 1980. Wolverhampton Wanderers, 1991. PRESTON NORTH END, 1996 (loan). Doncaster Rovers, 1996. Exeter City, 1997. Halesowen Town.

■ Paul Birch was a member of the Aston Villa FA Youth Cup-winning side

of 1980 and made his League debut in a 1–0 home win over Sunderland in August 1983. Over the next eight seasons, the popular midfielder went on to score 24 goals in 212 League and Cup appearances. He was transferred to Wolverhampton Wanderers for £400,000 in February 1991. Although he seemed to spend much of his time at Molineux on the treatment able, he had appeared in 166 games prior to joining North End on loan in March 1996. At Deepdale, he was used as cover for the injured Lee Cartwright and slotted in well in midfield. Widely experienced, his busy, bustling style helped put North End back on course for the Third Division Championship after they were faltering in the New Year. The second of his two strikes for Preston was the only goal of the game against Doncaster Rovers and gave the Deepdale club three precious points. In fact, the Belle Vue club were Paul Birch's next destination but after just less than a season with the Yorkshire club he signed for Exeter City on transfer deadline day in March 1997. Though he entertained the idea of going into

management when his League days were over, he left the Grecians to play non-League football for Halesowen Town.

BIRD, John Charles

Centre-half

Born: Doncaster, 9 June 1948.
Career: Doncaster United. Doncaster Rovers. PRESTON NORTH END, 1971. Newcastle United, 1975. Hartlepool United, 1980.

■ Central defender John Bird began his League career with his local club Doncaster Rovers and in 1968–69 he helped the Belle Vue side win the Fourth Division Championship. He was transferred to Preston North End in March 1971 and appeared in seven games towards the end of the 1970–71 season as North End won the Third Division title. The following season, Bird was the club's only ever present as they struggled to avoid immediate relegation from Division Two. Bird missed very few games over the next couple of seasons but was unable to prevent the club's relegation in 1973–74. An ever present

during the club's Third Division campaign in 1974–75, he had appeared in 187 games for North End when he joined Newcastle United in September 1975, with Alex Bruce plus £60,000 returning to Deepdale. The move was shrouded in controversy for North End officials sold their star player and captain against the wishes of manager Bobby Charlton. The famous ex-England player resigned in protest but Bird arrived at St James' Park nevertheless. Though he found the transition from the lower Divisions to the top flight a handful at first, he quickly came to grips with the Magpies' defence. After Bird eventually lost his place to Stuart Boam, he moved on to Hartlepool United. On hanging up his boots, he remained at the Victoria Ground as coach before being appointed manager. Unable to lift the club to challenge for promotion, he left to manage York City but he had little success at Bootham Crescent and returned to Doncaster Rovers as coach.

BISHOP, Charles Darren

Defender

Born: Nottingham, 16 February 1968.
Career: Watford, 1986. Bury, 1987. Barnsley, 1991. PRESTON NORTH END, 1996 (loan). Burnley, 1996 (loan). Wigan Athletic, 1996. Northampton Town, 1997. Ilkeston Town.

■ After an apprenticeship at Stoke and a year at Watford without a League appearance, Charlie Bishop joined Third Division Bury in the summer of 1987. He helped the Shakers to the Play-offs in 1989–90, where Tranmere Rovers beat them, but after another season at Gigg Lane he was transferred to Barnsley for £50,000. Though he was a regular for most of his time at Oakwell, he did have a loan spell with Preston midway through their Third Division Championship-winning season of 1995–96. North End won three and drew one of Bishop's four games but when his loan expired he returned to Barnsley before joining Burnley on loan. Adrian Heath wanted to make the move a permanent one but Wigan Athletic quickly stepped in, paying £20,000 for his services. In only his second game – a League Cup-tie against North End –

Bishop snapped ankle ligaments but he returned to help the Latics win the Third Division Championship. He later played for Northampton Town before leaving to play non-League football for Ilkeston Town and helping to run his family business.

BLACKLEY, John Henderson

Central defender

Born: Polmont, 12 May 1948.
Career: Hibernian. Newcastle United, 1977. PRESTON NORTH END, 1979. Hibernian. Hamilton Academicals.

■ Scottish international John Blackley, who represented his country in the 1974 World Cup Finals, was a member of the Hibernian side that won the Scottish League Cup in 1972, beating Celtic 2–1. He was also on the losing side in the League Cup Finals of 1969 and 1974 as well as the 1972 Scottish Cup Final. Blackley was well known for his superstitious insistence on being the last to appear on the pitch and kicking the ball into the Hibernian net before kick-off. When he joined Newcastle United in October 1977 for a fee of £100,000 he was nearing the end of his career, but he still displayed his almost casual, arrogant approach to the game. Although he was voted Player of the Year, he was unable to halt the Magpies' slide into Division Two. On leaving St James' Park, Blackley

joined Preston North End and, though his experience initially proved invaluable at the heart of the Deepdale club's defence, most of his two-and-a-half seasons were spent on the treatment table. He later rejoined Hibernian, eventually making 276 appearances in his two spells, before becoming player-manager of Hamilton Academicals. He later managed his beloved Hibernian, and Cowdenbeath, before coaching both Dundee and Dundee United.

BLEASDALE, David George

Midfield

Born: St Helens, 23 March 1965.
Career: Liverpool. PRESTON NORTH END, 1983.

■ Midfielder David Bleasdale was an amateur with Liverpool prior to signing for Preston North End in the summer of 1983. After making his debut in a 3–3 home draw against Brentford, he helped to make both Steve Elliott's goals in a 4–1 defeat of Southend United. Bleasdale, who appeared in four League games, also appeared in a goalless League Cup-tie against Tranmere and a 3–0 win over Rochdale in the Associate Members Cup, thus never played on a losing North End side.

BLESSINGTON, James

Inside-right

Born: Linlithgow, 28 February 1874.
Career: Leith Hibernian, 1888. Hibernian, 1889. Leith Athletic, 1891. Glasgow Celtic, 1892. PRESTON NORTH END, 1897. Derby County, 1899. Bristol City, 1899. Luton Town, 1900. Leicester Fosse, 1903.

■ James Blessington had been a member of three Celtic Championship-winning teams, picked up two Scottish Cup runners'-up medals and earned four full Scottish caps and five selections for the Scottish League side before he crossed the border to sign on at Deepdale. After playing in five games towards the end of the 1897–98 season, he netted his only goal for the club during the early part of the following campaign in a 2–2 draw at Nottingham Forest. On leaving North End, he had a brief spell with Derby County before lighting up the forward line of his two Southern League clubs, Bristol City and Luton Town. He later joined Leicester Fosse and became that club's first-ever team manager. In 1911 he became trainer to Cliftonville and two years later was appointed coach to Belfast Celtic. He was about to take up a coaching appointment in Germany but war broke out and he joined the Merchant Navy. After a spell managing Abertillery he became a licensee in Guernsey and the West Country.

BLYTH, James Anton

Goalkeeper

Born: Perth, 2 February 1955.
Career: PRESTON NORTH END, 1972. Coventry City, 1972. Hereford United, 1975 (loan). Birmingham City, 1982. Nuneaton Borough.

■ Due to the form of Alan Kelly, goalkeeper Jim Blyth made just one appearance for Preston North End – in a 2–2 home draw against Swindon Town on the final day of the 1971–72 season. The following October, Coventry City paid £20,000 for his services, with an extra £10,000 due when he played in the Sky Blues' League side. It was three years in coming as he understudied first Bill Glazier and then Bryan King. Once established, his displays led to a call-up

to the full Scotland side against Bulgaria, but a misunderstanding with Willie Donachie, who put through his own goal, probably cost him his place in Scotland's World Cup squad. Though Blyth later shared the goalkeeping duties with Les Sealey, he went on to appear in 174 League and Cup games before a loan spell with Hereford United was followed by him joining Birmingham City. Unable to displace either Tony Coton or David Seaman, he left to play non-League football for Nuneaton Borough.

BLYTH, Robert

Wing-half, outside-left

Born: Glenbuck, 1870.
Died: 1941.
Career: Glenbuck Athletic. Middlesbrough Ironopolis. Glasgow Rangers. Dundee. PRESTON NORTH END, 1894. Portsmouth.

■ Bob Blyth was able to play in a variety of positions. He had played his early football for Middlesbrough Ironopolis prior to spells with Scottish clubs Rangers and Dundee. It was from the Firs Park club that he joined Preston shortly before the start of the 1894–95 season, making his debut on the opening day of the campaign in a 3–1 win at Wolverhampton Wanderers. He was ever present in each of the following two seasons, with his best return in terms of goals scored coming in 1895–96, when his total of five included a brace in a 4–3 defeat of Sheffield United. Towards the end of his time at Deepdale, he captained the side before leaving to play Southern League football for Portsmouth. Blyth appeared in 124 League and Cup games for North End.

BLYTH, William J.

Right-half

Born: Portsmouth.
Career: Portsmouth. PRESTON NORTH END, 1905.

■ William Blyth had been playing Southern League football for his home-town club Portsmouth when North End signed him in the summer of 1905. An attacking right-half, he had produced several outstanding performances for the club's reserve side when he appeared against Sunderland at Roker Park in what proved to be his only first-team game for the Lilywhites. The match finished as a 2–0 win to the Wearsiders in a season that North End ended as runners-up in Division One.

BOGAN, Thomas

Inside-forward

Born: Glasgow, 18 May 1920.
Died: 23 September 1993.
Career: Hibernian. Glasgow Celtic.
PRESTON NORTH END, 1948.
Manchester United, 1949. Aberdeen, 1950.
Southampton, 1951. Blackburn Rovers,
1953.

■ Thomas Bogan was a Scottish wartime international. He was capped against England at Hampden Park in April 1945 but twisted his knee when he somersaulted over Frank Swift in a lightning first-minute attack and was carried off. He had started his career with Hibernian prior to the hostilities but joined Celtic in February 1946. In his early days at Parkhead he suffered a broken leg, but bounced back in 1947–48 to have an outstanding season. Initially he refused a transfer to Deepdale but eventually signed for the Lilywhites in

September 1948. He made his North End debut in the derby game with Blackpool but was on the losing side as the Seasiders won 3–1 at Deepdale. Unable to command a regular first-team spot, he left towards the end of the 1948–49 relegation season to spend a season with Manchester United. Bogan scored seven goals in 29 games for the Reds before returning to Scotland with Aberdeen. Bogan later spent 18 months with Southampton before becoming Johnny Carey's first signing at Blackburn Rovers.

BOGIE, Ian

Midfield

Born: Newcastle, 6 December 1967.
Career: Newcastle United, 1985.
PRESTON NORTH END, 1989. Millwall,
1991. Leyton Orient, 1993. Port Vale,
1995. Kidderminster Harriers, 2000.
Bedlington Terriers.

■ When Ian Bogie started out with his home-town team, Newcastle United, he was dubbed the new Gazza but he never lived up to that unfair billing. Unable to stamp his authority on the games in

which he played, he was released and joined Preston North End in exchange for Gary Brazil plus a cash adjustment. After making his debut in a 1–1 home draw against Bristol Rovers in February 1989, Bogie became a regular member of the North End side and helped the club reach the Play-offs in his first season. After a 1–1 draw at Deepdale, North End lost 3–1 to Port Vale in the second leg. Bogie settled into a midfield role and had his best season in 1990–91, netting eight goals in 31 League outings, including two in the 4–3 defeat of Shrewsbury Town. A fee of £145,000 took him to Millwall but in his two seasons at The Den, Bogie spent much of his time on the treatment table. He later played for Leyton Orient before signing for Port Vale in March 1995. He soon endeared himself to the Vale fans by scoring the winner in each of the local derbies against Stoke City and in each of the epic FA Cup-ties against Everton. Bogie gave the Valiants five years of service, scoring 12 goals in 181 games before leaving to play for Kidderminster Harriers. Hampered by a back injury, he returned to the North East to play for Bedlington Terriers.

BOND, John

Outside-right

Born: Preston.
Career: PRESTON NORTH END, 1913.

■ Local-born winger John Bond made his only League appearance for North End in their First Division relegation season of 1913–14. Wearing the number-seven shirt, he lined up for the final game of the campaign at home to Manchester City and scored Preston's opening goal in a 2–2 draw.

BOND, Richard

Outside-right

Born: Garstang, 14 December 1883.
Died: 1955.
Career: Royal Field Artillery. PRESTON NORTH END, 1902. Bradford City, 1909. Blackburn Rovers, 1922. Lancaster Town. Garstang.

■ England international winger Dickie Bond began his career with Preston North End, making his debut in an FA Cup tie against Bishop Auckland in December 1902 and scoring in a 3–1 win. He kept his place in the side for the League match against Stockport County the following week and again found the net in a 6–1 defeat of the Hatters. Fast and direct, Dickie Bond became the finest outside-right in the country in a little over two years. He made his international debut for England against Ireland in February 1905 and went on to win eight caps, five during his time at Deepdale. Two months after he made his international bow, Bond netted a hat-trick in the First Division encounter with Sheffield United, a match North End won 4–0. The following season, Preston were runners-up to Liverpool in the League Championship with Bond ending the campaign as the club's leading scorer with 17 goals. Bond continued to play for North End until the end of the 1908–09 season and scored 37 goals in 163 League and Cup games before leaving to play for Bradford City. Though he went on to make 301 First Division appearances and score 60 goals, nothing could compensate him for missing the 1911 FA Cup Final against Newcastle United: Bond had been suspended for using 'improper language' to the crowd at Woolwich Arsenal. During World War One, Bond was taken prisoner by the Germans. However, on his return to League football in 1919, he scored 11 goals in 41 games. Later appointed captain of the Valley Parade club, he parted company with them following their relegation in 1921–22. He ended his career with Blackburn Rovers.

BOOTH, Thomas Anthony

Centre-half

Born: Manchester, 9 November 1949.
Career: Manchester City, 1967. PRESTON NORTH END, 1981.

■ Centre-half Tommy Booth had something of a meteoric rise to fame after making his debut for Manchester City in a 1–1 home draw against Arsenal in October 1968. He ended his first season with City by scoring the winning goal in the FA Cup semi-final against Everton at Villa Park and also won England Under-23 honours. His performances that season prompted Joe Mercer to describe him as being like 'Stan

Cullis and Neil Franklin rolled into one'. Booth was City's first-choice centre-half for seven seasons, missing very few games until the arrival of Dave Watson. However, following Colin Bell's injury, he showed his versatility by moving into midfield and producing some very effective performances. During his City career, he won several honours: an FA Cup-winners' medal, a European Cup-winners' Cup medal and two League Cup-winners' medals. He had appeared in 478 League and Cup games when he was allowed to join Preston North End for £30,000 in September 1981. After making his debut in a 1–0 League Cup defeat of Leicester City, he appeared in a couple of goalless draws before the side conceded its first goal with Booth in the side in a 1–1 draw with Burnley. In the next game, Booth left the field injured and North End lost 4–3 at Exeter! Injuries hampered his time at Deepdale, though he managed 95 League and Cup appearances before taking over as manager from Alan Kelly. He tried valiantly to halt the club's slide towards the Fourth Division but without success and, just days after North End's infamous home FA Cup defeat at the hands of non-League Telford United, he was sacked.

BOSBURY, Charles Edwin

Outside-right

Born: Newhaven, 5 November 1897.
Died: 1928.
Career: Pemberton Billings. Southampton, 1921. Birmingham, 1922. PRESTON NORTH END, 1925. Lincoln City, 1926.

■ Flying winger Charlie Bosbury, who was a fine sprinter on the athletics track,

started out with Southampton as the Saints began their first season of League football in 1920–21. Unable to break into the first team, he joined Birmingham but though he was tall and strongly built, he made just 15 appearances in three seasons at St Andrew's. He arrived at Deepdale in the summer of 1925 but had to wait until the turn of the year before making his debut in a 1–0 win over Wolves. His only other appearances in a North End shirt resulted in 4–1 defeats – against Blackburn Rovers in the FA Cup and Swansea Town. Bosbury moved on to Lincoln City, where he was a huge success, scoring 30 goals in 85 games and helping the Imps to finish runners-up in the Third Division North in 1927–28. Sadly, he died shortly afterwards, aged just 31.

BOURNE, Richard Arthur

Outside-left, inside-left

Born: Roundle, 1881.
Died: 1944.
Career: Roundle. Sheffield United, 1900. Barnsley, 1902. PRESTON NORTH END, 1902. Clapton Orient, 1905. West Bromwich Albion, 1906. Walsall.

■ Dickie Bourne was a speedy left-winger who began his League career with Sheffield United prior to moving on to another Yorkshire club, Barnsley. However, it was only when he signed for North End that he began to play first-team football on a regular basis. In 1903–04 he missed just one game as North End won the Second Division Championship; his accurate crosses helping Percy Smith score 26 League goals. Yet Bourne, who had scored seven goals in 70 games and created many more, was allowed to move on to Clapton Orient at the end of the following season. He later played for West Bromwich Albion before ending his playing days with Walsall.

BOYD, David

Inside-left

Born: Preston.
Career: PRESTON NORTH END, 1896.

■ Inside-left David Boyd topped North End's goalscoring charts in 1896–97 – his first season at Deepdale. His 14 goals included doubles in the 4–0 away win over Blackburn Rovers, the 3–2 home win against Nottingham Forest and the 4–0 home win over Wolverhampton Wanderers. Unfortunately he lost form the following season and also suffered a number of injuries that forced his premature retirement after just two seasons on the North End staff.

BRADFORD, John William

Wing-half, centre-half

Born: Peggs Green, 6 November 1903.
Career: Peggs Green Victoria. Birmingham, 1923. Brighton and Hove Albion, 1924. PRESTON NORTH END, 1925. Walsall, 1926.

Bill Bradford was a versatile player who was able to play in any of the half-back line positions. He played his early football with Peggs Green Victoria before joining local League side Birmingham. Unable to force his way into their team, he had a brief spell with Brighton and Hove Albion prior to making just one appearance for North End in a 2–0 reversal at Barnsley. After leaving Deepdale he returned to the Midlands to join Walsall. In 11 seasons with the Saddlers, he scored 21 goals in 318 League games and helped the club to a best finish of fourth in the Third Division North in 1933–34.

BRADLEY, Herbert

Outside-left

Born: Padiham, 1887.
Career: Colne. Bury, 1906. Notts County, 1910. PRESTON NORTH END, 1911.

Winger Herbert Bradley was discovered by Bury while playing non-League football for Colne, but he made just 18 appearances in three seasons at Gigg Lane. He was transferred to Notts County but again struggled to make much of an impact and in the summer of 1911 he joined Preston North End. With Herbert Danson producing some fine performances in the number-11 shirt, he was limited to just two first-team appearances – featuring in the victories over the two Merseyside clubs: Everton 2–1 and Liverpool 1–0. At the end of the season, his contract was not renewed and he parted company with the club, drifting into the local non-League scene.

BRAIN, Joseph

Centre-forward, inside-left

Born: Ebbw Vale, 28 January 1910.
Career: Ebbw Vale. Sunderland, 1930. Norwich City, 1931. Barrow, 1932. PRESTON NORTH END, 1933. Swansea Town, 1934. Bristol City, 1937.

Joe Brain played his early football with Ebbw Vale, his home-town team, before joining Sunderland in March 1930. He failed to secure a First Division place at Roker Park and moved to

Norwich City in May 1931. After a season at Carrow Road he joined Barrow and was their top scorer in 1932–33. Towards the end of that season, he was sold to North End for £300 and, though he only played in seven games during the club's promotion-winning season of 1933–34, he did score vital goals in the games against Notts County and Swansea Town. It was the Vetch Field club that Brain joined in August 1934 and he was their leading marksman in two successive seasons before he left to play for Bristol City. He was an influential figure as City just missed promotion and were Third Division South Cup finalists in 1937–38. Following the outbreak of war, he became a PE instructor in the Royal Artillery before later running a newsagent's kiosk.

BRANAGAN, James Patrick Stephen

Full-back

Born: Urmston, 3 July 1955.
Career: Oldham Athletic, 1973. Cape Town City (South Africa). Huddersfield Town, 1977. Blackburn Rovers, 1979. PRESTON NORTH END, 1987. York City, 1987. Chorley.

The son of former Manchester City and Oldham Athletic full-back Ken Branagan, James also joined the Latics but though he captained the club's reserve side, he could not break into the Boundary Park club's League side on a regular basis. After leaving to try his luck in South African football with Cape Town City, it was not long before he was back in England with Huddersfield Town. Again he was unable to hold down a regular spot and Blackburn Rovers paid £20,000 for his services in October 1979. He soon established himself and helped Rovers win promotion to the Second Division in 1979–80. A versatile player who could turn out in midfield as well as any of the defensive positions, he captained the side on a number of occasions. He had played in 332 League and Cup games when he signed for Preston North End in the summer of 1987. However, with the club winning just one of its opening 13 League Cup games, he appeared in just a h

of matches. His last appearance was against York City, who also happened to be his last League club when he left Deepdale in October 1987. He later had a spell playing non-League football for Chorley.

BRANDON, James

Centre-forward

Born: Preston.
Career: PRESTON NORTH END, 1890. The Wednesday. Bootle 1892.

■ Centre-forward James Brandon played his first game for North End on the opening day of the 1890–91 season when he scored in a 3–0 defeat of West Bromwich Albion. Midway through the following month he netted two goals in a 3–1 win at Accrington – he almost claimed a hat-trick but his goal-bound shot was helped over the line by Hugh Gallacher. Despite this promising start he could not win a regular place and moved to The Wednesday. Unable to break into the Yorkshire club's side, he joined Bootle and again proved he knew where the goal was with five strikes in eight appearances before a disagreement with the board produced a parting of the ways.

BRANSTON, James Hart

Goalkeeper

Born: Sutton-in-Ashfield, 22 February 1894.
Died: 1970.
Career: Grimsby Town, 1913. Sutton Junction. Rotherham County, 1919. PRESTON NORTH END, 1921.

■ Goalkeeper Jimmy Branston was unable to make the grade with Grimsby Town and returned to his native Nottinghamshire to play non-League football for Sutton Town. On the resumption of League football in 1919–20, he joined Rotherham County and appeared in 111 League games in three seasons before signing for Preston North End midway through 1921–22. Though he soon became the club's first-choice 'keeper, he was Cup-tied so when North End met Huddersfield Town in the FA Cup Final, Mitchell was recalled to the side. Branston was ever present in 1922–23 but the following season he was hampered by injuries and lost his place to new signing George Prout. The two of them shared the goalkeeping duties in 1924–25 but North End were relegated along with Nottingham Forest. After appearing in the opening four games of the 1926–27 season, Branston left following the signing of Tony Carr. He had taken his total of appearances to 136.

BRAZIL, Gary Nicholas

Forward

Born: Tunbridge Wells, 19 September 1962.
Career: Crystal Palace. Sheffield United, 1980. Port Vale, 1984 (loan). PRESTON NORTH END, 1985. Newcastle United, 1989. Fulham, 1990. Cambridge United, 1996. Barnet, 1996. St Albans City.

■ A former Crystal Palace apprentice, Gary Brazil was allowed to leave Selhurst Park in the summer of 1980 to join Sheffield United. Though he went on to appear in 78 games for the Bramall Lane club, almost half were when he came off the bench. Finding his first-team opportunities severely limited, he had a loan spell with Port Vale before joining North End, also on loan. However, the move was made permanent a few months later in a £12,500 deal. Although

he was unable to prevent the club from being relegated, he then began to form a prolific partnership upfront with John Thomas. Both players scored 18 goals in all competitions in 1985–86, but the season was a disaster as North End finished next to bottom in the Fourth Division. The pair continued to find the net the following season as the club won promotion from the League's basement. In 1987–88, following Thomas' transfer to Bolton Wanderers, Brazil became North End's leading scorer with 20 goals in all competitions. During the early stages of the following campaign he

netted his only hat-trick for the club in a 5–0 defeat of Gillingham. But after scoring 72 goals in 202 League and Cup games, he left Deepdale midway through the season to play for Newcastle United. Brazil struggled at St James' Park and in September 1990 he moved to Fulham for a fee of £110,000. A player who relied more on skill and pace than physical strength, the Cottagers moved him from the centre to wide on the left, providing support rather than being at the heart of the attack. Though this role did not seem to suit his predatory instincts, he still went on to score 60 goals in 254 games before joining Cambridge United. Unable to command a first-team place, he moved to Barnet where he scored twice before moving out of League football to join St Albans City.

BRIGHT, David

Full-back

Born: Hexham, 24 December 1946.
Career: West Wylan Juniors. Sunderland, 1965. PRESTON NORTH END, 1967. Oldham Athletic, 1969.

■ Full-back David Bright was spotted playing junior football for West Wylan by his local club Sunderland and signed for the Wearsiders in the summer of 1965. Despite some impressive displays in the club's reserve side he could not force his way into the League side and in July 1967 he joined Preston North End. His only appearance in North End's League side came in a 2–1 reversal at Oxford United and, though he was a consistent performer at Central League level, he was eventually allowed to join Oldham Athletic where he was more of a regular.

BRISCOE, James Edward

Centre-forward, outside-right

Born: Clock Face, 23 April 1917.
Died: 1981.
Career: St Helens Town. PRESTON

NORTH END, 1936. Heart of Midlothian. Northampton Town, 1946. Wolverton.

■ Signed from St Helens Town, James Briscoe was a versatile forward who appeared for North End in five games in 1936–37, but he never finished on the winning side. Indeed the club suffered heavy defeats against Wolves (0–5) and Manchester City (2–5) with Briscoe in their ranks. He tried his luck north of the border with Heart of Midlothian and in his first season at Tynecastle he helped the club finish runners-up in the Scottish League First Division. After World War Two, he returned to Football League action with Northampton Town, scoring 17 goals in 53 games before moving into non-League football with Wolverton.

BRISCOE, Lee Stephen

Left-back

Born: Pontefract, 30 September 1975.
Career: Sheffield Wednesday, 1994. Manchester City, 1998 (loan). Burnley, 2000. PRESTON NORTH END, 2003.

■ England Under-21 international left-back Lee Briscoe started out with Sheffield Wednesday where, in his early days with the club, he also appeared in midfield. A player with drive and pace, he did not make the progress expected of him at Hillsborough and he was loaned out to Manchester City in February 1998. While at Maine Road, he scored his first goal in the Football League at a rain-soaked Huddersfield Town. Though City manager Joe Royle was keen to sign him, he returned to Hillsborough and scored his first goal for the Owls in the match against Arsenal, though this was overshadowed by the antics of Paolo di Canio. He had made 90 appearances in all competitions for Wednesday when he was allowed to join Burnley on a free transfer. Hampered by injuries in his early days at Turf Moor, he came off the bench to score twice in the space of a few minutes against Walsall. A virtual ever present for the Clarets, he joined North End on a one-year deal in July 2003. A persistent hamstring injury led to an operation, so Briscoe did not make his first-team debut until the following March. Sadly a back injury in only his second start brought a premature end to a frustrating season, at the end of which he was forced to retire.

BROADBENT, William Henry

Right-half, right-back

Born: Oldham, 20 November 1901.
Died: 1979.
Career: Wellington Albion. Oldham Athletic, 1920. Brentford, 1924. Clapton Orient, 1925. PRESTON NORTH END, 1932.

■ Signed from local side Wellington Albion, Billy Broadbent began his League career with his home-town club Oldham Athletic but was never a regular. Following a season with Brentford, he signed for Clapton Orient and spent seven seasons with the club. Though he was unable to prevent their relegation from Division Two in 1928–29, he was one of the club's most consistent players and appeared in 198 games before moving to North End for the start of the 1932–33 season. Unable to oust the formidable Guy Nisbet at right-half, he made just two appearances before deciding to hang up his boots.

BROADHURST, Frederick

Full-back

Born: Aspull, 30 November 1888.
Died: 1953.
Career: Hindley Central. PRESTON NORTH END, 1910. Hindley Central. PRESTON NORTH END, 1911. Stalybridge Celtic, 1922. Stockport County, 1923. Barrow, 1924. Nelson, 1925. Chorley.

■ Fred Broadhurst was able to play in either full-back position. He started out with Hindley Central prior to playing two games for North End during the 1910–11 season. He rejoined Hindley for a brief spell before returning to Deepdale. However, it was 1913–14 before he won a regular place in the side, only for North End to suffer relegation to the Second Division. The club bounced back immediately, winning promotion as runners-up to Derby County with Broadhurst scoring his first goal for the club from the penalty spot in a 2–1 win over Hull City. He was the club's regular penalty-taker when League football resumed after the hostilities in 1919–20 and, though he was later a fringe player, he had played in 115 games before he left to play for Stalybridge Celtic. This was followed by a brief spell with Stockport County before he played for Barrow, Nelson and finally non-League Chorley.

BROOME, Thomas Alfred

Wing-half, centre-forward

Born: Pendleton, 1892.
Died: 1956.
Career: Rochdale. PRESTON NORTH END, 1913. Caernarvon United. Grimsby Town, 1920. Bolton Wanderers, 1920. Chesterfield, 1921.

■ Having impressed with Rochdale during their pre-League days, Tommy Broome joined North End prior to the start of the 1913–14 season. He was a versatile player and wore five different numbered outfield shirts while making 15 appearances in that relegation season. Broome served the club well the following campaign, making 31 appearances, again in a variety of positions, and scored his first goal for the Lilywhites while wearing the number-six shirt in a 1–0 win at Hull City. Those two points against fellow promotion contenders helped consolidate North End's position near the top of the table and they returned to the top flight as runners-up to Derby County. He was still a first-team regular in 1919–20 but left to play for Caernarvon United. He returned to League action with Grimsby Town and this was followed by a trial with Bolton Wanderers and a season playing for Chesterfield.

BROOMES, Marlon Charles

Centre-half

Born: Birmingham, 28 November 1977.
Career: Blackburn Rovers, 1994. Swindon Town, 1997 (loan). Queen's Park Rangers, 2000 (loan). Grimsby Town, 2001 (loan). Sheffield Wednesday, 2001. Burnley, 2002. PRESTON NORTH END, 2002. Stoke City, 2005.

■ A highly-rated central defender with Blackburn Rovers, Marlon Broomes was farmed out to Swindon Town in January 1997 for first-team experience. The highlight of his two-month stay was a long-range wind-assisted goal from 40 yards against Birmingham. The lowest point was a 7–0 defeat by First Division Champions Bolton Wanderers. Finally presented with first-team opportunities at Ewood Park, this England Under-21 international made his debut against Preston in the Coca-Cola Cup. Unfortunately, a freak pre-season injury in 1998 meant that his leg had to be put in plaster because of ligament damage. He returned to first-team action the following season but suffered a recurrence of the injury. It was ultimately

decided that it was being caused by a misalignment of his ankle. Having now slipped down the pecking order at Blackburn, Broomes had a loan spell with Queen's Park Rangers but although Gerry Francis wanted to make the deal a permanent one, the clubs could not agree terms. After another loan spell, this time with Grimsby Town, Broomes joined Sheffield Wednesday on a free transfer after appearing in just 38 games in seven years on the Rovers staff. He left Hillsborough in the summer of 2002 and spent the close season with Burnley before joining North End in readiness for the 2002–03 season. He made his debut at Gillingham and continued to feature regularly throughout the campaign, playing in a variety of defensive positions. A series of injuries and suspensions did not help him maintain a settled place in the side in 2003–04 and his longest run was only 12 games. Injuries decimated his appearances the following season, at the end of which he joined Stoke City.

BROWN, Alexander

Centre-forward

Born: Beith, 7 April 1879.
Career: Glenbuck. Kilsyth Wanderers. St Bernards. PRESTON NORTH END, 1896. Portsmouth. Tottenham Hostpur. Portsmouth. Middlesbrough, 1903. Luton Town. Kettering Town.

■ A prodigious goalscorer, 'Sandy' Brown joined Preston from Edinburgh club St Bernards in 1896 and made his debut in a goalless draw at Bury on the opening day of the 1896–97 season. In his first season at Deepdale he found himself in and out of the side, but in 1897–98 he was the club's leading scorer. Brown spent one more season at Deepdale, taking his tally of goals to 29 in 67 League and Cup games before leaving to play for Portsmouth. In his first season in the Southern League, Brown scored 34 of Pompey's 110 goals, including a hat-trick against Queen's Park Rangers. Spurs spotted his talents and his transfer was secured. Brown's impact was immediate, for it was his goals that were responsible for Spurs' first-ever FA Cup victory at the end of his initial season. He scored both Spurs' goals in the 1901 Final and added the deciding strike in the final replay to give him 15 goals and a goal in every round. Having played for the Anglo-Scots in an international trial, he was selected for the full Scotland side against England in 1902, but the ill-fated match was subsequently declared void due to the Ibrox disaster. In May 1902 he was allowed to return to Fratton Park and, though he only stayed one season, he proved his effectiveness by scoring 31 goals. He then joined Middlesbrough and at last won a Scottish cap. He later played for Luton Town before ending his career with Kettering.

BROWN, Arthur F.

Centre-forward

Born: Tamworth, 1879.
Career: Atherstone Star. Tamworth. Aston Villa, 1900. Southampton. Queen's Park

Rangers. PRESTON NORTH END, 1904. Blackpool, 1905.

■ 'Arthur Brown was known as the 'Tamworth Sprinter' because of his impressive speed and was also capable of a very hard shot. He had a brief spell with Aston Villa, scoring two goals in two games, before he moved into the Southern League with Southampton. He scored seven times during an 11–0 victory over Northampton in 1901 – a record that still stands today for a Saints player in a Southern League match. His spell at The Dell encompassed two seasons, in which time he helped the Saints reach the FA Cup final in 1902, scoring in the replay. Injuries cost him his place and, not content with reserve football, he joined Queen's Park Rangers. Soon afterwards he signed for Preston North End and scored on his debut against his former club, Aston Villa, on the opening day of the 1904–05 season – a match North End won 2–1 at Villa Park. Brown found the net on a regular basis in those opening games, including netting two penalties in a 3–1 defeat of Notts County. He scored on the opening day of the following season at Birmingham but then lost out to Percy Smith for the majority of a campaign in which the club finished runners-up to Liverpool. On leaving Deepdale, he had a brief spell with Blackpool before ending his involvement with the game.

BROWN, David James

Goalkeeper

Born: Hartlepool, 28 January 1957.
Career: Horden Colliery. Middlesbrough, 1977. Plymouth Argyle, 1979 (loan). Oxford United, 1979. Bury, 1981. PRESTON NORTH END, 1986. Scunthorpe United, 1989 (loan). Halifax Town, 1989.

■ Goalkeeper David Brown was spotted playing for Horden Colliery by Middlesbrough and given a chance at League level by the Ayresome Park club. Unable to displace Jim Platt, he had a loan spell with Plymouth Argyle before joining Oxford United in October 1979. His next club was Bury and he spent five seasons at Gigg Lane, helping them win promotion to the Third Division in 1984–85. He had appeared in 146 League

games for the Shakers when John McGrath brought him to Deepdale in the summer of 1986. He made his debut in a 1–1 draw at Tranmere on the opening day of the 1986–87 season, a campaign in which he played in 24 games and kept six clean sheets to help North End win promotion from the Fourth Division. The following season he continued to share the goalkeeping duties with Alan Kelly but was the manager's preference in the Sherpa Van Trophy in which they reached the Northern Area Final. In 1988–89 his confidence began to suffer and he lost his place for much of the season to Roy Tunks. Following a loan spell with Scunthorpe United, he joined Halifax Town and saw out his career with the Shaymen.

BROWN, Edwin

Centre-forward

Born: Preston, 28 February 1926.
Career: PRESTON NORTH END, 1948. Southampton, 1950. Coventry City, 1952. Birmingham City, 1954. Leyton Orient, 1959. Scarborough. Stourbridge. Bedworth Town. Wigan Athletic.

■ Edwin Brown was a one-time theological student who had studied in

the Channel Islands before being evacuated during the war. He was also one of the fastest strikers ever to wear the lilywhite of Preston North End. After making a handful of appearances in 1948–49, he top scored the following season with 13 goals as North End finished sixth in Division Two. Brown had scored two goals in the opening four games of the 1950–51 season when he was allowed to join Southampton as a replacement for Charlie Wayman, who had gone in the opposite direction. His stocky build and burst of speed meant that he was soon scoring goals with almost the same frequency as Wayman. However, he could not settle on the South Coast and, after scoring 32 goals in 57 games, he asked for a transfer and moved to Coventry City. Unable to prevent the Highfield Road club's relegation in 1951–52, he was their leading scorer for the next couple of seasons, finding the net 50 times in 85 games before moving to Birmingham City. He helped the Blues win the Second Division Championship in his first season at St Andrew's, netting a hat-trick in a 9–1 defeat of Liverpool. He continued to find the net regularly, scoring 74 goals in 158 games. He later ended his career at Leyton Orient, his fifth club, and took his tally of League goals to 190 in 399 games before playing non-League football for Scarborough,

Stourbridge, Bedworth Town and Wigan Athletic.

BROWN, James Keith

Midfield

Born: Bothwell, 3 October 1953.
Career: Aston Villa, 1970. PRESTON NORTH END, 1975. Ethnikos (Greece). Portsmouth, 1980.

■ Midfielder Jimmy Brown worked his way up through the ranks at Aston Villa to become a regular member of their side that won the Third Division Championship in 1971–72. He had appeared in 75 League games when manager Harry Catterick brought him to Deepdale in October 1975. Making his debut in a 1–0 defeat at Brighton, he certainly strengthened North End's midfield as they went on to finish eighth in Division Three. In 1976–77, his promptings led to both Bruce and Elwiss topping the 20–goal mark, with North End on the fringe of the promotion pack in sixth place. Though North End were promoted the following season, Jimmy Brown appeared in just a handful of League and Cup games at the start of the campaign before leaving to play in Greece for Ethnikos. He returned in February 1980 to see out his career on the South Coast with Portsmouth.

BROWN, John Christopher

Goalkeeper

Born: Bradford, 30 December 1947.
Career: PRESTON NORTH END, 1965. Stockport County, 1970 (loan). Stockport County, 1975. Wigan Athletic, 1976.

■ Goalkeeper John Brown attracted the interest of a number of League clubs while playing for Bradford schoolboys, whom he helped reach the semi-finals of the English Schools' Trophy. After working as an apprentice joiner, he signed for Preston North End and made his League debut as a 17-year-old in a 4–2 defeat by Bolton Wanderers, for whom Wyn Davies netted a hat-trick. He spent most of the 1960s as understudy to Alan Kelly in the Preston goal but took

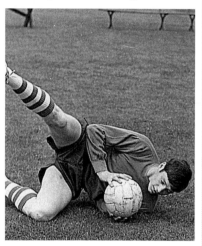

over in 1972 for two first-team seasons. He was released from Deepdale during Bobby Charlton's brief spell as manager to be replaced by Roy Tunks. Stockport County snapped him up but after being voted Player of the Season, he lost his place in the side through injury and moved on to Wigan Athletic. Though it looked like a backward step, his decision was vindicated when the Latics joined the Football League two seasons later. He kept a clean sheet in a goalless draw at Hereford United in the club's first-ever game in the competition and his experience and bravery served them well for their first two seasons of League football. He left Springfield Park at the end of the promotion-winning season of 1981–82 after being a rock for the team to build on in the drive to gain admission to the League and the subsequent quest for promotion.

BROWN, Michael Anthony

Winger

Born: Birmingham, 8 February 1968.
Career: Shrewsbury Town, 1986. Bolton Wanderers, 1991. Shrewsbury Town, 1992. PRESTON NORTH END, 1994. Rochdale, 1996 (loan). Shrewsbury Town, 1996. Boston United, 2001.

■ Winger Michael Brown served his apprenticeship with Shrewsbury Town, turning professional with them in February 1986. He made his League debut as a substitute against Blackburn Rovers the following August and went on to make 228 appearances before he and Tony Kelly joined Bolton Wanderers for a combined fee of £200,000. Much of his time at Burnden Park was spent on the treatment table and in December 1992 he rejoined Shrewsbury on loan, the deal later becoming permanent. He helped the Shrews win the Third Division Championship in 1993–94 before returning to the North West in November 1994 to play for Preston North End. Manager Gary Peters paid £75,000 for his services but injury meant that Brown had to wait nine months before making his debut. He had made just 10 appearances as North End went on to take the Third Division Championship in 1995–96. His only goal in that campaign came in the 5–0 rout of

Cardiff City on New Year's Day – it was scored just 30 seconds after he came on as a substitute. After a loan spell with Rochdale, he returned to Shrewsbury for a third time. When he played he continued to leave defenders in his wake, but he suffered more than his fair share of injuries. Though not a prolific scorer, he will never score a more important goal than in the last game of the 1999–2000 season against Exeter that secured Shrewsbury's League status. He went on to create a new club record of League appearances when he overtook Colin Griffith's tally of 406 before being released in the summer of 2001 to join Boston United.

BROWN, William

Centre-forward

Born: Preston, 1875.
Career: PRESTON NORTH END, 1895.
Tottenham Hotspur. Lincoln City, 1896.

■ Centre-forward William Brown appeared in just one Football League game for Preston North End: he played in the 1–1 home draw against Burnley in October 1895. Despite a sound display he returned to the club's reserve side before moving on to play for Spurs in the Southern League at the end of the season. His stay at White Hart Lane was brief and he returned to League football with Lincoln City but again made just one appearance before parting company with the Imps.

BROWN, William Falconer

Full-back

Born: Larkhall, 20 October 1922.
Died: 1978.
Career: Larkhall Thistle. PRESTON NORTH END, 1942. Queen of the South. Grimsby Town, 1951.

■ William Brown was a tough-tackling full-back who joined North End from Scottish junior club Larkhall Thistle during World War Two. Initially, he was unable to displace either Andy Beattie or Will Scott and he made his debut at centre-half in a 4–1 defeat at Wolves in March 1947. Though Beattie left to enter the world of management, his number-two shirt was worn for the majority of the following season by

David Gray and it was 1948–49 before Brown won a regular place in the Preston side. However, defensive frailties and the loss of Tom Finney with injuries for long spells saw North End relegated. Early the following season, Brown returned to Scotland to play for Queen of the South and in 1950–51 he helped them win the Scottish 'B' Division Championship. In the close season he signed for Grimsby Town and after finishing as runners-up in the Third Division North in his first season at Blundell Park, he helped them win the Championship in 1955–56. Brown, who scored just one goal in his time with the club, went on to appear in 265 League games for the Mariners before retiring.

BRUCE, Alexander Robert

Forward

Born: Dundee, 23 December 1952.
Career: PRESTON NORTH END, 1970. Newcastle United, 1974. PRESTON NORTH END, 1975. Wigan Athletic, 1983.

■ Striker Alex Bruce had always harboured dreams of becoming a professional footballer and after recom-

mendations from scout Jimmy Scott, he left his Dundee home to sign for Preston North End. He quickly graduated through the club's youth and reserve teams to make his debut as a 19-year-old against Swindon Town on the final day of the 1971–72 season. He made a good enough impression to remain on the first-team scene the following season, albeit on the bench for the first half of the campaign. It was the match against Orient in November 1972 when he finally hit the big time, coming on to replace Alan Tarbuck and score the winner in a 2–1 victory at Brisbane Road. The goals soon began to flow regularly and his exploits led to First Division Newcastle United paying out £150,000 for Bruce in the middle of the Magpies' 1974 FA Cup run to Wembley. As he was Cup-tied, he rarely received an opportunity in Joe Harvey's first team that season and afterwards found it almost impossible to break the Macdonald-Tudor front combination. He returned to Preston without reaching double figures in any of his seasons at St James' Park, though he did win Under-23 honours for Scotland while on United's books. North End fans were delighted to have Bruce back and he went on to top score for the club in five of the next six seasons. His partnership

with Mike Elwiss became the scourge of opposition defences throughout the League and Bruce's 26 goals in 1976–77 included his first hat-trick for the club in a 6–2 defeat of Peterborough United. The following season saw North End win promotion to the Second Division, with Bruce's total of 27 goals including all four in a 4–0 win over Colchester United. In 1977–78, Bruce was presented with an Adidas golden shoe award for being top goalscorer and only missed out on a second award the following season because less of his 26 goals were scored in the League than the winner, West Ham's 'Pop' Robson. Bruce went on to score 157 goals in 363 League matches; not far off Sir Tom Finney's club record. In August 1983 he moved to Wigan Athletic, finishing his playing days with 51 appearances for the Latics. On hanging up his boots, he returned to Preston where he was employed as a leisure centre manager.

BRUNTON, Matthew

Inside-right, centre-forward

Born: Burnley, 20 April 1878.
Died: 1962.
Career: South Lancs Regiment. PRESTON NORTH END, 1899. Accrington Stanley. Burnley, 1901. Accrington Stanley. Leicester Fosse, 1904. Nelson. Accrington Stanley. Oldham Athletic, 1907. Southport Central. Haslingden. Darwen. Accrington Stanley.

■ Though he scored in both of North End's opening games of the 1899–1900 season, it was in Lancashire Combination football that Matt Brunton excelled. After a spell with Burnley in which he appeared in all five forward positions, he joined Accrington Stanley. They became the first non-reserve side to win the Lancashire Combination Championship – in 1902–03 – with Brunton scoring 40 goals from the centre-forward berth. He then had unsuccessful spells with Leicester Fosse and Nelson before rejoining Accrington for another Championship win in 1905–06. He picked up his third Championship medal with Oldham, helping them subsequently gain election to the Football League. After brief spells with Southport Central, Haslingden,

Darwen and Accrington Stanley again, he became a swimming instructor. During World War One he suffered a serious leg wound while serving as a sergeant in the South Lancashire Regiment.

BRYSON, James Ian Cook

Winger

Born: Kilmarnock, 26 November 1962.
Career: Kilmarnock. Sheffield United, 1988. Barnsley, 1993. PRESTON NORTH END, 1993. Rochdale, 1997. Bamber Bridge.

■ Ian Bryson began his career with his home-town team, Kilmarnock, playing in 250 League and Cup games in a seven-year career at Rugby Park. In the summer of 1988, Sheffield United paid £40,000 for his services and his tenacity and powerful surges in support of the attack helped the Blades become a real force to be reckoned with. He went on to score 44 goals in 197 games before leaving to join Barnsley. His form continued to receive rave reviews in Yorkshire but after just three months at Oakwell, he was surprisingly allowed to move to Preston North End. He soon established himself at Deepdale, playing just in front of the defence from where he distributed the ball and began his surging runs forward. Soon afterwards he was appointed team captain and in 1995–96 he led the club to the Third Division Championship. Though he was now 33 years old, his form was good enough to see him elected to the PFA Division Three side on awards night. Though he remained an important member of the first-team

squad in 1996–97, he was more often on the bench. Having scored 21 goals in 179 games, he was released in the close season and joined Rochdale. Sadly injuries hampered his progress at Spotland and after two seasons of struggle, he was released, going on to play non-League football for Bamber Bridge.

BUCKLEY, Gary

Midfield

Born: Manchester, 3 March 1961.
Career: Manchester City, 1978. PRESTON NORTH END, 1981. Chorley. Bury, 1984.

■ Midfielder Gary Buckley began his career with Manchester City, making six League appearances during the 1980–81 season before being transferred to Preston North End in October 1981. He was thrust into an ailing North End side by manager Tommy Docherty but Buckley, who made his debut in a 1–0 League Cup victory over Leicester City, could not turn things around. Gordon Lee replaced Docherty after Alan Kelly had taken over team affairs for a week. Buckley appeared in 37 League and Cup games before leaving to play non-League football for Chorley. He later returned to the Football League with Bury and helped them win promotion to Division Three in his only season with the club.

BULMER, Peter

Full-back

Born: Liverpool, 31 August 1965.
Career: Chester City, 1983. Rhyl.
PRESTON NORTH END, 1986.

■ Full-back Peter Bulmer was a member of Chester City's Fourth Division side in the mid-1980s. He had made 71 League appearances for the Cestrians when he left to play non-League football for Rhyl. His consistent displays for the Welsh club led to a number of League clubs showing interest and in the summer of 1986 he joined Preston North End. In a campaign in which the Deepdale club won promotion from the Fourth Division as runners-up to Northampton Town, Bulmer made just four League appearances and played in three Littlewoods Cup games – all at the start of the campaign before losing out to the full-back pairing of Mick Bennett and Bob McNeil.

BURLEY, Craig William

Midfield

Born: Irvine, 24 September 1971.
Career: Chelsea, 1989. Glasgow Celtic, 1997. Derby County, 1999. Dundee, 2003. PRESTON NORTH END, 2004. Walsall, 2004.

■ A nephew of George Burley, the former Ipswich star and currently manager of Southampton, Craig joined Chelsea and, within a week of making his full Football League debut for the Stamford Bridge club, had been selected for the Scotland Under-21 team. A midfielder with great vision and long-range shooting ability, he suffered his fair share of injuries with the London club but still managed to impress Scotland manager Craig Brown, who rewarded him for his good displays in 1994–95 with the first of his 46 caps in the match against Japan. He also featured in the bizarre World Cup qualifier in Tallinn in October 1996 when Estonia failed to appear and the match was abandoned after three seconds. He went on to play in 137 games for Chelsea before a £2.5 million move to Celtic in the summer of 1997. In a little over two years at Parkhead, Burley helped the Bhoys win the Scottish Premier Division title and

the League Cup in the 1997–98 season. After an unhappy start to the 1999–2000 season, Burley joined Derby County in a £3 million deal and, along with Georgi Kinkladze, he was instrumental in the Rams maintaining their Premiership status. Injuries then hampered his progress and he missed much of County's relegation season. On leaving Pride Park he had a brief spell with Dundee before joining Preston on a short-term contract. He made four appearances for North End – three as substitute – but never really got the chance to show his undoubted pedigree. He declined the offer of an extension to his contract and joined Walsall, making his Saddlers debut at Deepdale. He made little impact at the Bescot Stadium and decided to hang up his boots.

BURNS, Francis

Left-back

Born: Glenboig, 17 October 1948.
Career: Manchester United, 1965. Southampton, 1972. PRESTON NORTH END, 1973. Shamrock Rovers.

■ Francis Burns was another in a long line of Manchester United players who came to maturity through the club's junior ranks. He arrived at Old Trafford as a 15-year-old in 1964 and three years later he was lining up at left-back as the Reds took on West Ham United. He went on to enjoy 45 outings that season, playing in most of the European Cup games but missing out at the end of United's great run through injury. Injuries, particularly cartilage trouble, dogged his career and over the next five seasons, his first-team appearances were dictated by his fitness. Burns, who played for Scotland against Austria in November 1969, left Old Trafford in 1972 to join Southampton for a fee of £60,000. He never really settled on the South Coast and after just 14 months at The Dell he jumped at the chance to return to the North West with Preston North End. At Deepdale he teamed up with his old Manchester United colleague, Bobby Charlton, who was manager at the time. Persistent injury problems again prevented Burns from regularly displaying his enormous talent but he was a member of the side that

won promotion to Division Two in 1977–78. His last season with North End was the relegation campaign of 1980–81 after which, having played in 306 games for the club, he left to end his career with Shamrock Rovers.

BURNS, Michael Thomas

Goalkeeper

Born: Leeholme, County Durham, 7 June 1908.
Died: Newcastle-upon-Tyne, September 1982.
Career: Chilton Colliery. Newcastle United, 1927. PRESTON NORTH END, 1936. Ipswich Town, 1938.

■ After once being converted to a forward for conceding too many goals, Mick Burns developed into a steady goalkeeper and served his first club, Newcastle United, for nine seasons. At a time when the Magpies had three or even four senior 'keepers on their books, Burns was never recognised as a first choice. He had played in 108 games for the North East club when he joined Preston North End in the summer of 1936. He had played in just seven League games when he found himself thrust into the biggest game of his life, as stand-in for Harry Holdcroft in the 1937 FA Cup Final against Sunderland. After another season at Deepdale, in which he continued to understudy Holdcroft, he left to play for Ipswich Town. He went straight into the club's first team for what was their first season of League football.

During the war years, he 'guested' for Town's greatest rivals, Norwich City, before returning to Portman Road for the start of the 1946–47 season. He played the last of his 176 games for Ipswich in an FA Cup tie at Gateshead in January 1952, when he was almost 44 years old. After retiring from the game, he worked as a caretaker in a Newcastle school.

BURTON, Simon Paul

Winger

Born: Farnworth, 29 December 1973.
Career: PRESTON NORTH END, 1992. Altrincham.

■ Simon Burton joined North End on a Youth Training Scheme basis after some impressive displays for the club's reserve side. He made his debut as a substitute for Tony Ellis in a 2–0 defeat at Brighton in September 1992. During the course of that 1992–93 season, Burton found himself in and out of the North End side, with his best performance coming in the game against Wigan Athletic at Springfield Park when he scored two and rattled the bar in a 3–2 win. Unable to build on his first season, he was released and moved into non-League football with Altrincham.

BUTLER, William

Full-back

Born: Doncaster, 1884.
Career: Doncaster Rovers, 1904. PRESTON NORTH END, 1906.

■ Full-back William Butler began his Football League career with his home-town club Doncaster Rovers, but in two seasons with the Yorkshire club, he made only seven appearances before switching to Preston North End. Replacing George Tod, he appeared in three games midway through the 1906–07 season. The last of these was a 6–1 defeat by Liverpool and, with Butler deemed to be at fault for a number of the goals, it proved to be his last appearance for the club.

BUTTERWORTH, Albert

Outside-right, inside-right

Born: Ashton-under-Lyne, 20 March 1912.
Died: 1991.

Career: Droylsden. Manchester United, 1930. Blackpool, 1932. PRESTON NORTH END, 1934. Bristol Rovers, 1936.

■ Unable to force his way into Manchester United's League side, Albert Butterworth moved on to Blackpool. However, despite scoring twice in a 4–1 defeat of Liverpool, he could not prevent the Seasiders' relegation to the Second Division. Midway through the following campaign, he joined Preston North End but made just a couple of appearances. In 1935–36, Butterworth found himself in and out of the North End side but netted a number of vital goals before being allowed to join Bristol Rovers at the end of the season. Butterworth was a much more regular player for Rovers, scoring 13 goals in 98 League games as the side struggled in the lower reaches of the Third Division South.

BYFIELD, Darren

Forward

Born: Sutton Coldfield, 29 September 1976.
Career: Aston Villa, 1994. PRESTON NORTH END, 1998 (loan). Northampton Town, 1999 (loan). Cambridge United, 1999 (loan). Blackpool, 2000 (loan). Walsall, 2000. Rotherham United, 2002. Sunderland, 2004. Gillingham, 2004.

■ Darren Byfield was a pacy striker who began his career with Aston Villa. He consistently found the net at youth and reserve team level and made his debut in the Premiership game at Leeds United in December 1997. Despite showing the potential to become a future star in the game, the following season was somewhat disappointing and in November 1998 he went on loan to Preston North End. He scored on his debut against Burnley but picked up a knee injury. He returned to Villa Park early after refusing a place on the bench against Wrexham at the end of December. This was followed by loan spells with Northampton, Cambridge United and Blackpool but with him clearly not being in manager John Gregory's plans, he joined Walsall on a free transfer. Displaying quick reactions in the box and with an eye for goal, he netted the winner in the second period of extra-time in the Play-off Final win against Reading that took the Saddlers back to Division One. He continued to find the net regularly but he left to join fellow relegation rivals Rotherham United towards the end of the 2000–01

season. On the opening day of the following campaign, he scored four goals in Rotherham's 6–0 defeat of Millwall, his form leading to him winning full international honours for Jamaica. His goalscoring exploits soon attracted the attention of other clubs and in February 2004 he moved on to Sunderland. Despite his good scoring ratio for the Black Cats, he left the Stadium of Light to continue his career with Gillingham.

CALLAGHAN, Aaron Joseph

Centre-half

Born: Dublin, 8 October 1966.
Career: Stoke City, 1984. Crewe Alexandra, 1985 (loan). Oldham Athletic, 1986. Crewe Alexandra, 1988. PRESTON NORTH END, 1992. Shelbourne. St Patrick's Athletic. Crusaders. Glenavon. Dundalk.

■ Aaron Callaghan was a Republic of Ireland Under-21 international who came through the ranks at Stoke City to make his first-team debut at the age of 18. However, he failed to sustain a permanent place in the team and after a loan spell at Crewe Alexandra, he was signed by Oldham manager Joe Royle for £10,000. When made available by the Latics, Crewe manager Dario Gradi took him on a permanent basis to Gresty Road and he soon became a fixture in the Railwaymen's side. After helping Crewe win promotion to the Third Division in 1988–89, his first season with the club, he went on to appear in 158 League games before leaving to join Preston in the summer of 1992. Though he played in the majority of games in his first season at Deepdale and scored some spectacular goals – notably against his first club Stoke – he fell out of favour during the early stages of the 1993–94 season and returned to Ireland to play for Shelbourne. After helping the Shels win the FAI League Cup, he had a brief spell with St Patrick's Athletic before going north of the border to help Crusaders win two Irish League Championships. He then played for Glenavon before signing for Dundalk and helping them win the FAI Cup. Callaghan is now assistant manager of Longford Town.

CALVERLEY, Alfred

Winger

Born: Huddersfield, 24 November 1917.
Died: 1991.
Career: Huddersfield Town, 1943. Mansfield Town, 1946. Arsenal, 1947. PRESTON NORTH END, 1947. Doncaster Rovers, 1947.

■ Winger Alf Calverley joined his home-town team Huddersfield Town during World War Two and, in his very first wartime game, netted a hat-trick in a 3–0 defeat of Leeds United. However, by the time League football resumed in 1946–47, he had joined Mansfield Town. Towards the end of his first season at Field Mill, Calverley was signed by First Division Arsenal for £5,000 and made the first of 11 appearances against North End, a match the Gunners won 4–1. At the end of that season, he left Highbury to join Preston. After appearing in the opening 13 games of the 1947–48 campaign, when his pin-point crosses provided numerous goalscoring opportunities for McIntosh and McLaren, he fell out of favour and was transferred to Doncaster Rovers. At Belle Vue, he was a regular in the Rovers' side, scoring 11 goals in 142 League games before hanging up his boots.

CAMERON, Daniel

Full-back

Born: Dundee, 9 November 1953.
Career: Sheffield Wednesday, 1971. Colchester United, 1975 (loan). PRESTON NORTH END, 1976.

■ Dundee-born full-back Danny Cameron began his career with Sheffield Wednesday but, though he never let the side down when he played, he could not hold down a regular first-team place. Following a loan spell with Colchester United and Wednesday's relegation to the Third Division, Cameron joined Preston North End in April 1976 and made his debut off the bench in the final game of the season at Hereford United. It was 1977–78 before Cameron established himself as a first-team regular, playing in 40 games and helping North End win promotion to Division Two. He continued to give 100 per cent effort in the higher grade of football for

the next few seasons before parting company with the club.

CAMERON, Kenneth

Inside-forward, outside-left

Born: Hamilton, 1905.
Career: Parkhead. PRESTON NORTH END, 1926. Middlesbrough, 1929. Bolton Wanderers, 1933. Hull City, 1935. Queen's Park Rangers, 1936. Rotherham United, 1937.

■ Signed from Scottish junior football, inside-forward Ken Cameron made a handful of appearances in 1926–27, scoring his first goal for the club in a 4–1 home win over Blackpool. Though he only made four appearances the following season he scored four goals, including a hat-trick on the final day of the season at Grimsby Town. This was an unusual match as, with just over five minutes left, North End led 6–0. Joe Robson then netted a three-minute hat-trick and, with the Preston defence all at seas, Bestall claimed a fourth goal with the last kick of the game. Unable to reproduce his goalscoring form the following season, Cameron was allowed to join Middlesbrough. His three seasons at Ayresome Park were all spent in Division One, where he scored 30 goals in 99 games. He later had spells with Bolton Wanderers, Hull City and Queen's Park Rangers before joining Rotherham United, where he ended his career before being given a first-team opportunity.

CAMERON, Stuart John

Goalkeeper

Born: Liverpool, 28 November 1966.
Career: PRESTON NORTH END, 1983.

■ YTS trainee goalkeeper Stuart Cameron played his one and only League game for North End during the course of the 1983–84 season, when he replaced Peter Litchfield for the home fixture against lowly Scunthorpe United. Despite having a good game and keeping a clean sheet in a 1–0 win for North End, he was released at the end of the season.

CAMPBELL, Anthony Glen

Goalkeeper

Born: Leyland, 26 February 1965.
Career: PRESTON NORTH END, 1983.

■ Goalkeeper Glen Campbell made his North End debut in a 1–1 draw with Chesterfield in November 1982 but, as he was third in the pecking order behind Peter Litchfield and Stuart Cameron, he did not appear at all in 1983–84. The following season, which saw North End relegated to the League's basement, Campbell appeared in 17 games, sharing the goalkeeping duties with Litchfield, Wealands and Platt. Though Campbell was between the posts in a number of heavy defeats – York City (2–4 at home), Swansea City (1–4 away), Bristol City (0–4 away), Hull City (1–4 at home) and Wigan Athletic (2–5 at home) – he kept a clean sheet on his final appearance for the club in a 1–0 win at York City.

CAMPBELL, Leslie

Outside-left

Born: Wigan, 26 July 1935.
Career: Wigan Athletic. PRESTON NORTH END, 1953. Blackpool, 1960. Tranmere Rovers, 1961. Wigan Athletic.

■ After just a handful of appearances in Wigan Athletic's Lancashire Combination Championship-winning side of 1952–53, winger Les Campbell joined North End. Deputising for the injured Tom Finney, he made his debut

in a 1–0 defeat at Champions-elect Wolverhampton Wanderers. Though he went on to appear in 14 games, creating a number of goals for the likes of Charlie Wayman and Jimmy Baxter, he was not considered for any of the FA Cup games which saw North End reach the Final. Able to play on either flank, Campbell spent the next few seasons as understudy to both Finney and Morrison. By the time he left Deepdale in the summer of 1960, he had made just 64 League appearances. It was a similar story at his new club Blackpool and after one season at Bloomfield Road, he moved on to Tranmere Rovers. After injuries hampered his first season at Prenton Park, Campbell missed few games over the following two seasons before leaving to rejoin Wigan Athletic, whom he helped win the 1964–65 Cheshire League title.

CAMPBELL, William Cecil

Inside-forward

Born: London.
Career: Royal Arsenal. PRESTON NORTH END, 1890. Middlesbrough. Darwen, 1892. Blackburn Rovers, 1893. Newton Heath, 1893. Notts County, 1893. Newark.

■ Able to play in a variety of forward positions, William Campbell joined North End midway through the 1890–91 season from Royal Arsenal. After making his debut in a 1–0 win at Everton, he played in the first-round FA Cup defeat at Stoke before scoring four goals in the next three games, including a brace in the 7–0 rout of Burnley. Despite North End finishing runners-up to Everton in the Football League, Campbell moved on to Middlesbrough and shortly afterwards to Darwen. He later had spells with Blackburn Rovers, Newton Heath and Notts County before seeing out his career with Newark.

CARLIN, John

Inside-forward, outside-left

Born: Liverpool, 1882.
Career: Liverpool, 1902. PRESTON NORTH END, 1907.

■ Inside-forward John Carlin started out with his home-town team Liverpool

and, though he was not a first-team regular, he made some vital contributions to the club's successive League Championship wins in 1904–05 and 1905–06. He left Anfield to join Preston North End in 1907. Given quite an extensive run in the Deepdale club's first team, he opened his goalscoring account with two goals in the space of five minutes in a 3–0 defeat of Woolwich Arsenal. Despite continuing to look threatening, he lost out to James Wilson and decided to retire at the end of the 1908–09 season.

CARMICHAEL, Matthew

Centre-half, forward

Born: Singapore, 13 May 1964.
Career: Basingstoke Town. Lincoln City, 1989. Scunthorpe United, 1993. Barnet, 1994 (loan). PRESTON NORTH END, 1995. Mansfield Town, 1995. Doncaster Rovers, 1995. Darlington, 1996.

■ Singapore-born Matt Carmichael played his early football for non-League Basingstoke Town before being given his chance in the Football League with Lincoln City in the summer of 1989. A virtual ever present in the Imps' Fourth Division side, he had scored 21 goals in 156 games when he left to play for Scunthorpe United in July 1993. He found the net with greater consistency for the Irons with 27 goals in 76 games yet, following a loan spell with Barnet, he was allowed to join North End on a free transfer. The former squaddie scored twice on his Preston debut in a 5–0 win over Bury. Strong on the ball and in the air, he added a further goal in a 1–1 draw against Gillingham but was released at the end of the season. He spent a week on trial at Mansfield Town prior to signing for Doncaster Rovers. At Belle Vue he appeared in a variety of positions before midway through the season he moved to Darlington, where his best displays were as a central defender. Despite helping the Quakers to the Play-off Final, he parted company with the Feethams club.

CARR, Anthony Grey

Goalkeeper

Born: Old Hartley, 18 May 1901.
Died: 1968.
Career: Seaton Delaval Villa. Newport

County, 1922. Sheffield Wednesday, 1924. Seaton Delaval Villa. PRESTON NORTH END, 1926. South Shields, 1929. Gateshead, 1930. New Brighton, 1934.

■ Goalkeeper Tony Carr began his Football League career with Newport County, making 80 appearances before moving to First Division Sheffield Wednesday. Injuries hampered his progress with the Owls and he returned to non-League football with his first club, Seaton Delaval Villa. Preston manager Frank Richards offered Carr the chance to resurrect his League career and he joined the Deepdale club in readiness for the 1926–27 season. Carr did not have the best of debuts as North End went down 5–1 at Oldham Athletic and, though he was on the end of a few more heavy defeats – notably a 7–0 mauling at Nottingham Forest – his displays helped the club finish fifth in Division Two. With Carr in outstanding form, North End were again pushing for promotion to the top flight in 1927–28 but the arrival of Frank Moss saw Carr move to South Shields. His form for the North East club was good and helped them to seventh place in the Third Division North. Carr later ended his career with New Brighton.

CARRICK, Matthew David

Winger

Born: Evenwood, 5 December 1946.
Died: 1989.
Career: Wolverhampton Wanderers, 1964. Wrexham, 1966. Altrincham. Port Vale, 1969. Stalybridge Celtic. Witton Albion. PRESTON NORTH END, 1973. Rochdale, 1974. Altrincham.

■ Versatile forward David Carrick was on the books of Wolverhampton Wanderers before he switched to Wrexham, where he made his Football League debut on the opening day of the 1966–67 season. As well as creating goals for teammates Albert Kinsey and Sammy McMillan, Carrick scored a handful of spectacular goals himself that season, helping the Robins to finish seventh in Division Four. Surprisingly released midway through the following season, he joined non-League Altrincham before moving on to Port Vale. Unable to make much impact at Vale Park, he had spells

with Stalybridge Celtic and Witton Albion before arriving at Deepdale in November 1973. He made his debut as a substitute for Graham Hawkins in a 1–1 draw at Oxford United and came off the bench again in the following game, replacing Nobby Stiles in another draw, 2–2 with Luton Town. These were his only appearances in what was a miserable season as North End were relegated to Division Three and deducted a point by the FA as Carrick was classed ineligible when he made his debut. He ended his first-class career with Rochdale before returning to Altrincham to end his playing days.

CARTWRIGHT, Lee

Midfield

Born: Rawtenstall, 19 September 1972.
Career: PRESTON NORTH END, 1991. Stockport County, 2004.

■ Midfield dynamo Lee Cartwright quickly forged a reputation as a very fast winger, with the ability both to create and score goals. He made his North End

debut in a 1–0 win at Shrewsbury Town in March 1991 and continued to show promise over the next few seasons, helping North End reach the Third Division Play-offs in 1993–94 and 1994–95. Cartwright's move from the centre of Preston's midfield to the wide right in 1995–96 was an inspired move: his pace and accurate crossing led to many goals for the strikers. It was a tragedy for himself and North End when a serious knee injury at Scunthorpe in February sidelined him for the rest of the campaign, although by then he had played enough games to qualify for a Third Division Championship medal when the title was eventually won. His return to first-team action exactly a year later ended his nightmare following a cruciate ligament operation. His speed and penetration on the right side of midfield had been sorely missed. Though he scored his first double for the club in a 4–1 away win at Wigan in 1997–98, he also picked up a niggling injury, which did not help in his attempts to find some consistent form. Though 1998–99 was a miserable season for the club's longest-serving player for a number of reasons – injuries and a loss of pace and the ability to beat his marker

– he did reach his 250th League and 300th career games (the first North End player to do so since the 1980s). Injuries continued to blight his career – a cartilage operation in 1999–2000 as North End won the Second Division Championship, followed by a knee operation in the close season which meant he missed the start of the following season. He started the 2001–02 campaign with a testimonial against Middlesbrough before playing his 400th senior game for North End, later briefly returning to his original central midfield role. Over the next couple of seasons, his appearances became less frequent and his last game for the club against Gillingham in December 2003 saw him become only the fourth player ever to make 100 substitute appearances for a single club. Moving on to Stockport County, he quickly settled in at Edgeley Park, becoming a regular on the right-hand side of midfield and playing a key role in the club's successful fight to avoid relegation. However, in 2004–05 he picked up a serious injury that ruled him out for much of the campaign.

CATTERALL, John

Inside-left, outside-left

Born: Leyland, 1883.
Career: PRESTON NORTH END, 1904.

▮ Leyland-born winger John Catterall made four appearances in the number-11 shirt during the 1904–05 season – the club's first season back in the top flight for three years – but was never on the winning side. Though he remained at Deepdale for a further five seasons, he did not figure in the first team until October 1909 when he scored North End's goal in a 3–1 defeat at Bury. Released at the end of the season, he drifted into local non-League football.

CAUSER, Arthur Hayden

Goalkeeper

Born: Wolverhampton, 1890.
Career: Glossop North End, 1912. PRESTON NORTH END, 1919. Shrewsbury Town.

▮ Goalkeeper Arthur Causer holds a unique record as he is the only player to have played for two League teams called

North End. Before World War One, he made 109 appearances for Glossop North End, always reserving his best for games against Preston. John Morley netted a hat-trick for the Lilywhites in a 3–2 win at Devil's Elbow on New Year's Day 1913. In the last season before the hostilities – when Preston won the Second Division Championship and Glossop finished bottom of the League – Causer had outstanding games in the two 1–0 defeats. After joining Preston, Causer made his debut in the opening game of the 1919–20 season, a 4–0 defeat at Blackburn Rovers, but over the next couple of seasons he found himself sharing the goalkeeping duties with a number of other 'keepers including Whalley, Foot, Jones, Wilcock, Mitchell and Elliott. He later left Deepdale to continue his career with Shrewsbury Town.

CHADWICK, Thomas

Wing-half, centre-half

Born: Blackburn, 2 March 1882.
Died: 1960.
Career: Blackburn Rovers, 1900. Everton, 1901. PRESTON NORTH END, 1908.

▮ Able to play in any of the half-back positions, Tom Chadwick was on the books of Blackburn Rovers just after the turn of the century but he moved to Everton after being unable to break into the club's League side. He was at Goodison Park for seven seasons, but he made just 21 League appearances in all that time. Chadwick joined North End prior to the start of the 1908–09 season and made his debut in the opening game of the campaign in a goalless draw at Chelsea. With the half-back line of Holdsworth, McCall and Lyon well established, Chadwick made just nine appearances before parting company with the club.

CHALLENDER, Gregory Louis

Midfield

Born: Rochdale, 5 February 1973.
Career: Mossley. PRESTON NORTH END, 1993. Southport.

▮ Midfielder Greg Challender arrived at Deepdale from non-League Mossley in

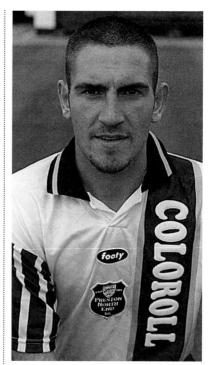

the summer of 1993. After some impressive displays in the club's reserve side, he made his League debut in a 4–1 home win over Chesterfield when he helped make two of Tony Ellis' hat-trick goals. He was unable to hold down a regular place, though, and netted his only North End goal in the 3–2 home defeat by Wycombe Wanderers. Challender remained at Deepdale for another season before leaving to play for Southport.

CHALMERS, James

Outside-left, inside-left

Born: Old Luce, 3 December 1877.
Career: Clyde. Greenock Morton. Sunderland, 1897. PRESTON NORTH END, 1898. Notts County, 1899. Partick Thistle. Watford. Tottenham Hotspur. Swindon Town. Norwich City. Bristol Rovers.

▮ Prematurely grey-haired when scarcely out of his teens, Jimmy Chalmers had played for both Clyde and Morton before joining Sunderland for the 1897–98 season. During the course of the campaign, he scored some vital goals including two in a 4–0 defeat of Nottingham Forest on the final day of the season to help the Wearsiders to the runners'-up spot in Division One. Early the following season, he moved to

Preston North End but failed to make the impact he had at Roker Park, scoring twice in 10 games as the Lilywhites just avoided relegation to Division Two. Thereafter, he moved freely from club to club, playing for Notts County, Partick Thistle, Watford, Spurs, Swindon Town, Norwich City and Bristol Rovers – his style once being described as 'impetuous and dashing'.

CHANDLER, Sidney Ellis

Right-half, inside-right

Born: London, 30 May 1901.
Died: 1961.
Career: Aston Villa, 1925. PRESTON NORTH END, 1926. Reading, 1928. Canterbury Waverley.

■ Unable to force his way into Aston Villa's League side, inside-forward Sidney Chandler joined Preston North End just days before the start of the 1926–27 season. He played his first game in the number-four shirt in a 2–2 draw with Clapton Orient on the opening day of the campaign, later switching to inside-right after a handful of displays at right-half. Missing just one game, a 2–1 home defeat at the hands of Portsmouth, he was second-top scorer to Tommy Roberts with 11 goals – a total which included doubles against Blackpool, Reading and South Shields. He continued to alternate between right-half and inside-right the following season before playing in just a handful of games at the start of the 1928–29 campaign. He moved on to Reading but following their relegation from Division Two in 1930–31, he left to play non-League football for Canterbury Waverley.

CHAPMAN, Leslie

Midfield

Born: Oldham, 27 September 1948.
Career: Oldham Athletic, 1967. Huddersfield Town, 1969. Oldham Athletic, 1974. San Jose Earthquakes (US, loan). Stockport County, 1979. Bradford City, 1980. Rochdale, 1983. Stockport County, 1985. PRESTON NORTH END, 1986.

■ In May 1989, Les Chapman completed 22 seasons of League soccer,

which made him the game's second longest-serving player behind Swansea's Tommy Hutchison. Chapman was working as a trainee accountant when his home-town team Oldham Athletic signed him in January 1967. He was transferred to Huddersfield Town – with whom he had once been on amateur forms – in September 1969. He featured in Town's Second Division Championship side that season and in January 1971 his opening goal in the televised 2–1 victory over Arsenal was voted Goal of the Month. In December 1974, with Town dropping into Division Three, he rejoined Oldham. In almost four and a half years with the Latics – he had a loan spell in the US with San Jose Earthquakes in 1978 – Chapman missed only five Second Division games. His free transfer to Stockport County in May 1979 came as a shock to Latics fans. Bradford City signed him for £10,000 in February 1980 and two years later he helped them out of Division Four. He joined Rochdale in June 1983 and later served them as player-manager and assistant manager. In July 1985, Chapman became player-manager at Stockport, relinquishing the post 12 months later to join Preston North End as player-assistant manager. During the course of that 1986–87 season, a campaign in which North End won promotion to the Third Division, a rare Chapman goal in a 2–1 win at Orient clinched the club's elevation into a higher grade of football. His appearance at Swansea's Vetch Field on 17 January 1987 was of special significance to Les Chapman because it meant that the veteran player had played at all 92 League grounds. After playing for one more

season, he retired to take up the role of coach with the club. In February 1990, he was appointed team manager after the departure of John McGrath. His new job coincided with a decent run of form, which was timely, especially after the team had flirted with relegation for much of the campaign. But the team's form began to falter once more and Les Chapman was relieved of the manager's job in September 1992.

CHARLTON, Robert

Inside-forward

Born: Ashington, 11 October 1937.
Career: Manchester United, 1954. PRESTON NORTH END, 1974.

■ In February 1958, after a European Cup-tie in Belgrade, Manchester United's plane crashed in thick snow at Munich Airport. Bobby Charlton was thrown 50 yards and escaped with just a deep cut to his head. After his return to Old Trafford, though, it did not take long for him to reach the footballing heights – within a little over two months, he made his international debut against Scotland, marking the occasion with a spectacular goal. By 1966 and the World Cup Finals in England, Charlton's skills had reached their full maturity. He opened England's scoring with a typical long-distance blast and went on to score some thrilling goals in the tournament, including both goals in England's 2–1 semi-final win over Portugal. At the end of that season, he won both the Footballer of the Year and European players' awards. In May 1968 he scored two goals in the emotionally charged European Cup Final against Benfica at Wembley as United won 4–1. After 106 caps and 49 goals his international career ended in Mexico in dramatic fashion. He was substituted in order to keep him fresh for the semi-finals as England led West Germany 2–0, but it was not to be, as the Germans ran out 3–2 winners. He pulled on a Manchester United shirt for the last time at Stamford Bridge in 1973, setting appearance records for both club and country. Charlton joined Preston North End as manager in the summer of 1973 but his first season in charge at Deepdale ended in relegation and he decided to put his boots back on to take on the

Wrexham, 1968. Bradford Park Avenue, 1969.

■ Ray Charnley was playing non-League football for Morecambe when Blackpool manager Joe Smith persuaded him to join the Seasiders in the summer of 1957. In his first season with the club he scored twice in Blackpool's biggest-ever home victory, 7–0 over Sunderland, before going off with a gashed forehead. Charnley topped the Blackpool scoring charts for the first of five consecutive seasons in 1958–59 with a best of 36 goals in 1961–62. During the course of that season he netted four of Blackpool's goals in a 7–2 home win over Wolverhampton Wanderers and scored hat-tricks in the defeats of Chelsea and Leyton Orient. This form led to his only full international cap for England in the match against France at Hillsborough. Charnley scored 10 hat-tricks for the Bloomfield Road club in a total of 222 goals in 407 games before Stan Mortensen made the unpopular decision to transfer him to rivals Preston North End in December 1967. Just nine days after putting pen to paper Charnley, who made his North End debut against Millwall, returned to Bloomfield Road and scored against his former club, although Preston went down 4–1. With

player-manager's role. During the 1974–75 season Charlton, who played in 38 games, did not let the fans down and one of the features of the campaign was to see his famous shooting power. Towards the end of the season, he hung up his boots again, this time for good, but his time with the team will always be remembered with great affection and there is no doubt his skills helped the youngsters take first-team football in their stride. The following season, however, he resigned after the board went behind his back to sell John Bird to Newcastle United. His integrity and respect had been compromised. He was an active director of Wigan Athletic,

whom he managed for a brief spell towards the end of the 1982–83 season before establishing the famous Bobby Charlton soccer schools for children. Knighted for his services to football, he has helped make Manchester United the most famous club in the world and was without doubt one of the most talented and popular footballers of all-time.

CHARNLEY, Raymond Ogden

Centre-forward

Born: Lancaster, 29 May 1935.
Career: Morecambe. Blackpool, 1957.
PRESTON NORTH END, 1967.

the midfield failing to create goalscoring chances, Charnley struggled to find the net with his usual regularity, although he did score twice in a 3–1 FA Cup third-round win at Queen's Park Rangers just a week after they had lost there in the League. At the end of the season, Charnley moved on to Wrexham before later ending his career with Bradford Park Avenue.

CHESTER, Albert

Inside-left

Born: Hexham.
Career: Wingate Albion. PRESTON NORTH END, 1910. Croydon Common. Queen's Park Rangers. Brentford.

■ Inside-forward Albert Chester joined North End from Wingate Albion and made his debut in a 2–0 defeat at Woolwich Arsenal towards the end of the 1910–11 season. His second and final appearance came on the last day of the season when he scored in another 2–0 defeat, this time of Bradford City. He left Deepdale to play Southern League football for Croydon Common. He later turned out briefly for Queen's Park Rangers in the same competition before ending his playing days with Brentford.

CHIPPENDALE, Brian Albert

Midfield

Born: Bradford, 29 October 1964.
Career: Bradford City. York City, 1983. Halifax Town, 1984 (loan). Burnley, 1985. PRESTON NORTH END, 1985. Farsley Celtic.

■ Unable to make the grade with his home-town club, Bradford City, midfielder Brian Chippendale had spells with York City and Halifax Town before appearing briefly in the Burnley side at the start of 1985–86, the Clarets' first-ever season in Division Four. He was released after a handful of games and joined Preston North End in October 1985. He made his debut in a 6–3 home defeat by Chester City and in fact was never on the winning side in any of his six League appearances. It was not the best season for the club as they finished just one place above the foot of the Fourth Division. He later played for

Farsley Celtic in the Northern Counties East League.

CHRISTIE, David

Winger

Born: Salford, 26 February 1973.
Career: PRESTON NORTH END, 1991. Halifax Town, 1993.

■ YTS trainee winger David Christie played his first game for Preston North End when he came off the bench to replace Lee Ashcroft in a 2–1 home win over Leyton Orient in April 1992. There followed a couple more appearances as a substitute before he eventually made his first start early the following season in a 2–0 defeat at Brighton. Midway through that 1992–93 season, Christie joined Halifax Town but was unable to prevent them losing their Football League status.

CLARK, Clive

Outside-left

Born: Leeds, 19 December 1940.
Career: Leeds United, 1958. Queen's Park Rangers, 1958. West Bromwich Albion, 1961. Queen's Park Rangers, 1969. PRESTON NORTH END, 1970. Southport, 1973. Telford. Washington Diplomats (US). Philadelphia Fury (US).

■ One of the game's fastest-ever wingers, Clive Clark began his first-class

career with Queen's Park Rangers before signing for West Bromwich Albion in January 1961. A superb goalscorer as well as provider, Clark was a virtual ever present in the Albion side from his arrival at the Hawthorns until he returned to Loftus Road in the summer of 1969. He was a member of the Albion side that reached Cup finals in three successive years – 1966, 1967 and 1968 – collecting winners' medals in the League Cup Final against West Ham in the first and in the FA Cup Final against Everton in the last. In the run to the League Cup Final of 1967, Clark became the only player ever to score in every game of the tournament, including the two goals that gave Albion a handsome half-time lead against Queen's Park Rangers, only to see the match end in disappointment when Albion lost 3–2. In around 350 games for Albion, Clark scored nearly a hundred goals and was the club's top scorer in 1966–67 with 19 League goals. His second spell at Loftus Road was brief and in January 1970 he joined Preston North End. Though he was unable to halt the club's slide into the Third Division, he was a revelation in 1970–71 as his crosses provided Gerry Ingram and Bobby Ham with numerous goalscoring oppor-tunities in a campaign in which North End won the Division Three title. Injuries then began to restrict Clark's first-team appearances and he left Deepdale to assist Southport and then Telford before winding down his career in the NASL with Washington Diplomats and Philadelphia Fury.

CLARK, Jonathan

Midfield

Born: Swansea, 12 November 1958.
Career: Manchester United, 1975. Derby County, 1978. PRESTON NORTH END, 1981. Bury, 1986. Carlisle United, 1987. Morecambe. Rhyl.

■ Jonathan Clark was a Welsh Under-21 international midfielder who had made one substitute outing for Manchester United when former United boss Tommy Docherty paid £50,000 for him to move to Derby County in September 1978. Docherty's advance praise – 'the best thing to come out of Wales since coal' – did him no favours and though he was a wholehearted performer, he found it hard to make any impact in a struggling Rams side. He also had the misfortune to be sent off when he played his first League game in his native Swansea in October 1980. He joined Preston North End in the summer of 1981 and made his debut in a 2–1 defeat at Millwall on the opening day of the 1981–82 season. Injuries then hampered his progress at Deepdale and it was only midway through the 1983–84 campaign that he began to make his mark on the side. Clark's best season in North End colours was 1984–85 but sadly it also coincided with the club's relegation to the Fourth Division for the first time in their history. The 1985–86 season was the worst in the club's history and it was not until mid-March that anything like a decent run was put together. This coincided with Jonathan Clark being appointed caretaker manager in place of Brian Kidd. Suddenly, North End managed five wins on the trot, including three successive 3–2 victories, but then a home defeat by Orient and a 4–0 beating at Colchester brought everyone back down to earth. Only Torquay United's failings saved North End from the dreaded last

position in the Football League and that in itself was complete humiliation as the League's first winners had to apply for re-election. John McGrath was appointed manager and in December 1986, Clark joined Bury. He later played for Carlisle United prior to appearances for non-League sides Morecambe and Rhyl.

CLARKE, Thomas

Goalkeeper

Born: Ardrossan, 12 April 1946.
Career: Airdrieonians. Carlisle United, 1970. PRESTON NORTH END, 1975.

■ Goalkeeper Tom Clarke began his career in the Scottish League with Airdrie, helping them win the Scottish League First Division in 1965–66. His performances north of the border had attracted the attention of a number of English clubs and in July 1970 he joined Carlisle United. Most of his time at Brunton Park was spent as understudy to long-serving Alan Ross as the Cumbrian club continually challenged for promotion to the top flight. Clarke joined North End in the summer of 1975 as cover for Roy Tunks. He made three appearances for the club midway through the campaign, with the last bringing a 3–2 victory over Rotherham United. He was probably a little unlucky to lose his place to Tunks because North End's regular 'keeper, who had been dropped, conceded eight goals on his last appearance for the reserves in a home Central League match against Liverpool.

CLEMENT, Neil

Defender, midfield

Born: Reading, 3 October 1978.
Career: Chelsea, 1995. Reading, 1998 (loan). PRESTON NORTH END, 1999 (loan). Brentford, 1999 (loan). West Bromwich Albion, 2000.

■ Son of the late Queen's Park Rangers and England full-back Dave Clement, Neil began his career with Chelsea where his potential was recognised by then England boss, Glenn Hoddle. He was one of two Youth internationals called up to join the England squad's preparation for the World Cup qualifier against Italy. After a couple of substitute appearances in the

League Cup, Clement joined Reading on loan but a dip in form and an excessive transfer fee demand by the London club meant that no permanent deal was arranged. Unable to get further games at Chelsea, he joined Preston during transfer deadline week in March 1999. He made a memorable debut at Colchester United, when he was sent off for two bookable offences. Following his four appearances for North End, where he was never on the winning side, he had loan spells with Brentford and West Bromwich Albion before joining the Baggies on a permanent basis. A stylish left-wing-back, he was deservedly voted Albion's Player of the Year in his first season at the Hawthorns and named in the PFA Division One team of the season in 2001–02. He later helped Albion win promotion to the Premiership and his consistency both in midfield and at the heart of the Albion defence ensured that they retained their top-flight status until they were relegated at the end of the 2005–06 season.

CLIFTON, William

Outside-right

Born: Preston, 1891.
Career: PRESTON NORTH END, 1914. Rochdale, 1921.

■ Local-born winger William Clifton appeared for Preston either side of World War One, making his debut in a 1–1 draw at Clapton Orient towards the end of the 1914–15 season. With North End winning promotion that season, his next games in 1919–20 were in the First Division but he was only on the winning side on the final day of the campaign, when they needed to win at Everton to avoid the drop. It was Clifton who provided the cross for Roberts to score the only goal of the game. Unable to force his way back into the first team the following season, he joined Rochdale for their first season in the Football League.

COCHRANE, John

Forward

Born: Bellshill, 27 April 1959.
Career: PRESTON NORTH END, 1977.

■ Scottish-born forward John Cochrane was just 18 years 17 days old when he made a goalscoring debut for Preston North End in a 2–1 win at Shrewsbury Town on the final day of the 1976–77 season. Despite this promising start, he was unable to force his way into the North End side during the club's promotion-winning season of 1977–78 and it was the following season before he added to his first-team appearances, netting another goal against Brighton. With the likes of Alex Bruce and Michael Robinson in the side, Cochrane was allowed to leave the club.

COLEMAN, Anthony George

Outside-left

Born: Ellesmere Port, 2 May 1945.
Career: Stoke City. Tranmere Rovers, 1962. PRESTON NORTH END, 1964. Bangor City. Doncaster Rovers, 1965. Manchester City, 1967. Sheffield Wednesday, 1969. Blackpool, 1970. Durban City (South Africa). Southport, 1973. Stockport County, 1974.

■ Much-travelled winger Tony Coleman was an apprentice on Stoke City's books but opted for a move to Tranmere Rovers when he was unable

to make much progress at the Victoria Ground. It was from the Prenton Park club that Coleman joined North End in the summer of 1964 and, though he spent most of his time at Deepdale as understudy to Doug Holden, he played in five consecutive games midway through the season, scoring in a 6–1 defeat of Portsmouth. After a spell in non-League football with Bangor City, he returned to League action with Doncaster Rovers, helping them win the Fourth Division Championship in 1965–66. His displays for the Belle Vue club led to him joining Manchester City where he won a League Championship medal in 1967–68 and an FA Cup winners' medal in 1969 after City had beaten Leicester 1–0 in the Final. Shortly after this success, Coleman joined Sheffield Wednesday but following their relegation from the top flight he moved to Blackpool. After a spell playing for Durban City in South Africa, Coleman played for Southport before ending his career with Stockport County.

COLEMAN, Gordon Michael

Midfield

Born: Nottingham, 11 February 1954.
Career: Padstow YC. PRESTON NORTH END, 1973. Bury, 1983.

■ Gordon Coleman arrived at Deepdale after being plucked from Nottinghamshire amateur football where he banged in the goals on a regular basis for his local side. The two Nottingham clubs, Forest and County, had been put off by the fact that Coleman had been deliberating on whether to become a professional footballer or not. But eventually the lure of the game became too much for the youngster and he set his sights on making a success of his football career with Preston North End. He made his League debut as a 17-year-old in a 3–1 defeat of West Bromwich Albion in October 1973 and appeared in a further six games during that relegation season. His first goal came the following season in a 1–1 draw with Crystal Palace after which he established himself as a quality player with an eye for goal. Over the next 10 seasons, Coleman missed very few

games, helping North End win promotion to Division Two in 1977–78. Though he suffered a spate of niggling injuries towards the end of his stay at Deepdale, he had scored 30 goals in 301 League and Cup games before he left to join Bury in August 1983.

COMMON, Alfred

Forward

Born: Millfield, County Durham, 25 May 1880.
Died: 1946.
Career: South Hylton. Jarrow. Sunderland, 1900. Sheffield United, 1901. Sunderland, 1904. Middlesbrough, 1904. Woolwich Arsenal, 1910. PRESTON NORTH END, 1912.

■ Alf Common started his footballing career playing junior football with South Hylton and Jarrow before he joined Sunderland in 1900. He soon won a regular place and helped the club to the runners'-up spot in the First Division in his first season. However, with the Wearsiders having a surplus of inside-forwards, he was allowed to join Sheffield United. In his first season with the Bramall Lane club he became a folk hero by scoring the winning goal in the 1902 FA Cup Final against Southampton. He stayed at Bramall Lane for a further two seasons and also won the first of his three England caps against Ireland in February 1904. He moved back to Sunderland for the start of the 1904–05 season before making football history by becoming the first-ever player to be transferred for a four-figure sum when he joined Middlesbrough for £1,000 in February 1905. In his first full season he was the club's top scorer with 24 goals, netting hat-tricks against Stoke and Brighton. Forming a good strike partnership with Steve Bloomer, he scored another treble for Boro in a 4–2 win at Liverpool in April 1907. Early the following season he lost the Middlesbrough captaincy following drunkenness and violent behaviour. Three years later he joined Woolwich Arsenal after scoring 65 goals in 178 games. In 1911–12 he was the club's leading scorer but shortly afterwards he left to play for Preston North End. Not only did the signing create huge interest in the town but it also lifted the other members of the team to know that players of his quality were being brought in. His seven goals in 21 games helped North End to win the Second Division Championship as they finished three points clear of Burnley. Though he scored on the opening day of the 1913–14 season in a 2–2 draw against his former club, Sunderland, he began to struggle against the top-flight opposition and retired.

COMMON, Edward Winchester

Full-back

Born: Seaton Delaval, 25 January 1904.
Career: Blyth Spartans. Everton, 1928. PRESTON NORTH END, 1933. Chester, 1935.

■ Full-back Ted Common had played non-League football for Blyth Spartans prior to joining Everton. However, he failed to win a regular place in the Blues side, last appearing in a handful of games during the club's relegation season of 1929–30. He remained at Goodison Park until November 1933 when he joined Preston North End. Common's only

appearance for the Lilywhites came on Christmas Day when North End lost 3–2 at Brentford. He later signed for Chester and in his first season, 1935–36, helped them finish runners-up in the Third Division North. He eventually made 142 appearances for the Cestrians.

CONNOR, David Richard

Full-back

Born: Wythenshawe, 27 October 1945.
Career: Manchester City, 1962. PRESTON NORTH END, 1972. Macclesfield Town.

■ Beginning his career with Manchester City, Dave Connor was one of the Maine Road club's greatest utility players. He made his debut against Charlton Athletic in August 1964 and then appeared in every first-team position except goalkeeper for City, eventually making 165 League and Cup appearances. In January 1972 he joined Preston North End. He played his first game in a 1–1 home draw against Orient and appeared in the majority of the remaining games in that 1971–72 campaign. Though he only made 29 League appearances in a season and a half at Deepdale, he wore six different numbered outfield shirts. Connor later rejoined Manchester City and was a regular in the club's Central League side. Unable to force his way into the City first team, he joined Macclesfield Town, later becoming the Silkmen's manager.

CONNOR, Edward A.

Inside-right

Born: Preston, 1872.
Career: PRESTON NORTH END, 1893. Liverpool, 1894.

■ Local-born forward Edward Connor was given his North End debut during the course of the 1893–94 season when the club just avoided relegation from the First Division. In what was his only appearance, he replaced the injured Jimmy Ross in the match against Champions-elect Aston Villa and, though he made a goal for Frank Becton, North End lost 5–2. At the end of that season he joined Liverpool but could not force his way into the Anfield club's League side.

CONROY, Michael Kevin

Forward

Born: Glasgow, 31 December 1965.
Career: Clydebank. St Mirren. Reading, 1988. Burnley, 1991. PRESTON NORTH END, 1993. Fulham, 1995. Blackpool, 1998. Chester City, 1998 (loan). Chester City, 1999 (loan).

■ Having begun his career as an apprentice with Coventry City, Michael Conroy returned to his native Scotland in 1984 without having made a breakthrough at Highfield Road and joined Clydebank. Immediately the goals started flowing and Conroy finished as top scorer in each of his four seasons at Kilbowie Park. After a short spell at St Mirren, he joined Reading in September 1988 for £40,000 but after being used mainly as a utility player, he left Elm Park for Burnley. In 1991–92, his first season at Turf Moor, Conroy scored goals as though they were going out of fashion – 24 in the League and six in Cup matches – as the Clarets won promotion from the Fourth Division as Champions. The following season was a little disappointing for Conroy, for in a season of consolidation, he was unable to recapture his deadly goalscoring form. Unable to agree terms with Burnley manager Jimmy Mullen in the close

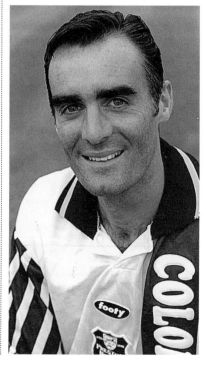

season of 1993, he left Turf Moor as the following campaign got underway, joining Preston for £85,000. In his first full League start, Conroy netted a hat-trick in a 6–1 defeat of Shrewsbury Town and finished the season as second top scorer behind Tony Ellis. However, his goals dried up towards the end of the campaign and he played no part in North End's Play-off defeat by Wycombe Wanderers. His 10 goals during 1994–95, which included two in the 2–1 win at Mansfield and the winner in the televised FA Cup tie against Blackpool, made him top scorer as Preston reached the Play-offs again, this time falling to Bury in the semi-final. He moved to Fulham in August 1995 and once again emerged as his team's top scorer. His first League goal for the Cottagers was the 100th of his senior career. When Fulham won promotion in 1996–97, Conroy was again the Cottagers' leading scorer. His performances won him selection in the PFA divisional team and the club's Player of the Year award. Injuries then restricted his appearances and after scoring 42 goals in 115 games he joined Blackpool. Unable to win a regular spot in the Seasiders' team, he spent two spells on loan at Chester City before hanging up his boots.

COOK, George

Full-back, left-half

Born: Shankhouse, 20 November 1904.
Career: Bedlington United. Gillingham, 1924. PRESTON NORTH END, 1924. Torquay United, 1927. Carlisle United, 1928. Sittingbourne. Everton, 1930. Tranmere Rovers, 1931. Carlisle United, 1932.

■ Full-back George Cook joined North End from Gillingham prior to the start of the 1924–25 season and made his debut in a 3–1 defeat of Nottingham Forest. He kept his place in the side until James Phizacklea replaced him towards the end of that relegation campaign. The following season saw Cook in and out of the North End side. In the summer of 1926 he moved to Torquay United and played in their first season of League football. He then joined Carlisle United and completed a remarkable double by appearing for the Cumbrian side on their entry into the Football League.

After a season at Everton in which he failed to break into their League side, he had a brief spell with Tranmere before rejoining Carlisle where he ended his career.

COOK, Lawrence

Outside-right, right-back

Born: Nelson, 1880.
Career: Nelson. Blackpool, 1904. PRESTON NORTH END, 1905.

■ Lawrence Cook was a versatile player who played his early football for his home-town team Nelson. He was given his chance at League level by Blackpool and in 1904–05 he made seven appearances for the Seasiders on the right-wing. He left Bloomfield Road in the close season and joined North End primarily as cover for a number of positions. His chance, in a season in which North End finished runners-up to Liverpool in the First Division, came against Notts County, a match Preston won 4–1. Though he still could not force his way into the North End side, he remained at Deepdale the following season, playing his last match at full-back in a 3–0 defeat at Manchester United before leaving to play in the local non-League scene.

CORBETT, William

Centre-half

Born: Falkirk, 31 August 1922.
Career: Dunipace Thistle. Maryhill Juniors. Glasgow Celtic, 1941. PRESTON NORTH END, 1948. Leicester City, 1949. Yeovil Town. Dunfermline Athletic. Morton.

■ 'Capped' in the wartime international against England in 1942, William Corbett also 'guested' for West Ham United, Cardiff City, Swansea Town and Southampton while on military service. A former motor mechanic, he returned to Parkhead after the war to continue his career with Celtic, where his performances almost led to him winning full international honours for Scotland. In 1947–48, Celtic were threatened with relegation for the first time ever and were desperate for points in one of their final matches at Falkirk. With the game goalless and time running out, Celtic

were awarded a penalty. Up stepped Corbett to secure a 1–0 win for Celtic. Nevertheless, he left Parkhead that summer to join Preston North End. Having made his debut in a 2–2 home draw against Portsmouth on the first day of the 1948–49 season, Corbett was the club's first-choice centre-half until midway through the season when, following a disastrous display against Bolton (a match the Wanderers won 5–3), he lost out to Paddy Waters. Leicester City manager Johnny Duncan took Corbett to Filbert Street but shortly afterwards the manager departed. Corbett followed after failing to convince new manager Norman Bullock that he could marshall City's defence as well as he had organised Celtic's. After a spell with Yeovil Town, he returned north of the border to play for Dunfermline Athletic and later Morton.

CORR, Peter Joseph

Outside-right

Born: Dundalk, 22 June 1923.
Career: Dundalk. PRESTON NORTH END, 1947. Everton, 1948. Bangor.

■ A former Gaelic football player, Peter Corr joined Preston North End from League of Ireland club Dundalk in April 1947. Understudy to the great Tom Finney, he was also unlucky with injuries during his time at Deepdale. As a result he appeared in just the last three games of the 1946–47 season. Following a campaign of Central League football, he moved to Everton. At Goodison Park he linked up with fellow-countrymen Tommy Eglington and Peter Farrell to form an attacking force bursting with ability and flair. Corr also possessed a great turn of speed, which enabled him to lose his marker. Though he won full international honours for the Republic of Ireland, he was no more than an occasional player in the Blues' First Division side, making 24 appearances in two seasons before leaving for Bangor in 1949.

COWAN, John

Winger

Born: Dumbarton, December 1870.
Died: 1937.
Career: Vale of Leven. PRESTON NORTH

END, 1892. Glasgow Rangers. Aston Villa, 1895. Dundee Harp.

█ Able to play on either flank, winger John Cowan joined North End from Scottish side Vale of Leven in the summer of 1892 and scored on his home debut in a 4–1 win over Sheffield Wednesday. Though it was his only goal in 26 League games that season, it was a different story in the FA Cup where he scored four goals in six games. This included two in a 4–1 win at Accrington and the club's second goal in the first semi-final meeting with Everton. Cowan scored a number of spectacular goals in his second season with the club, cutting in from the flank and unleashing unstoppable drives, but he is best remembered for netting four of North End's goals in their 18–0 FA Cup first-round rout of Reading. At the end of the season he left to play for Rangers before later returning to the Football League with Aston Villa. In each of his two seasons at Villa Park, the club won the League Championship. Cowan scored 25 goals in 69 games before leaving to see out his career in his native Scotland with Dundee Harps.

COX, John

Left-half

Born: Darvel 1911.
Career: Darvel Juniors. Hamilton Academicals. PRESTON NORTH END, 1938.

█ Wing-half Jackie Cox was spotted playing Scottish junior football for Darvel Juniors by Hamilton Academicals and signed for the successful Scottish

First Division side in 1934. For three consecutive seasons, Cox helped the Accies finish in the top half of the table before joining Preston North End in the summer of 1938. Signed primarily as cover for Bill Shankly and Jimmy Milne, he made his debut in a 2–1 defeat at Leicester City in the club's fifth game of the season before scoring the following week against Middlesbrough. Because of the fine form of Docherty and Milne, Cox made just five appearances before later returning north of the border.

CRANSTON, William

Wing-half

Born: Kilmarnock, 18 January 1942.
Career: Saxone YC. Blackpool, 1960. PRESTON NORTH END, 1964. Oldham Athletic, 1970.

█ Bill Cranston began his League career with Blackpool, making his Seasiders' debut in a 7–2 defeat of the mighty Wolverhampton Wanderers in January 1962. Over the next couple of seasons, he made just a handful of appearances before establishing himself in 1963–64. Yet early the following season, he was allowed to leave Bloomfield Road to join Preston North End. His early displays were very promising and over the next five seasons, he proved himself a most valuable member of the North End squad. During that time, his only League goal came in the 3–2 defeat of Hull City in October 1967 when he came off the bench to replace Jimmy McNab and headed the winner. In July 1970, Cranston moved to his third Lancashire club, Oldham Athletic, where he clocked up exactly 100 League appearances. In his first season at Boundary Park he helped the Latics win promotion to the Third Division.

CRAVEN, Joseph Gerard

Centre-half

Born: Preston, 28 December 1903.
Died: 1972.
Career: St Augustine's. Stockport County, 1923. PRESTON NORTH END, 1925. Swansea Town, 1931. Port Vale, 1934. Newport County, 1935. Accrington Stanley, 1936. Leyland Motors.

█ Though he was born in Preston,

much-travelled centre-half Joe Craven began his League career with Stockport County. He joined North End in 1925 and made his debut against high-flying Wolverhampton Wanderers. Craven scored the only goal of the game but, despite this impressive start, it was his only appearance of the season. After appearing twice in 1926–27, he failed to appear at all the following season and just once in 1928–29. In fact, it was 1929–30 before he won a regular place in the Preston side but after one more season of first-team football, he left to join Swansea. After three seasons at the Vetch, he signed for Port Vale but injuries hampered his progress with the Valiants and at the end of 1934–35 he signed for Newport County. He later played for Accrington Stanley before ending his career with Leyland Motors.

CRAWFORD, Robert

Left-half

Born: Glespin, 4 January 1901.
Died: 1965.
Career: Glenbuck Cherrypickers. Raith Rovers. PRESTON NORTH END, 1921. Blackpool, 1932. Blackburn Rovers, 1934. Southport, 1936. Lancaster City.

█ One of North End's all-time greats, Bobby Crawford played his early football for Glenbuck Cherrypickers prior to joining Raith Rovers. He signed for Preston during the 1921–22 season and made his debut in a goalless home draw against Oldham Athletic. Midway through the following season, Crawford made the number-six shirt his own yet, despite coming into the side almost by default, he quietly and commandingly held his place. There were times when he was faulted for attacking too much and neglecting his defensive duties. But during the 1929–30 season, manager Alex Gibson tried Crawford at centre-forward and he responded with two goals in his first game and four goals in his second as Stoke were beaten 5–1. At dead-ball situations, he was one of the fiercest strikers of a ball and the majority of his 17 goals for the club came from such a situation. During his North End career he missed just one game in seven seasons and holds the record for the most consecutive appearances with 194 between February 1928 and September 1932. He left to play for Blackpool but could not prevent the Seasiders from losing their top-flight status. A brief spell with Blackburn Rovers was followed by a couple of seasons playing for Southport before he ended his playing days with non-League Lancaster City.

CRAWLEY, Thomas

Centre-forward, centre-half

Born: Hamilton, 10 November 1911. Died: 1977.
Career: Blantyre Victoria. Hamilton Academicals. Motherwell. PRESTON NORTH END, 1935. Coventry City, 1935.

■ Thomas Crawley was a player who could operate at both centre-half and centre-forward. He began his career with Hamilton Academicals and then Motherwell, helping the Steelmen to finish runners-up in the Scottish First Division before he joined North End in the summer of 1935. He played in a couple of games during the early part of the 1935–36 season, replacing the injured Bud Maxwell but, though he was not on the losing side, he failed to find the net. Despite some promising displays for the club's reserve side, he left Deepdale just nine months after arriving to sign for Coventry City, helping them win the Third Division South Championship in his first season with the club.

CRESSWELL, Richard Paul Wesley

Forward

Born: Bridlington, 20 September 1977.
Career: York City, 1995. Mansfield Town, 1997 (loan). Sheffield Wednesday, 1999. Leicester City, 2000. PRESTON NORTH END, 2001. Leeds United 2005.

■ Richard Cresswell began his career with York City and had a brief loan spell with Mansfield Town in order to gain some League experience. It certainly helped as he soon began to fulfil the promise he had shown on his arrival at Bootham Crescent. In 1998–99 he became the first York player to be capped for England at Under-21 level. His form during that campaign led to Sheffield Wednesday paying £950,000 for his services. With both pace and confidence and keen to be involved in build-up play, Cresswell soon became a huge favourite of the Wednesday fans. However, most of his appearances for the Owls were from the bench and in September 2000 he returned to the Premiership with Leicester City. Unable to establish himself at Filbert Street, he went on loan to Preston North End in March 2001. He scored on his debut just four minutes after coming on as a substitute against Wolves. Having combined well with Macken and Healy, the move was made permanent in the close season with North End paying £500,000 for his signature. Though he started the 2001–02 season on the bench, he showed his worth by scoring four times in three substitute appearances. Despite hamstring problems, he returned to assume the mantle of the club's main striker and ended the campaign as the leading scorer with 16 goals. He was North End's leading scorer again in 2002–03 in spite of suffering a spate of injuries – including one when he was lucky to avoid serious facial injuries after colliding with the perimeter fence at

Bradford. Injuries and a loss of form hampered his progress the following season but he rediscovered his goalscoring touch in 2004–05. He netted 21 goals all told, including a hat-trick in a 3–2 Carling Cup win over his former club Leicester City at the Walkers Stadium. He obviously enjoyed the feat as he repeated it with another treble on New Year's Day against promotion rivals Sunderland. Paramount in North End reaching the season's Play-offs, he had scored 58 goals in 203 games when he was surprisingly allowed to join Leeds United for £1.5 million. Despite being the club's leading scorer in 2004–05, he had made just three appearances when he left Deepdale. It had looked as though he would be joining Sheffield United, but it was Leeds United who splashed out £1.15 million to prise him away from North End. After being hampered by ruptured knee ligaments, he returned to the Leeds side for the Play-off semi-final with Preston. After infuriating fans in the first leg at Elland Road, he received his marching orders in the final minute of the second leg at Deepdale.

CRITCHLEY, Edward

Outside-right

Born: Ashton-under-Lyne, 31 December 1903.
Career: Witton Albion. Stockport County, 1922. Everton, 1926. PRESTON NORTH END, 1934. Port Vale, 1934.

■ By the time he was 20, Ted Critchley was Stockport County's first-choice outside-right, developing an expert control and a quick turn of speed which embarrassed many an experienced full-back in the strong Second Division of that era. In Critchley's three full seasons at Edgeley Park, County struggled to maintain their status, continuing their necessary policy of selling their best players. Therefore, it came as no surprise when he was transferred to Everton in December 1926. Within three days, he had made his debut in front of a Christmas Day crowd of 37,500 at Goodison Park, providing the service for Dixie Dean to score four goals in a 5–4 win against Sunderland. In Critchley's first full season, Everton won the League Championship and he played a large part

by providing the ammunition for the immortal Dixie Dean to score a record-breaking 60 League goals. Critchley's eight seasons with Everton were anything but dull – relegation in 1929–30, the Second Division Championship in 1930–31 and the First Division title again the following season. Having been injured for the 1929–30 FA Cup semi-final, he played in the 1932–33 semi-final, only to lose his place for the Wembley victory against Manchester City. Regarded as one of the best wingers never to have been capped, he had scored 42 goals in 229 games for Everton when he moved to Preston North End in June 1934. He played in the opening 11 games of the 1934–35 season, scoring his only goal in the 2–0 win over Huddersfield Town, but on losing his place to George Bargh, he left Deepdale to play for Port Vale, where he ended his career.

CROFT, Henry

Inside-left, outside-left

Born: Bolton, 1900.
Career: PRESTON NORTH END, 1920. Portsmouth, 1922. Atherton.

■ Harry Croft spent two seasons at Deepdale shortly after football resumed following World War One, making a single appearance in each campaign. Unable to oust Peter Quinn, his two games saw North End suffer heavy defeats against Manchester City by 1–5 in April 1921 and West Bromwich Albion by 0–3 in February 1922. Croft moved on to Portsmouth but following a handful of League appearances for the South Coast club, he returned to the North West to play non-League football for Atherton Collieries.

CROSS, Graham Frederick

Centre-half, wing-half

Born: Leicester, 15 November 1943.
Career: Leicester City, 1960. Chesterfield, 1976 (loan). Brighton and Hove Albion, 1976. PRESTON NORTH END, 1977. Enderby Town. Lincoln City, 1979.

■ Graham Cross was Leicester City's most consistent servant ever and during his 16 seasons at Filbert Street he also proved himself one of the most versatile. Though he won 11 caps for England at Under-23 level, it was said that his regular switching of position cost him a full international cap. Four Cup Final appearances, a Second Division

Championship medal and a 1973 testimonial game were the tangible memories of his Leicester career. He was also a county cricketer with Leicestershire. Cross, who holds City's records for most appearances in each of the two major Cup competitions, appeared in 599 first-team games before leaving the Foxes to play for Brighton and Hove Albion. He was ever present in Brighton's runaway rise from Third Division to Second Division in 1976–77. A year later as North End sold both Gary Williams and Mark Lawrenson to the Seagulls, the cash plus player deal meant that Graham Cross and Harry Wilson came in as straight replacements for the two talented youngsters. Cross played in 40 games for North End in 1977–78, helping them win promotion from the Third Division. His only goal proved to be the winner in a 2–1 defeat of Sheffield Wednesday. Cross left Deepdale early the following season and had a brief spell with Enderby Town before joining Lincoln City. It was wholly unfitting that when he answered the Imps' emergency call in 1979, he could not save them from relegation. A spell managing Hinckley Athletic marked the final phase of his soccer involvement. Sadly, in 1993 he was back in the news when he was jailed for nine months for theft and false accountancy after using Post Office funds in his care to cover serious gambling debts.

CROSS, Paul

Left-back

Born: Barnsley, 31 October 1965.
Career: Barnsley, 1983. PRESTON NORTH END, 1991 (loan). Hartlepool United, 1992. Darlington, 1993.

■ Barnsley-born full-back Paul Cross started out with his home-town club and appeared in 143 League and Cup games in eight seasons at Oakwell. Towards the end of his time with the Tykes, he had a brief loan spell with Preston North End. Following a disappointing debut at Birmingham City, Cross was outstanding in the number-three shirt as North End won three games in succession: 2–0 at home against West Bromwich Albion, 3–2 away at Bury and 1–0 at home to Huddersfield Town. Shortly after returning to Oakwell, Hartlepool United paid £20,000 for his services. During his time at the Victoria Ground, Cross netted his first League goal but in November 1993 he left to join Darlington where he was immediately made club captain. His steadying influence was sorely missed when a serious knee injury forced him to leave the Feethams.

CROSSAN, Bernard

Inside-left

Born: Preston, 1870.
Died: 1918.
Career: PRESTON NORTH END, 1890.

■ North End had just won the Football League Championship for a second successive season when inside-forward Bernie Crossan joined them. Though Everton pipped North End by two points in 1890–91, the Deepdale club did the double over the Merseysiders: in the game at Goodison Park, Crossan scored the only goal of an exciting encounter. In North End's next game, he netted twice in a 4–1 defeat of Aston Villa but though he held his place for all but the final game of the season, they turned out to be his only appearances for the club.

CROSSLEY, Paul

Winger

Born: Rochdale, 14 August 1948.
Died: 1996.
Career: Rochdale, 1965. PRESTON NORTH END, 1966. Southport, 1968 (loan). Tranmere Rovers, 1969. Seattle Sounders (US). Chester City, 1975.

■ Rochdale-born winger Paul Crossley began his career with his home-town club before moving to Preston North End in November 1966. However, he had to wait until the final game of that 1966–67 season before making his North End debut in a 1–1 draw at Carlisle United. He appeared in a couple of games the following season but as he was unable to win a regular place he went on loan to Southport before Tranmere Rovers paid £5,000 to take him to Prenton Park in the summer of 1969. In his first game for Tranmere, he had a hand in each of George Yardley's goals as

he netted a hat-trick in a 3–2 defeat of Bury. Over the next five seasons, Crossley became noted for his pin-point crosses which Eddie Loyden, amongst others, put away in style. However, Crossley also knew where the net was and in 1973–74 and 1974–75 he was Rovers' top scorer. In 1975 he spent the summer playing for Seattle Sounders in the NASL but on arriving back late for the start of the new season, he lost his place. Crossley, who had scored 45 goals in 229 games, later joined Chester City with whom he enjoyed three good seasons.

CUNNINGHAM, John

Inside-forward

Born: Glasgow, 1873.
Career: Glasgow Celtic. Partick Thistle. Heart of Midlothian. Glasgow Rangers. Glasgow Thistle. PRESTON NORTH END, 1893. Sheffield United, 1897. Aston Villa, 1898. Newton Heath, 1898. Wigan County. Barrow.

■ John Cunningham first turned out for Celtic against Bolton Wanderers on 23 May 1889 and two days later proved himself against Preston North End. He then had spells with a number of other Scottish clubs including Partick Thistle, Hearts, Rangers and Glasgow Thistle before joining North End in September 1893. Able to play in a variety of forward positions, he made his Preston debut in a 4–1 reversal at Burnley. Later that season he scored North End's winner in a 3–2 defeat of Everton at Goodison Park. Unable to force his way into the Preston side on a regular basis, he had to wait until towards the end of the 1894–95 season before making his mark. Playing in the last seven games, he scored five goals including a brace in the 4–0 win over Burnley. One of his best games for the club came the following season against Champions-elect Aston Villa. Cunningham scored one and had a hand in the three other goals in a 4–3 win. On leaving Deepdale, he joined Sheffield United and was in the side that beat Celtic in 1898 to win the first unofficial British Championship. A brief spell at Villa Park, where he did not appear in the first team, was followed by periods with Newton Heath, Wigan County and Barrow before he decided to hang up his boots.

CUNNINGHAM, William Carruthers

Full-back

Born: Cowdenbeath, 22 February 1925.
Died: November 2000.
Career: Dunfermline Athletic. Airdrieonians. PRESTON NORTH END, 1949. Southport, 1964.

■ Willie Cunningham, one of Preston North End's most famous sons, came through his local sides with his cousin Jimmy Baxter to play in the same team. Playing at centre-half, Cunningham joined Dunfermline Athletic as a part-timer. He was 18 years old and had been working down the pit for almost four years. He continued to combine soccer with mining for a further six years but by now had moved to Airdrie. In July 1949, a £5,000 bid brought him to Deepdale and he remained a fixture in the North End side until 1963. Cunningham made his Preston debut in a 2–0 home win over Grimsby Town and though injuries forced him to miss a number of games in his first two seasons with the club, he helped North End win the Second Division Championship in 1950–51. Towards the end of the following season, in which he was one of four ever-presents, Willie Cunningham was appointed captain in his 99th League appearance for the club. He played for North End in the 1954 FA Cup Final defeat by West Bromwich Albion and won eight full caps for Scotland, captaining them during the 1954 World Cup Finals in Switzerland. Cunningham seemed more injury-prone playing international football than he did turning out for North End. An injury sustained in the April 1955 meeting against England caused him to miss the last eight games of that season. Cunningham went on to appear in 487 League and Cup games for North End before he left Deepdale for a short spell as player-manager of Southport. The lure of Deepdale was much too strong, though, and he had no hesitation in returning to North End when asked to take the job of reserve team trainer soon afterwards. In the years of his greatness, Willie Cunningham meant as much to North End's defence as Tom Finney did to the attack, but he got far less praise.

Certainly there was no shrewder tactician at full-back than Willie Cunningham – a truly formidable defender.

CURTIS, John Charles Keyworth

Full-back

Born: Nuneaton, 3 September 1978.
Career: Manchester United, 1995. Barnsley, 1999 (loan). Blackburn Rovers, 2000. Sheffield United, 2003 (loan). Leicester City, 2003. Portsmouth, 2004. PRESTON NORTH END, 2004 (loan). Nottingham Forest, 2005.

■ A former England Youth team captain, John Curtis made his debut for England at Under-21 level before making his full debut for Manchester United. Voted United's Young Player of the Year for 1997, his only minor transgression in his early days at Old Trafford came when he was sent off while playing for Young England against Greece. Finding the competition for places at Old Trafford tough, he went on loan to Barnsley where he scored a goal in the game against Manchester City. In the summer of 2000, Curtis left the Reds to join Blackburn Rovers in a £1.5 million deal. He quickly settled into the Ewood Park club's team, producing consistent displays week in,

week out. Unfortunately, injuries hampered his progress and he went on loan to Sheffield United, helping them to reach the FA Cup semi-final and First Division Play-offs in 2002–03. He then joined Leicester City but struggled as the Foxes fought to find a winning formula and it was not long before he was on the move again – this time to Portsmouth. In September 2004 he joined North End on loan and impressed the Deepdale fans with his obvious ability. However, a permanent move fell through following a change of management at Fratton Park. Having made 12 appearances for North End, he returned to the South Coast club before moving to Nottingham Forest, but he was unable to prevent them from being relegated to Division Two.

DAGGER, John Leslie

Outside-right

Born: Longtown, 25 April 1933.
Career: West Auckland. PRESTON NORTH END, 1956. Carlisle United, 1961. Southport, 1963.

■ Spotted playing non-League football for West Auckland, winger Les Dagger replaced Les Campbell midway through the 1956–57 season, making his debut in a 6–0 rout of Sunderland. In that game, Tommy Thompson netted a

hat-trick, latching on to a couple of Dagger's pin-point crosses to fire home from close range. That season, North End finished third in Division One. Dagger's first goal for the club proved to be a winner in the 4–3 defeat of Charlton Athletic at The Valley. North End were runners-up in 1957–58 but for much of the season Dagger lost out to Derek Mayers. Injuries hampered his progress over the next couple of seasons and at the end of 1960–61, following North End's relegation from the top flight, he left to play for Carlisle United. In his first season at Brunton Park, he helped the Cumbrian outfit win promotion from Division Four but in the summer of 1963 he moved to Southport, where he later ended his career.

DAINTY, Albert

Centre-forward

Born: Lancaster, 4 December 1923.
Died: 1979.
Career: Standfast Dyers. PRESTON NORTH END, 1942. Stockport County, 1947. Southport, 1949.

■ Versatile forward Albert Dainty scored in his only League game for North End as Grimsby Town were beaten 3–0 in January 1947. Allowed to leave Deepdale the following April, he joined Stockport County and scored twice on his debut for the Hatters on the final day of the season against York City. In 1947–48, Dainty was County's top scorer with 12 goals, including eight in the final seven games of the campaign. Halfway through the following season he signed for Southport but though he continued to score fairly regularly, the Sandgrounders struggled in the lower reaches of the Third Division South.

DALEY, Omar

Winger

Born: Jamaica, 25 April 1981.
Career: Portmore United (Jamaica). Reading, 2003. PRESTON NORTH END, 2004.

■ Omar Daley is a Jamaican international who made his Football League debut for Reading, having joined the Royals from Portmore United in the summer of 2003. Unable to hold down a

regular spot at the Madejski Stadium, he joined North End on a season-long loan prior to the start of the 2004–05 campaign. Having made his debut as a replacement for Eric Skora in a 1–0 defeat at Brighton, the Jamaican winger's only starts came in a Carling Cup-tie at Mansfield in which he recorded his only goal of the campaign in a 4–0 win and the home draw with Millwall. Sadly, his contract was cancelled on transfer deadline day.

DANIEL, David

Left-half, centre-forward

Born: Porth, 1905.
Career: PRESTON NORTH END, 1925. Mid-Rhondda United. Torquay United, 1927.

■ David Daniel joined North End in the weeks following their relegation from the First Division in 1924–25. He made what turned out to be his only appearance in North End colours, early the following season in a 3–2 win over Portsmouth. In spite of this promising debut, he went back to the reserves before leaving to play non-League football for Mid-Rhondda United. Daniel later returned to League action in 1927 with Torquay United, who were playing their inaugural season in the competition.

DANIELS, George

Outside-left

Born: Chorlton, 1899.
Career: PRESTON NORTH END, 1919. Bury, 1920. Rochdale, 1921.

■ Winger George Daniels was one of 24 North End debutants during the 1919–20 season. Though he did not have the best of debuts as North End crashed 5–1 at Bradford City, he went on to make 12 appearances, scoring his only goal for the club in a 1–1 draw at high-flying Burnley. He left Deepdale in the close season to join Bury but on being unable to break into the Shakers' League side, he signed for Rochdale who were playing their first season of League football in the Third Division North.

DANSON, Herbert

Inside-left, outside-left

Born: Preston, 21 June 1883.
Died: 1963.
Career: PRESTON NORTH END, 1902. Lancaster Town.

■ Herbert Danson made his North End debut in an FA Cup tie at Millwall in February 1903 but did not make his League debut for another two years. During the course of that 1905–06 season Danson, who favoured the left-wing position, turned out twice in the number-seven shirt, finding the net on each occasion. Over the next few seasons, Danson found himself in and out of the North End side until in 1908–09 he appeared on a much more regular basis. That season saw him switched to inside-left and in the game against Manchester City he netted twice and struck the upright in a 3–0 win. The following season he reverted to outside-left and hit another double in a 4–0 defeat of Notts County. 'Chippy' Danson, as he was known, put in a transfer request in November 1911, as he said that he had had a verbal promise of a benefit game, but this had not materialised. He left the club at the end of the season to play non-League football for Lancaster Town.

DARBY, Julian Timothy

Midfield

Born: Farnworth, 3 October 1967.
Career: Bolton Wanderers, 1985. Coventry City, 1993. West Bromwich Albion, 1995. PRESTON NORTH END, 1997. Rotherham United, 1998 (loan). Carlisle United, 2000.

■ Julian Darby began his career with Bolton Wanderers as a midfielder but he later became more of a utility player. In

1986–87, his first full season in the Bolton side, he wore nine different outfield shirts. In 1988–89 he managed to score for the club in every competition, but the most memorable was his 27th-minute Wembley equaliser against Torquay United in the Sherpa Van Trophy Final. He was ever present in the number-11 shirt during 1989–90 as the Wanderers reached the Play-offs and the following season he missed just one game as the Wanderers again reached Wembley. Having helped Bolton win promotion from the Second Division in 1992–93, Darby joined his former manager Phil Neal at Coventry City. He had scored 52 goals in 345 games during his time with Bolton. Injuries hampered his progress during two years at Highfield Road but West Bromwich Albion paid £250,000 for his services in November 1995. After helping the Baggies retain their First Division status, he returned to the North West in the summer of 1997 when he signed for Preston North End in a player-exchange deal involving Kevin Kilbane. Unable to establish a regular first-team place, he went on loan to Rotherham United. Set to join earlier, he suffered an ankle injury before the forms could be completed but finally arrived at Millmoor just before the deadline. Darby had to bide his time for a first-team chance at Deepdale in 1998–99 but, following two earlier substitute appearances, he netted against Ford United in the FA Cup and Hartlepool in the Auto Windscreens

Shield. He later deputised for the injured Gary Parkinson at right-back but, despite giving a good account of himself, he lost out to new signing Graham Alexander. After rejecting a move to Shrewsbury, he combined a coaching post at the club's School of Excellence with captaining the reserves, where his experience was passed on to North End's emerging stars. He later joined Carlisle United as player-coach before deciding to retire.

DAVEY, Simon

Midfield

Born: Swansea, 1 October 1970.
Career: Swansea City, 1989. Carlisle United, 1992. PRESTON NORTH END, 1995. Darlington, 1997 (loan).

■ Midfielder Simon Davey started out with his home-town club Swansea City, making 58 appearances for the Vetch Field club before joining Carlisle United on a free transfer in the summer of 1992. Davey was a virtual ever present in his time at Brunton Park, clocking up a total of 137 first-team appearances in which he scored 23 goals before Preston paid £125,000 for his services in February 1995. After making his North End debut in a 2–2 draw at Walsall, he scored in his first match at Deepdale when the match against Doncaster Rovers ended in the same scoreline. That season, North End finished fifth but Davey won a Third Division Championship medal, having previously helped Carlisle to top spot. He won another Third Division Championship medal in 1995–96 as North End finished three points ahead of Gillingham. Davey scored 10 goals, many of them vital, and was elected to the PFA award-winning divisional team. Bringing aggression to his ball-winning skills, he was very dangerous when running at players and his passing ability opened up many an opposition defence. Though he temporarily lost his place midway through the following season, he returned to display his tenacity and contribute his usual quota of valuable goals. These included a brace at Millwall and winners against Gillingham and Wycombe Wanderers. After suffering a spate of niggling injuries, he was loaned out to Darlington but under new manager David Moyes he returned to the

side to demonstrate that he remained an energetic 'box-to-box' player. Davey played his last game for the club against Bristol City on the final day of the 1997–98 season.

DAVIDSON, Callum Iain

Full-back, wing-back

Born: Stirling, 25 June 1976.
Career: St Johnstone, 1994. Blackburn Rovers, 1998. Leicester City, 2000. PRESTON NORTH END, 2004.

■ Callum Davidson began his career with St Johnstone, where his displays led to a number of top clubs north and south of the border showing an interest in his future. Signed by Blackburn Rovers for a fee of £1.75 million in February 1998, he arrived at Ewood Park with hamstring trouble and then developed a septic toe. When given his Football League debut against Arsenal after eight weeks, he promptly pulled a muscle after an hour and did not play again for the rest of the season. Nevertheless, his form the following season led to him winning full international honours for Scotland but, after becoming a victim of foul play, recurring headaches forced him to miss

games for Rovers. In July 2000, Davidson joined Leicester City for £1.7 million and his presence provided the Foxes' defence with a more solid look before injuries kept him out of contention for a place at both club and international level. Davidson made the headlines in the summer of 2002 when he suffered a broken jaw in a much-publicised incident, but he received a hero's welcome when he returned to first-team action with the Foxes. His form for Leicester prompted Berti Vogts to recall him to the Scotland team but after appearing in 114 games he was released by new City boss Micky Adams. He joined North End in the summer of 2004 but sadly his first season with the club saw him suffer a catalogue of injuries. Only able to show his defensive qualities in short bursts, he twice had to leave the field in the opening quarter of an hour, while in the match against Cardiff City he had to withdraw during the pre-match warm-up. Despite his lack of appearances, he managed his first goal

for the club – the winner over Crewe Alexandra. Davidson, who scored in three successive matches and then netted against Champions elect Reading, is considering bringing out a fun goal compilation after beating his usual total of a goal a season!

DAVIDSON, Ian

Wing-half

Born: East Lothian, 8 September 1937.
Career: Kilmarnock. PRESTON NORTH END, 1962. Middlesbrough, 1965. Darlington, 1967.

■ A tall, gangly wing-half, Ian Davidson had twice helped Kilmarnock finish runners-up in the Scottish First

Division before joining Preston North End in December 1962. Having made his debut in a 1–1 draw at Swansea, Davidson played in the majority of the remaining games that season. His signing, along with that of Doug Holden from Bolton Wanderers, helped the Deepdale club retain its Second Division status. His performances in 1963–64 were outstanding and he scored his only goal for the club in a 4–0 win over Cardiff City. However, the club dropped a bombshell by leaving Davidson out of their FA Cup Final side to face West Ham United, replacing him with Howard Kendall, who became the youngest player to appear in a Final. Davidson returned to first-team action midway through the following season but in February 1965 he left to join Middlesbrough. In 1966–67 he helped Boro win promotion from the Third Division but then promptly departed to sign for Darlington, who were relegated from the same Division in his only season with the Quakers.

DAVIDSON, Jonathan Stewart

Defender

Born: Cheadle, 1 March 1970.
Career: Derby County, 1988. PRESTON NORTH END, 1992. Chesterfield, 1993 (loan). Telford. Dagenham and Redbridge. Ilkeston Town. Nuneaton Borough.

■ Jonathan Davidson was one of a number of young players pushed into senior action in a Derby County team severely depleted by injuries and suspensions. Davidson, who was captain of the Rams' youth and reserve teams at the Baseball Ground, could not hold down a regular first-team place and in July 1992 he joined Preston North End. Davidson, who was able to play in either of the full-back positions, played in the majority of games in the first half of the 1992–93 season, scoring his first League goal against Plymouth and finding the net in the epic 5–4 FA Cup replay defeat against Bradford City. While at Deepdale he suffered a serious knee injury and, though he had a loan spell at Chesterfield, the treatment did not solve the problem. He left Preston at the end of that relegation season and played non-

League football for Telford, Dagenham and Redbridge, Ilkeston Town and Nuneaton Borough before returning to Derby as kit man.

DAVIE, James Graham

Wing-half

Born: Cambuslang, 7 September 1922.
Died: 1984.
Career: Kilmarnock. PRESTON NORTH END, 1948. Northampton Town, 1950. Shrewsbury Town, 1953.

■ Wing-half Jim Davie arrived at Deepdale from Kilmarnock in June 1948 and played his first game for the club on the opening day of the 1948–49 season in a 2–2 home draw with Portsmouth. After some initially good displays, he lost his place in the team and as North End slipped towards the relegation zone, he found it difficult to win back his place on a regular basis. Despite some sterling efforts during the early weeks of North End's 1949–50 Second Division campaign, Davie was allowed to leave Deepdale and joined Northampton Town. He spent a couple of seasons at the County Ground, scoring his first League goal before moving to Shrewsbury. Unfortunately he suffered a serious knee injury during pre-season training at Gay Meadow and retired without having played for the Shrews' League side.

DAVIES, Roger

Forward

Born: Wolverhampton, 25 October 1950.
Career: Bridgnorth Town. Worcester City. Derby County, 1971. PRESTON NORTH END, 1972 (loan). Bruges (Belgium). Leicester City, 1977. Tulsa Roughnecks (US). Derby County, 1979. Seattle Sounders (US). Fort Lauderdale Strikers (US). Burnley, 1983. Gresley Rovers, 1983. Darlington, 1983.

■ Roger Davies joined Derby County from Worcester City of the Southern League in September 1971 for £12,000, which was then a record for a non-League player. Unable to break into the Rams side, he joined Preston on loan at the beginning of the 1972–73 season but after two fruitless games against Queen's Park Rangers and Burnley he was recalled by Derby. After returning to the

Baseball Ground, Davies, who had been in County's Central League-winning team of 1971–72, forced his way into the Derby side. He scored a spectacular hat-trick in a great FA Cup replay recovery at Tottenham and was sent off in the European Cup semi-final against Juventus after reacting to provocation. Davies earned an England Under-23 cap and was a regular member of County's 1974–75 League Championship-winning side. That season he scored all five goals against Luton Town. In August 1976, Davies signed for Bruges for £135,000. He helped them to a Belgian League and Cup double and then signed for Leicester City. Between two spells in the NASL, when he appeared as a substitute in the Soccer Bowl, Roger Davies returned to the Baseball Ground but could do nothing to prevent the club's relegation from Division One.

DAVIES, Stanley Charles

Centre-forward, inside-forward

Born: Chirk, 24 March 1898.
Died: 1972.
Career: Chirk. Rochdale. PRESTON NORTH END, 1919. Everton, 1920. West Bromwich Albion, 1921. Birmingham, 1927. Cardiff City, 1928. Rotherham United, 1929. Barnsley, 1930. Manchester Central. Dudley Town.

■ During the course of World War One, Stan Davies, who had worked in the coal mines at Chirk, was wounded at Cambrai. On discharge from hospital he joined the Army Signalling School at Dunstable. He ended the war with the Military Medal and the Belgian Croix de Guerre. Having made a few wartime appearances for Rochdale, he joined North End after the cessation of hostilities. Stan Davies had a lot of stamina and could hit a ball hard and true, but after making his debut in a 4–0 defeat at neighbours Blackburn Rovers at the start of the 1919–20 season, he only made 26 League and Cup appearances and scored 11 goals in two years at Deepdale. The club were not prepared to persist with him and he was transferred to Everton for £4,000. He scored a hat-trick for Everton in a 5–0 win over Manchester United on the opening day of the 1921–22 season and had scored 10 goals in 22 games when the Blues surprisingly let him join West Bromwich Albion. A most versatile player, Davies made 18 full international appearances for Wales, 11 of them while with Albion. He was the Baggies' leading scorer for three successive seasons. Although he made appearances at both centre-half and right-wing, he had scored 77 goals in 147 games before he left to spend a season at Birmingham. Later he was appointed player-manager of Cardiff City before taking up a similar position with Rotherham United. Lack of success turned a section of the supporters against him and he resigned to play for Manchester Central in the Lancashire Combination before being reinstated as an amateur in 1933 and ending his playing days with Dudley Town.

DAVIS, Claude

Defender

Born: Jamaica, 6 March 1979.
Career: Portmore United (Jamaica). PRESTON NORTH END, 2003.

■ Initially signed on a season-long loan, the big Jamaican international defender made an instant impression with a powerful display at the heart of the North End defence against West Bromwich Albion at the Hawthorns. A series of niggling injuries prevented him

from claiming a regular place but North End fans were happy when the move became permanent in March 2004. Despite a couple of periods when he was again injured, Davis was a regular in the Preston side for the first half of the 2004–05 season. Incredibly strong at holding players at bay, he has great pace in recovery and an almost telescopic tackling ability. He returned to first-team action towards the end of the season and was voted Man of the Match in two of the club's Play-off games. The central defender scored his first goal for two seasons in the 1–1 draw at Derby County and this led to him scoring two others in the wins over Millwall and Luton Town. However, on the down side, he, along with Danny Dichio, was dismissed in the game with Crystal Palace.

DAWSON, Alexander Downie

Centre-forward

Born: Aberdeen, 21 February 1940.
Career: Manchester United, 1957. PRESTON NORTH END, 1961. Bury, 1967. Brighton and Hove Albion, 1968. Brentford, 1970 (loan).

■ Aberdeen-born Alex Dawson was playing for Hull Schools when Manchester United spotted him. He came through the club's junior ranks and signed professional forms shortly after his 17th birthday in May 1957. The previous month he had scored on his League debut in a 2–0 defeat of Burnley. After the Munich disaster, the bustling centre-forward commanded a regular place and was one of the inspirations behind United's march to the 1958 FA Cup Final. He scored five goals in six matches including a hat-trick in the 5–3 semi-final win over Fulham. After United signed David Herd in the summer of 1961, Dawson found it difficult to get into the side and in October 1961 he moved to Second Division Preston North End for £18,000. He netted on his debut in a 2–2 draw at Rotherham and scored on a regular basis over the next few seasons. He was the club's leading scorer in four of his five seasons at Deepdale, netting five hat-tricks. The first of these came in 1962–63 as Swansea Town were beaten 6–3. His best season in terms of

goals scored was 1963–64 when his total of 36 League and Cup goals included another hat-trick against Swansea and a goal in the FA Cup Final defeat by West Ham United. In fact, Dawson scored 13 goals in the first nine games of the season and cannot have been far away from winning full international honours for Scotland. In 1964–65, Dawson netted three hat-tricks – in the games against Charlton Athletic (3–2 away), Portsmouth (6–1 at home) and Manchester City (3–4 away). However, the team's poor form over the next couple of seasons began to affect Dawson's output, though by the time he left Deepdale following a disagreement with the club, the 'Black Prince' had found the net 114 times in 197 games. Transferred to Bury, he later played for Brighton and Hove Albion and went on loan to Brentford before hanging up his boots. His career spanned 13 years and 394 League games in which he scored 212 goals.

DAWSON, Charles

Winger, inside-left

Born: Preston, 1886.
Career: PRESTON NORTH END, 1906.

■ Charlie Dawson ended his first season, 1906–07, as the club's leading scorer with 11 goals. He netted a hat-trick in his first game for a North End XI – a Lancashire Cup-tie at Colne which Preston won 4–1. He also scored two in the next round against Blackpool and another in the semi-final against Liverpool. The highlight of his League career came in the match against League Champions-elect Newcastle United when he scored both Preston's goals in a 2–2 draw. Though not as prolific over the next few seasons, he did net a hat-trick in a 6–0 defeat of Chelsea during the early stages of the 1908–09 campaign. However, injuries restricted his appearances and the versatile forward was forced to retire prematurely.

DAWSON, George

Left-half, outside-left

Born: Bedlington, 1891.
Died: 1927.
Career: Bedlington United. PRESTON NORTH END, 1912.

Discovered playing for Bedlington United, George Dawson played his first game in North End colours in a 4–0 win over Barnsley in November 1912. The strong-tackling left-half did not miss a game for the remainder of the season as Preston won the Second Division Championship, finishing three points clear of Burnley. His only goal that campaign rescued a point for North End against Barnsley. Though he certainly was not out of place in the top flight, he could do nothing to prevent North End's relegation after one season of First Division football. In 1914–15, Dawson netted again in the match against Barnsley, helping Preston bounce back to the top flight with immediate effect as runners-up to Derby County. When League football resumed in 1919–20, Dawson was again a key member of the North End side, his experience helping the club avoid relegation. Injuries and illness began to take their toll and at the end of the following season he hung up his boots.

DAY, Christopher Nicholas

Goalkeeper

Born: Walthamstow, 28 July 1975.
Career: Tottenham Hotspur, 1993. Crystal Palace, 1996. Watford, 1997. Lincoln City, 2000 (loan). Queen's Park Rangers, 2001. Aylesbury United (loan). PRESTON NORTH END, 2005 (loan).

Agile shot-stopper Chris Day, an England Under-21 international goalkeeper, left Spurs in the 1996 close season to sign for Crystal Palace for a fee of £225,000. He had an outstanding first season with the Eagles, helping the club have one of the best defensive records in the First Division. Surprisingly allowed to leave Selhurst Park, he joined Watford in a deal that took Kevin Miller in the opposite direction. However, due to the consistency of Alec Chamberlain, Day was confined to the Hornets' reserve side. In fact, he spent three seasons as Chamberlain's understudy until spending an extended period on loan with Lincoln City. Transferred to Queen's Park Rangers in the summer of 2001, he soon became a great crowd favourite until suffering a double fracture of the right leg in a game against Oldham. On recovery he had a spell on loan at Aylesbury United of the Ryman League. He then won back his place with Rangers until losing out to Simon Royce midway through the 2004–05 season. In February 2005, he was loaned out to

North End to cover for injuries. He impressed during his stay at Deepdale, being on the losing side just once in his six-match stint. Unfortunately a longer-term deal could not be arranged and he returned to Loftus Road.

DERBYSHIRE, Joseph Edward

Right-back

Born: Turton.
Career: Darwen. PRESTON NORTH END, 1902. Darwen.

Right-back Joe Derbyshire joined Preston from Darwen midway through the 1902–03 season. He made his debut in the local derby against Blackpool, which ended all square at 2–2, and kept his place for the remainder of the season. He was ever present in 1903–04 as North End won the Second Division Championship. Derbyshire had played in 70 consecutive League games following his debut until he suffered an injury against Aston Villa in December 1904. The following season, Preston finished runners-up to Liverpool in the First Division and Derbyshire scored his first goal for the club from the penalty spot in a 1–0 win over Bury. Injuries and a loss of form then began to affect his progress at Deepdale, though in 1907–08 he scored five times from the penalty spot. His last game in North End colours on 17 March 1909 saw him score two penalties in a 3–2 win at Bristol City. On leaving Deepdale, Joe Derbyshire rejoined his first club, Darwen.

DEVLIN, James Thomas

Inside-forward, outside-right

Born: Bellshill, 2 October 1904.
Career: Kilsyth Rangers. Third Lanark. Birmingham, 1924. PRESTON NORTH END, 1925. Liverpool, 1927. Swindon Town, 1928. Brooklyn Wanderers (US). Aberdeen. Walsall, 1932. Zürich (Switzerland). Fleetwood Town. Oldham Athletic, 1934.

Much-travelled inside-forward Tom Devlin played football in four countries. A ball-playing forward, he was direct and forceful in the traditional Scottish mould. He started his first-class career with Third Lanark before joining

Birmingham in September 1924. On his arrival at St Andrew's, he found that his chances of first-team football were limited and he moved on to Preston North End. He scored on his debut for the Lilywhites in a 2–1 win over Oldham Athletic but it proved to be his only goal for the club in two seasons at Deepdale. After brief spells with Liverpool and Swindon Town, he went to play in the US for Brooklyn Wanderers where he was hugely successful. Following a brief spell with Aberdeen, he turned out for Walsall before trying his luck in Switzerland with Zürich. He later returned to the North West to play for Fleetwood Town prior to winding down his career with Oldham Athletic.

DEWHURST, Frederick

Inside-left, centre-forward

Born: Fulwood, 16 December 1863.
Died: 1895.
Career: Preston Juniors. PRESTON NORTH END. Corinthians. PRESTON NORTH END. Corinthians. PRESTON NORTH END, 1888. Corinthians. PRESTON NORTH END, 1889.

■ Fred Dewhurst was the first North End player to play representative football for Lancashire when he took part in the game against London for the benefit of

the Moorfield Colliery Relief Fund. Dewhurst was a schoolmaster at the Catholic college in the town and one of the first secretaries. He was also a man renowned for testing his physical prowess against rival goalkeepers. Prior to the inauguration of the Football League, North End were anxious to prove their worth against the Corinthians. Having beaten them 3–1 at the Kennington Oval, they defeated them 4–3 at Deepdale in the return, with Fred Dewhurst netting a hat-trick. In North End's first-ever Football League game against Burnley, Fred Dewhurst scored the club's opening goal in a 5–2 win: after just a couple of minutes he dribbled his way through a static Clarets defence before shooting inside the post. The North End captain also scored the club's last goal and had a goal disallowed for an infringement off the ball. Fred Dewhurst scored in all but one of his nine international appearances for England. In his final game he scored along with his North End teammate John Goodall in a 4–1 defeat of Wales. In the FA Cup Final of 1889 against Wolverhampton Wanderers, Fred Dewhurst scored North End's first goal in a 3–0 victory. The Preston captain, followed by Major Sudell, collected the trophy from Major Marindin, who diplomatically hid his distaste at seeing the trophy pass into the hands of a side made up almost entirely of Scotsmen!

DEXTER, George

Right-back

Born: Hucknall Torkard, 28 July 1895.
Career: Bestwood Colliery. Coventry City. PRESTON NORTH END, 1914.

■ Tough-tackling full-back George Dexter was spotted by Coventry City playing for Bestwood Colliery. His displays for the Southern League club led to a number of top teams pursuing his signature. As it was Dexter joined North End during the club's Second Division promotion-winning season of 1914–15. However, with Broadhurst and Holbem, the club's regular full-back pairing, playing well his only appearance for the club came in a 3–0 defeat of Grimsby Town during the early stages of the campaign.

DIAF, Farid

Midfield

Born: France, 19 April 1971.
Career: Stade Rennais (France). PRESTON NORTH END, 1999.

■ Following an outstanding trial period with North End in 1998–99, Frenchman Farid Diaf signed an initial three-month contract in the summer of 1999, which was later extended to the end of the season. After impressing in pre-season training, he suffered a torn groin muscle two days before the start of the campaign. After a lengthy recovery, the cultured left-sided midfielder made his debut off the bench against Bournemouth. His full debut at Colchester in the next match saw him sustain a cheekbone fracture. He refused a second operation and was back on the bench in a matter of weeks. However, his Gallic flair and ball-playing talents failed to win him a regular first-team place and he was released in the summer.

DICHIO Daniele Salvatore Ernest

Forward

Born: Hammersmith, 19 October 1974
Career: Queen's Park Rangers 1993; Barnet (loan) 1994; Sampdoria (Italy) 1997; Lecce (Italy) (loan) 1998; Sunderland 1998; West Bromwich Albion 2001; Derby County (loan) 2003; Millwall 2004; PRESTON NORTH END 2005.

■ Very good in the air and a player who utilises his teammates as well,

Danny Dichio scored on his League debut for Queen's Park Rangers against Aston Villa at Loftus Road before making way for the returning Les Ferdinand. However by the start of the 1995–96 season, Ferdinand had joined Newcastle and Dichio was partnering Kevin Gallen up front. After a slow start he scored two at Leeds and then netted seven goals in a spell of six games. Capped by England at Under-21 level, he was voted the club's Young Player of the Season. After another season at Loftus Road, Dichio's contract expired and he left to play his football with Sampdoria in Italy. He later joined Lecce on loan but after a frustrating seven months abroad, the tall striker joined Sunderland as cover for Niall Quinn. Though he made more appearances from the bench than starts in 1998–99, he played an extremely important role in Sunderland's promotion to the Premiership, netting 12 goals and collecting a deserved First Division Championship medal. He was then hampered by a back injury which restricted his first-team opportunities to League Cup ties and appearances from the bench. After a brief loan spell with West Bromwich Albion, he joined the Baggies permanenly and contributed some vital goals as the club won promotion. In 2002–03 he was the club's leading marksman in the Premiership with eight goals, and netted a hat-trick in the FA Cup win over Bradford City. Unable to repeat his scoring feats the following season, he went out on loan to

Derby before signing for Millwall. Having netted some valuable goals for the Lions, he opted to join Preston in the summer of 2005. Though almost half his League appearances for North End in 2005–06 were from the bench and he failed to find the net, he did create numerous chances for his teammates and more than played his part in the club reaching the Play-offs.

DICKIE, George James

Outside-left

Born: Montrose, 22 September 1903.
Died: 1960.
Career: Buckie Thistle. PRESTON NORTH END, 1923 (trial). Buckie Thistle. Stoke City, 1925. PRESTON NORTH END, 1925. Forres Mechanics. St Johnstone. New Brighton, 1927. Bristol City, 1928. Chester. Macclesfield. Chester, 1932. New Brighton, 1932.

■ Initially with Buckie Thistle, winger Jim Dickie had a trial with North End but, having failed to impress, returned north of the border until he was signed by Stoke City in the summer of 1925. He had made just one appearance for the Potters when he switched to North End, making his debut in a 1–0 defeat of Wolverhampton Wanderers. He scored the winner in his next game against Fulham but after just one more appearance in the North End colours, he left to play for Forres Mechanics and later St Johnstone before signing for New Brighton. Dickie was ever present in 1927–28, but moved to Bristol City midway through the following season. This was followed by two brief periods at Chester that sandwiched a spell at Macclesfield. He returned to New Brighton but, despite taking his tally of goals to 19 in 83 games, he was unable to prevent them having to apply for re-election in 1932–33.

DICKINSON, Thomas John

Outside-right

Born: Preston, 1889.
Career: PRESTON NORTH END, 1910.

■ Winger Thomas Dickinson was one of six local-born players who made just a single Football League appearance for Preston North End during the 1910–11

season. Dickinson played in the 1–0 defeat at high-flying Aston Villa in December 1910 but, despite giving a good account of himself, he lost out to a fully recovered John Thompson.

DICKSON, Charles

Winger

Born: Dundee, 1871.
Career: Dundee. PRESTON NORTH END, 1893. Newcastle United, 1894. Loughborough Town, 1895.

■ Signed from his home-town club Dundee, fleet-footed winger Charlie Dickson was unable to gain a regular place in the fine North End side that made a big impact in the early days of the Football League. Signed in readiness for the start of the 1893–94 season, he made just three appearances, though he did score in a 3–1 win at Newton Heath. However, when he moved to Newcastle United he made a headlining start, scoring on his debut against Burslem Port Vale and powering in goals in each of his next three outings as well. When United failed to gain promotion at the end of the 1894–95 season, he joined League newcomers Loughborough Town where he saw out his playing days.

DOBSON, Samuel

Inside-forward

Born: Preston, 1870.
Career: PRESTON NORTH END, 1890. Sheffield United, 1892.

■ Local-born inside-forward Sammy Dobson made eight appearances for North End during the 1890–91 season when they finished runners-up in the Football League to Everton. Having scored on his debut in a 3–1 win at Derby County, Dobson netted twice on his next outing as Wolverhampton Wanderers were beaten 5–1. He went on to score five goals but then inexplicably was allowed to join Sheffield United for their first season in League football.

DOCHERTY, Thomas Henderson

Wing-half

Born: Glasgow, 24 August 1928.
Career: Glasgow Celtic. PRESTON

NORTH END, 1949. Arsenal, 1958. Chelsea, 1961.

■ The irrepressible Tommy Docherty, one of the best known characters in soccer, has now come to the end of his football career, but in his day he was dedicated, dynamic, reckless, ruthless, seldom predictable and always controversial. After National Service with the Highland Light Infantry – he played for the regiment in Palestine – he signed for Glasgow Celtic in June 1948. At Parkhead he was in the shadow of the great Bobby Evans and soon joined North End, primarily as a replacement for Bill Shankly, who had retired a year earlier to take up coaching duties with North End's reserve side. His North End debut on Christmas Day 1949 created scarcely a ripple – starting at outside-left, he was soon dropped. He lost his place again after deputising for Finney at Deepdale in a farcical Cup replay won by Watford. Soon he got in at right-half and was never dropped again. A terror in the tackle, the 'Doc' was no angel, but his hard tackling was usually fair. The Scottish international selectors were greatly impressed by his displays at wing-half and, after making his debut against Wales in 1952, he went on to win 25 caps. Docherty had been at Deepdale eight seasons when North End manager Cliff Britton bowed to the Scotsman's persistent and mystifying requests for a

move, transferring him to Arsenal for £28,000 in August 1958. Docherty had appeared in 323 of a possible 356 League games for North End – missing 21 through injury and seven through international calls. Only Shankly with 294 games had a comparable record as a North End right-half. It was tragically ironic that Docherty had the misfortune to break a leg while playing for the Gunners against North End. After joining Chelsea as player-coach, he later became manager. Though he could not prevent their relegation, they bounced straight back the following term. The League Cup was won in 1965 and the Doc also took Chelsea to their first FA Cup Final. Docherty resigned as Chelsea boss in October 1967 and later managed Rotherham United, Queen's Park Rangers and Aston Villa before taking charge of Portuguese side Porto. In September 1971 he became Scotland's national team manager and restored the nation's pride. But in December 1972, he accepted the offer to manage Manchester United. He assembled some exciting sides in his time at Old Trafford and, though they dropped into Division Two, they won the title at the first attempt in 1974–75. The following season they finished third in Division One and reached the FA Cup Final only to lose to Southampton. In 1976–77 they won the trophy by beating Liverpool 2–1. After losing his job as the result of an affair with the wife of United's physiotherapist Laurie Brown, he managed Derby County, Queen's Park Rangers and Australian side Sydney Olympic before taking charge of Preston North End for just six months. He later managed Wolves and had a brief spell in charge of Altrincham, but now earns his money as an after-dinner speaker with engagements all over the world.

DONALDSON, John

Left-half

Born: Liverpool, 1884.
Career: Everton, 1905. PRESTON NORTH END, 1907. Bradford Park Avenue, 1908.

■ Left-half John Donaldson spent a season at Everton but made just a couple of appearances. His debut coincided with

Jack Sharp netting a hat-trick in a 3–2 defeat of Sheffield United. He was signed by Preston, but his only appearance for the Lilywhites came midway through the 1907–08 season in a 2–0 defeat at Bolton. Leaving Deepdale in the summer, he had a season with Bradford Park Avenue before returning to Merseyside to play in the local non-League scene.

DONNELLY, John

Full-back

Born: Broxburn, 17 December 1936.
Career: Glasgow Celtic. PRESTON NORTH END, 1962.

■ John Donnelly looked set to be Celtic's right-back for many years following his debut against Rangers in August 1957, but he was called-up for National Service in mid-July 1958 and was replaced by Dunky Mackay. Though he was occasionally exposed by very fast wingers, he made 43 appearances for the Parkhead club before signing for Preston North End in April 1962. He made his debut in the third match of the following season but did not have the best of times as North End lost 4–1 at Walsall. Donnelly went on to play in 26 games that season. Although he got his name on the score sheet, it was in another heavy defeat as Cardiff City won 6–2 at Deepdale. Over the next few seasons he found himself understudy to the ever-dependable George Ross and, when he did win a place in the side, it was at left-back. Donnelly spent five seasons at Deepdale but only made 57 League appearances. The last was in a 3–1 defeat of Norwich City in February 1967.

DOOLAN, Alexander

Full-back

Born: Tarbolton, 7 August 1889.
Died: 1937.
Career: Annbank. Kilmarnock. Beith (loan). Bradford City, 1912. PRESTON NORTH END, 1920. Mold Athletic.

■ Full-back Sandy Doolan joined Bradford City from Kilmarnock in 1912, but found himself in and out of the Bantams' side in the seasons leading up to World War One. After the hostilities, he spent one more season at Valley Parade before signing for Preston before the start of the 1920–21 campaign. A last-minute goal-line clearance in a goalless draw at Middlesbrough on debut endeared him to the North End fans and he went on to appear in both full-back berths that season while making 31 appearances. Doolan was a mainstay of the North End defence for the next season and a half before leaving Deepdale to play non-League football for Mold Athletic.

DOUGAL, James

Inside-forward

Born: Denny, 3 October 1913.
Died: 17 October 1999.
Career: Falkirk. PRESTON NORTH END, 1934. Carlisle United, 1946. Halifax Town, 1948. Chorley.

■ Jimmy Dougal joined Preston North End from Falkirk midway through the 1933–34 season and made his debut in a 3–1 home win over West Ham United. He was a tricky customer for left-backs to cope with because of his elusiveness and sudden darts into the danger zone – the right-winger, as he was in those days, became known as the 'Galloping Ghost'. After helping North End win promotion to the top flight in his first season with the club, he was switched to inside-forward before a new style of forward play was adopted to beat the stopper centre-half and Jimmy Dougal was the man selected. Jimmy Dougal was successful in a team which came near to pulling off the League and Cup double in 1937–38. He played in all the rounds of that season's FA Cup competition but unfortunately missed the Wembley Final against Huddersfield Town. Indeed, he never quite recovered from the injury sustained against Aston Villa in the semi-final and which had kept him out for a month. In 1938–39, Jimmy Dougal was the club's leading scorer with 19 goals, including five 'doubles'. He also won his only full cap for Scotland against England, scoring his side's goal in a 2–1 defeat. Nevertheless, despite his successful campaign, there were occasions when Dougal would frustrate not only sections of the crowd but also his own teammates with his over-elaboration on the ball. During the war years Jimmy Dougal, who was a

member of the North End side that won the League Cup Final against Arsenal at Wembley, was a prolific scorer, netting 96 goals in 154 appearances. This total included four of Preston's goals in a 10–1 win over Accrington Stanley in May 1940. Later during the hostilities he netted a hat-trick in a 6–0 defeat of Chester. He also scored for Scotland against England at Hampden Park in a Victory International in May 1940. Dougal made a handful of League appearances in 1946–47 before moving on to Carlisle United. He spent two fairly successful years at Brunton Park before joining Halifax Town in October 1948 where he ended his League career.

DOUGAL, William

Wing-half

Born: Falkirk, 30 October 1923.
Career: Glasgow Rangers. PRESTON NORTH END, 1947. Barnsley, 1952.

■ Signed from Glasgow Rangers midway through the 1947–48 season, wing-half Willie Dougal had to wait three months before making his League debut in a 2–0 win at Sunderland. He spent the rest of that campaign sharing the number-six shirt with Bill Shankly but by the opening game of 1948–49, he had been switched (albeit temporarily) to inside-right and scored in the 2–2 draw with Portsmouth. Replaced by a fit again Andy McLaren, he spent much of the campaign in the reserves, though he did find the net again in a 4–1 defeat of Sheffield United. Although he never appeared in North End's first team again, he remained at Deepdale for a further three seasons before joining Barnsley. The club were relegated to the Third Division North in his only season at Oakwell.

DOYLE, Stephen Charles

Midfield

Born: Neath, 2 June 1958.
Career: PRESTON NORTH END, 1975. Huddersfield Town, 1982. Sunderland, 1986. Hull City, 1989. Rochdale, 1990.

■ Welsh Under-21 midfielder Steve Doyle was renowned in the game as a strong-running, tenacious ball-winner. Doyle's first senior taste of football came

with Preston North End when, at the age of 16 years 166 days, he made his League debut in a 3–1 defeat at Tranmere Rovers in a Third Division fixture in November 1974. Doyle was still an apprentice but the newly-relegated Deepdale club obtained his signature on a professional contract the following June – one of Bobby Charlton's last major pieces of business before his resignation three months later. Doyle went on to give North End eight seasons of consistent performances. During this time Preston won back their Second Division place in 1977–78 only to lose it again by the end of the 1980–81 campaign. Despite managerial changes, Steve Doyle chose to remain with Preston, but just when it looked as if Gordon Lee was about to resurrect the club's playing fortunes, he became anxious for a move to fresh pastures. In October 1982, he joined Huddersfield Town after an unproductive six-week trial at Newcastle. A highly popular and dependable player at Huddersfield, he helped the club win promotion from the Third Division in his first season at Leeds Road. In September 1986 he was transferred to Sunderland but, despite suffering relegation from the Second Division in 1987 via the Play-offs, he was part of the Wearsiders' team that bounced straight back as Third Division Champions. On leaving Roker Park, Hull City paid £75,000 for his services before he later ended his career with Rochdale.

DRUMMOND, George

Winger, centre-forward

Born: Edinburgh, 1865.
Died: Preston, 1914.
Career: St Bernard's. PRESTON NORTH END, 1883.

■ Having learnt his football with St Bernard's, George Drummond won a county cap for Edinburgh against representatives of Glasgow, London and Sheffield. He was only 18 years old when he moved south to Preston but impressed immediately with a hat-trick in a 4–4 draw against Accrington in September 1883. A versatile footballer, he settled into the North End side at inside-right before playing on both wings, centre-forward, half-back and

full-back. In 1893 he even played in two FA Cup ties against Middlesbrough in goal. When League football got underway in 1888, Drummond had settled into the outside-left position and helped North End win two League Championships, in 1888–89 and 1889–90, having already won FA Cup-winners' medals. Towards the end of his first-team career, he began to train the successful North End reserve team and in 1900 he was awarded a testimonial game when almost 6,000 paid to see North End take on the 'Old Invincibles'. In 1902 he was appointed as the Deepdale club's first-team trainer, a position he later held at Burnley and Falkirk. While in Scotland he fell ill and returned home to Preston in the autumn of 1913, but a year later he died from cancer aged 49.

DRUMMOND, John

Winger

Born: Edinburgh.
Career: Partick Thistle. PRESTON NORTH END, 1890. Sheffield United, 1892. Liverpool, 1894. Barnsley St Peter's.

■ Attracted by his goalscoring feats for Partick Thistle, North End signed Jack Drummond in the summer of 1890 and he scored on his debut on the opening day of the 1890–91 season as Preston beat West Bromwich Albion 3–0. Unable to hold down a regular spot, he scored four goals in 11 League games before leaving to play for Sheffield United. When he arrived at Bramall Lane, the Blades were a Midlands Counties League side, moving into the Northern League for 1891–92. The following season was United's first in the Football League and after finishing as runners-up in Division two, were promoted after a 'test match'. He had scored nine goals in 40 League games for the Yorkshire side when he left for a brief spell with Liverpool prior to ending his career with Barnsley St Peters.

DUGGINS, Alfred Edward

Outside-left

Born: Aston.
Career: Redditch Town. Aberdeen. Heart of Midlothian. PRESTON NORTH END, 1923. Walsall, 1924. New Brighton, 1925.

■ Though he had first impressed in Scottish League football with Aberdeen, Alf Duggins was playing for Hearts when he left to join Preston North End towards the end of the 1923–24 season. After playing in two games against Bolton and West Ham United, neither of which was won, he left Deepdale in the close season to join Walsall. After one season with the Saddlers, he moved to New Brighton where he scored his first Football League goals.

DUNN, Barry

Winger

Born: Sunderland, 15 February 1952.
Career: Blue Star. Sunderland, 1979. PRESTON NORTH END, 1981. Darlington, 1982.

■ Winger Barry Dunn's performances for Blue Star alerted Sunderland manager Ken Knighton and he joined the Wearsiders in September 1979. Dunn made his Football League debut against North End as the sides played out a 1–1 draw at Deepdale. Providing the ammunition for 'Pop' Robson and John Hawley, as well as scoring a couple of vital goals himself, Dunn helped Sunderland win promotion to the First Division in his first season at Roker Park.

Unable to force his way into the side once the North East club were in the top flight, he moved to Preston in October 1981. He appeared in eight League games, scoring on his final League appearance in a 3–2 defeat at Wimbledon. Although he played in the club's next game, an FA Cup first-round defeat by Chesterfield, this signalled the end of his time in North End's first team. At the end of the season, he joined Darlington, who were then members of the Fourth Division.

DUNN, Hugh

Full-back

Born: Renfrew, 1875.
Career: Minerva. PRESTON NORTH END, 1893. Bristol Rovers. Burslem Port Vale, 1906.

■ Signed from the Minerva side of Renfrewshire, full-back Hugh Dunn gave North End seven years' service. He played his first game against West Bromwich Albion in March 1894 and making the last of his 180 appearances in a 6–1 defeat at Notts County in 1901. Without doubt his best season in North End colours was 1899–1900, when he was both ever present and captain. He then rather surprisingly left to play Southern League football for Bristol Rovers before joining Port Vale in August 1906. He was a regular in the Valiants side in 1906–07 but was released when Vale faced a financial crisis that led to the club's liquidation.

DUNN, Joseph

Centre-half

Born: Glasgow, 20 September 1925.
Career: Clyde. PRESTON NORTH END, 1951.

■ Joe Dunn joined Preston North End from Clyde for £1,500 in the summer of 1951. However, his arrival at Deepdale coincided with a fabulous run of form from club stalwart Willie Forbes and he had to wait until February 1952 before making his debut against Manchester United. During his early years with the club, Dunn only played on the rare occasions that his rival had to bow out through injury. A bad leg injury to Forbes allowed Dunn a consecutive run in the first team in 1952–53 but he lost his place on Forbes' return to action. In fact, Dunn did not gain a regular place in the North End side until some months after Joe Marston's return to his native Australia in May 1955. The following season he found himself on regular first-team duty but after a 5–0 defeat to Newcastle United on Christmas Eve, things got worse with five successive defeats. North End were flirting with relegation but a 3–3 draw against Blackpool at Deepdale saved them. During the course of that campaign, Joe Dunn showed remarkable determination and defensive skills as he helped the club hold on to their top-flight status. After that season, Dunn became the club's regular centre-half and earned himself a reputation as a no-nonsense defender with good heading and tackling abilities. He remained in the Preston side until the 1960–61 season, but he was dropped after the club had opened the campaign with three successive defeats. It was only when Tony Singleton was injured that he managed to get another game – unfortunately the belated appearance coincided with a 5–1 defeat to Sheffield Wednesday. This was Joe Dunn's final match for North End. Dunn, who had made 239 League and Cup appearances, the majority during his last five years at the club, had served North End with distinction and loyalty for many years.

DUXBURY, Thomas

Right-half

Born: Accrington, 1895.
Career: Accrington Stanley. PRESTON NORTH END, 1920. Leeds United, 1924. Fleetwood Town.

■ Wing-half Tom Duxbury played his early football for his home-town club Accrington Stanley but sprang to prominence at Preston, whom he joined in December 1919. He had to wait until towards the end of the following season before making his debut in a 3–0 defeat at Bolton. In 1921–22, Duxbury played in the majority of games, excelling during the club's run to the FA Cup Final, where he was one of North End's better players in their 1–0 defeat by Huddersfield Town. He remained at Deepdale until June 1924, when he left to continue his career with Leeds United. His time at Elland Road was not successful and he left to end his career playing non-League football for Fleetwood Town.

EASTER, Graham Paul

Winger

Born: Epsom, 26 September 1969.
Career: West Bromwich Albion, 1988. Huddersfield Town, 1989. Crewe Alexandra, 1989. Helsinki (Finland). PRESTON NORTH END, 1990.

■ Winger Graham Easter failed to make the grade with either of his first two clubs – West Bromwich Albion and Huddersfield Town. Indeed, when he joined Crewe his only League appearances were made from the bench. Disillusioned with life in the Football League, he tried his luck in Finland before joining North End as a non-contract player in October 1990. While with Preston he did start a League game – a 2–1 home defeat by Reading – but it proved to be his only appearance in that competition and he left to play non-League football for a number of clubs.

EASTWOOD, Cecil Milner

Left-half

Born: Tadcaster, 7 June 1894.
Career: Castleford Town. Plymouth Argyle, 1920. PRESTON NORTH END, 1925. Stoke, 1926. Stockport County, 1927.

■ Cecil Eastwood was a Yorkshireman whose displays at left-half for non-League Castleford Town persuaded Plymouth Argyle to give him a chance at League level. Eastwood was a revelation and went on to appear in 108 League games for the Pilgrims as they finished runners-up in the Third Division South in six consecutive seasons. Eastwood only played in four of those seasons as he had joined North End in the summer of 1925. The majority of his 20 appearances in a North End shirt in 1925–26 were at centre-half but, though he scored a couple of spectacular goals, he eventually lost his place to David Morris before signing for Stoke. His consistent performances helped the Potters win the Third Division North Championship in 1926–27 but after one more season he left to play for Stockport County, where he failed to break into the first team.

EATON, Adam Paul

Left-back

Born: Wigan, 2 May 1980.
Career: Everton, 1997. PRESTON NORTH END, 1999. Mansfield Town, 2002 (loan). Mansfield Town, 2003.

■ Adam Eaton signed for Preston from Everton, with whom he had won an

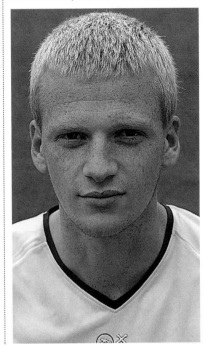

FA Youth Cup-winners' medal. He broke a toe in pre-season training but it did not hinder him too much as he impressed in the reserves. After sitting on the bench several times, he came on as substitute in the Auto Windscreens Shield match against Wrexham, which North End won 4–1. He continued to develop and made an impressive full debut at left-back in the FA Cup tie against Stockport County the following season. Although Rob Edwards' consistent form restricted his further involvement, he did make his League debut against West Bromwich Albion on the final day of the campaign. Eaton made steady progress in 2001–02 and was unfortunate not to score on the occasions he played in the League side. Surprisingly loaned to Mansfield, he later joined the Stags on a permanent basis before suffering a groin injury which required a period of rehabilitation at Lilleshall. Unfortunately, after recovering he suffered more bad luck and required two operations on a hip.

EAVES, David Michael Curtis

Midfield

Born: Blackpool, 13 February 1973.
Career: PRESTON NORTH END, 1991.

■ Blackpool-born midfielder David Eaves worked his way up through the

ranks at Deepdale to make his debut in a 2–0 defeat at Brentford in March 1991. He made a couple of further appearances off the bench that season but did not appear at all in 1991–92. The following season he made a handful of appearances but then parted company with the club.

ECCLESTON, Thomas

Wing-half

Born: Preston, 1874.
Career: PRESTON NORTH END, 1895.

■ Wing-half Tommy Eccleston spent six seasons at Deepdale but in that time he made just 26 League appearances. He scored goals in the 2–0 home win against Blackburn Rovers on the final day of the 1899–1900 season and the winner in a 3–2 victory against Derby County during the early stages of the following campaign. Often finding himself in the shadow of his brother, William, there were just three occasions when the two of them played in the same team. During his penultimate season with the club, William played instead of Tommy in the semi-final replay of the Lancashire Cup but Tommy returned for the Final.

ECCLESTON, William

Right-half, inside-right

Born: Preston, 1873.
Died: 1937.
Career: PRESTON NORTH END, 1893. Grimsby Town, 1894. PRESTON NORTH END, 1895.

■ Originally on the books of Preston North End, William Eccleston was one of the game's earliest versatile players. However, he could not force his way into the club's League side and left to play for Grimsby Town. In his only season for the Mariners he scored 13 goals in 29 games to help the club finish ninth in Division Two. Returning to Deepdale in time for the 1895–96 season, he made his long-awaited debut in a 1–0 defeat of Nottingham Forest before scoring the winner in his first game at Deepdale as North End beat Sheffield United 4–3. Towards the end of his stay at North End he played all his games at right-half, but during his five seasons with the club he had worn five different numbered outfield shirts.

EDWARDS, John

Outside-left

Born: Preston, 1867.
Died: 1960.
Career: PRESTON NORTH END, 1888.

■ In 1888–89, the inaugural season of League football, Preston North End won the League Championship and completed the double by beating Wolves in the FA Cup Final. Geordie Drummond was the outside-left in that side and, when he was injured, Sam Thomson replaced him. Jack Edwards was also an outside-left and so his appearances were restricted. He did score three goals in just four appearances though – including two in a 4–1 defeat of Notts County – but he never played for the club again.

EDWARDS, Robert William

Defender, midfield

Born: Kendal, 1 July 1973.
Career: Carlisle United, 1990. Bristol City, 1991. PRESTON NORTH END, 1999. Blackpool, 2004.

■ Rob Edwards began his career with his local club Carlisle United before a £135,000 transfer took him to Bristol City in March 1991. Although he initially found it difficult to hold down a first-team place, he found his form only for the club to be relegated to the Second Division in 1994–95. Early the following season, illness in the guise of glandular fever intervened, but in 1996–97 he was back to his best and was called into the full Wales squad after playing in the Under-21 and 'B' sides. After a couple of international appearances, he began to suffer from a spate of niggling injuries and missed a number of games in which his experience would have helped the side. In the summer of 1999, Edwards declined a new contract and joined Preston North End after appearing in 263 games for the Robins. At Deepdale he was used more as a left-back than in his usual midfield position, but he ended his first season with the club by winning a Second Division Championship medal. The following season his experience proved vital in helping the club adapt to the higher grade of football. Injuries such as a broken rib and a punctured lung forced him to miss matches, including an

international call-up in August 2001. A broken hand then disrupted his progress before new manager Craig Brown used him in a three-man central defensive formation, but in the summer of 2004 he was allowed to join Blackpool. Forming a solid partnership with Peter Clarke at the heart of the Seasiders' defence, his efforts were rewarded with an extension to his contract.

ELLIOTT, John William

Goalkeeper

Born: Scotswood, 21 May 1899.
Career: PRESTON NORTH END, 1920.
Scotswood. Ashington, 1925.

■ Goalkeeper John Elliott played a handful of matches for North End in 1920–21 as understudy to Arthur Causer. In the last of these he conceded six goals at Bradford City. He started the following season as the club's first-choice

'keeper but kept only one clean sheet in the openings seven games and lost out to Mitchell. He made one more appearance midway through the campaign but conceded three goals at home to West Bromwich Albion. After a spell playing for his home-town team of Scotswood, he joined Ashington and played in 56 League games for the Third Division North club.

ELLIOTT, Joseph

Wing-half

Born: Preston, 1877.
Career: PRESTON NORTH END, 1898.
New Brompton.

■ Wing-half Joe Elliott made his North End debut in a 3–1 defeat at Burnley in the second game of the 1898–99 season but it was his only appearance of the campaign. However, the following season he missed just the two opening games and he also scored his first goal for the club at Manchester City. He continued to be a first-team regular at Deepdale throughout the club's relegation season of 1900–01, netting goals in both matches against Bury. He was impressive in North End's 1901–02 Division Two campaign, the club just missing out on promotion back to the top flight, but was then surprisingly allowed to leave and join New Brompton.

ELLIOTT, Stephen Blair

Forward

Born: Haltwhistle, 15 September 1958.
Career: Nottingham Forest, 1976.
PRESTON NORTH END, 1979. Luton Town, 1984. Walsall, 1984. Bolton Wanderers, 1986. Bury, 1988. Rochdale, 1989. Guiseley.

■ After serving his apprenticeship at Nottingham Forest under the watchful eye of Brian Clough, Stephen Elliott turned professional and wore the number-nine shirt vacated by Peter With. After a handful of First Division games for Forest, all of which were goalless draws, he lost his place to Gary Birtles prior to joining Preston North End for a then club record fee of £95,000. He was ever present in 1979–80, his first full season at the club, and ended the campaign as North End's leading scorer

with 16 League goals. Elliott remained a regular in the Preston side over the next few seasons and in 1982–83 again topped the club's scoring charts. His total of 23 League and Cup goals included his only hat-trick for the club against Millwall on the opening day of the season. Elliott also scored in six consecutive games and in doing so took his tally of goals to 11 in the opening 10 games. Having scored 74 goals in 225 games for North End he then returned to the First Division with Luton Town. His stay at Kenilworth Road was brief and he then spent two seasons with Walsall before returning to the north-west with Bolton Wanderers. Unable to prevent their relegation, he

then found his first-team opportunities limited and made the short journey to Bury before ending his League career with Rochdale. Having taken his tally of League goals to 125, he joined HFS Loans side Guiseley.

ELLIS, Anthony Joseph

Forward

Born: Salford, 20 October 1964.
Career: Horwich RMI. Oldham Athletic, 1986. PRESTON NORTH END, 1987. Stoke City, 1989. PRESTON NORTH END, 1992. Blackpool, 1994. Bury, 1997. Stockport County, 1999. Rochdale, 1999. Burnley, 2001. Mossley.

■ Salford-born striker Tony Ellis was playing non-League football for Horwich RMI when Oldham Athletic took him on as a full-time professional.

Finding it difficult to hold down a regular first-team place at Boundary Park, he left the Latics in October 1987 and joined Preston North End for a fee of £20,000. He proceeded to give good value for money at Deepdale. In 1988–89, his first full season, he was the club's leading scorer with 20 League goals including a hat-trick in the 6–0 rout of Chesterfield. In December 1989, Ellis joined Stoke City for £250,000 but he never really settled at the Victoria Ground and in the summer of 1992 he was given the opportunity to return to his old hunting ground at Deepdale in a big-money part-exchange deal also involving Graham Shaw. Though North End were relegated, Ellis was top scorer with 25 League and

Cup goals, including a hat-trick in a 3–2 win over rivals Blackpool at Bloomfield Road and another treble in a 5–2 defeat of Rotherham United. In 1993–94, Ellis scored 31 goals in all competitions – hitting another hat-trick against Chesterfield. Ellis, who had scored all his Deepdale goals on the plastic pitch, had netted 88 goals in 194 games in his two spells before signing for Blackpool for £165,000 in July 1994. Ellis consistently found the net throughout his stay at Bloomfield Road, scoring 65 goals in 172

games before joining Bury. Not part of Neil Warnock's plans at Gigg Lane, he moved to Stockport County, Rochdale and Burnley before playing in Australia prior to joining non-League Mossley.

ELSE, Frederick

Goalkeeper

Born: Golborne, 31 March 1933.
Career: Wigan Athletic. PRESTON NORTH END, 1953. Blackburn Rovers, 1961. Barrow, 1966.

■ Fred Else began his Football League career with Preston North End after impressing for Axwell Park Colliery Welfare while doing his National Service. He made his League debut for the Lilywhites in a 4–0 win against Manchester City at Deepdale in March 1954, following an injury to George Thompson. By 1956–57, Else was North End's first-choice 'keeper and in his first full season was ever present as the Deepdale club finished third in Division One. In fact, he impressed so much that he played for England 'B' and was unlucky not to win full international honours. A firm favourite with the North End fans, he was surprisingly sold to Blackburn Rovers for £17,000 in August 1961 after failing to agree terms. The very same evening that he put pen to paper, he played for Rovers against North End in a

pre-season friendly. Else was Blackburn's first-choice goalkeeper for five seasons and was ever present in 1963–64 when Rovers finished seventh in the top flight. A broken collarbone in the derby with Burnley forced him to miss a number of games, but on his return he proved he had lost none of his sharpness. Following Rovers' relegation in 1965–66, Else, who had appeared in 221 games, left to play for Barrow. While at Holker Street, he became the club's manager for a short spell before their demise from the Football League.

ELWISS, Michael Walter

Forward

Born: Doncaster, 2 May 1954.
Career: Doncaster Rovers, 1971. PRESTON NORTH END, 1974. Crystal Palace, 1978. PRESTON NORTH END, 1980 (loan).

■ Having signed his former Old Trafford teammates Burns, Sadler and Stiles, North End manager Bobby Charlton went to Belle Vue, the home of Doncaster Rovers, to watch Mike Elwiss. Charlton liked what he saw and quickly set up a deal to take the centre-forward to Deepdale. Elwiss made his North End debut against Carlisle United in March 1974 and what a debut it was as he scored twice in the first half. Unfortunately, the Cumbrian outfit hit back in the second half to secure a point from a 2–2 draw. However, he was unable to prevent the Deepdale club's relegation to the Third Division, despite scoring both his side's goals on the final day against Middles-

brough, who had already won promotion. Elwiss had though begun to form a prolific strike partnership with Alex Bruce. He was ever present again in 1977–78, helping the club win promotion to Division Two before the club accepted a generous offer for his services from Crystal Palace. He became a great favourite at Selhurst Park before injuries hampered his progress. He returned to Deepdale on loan in an effort to prove his fitness and netted twice in a 2–1 win at Leicester in his first full game – thus securing a timely and well-deserved success for North End. Sadly, Mike Elwiss had to retire due to his recurring injuries, even though he was still only in his mid-twenties.

EMERSON, Dean

Midfield

Born: Salford, 27 December 1962.
Career: East Manchester. Stockport

County, 1982. Rotherham United, 1985. Coventry City, 1986. Hartlepool United, 1992. Stockport County, 1993. PRESTON NORTH END, 1994. Chorley.

■ The distinctive red-haired Dean Emerson began his career with Stockport County and developed into a fast-raiding midfield player with a strong tackle, powerful shot and the ability to make defence-splitting passes. However, with County's neverending parlous financial position, it was inevitable that he would not remain at Edgeley Park. After four seasons, County accepted Rotherham United's £30,000 bid for their Player of the Year. Emerson, who was still only 22, had made 172 appearances for County. After just over a year at Millmoor he joined First Division Coventry City in an exchange deal worth £100,000. He held down a regular place at Highfield Road before a serious knee injury in 1987 led to three operations, resulting in him missing the Sky Blues' only FA Cup success at Wembley. Freed by Coventry in 1992, he spent a season with Hartlepool United before returning to Stockport for a second spell. In November 1994 he joined Preston North End but, though he made a couple of appearances off the bench in the FA Cup and in a League match against Northampton Town, his only start came in a 1–0 defeat of Barnet. Emerson never really had the chance to show his abilities and moved on to non-League Chorley.

ENGLISH, John Charles

Full-back

Born: Hebburn, 13 December 1886.
Died: 1953.
Career: PRESTON NORTH END, 1910. Watford. Sheffield United, 1913. Darlington.

■ Full-back John English had played non-League football in his native North East for Hebburn and Wallsend Park before he joined North End in the summer of 1910. Though spending much of his time in the club's reserves, he was called into action for a three-game spell at the turn of the year after an injury to Charlie McFadyen. English also played in three games at the start of the 1911–12 season – his last appearance being in a 6–2 defeat at Tottenham Hot-

spur when he was deemed responsible for three of the goals. After a spell with Watford, who were then a non-League club, he joined Sheffield United and gave them good service in the two seasons prior to World War One. He was a member of the Blades' FA Cup-winning team of 1915. After the hostilities ended, he joined Darlington as player-manager and steered the club to the North Eastern League Championship in 1920–21. The Quakers joined the newly formed Third Division North the following season and finished runners-up. Darlington were Champions in 1924–25 and were promoted to Division Two. English later managed Nelson, Northampton Town and Exeter City but without much success.

ETUHU, Dickson Paul

Midfield

Born: Kano, Nigeria, 8 June 1982.
Career: Manchester City, 1999. PRESTON NORTH END, 2002.

■ Nigerian Dickson Etuhu began his career with Manchester City. He made his first-team debut against Birmingham in September 2001 when he linked up with another new boy in Ali Benarbia. He had a run of 11 games in City's midfield before losing his place. In January 2002, Etuhu was sold to Preston North End for a fee of £300,000 and instantly became popular with the fans for his powerful tackling and strong running in the centre of the park. After scoring his first goal on his second appearance at Deepdale in a 4–2 defeat of Sheffield Wednesday, he netted the only goal of the game against West Bromwich Albion. Though injuries hampered his progress in 2002–03, he turned in some stunning performances after the arrival of Brian O'Neil, who played alongside him in midfield. Using his height effectively, he scored with a number of near-post headers, while continuing to make surging runs to support the strikers. After lacking consistency in 2003–04, Etuhu underwent a hernia operation and the following season he made a steady start until being dismissed in the game against Wolverhampton Wanderers at Molineux. In last season's game against Wolves, Etuhu scored with a close-range header, having netted on the opening day of the season against Watford. He later lost his place in the North End side and went on loan to Norwich City, playing for the Canaries against Preston towards the end of the campaign.

EVANS, Raymond

Winger

Born: Preston, 21 June 1933.
Career: PRESTON NORTH END, 1951. Bournemouth 1959.

■ Local-born forward Ray Evans worked his way up through the ranks before making his debut in a 3–2 defeat at Arsenal in October 1953. Despite scoring the winner against Sheffield United the following match, North End had a settled side as they went on to play in that season's FA Cup Final. Evans did not appear again until towards the end of the following season when he netted at Leicester City. Though he failed to find the net again, he spent the next two seasons in and out of the North End side until he was transferred to Bournemouth in the summer of 1959. Evans spent a couple of seasons playing for the Cherries before drifting into non-League football.

EWART, John

Goalkeeper

Born: Oakbank, 14 February 1891.
Died: 1943.
Career: Douglas Park. Bellshill Rovers. Bellshill Athletic. Larkhall Thistle. Airdrieonians. Bradford City, 1912. Airdrieonians. Bradford City, 1927. PRESTON NORTH END, 1928.

■ Goalkeeper Jock Ewart played junior football in Scotland for a number of clubs, including Bellshill Athletic and Larkhall Thistle, before he signed for Airdrieonians in March 1909. His displays led to him winning representative honours for the Scottish League on two occasions before he joined Bradford City for a fee of £1,200 in May 1912. A popular goalkeeper with the City fans, his bravery and superb positional play saw him win full international honours for Scotland against England in a 1921 international. In 1923, Airdrieionians paid City £3,000 for Ewart's

return and he went on to help them beat Hibernian in the Scottish Cup Final. In May 1927, Bradford City re-signed Ewart as they tried to return to the Second Division but, having failed in their promotion push, Ewart, who had made 302 appearances for the Yorkshire club, was allowed to join Preston North End. Ewart made his debut on the opening day of the 1928–29 season, helping North End beat Blackpool 3–1 in front of a Deepdale crowd of 23,567. Sharing the goalkeeping duties with Frank Moss, he appeared in 31 games that season as North End finished mid-table in Division Two. He then toured North America with the Lilywhites but, after playing in a handful of games the following season, gave way to Des Fawcett. A few months into retirement, he was suspended indefinitely by the FA for his alleged involvement in a match-fixing affair surrounding a game between Bradford City and Bury. He later returned to the game as a trainer to New Brighton and eventually became a publican.

EYRES, David

Left-winger

Born: Liverpool, 26 February 1964.
Career: Rhyl. Blackpool, 1989. Burnley, 1993. PRESTON NORTH END. 1997. Oldham Athletic, 2000.

■ David Eyres was already 25 years old when Blackpool manager Jimmy Mullen signed him from Northern Premier League Rhyl for £10,000 in the summer of 1989. He soon established a regular place in the Seasiders' team but his first season at Bloomfield Road ended in disappointment as Blackpool were relegated to the Fourth Division. After losing to Torquay in the Play-offs in 1991, Blackpool beat Scunthorpe in the Play-offs the following year in a penalty shoot-out. Back in the new Second Division, Eyres was the club's leading scorer and it was this form that persuaded his former manager Jimmy Mullen, who had moved to Burnley, to splash out £90,000 for his services. It represented excellent value for money, for in his first season at Turf Moor he netted 29 goals in all competitions. His goals were instrumental in the Clarets'

run to the Play-offs and ultimate success against Stockport County. Despite relegation in 1994–95, Eyres' form was one of the key factors in the Clarets avoiding a second successive relegation. Eyres had scored 55 goals in 212 games for Burnley when in October 1997 he was transferred to Preston North End for £80,000. Though now at the veteran stage, he helped North End win the Second Division Championship in 1999–2000, netting twice against his first club Blackpool. Also among the highlights of that season, Eyres netted his first goal of the campaign in his 400th Football League game and made his 500th appearance at Millwall. Though he was rewarded with a one-year contract, he found that he had a permanent place on the bench at the start of the following season and, frustrated by his lack of action, he opted for a move to Oldham Athletic. In his first season at Boundary Park, he swept the club's Player of the Season awards and continued to be the Latics' most outstanding player, scoring a number of goals with trademark free-kicks. Eyres, who became the oldest outfield player in the Football League, had a spell as the Latics' caretaker manager and had appeared in 759 first-team games for his four Lancashire clubs.

FAGAN, William

Inside-forward

Born: Inveresk, 20 February 1917.
Died: 1992.
Career: Glasgow Celtic. PRESTON NORTH END, 1936. Liverpool, 1937. Weymouth.

■ Inside-forward Willie Fagan began his footballing days in his native Scotland with Celtic but, in October 1936, Tommy Muirhead took him to Deepdale to join the O'Donnells for a fee of £3,500. He made his North End debut in a 2–0 win at Stoke and went on to score six goals in 29 League games. He was also a member of the Preston side that lost 3–1 to Sunderland in that season's FA Cup Final. Early the following season, he left North End to join Liverpool. Fagan, a powerful, bustling player, would undoubtedly have gone on to score many goals for the Reds had it not been for the outbreak of war. As it was, he was barely 22 years old when hostilities began. During the war he 'guested' for a host of clubs, including Newcastle, Chelsea, Millwall and Reading, as well as playing in a number of wartime internationals for Scotland. At the end of the conflict, Fagan returned to Anfield and was a member of Liverpool's Championship-winning side of 1946–47. He also played in the side that lost to Arsenal in the 1950 FA Cup Final. However, his appearances became less frequent and in 1952 he joined Weymouth as player-manager. After ending his involvement with the game, he worked for Her Majesty's Prisons.

FAIRBROTHER, John

Goalkeeper

Born: Burton, 16 August 1917.
Career: Burton Town. PRESTON NORTH END, 1937. Newcastle United, 1947.

■ Jack Fairbrother was a well-built, confident and stylish goalkeeper who joined Preston North End from Burton

Town in March 1937. However, due to the onset of World War Two, he did not make his Football League debut until he was approaching 30 years of age. He had to be content with wartime football in which he was good enough to appear for the Football League's elect team. A former policeman during the war – for a time he wore white police gloves on the field as a gimmick – he made his Football League debut for North End on the opening day of the 1946–47 season as Leeds United were beaten 3–2. He missed just one game in that first season of League football following the hostilities, helping North End finish seventh in the First Division. In the close season, Newcastle United paid £6,500 to take him to St James' Park, where his early displays brought him close to winning full international honours. He was in goal in 1951 when the Magpies won the FA Cup by beating Blackpool 2–0 in the Final, but after four seasons as the club's first-choice 'keeper, he lost his place to Ronnie Simpson after breaking a collarbone. He was manager at Peterborough United during their great Midland League days when they shone as FA Cup giant-killers and his success at London Road led to him being appointed manager of Coventry City. The nephew of former North End and England winger George Harrison, he later had a second spell in charge of the Posh.

FARNWORTH, Simon

Goalkeeper

Born: Chorley, 28 October 1963.
Career: Bolton Wanderers, 1981. Stockport County, 1986 (loan). Tranmere Rovers, 1987 (loan). Bury, 1987. PRESTON NORTH END, 1990. Wigan Athletic, 1993.

■ Goalkeeper Simon Farnworth was originally on the books of Manchester United, during which time he was capped by England Schools. When the Reds did not take up their option, Bolton Wanderers stepped in and, under the watchful eye of Charlie Wright, he soon became the Trotters' first-choice 'keeper, ousting the more experienced John Platt. He appeared for the Wanderers in the 1986 Freight Rover Trophy Final at

Wembley but after losing his place in the side to Dave Felgate, he had spells on loan with Stockport County and Tranmere Rovers before joining Bury. Highly popular with the Shakers' fans, he had appeared in 124 games for the Gigg Lane club when in the summer of 1990 he moved to Preston North End. The Deepdale club went down 3–1 at home to Grimsby Town on the opening day of the 1990–91 season and Farnworth, who was injured in a Leyland Daf Cup game against Carlisle, found himself sharing the goalkeeping duties with Alan Kelly. It was a similar story in 1991–92 but, following Kelly's transfer to Sheffield United, Farnworth was the club's first-choice the following season. Despite some heroic displays, North End were relegated and Farnworth moved on to Wigan. A virtual ever present during his time at Springfield Park, the experienced 'keeper celebrated his 100th consecutive appearance at Walsall in April 1995 and later became the Latics' physiotherapist.

FARRALL, Alec

Wing-half

Born: Hoylake, 3 March 1936.
Career: Everton, 1953. PRESTON NORTH END, 1957. Gillingham, 1960. Lincoln City, 1965. Watford, 1966.

■ Wing-half Alec Farrall joined North End from Everton in the summer of 1957, having made just a handful of League appearances for the Merseyside club. He made his debut in a goalless draw at Sunderland, but scored on his home debut as high-flying West Bromwich Albion were beaten 3–1. However, he was unable to regularly oust Jim Baxter in a season in which North End were runners-up in the First Division. It was a similar story in 1958–59, though he did score in three consecutive games just after the turn of the year including the winner in the FA Cup fourth-round tie against Bradford City. Farrall's best performance in a North End shirt came towards the end of the following season when he netted twice and struck the woodwork in a 4–3 home defeat by Sheffield Wednesday. In the close season, he joined Gillingham and helped them win the Fourth Division Championship in 1963–64. He later played for Lincoln City and Watford before hanging up his boots.

FARRELL, Vincent

Inside-left, left-half

Born: Preston, 1909.
Died: 1987.
Career: Dick Kerr's XI. PRESTON NORTH END, 1930. Clapton Orient, 1934. Exeter City, 1937. Clapton Orient, 1938.

■ Able to play in a number of positions, Vincent Farrell played his early football for Dick Kerr's XI before joining North End prior to the start of the 1930–31 season. During his first campaign with the club, Farrell netted a hat-trick in the 4–1 win over Charlton Athletic, having already scored against the Addicks at The Valley earlier in the season. Injuries hampered his progress the following season and he was allowed to leave Deepdale and join Clapton Orient. Here he rediscovered his form and scored 21 goals in 79 games for the Third Division South outfit. He later had a brief spell with Exeter City before rejoining Clapton Orient. However, he was badly injured in training and did not appear in their League side again.

FARRELLY, Michael

Midfield

Born: Manchester, 1 November 1962.
Career: PRESTON NORTH END, 1981.

■ Midfielder Mike Farrelly, who played semi-professional football for

England, joined North End in the summer of 1981 and made his debut as a substitute for Willie Naughton in a 1–1 home draw against Huddersfield Town. In his first two seasons at Deepdale, Farrelly made just a handful of appearances before winning a regular place in the side in 1983–84. The following season he missed very few games but North End struggled throughout the campaign. Indeed, they needed to beat Wigan at Deepdale in the penultimate game to have any chance of staying up. As it was, North End were beaten 5–2 and relegated to the Fourth Division for the first time in their history. Mike Farrelly was one of a number of players who had worn the North End shirt for the last time.

FARRINGTON, George

Centre-forward

Born: Preston, 1884.
Career: PRESTON NORTH END, 1906.

■ Signed from local football, centre-forward George Farrington appeared in two games for North End during the 1906–07 season. Though the Lilywhites were struggling to avoid relegation from the First Division, Farrington was never on the losing side as Sheffield Wednesday were beaten 1–0 and already relegated Stoke came to Deepdale and drew 2–2 on the final day of the season. Farrington could have ended on a high note but blasted a last-minute shot wide when

Charlie Dawson, who had scored both North End's goals, was better placed.

FAWCETT, Desmond Hallimond

Goalkeeper

Born: Middlesbrough, 1907.
Died: 1968.
Career: Loftus Albion. Darlington, 1926. Nelson, 1928. PRESTON NORTH END, 1929. York City, 1932. Mansfield Town, 1934. Rochdale, 1936. Wellington Town.

■ Goalkeeper Des Fawcett was a member of the Darlington side relegated from the Second Division in 1926–27. He later played for Nelson before signing for Preston North End in 1929. He made his debut in a 2–0 defeat at Reading on the opening day of the 1929–30 season. It was not the best of seasons for North End and, though the defence conceded 80 goals, 21 of these were scored in the five matches that Fawcett was absent through injury. However, he lost his place the following season to John Hampton, who joined Preston from Derby County, and left to play for York City near the start of the 1931–32 campaign. After two seasons as the Minstermen's first-choice 'keeper, he had spells with Mansfield Town and Rochdale before leaving to play non-League football for Wellington Town.

FEE, Gregory Paul

Centre-half

Born: Halifax, 24 June 1964.
Career: Bradford City, 1983. Boston United. Sheffield Wednesday, 1987. PRESTON NORTH END, 1990 (loan). Northampton Town, 1990 (loan). PRESTON NORTH END, 1991 (loan). Leyton Orient, 1991 (loan). Mansfield Town, 1991. Chesterfield, 1992 (loan).

■ Central defender Greg Fee started out with Bradford City but left Valley Parade to play non-League football for Boston United after being unable to hold down a regular first-team spot. His consistent displays at the heart of the Lincolnshire club's defence prompted Sheffield Wednesday to give him another chance at League level. In September 1990, Fee joined North End on loan and he played his first game in a 3–2 defeat at

Southend. In that loan spell, Fee appeared in a further nine games but though the club only conceded four goals in that time, Fee returned to Hillsborough. He then went on loan to Northampton before returning to Deepdale for a second loan spell in the New Year. Despite some good displays, terms could not be agreed and after a further loan spell with Leyton Orient, he signed for Mansfield Town. Unable to prevent the Stags' relegation to Division Four, he was instrumental in them winning promotion at the first attempt in 1992–93 but later parted company with the club.

FENSOME, Andrew Brian

Full-back

Born: Northampton, 18 February 1969.
Career: Norwich City, 1987. Bury Town. Cambridge United, 1989. PRESTON NORTH END, 1993. Rochdale, 1996. Barrow.

■ Having been unable to make the grade with Norwich City, full-back Andy Fensome went to play non-League football for Bury Town before being given the chance to resurrect his League career with Cambridge United. Having helped United win promotion from the Fourth Division in his first season at the Abbey Stadium, he was outstanding in 1990–91 as the club won the Third Division Championship at the first attempt. The club almost made it three successive promotions as they finished fifth in Division Two in 1991–92. However, following the club's relegation the following season, Fensome joined Preston North End and made his debut in a 2–2 draw at Wigan in the Lancashire derby. He missed just one game after the derby and helped North End into the Play-offs where, after beating Torquay United, they lost 4–2 to Wycombe Wanderers in the Wembley Final. In 1994–95, Fensome was Preston's most improved player, gaining in confidence as the season progressed. Sound in defence and a long throw specialist, he once again helped North End reach the Play-offs and was ever present in all competitions. Despite being named Player of the Year for 1994–95, he found himself in and out of the Preston side the following season. However, he never let the club down from right-back and combined well with Lee Cartwright on that flank. His exclusion from the team in mid-season was a mystery to most North End fans. Despite winning a Third Division Championship medal, he was released in the close season and joined Rochdale. He gave the Spotland club two seasons of service and, despite Dale's up and down form, missed only a handful of games. Released in the summer of 1998, he went to play for Barrow.

FENTON, Frederick

Outside-left

Born: Gainsborough, 15 November 1878.
Career: Gainsborough Trinity, 1898. West Ham United. Gainsborough Trinity, 1901. PRESTON NORTH END, 1901. West Bromwich Albion, 1903. Bristol City, 1904. Swindon Town. Croydon Common.

■ Outside-left Fred Fenton began his career with his home-town club Gainsborough Trinity. He scored seven goals in 62 Second Division games for the Lincolnshire side in two spells with the club either side of a period playing Southern League football for West Ham United. In 1901, the diminutive winger joined Preston North End and played his first game in a 1–1 home draw with Blackpool. Given more of a run in the team in 1902–03, Fenton created many of the goals scored by Pearson and Smith and his exciting wing play prompted First Division West Bromwich Albion to take him to the Hawthorns. After a season gaining top-flight experience, Fenton moved to Bristol City and helped them win the Second Division Championship in 1905–06 prior to spells in the Southern League with Swindon Town and Croydon Common.

FERRIS, James

Inside-forward

Born: Belfast. 28 November 1894.
Died: Belfast, 1932.
Career: Distillery. Belfast Celtic. Chelsea, 1920. PRESTON NORTH END, 1921. Pontypridd. Belfast Celtic.

■ Northern Ireland international inside-forward James Ferris, who scored in the 1–1 draw with England in October 1919, played his early football in the Irish League with Distillery and Belfast Celtic before joining Chelsea in 1920. In his only season at Stamford Bridge, the London club struggled in the lower reaches of the top flight but Ferris, who continued to represent his country, scored eight goals in 33 games. Allowed to join Preston North End towards the end of the 1921–22 season, he made little impression but made amends when given an extended run in the side the following term. Towards the end of his stay with North End, Ferris netted a well-taken hat-trick in a 5–0 home win over Burnley. This was without doubt the highlight of a Preston career that saw the international forward score 11 goals in 53 League games. He later had a spell with Pontypridd before returning to Ireland to end his career with one of his former clubs, Belfast Celtic.

FIELDING, Mark John

Full-back

Born: Bury, 10 November 1956.
Career: PRESTON NORTH END, 1974.

■ Mark Fielding was a strong-tackling full-back who worked his way up through the ranks at Deepdale to make 13 League and Cup appearances during the 1974–75 season, when Bobby Charlton was North End's player-manager. Having made his debut in a 2–0 defeat at Bury, Fielding later had a run of nine consecutive games in the number-two shirt. He helped Preston beat non-League sides Blyth Spartans and Bishop Auckland in the FA Cup before they went out to Carlisle United in round three.

FINDLAY, Alex

Outside-right

Career: PRESTON NORTH END, 1896.

■ Outside-right Alex Finlay was called into the North End side in place of the injured Thomas Smith for the fourth game of the 1896–97 season. He had an impressive debut and scored one of his side's goals in a 5–3 defeat of Burnley. With Smith still receiving treatment, he kept his place in the side but with North End going down 3–1 to Bolton Wanderers that was the extent of his appearances for the Deepdale club.

FINNEY, Stephen Kenneth

Winger

Born: Hexham, 31 October 1973.
Career: PRESTON NORTH END, 1992. Manchester City, 1993. Swindon Town, 1995. Cambridge United, 1997 (loan). Carlisle United, 1998. Leyton Orient, 1999. Barrow. Chester City, 1999.

■ Winger Steve Finney was a youth trainee at Deepdale who, after impressing in the club's reserves, made a handful of appearances coming off the bench. In 1992–93, his second season with the club, he played in the Autoglass Trophy at Wigan. He kept his place in the side to make his first full start against Hull City but was substituted by Lee Fowler as the Tigers won 2–1. It proved to be Finney's only start for North End and he left to try his luck with Manchester City. Unable to make much headway at Maine Road, he joined Swindon Town in the summer of 1995 and had scored 15 goals before Christmas when he broke his leg at Burnley. A Second Division Championship medal went some way to rewarding him for his efforts. Despite making a full recovery from the injury, he lost his

goalscoring form. After a loan spell with Cambridge United, he was released by the Robins and returned to his native Cumbria to play for Carlisle United. While at Brunton Park, he netted Carlisle's 4,000th League goal but it also proved to be his swansong as he was transferred to Leyton Orient. His stay at Brisbane Road was brief and he played for Barrow prior to returning to League football with Chester City, who themselves were relegated to the Conference.

FINNEY, Thomas

Forward

Born: Preston, 5 April 1922.
Career: PRESTON NORTH END, 1940.

■ Tom Finney had just turned 38 when he played his last League match. It was not particularly important as Preston were comfortably placed in the First Division and the visitors Luton Town were already certain to be relegated. However, Finney's admirers proved their regard for him as 30,000 turned up to see him make his farewell a touching and memorable occasion. Their idol had been playing for some time at centre-forward – thereby creating a club record by playing and scoring in all five forward positions – but to please the fans he reverted to his original role of outside-right. For over a decade, Finney was Preston and Preston was Finney. There were other notable players – Quigley, Wayman, Docherty – but none were local, none stayed so long and none were ever in the same class. When he retired in 1960 he held all the long-term appearance and scoring records for North End and had played 76 times for his country – a number then exceeded only by Billy Wright, with whom he figured in all but two of his internationals. Like so many of his generation, Finney lost several of his most promising football years through war service. He was only 19 when he played brilliantly against Eddie Hapgood, Arsenal's long-established England full-back, in the 1941 War Cup Final at Wembley and contributed to Preston's victory in the replay at Blackburn. Towards the end of the war his exploits with other accomplished players at international level in Italy and Austria made it clear that England had found a winger of exceptional ability, possessing all the key attributes. Thus in September 1946 at Belfast, a month after his belated League debut at 24 for Preston in the First Division, he made his international debut. In his early days on the international scene, many would say, 'When will we see the Preston edition of him in an England shirt?' They certainly did at Hampden Park a number of times and he scored four goals in Lisbon in 1950 in what he considers his best international. In February 1950, Tom Finney achieved something for North End that he never achieved in the League or Cup for them: he scored a hat-trick, though it came in a friendly against Dundee as North End won 6–2. Having just missed a League Championship medal in 1952–53, when Arsenal edged

Tom Finney, playing for England.

North End into second place on goal average by winning their last match, Finney yearned to lead his side to a Wembley triumph in the Cup. So much was expected of him after a good season but his contribution to a mediocre final that West Bromwich Albion won 3–2 was a small one. Too much had been taken out of him by the stress of that week. Scores of friends and acquaintances badgered him for tickets; there were also interviews, photographic sessions and television appearances. One thing on which all who played with or against Tom Finney agree is that, in addition to all his skill, he never lacked courage. In his time he took a large amount of punishment. This is reflected in the fact that he missed 115 matches – most of them in ones, twos and threes – through injury of one kind or another. Bill Shankly used to say he would go through a mountain. Today he would be just as good as he was then – make no mistake about that. He was the greatest.

FITTON, George Arthur

Outside-left

Born: Melton Mowbray, 16 May 1902.
Died: 1984.
Career: Kinver Swifts. Cookley St Peter's. Kidderminster Harriers. West Bromwich Albion, 1922. Manchester United, 1931. PRESTON NORTH END, 1932. Coventry City, 1935. Kidderminster Harriers.

■ Fitton's impressive wing play for Kidderminster Harriers prompted West Bromwich Albion to give him a chance in League football in 1922. Though he stayed at the Hawthorns for almost eight years, helping them to finish runners-up in the First Division in 1924–25, he only made 96 League appearances, scoring 11 goals, in that time. He then had a brief spell with Manchester United before signing for Preston North End midway through the 1932–33 season. Though the Lilywhites lost 1–0 at Southampton in Fitton's first game for the club, the lively winger showed his worth by netting seven goals in the 15 games he played following his debut. In 1933–34, Fitton was outstanding. As well as scoring five goals in a 10–game spell, he also created numerous chances for the likes of Stephenson and Palethorpe as North End

went on to win promotion to the First Division as runners-up to Grimsby Town. He continued to impress in the top flight, scoring some vital goals along the way as North End consolidated their new status in mid-table. Surprisingly allowed to leave the club, he joined Coventry City and helped the Highfield Road club win the Third Division South Championship in his first season. The winger, who scored 52 goals in 224 games for his four League clubs, later ended his career back at Kidderminster Harriers.

FITZPATRICK, Paul James

Defender, midfield

Born: Oxford, 5 October 1965.
Career: Tranmere Rovers. Bolton Wanderers, 1985. Bristol City, 1986. Carlisle United, 1988. PRESTON NORTH END, 1988 (loan). Leicester City, 1991. Birmingham City, 1993. Bury, 1993. Hamilton Academicals. Northampton Town, 1994. Rushden and Diamonds.

■ Lanky utility player Paul Fitzpatrick was a former Tranmere Rovers junior player who was given his chance in League football by Bolton Wanderers in March 1985. Just over a year later he joined Bristol City and in 1987–88 helped the Ashton Gate club reach the Play-offs. Fitzpatrick later joined Carlisle United and featured in the Cumbrian club's promotion challenge in 1989–90. Prior to this, he had a loan spell with Preston North End. His first game was a 3–3 home draw with Cardiff City. He did not appear in either of the Sherpa Van Trophy ties with Bolton and Bury but returned to action for his second and last appearance in a North End shirt – a 2–1 defeat at Fulham. Fitzpatrick was Brian Little's first purchase as Leicester manager, paying Carlisle £40,000 for his signature. With competition for places at Filbert Street fierce, he opted for a free transfer to Birmingham City and later played for Bury, Hamilton Academicals, Northampton Town and Rushden and Diamonds.

FLEMING, Terence Maurice

Full-back, midfield

Born: Marston Green, 5 January 1973.
Career: Coventry City, 1991. Northampton Town, 1993. PRESTON NORTH

END, 1994. Lincoln City, 1995. Plymouth Argyle, 2000. Cambridge United, 2001. Grimsby Town, 2004.

■ Unable to hold down a regular first-team place at his first club, Coventry City, Terry Fleming joined Northampton Town on a free transfer in the summer of 1993. His consistent displays for the Cobblers during the 1993–94 season prompted North End manager John Beck to bring him to Deepdale. Able to provide cover at either full-back or on the wing, he was unable to secure a regular place in the Preston side until towards the end of the 1994–95 campaign. Even though he appeared in the opening games of the club's Third Division Championship-winning season, he was one of four North End players who left Deepdale to link up with former boss John Beck at Lincoln City. Putting his off-the-field problems behind him, he developed into one of the Imps' most creative players and his long throw-ins caused untold problems in the opposition's defence. In 1997–98 he helped Lincoln win promotion to the Second Division but, once in the higher grade of football, he let his disciplinary problems resurface, collecting 11 yellow cards throughout the 1998–99 campaign. Despite this, he was appointed Lincoln's captain and his combative style provided plenty of inspiration for his teammates. Unable to agree terms for a new deal, Fleming, who had appeared in 210 games for Lincoln, joined Plymouth Argyle. After struggling to win over the Home Park fans, he again linked up with John Beck, this time at Cambridge United. Giving United over three seasons of service, the versatile Fleming later moved to Grimsby Town where he was a regular in the Mariners' side.

FLITCROFT, David John

Midfield

Born: Bolton, 14 January 1974.
Career: PRESTON NORTH END, 1992. Bury, 1992 (loan). Chester City, 1993. Rochdale, 1999. Macclesfield Town, 2003. Bury, 2004.

■ David Flitcroft, the brother of Blackburn Rovers' Gary Flitcroft, began his career with Preston North End during the relegation season of 1992–93. The Bolton-born midfielder scored on

his debut in a 2–0 win over Reading and then after coming off the bench in a 4–2 defeat of Chester. Unable to force his way into the Preston side at the start of the following season, he spent a period on loan with Bury before signing for Chester City in December 1993. Employed to great effect on the right-hand side of the Cestrians midfield, much of his early time with the club was disrupted by injury. However, he recovered to play in 193 games before becoming Rochdale manager Steve Parkin's first signing. He was a key figure in the centre of the Spotland club's midfield and turned down a move to Shrewsbury to become Rochdale's Player of the Year in 2002–03. Surprisingly released, he was appointed team captain at Macclesfield before his contract was cancelled by mutual consent and he moved to Bury where he triggered an improvement in the Shakers' form.

FLYNN, Michael Anthony

Centre-half

Born: Oldham, 23 February 1969.
Career: Oldham Athletic, 1987. Norwich City, 1988. PRESTON NORTH END, 1989. Stockport County, 1993. Stoke City, 2002 (loan). Barnsley, 2002. Blackpool, 2003. Accrington Stanley.

■ Mike Flynn began his career with his home-town club, Oldham Athletic, before a big money deal took him into the top flight with Norwich City. Things did not work out for him at Carrow Road and he left without making a League appearance for the Canaries. Flynn signed for Preston North End in December 1989 for a fee of £125,000, making him then the most expensive player in the Deepdale club's history. The cultured defender came off the bench to make his North End debut in an embarrassing FA Cup defeat at the hands of non-League Whitley Bay. His next game was in the Leyland Daf Cup as Stockport County were beaten 4–2. Over the next few seasons, Flynn was outstanding at the heart of the North End defence but, towards the end of the club's relegation season of 1992–93, he was allowed to leave Deepdale to join Stockport County for a club record fee of £150,000. The club's only ever present in

1993–94, he skippered County to the Play-offs where they lost 2–1 to Burnley in the Wembley Final. Missing very few games, he led the club to promotion to the First Division and to the semi-finals of the League Cup in 1996–97. A committed and fearless defender whose long throws added to County's attacking options, he played in 460 first-team games for the Edgeley Park club before going on loan to Stoke City prior to joining Barnsley on a free transfer. Unable to prevent the Yorkshire club's relegation, he later found his first-team chances were becoming more limited, so he moved to Blackpool. Flynn, who helped the Seasiders win the LDV Vans Trophy at the Millennium Stadium, later moved into non-League football with Conference outfit Accrington Stanley.

FOLLY, Yoann

Midfield

Born: Togo, 6 June 1985.
Career: St Etienne (France). South-ampton, 2003. Nottingham Forest, 2005 (loan). PRESTON NORTH END, 2005 (loan).

■ French Youth international Yoann

Folly was also a member of the French squad for the prestigious under-21 international tournament in Toulon. He began his career with St Etienne before joining Southampton for £250,000 in the summer of 2003. New manager Paul Sturrock gave him his chance in the Saints' midfield and, though still a teenager, he responded to the challenge, appearing in nine Premiership games towards the end of the 2003–04 season. Surprisingly, he struggled to hold down a place the following season and, after a loan spell with Nottingham Forest, he joined Preston North End on a similar basis. Folly, who showed fine potential while at Deepdale, made just two appearances off the bench in the home games against Gillingham and Brighton and Hove Albion, with the South Coast club being beaten 4–0.

FOOT, George

Goalkeeper

Born: Heaton Park, 1888.
Career: Heaton Park. Bury, 1911.
PRESTON NORTH END, 1919.

■ Goalkeeper George Foot was spotted playing for Heaton Park by Bury in 1912 and was in the Shakers side that played North End towards the end of the Deepdale club's Second Division Championship-winning season. That day, Foot kept a clean sheet, producing save after save in a goalless draw. When football resumed after World War One, Foot joined Preston but was one of four

goalkeepers used by the club in that First Division campaign. Foot played in five games for North End and, though he was never on the winning side, only two of the games ended in defeat.

FORBES, William

Wing-half

Born: Glasgow, 25 May 1922.
Career: Dunfermline Athletic.
Wolverhampton Wanderers, 1946.
PRESTON NORTH END, 1949. Carlisle
United, 1956. Fleetwood Town.

■ Wing-half Willie Forbes played his early football for Dunfermline Athletic before Ted Vizard signed him for Wolverhampton Wanderers in September 1946. This reliable, hard-working and strong-tackling player scored 23 goals in 75 games for Wolves before North End manager Will Scott paid £18,000 for his services in December 1949. In 1950–51, his first full season with the club, Forbes was ever present as North End won the Second Division Championship. Throughout his time at Deepdale, Forbes was much respected for his fiery style of play in the centre of the park. Along with Tommy Docherty and Joe Marston, Forbes made up the club's most famous half-back line. Although his colleagues represented Scotland and Australia respectively, Forbes never won international honours. Forbes' fiery temper did once get him into trouble with the FA, who suspended him for his part in a feud with Blackburn Rovers' Alec Venters during a vital Championship game. A member of the Preston side beaten in the FA Cup Final of 1954, Forbes spent six seasons with the club before signing for Carlisle United. He continued to demonstrate his all-action style for the Cumbrian club before leaving Brunton Park to end his involvement with the game with a spell as player-manager of non-League Fleetwood Town.

FORD, John

Outside-right

Born: Wishaw, 1891.
Died: 1917.
Career: PRESTON NORTH END, 1913.

■ Signed from Scottish junior foot-

ball, outside-right John Ford made his North End debut in a 4–1 home win over Middlesbrough during the club's First Division relegation season of 1913–14. He scored two goals that campaign, both of them coming in a rare away win, 3–0 at Bolton Wanderers. In 1914–15, Ford proved himself to Second Division defences and his exciting wing play resulted in goalscoring opportunities for the likes of Osborn and Macauley and the club returning to the top flight at the first time of asking as runners-up to Derby County. Sadly, John Ford was killed during the latter stages of World War One.

FORREST, James

Centre-half, right-half

Born: Lesmahagow, 1 January 1899.
Career: Maryhill. Clyde. PRESTON
NORTH END, 1923. Cowdenbeath.

■ After impressing with Scottish League club Clyde, James Forrest joined North End midway through the 1923–24 season, playing in a couple of games as the club struggled in the lower reaches of the First Division. The following season he played alongside Joe McCall in the heart of the Preston defence but, though he gave some solid displays, he was unable to prevent the Deepdale club from losing their top-flight status. In and out of the side in 1925–26, he left Deepdale in the close season to return north of the border to continue his career with Cowdenbeath.

FORREST, James

Centre-forward

Born: Glasgow, 22 September 1944.
Career: Glasgow Rangers. PRESTON
NORTH END, 1967. Aberdeen. Hong
Kong Rangers.

■ Jim Forrest was one of the game's greatest goalscorers, as his goals-to-game ratio for Rangers – 145 in 164 games – testifies. He was capped five times by Scotland but failed to find the net. One of only a handful of players to score 100 League goals in the post-war years, his tally was 57 in 1965–66. Two seasons earlier he had helped Rangers win the League Championship and the League Cup when he scored a record four goals

in the 5–0 Final win over Morton. Jim Forrest scored four goals more than once and in October 1965 he scored five in a 7–1 win over Hamilton Academicals at Douglas Park. Forrest's Ibrox career ended under the cloud of the infamous Scottish Cup defeat by Berwick Rangers in January 1967. Unbelievably blamed for this surprise reversal, he was transfer listed and within weeks had joined Preston North End. Forrest scored on his Preston debut in a 2–0 win over Derby County and went on to find the net three times in eight appearances towards the end of the 1966–67 campaign. Unable to find the net in 18 League games the following season, he returned north to play for Aberdeen, helping the Pittodrie club win the 1970 Scottish Cup Final. He left the Dons in 1973 to see out his career with Hong Kong Rangers.

FORSHAW, Edward

Centre-half

Born: Preston, 1881.
Career: PRESTON NORTH END, 1901.

■ A towering centre-half who had impressed in local junior football, Edward Forshaw was given his chance in the North End side during the course of

the 1901–02 season as the club challenged for promotion to the First Division. Michael Good had worn the number-five shirt for most of that season but injury forced him to miss two games. Despite giving a good account of himself in wins over Stockport County and Burnley, Forshaw was released at the end of the season.

FOSTER, James

Goalkeeper

Born: Wigan, 1907.
Career: Washington Colliery. PRESTON NORTH END, 1929. Manchester Central. Crewe Alexandra, 1932. Barnsley, 1935. Wigan Athletic.

■ After some outstanding displays for non-League Washington Colliery, goalkeeper Jim Foster joined Preston North End in the summer of 1929 as cover for regular 'keeper Des Fawcett. In that season's Second Division campaign, Foster was called upon only once, playing what turned out to be his only game for the club in a 5–1 defeat at Blackpool. This was followed by a couple of seasons playing for Manchester Central before he returned to League action with Crewe Alexandra. He had two seasons in their Third Division North side before playing in a handful of games for Barnsley. Foster later returned to the North West to play a season of Cheshire League football for Wigan Athletic.

FOSTER, Robert John

Inside-forward

Born: Sheffield, 19 July 1929.
Career: Chesterfield, 1947. PRESTON NORTH END, 1951. Rotherham United, 1958.

■ A player guaranteed to score goals, Bobby Foster arrived at Deepdale from Chesterfield in July 1951. In his first couple of seasons with the club, Foster found himself in and out of the North End side and it was not until 1953–54, when he was a member of the FA Cup Final side, that he established himself fully. Alternating between different positions in the forward line Foster, who won England 'B' honours, occasionally deputised for Tom Finney and once

scored four goals in a spell of five games on the right-wing. Foster's best season in terms of goals scored was 1954–55 when he netted 13 goals in 28 games, including nine in the opening 12 games of the campaign. Towards the end of his stay at Deepdale, Foster lost his place to Tommy Thompson and was languishing in the reserves when the club sold him to Rotherham United in a deal which also took his North End teammate Ken Waterhouse to Millmoor in May 1958.

FOSTER, Wayne Paul

Forward, midfield

Born: Leigh, 11 September 1963.
Career: Bolton Wanderers, 1981. PRESTON NORTH END, 1985. Heart of Midlothian. Hartlepool United, 1994 (loan).

■ Wayne Foster made rapid progress as a youngster with Bolton Wanderers, whom he joined straight from school. In 1981–82, he forced his way into the club's League side with some deft and speedy performances in the Central League. He won England Youth honours and continued to make steady progress, but things were difficult in a struggling team. After the Wanderers were relegated to the

Third Division, competition for the forward places became more intense and Foster was allowed to join Preston North End on a free transfer in May 1985. His only season at Deepdale (1985–86) turned out to be the worst in the club's history. He kept his place in the side for most of the season and towards the end of the campaign he netted in a vital 3–2 win at Mansfield Town. North End finished just one place off the bottom of the Fourth Division and had to apply for re-election. Foster was freed and joined Hearts. His luck changed in the Scottish League as he was switched to a wider role with the Tynecastle club. Foster helped Hearts to finish runners-up to Celtic in the Scottish Premier Division and gave the club eight seasons of service. He played in 207 games before he left the game following a loan spell with Hartlepool United.

FOWLER, John Anthony

Midfield

Born: Preston, 27 October 1974.
Career: Cambridge United, 1992.
PRESTON NORTH END, 1993 (loan).
Cambridge City. Kettering Town.

■ Central midfield player John Fowler was born in Preston, but he began his career with Cambridge United. His opportunities of first-team football at the Abbey Stadium were limited so he opted for a loan spell at his home-town club and arrived at Deepdale in February 1993. During his time with North End, Fowler made five starts, but the only time he appeared on the winning side was in a 3–2 defeat of Wigan Athletic at Springfield Park. Allowed to return to Cambridge United, he had a loan spell with Cambridge City before joining Kettering Town.

FOWLER, Lee Edward

Left-back, midfield

Born: Eastwood, 26 January 1970.
Career: Stoke City, 1988. PRESTON NORTH END, 1992. Doncaster Rovers, 1993.

■ Able to play at both full-back and in midfield, Lee Fowler started out with Stoke City, appearing in 49 League games for the Potters at a time when they were

constantly challenging for promotion to Division Two. Fowler left the Victoria Ground at the end of the 1991–92 season and made his North End debut in a 1–1 draw at Bournemouth on the opening day of the 1992–93 campaign. Fowler was a regular member of the Preston side throughout that disappointing season, showing his versatility by appearing in four different numbered outfield shirts. However, following relegation, Fowler left the club to continue his career with a brief spell at Doncaster Rovers.

FOX, Frederick Samuel

Goalkeeper

Born: Highworth, 22 November 1898.
Died: 1968.
Career: Swindon Town. Abertillery. PRESTON NORTH END, 1921. Gillingham, 1922. Millwall, 1925. Halifax Town, 1927. Brentford, 1928.

■ Fred Fox began his career with his local club, Swindon Town, playing for the Robins during World War One. When the hostilities ceased, he had a brief spell with Abertillery before joining Preston North End in the summer of 1921. He made just three appearances and was never on the winning side, conceding four goals on his last appearance at Liverpool. Leaving North End to play for Gillingham, Fox's displays between the posts for the Kent club led to him winning full international honours for England when he played in a 3–2 win

over France in 1925. An outstanding 'keeper with a safe pair of hands and good anticipation, he appeared in 119 League games for the Gills before moving to Millwall. After two seasons at The Den, he played for Halifax Town before seeing out his first-class career with Brentford.

FRIAR, John

Outside-right

Born: Newmains, 22 July 1911.
Died: 1979.
Career: Carluke Rovers. Hibernian. Bradford City, 1930. Portsmouth, 1932. Bournemouth, 1933. Port Vale, 1934. PRESTON NORTH END, 1934. Norwich City, 1935. Ipswich Town, 1938.

■ John Friar was a powerful right-winger who played for Hibernian before coming south of the border to try his luck in the Football League with Bradford City. Unable to make much headway at Valley Parade, Friar joined Portsmouth but after making his first-class debut he moved further along the South Coast to Bournemouth. In his only season at Dean Court, he was the Cherries' leading scorer and this form prompted Port Vale to sign him in the close season. He was Vale's leading marksman when he was sold to Preston North End in exchange for Ted Critchley and a cash balance. Friar scored on his Preston debut in a 3–3 draw at Leeds United and found the net five times in his first six games for the club. As well as his goals, he created numerous goalscoring opportunities for Bud Maxwell, but after just three games of the 1935–36 season he was allowed to join Norwich City before ending his career with neighbours Ipswich Town.

FULLAM, John Rowan

Wing-half

Born: Dublin, 22 March 1940.
Career: Home Farm. PRESTON NORTH END, 1958. Shamrock Rovers, 1961. Bohemians, 1969. Shamrock Rovers, 197. Athlone Town, 1979.

■ Wing-half Johnny Fullam joined First Division Preston North End from Home Farm in October 1958. After spending a season in the club's Central

League side, he made his Football League debut in a 2–1 win at Newcastle United. The following season, despite some impressive individual displays in the club's midfield, North End finished bottom of the First Division and were relegated. Johnny Fullam returned to Ireland in 1961 to join Shamrock Rovers after scoring six goals in 56 League and Cup games during his stay at Deepdale. Fullam won five FAI Cup-winners' medals with the Hoops, scoring the winner in the 1965 replayed Final against Limerick, and one League Championship medal in 1963–64. His career seemed over in 1969 until he was snapped up by Bohemians, who discarded their amateur status and opened their doors to professionals. He captained Bohemians when they won the FAI Cup in 1976, collecting his second FAI Cup-winners' medal with Bohemians and his seventh in total. He also won a Championship medal with the club in 1974–75 and appeared in three League Cup finals, scoring in the victory over Finn Harps in 1975. He then rejoined Shamrock Rovers and won another League Cup-winners' medal in 1977. He was also a runner-up in the competition in 1979 – the only occasion in a major Final that he finished on the losing side. In November 1979, he joined Athlone Town just a few months before his 40th birthday and helped them to victory in the competition. Twice winner of the Irish Soccer Writers' Personality of the Year, Fullam collected 11 full caps for the Republic of Ireland, the first while with North End. As well as playing football, he ran two successful companies: a motor factors company and an industrial supply company.

FULLER, Ricardo Dwayne

Forward

Born: Kingston, Jamaica, 31 October 1979.
Career: Tivoli Gardens (Jamaica). Crystal Palace, 2001. Heart of Midlothian, 2001 (loan). PRESTON NORTH END, 2002. Portsmouth, 2004.

■ This exciting young Jamaican striker originally arrived in England for a trial with Charlton Athletic in December 1999. He was on the verge of signing for the Addicks when a routine medical revealed a back problem that required corrective surgery. Once he was fully fit, Fuller was released to join South London neighbours Crystal Palace shortly before the transfer deadline in February 2001. Though only 22, he was an experienced Jamaican international and joined the national squad in the New Year, contributing to their campaign to qualify for the 2002 World Cup Finals in the Far East. Leaving Selhurst Park to rejoin Tivoli Gardens in Jamaica, he signed for Preston North End in the summer of 2002 for a fee of £500,000 following a successful loan spell with Hearts. A natural entertainer, he became an instant hit with the North End fans. Hard to knock off the ball, Fuller proved to be lightning fast, packed a powerful shot and was good in the air. Fuller scored on his League debut for North End on the opening day of the 2002–03 season, but Preston lost 2–1 to his former club Crystal Palace. He scored 11 goals in 20 games including two in the Lancashire derby victory over Burnley and both goals in the 2–0 defeat of promoted Leicester City. A serious knee injury in the match at Coventry ended his season in December 2002 and put an end to fears that he might be lured away during the transfer window. In the first-half of

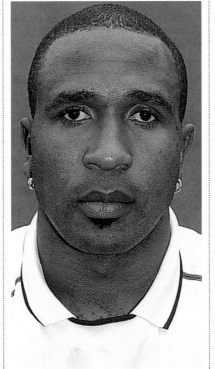

2003–04, Fuller scored nine goals in his first 16 games including a hat-trick against Burnley in which he demonstrated all his strengths – powerful heading ability, speed and clinical finishing. However, speculation over a possible transfer to a Premiership club seemed to unsettle him and he only scored a further three goals in the second half of the campaign. After scoring in North End's first away game of the 2004–05 season, Fuller joined Portsmouth and, though most of his appearances for the South Coast club came from the substitutes' bench, he remains a talented striker.

GAGE, Kevin William

Midfield, full-back

Born: Chiswick, 21 April 1964.
Career: Wimbledon, 1982. Aston Villa, 1987. Sheffield United, 1991. PRESTON NORTH END, 1996. Hull City, 1997.

■ Kevin Gage made his Football League debut for Wimbledon in the 4–2 defeat by Bury at Plough Lane on the last day of the 1980–81 season. He was still an apprentice and the youngest player to appear for the club. Despite that defeat, the Dons were able to celebrate promotion to the Second Division. Unfortunately relegation the following season saw them back in Division Three, but Gage helped Wimbledon win promotion back to the Second Division in 1983–84 and to the top flight in 1985–86. In the summer of 1987, Gage was transferred to Aston Villa for £100,000 after scoring 17 goals in 189 games. He was ever present in the Villa side promoted to the First Division in 1987–88 but then struggled to maintain his form. Finding himself in and out of the side, he was rescued from obscurity by his former manager Dave Bassett, who signed him for Sheffield United. It took him a while to settle at Bramall Lane but in 1994–95 he was voted the Yorkshire club's Player of the Year. He had made 131 appearances for the Blades when in March 1996 he left to join Preston North End on a free transfer. He appeared in seven of the club's last eight games and was on the losing side only once as North End won the Third Division Championship. Gage was injured in the first half of the opening

1–0 scoreline was repeated a week later against Sheffield Wednesday. However, his final appearance in North End colours was not so successful, as they lost 3–0 at Liverpool.

GALLACHER, Hugh M.

Outside-left, inside-left

Born: Girvan, 1 May 1870.
Career: Glasgow Celtic. PRESTON NORTH END, 1890. Sheffield United, 1892. Leicester Fosse, 1894. Nelson. New Brompton.

■ A fine outside-left who represented Celtic once during their initial Scottish League campaign, Hugh Gallacher joined Preston just as they were losing their 'Invincibles' tag. However, he still helped them to runners'-up spot in the Football League for three seasons running. In 1890–91 he was the club's leading scorer with just six goals, while the following season he was ever present. While with North End, Gallacher had become noted for the eccentricity of chewing his way through an ounce of 'twist' tobacco per game – a half-ounce each half! After leaving North End, he moved to Bramall Lane for the Blades' promotion run-in and played in the first Sheffield derby at League level. He then moved to Leicester Fosse but after two seasons he lost his place to Billy Dorrell, who had returned to the club from Aston Villa, and wound down his career with spells at Nelson and New Brompton.

GALLACHER, Kevin William

Forward

Born: Clydebank, 23 November 1966.
Career: Duntocher BC. Dundee United, 1983. Coventry City, 1990. Blackburn Rovers, 1993. Newcastle United, 1999. PRESTON NORTH END, 2001. Sheffield Wednesday, 2002. Huddersfield Town, 2002.

■ Kevin Gallacher, the grandson of the legendary Patsy Gallacher who played for Celtic between 1911 and 1925, began his career with Dundee United. He appeared in two Scottish Cup finals and the 1987 UEFA Cup Final for the Tannadice Park club before coming south of the border to join Coventry City for £900,000 in January 1990. He was

hampered by injuries during his time at Highfield Road but it did not deter Blackburn Rovers manager Kenny Dalglish from paying £1.5 million for his services in March 1993. Sadly, the versatile front-runner suffered a horrendous triple fracture of a leg against Arsenal in February 1994. After trying to make a comeback almost a year later, he ended up with his leg back in plaster after it was broken in the same spot. He fought his way back to fitness and won a regular place in 1996–97, scoring his first hat-trick for the club against Wimbledon. In 1997–98, Gallacher had his best-ever season for the club, scoring 20 goals in all competitions including another treble in the Premiership defeat of Aston Villa. Gallacher, who scored 52 goals in 161 games for Rovers, left Ewood Park to join Newcastle United in October 1999 for £700,000. Injuries hampered his progress at St James' Park and he eventually

game of the 1996–97 season at Notts County and was unable to regain a regular place at right-back for North End following further injuries and illness. In September 1997 he left to team up with former Wimbledon colleague Glyn Hodges at Hull City. Sadly, he was troubled by a calf injury that showed little sign of clearing up and he left to concentrate on his restaurant business in the Peak District.

GALBRAITH, David

Winger

Born: Preston, 1889.
Career: PRESTON NORTH END, 1909.

■ Able to play on either flank, diminutive winger David Galbraith appeared in a handful of games for Preston in the 1909–10 and 1910–11 seasons. On his debut in February 1910, it was his cross that David McLean converted to score the only goal of the game against Manchester United. The moved to Preston. The persistent injury problems continued to haunt him in 2001–02, his only season at Deepdale, and they restricted him to just a handful of first-team appearances. Gallacher though did get on the score sheet for North End in the 3–0 home win over Sheffield United before moving to Sheffield Wednesday on transfer deadline day. Capped 53 times by Scotland, he later ended his career with a brief spell at Huddersfield Town.

GALLIMORE, Frank

Right-back

Born: Northwich, 19 October 1908.
Career: Witton Albion. PRESTON NORTH END, 1931.

■ Signed by North End manager Alex Gibson from the obscurity of the

Cheshire League with Witton Albion, right-back Frank Gallimore made his debut in a 3–2 defeat of Charlton Athletic in September 1931. Although not tall or of powerful build, he was decisive, unflinching, determined and consistent. Never easily beaten, Gallimore recovered well and was fast and strong in the tackle. Ever-present in 1932–33, injuries hampered his progress over the next two seasons until in 1935–36 he again went through a season without missing a game. He played in the 1937 and 1938 FA Cup finals and helped North End finish third in Division One in the latter season. Gallimore was ever present for a third season in 1938–39, though his one regret must have been that he never got on the score sheet despite his regular attacking forays. The war ended his football career and, though he took charge of a town-centre public house, it never really suited him. When the war ended he emigrated to Canada.

GALLIMORE, Leonard

Left-back, left-half

Born: Northwich, 14 September 1913.
Career: Dick Kerr's XI. Bainton Victoria. PRESTON NORTH END, 1933. Liverpool, 1936. Watford, 1937.

■ The younger brother of Frank Gallimore, Leonard was on the books of both Liverpool and Huddersfield Town before playing for Dick Kerr's XI and Bainton Victoria. A well-built left-back, North End gave him his chance in League football. He played in four games during the club's Second Division promotion-winning season of 1933–34. Gallimore did not appear again in the North End first team until 1936–37 when he lined up alongside brother Frank in three of his five games. The last of these was a 5–0 defeat at Wolverhampton Wanderers. Gallimore joined Liverpool but did not appear in their League side before moving to Watford and playing for the Vicarage Road club either side of the war. When Arsenal turned up to play Watford in a friendly in 1945, they were two men short and so Gallimore was loaned to the Gunners. Uncharacteristically, he scored twice but Watford won 3–2. He was eventually sacked by the club and, while

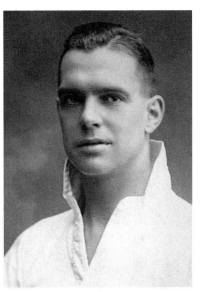

still living in Watford, was convicted several times of criminal offences and twice jailed.

GALLOWAY, David Wilson

Inside-forward

Born: Kirkcaldy, 6 May 1905.
Career: Wellesley Juniors. Raith Rovers. Aberdeen. PRESTON NORTH END, 1932. Port Vale, 1934. Carlisle United, 1935. Clapton Orient, 1938.

■ A crafty inside-forward, David Galloway played his early football for Raith Rovers before joining Aberdeen. It was from Pittodrie that he signed for North End in the summer of 1932. After a season in and out of the League side, he started the club's promotion-winning season of 1933–34 in fine style and scored what proved to be his only goal for the club in a 3–2 win over Burnley. However, he again lost his place and joined Port Vale in the close season. Released after the 1934–35 season, he moved on to Carlisle United and spent three seasons with the Cumbrian outfit before ending his playing days with Clapton Orient.

GALLOWAY, Thomas

Right-half, centre-half, inside-left

Born: Kilmarnock, 1887.
Career: Stockport County, 1907. PRESTON NORTH END, 1911. Portsmouth.

■ One of the game's earliest utility players, Tommy Galloway played wing-half, centre-half and inside-forward for his first club, Stockport County. He left Edgeley Park before the start of the 1911–12 season to play for Preston North End. Following his debut, a 2–1 defeat of Manchester City, Galloway performed manfully in whatever position he was asked to play but could not prevent the club from losing their top-flight status. The following season he appeared in just nine games and only finished on the losing side once as North End won the Second Division Championship. Galloway was not retained and left Deepdale to play Southern League football for Portsmouth.

GARA, Andrew

Inside-forward, centre-forward

Born: Ireland, 1875.
Career: Wigan County. PRESTON NORTH END, 1898. Nottingham Forest, 1902. Bristol City, 1902. Ashton Town.

■ Andrew Gara played football for a number of Irish junior clubs before crossing the water to play for Wigan County. He joined Preston North End in March 1899 and made seven appearances and scored three goals at the end of a campaign which saw the club just retain its top-flight status. He continued to score at the ratio of a goal every three games and when North End were relegated in 1900–01, he was the club's leading scorer with 11 goals. In the third game of the 1901–02 season, Gara netted a hat-trick in a 4–0 win at Barnsley. Sadly, injuries hampered his performances that season and at the end of that campaign, in which the club finished third in Division Two, he left Deepdale to play for Nottingham Forest. His stay at the City Ground was short-lived and he moved on to Bristol City where he rediscovered his goalscoring form. He later ended his career playing non-League football back in the North West with Ashton Town.

GARRETT, Archibald Campbell

Centre-forward, inside-left

Born: Lesmahagow, 17 June 1919.
Died: 1994.
Career: Heart of Midlothian. PRESTON
NORTH END, 1937. Heart of Midlothian. Northampton Town, 1946. Birmingham City, 1947. Northampton Town, 1948. Wisbech Town.

■ A highly talented forward, Archibald Garrett started his career in his native Scotland with Heart of Midlothian before coming south of the border to try his luck with Preston North End midway through the 1937–38 season. Having made his debut in a 2–0 win at Birmingham, Garrett netted twice on his next, and what turned out to be his last, appearance in a 4–1 defeat of Derby County. After another spell at Tynecastle, Garrett returned to Football League action after the war with Northampton Town and scored 35 goals in 51 games for the Cobblers before moving to Birmingham and helping them win promotion to the First Division. He later rejoined Northampton and took his tally of goals to 50 in 94 games before leaving to play non-League football for Wisbech Town.

GARTH, James Russell

Forward

Born: Glasgow, 1 May 1922.
Died: 1968.
Career: Morton. PRESTON NORTH END, 1946.

■ Forward Jimmy Garth arrived at Deepdale in November 1946 from Scottish League club Morton. Having made his debut in a 2–2 draw at Derby County and scored on his first home appearance in a 2–0 defeat of Arsenal, Garth had played in just four games when he was named as travelling reserve for Scotland's Home International Championship match against Northern Ireland. In that 1946–47 season, Garth scored eight goals in 21 games including two in each of the last two games of the campaign to help North End finish seventh in Division One.

GARVIE, John

Centre-forward

Born: Bellshill, 16 October 1927.
Died: 1996.
Career: Hibernian. PRESTON NORTH END, 1949. Lincoln City, 1950. Carlisle United, 1956.

■ John Garvie was a prolific goal-
scorer for Hibernian in the Scottish League prior to joining North End at the start of the 1949–50 season. Though he failed to find the net in his five appearances for the club, he set up both of Angus Morrison's goals on his debut as Grimsby Town were beaten 3–1. Unable to win a regular place, he moved on to Lincoln City and helped them win the Third Division North Championship in his second season at Sincil Bank. Garvie spent five seasons with the Imps, scoring 73 League goals in 183 games before leaving to end his career with Carlisle United.

GEMMILL, Archibald

Midfield

Born: Paisley, 24 March 1947.
Career: St Mirren. PRESTON NORTH END, 1967. Derby County, 1970. Nottingham Forest, 1977. Birmingham City, 1979. Jacksonville (US). Wigan Athletic, 1982. Derby County, 1982.

■ Archie Gemmill was a valued member of the Scotland squad and played 43 times for his country. No one who saw his goal against Holland in the 1978 World Cup will ever forget it. He had already scored from the penalty spot to give the Scots a 2–1 lead when he picked up the ball wide on the right in the 68th minute of this vital match. He threaded his way through the Dutch defence, evading three strong challenges before shooting home. Gemmill played his early football for St Mirren before arriving in England in June 1967 after

signing for Preston North End for £16,000. The combative midfielder made his debut as a substitute at Norwich City in the second game of the 1967–68 season, coming off the bench to score in a 3–1 win. Gemmill spent three seasons at Deepdale but, following the club's relegation to the Third Division, he joined Derby County for £60,000. It was under Brian Clough's management that his career really began to take off. He played a highly significant part in proceedings when the Rams won the League Championship in 1971–72 and he won a second League Championship medal in 1974–75 before moving across the East Midlands to Nottingham Forest in October 1977. He went straight into the Forest side and, in the 34 games he played, he was only on the losing side twice. At the end of the campaign, Gemmill picked up his third League Championship medal. In August 1979 he was allowed to leave Forest to join Birmingham City. He later played for Wigan Athletic before rejoining Derby County. Gemmill later shared the managerial duties at Rotherham United with former Forest colleague John McGovern, but is now involved in a talent-spotting role for the Scottish Football Association.

GERRARD, Edward D.

Right-half

Born: Hindley, 1 December 1903.
Career: Hindley Colliery. PRESTON NORTH END, 1925.

■ Right-half Edward Gerrard was spotted playing local non-League football for Hindley Colliery by North End manager Frank Richards and was given his chance in League football during the course of the 1925–26 season. The tough-tackling player appeared in 10 games and was only on the losing side twice. One of Gerrard's games was the 6–4 defeat of Blackpool in which 20,048 fans were treated to one of Deepdale's most memorable games.

GERRISH, William Webber Walter

Inside-forward

Born: Bristol, 28 December 1884.

Died: France, 1916.
Career: Bristol Rovers. Aston Villa, 1909. PRESTON NORTH END, 1912. Chesterfield.

■ Billy Gerrish was signed by Aston Villa from Bristol Rovers in the summer of 1909 to partner Harry Hampton, who was known as the 'Wellington Whirlwind'. But Hampton was injured and Gerrish found himself leading Villa's attack in his first few games. He scored on his debut in a 5–1 home win over Arsenal and in his next home game he a netted a hat-trick against Chelsea. At the end of his first season, Gerrish had scored 14 goals in 36 games and won a League Championship medal. Injuries then plagued his career but even when he had regained full fitness he found that he could not win a place due to the fine form of Bache, Hampton and Stephenson and the signing of Harold Halse. He left Villa for North End but appeared in just three games in their Second Division Championship-winning season of 1912–13 before joining Chesterfield. Gerrish was killed in action while serving with the Footballers' Battalion Middlesex Regiment in France in 1916.

GIBSON, David

Left-back

Born: Kilmarnock, 1898.
Died: 1964.
Career: Shawfield Juniors. Kilmarnock. PRESTON NORTH END, 1925. Springfield Babes (US). Fall River Marksmen (US). Providence Clamdiggers (US). Providence Gold Bugs (US). Fall River (US). Queen of the South.

■ David Gibson's consistent displays for home-town club Kilmarnock prompted North End to offer him the chance of League football in the summer of 1925. The burly left-back made his debut for the Deepdale club in disastrous circumstances as they went down 4–0 at home to South Shields. However, Gibson played in 15 consecutive League and Cup matches from his debut, forming a strong full-back pairing with Billy Wade. Surprisingly released in the close season, he went to play for a number of clubs in the US before returning to see out his career back in the Scottish League with Queen of the South.

GIBSON, Simon John

Centre-half

Born: Nottingham, 10 December 1964.
Career: Chelsea, 1982. Swindon Town, 1983. PRESTON NORTH END, 1984. Rochdale, 1986.

■ Unable to make the grade at Stamford Bridge, central defender Simon Gibson left Chelsea to play for Swindon Town in November 1983. In a side struggling near the foot of the Fourth Division, he was outstanding. Just over a year later he joined Preston North End. Gibson scored on his North End debut in a 1–1 home draw with Brentford but, though he gave some sterling displays, he could not prevent their relegation to the League's basement. In what turned out to be the worst season in the club's history, Gibson scored against Exeter City in the penultimate game of the campaign, helping to save Preston from finishing in the dreaded last position in the Football League. He moved on to play in a handful of games for Rochdale before moving into the local non-League scene.

GILCHRIST, John Wetherspoon

Right-half

Born: Glasgow, 30 March 1899.
Died: 1950.
Career: St Anthony's. Glasgow Celtic. PRESTON NORTH END, 1922. Carlisle

United. Third Lanark. Dunfermline Athletic. Bathgate. Brooklyn Wanderers (US). Chicago Bricklayers (US). J & P Coats (US).

■ Wing-half John Gilchrist began his career with Celtic where his displays led to him winning full international honours for Scotland against England at Villa Park in April 1922. Midway through the following season he was suspended indefinitely for 'wilful inattention to training' and, having played in 134 games for the Bhoys, he left Parkhead to join Preston North End for £4,500. The tough-tackling Scotsman celebrated his transfer with champagne but the moment he left the Parkhead club, his career went downhill fast. At Deepdale, Gilchrist was soon in trouble as his biting tongue manifested itself and after just nine months he was put up for transfer. He had a loan spell with Carlisle United before returning north of the border to play for Third Lanark and Dunfermline Athletic.

GILLESPIE, Thomas B.

Outside-right, inside-left

Born: Girvan, 26 February 1901.
Career: Hamilton Academicals. Queen of the South. PRESTON NORTH END, 1925. Bethlehem Steel (US). Newark Americans (US). PRESTON NORTH END, 1931.

■ Versatile forward Tom Gillespie played his early football north of the border with Hamilton Academicals and later Queen of the South before signing for North End in November 1925. He went straight into the Preston side for the visit of Port Vale and, though the Valiants were near the top of Division Two at the time, Gillespie laid on two of his side's goals in a 4–0 win. He scored his first goal for the club in the 6–4 defeat of Blackpool and netted again on the final day of the season against Barnsley. He then left Deepdale and had spells playing for Bethlehem Steel and Newark Americans before returning to play in a handful of games for North End in 1931–32.

GILLIBRAND, Charles S.

Outside-right

Born: Preston, 1887.

Career: PRESTON NORTH END, 1907. Blackpool, 1908.

■ Flying winger Charlie Gillibrand worked his way up through the ranks before making his debut in the abandoned FA Cup replay at home to Brighton in January 1908. He kept his place in the side to make his League debut two days later and scored in a 3–2 win over Sunderland. He played in five consecutive League and Cup games, and found the net again in a 3–1 defeat of Bristol City at Ashton Gate. Gillibrand was then surprisingly allowed to leave Deepdale to join North End's rivals Blackpool, but he could not force his way into the Seasiders' League side.

GILLOW, Wilfred Bernard

Right-half, inside-left

Born: Preston, 8 July 1892.
Died: 1944.
Career: Lancaster Town. PRESTON NORTH END, 1910. Fleetwood. Blackpool, 1912. PRESTON NORTH END, 1914. Grimsby Town, 1919. Lancaster Town.

■ Following impressive displays for Lancaster Town, Wilf Gillow joined his home-town team Preston North End in the summer of 1910. However, after being unable to break into the Deepdale club's side, he left to play non-League football for Fleetwood. His displays led to Blackpool offering him a chance of first-team football and he was a regular member of the Seasiders team that struggled in the lower reaches of Division Two in 1912–13. He rejoined Preston for the 1914–15 season and played in three games as the club won promotion to the First Division. He appeared in a handful of games for North End when League football resumed in 1919–20, before leaving to give Grimsby Town five seasons of service. Gillow ended his playing days back at Lancaster.

GODFREY, Brian Cameron

Inside-forward

Born: Flint, 1 May 1940.
Career: Flint Alexandra. Everton, 1958. Scunthorpe United, 1960. PRESTON NORTH END, 1963. Aston Villa, 1967. Bristol Rovers, 1971. Newport County, 1973.

■ Though he scored the goal that took North End to the 1964 FA Cup Final, Brian Godfrey was 12th man at Wembley. That was two years before substitutes were introduced and to his disappointment he did not receive a medal. Godfrey joined Preston from Scunthorpe United in October 1963, although he had started his career with Everton. During his time at Deepdale, Godfrey proved himself a prolific scorer and in 1964–65 he teamed up with Alex Dawson: the two of them scored 53 of North End's 80 League and Cup goals. Godfrey's share was 26 and included a hat-trick in a 5–1 win at Ipswich Town. The following season, Godfrey was the club's leading scorer with 20 goals. In the last game of the campaign, he netted the club's fastest-ever hat-trick: his three goals came in the space of just five minutes as North End beat Cardiff City 9–0. Later he joined Aston Villa and continued to score goals as if they were going out of fashion. It was with Villa that the Welsh international achieved his greatest moment in football when he returned to Wembley as captain of the Midlands club in the League Cup Final. Godfrey's midfield generalship had inspired the Third Division club to victory over Manchester United in the semi-final but there was no fairytale ending and Spurs defeated Villa in the Final. Godfrey later played for Bristol Rovers and Newport County before embarking on a career in management with Bath City, Exeter City, Weymouth and Gloucester City.

GOOCH, James Arthur George

Goalkeeper

Born: West Ham, 11 July 1921.
Career: Becontree. PRESTON NORTH END, 1942. Bradford City, 1953. Watford, 1954. Bath City. Yiewsley Town.

■ Formerly a London bobby, Jimmy Gooch joined North End during World War Two. Initially understudy to Jack Fairbrother, he made his debut during the 1946–47 season in a 2–2 draw with Wolverhampton Wanderers. It was his only appearance that season but, with Fairbrother leaving to play for Newcastle United, he became the club's first-choice 'keeper the following season. Injuries hampered his progress during North End's relegation season of 1948–49 and over the next couple of seasons he shared the goalkeeping duties with Malcolm

Newlands. He helped North End win the Second Division Championship in 1950–51. Gooch was a colourful character, often brilliant and occasionally erratic. In one game that North End lost 4–2 to Wolves in April 1948, Gooch gifted North End's opponents the winner when a 50–yard shot sailed over his head – he was covering its flight but he slipped and fell. Maine Road was not the happiest of grounds for Gooch: on two occasions he suffered a dislocated shoulder while playing there. On leaving North End, he had a season with Bradford City before joining Watford. He waited two seasons at Vicarage Road before making his debut but his patience was rewarded. He later had spells playing non-League football for Bath City and Yiewsley Town before working on North End's administrative staff until 1991.

GOOD, Michael HS

Centre-half, inside-right

Born: Airdrie, 30 July 1875.
Career: Airdrie Hill. Airdrieonians. Small Heath, 1896. Watford. PRESTON NORTH END, 1901. Bristol City, 1902. Reading. Brighton and Hove Albion. Southern United.

■ Mickey Good was playing football for his home-town team Airdrie when he was given the opportunity to play in the Football League for Small Heath. He spent most of his time with the Midlands club as an understudy to the Blues' main forwards. After switching to centre-half, Good joined Watford, who were then members of the Southern League. He was appointed club captain, but the Hornets only avoided relegation from the Southern League after a 'test match'. He joined North End in the summer of 1901 and made his debut in a 3–1 defeat at the eventual Champions, West Bromwich Albion, on the opening day of the 1901–02 season. Good, who scored in successive home games against Newton Heath and Barnsley, helped North End finish third in Division Two before leaving to play for Bristol City. He later had spells with Reading, Brighton and Hove Albion and Southern United. The FA suspended the latter until they paid what was due to Good under his contract.

GOODALL, Archibald Lee

Centre-half, centre-forward

Born: Belfast, 19 June 1864.
Died: 1929.
Career: Liverpool Stanley. St Jude's. PRESTON NORTH END, 1888. Aston Villa, 1888. Derby County, 1889. Plymouth Argyle. Glossop, 1903.

■ Born in Ireland and raised in Scotland, Archie Goodall played for several clubs before 1888. When the Football League was formed, he played for Preston North End. Goodall was as rumbustious as his brother John was gentle and played in just two League games for North End, scoring in the 4–0 win at Wolverhampton Wanderers on his League debut. His move from Preston to Aston Villa was the first transfer during a season to be approved by the League. In May 1889, he joined Derby County and was one of the greatest-ever characters to play for the club. He caused alarm before the 1898 FA Cup Final because he was outside trying to unload tickets on which he had speculated. On another occasion he refused to play extra-time in a Minor Counties League Cup Final because he said his contract ended after 90 minutes! He was suspended before the 1899 FA Cup Final against Sheffield United for 'insubordination and inattention to training' but the ban was lifted in time for him to play at Crystal Palace. Goodall scored 52 goals in 423 games for the Rams from his position of centre-half. He once toured Europe and America with a strongman act 'walking' around a giant metal hoop and was a great follower of country sports.

GOODALL, John

Centre-forward, outside-right

Born: Westminster, 19 June 1863.
Died: 1942.
Career: Kilmarnock Athletic. Great Lever. PRESTON NORTH END, 1888. Derby County, 1889. New Brighton Tower, 1899. Glossop, 1900. Watford. Racing Club Roubaix (France). Mardy (France).

■ The son of a corporal in the Scottish Fusiliers, John Goodall had a somewhat cosmopolitan background. He was born in London but raised in Ayrshire and his parents' travels were diverse enough to leave him with a younger brother, Archie, who was Irish. Having played for Kilmarnock Athletic, he later joined the exodus south and ended up at Great Lever. Shortly after his arrival at Deepdale, he scored nine goals in North End's 16–2 win in a friendly match against Dundee Strathmore. Yet when North End beat Hyde United 26–0 on 15 October 1887, John Goodall only claimed the last goal. During the club's run to the 1888 FA Cup Final, he scored a hat-trick in North End's 5–0 semi-final

win over Crewe Alexandra. Goodall ended North End's first season in the Football League as the club's leading scorer with 20 goals in 21 games, though surprisingly he did not score in the club's inaugural game in the competition as they beat Burnley 5–2. However, he did net successive hat-tricks in a 5–2 home victory over Wolves and a 7–0 away win at Notts County, and was instrumental in the club achieving the League and Cup double. At Preston, Goodall had assumed the responsibility of organising the attack and carried the side's development a stage further by instigating many ploys that would never have otherwise became part of the team's repertoire. By the time of his departure to Derby County, he had achieved all he could hope to do at Deepdale. John Goodall had scored five goals against Derby County in the Rams' first-ever game in 1884. The club were so pleased to have the services of the legendary Preston man that they sent

their secretary around the town to paste up notices announcing Goodall's arrival. Goodall went on to spend nine seasons at the Baseball Ground, scoring 76 goals in 211 games. The founder of scientific football, the on-field genius behind the scoring exploits of Steve Bloomer, he was also author of a book on the arts of the game. He also played first-class cricket for Derbyshire, represented England at bowls and was an excellent billiards player and a prize-winning cage-bird fancier.

GOODBURN, Harold

Outside-right

Born: Preston, 1885.
Died: 1907.
Career: PRESTON NORTH END, 1906.

■ Winger Harold Goodburn had just made it into the North End League side, playing in two 3–0 defeats at the hands of Aston Villa and Birmingham in the 1906–07 season, when he was taken ill. Sadly, he died shortly afterwards of pleuro-pneumonia. Quite understandably the remainder of the campaign petered out: North End were only able to win 2 of the remaining 15 games and they ended the season just above the relegation places.

GOODWIN, Ralph

Right-back

Born: Hanley, 1887.
Career: Stalybridge Rovers. Stockport County, 1907. PRESTON NORTH END, 1919. Stockport County, 1920.

■ Ralph Goodwin spent 13 seasons with Stockport County and developed into an unflappable right-back. He was wanted by a number of other clubs. A quiet and most reliable player, his best seasons were those when he was partnered by Stephen Fagan and then Tommy Roberts. He made 188 League and Cup appearances for County and played for them throughout World War One, making a further 136 appearances. On the resumption of League football, he had a brief spell with Preston North End, playing in seven games during the 1919–20 season. The Lilywhites lost 5–1 at home to Bradford City on Goodwin's debut and the strong-tackling defender

was never on the winning side during his time at Deepdale. He later returned to Edgeley Park, but made just one further appearance before retiring to the athletic outfitter's business he had first acquired in 1912.

GORDON, John B.

Outside-right

Born: Port Glasgow, 1863.
Career: PRESTON NORTH END, 1888. Loughborough Town, 1895. Wigan County.

■ One of the first Scotsmen to play for North End, Jack Gordon was working at Leyland as a joiner when he was first asked to play for the club in February 1882. He scored on his debut in a 7–0 win over Fishwick Ramblers, a local side who were then on a level with North End. Yet, despite impressing, he returned home to Port Glasgow where he worked in the shipyards and played football for Port Glasgow Athletic. Two years later he returned to Deepdale and after a handful of games at inside-right, switched to the wing where he teamed up with Jimmy Ross. He scored lots of goals in North End's pre-League days, including five in the 26–0 win over Hyde United. His pinpoint crosses led to Preston players scoring a large number of goals with their heads. He made his League debut for the club on the opening day of the

1888–89 season, scoring North End's second goal in the third minute of their 5–2 win over Burnley. In October 1891, he scored North End's first-ever penalty in a 4–2 win at Blackburn Rovers. Sadly, Jack Gordon developed congestion of the lungs and pleurisy and doctors had to battle for three days to save his life. Gordon played the last of his 113 League games at Derby County in November 1894, almost 13 years since his first appearance.

GORNALL, John

Centre-half

Born: Preston, 28 March 1941.
Career: PRESTON NORTH END, 1960.

■ Centre-half Jack Gornall was understudy to long-serving Tony Singleton. He made his debut in a 2–1 defeat at Scunthorpe United towards the end of the 1961–62 season. He appeared in a further three games the following campaign but was never on the winning side, although a goal-line clearance in his final game in North End colours ensured that the game against Grimsby Town remained goalless.

GOULD, Jonathan Alan

Goalkeeper

Born: Paddington, 18 July 1968.
Career: Clevedon Town. Halifax Town, 1990. West Bromwich Albion, 1992. Coventry City, 1992. Bradford City, 1996. Gillingham, 1996 (loan). Glasgow Celtic, 1997. PRESTON NORTH END, 2003. Hereford United, (loan). Bristol City, 2005.

■ Jonathan Gould, the son of Bobby Gould, was playing for Western League club Clevedon Town before he was signed by Halifax Town in 1990. Later released by the Shaymen, he was signed by his father for West Bromwich Albion but was not called upon for first-team action. After being dismissed by Albion, Bobby Gould took over the reins at Coventry City and his son was one of his first signings, as cover for Steve Ogrizovic. After making a spectacular debut in a 5–1 defeat of Liverpool, it all went wrong for him in the game against Wolves at Molineux. He came on as a substitute after Ogrizovic had been sent

off and conceded two goals in his first two minutes on the pitch. Shortly afterwards he joined Bradford City, but in the game at Molineux – not his happiest ground – he received 18 stitches in a face wound. In the summer of 1997 he joined Celtic and in his first season at Parkhead, he helped the Bhoys win the League Championship. The club's first-choice 'keeper for the next few seasons, he helped them win another League title in 2000–01 and the League Cup in 1997–98, 1999–2000 and 2000–01. His form was such that he won his first full cap for Scotland in the European Championship qualifier against Lithuania. After losing out to Rob Douglas, he followed Craig Brown to North End and made his debut against Ipswich Town in January 2003. He remained the club's first-choice 'keeper for the rest of that season but the following season, despite experiencing some personal highs, his campaign was disrupted by injury. One of the best 'keepers to have played for North End for many years, he was recalled to the Scotland squad for the Euro 2004 Play-offs on the back of some remarkable goalkeeping performances. Yet at the start of the 2004–05 season he found himself on the transfer list and his contract was cancelled after a loan spell at Hereford. Soon afterwards, he signed for Bristol City but did not add to his total of first-team appearances.

GOWLING, Alan Edwin

Forward

Born: Stockport, 16 March 1949.
Career: Manchester United, 1967. Huddersfield Town, 1972. Newcastle United, 1975. Bolton Wanderers, 1978. PRESTON NORTH END, 1982.

■ Alan Gowling began his career with Manchester United, winning England Schoolboy and England Amateur international honours and appearing in the 1968 Mexico Olympics. While learning the game, he became an economics graduate at Manchester University and found his way into United's team during 1968–69 in the era of Best, Charlton and Law. He appeared in 71 games and won an England Under-23 cap before signing for Huddersfield Town in a £60,000 deal in June 1972. Gowling became a regular goalscorer at Leeds Road but having just dropped out of the top flight, the Yorkshire club suffered a second successive relegation in 1972–73. After they dropped into the Fourth Division two years later, Gowling moved to Newcastle United for £70,000. At St James' Park, Gowling formed a spearhead with Malcolm Macdonald that won him a League Cup runners'-up medal in 1976. After scoring 52 goals in 123 senior appearances, he signed for Bolton Wanderers in March 1978 for what was then a club record fee of £120,000. He was the final piece in Ian Greaves' jigsaw that was to push Wanderers into the First Division. He certainly proved his worth the following season, when his striking partnership with Frank Worthington was the envy of other First Division clubs. In November 1980, Gowling was elected chairman of the Professional Footballers' Association. In the summer of 1982 he was given a free transfer after scoring 31 goals in 165 games. He joined Preston North End as a part-timer and played most of the first half of the 1982–83 season in defence before switching to attack. After scoring in a couple of games, he netted in each of the last three games of the campaign as Lincoln City, Reading and Wigan Athletic were all beaten. At the end of the season, Gowling retired to concentrate on his business interests.

GRAHAM, Deiniol William Thomas

Forward

Born: Cannock, 4 October 1969.
Career: Manchester United, 1987. Barnsley, 1991. PRESTON NORTH END, 1992 (loan). Carlisle United, 1993 (loan). Stockport County, 1994. Scunthorpe United, 1995.

■ Originally one of 'Fergie's Fledglings', the Welsh Under-21 international failed to make the grade at Old Trafford and joined Barnsley for £50,000 in the summer of 1991. Most of his appearances at Oakwell came from the bench and in October 1992 he spent a brief period on loan with Preston North End. Though he failed to score in any of his eight League appearances, he did find the net in the FA Cup replay at Bradford City, which North End lost 5–4. Graham also spent a month on loan at Carlisle United before signing for Stockport County. His stay at Edgeley Park was brief and after being released he joined Scunthorpe United on trial, but was judged not to be worth a full contract and was let go.

GRAHAM, John

Left-half

Born: Ayr, 23 February 1857.
Died: 1927.

Career: Annbank. PRESTON NORTH END, 1888.

■ Scottish international Johnny Graham, who was toughened by his job as a quarryman, joined Preston North End from Annbank during the 1884–85 season. The left-half was a member of the 'Invincibles' side, as Preston became the first Football League Champions and the first to achieve the League and Cup double. Though he never got on the score sheet for North End during their League days, he did create a number of goalscoring opportunities for the likes of John Goodall and Jimmy Ross with his long throws. Graham was a regular in the North End side until the latter stages of the 1888–89 season when a broken collarbone caused his retirement.

GRAHAM, William

Centre-half
Career: PRESTON NORTH END, 1888.

■ William Graham lined up at centre-half for Preston North End in their first-ever League match against Burnley at Deepdale. The Lilywhites won 5–2 but Graham was to play in only five games of their League Championship-winning season and did not appear in any of the FA Cup games. Always on the winning side, he lost out to the consistency of David Russell and parted company with the club at the end of the season.

GRANT, Anthony

Forward

Born: Drogheda, 20 August 1976.

Career: Leeds United, 1994. PRESTON NORTH END, 1995. Glenavon.

■ Republic of Ireland Youth international Tony Grant was signed from Leeds United in November 1995 and soon became a favourite in the club's reserve side as an aggressive, powerful forward. His displays led to him winning regular inclusion in the club's first-team squad, although usually on the bench. In fact, Grant's only appearance came when he replaced Kevin Kilbane in a 1–1 draw with Darlington during the club's Third Division Championship-winning season. He later had a spell on loan playing in the Irish League for Glenavon before joining them permanently.

GRANT, Duncan C.

Centre-forward

Born: Preston, 1892.
Career: PRESTON NORTH END, 1914.

■ Centre-forward Duncan Grant played in nine games for North End and scored three goals in the club's Second Division promotion-winning season of 1914–15. Having made his debut in a 1–1 draw at Nottingham Forest, he scored the winner on his home debut against Hull City and followed this up with goals in successive matches against Arsenal and the eventual League Champions, Derby County.

GRAY, Andrew David

Forward

Born: Harrogate, 15 November 1977.
Career: Leeds United, 1995. Bury, 1997 (loan). Nottingham Forest, 1998. PRESTON NORTH END, 1999 (loan). Oldham Athletic, 1999 (loan). Bradford City, 2002. Sheffield United, 2004.

■ The son of Frank and the nephew of Eddie, former Leeds United and Scottish internationals, Gray started out with the Elland Road club but the tricky right-winger failed to hold down a regular first-team spot and joined Bury on loan. In September 1998 he was transferred to Nottingham Forest for £175,000 but in a side struggling to come to terms with life in the Premiership, he lost his place and went to Deepdale on loan. In a season in which North End reached the Play-offs, Gray made five appearances. He created

three of the goals on his debut in a 5–0 mauling of Lincoln City. Another loan spell in the North West followed, this time with Oldham Athletic, before he returned to the City Ground. Over the next couple of seasons, his first-team outings were few and far between and, having made just 76 League and Cup appearances in four seasons, he was released and joined Bradford City. Gray enjoyed a terrific first season at Valley Parade, finishing as top scorer with 15 goals, and was voted the Bantams' Player of the Year. His reward for his great performances was his first full cap for Scotland against Lithuania. He was allowed to join Sheffield United where he was the Blades' top scorer in 2004–05 and was called up for the full Scotland international squad.

GRAY, David

Full-back

Born: Coupar Angus, 8 February 1922.
Career: Glasgow Rangers. PRESTON NORTH END, 1947. Blackburn Rovers, 1948.

■ Full-back David Gray joined Preston North End from Glasgow Rangers in the summer of 1947. Strong in the tackle and quick to recover, he looked an excellent prospect. He made his debut in a 3–1 reversal at Liverpool

on the opening day of the 1947–48 season and kept his place in the Preston side until near the end of the season when an injury in the home game with Portsmouth forced him to miss the next five games. He returned to the side against Derby County but, with young Joe Walton showing tremendous potential, he was allowed to move to neighbours Blackburn Rovers. Gray was a regular in the Ewood Park club's Second Division side and clocked up 105 League appearances before injury forced his premature retirement.

GRAY, Frederick John Swithin

Outside-left

Born: Walsall, 1868.
Career: PRESTON NORTH END, 1889.

■ Winger Freddie Gray from Walsall was one of a number of amateurs who came to help North End during their early years in the Football League. Although he was registered two weeks before he played – scoring in the game against Stoke – the move caused official displeasure. Unknown to Preston he was on the books of Aston Villa and, as North End had played him without transfer fee or formal clearance, it cost them a fine of £5.

GRAY, Terence Ian

Winger

Born: Bradford, 3 June 1954.
Career: Ashley Road. Huddersfield Town, 1972. Southend United, 1979. Bradford City, 1982. PRESTON NORTH END, 1984. Ossett Town.

■ Terry Gray, who was an England junior tennis player at Wimbledon when he was 15, signed for Chelsea on amateur forms shortly after leaving school and was with Leeds Ashley Road when he won England Youth caps and began to attract League scouts. He signed for Huddersfield Town where he proved to be an industrious player who was equally adept in a variety of positions. He started his career with the Yorkshire club in the Third Division and left them as a Fourth Division side. Their first season in the League's basement was his most successful as a goalscorer. Towards the

end of his days with Huddersfield he was appointed club captain. In June 1979 he moved to Southend United and after relegation in his first season at Roots Hall, he won a Fourth Division Championship medal with the Shrimpers in 1980–81. After one more season he joined Bradford City and won their Clubman of the Year award before moving to Preston North End in November 1984 for £5,000. After an impressive start he found himself in and out of the North End side, but he was retained despite the club being relegated to the Fourth Division. He did manage to find the net in that disastrous 1985–86 season as high-flyers Carlisle United were beaten 3–2. However, in the close season he was granted a free transfer. After an unproductive trial at Rochdale, he signed for Ossett Town in the Northern Counties (East) League.

GREATOREX, William Henry Alphonse

Right-back

Born: Preston, 3 January 1895.
Died: 1971.

Career: Preston Winckley. PRESTON NORTH END, 1919. Southport, 1921. Chesterfield, 1923. Morecambe.

■ Full-back Billy Greatorex joined North End from local side Preston Winckley in readiness for the first season of peacetime football after World War One. He played his first game in North End colours in a 1–1 draw at Burnley and played in all but a couple of games throughout the rest of the season. Preston just avoided relegation from Division One but Greatorex, who played in most of North End's early games in 1920–21, was allowed to join Southport for their first season of League football. Greatorex later helped Chesterfield finish third in Division Three (North) and ended his playing days with non-League Morecambe.

GREAVES, Steven Ronald

Defender

Born: Chelsea, 17 January 1970.
Career: Fulham, 1988. PRESTON NORTH END, 1990. Ipswich Town, 1991. Scunthorpe United, 1992.

■ Steven Greaves had just made one appearance as a substitute for Fulham when he joined North End prior to the start of the 1990–91 season. He made his debut in a 3–1 defeat at home to Grimsby Town on the opening day of the campaign, but found himself in the club's reserve side until he played his second game against Chester City midway through October. Unable to win a regular first-team place, he left Deepdale to join Ipswich Town. Greaves failed to play in a single first-team game at Portman Road and eventually left to join Scunthorpe United where he ended his first-class career.

GREEN, Benjamin Haigh

Inside-right

Born: Penistone, 23 February 1883.
Died: 1945.
Career: Penistone Juniors. Barnsley, 1901. Small Heath, 1903. Burnley, 1909. PRESTON NORTH END, 1911. Blackpool, 1913.

■ Having begun his career with Barnsley, Benny Green joined Small Heath where he teamed up with Billy 'Bullet' Jones to form a prolific goalscoring partnership. On Boxing Day 1905, Green scored five of the Blues' goals in a 7–0 home win over Middlesbrough. On 29 December 1906 he had the distinction of scoring the club's first-ever goal at St Andrew's in a 3–0 defeat for Preston North End, for which he won a piano! Having scored 46 goals in 198 games, he was sold to Burnley where he continued to find the net in his two seasons at Turf Moor. Despite his reputation as a troublemaker, Preston North End secured his services at the start of the 1911–12 season. He netted the only goal of the game on his debut as North End beat Sheffield Wednesday on the opening day of the season but, despite his 10 goals, he could not prevent the club losing their top-flight status. In 1912–13 he was Preston's top scorer with 13 goals, helping the club win immediate promotion as Second Division Champions. Finding goals hard to come by the following season, Green moved on to Blackpool and played for the Seasiders until the outbreak of World War One.

GREEN, Ellis

Outside-left

Born: Chorley, 1878.
Career: Chorley. PRESTON NORTH END, 1900. Brentford. Fulham.

■ Ellis Green was a left-winger who played his early football for Chorley. He joined the Lilywhites in October 1900 with a reputation for scoring spectacular goals. With North End struggling near the foot of the First Division, Green took a number of games before finding his feet. Having scored his first goal in a 1–1 draw with eventual runners-up Sunderland, Green netted four times in the space of six games near the end of the campaign; all four matches were won. But on the last day, Preston lost at home to already relegated West Bromwich Albion while their nearest rivals Stoke pulled off a surprise victory at Notts County. Green made a good start to life in Division Two, netting twice in a 5–0 defeat of Leicester Fosse, but on losing his place to Bob Jack, he left to play Southern League football for Brentford and later Fulham.

GREEN, James

Outside-right

Born: Wheelton, 1877.
Career: PRESTON NORTH END, 1898. Chorley.

■ The brother of Ellis Green, this Wheelton-born winger made his debut in a 2–1 defeat of Wolverhampton Wanderers midway through the 1898–99 season, but it was his only appearance of the campaign. James Green had a run of four consecutive games the following season but the club's only success in that spell was the 4–3 defeat of fellow strugglers Notts County. Not retained at the end of the season, Green joined non-League Chorley and gave the Victory Park club a few seasons of service.

GREEN, James

Outside-left, centre-forward

Born: Preston 1898.
Career: PRESTON NORTH END, 1919. Exeter City, 1921. Bideford Town.

■ Local-born forward James Green played football for a number of junior clubs before he was given his chance in the North End side midway through the 1919–20 First Division season. Having played in the 3–1 FA Cup defeat of Stockport County, Green appeared in four consecutive games and was never on the losing side, which was not a bad record as the Lilywhites finished just two places off the relegation zone. However, in 1920–21, Green played in three defeats – including a 6–0 thrashing at Liverpool – and North End did not score in any of the games in which he appeared. He later played for Exeter City before ending his playing career with non-League Bideford Town.

GREEN, Thomas

Outside-left

Born: Preston, 26 February 1900.
Died: 1973.
Career: Leyland. Hamilton Central. Dick Kerr's XI. PRESTON NORTH END, 1920. Southport, 1922. Dick Kerr's XI. Colne.

■ An outstanding player for local sides Leyland and Dick Kerr's XI, winger Tommy Green played in just one game for Preston North End during the

1920–21 season. Replacing the injured Peter Quinn on the final day of the campaign, it was his cross that Frank Jefferies converted in the 1–1 draw with Bradford City. Allowed to join Southport, he spent a season with the Sandgrounders before rejoining Dick Kerr's. He finished his career with Colne.

GREENALL, Colin Anthony

Centre-half

Born: Billinge, 30 December 1963.
Career: Blackpool, 1980. Gillingham, 1986. Oxford United, 1988. Bury, 1990 (loan). Bury, 1990. PRESTON NORTH END, 1992. Chester City, 1993. Lincoln City, 1994. Wigan Athletic, 1995.

■ Colin Greenall made his Blackpool debut against Huddersfield Town on 23 August 1980 at the age of 16 years and 237 days, thus becoming the Seasiders' youngest-ever League player. While with Blackpool he won England Youth honours and at the age of 20 was voted the Fourth Division's Player of the Year by the Professional Footballers' Association. However, following a contractual dispute, he moved to Third Division Gillingham for a fee of £40,000. Midway through the 1987–88 season, Oxford United paid £285,000 to take him to the Manor Ground. After a loan spell with

Bury, he joined the Shakers on a permanent basis but in March 1992 he moved to Preston North End. With relegation from the Third Division a distinct possibility, Greenall added some stability to a previously shaky back four and scored a vital goal to secure a point in a 1–1 draw with Swansea City. Injuries hampered his progress in 1992–93 and it was halfway through the season before he appeared in the North End side. After brief spells with Chester and Lincoln City, Greenall signed for Wigan Athletic. Appointed club captain, he was ever present in 1996–97 and instrumental in the club winning the Third Division Championship. Appointed the Latics' first-team coach, he came out of retirement to help the club and won the Man-of-the-Match award in the Auto Windscreens Shield Final success of 1999. He became acting manager following Bruce Rioch's departure before moving on to become youth-team coach at Rochdale.

GREENHALGH, Brian Arthur

Forward

Born: Chesterfield, 20 February 1947.
Career: PRESTON NORTH END, 1965. Aston Villa, 1967. Leicester City, 1969. Huddersfield Town, 1969. Cambridge United, 1971. Bournemouth, 1974. Torquay United, 1974 (loan). Watford, 1975. Dartford. Staines Town. Carshalton Athletic. Wealdstone.

■ Having impressed in the Central League, Brian Greenhalgh was called into the North End side for his debut against Bristol City in December 1965. Later that season, in what was only his fourth League appearance, he netted a marvellous hat-trick in a 3–1 win at Bolton Wanderers. Greenhalgh also scored twice on the final day of the campaign as Cardiff City were beaten 9–0 – a remarkable day in the club's history. Despite these performances, he only made eight appearances the following season and four in 1967–68 before being sold to Aston Villa. Having partnered Brian Godfrey in his Deepdale days, he lined up alongside the Welsh international at Villa Park and went on to score 12 goals in 40 games. After a

brief spell at Leicester City, he played for Huddersfield Town as they rose to the First Division. He rediscovered his long-dormant goalscoring touch at Cambridge United to net 47 in 116 games. He then commenced a series of southern travels, playing for Bournemouth, Torquay United and Watford before playing non-League football for Dartford, Staines Town, Carshalton Athletic and Wealdstone prior to becoming chief scout at Everton.

GREENWOOD, Nigel Patrick

Forward

Born: Preston, 27 November 1966.
Career: PRESTON NORTH END, 1984. Bury, 1986. PRESTON NORTH END, 1990. Halifax Town, 1992.

■ Nigel Greenwood was promoted from the reserves during the 1984–85 season, as the club were relegated to the Fourth Division. He made a most promising start, scoring four goals in four games shortly after making his debut, and it was hoped he would impress the following season in the League's basement. Despite this being the worst campaign in North End's history – finishing next to bottom of the Fourth Division and having to apply for re-election – Greenwood linked up well with both Thomas and Brazil to score

nine goals in 30 League games. He always worked hard up front but was fighting a losing battle for much of the season. He left to play for Bury and scored 24 goals in 110 games for the Shakers before returning to Deepdale in February 1990. At the end of the 1991–92 season, Greenwood left North End for a second time to play for Halifax Town where he ended his senior career.

GREER, William H.

Centre-half, right-half

Born: Preston, 28 February 1872.
Died: 1937.
Career: PRESTON NORTH END, 1891.
Darwen, 1898.

■ Wing-half Billy Greer joined North End from local junior football and, after impressing in the reserves, he was given a first-team outing on the final day of the 1891–92 season. Not overawed, he scored one of the goals in a 4–0 win over bottom-of-the-table Darwen. That day he wore the number-seven shirt and he kept it for the first game of the following season when North End beat Bolton 2–1. After that, he switched to right-half and was outstanding in a season in which the club finished runners-up in Division One. He was ever present in 1893–94 when he showed his versatility by playing

the majority of his games at centre-half. Over the next few seasons he missed very few games but midway through the 1896–97 campaign he was injured. After being unable to force his way back into the side, he moved to play for Darwen, where injury brought his career to an end.

GREGAN, Sean Matthew

Centre-half, midfield

Born: Guisborough, 29 March 1974.
Career: Darlington, 1991. PRESTON NORTH END, 1996. West Bromwich Albion, 2002. Leeds United, 2004.

■ Sean Gregan began his career with Darlington where he was the club's longest-serving player at the age of only 22. Gregan had a great game at Wembley in the Third Division Play-off Final in 1996 – a performance which prompted North End to pay £350,000 for his services in November of that year. Cool under pressure, a decisive tackler and commanding in the air, he scored his first goal for the club with a 30–yard thunderbolt at Shrewsbury. In fact, most of his goals were long-range spectacular efforts. Although Gregan's disciplinary record was a worry in his early days with the club, he was appointed captain midway through the 1997–98 season. Despite serving three suspensions the following season, he was named in the

PFA award-winning Second Division side and granted an extension to his existing contract. In 1999–2000, despite cracking a bone in his back in a tumultuous performance against Wigan at the JJB Stadium, he was once again selected for the PFA side and led North End to the Second Division Championship. In the higher grade of football, Gregan alternated between midfield and the centre of defence and, though he missed six weeks of the campaign following a cartilage operation, he did score the winner at Norwich with an amazing 50–yard lob. Like his teammates, Gregan suffered something of a hangover in 2001–02 from the previous season's Play-off disappointment, but he remained a firm favourite with fans and management alike. Despite this, Gregan was sold to West Bromwich Albion for £1.5 million in August 2002 after appearing in 251 games for North End. Bought to bolster the Baggies' midfield, he also appeared as a central defender. After being appointed the club captain, he led Albion to promotion to the Premiership. Gregan left the Hawthorns in September 2004 after Leeds United boss Kevin Blackwell paid £500,000 to take him to Elland Road – despite the Yorkshire club's precarious finances.

GRIERSON, George

Left-half

Born: Lesmahagow, 1903.
Career: PRESTON NORTH END, 1926.
Rochdale, 1930. Ashton National.

■ Though George Grierson spent four seasons at Deepdale, he made just five League appearances during that time. After replacing the injured Bobby Crawford in a 1–0 win over Southampton in February 1927, Grierson made another appearance towards the end of the season before returning to the reserves for the next two seasons. Three appearances in 1929–30 in which he experienced the highs and the lows – a 5–1 defeat of Stoke and a 4–0 reversal against Wolves – were Grierson's last appearances before he joined Rochdale. Unable to raise the Spotland club from the lower reaches of the Third Division North, he left to play non-League football for Ashton National.

GRIFFITHS, Frederick John

Goalkeeper

Born: Presteigne, 13 September 1873.
Died: 1917.
Career: South Shore. Clitheroe. South Shore. Blackpool. Stalybridge Rovers. Millwall Athletic. Tottenham Hotspur. PRESTON NORTH END, 1901. West Ham United. New Brompton. Middlesbrough, 1906.

■ Goalkeeper Fred Griffiths was the son of a Presteigne coal merchant. He started his career in junior football in his native Wales but it was while playing for South Shore and Blackpool (who amalgamated in 1899) that he really established his name, playing for his country against Scotland in February 1900 and England the following month. A fearless goalkeeper, he then had spells with Millwall and Spurs before he joined Preston North End in March 1902 following an injury to Peter McBride. The Scottish international 'keeper broke his collarbone in the match against Middlesbrough, so Griffiths played in the last 10 games of the season. Unfortunately, North End's season ended on a disappointing note as they lost their last three games. They had however secured enough points to hold on to third place in Division Two. At the end of the season, Griffiths returned to London to play for West Ham United where he stayed for two years before effectively finishing his footballing career with a two-year spell at New Brompton, although he was briefly on the books of Middlesbrough. Later working as a coalminer in Shirebrook, he died in France during the Great War while serving with the Sherwood Foresters.

GUDJONSSON, Thordur

Midfield

Born: Akranes, Iceland, 14 October 1973.
Career: IA Akranes (Iceland). KA Akureyar (Iceland). VfL Bochum (Germany). KRC Genk (Belgium). Las Palmas (Spain). Derby County, 2001 (loan). PRESTON NORTH END, 2002 (loan). VfL Bochum (Germany). Stoke City, 2005.

■ Icelandic international Thordur Gudjonsson had played for a host of

clubs on the continent when Derby County, who were struggling against relegation from the Premiership, decided they needed some variety to an injury-hit side. Jim Smith signed Gudjonsson on loan from Las Palmas but he failed to adapt to life in the top flight. He returned to the Spanish side after County decided not to pursue a permanent signing. He joined North End on a short-term contract in January 2002 but his debut was delayed due to a dispute between Las Palmas and the Spanish football association. His first three appearances came from the bench and his lack of match fitness was an obvious hindrance to him achieving his full potential. Failing to win a longer contract at Deepdale, Gudjonsson rejoined German club VfL Bochum before signing for Stoke City in January 2005.

GUNNLAUGSSON, Bjarke Bergman

Winger

Born: Akranes, Iceland, 6 March 1973.
Career: IA Akranes (Iceland). Feyenoord (Holland). IFC Nuremberg (Germany). Waldorf (Germany). Mannheim (Germany). Molde FK (Iceland). KR Reykjavik (Iceland). PRESTON NORTH END, 1999.

■ Bjarke Gunnlaugsson joined North End in the summer of 1999 shortly after

playing for KR Reykjavik in the Icelandic Cup Final and was a regular substitute for the Deepdale club. The twin brother of Arnar, who played for Bolton, Leicester and Stoke, he made his Preston debut against Enfield in the FA Cup and scored his first goal in the replay against the non-League club. In only his second start, the Icelandic international netted a hat-trick in a 4–1 win over Wrexham in the Auto Windscreens Shield. The tricky ball-playing winger, who was extremely hard to dispossess, ended his first campaign with a Second Division Championship medal. Eager to impress in the higher Division, he began the 2000–01 season with a niggling groin strain that was sustained the day before the campaign got underway. Out of action for over a month, he returned to score what proved to be his only goal of the season, an injury-time winner against Norwich City. Though obviously in pain, he struggled on through the campaign, making brief substitute appearances and thus delaying the operation on his injured hip until the close season. Unfortunately he failed to make a complete recovery and in December 2001, the popular Icelander was forced to retire. He had made just 58 League and Cup appearances in his two full seasons with the club, including 26 as substitute.

HAIR, Alexander

Centre-forward, inside-left

Born: Glasgow, 9 March 1902.
Career: Partick Thistle. PRESTON NORTH END, 1928. Shelbourne. Colwyn Bay United.

■ Alex 'Sandy' Hair's prolific goal-scoring feats north of the border for Partick Thistle prompted manager Alex Gibson to bring him to Deepdale at the start of the 1928–29 season. Hair certainly did not disappoint. He scored on his debut though the result, a 7–2 defeat at the hands of Bradford Park Avenue, was a great disappointment to the fans that had crossed the Pennines. Hair continued to find the net throughout the remainder of that season and his 19 goals in 31 games included a hat-trick in a 5–2 home win over Clapton Orient. He was not as prolific the following season and thus found himself in and out of the side. In the close season, he left Deepdale to try his luck in the League of Ireland with Shelbourne before returning to see out his career with Colwyn Bay United.

HALES, Herbert

Outside-left

Born: Kettering, 21 November 1908.
Died: 1982.
Career: Desborough Town. Nottingham Forest, 1928. Northampton Town, 1929. Peterborough and Fletton United. Stoke City, 1930. PRESTON NORTH END, 1931. Chesterfield, 1933. Stockport County, 1934. Rochdale, 1935. Burton Town. Kidderminster Harriers.

■ Outside-left Bert Hales was a much-travelled footballer who started his career with Nottingham Forest. Unable to make much progress at the City Ground, he had brief spells with Northampton, Peterborough and Stoke before arriving at Deepdale. After making his debut in a 2–2 draw at Oldham Athletic on the opening day of the 1931–32 season, Hales held his place on the left-wing for most of the campaign, scoring a number of vital goals. He continued this form into the following season and scored twice in the 5–5 draw at Grimsby Town, along with a number of other deadly strikes. Injury hampered his progress but on regaining full fitness he found that Arthur Fitton had taken his place. Hales moved on to Chesterfield and helped them finish as runners-up in the Third Division North in 1933–34. This was followed by spells at other League clubs Stockport County and Rochdale before he wound down his career with non-League Burton Town and Kidderminster Harriers.

HALL, John Edward

Outside-right

Born: Tyne Dock, 1885.
Career: Harton Star. Kingston Villa. Barnsley, 1905. Brighton and Hove Albion. Rochdale. South Shields. PRESTON NORTH END, 1910. Doncaster Rovers. Pontypridd. South Shields.

■ Jack Hall was a fast-raiding winger who began his first-class career with Barnsley. He played in 74 League games

for the Second Division club and scoring 14 goals, many of them spectacular. After a spell in the Southern League with Brighton & Hove Albion, he returned north to play for Rochdale and later South Shields before joining North End. He played his first game for the Lilywhites at Middlesbrough towards the end of the 1910–11 season and scored on his third appearance for the club in a 2–0 defeat of Notts County. Having played his part in ensuring the club retained its top-flight status, he appeared only spasmodically the following season, but did score the only goal of the game against Bury on his final outing for the club. On leaving Deepdale, he had spells with Doncaster Rovers and Welsh club Pontypridd before ending his career with a second stint at South Shields.

HALL, William Furness

Goalkeeper

Born: Walton-le-Dale, 6 February 1926.
Died: 1986.
Career: PRESTON NORTH END, 1948. Blackpool, 1949. Reading, 1953.

■ Goalkeeper Willie Hall acted as understudy to Jimmy Gooch during the 1947–48 season. He finally got his chance against Sunderland at Roker Park towards the end of the campaign and kept a clean sheet in a 2–0 win. Hall made seven appearances for North End in that campaign but will surely have wanted to forget what turned out to be his final outing for the club on the last day of the season. North End travelled to Blackpool and went down 7–0 to a Seasiders team that was missing Matthews and Mortensen. Unfortunately, Willie Hall was responsible for all but one of the goals. After a season in the reserves, Hall joined Blackpool as cover for George Farm. He later played for Reading, appearing in 16 games for the Third Division South club.

HALLIGAN, William

Inside-forward, centre-forward

Born: Athlone, 1886.
Died: 1950.
Career: Cliftonville. Belfast Celtic. Leeds City, 1909. Derby County, 1909. Wolverhampton Wanderers, 1911. Hull City, 1913. PRESTON NORTH END, 1919.

Oldham Athletic, 1919. Nelson, 1921. Boston Town. Wisbech Town.

■ Although he was perhaps a shade on the small side, Irish international Billy Halligan could play in any of the forward-line positions with equal facility. Capped twice by Ireland, against Wales in 1912 and England in 1912, he played his early football for Cliftonville and Belfast Celtic before joining Leeds City in the summer of 1909. Unable to make much headway with the Yorkshire club, he moved to Derby County where he won his first cap. With his next club, Wolves, Halligan netted 41 goals in 73 games. He was a craftsman of the highest class and a consistent marksman. He continued to find the net for his next club, Hull City, while during World War One he played in two victory internationals against Scotland. When League football resumed in 1919–20, Billy Halligan joined Preston North End but sadly age had caught up with him and he only managed 2 goals in his 16 games for the club. Remarkably though, these came in consecutive games against high-flying Liverpool, which resulted in two 2–1 wins for the Lilywhites. Halligan, who later had brief spells with Oldham Athletic and Nelson, scored over 100 League goals for his seven clubs.

HALLIWELL, Joseph Adam

Centre-forward, right-half, inside-forward

Born: Lostock Hall, 17 January 1894.
Career: Lostock Hall. PRESTON NORTH END, 1912. Barnsley, 1913. Nelson, 1927. Barnoldswick Town.

■ Joe Halliwell joined North End from Lostock Hall in 1912 and was one of the club's earliest utility players. He made his debut in a 2–0 home win over Bury and finished the season as the club's second-highest scorer with 10 goals in 22 games as North End won the Second Division Championship. Halliwell's tally included goals in three consecutive games just after the turn of the year and a brace in a 3–0 defeat of Leicester Fosse. However, he struggled in the higher grade of football and left to play for Barnsley. He gave the Oakwell club great service, scoring 83 goals in 312 games either side of the war. All of his time with Barnsley was spent in Division Two with the Yorkshire club's best performance being to finish third in 1914–15. After winding his League career down back in the North West with Nelson, he played non-League football with Barnoldswick Town.

HALSALL, Laurence

Outside-left, inside-left

Born: Blackpool, 1876.
Died: 1917.
Career: Blackpool, 1897. PRESTON NORTH END, 1897.

■ Signed from local rivals Blackpool during the 1897–98 season, Laurence Halsall played primarily on the left-wing. He made his debut in a 4–1 home defeat at the hands of Blackburn Rovers. In his next game at Deepdale, he scored in a 3–2 win over high-flying Aston Villa and was one of the successes in a campaign in which the Lilywhites just avoided losing their place in the top flight. Though not a prolific scorer, he netted twice in a 4–2 win over Stoke early the following season as the club again struggled to avoid the drop. After playing in the first nine games of the 1899–1900 season, Halsall was forced to retire through injury.

HAM, Robert Stanley

Forward

Born: Bradford, 29 March 1942.
Career: Bradford Park Avenue, 1961. Gainsborough Trinity. Grimsby Town, 1964. Bradford Park Avenue, 1964. Bradford City, 1968. PRESTON NORTH END, 1970. Rotherham United, 1971. Bradford City, 1973.

■ Bobby Ham has the unique distinction of having spent two separate spells with both Bradford City and Bradford Park Avenue. Born in Bradford, he was taken on the Park Avenue groundstaff when he was 15, but after just 3 months in the 'A' team, he moved to Huddersfield Town before joining City for the first time. He rejoined Park Avenue and signed professional forms in October 1961, but after an operation to cure a long-standing groin injury he left to play part-time with Gainsborough Trinity. Following a spell as Grimsby Town's reserve-team player-coach, he returned

to Park Avenue for a third time. In 1965–66 he scored 24 goals for Park Avenue including four in the match against Newport County. In February 1968, City paid their neighbours £2,750 for the inside-forward's services and at the end of the 1968–69 season Ham became the first Bradford-born player to top the club's goalscoring lists. During that season he scored four goals against York as the Bantams won 5–0. In January 1970 he hit a hat-trick against Bournemouth as City recorded their best Third Division win 8–1. After playing in 109 consecutive League games for the club, he joined Preston North End in October 1970 for a fee of £8,000. He scored on his debut in a 1–1 draw against Plymouth just five days after signing for the club. The goals continued to flow as Ham got his name on the score sheet in the next three games for North End. His signing was certainly timely because the team only lost three games that season after his arrival. Indeed, North End never lost a game when Ham scored. Though he never scored more than a single goal in a game – scoring 11 in 30 games – North End fans rightly hailed his predatory instincts. Having helped Preston win the Third Division Championship, Ham had made just 13 appearances the following season when he was allowed to join Rotherham United. After the Milers were relegated in 1972–73 he rejoined Bradford City for a third time and was their top goalscorer in 1974–75, his last season in the Football League.

HAMILTON, Herbert Harold

Right-back

Born: Wallasey, 27 March 1906.
Died: 1951.
Career: New Brighton Baptists. Harrowby. Poulton Rovers. New Brighton, 1923. Everton, 1926. PRESTON NORTH END, 1927. Chesterfield, 1931. Tranmere Rovers, 1937. Accrington Stanley, 1938. Bangor City. Marine.

■ After playing in the local junior leagues, right-back 'Duke' Hamilton was given his chance in the Football League by New Brighton, but made just one appearance in three years with the

club. Moving across the Mersey to play for Everton, he had also made just a single appearance for the Toffees when Preston North End signed him midway through the 1927–28 season. Having made his debut in a 4–2 win at Leeds, Hamilton then lost out to Frank Ward before appearing in the last five games, including a 6–4 win at Grimsby on the final day of the campaign. In and out of the side for much of the 1928–29 season, he made just a couple of appearances the following season before playing in five consecutive defeats in 1930–31. On leaving Deepdale, he joined Chesterfield and helped them win the Third Division North Championship in 1935–36. He later returned to the North West with Tranmere Rovers and Accrington Stanley before playing non-League football for Bangor City and Marine.

HAMILTON, Thomas

Full-back

Born: New Cumnock, 10 February 1893.
Died: 1959.
Career: Cronberry Eglington. Kilmarnock. PRESTON NORTH END, 1920. Manchester Central.

■ A stylish defender in the classical mould, Tommy Hamilton was able to play in either full-back berth. He joined North End from Kilmarnock for a fee of £3,100 in February 1921. Having made his Preston debut in a 1–0 home defeat by Arsenal, he initially struggled in the English game, though he developed into a wily, positional player much admired for his skilful passing. Hamilton was the central figure when North End lost by the only goal at Stamford Bridge in the 1922 FA Cup Final. As a last resort, he tripped Huddersfield's outside-left Billy Smith. The referee ignored the heated protests and awarded a penalty. Hamilton never denied his intention to stop Smith, but always maintained that the offence took place outside the penalty area. Appointed the club's captain, Hamilton was sent off in the 1–0 defeat at Birmingham in March 1923. Surprisingly he was not suspended and played in all of the remaining games that season. He missed very few games for North End over the next six seasons and was ever present in 1927–28 when the club finished fourth in Division Two, just missing out on a return to the top flight. Hugely popular with the Preston faithful, he had appeared in 284 League and Cup games when he left Deepdale to continue his career with Manchester Central.

HAMILTON, William

Wing-half

Born: Hamilton, 1 September 1918.
Career: Blantyre Celtic. PRESTON NORTH END, 1937.

■ Though he had signed for the club prior to World War Two, wing-half Willie Hamilton had to wait until the 1946–47 season before making his League debut for North End. It came in October 1946 when he replaced Willie Watson in a 1–1 draw against Manchester United at Old Trafford, after which he played in all the remaining games of the season. Though he did not score in those 37 games, he did find the net in the 6–0 rout of Barnsley in an FA Cup fourth-round tie. Having helped North End finish seventh in the First Division, Hamilton left Deepdale to continue his career back in his native Scotland.

HAMPTON, John William

Goalkeeper

Born: Wolverhampton, 1899.
Died: 1952.
Career: Wellington Town. Oakengates Town. Wolverhampton Wanderers, 1922. Derby County, 1927. PRESTON NORTH END, 1930. Dundalk.

■ Goalkeeper John Hampton joined Wolves from Oakengates Town as cover for the ever-reliable Noel George, having impressed greatly during his time in non-League football. In 1922–23, his first season in the side, he did well though he certainly had an off-day on Christmas Day, as Coventry put seven goals past him. Hampton remained loyal to the Molineux club until August 1927 when, having made 51 appearances, he joined Derby County. He signed for Preston North End in the summer of 1930 and played his first game for the club on the opening day of the 1930–31 season as Preston beat Southampton 5–0. Apart from three games midway through the

campaign when injury forced him to miss out, John Hampton was the club's first-choice 'keeper. Although he conceded five goals at Millwall in October 1930, North End still ran out winners 7–5. On leaving Preston, he crossed the water to play in the League of Ireland with Dundalk.

HANNAH, William King

Inside-forward

Born: Shotts, 6 August 1921.
Died: 1978.
Career: Albion Rovers. PRESTON NORTH END, 1947. Barrow, 1951.

■ Having impressed north of the border with Albion Rovers, inside-forward Willie Hannah signed for North End in December 1947. However, he had to wait until the following March before making his debut in a 2–0 win at Sunderland. He scored on his home debut the following week as Aston Villa, who were in the title-chasing group, were beaten 3–0. Hannah kept his place in the side for the rest of the season, scoring further goals against Wolves and Everton. Despite this promising start, Hannah made just a handful of appearances over the next couple of seasons and was eventually allowed to join Barrow. Though the club was struggling in the lower reaches of the Third Division North, Hannah was probably the club's most consistent player, appearing in 106 League games and scoring 16 goals for the Holker Street club.

HANNIGAN, Ernest

Winger

Born: Glasgow, 23 January 1943.
Career: Queen of the South. PRESTON NORTH END, 1964. Coventry City, 1967. Torquay United, 1969 (loan).

■ Having joined Preston from Queen of the South in the summer of 1964, Ernest Hannigan spent much of his first season with the club as understudy to Dave Wilson. In 1965–66, he appeared on a more regular basis and scored vital goals in both League and Cup matches. Having netted twice in a 3–2 win at Charlton Athletic in an FA Cup third-round tie, he then had an outstanding game against Bolton before netting in the

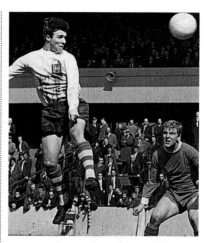

2–1 fifth-round defeat of mighty Spurs. Unfortunately, despite causing untold problems for Manchester United's defenders, Hannigan and his North End teammates lost 3–1 after taking the Red Devils to a replay. Hannigan, along with Godfrey, hit a hat-trick on the final day of the season as North End crushed Cardiff City 9–0 to ensure they would remain playing Second Division football the following season. Hannigan was ever present in 1966–67 and was the club's second-top scorer with 11 League goals but, early the following season, he left Deepdale to play in Coventry City's first season in the top flight.

HARGREAVES, Robert

Inside-forward

Born: Preston, 1876.
Career: PRESTON NORTH END, 1897.

■ Inside-forward Robert Hargreaves appeared in a handful of games at the start of the 1897–98 season, after which his appearances were few and far between. He was in the North End side on the final day of the campaign and set up both Sandy Brown's goals in a 5–0 defeat of Derby County. He made three appearances the following season, but in each game the Lilywhites failed to score. At the end of the campaign, in which North End just avoided relegation from Division One, he left to play in the local amateur leagues.

HARPER, Steven James

Midfield, defender

Born: Newcastle-under-Lyme, 3 February 1969.

Career: Port Vale, 1987. PRESTON NORTH END, 1989. Burnley, 1991. Doncaster Rovers, 1993. Mansfield Town, 1995. Hull City, 1999. Darlington, 2001. Kidsgrove Athletic.

■ Steve Harper broke into Port Vale's Third Division side in 1987–88 and scored twice in his first six matches, but they were to be the only goals of his Vale Park career. With Vale on their way to promotion via the Play-offs in 1989 without him, Harper joined North End. He scored 10 goals in 1989–90, the best return of his career. This total included a hat-trick in a 4–0 home win over Cardiff City but, despite his heroics, North End still ended the campaign just out of the Third Division relegation places. Although he scored against Rochdale in the Leyland Daf Cup, Harper failed to find the net in the League in 1990–91 and was offloaded to Burnley. Though never an automatic choice at Turf Moor, he did help them win the Fourth Division Championship in his first season with the club. On leaving the Clarets, he had a couple of seasons with Doncaster Rovers before joining Mansfield Town. A virtual ever present at Field Mill, he netted his second League hat-trick when the Stags beat Darlington 4–0 in 1997–98. Joining former Preston colleague Warren Joyce at Hull, Harper scored the third hat-trick of his career against Southend but, with the club having financial problems, he left to play for Darlington, where he ended his first-class career.

HARPER, Edward Cashfield

Centre-forward

Born: Sheerness, 22 August 1901.
Died: Blackburn, 22 July 1959.
Career: Whitstable Town. Sheppey United. Blackburn Rovers, 1923. Sheffield Wednesday, 1927. Tottenham Hotspur, 1929. PRESTON NORTH END, 1931. Blackburn Rovers, 1933.

■ A prolific marksman throughout his career, Ted Harper started with Whitstable and Sheppey before joining Blackburn Rovers where 43 goals in 37 games in 1925–26 won him an England cap against Scotland in April 1926. He moved to Sheffield Wednesday in November 1927 and scored a hat-trick on his debut in a 6–4 win at Derby County. Injuries hampered Harper's progress at Hillsborough and in March 1929 he moved to Tottenham Hotspur. In 1930–31 he set a new Spurs record with 36 goals in 30 matches. Had he not been injured at Swansea towards the end of the campaign and forced to miss six of the last eight games, he may well have set a record that even Jimmy Greaves could not have surpassed. Harper left White Hart Lane in December 1931 when he was allowed to join Preston in a £5,000 joint transfer with Dick Rowley. At the time of Harper's arrival, North End were third from bottom of Division Two but after scoring on his debut against Plymouth Argyle, the bustling centre-forward went on to score 24 League goals in 23 games to lift the club to a respectable mid-table position. The following season, 1932–33, Harper scored 37 League goals to set a new club record. By Christmas he had scored 19 goals including four against Burnley and a hat-trick against West Ham United. Another treble against Manchester United took his total to 25 before he netted another four against Lincoln City to break Tommy Roberts' record of 28 League goals. Harper also scored five goals in a Lancashire Cup replay against Everton and four more in a 9–2 victory over the Corinthians. Harper had a lethal shot and one of his penalties luckily missed the Wolves 'keeper before tearing a gaping hole in the net. The ball flew into the crowd at such a rate that most of the spectators thought he had shot wide.

At the start of the 1933–34 season, Harper's goals started to dry up and he was transferred back to Blackburn Rovers, his first League club, where he took his tally of goals in his two spells to 121 in 171 League games before retiring and joining the club's coaching staff.

HARRINGTON, Philip

Goalkeeper

Born: Bangor, 20 November 1963.
Career: Chester City, 1981. Blackpool, 1985. Burnley, 1985 (loan). PRESTON NORTH END, 1986 (loan). Rhyl.

■ A Welsh Youth international goalkeeper, Phil Harrington began his career at Chester City for whom he played the bulk of his League football. After a spell with Blackpool without a League appearance, he joined Burnley on loan following injuries to both Joe Neenan and Dennis Peacock. In February 1986 he joined North End on loan but in his second game for the club at Hereford United he suffered a badly fractured leg which sadly ended his Football League career at the age of only 22. He later played for Rhyl in the Northern Premier League.

HARRIS, Jason Andre Sebastian

Forward

Born: Sutton, 24 November 1976.
Career: Crystal Palace, 1995. Bristol Rovers, 1996 (loan). Lincoln City, 1997 (loan). Leyton Orient, 1997. PRESTON NORTH END, 1998. Hull City, 1999. Shrewsbury Town, 2001 (loan). Southend United, 2001. Harrogate Town. Nuneaton Borough.

■ One of a breed of young strikers to come out of the Crystal Palace youth team, Jason Harris was loaned to Bristol Rovers in order to gain further experience before returning to Selhurst Park. A loan spell with Lincoln City followed before he was transferred to Leyton Orient in September 1997. Unable to win a regular place in the Orient side, Harris joined North End in the summer of 1998 where he immediately impressed with his strength and aerial ability. He gained his first start at Maine Road but more often than not

was used from the bench with good effect, setting a new club record for substitute appearances in a season. Unluckily sent off at Northampton, he faded from the first-team scene for a while before returning to contribute several late point-saving goals. With still a year of his Preston contract to run Harris joined Hull City, who were managed by former North Ender Warren Joyce. Reputed to be one of the fastest players in the Football League, Harris suffered from a spate of niggling injuries. He had a loan spell with Shrewsbury before ending his League career with Southend United, prior to spells with non-League Harrogate Town and Nuneaton Borough.

HARRISON, Craig

Defender

Born: Gateshead, 10 November 1977.
Career: Middlesbrough, 1996. PRESTON NORTH END, 1999 (loan). Crystal Palace, 2000.

■ Craig Harrison made his Football League debut for Middlesbrough in 1997–98, contesting the left-back spot with Vladimir Kinder. The youngster was both competitive and gutsy in Boro's ongoing promotion battles and deservedly won the supporters' Young Player of the Year award. The following season he was loaned out to Preston North End to provide cover for both of the Deepdale club's injured left-backs. He gave an impressive performance on his debut against Luton and set up the equalising goal. His excellent composure and touch made a great impression on the North End fans before he returned to the Riverside after appearing in seven games. He missed the whole of the 1999–2000 season through illness and

injury before joining Crystal Palace for a fee of £200,000. His performances improved game by game for the Eagles until he suffered a double fracture of the leg in a match against Reading in January 2002. Unfortunately this forced his premature retirement from the game.

HARRISON, George

Outside-left

Born: Church Gresley, 18 July 1892.
Died: 1939.
Career: Gresley Rovers. Leicester Fosse, 1910. Everton, 1913. PRESTON NORTH END, 1923. Blackpool, 1931.

■ A hefty and direct left-winger, George Harrison demonstrated with Leicester Fosse, his first League club, that he was worthy of a much higher grade of football. After being ever present in 1912–13, Harrison signed for Everton where he demonstrated that he had one of the hardest shots in football and was a notable penalty-taker. Though he was not that successful in the role of out-and-out scorer, he made plenty of goals for other players, notably for Bobby Parker when Everton won the League Championship in 1914–15. He played wartime football with Everton and was a regular when the League resumed. His form for the Blues in the immediate post-war era led to him winning two England caps. Midway through the 1923–24 season, Harrison signed for Preston and made his debut in a 2–1 win at Chelsea. He was a virtual ever present in the Preston side for the next eight seasons, netting a hat-trick in a 4–2 defeat of Hull City in the first home game of the 1927–28 season and four goals, including two penalties, in the 5–2 win over Grimsby Town the following season. During his time at Deepdale, Harrison took 35 spot-kicks: he scored 29 and converted four of those that he missed at the second attempt. His method was simplicity itself – he aimed with all his strength at the goalkeeper, arguing that his intended victim instinctively would go one way or the other. George Harrison's stamina was almost as remarkable as his touchline skill and he was nearly 40 when he retired after a short spell with Blackpool. Initially he ran a pub in Preston but at the time of his early death, he was a licensee back in his native village.

HARTLEY, Percy

Wing-half

Born: Bolton, 1884.
Career: PRESTON NORTH END, 1905. Chorley. Exeter City. Rochdale.

■ Strong-tackling wing-half Percy Hartley was given his chance in the Football League during the course of the 1905–06 season. He made his only appearance in the penultimate game of the campaign in a 3–0 win at his home-town club, Bolton Wanderers. North End finished that season in the First Division as runners-up to Liverpool. Hartley made a couple of appearances at the start of the following season but then moved into non-League football to play for Chorley and later Exeter City and Rochdale.

HASELGRAVE, Sean Matthew

Midfield

Born: Stoke-on-Trent, 7 June 1951.
Career: Stoke City, 1968. Nottingham Forest, 1976. PRESTON NORTH END, 1977. Crewe Alexandra, 1981. York City, 1983. Torquay United, 1987.

■ Midfielder Sean Haselgrave began his career with his home-town club Stoke City and made 113 League appearances in a little over six seasons with the Potters. He was never a regular member of the side and missed out when Stoke beat Chelsea 2–1 to win the League Cup in 1972. He left the Victoria Ground in the summer of 1976 to join Brian Clough's Nottingham Forest but his stay was brief and in September 1977 he signed for Preston North End. He made his debut in a 2–0 home win over Cambridge United and kept his place in the side for the rest of the season, going on to make 38 League appearances. His presence certainly strengthened the midfield and helped the club win promotion to Division Two. His first goal for the club came the following season against Crystal Palace. It was also a campaign in which the midfielder won £100 in the club's lottery. He was a regular in the North End side until the 1980–81 season, when injuries disrupted his progress and he left Deepdale to join Crewe Alexandra. During his time at Gresty Road, the club struggled near the foot of the Fourth Division and he moved on to York City. In his first season

at Bootham Crescent, he helped the Minstermen win the Fourth Division Championship and later ended his career with a spell at Torquay United.

HATSELL, Dennis

Centre-forward

Born: Sheffield, 9 June 1930.
Died: 1998.
Career: PRESTON NORTH END, 1948. Chelmsford City.

■ On his arrival at Deepdale, Dennis Hatsell soon began to make a name for himself as a prolific goalscorer with the club's youth and reserve teams. It came as no surprise when he was given his first-team debut against Manchester United at a packed Old Trafford in September 1953, when he replaced the injured Bobby Foster. He scored on his home debut the following week as Bolton were beaten 3–1 and then netted twice in a 3–2 defeat at Arsenal in the following game. He completed his first season in the side with 11 goals in 17 games including a well-taken hat-trick in a 6–2 win over Spurs at White Hart Lane. Early the following season, Hatsell was selected for an FA XI against the RAF at Highbury in recognition of his

tremendous form at club level. However, over the next few seasons he was in and out of the North End side until 1958–59 when he had his best season for the club, scoring 16 goals in his 35 League games. After one more season at Deepdale he was allowed to leave the club and found himself playing non-League football for Chelmsford City. No doubt the North End board had their reasons for letting him leave, but nevertheless a lot of fans thought the club's decision to part company with Hatsell was an ill-thought move, especially with the club lurching through a major transitional period.

HAWKINS, Graham Norman

Centre-half

Born: Darlaston, 5 March 1946.
Career: Wolverhampton Wanderers, 1963. PRESTON NORTH END, 1968. Blackburn Rovers, 1974, Port Vale, 1978.

■ Graham Hawkins began his career with Wolverhampton Wanderers, helping the club win promotion from Division Two in 1966–67, but he left Molineux to join Preston North End in January 1968. Signed as a replacement for the long-serving Tony Singleton, he made his debut at Queen's Park Rangers but suffered an injury that curtailed his first-team appearances for a few weeks. On his return, the 22-year-old Hawkins was named as the club's captain – one of the youngest in North End's history. Unable to prevent the club's relegation in 1969–70, he led them to the Third Division Championship the following season when he was ever present. Hawkins was a firm favourite with the North End fans who appreciated his no-nonsense approach to defensive responsibilities, his ability to avert danger and the way that he created havoc in opposition penalty areas at set-piece situations. He left Deepdale in the summer of 1974 to join neighbours Blackburn Rovers and helped them win the Third Division title in his first season at Ewood Park. He ended his playing career with Port Vale. After a spell as assistant manager at Shrewsbury Town, he replaced Ian Greaves as manager of Wolves. Things sparked into life immediately for him and at the end of

his first season in charge, Wolves had gained promotion from Division Two. Then it all started to go wrong and he turned his back on British football and went to try his luck coaching in Saudi Arabia.

HAYES, William Edward

Goalkeeper

Born: Croston, 8 November 1895.
Career: Eccleston. PRESTON NORTH END, 1912. Chorley (loan). PRESTON NORTH END, 1914. Brighton and Hove Albion, 1920. Southend United, 1924. Accrington Stanley, 1926. Stockport County, 1927. Winsford United. Burscough Rangers. Stalybridge Celtic. Bacup Borough.

■ Goalkeeper Billy Hayes joined North End in 1912 but was unable to oust Bert Taylor so he went on loan to Chorley before returning to Deepdale in readiness for the 1914–15 season. He made his League debut for North End in a 1–1 home draw against Huddersfield Town and kept his place in the side for 10 matches before losing out to Charlie

Jones. He kept clean sheets in half of his appearances as North End went on to finish the campaign as runners-up to Derby County. Hayes joined Brighton and Hove Albion at the start of their 1919–20 season of Southern League football and was between the posts when they played their inaugural Football League game at Southend United. He missed just one game in 1920–21 and was ever present the following two seasons, helping the Seagulls finish fourth in the Third Division South in 1922–23, when he kept 19 clean sheets. Hayes was improving with every season and in 1923–24 kept a club record 21 clean sheets, including seven in a row. He made 225 appearances for Albion including 175 consecutive League and Cup games, which remained a record until broken by Eric Gill in 1956. He left to continue his career with Southend before playing for a number of clubs in his latter years.

HEALEY, Ronald

Goalkeeper

Born: Manchester, 30 August 1952.
Career: Manchester City, 1969. Altrincham (loan). Coventry City, 1971 (loan). PRESTON NORTH END, 1973 (loan). Cardiff City, 1974.

■ Ron Healey began his career with Manchester City where he was understudy to the England international Joe Corrigan. With his opportunities at Maine Road limited – he made 30 First Division appearances in four years with the club – he took the opportunity to go out on loan with a couple of clubs, the latter being Preston North End. Healey made the first of six appearances for the Deepdale club at Middlesbrough in December 1973, a game in which he suffered an early facial injury and had to go off for quarter of an hour for treatment. In that time, Boro scored past replacement 'keeper David Sadler and went on to win 3–0. Healey eventually joined Cardiff City and helped the Bluebirds win promotion to Division Two in 1975–76. While at Ninian Park, Healey won two full international caps for the Republic of Ireland, although the appearances were three years apart. Having made 216 League appearances for Cardiff he was forced into premature

retirement following a series of injuries. After ending his involvement with the game he returned to Manchester to work at the local airport.

HEALY, David Jonathan

Forward

Born: Downpatrick, 5 August 1979.
Career: Manchester United, 1997. Port Vale, 2000 (loan). PRESTON NORTH END, 2000. Norwich City, 2003 (loan). Leeds United, 2004.

■ David Healy began his career with Manchester United where he had a penchant for scoring goals. He had a disappointing introduction to first-team action in 1999–2000 when Aston Villa beat the Reds in the Worthington Cup competition. However, he really came to the fore when he made his international debut for Northern Ireland, scoring twice in a 3–1 win over Luxembourg. He also netted in his next international match as the Irish beat Malta 3–0. At club level he went on loan to Port Vale but, despite netting twice in his first four matches, he could not prevent the Valiants' relegation to Division Two. On his return to Old Trafford he signed a four-year contract but, although he continued to impress on the international front, he made little headway in United's first-team squad. In December 2000, Healy joined Preston North End for a club record fee of £1.5 million. He provided an immediate return on the club's investment by scoring after just four minutes of his debut against Sheffield United, a match North End lost 3–2 after being 2–1 ahead at half-time. Healy went on to score five times in his first seven outings for North End. Possessing an eye for goal, the nippy striker continued to find the net for Northern Ireland before netting his first senior hat-trick in a 6–0 win over Stockport County. However, during the early part of the 2002–03 season, Healy found himself on the bench and unable to displace Richard Cresswell or Ricardo Fuller. The young Irishman then spent a couple of spells on loan with Norwich City and during his time at Carrow Road he seemed to rediscover some of his confidence. Having almost left Deepdale, he worked hard to win back the home

HEATON, Charles

Outside-left

Born: Preston, 1868.
Career: PRESTON NORTH END, 1889.

■ Winger Charlie Heaton made a couple of appearances for North End in the 1889–90 season, scoring in the win over Burnley, but with stiff competition for places he was allowed to leave Deepdale and went to play in the local junior leagues.

HEATON, Frederick

Outside-right

Born: Westhoughton, 1904.
Career: Westhoughton Colliery. PRESTON NORTH END, 1929. Chorley.

■ Speedy right-winger Fred Heaton's displays for Westhoughton Colliery prompted North End manager Alex Gibson to give him a chance at Football League level. Heaton made his debut in a 2–2 home draw with Bradford City in October 1929 but could not win a regular place due to the form of Alex Reid. He did not play at all the following season but appeared in 11 games in 1931–32, scoring his only goal for the club and indeed the only goal of the game against Bradford Park Avenue. Released at the end of the campaign, he moved into non-League football with Chorley.

HENDERSON, Adam

Outside-left

Born: Darlington, 16 July 1873.
Career: Airdrie Fruitfield. Airdrieonians. PRESTON NORTH END, 1893. Glasgow Celtic. Bristol St George. PRESTON NORTH END, 1899.

■ Having played his early football north of the border with Airdrie, winger Adam Henderson joined Preston towards the end of the 1893–94 season. After a couple of League games, Henderson played in a relegation 'test match' against Notts County and scored in a 4–0 win that ensured the club kept their First Division status. Joint top scorer with David Smith in 1894–95, Henderson continued to find the net on a regular basis until in May 1897 he returned to Scotland along with

crowd, scoring in four consecutive games and totalling 15 goals in that 2003–04 season. The Northern Ireland striker made national headlines when he broke his country's goalscoring drought against Norway and in the summer he established a new career record of goals for the national team. After taking his tally of first-team goals to 45 in 158 games, Healy turned down a new deal with the Lilywhites and joined Leeds United after a lengthy transfer saga. He opened his scoring account for the Yorkshire club with a double strike in United's 4–2 win at Deepdale. The scorer of the goal that defeated England in the World Cup qualifier in Belfast, David Healy remains one of the best strikers outside the Premiership.

teammate Willie Orr to join Celtic. He played his first game in the Glasgow League against Rangers and scored Celtic's goal in a 1–1 draw. After a year at Parkhead, he left to play for Bristol St George before returning to Deepdale for a second spell in 1899. Although North End struggled in his first season back with the club, Henderson did net a hat-trick in a 5–2 home win over West Bromwich Albion and was the club's leading scorer with 13 goals. However, he was unable to prevent North End's relegation in 1900–01 and at the end of the season he decided to retire.

HENDERSON, George

Wing-half, centre-half

Born: Burnbank, 1876.
Career: Motherwell. Airdrieonians. PRESTON NORTH END, 1897. Swindon Town. Millwall Athletic. Nottingham Forest, 1901.

■ Able to play in a variety of positions, George Henderson had spells north of the border with Motherwell and Airdrieonians before joining Preston in 1897. He played his first game in a 3–0 defeat at Wolves on the opening day of the 1897–98 season and made just one more appearance in a 4–0 reversal at Aston Villa. He was not retained and had spells with Swindon Town and Millwall Athletic before joining Nottingham Forest in 1901. In his four seasons at the City Ground, Forest were continually challenging for League honours but he decided to hang up his boots after making 101 appearances.

HENDERSON, James Thomas

Wing-half

Born: Newcastle-upon-Tyne, 1877.
Career: Morpeth Harriers. Reading. Bradford City, 1904. Leeds City, 1905. PRESTON NORTH END, 1908. Clapton Orient, 1909. Rochdale.

■ A top-class sprinter with Morpeth Harriers, Jimmy Henderson once clocked 11 seconds for the 100 metres. He had spells with Reading and Bradford City before making 80 League and Cup appearances for Leeds City. He joined Preston North End at the start of the

1908–09 season and made seven appearances, the first in a 3–0 defeat of Manchester City. Henderson played in five defeats before his final game in North End colours brought a 3–2 win at Bristol City. Henderson went on to play for Clapton Orient before returning to the North West to see out his career with Rochdale.

HENDERSON, William

Centre-forward

Born: Edinburgh, 1898.
Died: 1964.
Career: St Bernard's. Airdrieonians. Manchester United, 1921. PRESTON NORTH END, 1924. Clapton Orient, 1925. Heart of Midlothian. Morton. Torquay United, 1928. Exeter City, 1929.

■ A big, bustling centre-forward, William Henderson shot to fame during the course of Manchester United's promotion-winning season of 1924–25 when he top scored with 14 goals including a hat-trick in a 3–0 defeat of Oldham Athletic. He had been at Old Trafford since 1921 but had failed to establish himself in his early years with the club. Henderson left United to join North End midway through the following season. The Lilywhites were going through a difficult time and Henderson, who scored North End's goal in a 1–1 draw with Everton, failed to prevent the club from being relegated to Division Two. He left Deepdale in the close season and spent a season with Clapton Orient before returning to Scotland for spells with Hearts and Morton. He later played for Torquay and Exeter before deciding to retire.

HENDERSON, William M.

Left-half

Born: Houghton-le-Spring, 1891.
Career: PRESTON NORTH END, 1913.

■ Spotted playing junior football in his native North East, William Henderson joined North End in readiness for the start of the 1913–14 season. The attacking left-half made his debut in a 2–1 home win over Burnley. He went on to appear in seven consecutive games following his debut and scored in a 4–1 defeat of Middlesbrough.

Unable to prevent the club losing its top-flight status, he made just a couple of appearances in 1914–15 as they won promotion at the first attempt. When League football resumed in 1919–20, Henderson wore the number-six shirt in the club's first game, a 4–0 reversal at Blackburn Rovers, but this turned out to be his last appearance for the Deepdale club.

HENDRY, Edward Colin James

Centre-half

Born: Keith, 7 December 1965.
Career: Islavale. Dundee, 1983. Blackburn Rovers, 1987. Manchester City, 1989. Blackburn Rovers, 1991. Glasgow Rangers, 1998. Coventry City, 2000. Bolton Wanderers, 2000. PRESTON NORTH END, 2002 (loan). Blackpool, 2002.

■ Colin Hendry was playing for Dundee when Blackburn Rovers' manager Don Mackay took him to Ewood Park for a fee of £30,000 in March 1987. The Scottish club had a few reservations about letting Hendry go south of the border and insisted that they receive half of any subsequent transfer fees. Having made his debut in defence, he moved to the attack following Glenn Keeley's recovery. It was in this position that he endeared himself to Rovers fans when he scored the only goal of the Full Members Cup Final win over Charlton

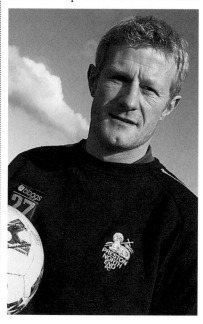

Athletic. His performances led to a number of top clubs following his progress and in November 1989 he left to join Manchester City for £700,000. Despite being a great favourite at Maine Road he returned to Ewood Park when Keith Curle arrived at the club. Under the guidance of Rovers' new manager, Kenny Dalglish, Hendry became a much more polished defender than he had been in his first spell at the club. He was outstanding during Rovers' Premier League Championship-winning season of 1994–95. Hendry, who won 51 caps for Scotland, continued to display his last-ditch tackles and brave headers at Ewood Park until 1998 when after scoring 34 goals in 384 League and Cup games, he left to play for Rangers. After an unhappy time at Ibrox he returned to Premier League action with Coventry City but soon fell out of favour and joined Bolton Wanderers. Despite being a valued member of the Wanderers squad, he was loaned out to Preston North End as cover for injuries. He made an uncompromising debut at Birmingham before a first-half calf injury in his next game against Millwall meant he was unavailable for the rest of his month-long loan spell. Hendry went on to play for Blackpool and later managed the Seasiders.

HENDRY William Harold

Centre-half, centre-forward

Born: Dundee, 20 June 1864.
Died: Shrewsbury, 4 May 1901.
Career: Dunblane Thistle. Dundee Wanderers. West Bromwich Albion, 1888. Stoke, 1888. Kidderminster Harriers. PRESTON NORTH END, 1889. Sheffield United, 1892. Dundee. Bury, 1896. Brighton United. Watford. Shrewsbury Town.

■ Billy Hendry was one of a number of Scots attracted to League football as the professional game started to proliferate in the wake of the advent of the Football League. He had a brief spell with West Bromwich Albion before joining Stoke. After playing for Kidderminster Harriers, Hendry signed for North End and played in 14 games during the 1890–91 season when the club finished runners-up to Everton in

the Football League. He then joined Sheffield United and captained the side to promotion before rejoining his home-town club. Brief spells with Bury, Brighton and Watford followed before he left to play for Shrewsbury. Sadly, the journeyman player died of a heart attack at the end of his second season with the club.

HEPPOLETTE, Richard Alfred William

Midfield

Born: India, 8 April 1949.
Career: PRESTON NORTH END, 1964. Leyton Orient, 1972. Crystal Palace, 1976. Chesterfield, 1977. Peterborough United, 1979.

■ When Ricky Heppolette stepped onto the pitch for his North End debut against Middlesbrough in April 1968, he became the first-ever Indian-born player to play in the Football League. Heppolette was a fine midfielder, possessing silky smooth passing skills and an eye for goal. Though he was unable to prevent the club being relegated to the Third Division in 1969–70, he was instrumental in winning promotion at the first time of asking when they were crowned Third Division Champions in 1970–71. It was Heppolette's best season in terms

of goals scored as he netted eight, including one on the opening day of the season against Halifax and both goals in a 2–1 win over promotion challengers Mansfield Town. North End fans appreciated the great contribution he made to Preston North End and were disappointed when he left Deepdale in December 1972 to play for Leyton Orient. He played in 113 League games for the Brisbane Road club and helped them finish fourth in Division Two in 1973–74. He moved on to Crystal Palace and later played for Chesterfield before ending his playing days with a stint at Peterborough United.

HETHERINGTON, James

Centre-forward, inside-right

Born: Sunderland, 11 April 1892.
Died: 1971.
Career: Sunderland Royal Rovers. Southwick. South Shields, 1920. PRESTON NORTH END, 1924. Lincoln City, 1925. Durham City, 1926. Norwich City, 1927. Guildford City. Walker Celtic.

■ Jos Hetherington played his early football in the League for South Shields where he netted 15 goals in 64 games in three seasons with the club. He arrived at Deepdale days before the start of the 1924–25 season and made his debut in a 1–0 defeat at West Ham United on the opening day of the campaign. He made just a handful of appearances for North End in that relegation season but did not find the net. In the close season he left to play for Lincoln City. He made little progress at Sincil Bank, or at League clubs Durham City and Norwich City, before leaving to play non-League football for Guildford Town and Walker Celtic.

HETHERINGTON, John Arthur

Outside-left, inside-forward

Born: Rotherham, 7 August 1906.
Died: 1977.
Career: Dalton United. Wolverhampton Wanderers, 1928. PRESTON NORTH END, 1935. Swindon Town, 1936. Watford, 1937.

■ A free-scoring winger with Wolverhampton Wanderers, Arthur Hetherington scored 24 goals in 94 League games for the Molineux club and helped them win the Second Division Championship in 1931–32. In January 1935, Hetherington joined Preston North End and made his debut in an exciting 4–3 win at Huddersfield Town. He scored in his next game, a 2–0 FA Cup fourth-round win over Swindon Town, and his wing play helped the club reach the quarter-finals where they went down to the only goal of the game against West Bromwich Albion at the Hawthorns. Though his appearances became limited in 1935–36, Hetherington still managed to find the net and it was a surprise to see him leave for Swindon Town. He spent almost two seasons at the County Ground before leaving to play for Watford, where injuries hampered his progress.

HEYES, Kenneth

Full-back

Born: Haydock, 4 January 1936.
Career: Everton, 1953. PRESTON NORTH END, 1957.

■ England Youth international full-back Ken Heyes joined Everton straight from school but, despite his impressive displays in the club's Central League side, he could not force his way into the Blues' side. In the summer of 1957 he joined Preston but his opportunities at Deepdale were limited due to the fine form of Cunningham, Wilson and Walton. Heyes made the first of three appearances for North End in a 1–1 draw at Manchester United in February 1960. Later in the season he appeared in a further two games including a 5–3 defeat of Blackburn Rovers. Released at the end of the season, he drifted into the local non-League scene.

HIBBERT David John

Forward

Born: Eccleshall, 28 January 1986
Career: Port Vale 2004; PRESTON NORTH END 2005

■ The tall striker experienced the highs and lows of football during the 2004–05 season, his first with his local club, Port Vale. He made his debut for the Valiants off the bench at Chesterfield

before impressing on his full debut against Barnsley in the LDV Vans Trophy. Unfortunately, he then damaged a knee ligament which kept him out of action for over four months. On his return he made a sensational League debut against Luton Town, scoring twice in a 3–1 win. A couple of weeks later he was knocked unconscious during the game at MK Dons and had to be airlifted to hospital in an air ambulance. Though he was forced to miss the end of the season there was no lasting damage and in the close season he joined Preston North End for a tribunal-set fee of £85,000. His only start for the club came in the FA Cup tie against Crystal Palace when, on his 20th birthday, he replaced the suspended David Nugent. Manager Billy Davies hailed his performance, saying with any

luck he could have scored three goals as North End's makeshift side battled to hold their promotion rivals. Though all his League appearances have come from the bench, there is little doubt that Dave Hibbert is a confident and good young talent.

HICKS, Stuart Jason

Centre-half

Born: Peterborough, 30 May 1967.
Career: Peterborough United, 1984. Wisbech Town. Colchester United, 1988. Scunthorpe United, 1990. Doncaster Rovers, 1992. Huddersfield Town, 1993. PRESTON NORTH END, 1994. Scarborough, 1995. Leyton Orient, 1997. Chester City, 2000. Mansfield Town, 2000. Hucknall Town.

■ Unable to make much headway with his home-town club, Peterborough United, defensive strongman Stuart Hicks played non-League football for Wisbech Town before joining Colchester United in March 1988. Following the

Layer Road club's demotion to the Conference, Hicks joined Scunthorpe United and in 1991–92, his final season with the club, led them to promotion from the Fourth Division via the Play-offs. Hicks then played for Doncaster Rovers and Huddersfield Town before joining North End towards the end of the 1993–94 season. Unfortunately, North End did not win any of the four games in that season's run-in which Hicks appeared in. He played in the 4–1 Play-off semi-final second leg against Torquay United, the last game on the Deepdale plastic pitch, but did not make the side for the Wembley final against Wycombe Wanderers. He started the following season as the club's first-choice centre-half but left to play for Scarborough. He proceeded to give the Yorkshire club great service and was their Player of the Year in 1995–96. Hicks' next club was Leyton Orient and he helped them reach the Play-off Final in 1998–99. He left Orient to join Chester City despite being hugely popular at Brisbane Road. Unable to prevent the Cestrians' demotion to the Conference, he left for Mansfield Town. Sadly he suffered a cruciate knee ligament injury and was out of action for a long time before leaving Field Mill.

HICKS, Thomas George

Left-back

Born: Trehafod, 1903.
Career: Pontypridd. PRESTON NORTH END, 1924. Nottingham Forest, 1927. Northampton Town, 1928. Chester.

■ Tommy Hicks arrived at Deepdale in 1924 after attracting the attention of a number of top League clubs. He made his debut in a 2–0 home defeat at the hands of Burnley during the early part of the 1924–25 campaign. After playing in a 4–0 defeat at Leeds a week later in which he was deemed responsible for two of the Yorkshire club's goals, he was dropped. Hicks did not appear again until the following season when he played in a handful of games. He played his last game in February 1927 and left to continue his career with Nottingham Forest. He then had a spell with Northampton Town, helping them finish third in the Third Division South in 1928–29, before seeing out his career with Chester.

HIGHAM, Peter

Centre-forward

Born: Wigan, 8 November 1930.
Career: Wigan Athletic. Portsmouth, 1949.
Bolton Wanderers, 1950. PRESTON
NORTH END, 1952. Nottingham Forest,
1955. Doncaster Rovers, 1958.

■ Peter Higham made just a handful of appearances for his home-town team, Wigan Athletic, before he joined Portsmouth. The competition for forward places was tough at Pompey and he made just one League appearance for the South Coast club before returning to the North West with Bolton Wanderers. Unable to break into the Burnden Park club's side, he left to try his luck with Preston. After a season in the club's Central League side, he made his debut in a 3–1 win at his former club Portsmouth midway through the 1953–54 season. The following season, Higham scored 10 goals in 14 League games including a spectacular hat-trick in a 6–0 defeat of Sheffield Wednesday. Despite this good goalscoring ratio, he could not hold down a regular place and moved to Nottingham Forest, where he helped Forest win promotion to the First Division in 1956–57. After almost three years at the City Ground in which he scored 20 goals in 61 games, Higham left to end his playing days at Doncaster Rovers.

HILDERSLEY, Ronald

Midfield

Born: Kirkcaldy, 6 April 1965.
Career: Manchester City, 1983. Chester
City, 1984 (loan). Chester City, 1984.
Rochdale, 1985. PRESTON NORTH
END, 1986. Cambridge United, 1988
(loan). Blackburn Rovers, 1988. Wigan
Athletic, 1990. Halifax Town, 1991.

■ Much-travelled midfielder Ronnie Hildersley worked his way up through the ranks at Maine Road and made his Football League debut for Manchester City in a 4–1 reversal at Swansea in March 1983. Midway through the following season, he went on loan to Chester City before joining the Cestrians on a permanent basis in the summer of 1984. After an injury-hit season at Sealand Road, Hildersley joined

Rochdale on a non-contract basis before signing for North End in June 1986. After making his debut on the opening day of the 1986–87 season in a 1–1 draw at Tranmere Rovers, he went on to appear in 33 League games as the club won promotion from the Fourth Division as runners-up to Northampton Town. He was a regular the following season as North End consolidated their position in the higher grade of football but, following a loan spell with Cambridge, he signed for North End's rivals, Blackburn Rovers. Despite injuries hampering his progress at Ewood Park, when he did play he continued to play every game to the best of his ability as Rovers challenged for a place in the top flight. Hildersley later had a brief spell with Wigan Athletic before ending his first-class career with Halifax Town.

HILL, Matthew Clayton

Defender

Born: Bristol, 26 March 1981.
Career: Bristol City, 1999. PRESTON
NORTH END, 2005.

■ Matthew Hill graduated from Bristol City's successful academy set-up and made his first-team debut in the

Ashton Gate club's demoralising 5–0 home defeat by Wolves in the 1999–2000 season. The following season he was voted the club's Young Player of the Year after impressing with his tigerish tackling and speedy recovery. Despite suffering knee ligament damage in 2001–02, Hill was voted City's Player of the Year and, for the second successive season, the Young Player of the Year. The following season Hill helped the Robins to victory in the 2–0 LDV Vans Trophy Final success over Carlisle United and in 2003–04 he was one of the club's most consistent players as they came near to promotion via the Play-offs. He had appeared in 246 games for Bristol City when he was sold to Preston North End for £100,000 in January 2005. Comfortable anywhere in the back four or on the left side of midfield, he shared the left-hand side with Callum Davidson and Eddie Lewis and built up excellent partnerships with both players. Matt Hill suffered a number of injuries throughout the 2005–06 season, none worse than the sickening clash of heads with Plymouth's Paul Connolly. The horrendous injury ruled him out of action for a while, though he was in the North End side for the first leg of the Play-off semi-final against Leeds.

HINDLE, John

Goalkeeper

Born: Preston, 10 November 1921.
Died: 1987.
Career: Clifton BC. PRESTON NORTH
END, 1946. Barrow, 1948. Aston Villa,
1950. Barrow, 1951.

■ Goalkeeper Jack Hindle found his path blocked at Deepdale by both Jack Fairbrother and Jimmy Gooch and after just one League appearance in a 2–1 defeat of Grimsby Town, he decided to move to Barrow. He had though already made his first-team debut for Preston the previous week as deputy for the injured Gooch in the FA Cup sixth-round tie at Manchester United, which the Reds won 1–0. Hindle's impressive displays for Barrow prompted First Division Aston Villa to secure his services and he played in 15 games in his only season with the Midlands club. He later rejoined Barrow and took his total of League appearances in his two spells for the club to 266 before deciding to retire.

HINNIGAN, Joseph Peter

Full-back

Born: Liverpool, 3 December 1955.
Career: South Liverpool. Wigan Athletic,
1975. Sunderland, 1980. PRESTON
NORTH END, 1982. Gillingham, 1984.
Wrexham, 1987. Chester City, 1988.

■ After being released by both Everton and Aston Villa, a coach of the Kirkby Sunday League side took Joe Hinnigan to South Liverpool. Here he played for the club's youth XI and helped them reach three finals, one of which was against Wigan Athletic. Within a matter of months he was playing in the Northern Premier League where more impressive performances led to him joining the Latics in the summer of 1975. After appearing in 120 Northern Premier League games for Wigan, he made his Football League debut on the opening day of the 1978–79 season at Hereford United. Hinnigan wrote himself into the Latics' history books when he scored the club's first Football League goal in a 3–2 defeat at home to Newport County. On leaving Springfield Park, he joined Sunderland for £135,000 and appeared in the last 14 games of the 1979–80

season, helping the Wearsiders win promotion to the top flight and never playing in a losing side. In December 1982, Hinnigan joined Preston North End and made his debut in a 2–1 home win over Cardiff City. Again he seemed to bring good luck as he was only on the losing side once in 13 games. He missed very few games in 1983–84 until he was surprisingly allowed to join Gillingham whom he helped finish near the top of the Third Division for three consecutive seasons. After a season with Wrexham, Hinnigan ended his career with Chester City. He later became the club's physiotherapist, a position he later held with Wrexham.

HIRST, Henry

Full-back

Born: Horbury, 24 October 1899.
Career: Rotherham County, 1921.
PRESTON NORTH END, 1924. Queen's
Park Rangers, 1925. Charlton Athletic,
1926. Thames.

■ Unable to win a regular place at his first club, Rotherham County, Harry Hirst joined the Lilywhites in the summer of 1924. Although he was a strong-tackling full-back, he made his two appearances for North End at right-half. His last game in Preston colours came in a 4–0 defeat at Arsenal, the club that finished the 1924–25 season just one

place above the relegated Deepdale club. He did not have any better luck at his next club, Queen's Park Rangers, who finished bottom of the Third Division South in Hirst's only season at the club. He later had spells with Charlton Athletic and Thames before hanging up his boots.

HODGE, Martin John

Goalkeeper

Born: Southport, 4 February 1959.
Career: Plymouth Argyle, 1977. Everton,
1979. PRESTON NORTH END, 1981
(loan). Oldham Athletic, 1982 (loan).
Gillingham, 1983 (loan). PRESTON
NORTH END, 1983 (loan). Sheffield
Wednesday, 1983. Leicester City, 1988.
Hartlepool United, 1991. Rochdale, 1993.
Plymouth Argyle, 1994.

■ Martin Hodge was an underrated goalkeeper who was signed by Everton manager Gordon Lee from Plymouth Argyle for a fee of £135,000 in the summer of 1979. Initially understudy to George Wood, he ousted the Scottish international and played for Everton in the following season's FA Cup semi-final against West Ham United. The breakthrough was temporary as Jim McDonagh, Jim Arnold and then Neville Southall took over between the posts. Predictably, Hodge had four periods on loan, two of them with Preston North End. His first stint began in December 1981 and he made his debut in a goalless draw at Chesterfield. Hodge appeared in 28 League games and kept 12 clean sheets for a Preston side that finished the campaign in mid-table. His second loan spell at Deepdale came in February 1983 when he replaced the injured Peter Litchfield. He managed seven clean sheets in his 13 games. After these loan spells, he opted for a fresh start with another club and joined Sheffield Wednesday for £50,000. He took the chance of the Owls number-one shirt with both hands. As Wednesday tore into the First Division after storming to promotion in 1983–84, he proved a revelation between the posts. His fine form put him in line for a call-up to the England squad for the 1986 World Cup, but he missed out at the last minute. He later served Leicester City with distinction and had spells with

Hartlepool and Rochdale before ending his first-class career back at Home Park with his first club, Plymouth Argyle.

HODGSON, Thomas

Right-half, centre-half

Born: Preston, 1878.
Career: PRESTON NORTH END, 1899.

■ Tommy Hodgson made just four appearances for Preston North End over two seasons with the Deepdale club, but was never on the winning side. The nearest he came was in a 1–1 draw against soon-to-be-relegated Burnley at home in December 1899. He played in two successive games in 1900–01 but the club released him at the end of a season in which they lost their First Division status.

HODGSON, William H

Inside-left

Born: Preston, 1887.
Career: PRESTON NORTH END, 1908.

■ Inside-left Billy Hodgson's only appearance in the 1908–09 season came in a 1–1 home draw against Middlesbrough. His two appearances the following season also ended in draws, but despite his promise he could not force his way into the side due to the form of Arthur Mountenay. In the close season, he parted company with the Lilywhites.

HOLBEM, Walter

Left-back, centre-half

Born: Sheffield, 1884.
Died: 1930.
Career: Heeley Friends. Sheffield Wednesday, 1906. Everton, 1911. St Mirren. PRESTON NORTH END, 1913.

■ Versatile defender Walter Holbem began his career with Sheffield Wednesday, helping them to finish fifth in the First Division in seasons 1907–08 and 1908–09. He had played in 86 League games in five seasons with the Owls when he left to play for Everton. Unable to win a permanent place in the Merseyside club's side, he tried his luck north of the border with St Mirren before returning to Football League action with Preston North End. Holbem made his first appearance for the Lilywhites in a 1–0 defeat at West Bromwich Albion midway through the 1913–14 season but, despite some good individual performances, he could not prevent the club's relegation to the Second Division. He continued to make telling contributions the following season and helped North End win promotion back to the top flight at the first attempt. During World War One, Holbem was arrested for being an absentee under the Military Services Act and after being fined was handed over to the Army authorities.

HOLDCROFT, George Henry

Goalkeeper

Born: Burslem, 23 January 1909.
Died: 1983.
Career: Biddulph. Norton Druids. Whitfield Colliery. Port Vale, 1926. Darlington, 1928. Everton, 1931. PRESTON NORTH END, 1932. Barnsley, 1945. Morecambe. Chorley. Leyland Motors.

■ Burslem-born goalkeeper Harry Holdcroft had played for a number of local clubs – Biddulph, Norton Druids and Whitfield Colliery – before signing for Port Vale. Unable to gain a regular place in the Valiants' side, he was quickly snapped up by Darlington before being transferred to Everton as cover for Ted Sagar. In December 1932, the North End management team produced a brilliant stroke by signing both Holdcroft and hard-tackling full-back Harold Lowe for a bargain price from the Goodison club. After making his debut in a 1–0 defeat at Southampton on Christmas Eve 1932, Holdcroft went on to play in 172 consecutive League and Cup games following his debut. In his first full season he helped North End win promotion to the First Division with a series of outstanding displays between the posts. Ironically, the first time Holdcroft was missing from the North End line up, against Stoke, was due to the fact that he was playing for England against Wales on 17 October 1936. That same season, North End reached the FA Cup semi-final but Holdcroft broke a finger against Middlesbrough the week before the game and missed the semi-final and the Final itself against Sunderland. The following season, North

End returned to Wembley and defeated Huddersfield Town 1–0 in the Final. Harry Holdcroft was in goal keeping yet another clean sheet. After 289 League and Cup games 'Handsome Harry', as he was known, found his life interrupted by World War Two just as he was in his

prime. Although he played occasionally during the war, 'guesting' for Burnley, Oldham Athletic and Manchester United amongst others, his North End career was at an end. He later signed for Barnsley before playing non-League football with Morecambe, Chorley and Leyland Motors.

HOLDEN, Albert Douglas

Winger

Born: Manchester, 28 September 1930.
Career: Bolton Wanderers, 1950. PRESTON NORTH END, 1962.

■ Able to play on either flank, Doug Holden joined Bolton Wanderers as an amateur in 1948 and appeared for the England Youth side before completing his National Service. He made his League debut for the Trotters in a 1–1 draw against Liverpool at Anfield in November 1951 and quickly proved that he possessed the temperament for the big occasion. Holden had only made 12 Central League appearances before his promotion to the first team. Though he played primarily on the left-wing, it was on the opposite flank that he made a name for himself in the 1953 FA Cup Final. Five years later he reverted to the left-wing for the 1958 FA Cup Final against Manchester United which Bolton won 2–0. Holden and Nat Lofthouse were the only Bolton players to appear in both finals. In March 1959 he played for the Football League against the Irish League and, after impressing in that match, he was selected for the full England side against Scotland at Wembley. In November 1962 he left to join Preston North End after scoring 44 goals in 463 games for the Wanderers. He made his North End debut in a 2–1 reversal at Sunderland and soon proved himself a worthy addition to a lengthy list of mature, ready-made players who went to Preston after earning their reputations elsewhere. He fitted ideally into the intended role. At the small fee he cost, Holden was a bargain. He showed he had not lost his craft and know-how with a brilliant performance in the FA Cup semi-final win over Swansea and a goal in the 3–2 defeat by West Ham United in the Final. Doug Holden was one of the unluckiest players when

shooting. Often the ball somehow managed to find its way onto the woodwork or else a defender miraculously got in the way. His chief asset was his ability to work in a confined space. Often there did not seem room to squeeze a football between the line and the full-back but somehow he got through. After ending his League career at Deepdale, he emigrated to Australia where he played for the national side.

HOLDEN, Melville George

Forward

Born: Dundee, 25 August 1954.
Died: 1981.
Career: PRESTON NORTH END, 1972. Sunderland, 1975. Blackpool, 1978.

■ Mel Holden made his North End debut towards the end of the 1972–73 season after which he was a regular in the Deepdale club's side. His best season in terms of goals scored was 1974–75 when he topped the club's scoring charts with 22 goals in all competitions. This total included his first hat-trick for the club in a 5–1 FA Cup first-round replay win over non-League Blyth Spartans. Holden came close to netting another treble in North End's next match but, after scoring twice in a 4–0 defeat of Huddersfield Town, his last-minute header struck the bar. This form prompted Sunderland to pay

£120,000 for his services in the close season. In his first season at Roker Park, he netted 13 goals and helped the Wearsiders win promotion to the First Division. Though the North East club were relegated after just one season in the top flight, Holden more than held his own, scoring 10 goals. He had scored 26 goals in 94 games for Sunderland when Blackpool paid £60,000 in the summer of 1978 to take him to Bloomfield Road. Mel Holden fell ill while with the Seasiders and sadly died from motor neurone disease at the age of only 26.

HOLDSWORTH, Edward

Right-half

Born: Halifax, 1884.
Career: Southport Central. PRESTON NORTH END, 1907. Swansea Town, 1920.

■ Signed from Southport Central, right-half Eddie Holdsworth played his first game in North End colours at the latter end of the 1907–08 season as they were held to a goalless draw at home to Sheffield United. Though he won a regular place in the side the following season, there was one occasion when he did not please the club's management. On New Year's Day, North End visited Ewood Park for the local derby against Blackburn Rovers and Holdsworth did not set foot on the pitch until the game had been underway for over five minutes. The result was a 1–1 draw but Holdsworth was fined one guinea for his late appearance. Over the next few seasons, Holdsworth worked hard in midfield trying to prompt the club's attack but even he could do little to prevent North End from being relegated in 1911–12. His best season in North End colours came in 1912–13 as the club returned to the top flight as Champions of the Second Division. He was ever present and two of his career total of three League goals were scored during this campaign. With Holdsworth still an important member of the side, North End were again relegated in 1913–14 but they repeated the achievement of two seasons previous by winning promotion at the first attempt. When League football resumed in 1919–20, Holdsworth was still a member of the club's First Division side but parted company with the Lilywhites midway through the season to see out his career with Swansea Town.

HOLLAND, Christopher James

Midfield

Born: Whalley, 11 September 1975.
Career: PRESTON NORTH END, 1993. Newcastle United, 1994. Birmingham City, 1996. Huddersfield Town, 2000. Boston United, 2004.

■ Chris Holland's only appearance in North End's League side was as a substitute for Trevor Matthewson in a 2–2 draw at Wigan Athletic in October 1993. However, he had given Newcastle United's management team glimpses of a talented repertoire which prompted the Magpies to pay £100,000 for his signature. An unpleasant incident in a nightclub in which ammonia was thrown in his face almost cost him the sight in his right eye. Happily he recovered and won selection for the England Under-21 side. In December 1995 he was called up to train with the full England squad. Finding his first-team opportunities at St James' Park limited, Holland moved to Birmingham City for £600,000 in September 1996. A busy and inventive player, he played for

the Football League Under-21 side that drew with Italian Serie 'B' in February 1997. Injuries hampered his progress and he became more of a fringe player. In February 2000 he moved to Huddersfield Town for a fee of £150,000. He brought a new dimension to the Terriers' midfield until he was sidelined by an Achilles injury, a broken toe and finally a hernia. He left the McAlpine Stadium to join Boston United where, after a first good season, he struggled to hold down a first-team place.

HOLLAND, John

Inside-forward

Born: Preston, 3 April 1901.
Career: PRESTON NORTH END, 1920. Swansea Town, 1923. Wrexham, 1925. Crewe Alexandra, 1925. Newport County, 1926. Clapton Orient, 1927. Carlisle United, 1929. Barrow, 1930. Darvel. Blackpool, 1932.

■ Much-travelled inside-forward Jack Holland played locally with Roebuck schoolboys under the tuition of former North End full-back Jack Winchester. He started his League career with his home-town club, Preston North End, making the first of six League appearances in a 1–1 draw at Derby County in January 1921. He went on to appear in a handful of League and Cup games that season. He appeared in a couple of games the following season but, unable to displace Jefferies or Woodhouse, he moved on to Swansea Town. In his second season at the Vetch Field, he helped the Swans win the Third Division South Championship. Holland then had season-long spells with Wrexham, Crewe, Newport and Clapton Orient, before joining Carlisle United where he had his best return of goals scored – 13 in 33 games – before seeing out his career with Barrow and finally Blackpool.

HOLMES, John

Wing-half

Born: Preston, 1870.
Career: PRESTON NORTH END, 1891. Liverpool, 1895. Burton Swifts, 1898. New Brighton Tower, 1899.

■ Wing-half John Holmes played his first game for the Lilywhites in a 3–0 win

over Derby County in what was his only appearance of the 1891–92 season. He played on a more regular basis the following season as Preston finished runners-up in the First Division for the second consecutive campaign. With North End struggling to hold on to their top-flight status in 1893–94, Holmes left Deepdale to continue his career with Liverpool. In his first season with his new club, he helped them win the Second Division Championship. He went on to play in 42 League games before moving on to Burton Swifts and finally New Brighton Tower, both of whom were struggling at the foot of the Second Division table.

HOLMES, Robert

Full-back

Born: Preston, 23 June 1867.
Died: November 1955.
Career: Preston Olympic. PRESTON NORTH END, 1888.

■ Bob Holmes was the longest-serving survivor of the Preston North End team known as the 'Invincibles' when he died aged 88 in November 1955. Holmes made his Football League debut in the first-ever League game against Burnley, although he had already played in North End's FA Cup Final defeat of 1888 and represented England. He played in all 22 of Preston's 1888–89 League Championship-winning matches and 19 the following season when they retained the title. As well as his seven appearances for England, all at left-back, he appeared in two Cup finals for his club, gaining a winners' medal in 1889. Holmes, who was never on the losing side in his seven appearances for England, also represented the Football League but his greatest accolade came on 13 March 1894 when he captained his country in the 6–0 defeat of Wales. Holmes, who later became President of the Football Players' Union, retired at the end of the 1899–1900 season but was retained on the club's books as an amateur. He actually played the last of his 300 League games on Boxing Day 1902, when North End went down 2–0 to Manchester City. His only League goal for the club came in a 1–1 draw against Burnley on 19 October 1895, though he

did score against Birmingham in North End's FA Cup-winning season of 1888–89. On hanging up his boots he took up refereeing but in December 1903 he resigned his position after securing a business in Preston town centre. In April 1908 he was appointed trainer to the England amateur international team to play in Belgium and Germany over Easter of that year.

HOLMES, Steven Peter

Centre-half, midfield

Born: Middlesbrough, 13 January 1971.
Career: Lincoln City, 1989. Gainsborough Trinity. Guisborough Town. PRESTON NORTH END, 1994. Hartlepool United, 1995 (loan). Lincoln City, 1995 (loan). Lincoln City, 1996. Dunston FB.

■ Unable to make the grade initially with Lincoln City, central defender Steve Holmes drifted into non-League football with Gainsborough Trinity and then Guisborough Town. North End manager John Beck gave him his chance at League level when he signed for the Lilywhites in March 1994. Holmes made his Preston debut in a 1–0 home defeat at the hands of lowly Exeter City – a match in which he could have scored a hat-trick – before scoring his only goal for the club in a 3–0 win over Hartlepool United. This result helped clinch the club's place in the

1994–95 Play-offs. He appeared in eight games during North End's Third Division Championship-winning season before he had loan spells with Hartlepool and Lincoln City. Holmes then joined the Imps on a permanent basis. While at Sincil Bank, he played a number of games in central midfield. In 1998–99 he was voted the club's Player of the Season. Later appointed Lincoln's captain, he suffered a slipped disc in his neck but recovered to end the 2000–01 season as the club's leading scorer with the remarkable tally for a defender of 11 goals. Eventually injuries caught up with him, but by the time he parted company with the club in the summer of 2002 he had appeared in 230 League and Cup games.

HOLT, Michael Andrew

Forward

Born: Burnley, 28 July 1977.
Career: Blackburn Rovers, 1995. PRESTON NORTH END, 1996. Macclesfield Town, 1998 (loan). Rochdale, 1998. Northwich Victoria (loan). St Patrick's Athletic.

■ A young striker signed by Preston from rivals Blackburn Rovers during the summer of 1996, Michael Holt received an early chance in the 1996–97 season through injuries to senior players. He

scored a 90th minute equaliser on his full debut against Spurs in the Milk Cup and became an immediate hit with the fans. During a good run in the first team, he demonstrated an all-action style, though he was occasionally a little over-enthusiastic in his attempts to close down defenders. After missing the target during the home defeat by Bournemouth in 1997–98, Holt went on loan to Macclesfield at the start of the following season before joining Rochdale. He ended his first season at Spotland as joint-top scorer but then struggled to find the net, although he did score when he came on as a substitute in the Auto Windscreens Shield Northern Final. Released in the close season he went to try his luck in the League of Ireland with St Patrick's Athletic.

HORNE, Alfred

Outside-right, inside-forward

Born: Birmingham, 1903.
Died: 1976.
Career: Alvechurch. West Bromwich Albion, 1923. Stafford Rangers. Hull City, 1925. Southend United, 1927. Manchester City, 1927. PRESTON NORTH END, 1929. Lincoln City, 1932. Mansfield Town, 1936.

■ Alf Horne was unable to make the grade with West Bromwich Albion and moved into non-League football with Stafford Rangers where his goalscoring exploits attracted the attention of Hull City. He failed to deliver the goods at Boothferry Park and joined Southend United whom he helped challenge for promotion from the Third Division South. After a brief spell with Manchester City, Horne arrived at Deepdale before the start of the 1929–30 season. Although he did not score on his debut he created three of Bobby Crawford's four goals in a 5–1 defeat of Stoke. He did score both of North End's goals in a 2–2 draw against Bradford City as the two clubs fought out a relegation battle. Injuries curtailed his appearances the following season and he later left the club to play for Lincoln City. Horne spent five seasons at Sincil Bank, scoring 36 goals in 166 League games and helping the Imps finish fourth in the Third Division South in consecutive seasons. He later ended his career with Mansfield Town, his seventh League club.

HORTON, Joseph Kenneth

Wing-half, inside-forward

Born: Preston, 26 August 1922.
Career: PRESTON NORTH END, 1945. Hull City, 1952. Barrow, 1955.

■ Ken Horton worked his way up through the ranks of his home-town club to make his debut in the number-four shirt for North End's first League game following World War Two – a 3–2 win over Leeds United. Bill Shankly returned to the side for the following game and it was 1947–48 before Horton won a regular place in the side. That season he missed just one game but still did not get on the score sheet. In 1948–49 he was powerless to stop the club from being relegated. In his first game as an inside-forward, Horton scored the winner in a 3–2 defeat of Queen's Park Rangers. In North End's Second Division Championship-winning season of 1950–51, he scored 23 goals. Forming a formidable strike partnership with Charlie Wayman, who netted 29 goals, Horton netted his first hat-trick for the club in the 7–0 demolition of Barnsley.

During the early part of the 1952–53 season, Horton moved to Hull City and spent three seasons playing for the Tigers before ending his first-class career with a season at Barrow.

HOSKER, John

Inside-left

Born: Preston, 15 February 1894.
Career: Lancaster Town. PRESTON NORTH END, 1919. Accrington Stanley, 1921. Morecambe.

■ A prolific scorer with Lancaster Town, inside-left John Hosker joined Preston for the start of the club's 1919–20 season of First Division football. After making his debut in a 2–1 home win over Oldham Athletic, he netted his first goal for the club in the return game at Boundary Park a week later, a match the Latics won 4–1. Hosker never really came to terms with First Division football and early the following season he moved to Accrington Stanley, who were playing in the Third Division North in what was their first season of League football following the re-formation of the club. Hosker helped them finish fifth in that 1921–22 season and went on to score 29 goals in 104 games before ending his playing days with another spell of non-League football, this time with Morecambe.

HOUGH, William Arthur

Right-back, wing-half

Born: Greenfield, 4 March 1908.
Career: Holywell Arcadians. New Brighton, 1930. PRESTON NORTH END, 1931. Blackburn Rovers, 1937.

■ Billy Hough had played just a handful of League games for New Brighton when he arrived at Deepdale for the 1931–32 season. Over the next couple of campaigns, Hough showed his versatility by playing in a number of positions but he was wearing the number-two shirt by the time of North End's Second Division promotion-winning season of 1933–34. An injury in the 5–3 defeat by Arsenal at Highbury midway through the following season kept Hough on the sidelines for a while and he did not play at all in 1935–36. Following a handful of appearances the

following season, he left Deepdale to join Blackburn Rovers. In the seasons leading up to the outbreak of World War Two, he played in 52 games and helped the club win the Second Division Championship in 1938–39.

HOUGHTON, Peter

Forward

Born: Liverpool, 30 November 1954.
Career: Prescot Town. South Liverpool. Wigan Athletic, 1978. PRESTON NORTH END, 1983. Wrexham, 1984 (loan). Chester City, 1985. Runcorn.

■ A member of the Liverpool Schools' Football Association squad which won the English Schools' Trophy, Peter Houghton joined Prescot Town where he won a Mid-Cheshire League Championship medal. He later moved to South Liverpool from where he was eventually signed by Wigan Athletic in January 1978. After helping the Latics finish runners-up to Boston in that seasons Northern Premier League, he made his Football League debut in the club's first-ever game in the competition at Hereford on the opening day of the 1978–79 season. Despite being handicapped by injuries he ended the season as the club's leading scorer with 14 goals including a hat-trick in a 5–3 defeat of Port Vale. Houghton topped the club's charts again the following season while in 1980–81 he netted his second treble in a 3–2 win at Tranmere Rovers. He formed a formidable strike force with Les Bradd that helped Wigan win promotion to the Third Division in 1981–82. Houghton's 17 goals included another hat-trick in a 6–3 win at Doncaster Rovers. In October 1983 he was allowed to leave Springfield Park to play for Preston North End. Following a disappointing debut in a 2–0 defeat at Gillingham, Houghton scored six goals in a 10–game spell midway through the season. Though he only played in 24 games in the club's relegation season of 1984–85, he still ended the campaign as leading scorer with just six goals. He later played for Chester City, whose manager was former Wigan boss Harry McNally, before ending his playing days with non-League Runcorn. Houghton later worked in the car manufacturing industry.

HOUSTON, Graham Robert

Winger

Born: Gibraltar, 24 February 1960.
Career: PRESTON NORTH END, 1978.
Burnley, 1985. Wigan Athletic, 1986.
Northwich Victoria. Carlisle United, 1987.

■ Gibraltar-born winger Graham Houston began his Football League career with Preston North End after working his way up through the ranks at Deepdale. He made his debut for the Lilywhites as a substitute for Brian Taylor in a 3–0 home defeat by Queen's Park Rangers in February 1980 before establishing himself as a first-team regular towards the end of the following season. After that he was an important member of the North End squad until the club's relegation in 1984–85 when he left to join Burnley as a non-contract player. Unable to break into the Clarets' first team he spent a season languishing in the club's Central League side before moving to Wigan Athletic. Released at the end of his only season with the Latics, he had a spell playing non-League football with Northwich Victoria before ending his first-class career with Carlisle United.

HOWARTH, Robert Henry

Full-back

Born: Preston, 1865.
Died: 1938.

Career: PRESTON NORTH END, 1888.
Everton, 1891. PRESTON NORTH END,
1894.

■ A former Excelsior rugby player, Bob Howarth made his first-team debut for North End on Shrove Tuesday 1883 against Battersea Old Collegians, a match the Lilywhites won 18–3. A powerful and formidable full-back, he soon established his reputation and within two years had played for Lancashire. In 1886 he represented the North against the South in one of the game's top fixtures of the day. By the time he made his Football League debut for North End, he had already appeared in two FA Cup semi-finals, a Final and played for England. While in the club's reserves he began to forge a great partnership with Bob Holmes and, although they were parted by Howarth's graduation to first-team football, they were soon to become a renowned combination for both North End and England. Indeed the names of Howarth and Holmes were inseparable for a good number of years – Howarth eventually qualifying as a solicitor and working in the town and Holmes becoming trainer of rivals Blackburn Rovers. Howarth had made 50 League appearances for North

End when in November 1891 he left Deepdale to join Everton. He played in another losing FA Cup Final, captaining the Blues when they lost 1–0 to Wolves. Like Nick Ross before him, he later returned to Deepdale but was only really used in an emergency. Playing his last game against Notts County in March 1899, some 16 years after making his debut, he then concentrated on his solicitor's practice.

HOWELL, Rabbi

Wing-half

Born: Wincobank, 12 October 1867.
Died: 1937.
Career: Ecclesfield. Rotherham Swifts.
Sheffield United, 1892. Liverpool, 1897.
PRESTON NORTH END, 1901.

■ Despite standing only 5ft 5in, Rabbi Howell started his career as a rather diminutive centre-half before he was converted to a wing-half by Sheffield United. Howell was a gypsy, born in a caravan and perhaps the only British gypsy to earn a full international cap for England. During his last season with the Blades, he helped them finish runners-up in the First Division but then joined Liverpool. In his last season with the Reds he went one better by helping them win the First Division Championship. Transferred to Preston, he made his Lilywhites debut on the opening day of the 1901–02 season as North End went down 3–1 at West Bromwich Albion. Howell played in 26 games that season and scored his only goal for the club in the 8–0 mauling of Lincoln City. He missed very few games the following season but in September 1903 he broke his leg after just five minutes of the home match with Burnley. The North End fans were so upset that a collection was immediately taken at the ground. Though Howell never played football again, North End went on to win that season's Second Division Championship.

HUDSON, Gary

Goalkeeper

Born: West Auckland, 1 November 1955.
Career: PRESTON NORTH END, 1973.

■ In 1973–74, a season that North End had the services of three experienced goalkeepers in Alan Kelly, John Brown and Ron Healey, young Gary Hudson played his only Football League match for the Deepdale club in the local derby against Bolton Wanderers. He certainly did not let the side down, making a number of vital saves in a 2–1 win for North End.

HUGHES, Adrian Francis

Centre-half

Born: Billinge, 19 December 1970.
Career: PRESTON NORTH END, 1989.

■ YTS trainee Adrian Hughes made his debut for North End in a 2–1 reversal

at home to Notts County on the final day of the 1987–88 season. He played in almost half the club's games the following season. Hughes was an important member of the Preston side for the next couple of seasons, appearing in exactly 100 League games. More than useful at set pieces, he scored the first of nine League goals in a 3–1 defeat of neighbours Bolton Wanderers midway through the 1988–89 season. However, he also suffered more than his fair share of injuries and in 1992 he parted company with the club.

HUGHES, David Robert

Winger

Born: Blackburn, 7 September 1948.
Career: PRESTON NORTH END, 1965. Southport, 1972. Bury, 1973. Southport, 1973. Crewe Alexandra, 1978.

■ Winger David Hughes spent five seasons at Deepdale, but during that time he made just 31 League appearances following his debut in a 4–0 defeat at Cardiff City in April 1967. His greatest number of appearances came in 1970–71 when he played in 19 games of North End's Third Division Championship-winning season. Though he never got on the score sheet himself, he laid on a number of crosses for Gerry Ingram and Bobby Ham to take advantage of. After one more season at Deepdale he left to play for Southport, helping them to win the Fourth Division title in his first season at Haig Avenue. His form for the Sandgrounders led to Bury taking him to Gigg Lane in the summer of 1973, but he never really settled there and rejoined Southport. Hughes took his total League appearances in his two spells to 153 before ending his career at Crewe Alexandra.

HUGHES, George

Goalkeeper
Career: Runcorn. PRESTON NORTH END, 1931.

■ With North End conceding far too many goals at the start of the 1931–32 season, manager Lincoln Hyde signed Runcorn goalkeeper George Hughes. However, on his debut at home to Port Vale he too was beaten with ease as the

Valiants won 4–1. Hughes though kept his place in the side for a run of 11 games. He kept two clean sheets but conceded four goals in a game on three occasions. George Wolf, who had lost his place to Hughes, returned to the side and Hughes moved on to pastures new.

HUMES, James

Winger

Born: Carlisle, 6 August 1942.
Career: PRESTON NORTH END, 1959. Bristol Rovers, 1962. Chester City, 1963. Barnsley, 1967.

■ Winger Jimmy Humes replaced the injured Sammy Taylor for the visit to Nottingham Forest in March 1960, a game that North End drew 1–1. He also appeared just once the following season as North End lost their First Division status, but played on a more regular basis in 1961–62, scoring his only goal for the club in a 3–2 home win over Leyton Orient. Humes left Deepdale in search of regular first-team football but made only a couple of appearances at his next club, Bristol Rovers, and moved on to Chester City. At Sealand Road he scored 31 goals in 124 League games, helping the Cestrians to a best finish of seventh in Division Four in 1965–66. He later ended his career with Barnsley.

HUNTER, Christopher Paul

Forward

Born: Hong Kong, 18 January 1964.
Career: PRESTON NORTH END, 1981. Chorley. PRESTON NORTH END, 1984.

■ Chris Hunter worked his way up through the club's junior and reserve sides to replace an injured Alex Bruce in a 3–0 defeat at Newport County in February 1983. With fierce competition for places in North End's forward line, Hunter left Deepdale to play non-League football for Chorley where he rediscovered his shooting boots. Hunter rejoined the Lilywhites before the start of the club's relegation season of 1984–85 and, though he failed to find the net in his six League outings, he did score North End's goal in the humiliating 4–1 FA Cup home defeat at the hands of Telford United.

HUNTER, John

Right-half

Career: Troon. PRESTON NORTH END, 1897. Portsmouth.

■ Right-half John Hunter was one of many Scots playing for North End around the end of the 19th century. He played his first game for the Lilywhites in a 1–1 draw at Notts County during the early stages of the 1897–98 season and went on to play in exactly half the League games in a campaign in which the club just managed to avoid relegation. With William Eccleston taking over the number-four shirt for the following season, Hunter appeared in just one game, a 1–0 win over Nottingham Forest, before leaving the club in the close season.

HUNTER, John

Centre-half

Born: Preston, 1881.
Died: 1928.
Career: PRESTON NORTH END, 1902.

■ Local-born defender John Hunter played his first game for Preston North End on the opening day of the 1902–03 season in a 2–2 draw at home to Woolwich Arsenal. He missed just one game in a campaign in which the club finished seventh in Division Two. Hunter's form at the heart of the North End defence continued to improve and in 1903–04 he was instrumental in the club winning the Second Division Championship. He scored his first goal for the club the following season in a 3–0 defeat of Woolwich Arsenal and certainly looked comfortable in the higher grade of football. In 1905–06, North End finished runners-up to Liverpool in the First Division and, though he only netted one goal, it secured a point in a 1–1 draw with Sunderland. Hunter missed very few games in his time with North End but, after appearing in 186 League games, he was injured in the game at Nottingham Forest in December 1907 and forced to retire.

IBBOTSON, Daniel

Winger

Born: Morecambe, 5 October 1968.
Career: PRESTON NORTH END, 1985.

■ YTS trainee winger Danny Ibbotson played in just one game for North End. This came in the final game of the disastrous 1985–86 season when the club finished one place off the bottom of the Fourth Division. Ibbotson, who did not sign professional forms, played in the 4–0 defeat at Aldershot but will not have the shirt to remember his debut as all the players threw their shirts to the North End fans who never stopped singing and chanting for their side.

INGLIS, John

Inside-right

Career: PRESTON NORTH END 1888.

■ Jock Inglis appeared in just one game during the club's inaugural season of League football, when he scored in a 5–0 defeat of Derby County. He also made a couple of appearances in 1889–90 when he again found the net. However, Inglis could not dislodge either Fred Dewhurst or Jimmy Ross and in the summer of 1890 he left the club.

INGRAM, Gerald

Forward

Born: Beverley, 19 August 1947.
Career: Hull Brunswick. Blackpool, 1967. PRESTON NORTH END, 1968. Bradford City, 1972.

■ Having made his mark in the local Humberside junior leagues, Gerry Ingram's talent for scoring goals was spotted by local amateur side Hull Brunswick. It was from here that he joined Blackpool, becoming manager Stan Mortensen's first signing. In 1967–68 he was the Seasiders joint-top scorer in the League with 17 goals and helped the club finish third in Division Two. In September 1968, Ingram left Bloomfield Road to sign for North End but the fans had to wait 10 games for the big striker to register his first goal for the club in a 1–0 win over Hull City. A couple of disappointing seasons followed for Ingram: he failed to find the net on a regular basis and North End were relegated to the Third Division. In 1970–71, North End won promotion as the Third Division Champions and Gerry Ingram was the club's leading scorer with a total of 24 League and Cup goals. His total included 10 goals in a six-game spell at the start of the season and a hat-trick in a 4–1 defeat of Reading. He left Deepdale in March 1972 to join Bradford City where he continued to find the net on a regular basis. In six seasons at Valley Parade, Ingram scored 60 goals in 174 League games and helped them win promotion from the Fourth Division in 1976–77.

IRVINE, William John

Centre-forward

Born: Carrickfergus, 18 June 1943.
Career: Burnley, 1960. PRESTON NORTH END, 1968. Brighton and Hove Albion, 1971. Halifax Town, 1972.

■ Willie Irvine was a prolific goalscorer throughout his entire Football League career. His most productive period for finding the net was at Burnley where he helped the reserves win the Central League Championship in 1962–63 before making his first-team debut. In fact, Irvine won the first of his 23 caps for Northern Ireland before he won a place in the Clarets' League side. After scoring on his Burnley debut in a 3–2 defeat of Arsenal, he followed that up three days later with a hat-trick in a 3–1 victory over Birmingham City. Forming a formidable strike partnership with Andy Lochhead, he scored 29 goals in 1965–66 (37 in all competitions) – a total that has only been exceeded for Burnley by Bert Freeman and George Beel. A broken leg signalled a downturn in Irvine's Turf Moor career and he was allowed to join Preston North End. Willie Irvine arrived at Deepdale in March 1968 and soon became a folk hero to the Preston faithful, especially after scoring on his debut in a 2–1 win over Aston Villa. In his next game in Preston colours, the Irishman netted a hat-trick in a 3–1 win over Huddersfield Town. He had helped transform the club's season and an eight-game unbeaten run took them to mid-table security. Irvine certainly found his goal touch at the start of the 1968–69 season, scoring 16 goals in the first 17 games. However, a knee injury against Chelsea forced him to miss much of the second half of the campaign. As he was not a regular in North End's Third Division Championship-winning side of 1970–71, he had a spell on loan with

Willie Irvine

JACK, Robert

Outside-left

Born: Alloa, 4 April 1876.
Died: Southend, 1943.
Career: Alloa Athletic. Bolton Wanderers, 1895. PRESTON NORTH END, 1901. Glossop, 1902. Plymouth Argyle. Southend United.

■ Bob Jack began his career with his home-town team, Alloa Athletic, before joining Bolton Wanderers in 1895. After making his debut in a 2–1 win at Small Heath, he quickly established himself with some exciting wing play. He was a member of the team that reached the 1896 FA Cup semi-final and was Bolton's leading scorer from outside-left a year later. He helped the Wanderers win back First Division status in 1899–1900, but within a year he had lost his place to William Tracey and joined Preston North End. He made his debut in a 3–0 win at Burnley and scored his first goal for the club on his fifth appearance as North End beat Blackpool 4–1 at Bloomfield Road. That season Jack scored six goals in 22 games as North End just missed out on promotion to the First Division, but he left almost immediately to play for Glossop. He later moved into the Southern League with Plymouth Argyle and became their manager before going to Southend in a similar capacity. Jack became secretary-manager at Plymouth for a second time between 1910 and 1938. His three sons all played for Bolton, with David, the most famous, being a member of the Wanderers' 1923 and 1926 FA Cup-winning sides.

JACKSON, Harry

Centre-forward

Born: Blackburn, 30 December 1918.
Died: 1984.
Career: Darwen. Burnley, 1942. Manchester City, 1946. PRESTON NORTH END, 1947. Blackburn Rovers, 1948. Chester City, 1949.

■ Though he had played for Burnley during World War Two, Harry Jackson was playing for Manchester City when League football resumed in 1946–47. Unable to hold down a regular place in City's side, he joined North End in

Brighton before joining the Seagulls on a permanent basis. In his second season at the Goldstone Ground, he helped Albion win promotion to Division Two before leaving to end his League career with Halifax Town.

IRVING, Joseph

Left-half

Born: Hobson, 1899.
Career: Langley Park. PRESTON NORTH END, 1921. Arsenal, 1922. Aberdare Athletic, 1925.

■ Left-half Joe Irving's only season playing for North End was 1921–22. He arrived at Deepdale on the back of some impressive displays for Langley Park and replaced Billy Mercer for the game at Newcastle United, but Preston lost 3–1. Irving went on to make 15 League appearances over the course of the campaign and appeared in the FA Cup third-round side that gained revenge by beating the Magpies 3–1. Though he never got on the score sheet, Irving created numerous chances for Roberts and Woodhouse and it was a surprise when he was allowed to leave the club in the close season. Irving joined Arsenal but was unable to break into the Gunners' League side, so he moved to Aberdare Athletic who were playing in the Third Division South at the time.

December 1947 and made a goalscoring debut in a 3–2 defeat of Burnley. He appeared in 10 games before the end of the season but could not really shake off Willie McIntosh with whom he shared the number-nine shirt. In 1948–49, Jackson scored in each of his first two appearances in the North End side – both against former club Manchester City and both ending in defeats. Jackson left Deepdale for Blackburn but his stay was brief and he ended his career with Chester City in the Third Division North, scoring 10 goals in 21 games.

JACKSON, Mark Philip

Midfield

Born: Preston, 3 February 1986.
Career: PRESTON NORTH END, 2004.

■ Mark Jackson was called into the club's first-team squad during an injury crisis towards the end of the 2003–04 season. His second inclusion on the bench led to him making his debut in a 5–1 defeat at Derby County. He continued to make steady development in the club's reserves and the following season he made a handful of appearances in all competitions. The highlight came

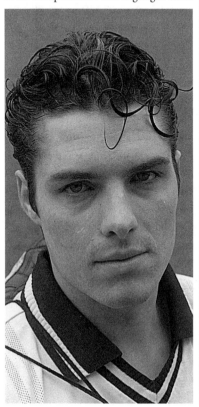

when he made his full debut at Leicester City in the Carling Cup, playing up front in North End's 3–2 win.

JACKSON, Matthew Alan

Right-back

Born: Leeds, 19 October 1971.
Career: Luton Town, 1990. PRESTON NORTH END, 1991 (loan). Everton, 1991. Charlton Athletic, 1996 (loan). Queen's Park Rangers, 1996 (loan). Birmingham City, 1996 (loan). Norwich City, 1996. Wigan Athletic, 2001.

■ An England Under-21 international, Matt Jackson began his career

with Luton Town before joining North End on loan in March 1991. He made his debut coming off the bench to replace Jeff Wrightson in a 5–1 win over Crewe Alexandra. He started three games and starred in the 1–0 Leyland Daf Cup win over Tranmere Rovers before an injury in the game at Swansea forced his loan to end prematurely. Jackson then joined Everton where he won a place in the Blues' team that won the 1995 FA Cup, beating Manchester United 1–0 in the Final. After losing his place in the Everton side to Marc Hottiger he had loan spells with Charlton, Queen's Park Rangers and Birmingham City before joining Norwich for a fee of £450,000. Shortly after his arrival at Carrow Road,

Jackson was appointed the club's captain and went on to appear in 172 games for the Canaries before his transfer to Wigan Athletic in October 2001. He showed his versatility at Wigan, playing at both right-back and in central defence, until dislocating his kneecap. He returned to help the Latics win the Second Division Championship in 2002–03 and, though he suffered an Achilles injury, he returned to the side to captain the club to promotion to the Premiership, where he has since demonstrated his ability to play at the highest level.

JACKSON, Michael James

Centre-half

Born: Runcorn, 4 December 1973.
Career: Crewe Alexandra, 1992. Bury, 1993. PRESTON NORTH END, 1997. Tranmere Rovers, 2002 (loan). Tranmere Rovers, 2004.

■ An England Youth international, Michael Jackson began his career with Crewe Alexandra but left to play for Bury after just a handful of League appearances for the Railwaymen. At Gigg Lane, Jackson struck up a superb partnership alongside Chris Lucketti at the heart of the Shakers' defence. He had played in 149 games for Bury when on transfer deadline day in March 1997 he moved to Preston for the ridiculously low fee of £125,000. He made his Preston debut in a 2–0 win over Notts County and soon slotted comfortably into the centre-back position. Strong and effective in the tackle and producing powerful headers at both ends of the park, his value to the side was shown in 1997–98 when he missed a five-match spell through injury and four of the games were lost. The following season he finally found his goalscoring range and became a potent threat at set pieces. In 1999–2000 he played a leading role in North End's Second Division Championship triumph, scoring the first of five goals against his former club Bury and netting after just 88 seconds of the local derby against Burnley. Not surprisingly his performances were recognised by selection for the PFA award-winning Second Division side. Injuries and suspensions hampered his progress the following season and in

2001–02 he found it difficult to displace either Chris Lucketti or Colin Murdock. Following a loan spell with Tranmere Rovers, Jackson returned to Deepdale to become part of a three-man central defensive set-up. In the summer of 2004 he joined Tranmere Rovers on a permanent basis after appearing in 283 first-team games for North End.

JACKSON, Walter E.

Centre-forward, outside-right

Born: Renton, 19 January 1897.
Career: Yoker Athletic. Kilmarnock. Bethlehem Steel. Aberdeen. PRESTON NORTH END, 1925. Bethlehem Steel. Philadelphia Centennials (US).

■ Walter Jackson was a prolific goalscorer in his days north of the border with Kilmarnock and Aberdeen. He joined Preston before the start of the 1925–26 season. Though he did not get on the score sheet on his debut in a 4–0 win over Hull City, he netted a hat-trick on only his ninth appearance for North End as Clapton Orient were beaten 4–1. Jackson scored 12 goals in 26 League and Cup games but, though he played in a similar number of games the following season, the goals dried up. After returning to play for Bethlehem Steel, he went to the US to play for Philadelphia Centennials.

JAMES, Alexander Wilson

Inside-left

Born: Mossend, 14 September 1901.
Died: 1953.
Career: Brandon Amateurs. Orbiston Celtic. Glasgow Ashfield. Motherwell. Raith Rovers. PRESTON NORTH END, 1925. Arsenal, 1929.

■ Arguably the finest inside-forward of all time, Alex James avoided learning a trade, preferring to dedicate himself to football. After succeeding in securing a trial for Ashfield in the Glasgow Junior League, he began to attract serious attention. After joining Raith Rovers, he made his debut in Scottish football in September 1922 against Celtic. Preston North End always enjoyed strong links north of the border and, in an effort to regain their First Division status, they signed James along with teammate

David Morris during the early part of the 1925–26 season. Following the signing of James, North End were fined 10 guineas for an irregularity in relation to the transfer form for the little Scot. After making his debut in a 5–1 defeat at Middlesbrough, James scored in each of his next four games and this lead to him winning the first of eight Scottish caps. The scorer of spectacular goals, he hit two specials in the 5–1 demolition of England at Wembley on a rain-soaked afternoon in April 1928 and these immortalised him. After topping North End's scoring charts for three successive seasons, he became frustrated by Preston's continued failure to gain promotion during his four-year spell at Deepdale and early in 1929 he was transfer-listed. When the Arsenal manager Herbert Chapman approached him to sign for the Gunners, James was quick to point out that it was not to his advantage to uproot his family to move south where the cost of living was so much higher. Chapman found a loophole in the League regulations which entitled a player to both work and play. He fixed James up as a football demonstrator with Selfridges while an evening paper agreed to take a weekly 'ghosted' article from the tiny Scot and

pay him a salary for the privilege of using his by now famous name. Typically, he reserved his first goal for his new club for a very special event – the 1930 FA Cup Final against Huddersfield Town. Arsenal's success heralded the start of one of the most amazing runs of success any English League club has ever known – four League titles and two FA Cup wins in only six seasons. After playing his last match for the Gunners in 1937, James worked as a pools promoter and as a reporter on a Sunday newspaper before returning to Highbury after the war to coach the club's youngsters. In 1953 he fell gravely ill with cancer and his death at the age of 51 shocked the whole of the football world.

JAMES, Julian Colin

Full-back

Born: Tring, 22 March 1970.
Career: Luton Town, 1988. PRESTON NORTH END, 1991 (loan).

■ Defender Julian James joined the Hatters from his home-town club, Tring Tornadoes, and worked his way up through the ranks at Kenilworth Road before making his debut at Southampton in May 1988. However, it was midway through the 1989–90 season before he established himself in the Luton side. Strong in the tackle and good in the air, he only ever missed games through minor injuries or suspensions – although he did have a loan spell with Preston North End at the start of the 1991–92 season. James made six appearances for North End following his debut in a 2–2 draw at Swansea and was only on the losing side once in that spell. After his return to Luton, James scored a number of vital goals for the club and in 1996–97 he played a major role in keeping the club on course for promotion. Unfortunately the term ended on a disappointing note when he was sent off in the first semi-final Play-off against Crewe, allowing the Railwaymen to dominate a game they could easily have lost. The following season the former England Under-21 defender suffered a double fracture of the leg and he was forced to retire after scoring 14 goals in 334 games for the Hatters.

JAMES, Martin Joseph

Outside-left, left-back

Born: Crosby, 18 May 1971.
Career: PRESTON NORTH END, 1989. Stockport County, 1993. Rotherham United, 1994.

■ Martin James played his first senior game in North End colours in the League Cup victory over Chester City at the start of the 1990–91 season and kept his place in the side to make his League debut four days later in a 3–3 draw at Reading. A regular for most of the next three seasons, James scored a number of spectacular long-range goals for the club. Towards the end of the club's relegation season of 1992–93 he left Deepdale to play for Stockport County. Though the Edgeley Park club enjoyed some success in both the League and the Autoglass Trophy during his time with the club, Martin James was on the fringes of the County side and signed for Rotherham United in the summer of 1994. Hugely popular with the Millmoor fans, his career was brought to a premature end following a serious back injury.

JAMES, Ralph

Goalkeeper

Born: Preston, 1879.
Career: PRESTON NORTH END, 1900.

■ Goalkeeper Ralph James made three League appearances for North End during the early stages of the 1900–01 season following an injury to Scottish international 'keeper Peter McBride. Though he was playing behind a rather shaky North End defence, he made an encouraging debut in a 2–2 draw at Wolverhampton Wanderers. Ralph James' other two appearances for the club ended in defeat as Aston Villa won 2–0 at Deepdale and Liverpool triumphed in an exciting game at Anfield by the odd goal in five.

JARRETT Jason Lee Mee

Midfield

Born: Bury, 14 September 1979
Career: Blackpool, 1998. Wrexham, 1999. Shelbourne (loan). Bury, 2000. Wigan Athletic, 2002. Stoke City (loan), 2005. Plymouth Argyle, 2005. Norwich City, 2005. PRESTON NORTH END (loan), 2006.

■ Having come through the junior ranks at Blackpool, Jason Jarrett made his first-team debut for the Seasiders when coming off the bench in an FA Cup tie at Wigan in November 1998, a match the Latics won 4–3. Though he showed much promise, Blackpool decided to release him and in the close season he joined Wrexham. Unable to win a regular place in the Robins' side, he had a period on loan with League of Ireland side Shelbourne, before joining his home-town team Bury. An attacking midfield player, who excels at linking defence and attack, he was a fixture in the Bury side in 2001–02 but with the club in financial difficulties, he was sold to Wigan for a bargain price of £75,000. He was a regular in the Latics' side until the turn of the year in the club's Second Division Championship-winning season of 2002–03. Though he remained a valuable member of Paul Jewell's squad, he then broke a leg in a pre-season friendly and on his recovery, was loaned out to Stoke City to improve his fitness. He later returned to the JJB Stadium and played in the last three games as Wigan won promotion to the Premiership. Though he was offered a new contract, he saw his future away from the JJB and joined Plymouth Argyle before signing for relegated Norwich City. Injuries and a loss of form at Carrow Road saw him lose his first-team place and he joined

North End on loan. The energetic box-to-box player's only goal for the club was the winner at Leicester when he headed home from close range after Claude David had flicked on Chris Sedgwick's corner. That goal was enough to ensure that Preston had secured a place in the Play-offs.

JEFFELS, Simon

Centre-half

Born: Barnsley, 18 January 1966.
Career: Barnsley, 1984. PRESTON NORTH END, 1987 (loan). Carlisle United, 1988.

■ Central defender Simon Jeffels appeared in 42 League games for his home-town club Barnsley during their Second Division days in the mid-1980s before going on loan to Preston North End in October 1987. His only appearance in a North End shirt came in a 1–0 defeat at Walsall, after which he was not selected again, even for the bench. He returned to Oakwell before signing for Carlisle United in the summer of 1988. He spent three seasons at Brunton Park and appeared in 77 Fourth Division games for the Cumbrian side.

JEFFERIS, Frank

Inside-forward

Born: Fordingbridge, 3 July 1884.
Died: 1938.
Career: Fordingbridge Turks. Southampton. Everton, 1910. PRESTON NORTH END, 1919. Southport, 1923. PRESTON NORTH END, 1925. Southport, 1926.

■ Spotted while playing for his home-town team, Fordingbridge Turks, Frank Jefferis was invited to The Dell by Southampton and capped a clever display by scoring a hat-trick in a match against the Corinthians. He soon won a regular place in the Saints side by his graceful and neat ball play and his ability to bring the best out of his fellow forwards. In the six seasons he spent at The Dell he was a firm favourite and it came as a nasty shock when he was transferred to Everton. At Goodison he created goals for players like Browell and Bradshaw and in 1914–15 he won a League Championship medal. He was capped twice for England shortly after joining the club, playing as a scheming inside-forward against Wales and Scotland in 1912. After playing wartime football for Everton, Jefferis joined Preston North End who, at the time of his joining, were in danger of relegation to Division Two. Jefferis scored on his debut in a 3–1 defeat of Middlesbrough and was on the winning side in his first four games before being injured – North End gained just three points out of the next seven matches. On his return they won three and drew three of the remaining seven fixtures and avoided relegation by winning at Everton in the last match of the season. The following season North End reached the FA Cup semi-final while in 1921–22 they went one better and reached the Final only to lose 1–0 to Huddersfield Town. After playing his part in making Tommy Roberts a star, Frank Jefferis left Deepdale to become Southport's player-coach. Though he retired in 1925 he was later called back into action by the Haig Avenue club when they were short of players. In 1936 he became trainer at Millwall and remained there until his death two years later.

JEMSON, Nigel Bradley

Forward

Born: Preston, 10 October 1969.
Career: PRESTON NORTH END, 1987. Nottingham Forest, 1988. Bolton Wanderers, 1988 (loan). PRESTON NORTH END, 1989 (loan). Sheffield Wednesday, 1991. Grimsby Town, 1993 (loan). Notts County, 1994. Watford, 1995 (loan). Rotherham United, 1996 (loan). Oxford United, 1996. Bury, 1998. Ayr United, 1999. Oxford United, 2000. Shrewsbury Town, 2000.

■ Nigel Jemson was a prolific scorer at schoolboy level before North End stepped in to sign him as a junior. He made rapid progress through the club's youth and reserve teams to make his League debut as a 16-year-old substitute in the 4–0 defeat at Aldershot on the final day of the 1985–86 season. In January 1987, he played his first full game for the Lilywhites, scoring a tremendous goal in a 1–1 draw against Swansea City at the Vetch. Jemson also

found the net in the following two matches against Lincoln City and Halifax Town. Nottingham Forest manager Brian Clough spotted Jemson's potential and so in March 1988, after he had scored eight goals in 32 League games, he paid North End £150,000 to take the youngster to the City Ground. He struggled to make an impact with Forest and was allowed to join Bolton on loan. His Wanderers debut came at Deepdale as North End won 3–1. He returned to Forest before being loaned back to Preston in March 1989. After scoring twice in six League games, he returned to the City Ground and earned a regular place in the side in 1989–90. He scored the winner in the League Cup Final against Oldham Athletic and also won an England Under-21 cap. In September 1991, Sheffield Wednesday paid £800,000 to take him to Hillsborough but he was unable to settle and moved to Notts County after a loan spell with Grimsby. Loan spells with Watford and Coventry City followed and then again with Rotherham United. At the latter he scored two goals as the Millers beat Shrewsbury 2–1 to win the Auto Windscreens Shield. Jemson then joined Oxford United and was their leading scorer in his first season at the Manor Ground. He later played for Bury and Ayr United before a second spell with Oxford was followed by him signing for Shrewsbury Town. Jemson was appointed the Gay Meadow club's captain and he hit the headlines after a hat-trick against former club Bury was followed by a brace that knocked Premiership Everton out of the FA Cup.

JENNINGS, John

Right-half, full-back

Born: Platt Bridge, 27 August 1902.
Died: 1997.
Career: Wigan Borough, 1923. Cardiff City, 1925. Middlesbrough, 1929. PRESTON NORTH END, 1936. Bradford City, 1937.

■ A railway fireman, Jack Jennings started out with local side Wigan Borough before signing for Cardiff in 1925. He played his first game for the Bluebirds at right-half but, due to the wealth of international defenders at the

club, he seldom got a first-team game. In 1926 he was chosen to tour Canada with the Football Association and then in 1927–28 he grabbed the opportunity of a full-back berth with City. He remained a virtual ever present in the Cardiff side until 1929 when he figured in a triple transfer with Joe Hillier and Freddie Warren that took all three players to Middlesbrough. Jennings became a first-team regular at Ayresome Park for the next six seasons and captained Boro for much of that time. Having played in 205 games for Boro, he left to join Preston North End in 1936. In a season in which the Lilywhites finished mid-table in the First Division and reached the FA Cup Final – where they lost 3–1 to Sunderland – Jennings played in 20 League and Cup games. He scored his only goal from the penalty spot in a 1–1 draw with Portsmouth. After ending his career with Bradford City, he worked as a masseur with the Northamptonshire county cricket team, and coached the England amateur international side and a number of British athletes.

JEPSON, Ronald Francis

Forward

Born: Stoke-on-Trent, 12 May 1963.
Career: Nantwich Town. Port Vale, 1989. Peterborough United, 1990 (loan). PRESTON NORTH END, 1991. Exeter City, 1992. Huddersfield Town, 1993. Bury, 1996. Oldham Athletic, 1998. Burnley, 1998.

■ Bustling striker Ronnie Jepson started out with non-League Nantwich Town before joining Port Vale in March 1989. Unable to gain a regular place, he was loaned to Peterborough United before joining Preston for £80,000 in February 1991. Jepson made his North End debut in a 1–0 defeat at Huddersfield Town, but three days later he netted a first-half hat-trick in a 6–1 Leyland Daf Cup victory over Burnley. Jepson never hit those heights again, although he did net two goals in each of the victories over Hull City and Darlington in 1991–92. He moved on to Exeter City where he scored on a more regular basis. This form prompted Huddersfield Town to pay £80,000 for his services in December 1993. His strike

partnership with Andy Booth flourished and he scored 42 goals in 124 games before returning over the Pennines to play for Bury. Despite a troublesome hamstring and an inflamed disc in his back, he helped the Shakers win the Second Division Championship in 1996–97. It was not long before 'Rocket Ronnie' was on the move again, this time to Oldham Athletic. However, his stay at Boundary Park was brief and he moved to Burnley, his eighth and final League club, where he spent most of his time on the substitutes' bench before hanging up his boots .

JESSOP, William

Outside-left

Born: Preston, 2 April 1922.
Died: 1994.
Career: PRESTON NORTH END, 1940. Stockport County, 1947. Oldham Athletic, 1948. Wrexham, 1951.

■ Winger Willie Jessop played for North End during World War Two but

when League football resumed in 1946–47, he only appeared in four games; the first was a 2–0 defeat at Middlesbrough. Jessop, whose last appearance for the Lilywhites was in the number-nine shirt, moved on to Stockport County but he stayed at Edgeley Park for just one season. He had his greatest success at his next club, Oldham Athletic, where he scored 16 goals in 94 games during three and a half seasons at Boundary Park before ending his playing days with Wrexham.

JOHNROSE, Leonard

Midfield, forward

Born: Preston, 29 November 1969.
Career: Blackburn Rovers, 1988. PRESTON NORTH END, 1992 (loan). Hartlepool United, 1992. Bury, 1993. Burnley, 1999. Bury, 2002. Swansea City, 2003. Burnley, 2004.

■ Lenny Johnrose impressed as a goal poacher in his early days with Blackburn Rovers until he was sidelined by injury. Unable to win back a place on a regular basis, he joined Preston on loan in January 1992. His only start came in a 1–0 defeat at Brentford, but he did score when he came off the bench to replace Adrian Hughes in a 2–1 reversal against Fulham at Deepdale. A year later and

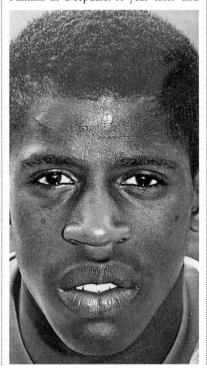

Johnrose was on his way to Hartlepool United for a fee of £50,000 but after a good first season at the Victoria Ground he joined Bury. His non-stop running, ability to time his tackling to perfection and some vital goals made sure that the 1996–97 Second Division Championship went to Gigg Lane. Very popular with Bury fans, he had scored 24 goals in 224 games for the Shakers when he joined a number of ex-Bury players at Burnley. He continued to demonstrate his never-say-die approach and was instrumental in the club winning promotion to the First Division in 1999–2000. However, the following season he suffered an Achilles tendon injury which forced him to miss a number of matches. He returned briefly to Gigg Lane before helping Swansea City avoid the drop into the Conference. An influential figure in the Swans' exciting FA Cup run, he later returned to Turf Moor for a third spell with the Clarets prior to hanging up his boots.

JOHNSON, Alan Keith

Centre-half

Born: Wigan, 19 February 1971.
Career: Wigan Athletic, 1989. Lincoln City, 1994. PRESTON NORTH END, 1995 (loan). Rochdale, 1996.

■ England Youth international Alan Johnson made his debut for his home-town team, Wigan Athletic, in a 1–0 win at Mansfield Town in January 1989. Useful at set pieces he scored his first goal for the club towards the end of that first season in a 1–0 defeat of Bury, a result that ensured the Latics would play Third Division football the following season. Over the next four seasons he missed very few games, but he failed to agree terms after the Latics were relegated in 1992–93. Signing a week-to-week contract, he joined Lincoln City in February 1995 for a tribunal-set fee of £65,000. His progress at Sincil Bank was hampered by a spate of niggling injuries and in September 1995 he joined North End on loan. In what turned out to be the club's Third Division Championship-winning season, Johnson played in two games, a 1–0 win at Hereford and a 2–2 draw at Colchester. Johnson later left Lincoln and joined Rochdale. An ever

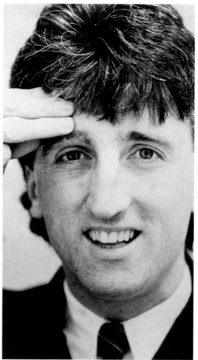

present and Player of the Year in his first season at Spotland, he missed the whole of the 1997–98 season through injury before being released.

JOHNSON, David Edward

Forward

Born: Liverpool, 23 October 1951.
Career: Everton, 1969. Ipswich Town, 1972. Liverpool, 1976. Everton, 1982. Barnsley, 1984. Manchester City, 1984. Tulsa Roughnecks (US). PRESTON NORTH END, 1984.

■ David Johnson began his Football League career with Everton but despite his early successes, which included a hat-trick in an 8–0 romp over Southampton, he was transferred to Ipswich Town in October 1971. At Portman Road he matured into a useful centre-forward, winning eight England caps. The first was against Wales in 1975 when he scored both England's goals in a 2–2 draw. In August 1976 he joined Liverpool for a club record £200,000. Johnson's courageous approach and his speed, skill and unselfishness instantly endeared him to the Kop. Despite niggling injuries during his early days at Anfield, he managed to collect a League Championship-winners' medal and figured in the Wembley defeat by Manchester United, but he missed out on European glory. Just when it seemed

Liverpool were going to discard him, his luck changed. After striking up a good understanding with Kenny Dalglish, he won a European Cup-winners' medal and four League Championship medals. In the summer of 1982, Johnson's colourful career came full circle when he rejoined Everton for £100,000. Unable to reproduce his form of old, he had brief spells with Barnsley and Manchester City before trying his luck in the US with Tulsa Roughnecks. Johnson joined Preston North End in October 1984. Like his strike partner, Nigel Greenwood, he found the net on occasions, but it was not enough to save the Deepdale club from relegation to the Fourth Division. Johnson holds a unique place in Merseyside folklore: he is the only player to have scored a derby winner for both Everton and Liverpool.

JOHNSON Jermal Pierre

Forward

Born: New Jersey, United States, 3 May 1984
Career: Blackburn Rovers 2002; PRESTON NORTH END (loan) 2006.

■ The quick-footed young striker was added to Blackburn Rovers' first-team squad around the midway point of the 2004–05 season and scored on his first

full start in the FA Cup fourth-round tie against Colchester United. Adept at holding up the ball under pressure and linking the play, he joined Preston on a month's loan in January 2006. Manager Billy Davies gave the American-born striker his debut in the home game against Leicester City. The 20-year-old took just 11 minutes to make his name known – but for all the wrong reasons! He was booked for a ridiculous dive over the hands of Foxes 'keeper Rob Douglas in what looked like a bid to earn North End a penalty. He continued to labour after the break and was eventually substituted. But two days later, in the game against Hull City, he opened the scoring on the hour mark and this led to North End running out 3–0 winners. At the end of his time at Deepdale, Johnson rejoined Rovers.

JOHNSTON, James

Right-half

Born: Forfar, 1890.
Career: PRESTON NORTH END, 1911.

■ James Johnston spent three seasons at Deepdale but in that time he only managed to make 10 League appearances for the Lilywhites. He made his debut in the local derby against Blackburn Rovers on Boxing Day 1911, a match that ended all square at 2–2. He did not appear at all in 1912–13 as the club won the Second Division Championship, but made seven appearances the following season as North End were relegated after just one season back in the top flight.

JOHNSTONE, Glenn Paul

Goalkeeper

Born: Kenya, 5 June 1967.
Career: Lancaster City. PRESTON NORTH END, 1993.

■ In 1992–93, a season in which Preston lost their Second Division status, goalkeeper Glenn Johnstone acted as understudy to the club's first-choice 'keeper, Simon Farnworth. When he was called upon, Johnstone played well behind a defence that leaked goals, keeping a clean sheet in a 1–0 win over Brighton and making a couple of important saves in the 3–3 draw with local rivals Blackpool.

JOHNSTONE, William

Inside-left

Career: PRESTON NORTH END, 1889.

■ Little is known about William Johnstone, except that he played in a couple of games during North End's second season of League football without finding the net. Unable to dislodge the likes of Jimmy Ross and Fred Dewhurst, he parted company with the club at the end of a season in which the club retained its League title.

JONES, Alexander

Centre-half

Born: Blackburn, 27 November 1964.
Career: Oldham Athletic, 1982. Stockport County, 1984 (loan). PRESTON NORTH END, 1986. Carlisle United, 1989. Rochdale, 1991. Motherwell. Rochdale, 1992. Halifax Town. Stalybridge Celtic. Chorley. Southport. Lancaster City.

■ Towering central defender Alex Jones started out with Oldham Athletic. As he was unable to force his way into the Latics side on a permanent basis, Jones went on loan to Stockport before joining Preston in the summer of 1986. He made his North End debut on the opening day of the 1986–87 season in a 1–1 draw at Tranmere before going on to be the club's

only ever present as they won promotion to the Third Division as runners-up to Northampton Town. Jones' first goal for the club, and his only one in the League that season, came in a 2–0 win at Torquay United. The commanding centre-half was hampered by injuries though he did net Preston's goal in a 1–1 draw with Champions-elect Sunderland. One of the best central defenders in the lower Divisions, he left Deepdale after making exactly 100 starts at League level to play for Carlisle United. This was followed by a brief spell with Rochdale before Motherwell paid £35,000 to take him to Fir Park. Jones found some of the nippy Scottish strikers a handful and rejoined Rochdale before seeing out his career with a number of non-League clubs.

JONES, Charles Edward

Goalkeeper

Born: Manchester, 1889.
Career: Northwich Victoria. PRESTON NORTH END, 1913.

■ Following an injury to regular goalkeeper Bert Taylor towards the end of the 1913–14 season, North End signed Charlie Jones from non-League Northwich Victoria. Jones played in the final two games of the campaign, keeping a clean sheet in a 1–0 win at already relegated Derby County and then producing a number of fine saves in a 2–2 draw with Manchester City. Unfortunately his displays were not enough to save the Lilywhites who were relegated along with Derby. In 1914–15, Hayes and Newton shared the goalkeeping duties until the turn of the year when Charlie Jones became the club's first-choice 'keeper. He played very well, keeping 10 clean sheets in 22 League and Cup appearances and helping the club return to the top flight at the first attempt. When League football resumed in 1919–20, Jones was one of four goalkeepers used by North End but at the end of the season he parted company with the club.

JONES David Frank Llwyd

Midfield

Born: Southport, 4 November 1984
Career: Manchester United 2003; PRESTON NORTH END (loan) 2005; NEC Nijmegen (Holland) (loan) 2006.

■ An England Under-21 international, David Jones is a hardworking midfielder who made great strides in his early seasons with Manchester United. As well as captaining the Old Trafford club's reserve side in 2004–05, he made his senior bow in the Reds' goalless FA Cup third-round tie against non-League Exeter City. Jones, who was looking to appear in United's first team on a more regular basis in 2005–06, was advised by manager Alex Ferguson to have a season's loan with a Championship club. Like David Beckham before him, he opted for Preston North End. During his time at Deepdale, the United starlet ran the midfield for North End and caused the opposition all sorts of problems with his dangerous set-pieces. His free-kick for the opener in the win at Millwall was an absolute gem! He had scored three goals in 22 games for Preston, for whom he was totally committed, when the Deepdale club were thwarted in their efforts to extend the loan star's stay until the end of the campaign. The midfielder opted to head off out of Deepdale to link up with NEC Nijmegen in Holland.

JONES, David Ronald

Centre-half

Born: Liverpool, 17 August 1956.
Career: Everton, 1974. Coventry City, 1979. Seiko (Hong Kong). PRESTON NORTH END, 1983.

■ A former captain of the England Youth team, David Jones made his senior debut for Everton as a 19-year-old and was capped shortly afterwards by England at Under-21 level. He first settled into the Everton side at left-back and, though he appeared rather ponderous, his deceptively long stride covered the ground quickly. After switching to the right to accommodate Mike Pejic in 1977, he held his place until Achilles tendon trouble and a broken elbow laid him low in 1978. On regaining fitness, Jones was recalled before moving to Coventry City for £275,000 in the summer of 1979. His time at Highfield Road was dogged by injuries and after trying his luck in Hong Kong he joined North End in August 1983. He was outstanding on his debut on the opening day of the 1983–84 season as North End won 1–0 at Bournemouth and went on to play in 37 games as the side finished mid-table in the Third Division. Injuries hampered his progress the following season and he decided to retire at the end of a campaign in which the club were relegated to the League's basement. As a manager he worked his way up from the bottom. He was with Morecambe, Southport and Mossley before taking charge at Stockport County. In his first full season in charge he took County to the semi-finals of the League Cup and to promotion to the First Division. He later managed Southampton and Wolverhampton Wanderers and is now in charge of Cardiff City.

JONES, Eric

Winger

Born: Ulverston, 23 June 1931.
Career: Notts County. PRESTON NORTH END, 1952. Nottingham Forest, 1955. Doncaster Rovers, 1958. Accrington Stanley, 1959. Southport, 1960.

■ Having played as an amateur with Notts County, winger Eric Jones had to wait almost two years before making his North End debut on Christmas Day 1953 in a 2–1 defeat at Burnley. Jones kept his place in the side and on Boxing Day he helped the Lilywhites reverse the result: his crosses provided the goals for Charlie Wayman. Able to play on either flank, he made a handful of appearances in 1954–55 before leaving to play for Nottingham Forest. In his second season at the City Ground, he helped Forest win promotion to the First Division but was transferred to Doncaster Rovers before their season in the top flight began. In his

only season at Belle Vue, the Yorkshire club were relegated, as were his next team Accrington Stanley in 1959–60. Jones' last port of call was Southport, where he scored 18 goals in 76 games for the Sandgrounders before hanging up his boots.

JONES, Harry Joseph

Centre-forward, inside-forward

Born: Haydock, 2 October 1911.
Died: 1957.
Career: Haydock Athletic. PRESTON NORTH END, 1932. West Bromwich Albion, 1934.

■ Harry 'Popeye' Jones joined North End in 1932 from his local club, Haydock Athletic, as understudy to the prolific Ted Harper. His only game that season – and as it transpired his only game in Preston colours – was the home match against Charlton Athletic when he scored in a 4–2 win. Unable to make further inroads, Jones joined West Bromwich Albion where he was seen as an eventual replacement for 'Ginger' Richardson. After some prodigious scoring for Albion's Central League team, he forced his way into the senior team. In 1936–37 he even managed to outscore Richardson to finish as the club's leading scorer with 17 goals. Top scorer in each of the next two seasons, his best years were lost to the war. In the first season of wartime regional football he scored 52 goals, including a club record run of a goal in 11 consecutive games. He later 'guested' for Everton and Blackburn until injury forced him to retire at the age of only 31.

JONES, Mark Thomas

Full-back

Born: Liverpool, 16 September 1960.
Career: Runcorn. PRESTON NORTH END, 1984.

■ Attacking full-back Mark Jones joined Preston from non-League Runcorn in February 1984, making his debut in a 3–1 home win over Orient a couple of months after putting pen to paper. In 1984–85, Jones played in 35 games of a season that ended with the club being relegated to the Fourth Division for the first time in their history. One of the highlights of that

disastrous campaign was Mark Jones' goal in the 2–1 win at high-flying Hull City, which was featured on *Match of the Day*. Able to play in either full-back berth, Jones was one of the club's most consistent players the following season when only a poor Torquay United side prevented North End finishing in the dreaded last position of the Football League. Even so, Jones was one of a number of players not retained by the club.

JOY, William Joseph

Goalkeeper

Born: Preston, 1864.
Died: 1947.
Career: PRESTON NORTH END, 1895. Blackburn Rovers, 1896. Darwen, 1897.

■ Goalkeeper Billy Joy joined North End for the 1895–96 season as cover for Welsh international James Trainer and made nine appearances during the course of the campaign. The first of these came in a 4–3 home win over Sheffield United, a scoreline that was repeated in Joy's next game as eventual Champions Aston Villa were beaten at Deepdale. Joy kept goal well until in the first round of the FA Cup he was deemed to be at fault for all Sunderland's goals in a 4–1 defeat for the Lilywhites. After leaving Preston, Joy remained in the North West and played in a handful of League games for both Blackburn Rovers and Darwen.

JOYCE, Warren Garton

Midfield

Born: Oldham, 20 January 1965.
Career: Bolton Wanderers, 1982.
PRESTON NORTH END, 1987.
Plymouth Argyle, 1992. Burnley, 1993.
Hull City, 1995 (loan). Hull City, 1996.

■ The son of Walter Joyce, who played for Burnley, Blackburn Rovers and Oldham Athletic, Warren Joyce chose football as his preferred sport after playing cricket and rugby at county level. He began his career with Bolton Wanderers and established himself as a Third Division regular in 1983–84. He was a virtual ever present until injury kept him out of the Wanderers side in early 1986, forcing him to miss the Freight Rover Trophy Final against Bristol City at Wembley. After Bolton's relegation to the Fourth Division in

1986–87, Joyce joined Preston North End for £35,000 after scoring 21 goals in 221 games. He made his debut in a goalless draw at Brighton and added some extra bite into the club's midfield. He was soon also appointed captain. Hugely popular with the North End fans due to his never-say-die attitude on the pitch, Joyce found goals easier to come by at Deepdale and in 1989–90 he was the

club's leading scorer with 11 goals. In May 1992 ambitious Plymouth Argyle paid £160,000 for his services but after only a year at Home Park, Joyce returned to the North West with Burnley. The tenacious midfielder made a dramatic start to his Turf Moor career, scoring twice on his debut against Port Vale. He later joined Hull City where his wholehearted performances during his first season led to him sweeping the board with the club's Player of the Year awards. Later appointed the Tigers' player-manager, Joyce moved on to join the coaching staff at Leeds United.

KAILE, Gordon Walter

Outside-left

Born: Blandford Camp, 7 December 1924.
Died: 1969.
Career: Nottingham Forest, 1945.
PRESTON NORTH END, 1951. Exeter City, 1954.

■ Flying winger Gordon Kaile began his Football League career with Nottingham Forest but, though he spent five seasons at the City Ground, he only made 65 appearances. Nevertheless, he was an important member of the Forest side that won promotion to the Second Division in 1950–51 as Champions of the Third Division South. That season Forest

scored 110 League goals and while Kaile scored a number of spectacular goals, it was his crosses that provided the ammunition for the likes of Wally Ardron and Tommy Capel. Transferred to Preston North End of the First Division, Kaile appeared in a couple of League games in 1951–52 as replacement for the injured Tom Finney. He did not play at all the following season before scoring his only goal for the club in September 1953 in a 5–1 win at Anfield. Kaile left Deepdale in the following summer to see out his career with Exeter City.

KANE, Leonard Russell

Full-back

Born: Belfast, 27 January 1926.
Career: Glentoran. PRESTON NORTH END, 1947. Plymouth Argyle, 1950.

■ Signed from Irish League side Glentoran, full-back Len Kane spent a season in North End's Central League side before making his debut in a 3–2 home defeat of Liverpool midway through the 1948–49 season. An understudy to players of the calibre of Brown, Scott and Walton, he made just a handful of League appearances in his time at Deepdale. On leaving Preston, he joined Plymouth Argyle but could not force his way into the Pilgrims' League side.

KAY, John

Right-back

Born: Great Lumley, 29 January 1964.
Career: Arsenal, 1981. Wimbledon, 1984.
Middlesbrough, 1985 (loan). Sunderland,
1987. Shrewsbury Town, 1996 (loan).
PRESTON NORTH END, 1996.
Scarborough, 1996. Workington.

■ John Kay started his career with Arsenal as a skilful midfield player but was converted to full-back after his promotion to the Gunners' reserve team. He made his Football League debut against West Bromwich Albion in February 1983 but he was released on a free transfer after making 14 appearances and joined Wimbledon. During three seasons with the Dons he played in 70 games and helped them win promotion. In the summer of 1987, Sunderland paid £22,500 to take Kay to Roker Park. After making his debut in a 1–0 win at Brentford in the club's first-ever Division Three game, he was ever present and won a Third Division Championship medal as the Wearsiders finished nine points ahead of runners-up Brighton. Kay helped the Wearsiders win promotion to the First Division in 1989–90 and went on to play in 236 games. After a loan spell with Shrewsbury, he joined Preston North End who had just won promotion to Division Two. He made his debut in a goalless home draw against Bristol Rovers and appeared in 10 consecutive League and Cup games before he was

allowed to join Scarborough. He made the right-back position there his own and was voted the club's Player of the Year in his first season. Kay was 35 when his League career ground to a halt and he left to play non-League football for Workington.

KEANE, Michael Thomas Joseph

Midfield

Born: Dublin, 29 December 1982.
Career: PRESTON NORTH END, 2000.
Grimsby Town, 2003 (loan). Hull City,
2004. Rotherham United, 2005.

■ A tough-tackling all-action midfielder, Michael Keane stepped up from the club's reserve side to make his senior debut against Blackburn Rovers in the penultimate match of the 2000–01 season. Predominantly left-footed, he progressed through the Republic of Ire-

land ranks and was called up to the Under-21 team while only 18. It was a similar story at club level, where his celebratory run following his first goal against Wimbledon will be long remembered. In early 2002–03 a foot injury led to a screw being fitted in a broken bone and this looked like keeping him out for the season. However, he recovered quicker than expected and went on loan to Grimsby where he performed with great commitment but was unable to prevent the Mariners being relegated. Having turned down a move to Grimsby, he remained at Deepdale and went on to appear in 65 games before making a £50,000 move to Hull City. He started well with the Tigers but after falling out of favour he was allowed to join Rotherham United.

KEEN, Nigel

Midfield

Born: Barrow, 23 October 1961.
Career: Manchester United, 1979. Barrow.
PRESTON NORTH END, 1985.

■ Unable to make the grade with Manchester United, midfielder Nigel Keen joined his home-town club Barrow where his impressive displays led to North End manager Tommy Booth signing him in the summer of 1985. Keen played his first game in North End colours on the opening day of the 1985–86 season in a 4–2 home defeat by Peterborough United. He went on to make 24 appearances as the

club struggled at the foot of the Fourth Division for most of the campaign. He failed to find the net in League games but did score in his second senior outing, a 2–1 Milk Cup win over rivals Blackpool. Like a number of players he was released at the end of this most disappointing campaign.

KELLY, Alan James Alexander

Goalkeeper

Born: Dublin, 5 July 1936.
Career: Drumcondra. PRESTON NORTH END, 1958.

■ Alan Kelly is the Republic of Ireland's most capped goalkeeper after Paddy Bonner – only a serious injury in September 1973 in a game against Bristol City prevented him from winning more caps. At the time of his injury, Kelly had made 47 international appearances for the Republic of Ireland and until recently was the only 'keeper to have captained the national side. The shoulder injury he sustained led to serious complications: he lost the power in his right hand and had to learn to write with his left. As a youngster he was snapped up by League of Ireland club Drumcondra where he won an FAI Cup-winners' medal in 1957 when they beat Shamrock Rovers 2–0 in the Final. A year later he was on his way to Deepdale. When Alan Kelly made his debut for North End in the FA Cup fourth-round tie at Swansea, it was a late decision to play him after Fred Else fell ill. Kelly's first two League games, against Sheffield Wednesday and Spurs, saw him concede five goals. In 13 seasons as a player at Deepdale, Alan Kelly experienced all the traumas, exaltations and drama normally associated with a top-flight club. He saw the club slide from a peak of second place in Division One in 1957–58 to Division Three for the first time in their history at the end of the 1969–70 season. However, they did win the Third Division Championship title the following season and were narrowly defeated 3–2 by West Ham United in the 1964 FA Cup Final. His consistency is demonstrated by the fact that in five successive seasons from 1966 he missed just five out of a possible 214 League games and was never dropped. When he was forced to retire, Kelly remained loyal to Preston. He became assistant manager and in 1983 became manager. He resigned the post in February 1985 and was later attached to the coaching staff at Everton. He went on to run goalkeeping clinics in Washington DC. He returned to Deepdale in 2001 as guest of honour when the Alan Kelly Town End was opened.

KELLY, Alan Thomas

Goalkeeper

Born: Preston, 11 August 1968.
Career: PRESTON NORTH END, 1985. Sheffield United, 1992. Blackburn Rovers, 1999. Stockport County, 2001 (loan). Birmingham City, 2001 (loan).

■ Alan Kelly, the son of the goalkeeping legend of the same name, followed in his father's footsteps when he joined Preston North End. After making his League debut against Crewe Alex-

andra in March 1986, he kept his place until the end of the season when North End reached their nadir – 23rd in Division Four. In 1986–87 he shared the goalkeeping duties with David Brown as Preston enjoyed a remarkable turn-around and won promotion to the Third Division. A long-term injury then kept Kelly out of action before he returned to contest the number-one jersey, first with Brown and then Simon Farnworth. After such a stop-start career with North End, who were then a struggling Third Division club, it came as a surprise when Dave Bassett signed him for Premier League Sheffield United as cover for Simon Tracey in the summer of 1992. Kelly became the first-ever substitute goalkeeper under new Premier League rules when he replaced Tracey for the last 10 minutes of the game against Spurs at White Hart Lane. With Tracey ruled out for the rest of the season, Kelly acquitted himself well and was called up into Jack Charlton's Republic of Ireland squad. Mainly used as an understudy to Paddy Bonner, he won a place in the Republic's squad for the 1994 World Cup Finals, though he remained on the bench throughout. Kelly later replaced Bonner as the Republic's first-choice 'keeper and went on to win 34 international caps. Back at Bramall Lane, he was elected to the 1995–96 PFA First Division team by his fellow professionals – a feat he achieved for the next two seasons. He was then hit by injuries and in the summer of 1999 he left the Blades, joining Blackburn Rovers for £675,000. Despite still appearing for the Republic of Ireland, Kelly dropped down the pecking order at Ewood Park behind Filan and Friedel. After loan spells with Stockport County and Birmingham City, he decided to retire.

KELLY, Hugh

Outside-left

Born: Preston, 1892.
Career: PRESTON NORTH END, 1914.

■ Hugh Kelly made a goalscoring debut on the opening day of the club's promotion-winning 1914–15 season when the Lilywhites drew 2–2 at Grimsby Town. He kept his place in the side for the opening three games before losing out to George Barlow. He returned to the side for the Boxing Day encounter against Lincoln City but was then relegated to the club's reserve side, having played in four games and not once been on the losing side.

KELLY, John

Winger, midfield

Born: Bebington, 20 October 1960.
Career: Cammell Laird. Tranmere Rovers, 1979. PRESTON NORTH END, 1981. Chester City, 1985. Swindon Town, 1987. Oldham Athletic, 1987. Walsall, 1989. Huddersfield Town, 1990 (loan). Huddersfield Town, 1991. Chester City, 1992.

■ John Kelly, a Republic of Ireland Under-21 international, began his League career with Tranmere Rovers after a number of impressive performances for local side Cammell Laird. Kelly spent a couple of seasons at Prenton Park before signing for Preston North End in October 1981. He made his debut for the Deepdale club in a goalless draw at Bristol City and went on to score five goals in 30 League games in that

1981–82 season. This included four in successive games towards the end of the campaign. Kelly's best season in terms of goals scored was 1983–84 when he netted 14 goals in all competitions including braces in the games against Brentford and Exeter City. At the end of North End's relegation season of 1984–85, Kelly left Deepdale to join Chester City. In his first season with the Cestrians he helped them win promotion from the Fourth Division. Following a brief spell with Swindon Town, he played for Oldham Athletic, Walsall and Huddersfield Town before rejoining Chester. He took his tally of goals in his two spells for the Sealand Road club to 18 in 116 League games before hanging up his boots.

KELLY, Robert

Inside-right, outside-right

Born: Ashton-in-Makerfield, 16 November 1893.
Died: 1969.
Career: Ashton White Star. Ashton Central. Earlstown Rovers. St Helens Town. Burnley, 1913. Sunderland, 1925. Huddersfield Town, 1926. PRESTON NORTH END, 1932. Carlisle United, 1934.

■ Former miner Bob Kelly was one of the most durable players in British football, making 601 League appearances in a career which spanned two decades either side of World War One. Originally a full-back with Ashton White Star and Ashton Central, Kelly converted to inside-forward after joining Liverpool County Combination club Earlstown Rovers in 1912. In August 1913 he signed for St Helens Town and three months later joined Burnley. Within a fortnight he was in their League side. After war service, he played in 27 of their record run of 30 undefeated League matches in 1920–21 en route to the League Championship. Kelly won the first of 14 full caps for England when he scored twice in a 5–4 win over Scotland at Sheffield. That season his total of 20 goals included four in a 7–1 win over Oldham Athletic. By the time he left Turf Moor to join Sunderland for a British record fee of £6,550 in December 1925, he had scored 97 goals in 299 League and

Cup games. In his first season at Roker Park he helped the Wearsiders to third place in Division One, but in February 1927 he moved to Huddersfield Town. With the Terriers he gained two FA Cup runners'-up medals and scored 42 goals in 213 games before in the summer of 1932, at the age of 38, he was transferred to Preston North End as a replacement right-winger for Alec Reid. Having made his debut in a 3–2 home defeat at the hands of Bradford Park Avenue on the opening day of the 1932–33 season, Kelly scored in his next games as Burnley, one of his former clubs, were beaten 6–1. The following season he helped North End win promotion to the First Division as runners-up to Grimsby Town. After a spell as player-manager of Carlisle United, he managed Stockport County to the Third Division title, but they were relegated 12 months later. After World War Two he coached in Portugal, Switzerland and the Channel Islands and managed Barry Town.

KELSO, Robert Robinson

Right-back, right-half

Born: Cardross, 2 October 1865.
Died: 1942.
Career: Renton. Newcastle West End. Everton, 1888. PRESTON NORTH END, 1889. Everton, 1891. Dundee. Bedminster.

■ Bob Kelso came from the famous Scottish football breeding ground of the 1880s and first made his name with Renton when they were a prominent force in football north of the border. He moved to Newcastle West End in the close season of 1888. Kelso made one appearance for Everton in the League's first season of 1888–89 against Preston North End, a match the Lilywhites won 2–0. He joined North End in readiness for the following season and missed just two games as the club retained the League Championship. In 1890–91, Preston finished runners-up to Everton and the Scottish international opted for a return to the Merseyside club. They persuaded him to convert to full-back with good effect. Strong-tackling and hard-kicking, he was in the Everton team which lost the 1893 FA Cup Final to Wolves at Fallowfield and also played in the side which came second in the First

Division two seasons later. In the summer of 1896, Kelso moved to Dundee where he won a recall to the national side 10 years after his last appearance.

KENDALL, Howard

Midfield

Born: Ryton-on-Tyne, 22 May 1946.
Career: PRESTON NORTH END, 1963. Everton, 1967. Birmingham City, 1974. Stoke City, 1977. Blackburn Rovers, 1979. Everton, 1981.

■ Howard Kendall was the youngest-ever player to appear in an FA Cup Final when, at the age of 17 years and 345 days,

he played for Preston North End against West Ham United in 1964.

He had played in just 13 League and Cup games. Kendall scored the only goal of the third-round replay against Nottingham Forest and netted his first League goal on only his second appearance in a 5–4 defeat of Southampton at The Dell. Over the next couple of seasons, Kendall demonstrated what a great player he was going to be and, while there was plenty of transfer speculation during the 1965–66 season, it was halted by the fact that North End again embarked on a thrilling FA Cup run. In March 1967, Everton manager Harry Catterick paid Preston £80,000 for the

21-year-old. He went on to be part of one of the most influential midfield combinations that Everton have ever had. Along with Ball and Harvey, he helped the Blues to an emphatic Championship success in 1969–70. He collected Football League representative honours and Under-23 caps and was unlucky not to get into the senior side. He was certainly good enough to have played for England, as his influence in midfield at Everton was often quite awesome. In February 1974 he was part of a complex transfer package which took Bob Latchford from Birmingham to Everton while Kendall made the opposite journey. He proved a reliable buy for the St Andrew's club, helping to stabilise them in the First Division and also taking them to the 1975 FA Cup semi-finals. In August 1977 he joined Stoke City and helped them win promotion to the First Division in 1978–79. In the close season he arrived at Ewood Park as Blackburn's player-manager. He helped take the club from the Third Division to the brink of the top flight, but perhaps the least surprising event of his career was when he returned to Goodison as player-manager in 1981. In 1983–84 the club won the FA Cup and reached the Final of the League Cup. The following season Everton won the League Championship and the European Cup-winners' Cup as well as reaching the FA Cup Final. Kendall was named Manager of the Year. After Everton won the League title in 1986–87 Kendall felt he could do no more and left to manage Athletico Bilbao. He later managed Manchester City, Everton for a second time, Notts County, Sheffield United, and Everton for a third time.

KENDALL, John William

Goalkeeper

Born: Broughton, 9 October 1905.
Died: 1961.
Career: Broughton Rangers. Lincoln City, 1922. Everton, 1923. PRESTON NORTH END, 1927. Lincoln City, 1928. Sheffield United, 1929. Peterborough United.

■ Having impressed with his local club, Lincoln City, goalkeeper John Kendall was transferred to Everton in the summer of 1923 as cover for Tom Fern,

who had also signed from the Imps. Due to Fern's consistency, Kendall made just one appearance in that 1923–24 season in the penultimate match of the campaign, a 4–2 win over Spurs. He started the following season as Everton's first-choice 'keeper but injuries and loss of form saw him lose his place. He moved to Preston in 1927 having made just 23 League and Cup appearances in four years at Goodison. With Tony Carr in outstanding form, Kendall made just two appearances for North End, the latter a 3–0 home defeat by fellow promotion-contenders Chelsea. He left Deepdale to rejoin Lincoln but a year later moved to Sheffield United where he played in 80 games for the Blades before moving into non-League football with Peterborough United.

KENNEDY, James

Inside-right

Born: Preston, 1891.
Career: PRESTON NORTH END, 1913.

■ During the club's relegation season of 1913–14, James Kennedy was one of a number of local players used by the club as they strove to avoid the drop into Division Two. He scored on his Preston debut but the Lilywhites were beaten 4–1 by high-flying Middlesbrough. After another couple of appearances – one of

which was a 2–1 win over Bradford City – the club released him.

KERFOOT, Jason John Thomas

Midfield

Born: Preston, 17 April 1973.
Career: PRESTON NORTH END, 1991.

■ Local-born midfielder Jason Kerfoot made four appearances off the bench during the course of the 1991–92 season, the first when he replaced Graham Shaw in a 1–0 defeat at Bournemouth. In fact, not only did North End lose each of the games that Kerfoot played in but they also failed to register a single goal.

KERR, Edward John

Outside-left

Born: Preston, 1898.
Career: PRESTON NORTH END, 1919.

■ Winger Edward Kerr played in a couple of games in 1919–20, the first season of League football after World War Two. The first ended all square at 3–3 with Bradford Park Avenue, with Kerr making both of Stan Davies' goals. On his second appearance in North End colours, Preston were well beaten 4–1 by Bolton Wanderers.

KERR, Jasper

Full-back

Born: Burnbank, 1 January 1903.
Career: Larkhall Thistle. Bathgate. Everton, 1924. PRESTON NORTH END, 1927. New Brighton, 1933. Lancaster Town.

■ Having impressed north of the border, full-back Jasper Kerr joined Everton before the start of the 1924–25 season but both his appearances in that campaign ended in 3–0 defeats. After a single appearance the following season he played in the majority of the games in the first half of the 1926–27 campaign, scoring from long distance at Burnley, before being allowed to join North End. Over the next four seasons, Kerr missed very few games and his consistency at right-back and left-back was a feature of North End's play. He had appeared in 121 League games for the Deepdale club

when he broke his left leg in the goalless home draw against Notts County in December 1931. As it happened, he never played for North End again. Although he tried to make a comeback in the League with New Brighton, it did not work out and he finished his playing days with Lancaster Town.

KIDD, Ryan Andrew

Defender

Born: Radcliffe, 6 October 1971.
Career: Port Vale, 1990. PRESTON NORTH END, 1992.

■ Despite promises of a schoolboy contract at Deepdale, Ryan Kidd was shown the door and ended up at Port Vale. After two years at Vale Park in which he made just one League appearance, Kidd was given a free transfer and joined North End. He made his debut as a substitute for Lee Fowler in the derby match with Blackpool in October 1992 – a game in which Tony Ellis netted a hat-trick in a 3–2 win for Preston. The predominantly left-footed defender settled in well into the North End side and helped the club reach the Play-offs the following season. He was suspended for the first leg of the semi-final at Torquay but returned to help the club reach the Final with a 4–1 extra-time second-leg victory. Unfortunately,

Preston lost 4–2 to Wycombe Wanderers in the Final. Though he temporarily lost his place in 1995–96 following his sending off at Colchester, he regained his spot and helped the club win the Third Division Championship. Kidd was a key figure in the adoption of the wing-back system by manager Gary Peters before his absence with a groin injury coincided with a poor run of results. He continued to prove himself North End's most consistent performer and only missed matches through injury or suspension. Operations on a troublesome ankle reduced his appearances, though whenever he did pop up to score a goal, they were usually with his right foot. An operation in summer 1999 to relieve a breathing problem was a precursor to his early season at Deepdale in 1999–2000 – he missed games through another ankle injury, illness and a broken hand. Thankfully, Kidd returned towards the end of the campaign to play in enough games to warrant a Second Division Championship medal. Diagnosed with a serious neck injury at the end of the season, he underwent surgery during the summer and was out of action for most of 2000–01. Kidd then underwent an operation for the fourth consecutive summer – this time on his knee – but, though he later returned to action, he suffered a recurrence of the neck problem in the game against Barnsley and was forced to retire. He is best remembered for his consistency over a 10-year period at both left-back and centre-half.

KILBANE, Farrell Noel

Centre-half

Born: Preston, 21 October 1974.
Career: Cambridge United. PRESTON NORTH END, 1993.

■ Formerly a youth trainee with Cambridge United, central defender Farrell Kilbane made just one substitute appearance for Preston North End. This came during the 1993–94 season when the club reached the Play-off Final. Kilbane came off the bench to replace Mickey Norbury in a 3–1 home win over Torquay United – the club's opponents in the Play-off semi-final.

KILBANE, Kevin Daniel

Left-winger, midfield

Born: Preston, 1 February 1977.
Career: PRESTON NORTH END, 1995. West Bromwich Albion, 1997. Sunderland, 1999. Everton, 2003.

■ Kevin Kilbane came up through the ranks at Preston North End and made his debut in 1995–96 as a substitute for Graeme Atkinson in a 4–0 win at Torquay. In his very first season in the side his ability to beat men at pace and whip in dangerous crosses led to him being called up to the Republic of Ireland Under-21 squad. His form the following season saw North End receive a bid of £900,000 from West Bromwich Albion and, though this was rejected, the Baggies splashed out a club record £1 million in the close season to take him to the Hawthorns. Kilbane quickly became a crowd favourite and was also elevated to the Republic of Ireland senior team. Though he occasionally lacked consistency when playing for Albion, he did score the 'Goal of the Season' against Bolton Wanderers and net the winner in the derby game with Wolves. His much-improved performances prompted Sunderland to pay £2.5 million for his services. It took Kilbane some time to adapt to his new surroundings and the step up into the Premiership. However, he continued to be a regular for the Republic of Ireland, helping them qualify for the 2002 World Cup Finals. In September 2003, Everton paid the Black Cats £750,000 for the Irishman. The following season Kilbane, who has won 64 caps for the Republic, became the first

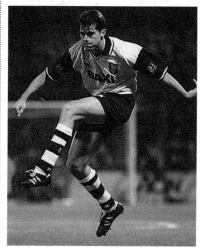

outfielder to figure in every Everton League game for 13 years. His consistent displays in a more central role also saw him voted as the Republic of Ireland's Player of the Year.

KIRBY, William

Inside-left

Born: Preston, 1882.
Career: Swindon Town. West Ham United. Swindon Town. Portsmouth. PRESTON NORTH END, 1911. Exeter City. Merthyr Town. Croydon Common. Brentford.

■ Bill Kirby was a prolific goalscorer in the Southern League for a number of clubs either side of his two seasons in the Preston side. He was ever present in 1911–12, his first season with the club, and was also the club's leading goalscorer with 14 goals but this could not prevent North End losing their top-flight status. The following season he scored braces in the 3–2 win over Leeds City and the 4–2 victory against Bradford Park Avenue, but then lost out to new signing Alf Common. Having scored eight goals in his 17 games, he certainly played his part in the club returning to the First Division as Champions of Division Two.

KNIGHT, John

Inside-left

Born: Bolton, 12 September 1922.
Died: 1996.
Career: Burnley, 1945. PRESTON NORTH END, 1948. Chesterfield, 1951. Exeter City, 1952. Bath City.

■ John Knight was a player of boundless energy who packed a ferocious shot. He followed his older brother George to Turf Moor as a junior in 1938 but, because of World War Two, it was not until 1947 that he tasted Football League action. He spent his time with Burnley mainly on the fringes of the first team but was good enough to deputise for the injured Billy Morris for a large part of the 1947–48 season. In December 1948 he joined Preston with Scottish international Andy McLaren moving in the opposite direction. After the club suffered relegation from the First Division in his first season at Deepdale, Knight became more of a regular in the North End side in 1949–50, creating a number of goals for both Finney and Eddie Brown. Unable to break into the club's League side during the Second Division Championship-winning season of 1950–51, Knight moved on to Chesterfield. He spent just one season at Saltergate before finishing his League career with Exeter, prior to playing non-League football for Bath City.

KNIGHT, John Herbert

Outside-left

Born: Manchester, 1891.
Career: Glossop, 1913. PRESTON NORTH END, 1919. Wigan Borough, 1921.

■ One of 24 players to make his Football League debut for North End during the 1919–20 season, winger John Knight had spent two seasons before World War One playing League football for Glossop. Once they had failed to gain re-election at the end of the 1914–15 season, Knight realised he would have to find a new club if he wanted to continue playing League football. He was an experienced player when he arrived at Deepdale, as he had appeared in 165 games for Glossop. He struggled to win a regular place at Preston, appearing in just three games over two seasons with the club. The first was in 1919–20 in a 1–1 draw with Derby County and the other two were in the following season

when North End beat Everton 1–0 and drew 2–2 with Sunderland. On leaving Deepdale, Knight made 15 appearances for Wigan Borough, another club that later folded.

KNIGHTON, Kenneth

Midfield

Born: Darton, 20 February 1944.
Career: Wolverhampton Wanderers, 1961. Oldham Athletic, 1966. PRESTON NORTH END, 1967. Blackburn Rovers, 1969. Hull City, 1971. Sheffield Wednesday, 1973.

■ Ken Knighton's early football experience was limited to Texborough near Barnsley but the youngster was

saved from a career in mining by joining Wolverhampton Wanderers as an apprentice professional. Switching from inside-left to wing-half, he made 16 League appearances before moving to Oldham Athletic in November 1966. At Boundary Park, he caught the eye of a number of talent spotters and a year later he joined Preston North End. Knighton made his debut the following month in a 4–1 home win over Charlton Athletic and went on to play in 20 games in a season that the club just avoided relegation to the Third Division by the skin of their teeth. He was ever present in 1968–69 as his non-stop endeavour earned him popularity with the Deep-

dale fans, but after he toured New Zealand with an FA party in the summer he left North End to join Blackburn Rovers. After a couple of seasons at Ewood Park, he returned to Yorkshire to play for Hull City before a move to his sixth and final League club, Sheffield Wednesday. At the end of his first season at Hillsborough, the Owls were desperately trying to avoid relegation and it took a Knighton goal four minutes from the end of their final game of the season against Bolton Wanderers to save them. However, even Knighton's grit and determination could not save them the following season. Knighton retired in 1976 to become Wednesday's youth-team coach. He later managed Sunderland to promotion to the First Division but was dismissed in April 1981 after being considered inflexible. He later managed Leyton Orient before moving into non-League football.

KNOWLES, James

Goalkeeper

Born: Preston, 31 July 1934.
Career: PRESTON NORTH END, 1957; Barrow, 1958.

■ In 1957–58, when North End finished the campaign as runners-up in the First Division to mighty Wolves, goalkeeper James Knowles played in two games as deputy for the ever-dependable Fred Else. His first game for the club saw him keep a clean sheet in a 2–0 win over Nottingham Forest but four days later he was between the posts on Christmas Day when North End drew 4–4 at Sheffield Wednesday. Knowles returned to the reserves before making the move to Barrow in the close season. He spent a couple of seasons at Holker Street but again was never first choice.

KOUMANTARAKIS, George

Forward

Born: Athens, Greece, 27 March 1974.
Career: AmaZulu (South Africa). Manning Rovers. Supersport United (South Africa). Lucerne (Switzerland). Basle (Switzerland). PRESTON NORTH END, 2003. RW Erfurt (Germany).

■ South African international George Koumantarakis joined North End from

Swiss club Basle in January 2003 on a contract until the end of the season. He made his League debut in a 1–1 home draw against Nottingham Forest at the end of the month. However, a lack of match fitness meant that he took quite a while to settle into the Deepdale club's style of play. Having opened his goalscoring account in the 4–2 win over Derby County, he netted a brace in the 5–0 rout of Walsall. He seemed to have developed a real understanding with his strike partner Richard Cresswell, who also scored in those two victories, but this was brought to an abrupt end when Koumantarakis suffered a serious knee injury while on international duty with South Africa. The big striker signed a one-year deal with North End following his previous season's loan but, because of the injury, was not seen in first-team action until the New Year. Koumantarakis was rather controversially called up by South Africa for the African Nations' Cup, despite not playing for nine months, but was sent back after the coach was suspended. After an appearance off the bench, he scored in his first start in the FA Cup replay at Reading. However, after two injury-hit seasons at Deepdale he left to continue his career in Germany with RW Erfurt.

KOZLUK, Robert

Right-wing back

Born: Mansfield, 5 August 1977.
Career: Derby County, 1996. Sheffield United, 1999. Huddersfield Town, 2000 (loan). PRESTON NORTH END, 2005 (loan).

■ A talented right-wing back, Rob Kozluk came through the ranks at Derby County, with whom he made a couple of appearances for the England Under-21 side in the Toulon tournament. Although he was voted County's Young Player of the Year in 1997–98, he found it difficult to break into the Rams side on a permanent basis and joined Sheffield United in March 1999. He made a most encouraging start at Bramall Lane and, following the appointment of manager Neil Warnock, his career flourished even more. His attacking play and crosses regularly set up chances for the forwards while his long throw into the penalty area

was often used as an attacking ploy. Following the arrival of Gus Uhlenbeek he went out on loan to Huddersfield where he made a tremendous impact before rejoining the Blades. Having suffered serious knee ligament damage, he eventually returned to action and scored his first senior goal at Grimsby in 2002–03. He continued to be a regular member of the team until a foot injury ruled him out of action at the start of the 2004–05 season. On returning to full fitness he joined North End on loan but after a substitute appearance in the League in a 2–0 win at Plymouth Argyle and starting the FA Cup defeat by Premiership West Bromwich Albion, he returned to Bramall Lane to cover an injury crisis.

LAIRD, Alexander

Inside-forward

Born: Denny, 1895.
Career: Glasgow Rangers. PRESTON NORTH END, 1922. Falkirk.

■ Inside-forward Sandy Laird arrived at Deepdale with a reputation as a prolific goalscorer following his time in Scotland with Rangers, but during two seasons at Deepdale he disappointed. He made his North End debut in a 1–1 draw at Blackburn Rovers on Christmas Day 1922 and appeared in 17 League games.

The first of his two League goals came in sensational fashion. North End beat Stoke 4–2 with Laird netting his side's third goal just a few seconds after the start of the second half. The following season he looked a little sharper in front of goal and scored against Liverpool and

Aston Villa, but both matches ended in heavy defeats and he left Deepdale to return to Scotland with Falkirk, who were struggling near the foot of the Scottish First Division at the time.

LAMB, Alan David

Midfield

Born: Falkirk, 3 July 1952.
Career: PRESTON NORTH END, 1970. Port Vale, 1977. Dundee, 1978.

■ Scottish Under-23 international midfielder Alan Lamb worked his way up through the juniors and reserve sides to make his North End debut in a 2–1 defeat at Charlton Athletic midway through the 1971–72 season. He scored his first goal for the club on the final day of that campaign in a 2–2 draw at home to Swindon Town. During the next few years, Lamb appeared in more games each season, but in 1973–74 he was powerless to prevent the club's relegation to the Third Division. Injuries and a loss of form then saw his appearances diminish for the senior side and in

March 1977 he moved on to Port Vale. He was a regular in the Valiants' midfield for a season and a half before returning to Scotland to continue his career with Dundee.

LAMBERT, John Gilbert

Inside-left, outside-left

Born: Preston, 16 March 1937.

Died: 1986.
Career: PRESTON NORTH END, 1955.

■ Gil Lambert impressed in the Deepdale club's reserve side for a couple of seasons before he was given his first opportunity in League football in September 1958. Following his debut against Birmingham, he scored on his next outing two days later as Leicester City were beaten 3–1. The following season, the fast-raiding winger netted twice in just three games but in what was Tom Finney's last season, he could not win a regular place. He spent one more season with North End, taking his tally of League goals to six in 22 appearances, but was not retained after the club lost its top-flight status.

LAMBERT, Matthew Roy

Defender

Born: Morecambe, 28 September 1971
Career: PRESTON NORTH END, 1990.
Bury, 1992.

■ Substituted on his League debut as North End lost 2–0 at Brentford, defender Matt Lambert appeared in three successive games at the end of the 1990–91 season – a campaign in which the club finished in mid-table in the Third Division. He appeared a little more frequently the following season and scored goals against Exeter City and Reading but, even so, he was released at the end of the season and joined Bury. Unable to break into the Shakers' League side, he drifted into non-League football.

LANCASHIRE, Graham

Forward

Born: Blackpool, 19 October 1972.
Career: Burnley, 1991. Halifax Town, 1992 (loan). Chester City, 1994 (loan). PRESTON NORTH END, 1994. Wigan Athletic, 1996. Rochdale, 1997. Hednesford Town.

■ Graham Lancashire burst onto the Football League scene with a vengeance in 1991–92 when he deputised for Mike Conroy in the Burnley side. In the four games that Conroy missed, Lancashire scored six goals including a hat-trick in a 6–2 victory at Wrexham. However, he was still unable to win a regular place in the Clarets side and after loan spells with

Halifax Town and Chester City, he was transferred to Preston North End for £5,000. He was not a regular in the Preston side that reached the Play-offs in 1994–95 or the side that performed even better the following season to win the Third Division Championship. As a result Lancashire, whose only goals had come after coming off the bench, joined Wigan Athletic. After scoring three goals in four games he damaged knee ligaments towards the end of the 1995–96 season. Lancashire started the following season in tremendous form, scoring 10 goals in the opening 12 games including a hat-trick in a 4–4 League Cup draw at Preston. Despite another knee injury he helped the Latics win the Third Division title but surprisingly in October 1997 he was sold to Rochdale for £40,000. Injuries hampered his progress at Spotland and after he was out of contract in 2001 he moved into non-League football with Hednesford Town.

LANGMEAD, Kelvin Steven

Forward

Born: Coventry, 23 March 1985.
Career: PRESTON NORTH END, 2004. Tamworth, 2004 (loan). Carlisle United, 2004 (loan). Kidderminster Harriers, 2004 (loan). Shrewsbury Town, 2004.

■ Kelvin Langmead was a regular goalscorer for North End's Under-19 and

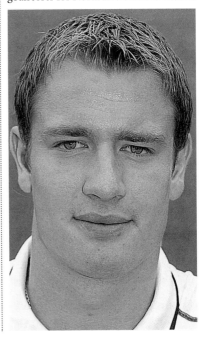

reserve teams during the 2003–04 season. He had loan spells with non-League Tamworth and Carlisle United, but was used as a substitute for most of his time at Brunton Park. He scored his first senior goal in a 3–2 defeat of Mansfield before returning to Deepdale where he received North End's Star of the Future award for being the club's most promising youngster. After another loan spell, this time at Kidderminster, he returned to Deepdale to make his debut for North End as a substitute in the home draw against Millwall. Shortly afterwards he was allowed to move to Shrewsbury where he created an immediate impression.

LANGTON, Robert

Outside-left

Born: Ormskirk, 8 September 1918.
Died: 1996.
Career: Burscough Victoria. Blackburn Rovers, 1938. PRESTON NORTH END, 1948. Bolton Wanderers, 1949. Blackburn Rovers, 1953. Ards. Wisbech Town. Kidderminster Harriers. Colwyn Bay.

■ Within 12 months of joining Blackburn Rovers from Southport League side Burscough Victoria, Bobby Langton had established himself in Rovers' first team. In the club's Second Division Championship-winning campaign of 1938–39, he scored 14 goals in 37 appearances. During the war he was an infantryman in India and represented the Army in practically every game they played. Having appeared for Rovers in the 1940 War Cup Final, which they lost 1–0 to West Ham United, he was restored to the Blackburn side at the end of the hostilities. In September 1946 he won the first of 11 England caps. Blackburn's fortunes began to wane and in August 1949 he was transferred to Preston North End for £16,000. In one of his early games against Manchester City, Langton scored after just seven seconds and finished his first season at Deepdale as the club's leading scorer with 12 goals. Unfortunately though he could not prevent North End from being relegated to Division Two. Sadly, his North End career never took off and after just 57 League and Cup games for Preston, he joined Bolton Wanderers for what was

then a club record fee of £20,000. He remained with the Trotters long enough to play in the famous 1953 FA Cup Final against Blackpool before returning to play at Ewood Park in September of that year. Although his speed had diminished in his second spell at Blackburn, he added a great deal of guile and cunning to his play. He had scored 58 goals in 230 League and Cup games for Rovers when he left to play in Ireland with Ards. Langton then entered non-League football with Wisbech Town before playing for Kidderminster Harriers and Colwyn Bay. After spells as trainer-coach at Kings Lynn and Wisbech, Langton returned to his roots and became manager of Burscough Rangers.

LAPOT, Stanley

Wing-half

Born: Edinburgh, 20 January 1944.
Career: Smeaton BC. PRESTON NORTH END, 1962.

■ After playing in the opening two games of the 1962–63 season, wing-half Stan Lapot found himself back in the club's reserves after the latter of these two outings saw North End crash 7–1 at Plymouth Argyle. He returned to the side for the final two games of the campaign and after beating Derby County 1–0 on the final day the club managed to

leapfrog their Second Division basement rivals. Lapot did not play at all the following season and made just a couple of appearances in 1964–65. He scored a couple of goals in successive wins over Derby and Cardiff midway through the following campaign. Still unable to establish himself in the North End side, he was released in the summer of 1967.

LATHAM, Nicholas

Inside-right

Born: Tarleton, 1900.
Career: PRESTON NORTH END, 1921.

■ Inside-forward Nick Latham appeared in just one game for the Lilywhites during the course of the 1921–22 First Division season. It was certainly not the best of debuts as North End went down 5–0 against Spurs at White Hart Lane. Though the North London club completed the double over Preston and finished runners-up in the League, Preston beat them 2–1 in that season's FA Cup semi-final.

LAVERY, William

Right-back

Born: Fleetwood, 1887.
Career: PRESTON NORTH END, 1906. Leicester Fosse. PRESTON NORTH END, 1908. West Ham United.

■ Tough-tackling full-back Bill Lavery started out with Preston in the 1906–07 season, appearing in 15 consecutive League and Cup games. His impressive displays prompted Leicester Fosse to sign him but during his time there he suffered a knee injury which meant that he was unable to break into their League side. He returned to Deepdale for the 1908–09 season but after some solid displays he lost out to John Winchester and left to play Southern League football for West Ham United.

LAWRENSON, Mark Thomas

Defender

Born: Preston, 2 June 1957.
Career: PRESTON NORTH END, 1974. Brighton and Hove Albion, 1977. Liverpool, 1981.

■ One of the most stylish and polished defenders of the modern era, Mark Lawrenson was born just a stone's throw away from North End's Deepdale ground. He followed in his father Tommy's footsteps by joining the Lilywhites, having rejected the opportunity to pursue a cricketing career with Lancashire. He signed professional forms for North End in August 1974 and, after some impressive displays in the club's Central League side, he made his Football League debut in a 2–2 draw against Watford towards the end of the 1974–75 season. At Deepdale a chance conversation with former Preston favourite Alan Kelly, who was then coach to both North End and the Republic of Ireland, led to Lawrenson winning the first of 38 full caps for the Republic. In three seasons in North End's first team, he appeared in 80 League and Cup games. His defensive play was immaculate and it was not long before the scouts were flocking to Deepdale. In July 1977, Brighton, who were newly promoted to Division Two, snapped him up for a fee of £100,000. He did not want to leave the club but North End needed the money and were thus forced to cash in their most valuable asset. At the time the deal went through, he was on holiday and agreed the transfer in a café on the sea front in Benidorm. He spent four years on the South Coast and helped the Seagulls win promotion to Division One in 1978–79 for the first time in their history. In August 1981 he moved to Liverpool for a record-breaking £900,000 fee. Lawrenson reached the pinnacle of his career on Merseyside. He remained a regular in the side in various positions throughout the decade and picked up League Championship and League Cup winners' medals in successive seasons in 1981–82, 1982–83 and 1983–84. He won a European Cup medal in 1984 and was a double winner in 1985–86 when Liverpool won both the League and the FA Cup. Another League Championship medal was added to the collection in 1987–88, his last season with the club. Lawrenson was forced into retirement because of an Achilles tendon injury. He later managed Oxford United and Peterborough United and a number of non-League sides before becoming a prominent TV and radio personality.

LAWRENSON, Thomas

Winger

Born: Preston, 24 May 1929.
Died: 1996.
Career: Leyland Motors. PRESTON NORTH END, 1949. Southport, 1955.

■ Winger Tommy Lawrenson joined North End from Leyland Motors in April

1949, but he had to wait over five years before making his debut in a 3–1 defeat against Spurs at White Hart Lane midway through the 1954–55 season. Unable to displace Angus Morrison, he joined Southport. In his first season at Haig Avenue, he helped the Sandgrounders finish fifth in the Third Division North, their highest position since 1924–25.

LAWTON, Norbert

Midfield

Born: Manchester, 25 March 1940.
Career: Manchester United, 1958. PRESTON NORTH END, 1963. Brighton and Hove Albion, 1967. Lincoln City, 1971.

■ Inspirational captain Nobby Lawton joined Preston from Manchester United in March 1963 at a time when the Deepdale club were struggling in the

lower reaches of the Second Division. Signed by Jimmy Milne for just £11,000, Lawton, who had appeared in 36 League games for United, made his Preston debut in a 4–2 home win over Walsall. The following season he helped North End finish third in Division Two and reach that season's FA Cup Final where they lost 3–2 to First Division West Ham United. Lawton was outstanding throughout the campaign. He scored one of the goals in the fourth-round replay win over neighbours Bolton Wanderers and it was his role in the Wembley showdown which captured many people's attention. Lawton never stopped running, cajoling and urging his teammates on, though it was to no avail as the Hammers ran out victors. Lawton spent three more seasons at Deepdale during which he missed very few games. Although he was never a prolific scorer, he did net seven goals in the space of 12 League games midway through the 1966–67 season. A born leader, he was allowed to join Brighton and Hove Albion in September 1967 and later ended his first-class career with Lincoln City.

LEE, Francis

Winger

Born: Chorley, 17 February 1944.
Career: PRESTON NORTH END, 1961.
Southport, 1970. Stockport County, 1974.

■ An outstanding schoolboy footballer, winger Frank Lee initially signed amateur forms with North End before putting pen to paper on a semi-professional contract with the club. He made his League debut in a 2–0 home defeat at the hands of Derby County in February 1964 even though he was still bound by the semi-professional contract he had signed a couple of years earlier. He eventually signed a full professional

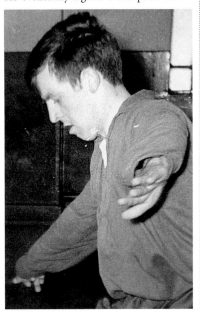

contact in April 1965 and during that season he appeared in 30 League games. Incredibly skilful with the ball at his feet, Lee possessed amazing speed and the ability to beat the best of defenders with tricky footwork. Though more of a provider than goalscorer, he did net nine goals in 1966–67, including five in the opening 11 games of the campaign. Over the next few seasons, Lee was an important member of the North End side but in November 1970 he was allowed to join Southport. During his time at Haig Avenue he helped the Sandgrounders win the Fourth Division Championship in 1972–73. He went on to score 21 goals in 115 games before ending his career with Stockport County.

LEES, John William

Right-back, right-half

Born: Northwich, 28 July 1895.
Career: Northwich Victoria. PRESTON NORTH END, 1919. Halifax Town, 1922.

■ After impressing for his home-town side, Northwich Victoria, John Lees joined North End midway through the 1919–20 season and made his debut in a 3–3 draw at Bradford Park Avenue. Injured on his home debut against Burnley, he missed a handful of games before returning to play in 21 consecutive League and Cup games until the end of the season. His form was one of the reasons that North End lost just one of their last seven games and avoided relegation. Lees started the following season in fine form but injuries took their toll and he lost his place to George Waddell. He moved to Halifax Town and spent eight seasons at The Shay, appearing in 248 League games.

LEONARD, Mark Anthony

Forward

Born: St Helens, 27 September 1962.
Career: Witton Albion. Everton, 1982. Tranmere Rovers, 1983 (loan). Crewe Alexandra, 1983. Stockport County, 1985. Bradford City, 1986. Rochdale, 1992. PRESTON NORTH END, 1992. Chester City, 1993. Wigan Athletic, 1994. Rochdale, 1996.

■ After a series of impressive displays for non-League Witton Albion, Everton

gave Mark Leonard the chance to turn professional. Unable to make the grade with the Goodison club, he went on loan to nearby Tranmere Rovers, making his League debut in a 1–0 defeat at Darlington. At the end of the 1983–84 season he joined Crewe and was a shining light in the Railwaymen's side as they finished mid-table in Division Four. In February 1985 he joined Stockport County and was the club's leading scorer with 23 goals in his first full season at Edgeley Park. This prompted Bradford City to pay £40,000 for him and, though most of his first-team appearances were from the bench, he still continued to find the net until a move to Rochdale. Leonard's stay at Spotland was brief and in the summer of 1992 he joined Preston North End, again for a fee of £40,000. He made his debut on the opening day of the 1992–93 season in a 1–1 home draw against Bournemouth but never really produced the form he was capable of. His only goal in 22 League games came in a 4–3 defeat of Chester City. The Cestrians were Leonard's next club prior to a move to Wigan Athletic. At Springfield Park he rediscovered his shooting boots as well as laying chances on for others. He rejoined Rochdale for a second spell before injury forced his retirement.

LEWIS, Derek Ivor Edwin

Inside-forward

Born: Edmonton, 10 June 1929.
Died: 1953.
Career: Fulham. Gillingham, 1950.
PRESTON NORTH END, 1952.

■ Derek Lewis had been on Fulham's books as an amateur prior to joining Gillingham in May 1950. Though they finished near the bottom of the Third Division South in each of his two seasons with the Kent club, Lewis proved himself a prolific scorer with 31 goals in 48 League outings. North End signed him in February 1952 and he replaced Bobby Foster in the 1–1 draw with Manchester City. He scored two goals that season, against Aston Villa and Portsmouth – both sides that finished above seventh-placed North End. In 1952–53, Lewis netted 12 goals in 29 League games to help North End finish as runners-up to First Division Champions Arsenal. This included four in successive games and a spell of eight in nine games. One of the club's most promising young players, he sadly died of a brain haemorrhage in the close season. The whole town mourned his passing.

LEWIS, Edward

Full-back, forward

Born: Manchester, 3 January 1935.
Career: Manchester United, 1952.
PRESTON NORTH END, 1955. West Ham United, 1956. Leyton Orient, 1958.

■ Eddie Lewis was a confident footballer who began his career with Manchester United by scoring almost a goal every other game in his time at Old Trafford. He spent almost five years at Busby's academy before transferring to Preston North End in December 1955. He went straight into the Deepdale club's side and made a goalscoring debut, albeit in a 3–2 defeat at Aston Villa. He also scored against his former club as North End beat Manchester United later in the season. Unable to make much headway during the early stages of the 1956–57 season, he left to play for West Ham United. Again he proved his worth in front of goal before moving across London to Leyton Orient in the summer of 1958. Here he was switched to a full-back role and was impressive in that position for the next five seasons, helping Orient win promotion to the First Division in 1961–62.

LEWIS, Edward James

Left-winger

Born: Cerritos, US, 17 May 1974.
Career: San Jose Clash (US). Fulham, 2000. PRESTON NORTH END, 2002. Leeds United, 2005.

■ Spotted by Fulham scouts while playing for the US in the CONCACAF Cup, Eddie Lewis joined the Cottagers from San Jose Clash just before the transfer deadline day in March 2000 for £1.3 million. Described as the 'American David Beckham', despite having modelled his game on Ryan Giggs, Lewis failed to make the impact he had hoped as Fulham missed out on the Play-offs. After the appointment of Jean Tigana most of his appearances came in the Worthington Cup. His pace and accurate crossing caused problems at reserve-team level and he netted successive hat-tricks against Swindon Town and Oxford United. In 2001–02 he appeared only once for Fulham, lining up in the final

Premiership game of the season, though he did secure a place in the US's World Cup squad, helping his side reach the quarter-finals where they lost to Germany. Eddie Lewis signed for North End in August 2002, but his debut for the Deepdale club was delayed due to work permit problems and the fact that he was not fully match fit. Though he took some time to settle, once he had he made steady progress throughout the campaign on the left flank, producing his best performance in the 3–1 defeat of Burnley. He went on to score six goals in 43 League and Cup outings. He also created a number of goals for his teammates as his telling crosses delivered by either foot gave the likes of Cresswell and Fuller ideal opportunities to find the net. After playing for his country in the summer's Gold Cup, he could have been excused for starting the 2003–04 campaign slowly, but this was not the case as he scored the first goal of the new campaign after just 92 seconds in the early kick-off against West Ham United. A hernia operation brought about a much-needed rest but he surprised everyone by returning for the final few games and scoring against Cardiff. The following season was a similar story: after an emergency appendix operation, he was back in time for the Play-offs.

LINDLEY, Tinsley

Centre-forward

Born: Nottingham, 27 October 1865.
Died: 1940.
Career: Nottingham Forest. Cambridge University. Corinthians. Casuals. Crusaders. Notts County, 1889. Nottingham Forest. Swifts. Nottingham Forest. PRESTON NORTH END, 1891.

■ One of the most famous amateur players of his generation, Tinsley Lindley made his England debut in 1886, scoring in a 6–1 win over Ireland in Belfast. He was a Cambridge Blue and a centre-forward with the great Corinthians side. He also played for Casuals, Crusaders and Notts County as well as Forest, though it is unclear which club he was attached to and at what time. Something of a character, he always refused to wear football boots, claiming they reduced his speed – he preferred to wear ordinary walking shoes instead! He scored four times when Forest beat Clapton 14–0 in January 1891 and managed 15 FA Cup goals in 25 appearances in the competition. His one and only game in Preston colours came in March 1892 when the club were beaten 4–1 by Sunderland. In 1899 he was called to the bar and lectured on law at Nottingham University before becoming a county court judge. In 1918 he was awarded an OBE for his work as chief officer of Nottinghamshire's Special Constabulary.

LITCHFIELD, Peter

Goalkeeper

Born: Manchester, 27 July 1956.
Career: Droylsden. PRESTON NORTH END, 1979. Bradford City, 1985. Oldham Athletic, 1988 (loan). Scunthorpe United, 1989.

■ Goalkeeper Peter Litchfield, who wore contact lenses, began his career at non-League Droylsden. He made an unforgettable debut for North End in a match against Chelsea in February 1981 – he just could not be beaten as North End won 1–0. Litchfield's display between the posts won him *The Sun* Match winner award – a cheque for £1,000 which he promptly gave to Mel

Holden's widow, choosing the Motor Neurone Disease Association in the former player's honour. Unfortunately, the club lost their Second Division status that season. Litchfield played in all of the games in the first half of the 1981–82 season before losing out to loan signing Martin Hodge. It was a similar story the following season as an injury to Litchfield saw Hodge return to Deepdale, again on loan. In 1983–84, Litchfield missed just one game as North End struggled in the lower reaches of the Third Division. The following season saw North End relegated to Division Four but Litchfield, who kept goal for the first half of the campaign, had been transferred to Bradford City. He was the Bantams' first-choice 'keeper for almost three seasons before leaving to end his first-class career with Scunthorpe United.

LLOYD, Norman William McLean

Midfield

Born: Torrance, 6 September 1949.
Career: PRESTON NORTH END, 1966. Stockport County, 1971 (loan). Southport, 1971. Stockport County, 1974.

■ Norman Lloyd's first game in North End colours came towards the end of the 1968–69 season in a 3–0 home win over Bury. The following term he appeared on a more regular basis and netted five goals in his 12 starts including a brace in a 4–1 defeat of Charlton Athletic. However, with players of the calibre of Wilson, Ham, Ingram and Irvine in the side, as North End went on to win the Third Division title, Lloyd joined Southport following a loan spell with Stockport County. He helped the Haig Avenue club win the Fourth Division Championship in 1972–73. He finished his career with Stockport County who ended his only season at Edgeley Park near the foot of the League's basement.

LOCKETT, Arthur H

Outside-left, right-back

Born: Alsagers Bank, 30 August 1875.
Died: 1957.

Career: Crewe Alexandra. Stoke, 1900. Aston Villa, 1902. PRESTON NORTH END, 1905. Watford. Mardy.

■ England international Arthur Lockett started his career as an outside-left and had a reputation for bamboozling a full-back twice. Having started out with his local club, Crewe Alexandra, he joined Stoke in 1900 before moving to Aston Villa. In his first season with the Midlands club he helped them finish runners-up in the First Division before injuries and a loss of form prompted him to move to North End in readiness for the 1905–06 season. His first campaign at Deepdale was outstanding as he more than played his part in helping the club finish runners-up to Liverpool in the First Division. Midway through the following season, Lockett was switched to full-back and played with great distinction until leaving to play Southern League football for Watford. He was so popular at the club's Cassio Road ground that his release after four seasons prompted a petition urging reconsideration, but the position stood and he went to play with John Goodall at Mardy.

LODGE, Paul

Midfield

Born: Liverpool, 13 February 1961.
Career: Everton, 1979. Wigan Athletic, 1982 (loan). Rotherham United, 1983 (loan). PRESTON NORTH END, 1983. Bolton Wanderers, 1984. Port Vale, 1984

(loan). Stockport County, 1985. Southport.

■ England Schoolboy international Paul Lodge played his early football with Everton, making his debut as a substitute in a 3–1 home defeat by Aston Villa. His first full appearance for the Blues was in the Merseyside derby against Liverpool, a match Everton lost 1–0. The midfield playmaker was unable to hold down a regular place at Goodison due to the fine form of Asa Hartford, Steve McMahon and Howard Kendall and he went on loan to both Wigan Athletic and Rotherham United. He joined Preston North End in February 1983 and was on the losing side on his debut as Preston crashed 3–0 at Newport County. Lodge kept his place in the side for the remaining 19 games of the season and appeared in every League and Cup game in the first half of the following campaign before joining Bolton Wanderers. Following a loan spell with Port Vale, he played for Stockport County before moving into non-League football with Southport.

LONERGAN, Andrew

Goalkeeper

Born: Preston, 19 October 1983.
Career: PRESTON NORTH END, 2000.
Darlington, 2002 (loan).

■ Called up in an injury crisis, goalkeeper Andy Lonergan made his North End debut at Coventry in the 2000–01 Worthington Cup-tie at Coventry City when he was just 16 years old. Previously capped by the Republic of Ireland in an Under-16 friendly, it was a season in which he made two appearances for England Under-17s as well as making his League debut in the 3–2 home win over Watford. Lonergan was out of the first-team picture for the next couple of seasons, so he went on loan to Darlington before making the England Under-20 squad for the Toulon tournament in the summer of 2003. On the back of these performances, he moved back up to become the club's second-choice 'keeper and had a run of eight consecutive appearances until a broken hand allowed Jonathan Gould back into the side. He started the 2004–05 season as the club's first-choice

'keeper and, after saving a penalty on the opening day of the campaign, capped that by scoring with a long clearance at Leicester City.

LONSDALE, George

Centre-forward

Born: Preston, 1874.
Career: PRESTON NORTH END, 1895.

■ George Lonsdale was a big, bustling centre-forward who had impressed in local junior football. North End gave him his chance in League football during the 1895–96 season. After making his debut in a 2–1 defeat at Sheffield United he scored on his next, and what transpired to be his final, appearance in Preston colours in a 3–2 victory over Small Heath.

LORMOR, Anthony

Forward

Born: Ashington, 29 October 1970.
Career: Newcastle United, 1988. Lincoln City, 1990. Peterborough United, 1994. Chesterfield, 1994. PRESTON NORTH END, 1997. Notts County, 1998 (loan). Mansfield Town, 1998. Hartlepool United, 2000. Shrewsbury Town, 2002 (loan). Telford United.

■ Tony Lormor made his debut for the Magpies when still on a youth training scheme, standing in for Brazilian international Mirandinha. He scored in each of his first two full appearances for the club and looked set to have a bright future in the North East. However, it was not to be and Lormor moved on to Lincoln City where he was the club's leading scorer for three consecutive seasons. A brief stay with Peterborough was followed by a move to

Chesterfield. From his debut the Spireites went 21 games unbeaten, such was his impact, and he scored the first Play-off goal at Wembley as Chesterfield rejoined the Second Division. At Saltergate, Lormor was a key part of the club's direct style and instrumental in the club's exciting run to the FA Cup semi-finals. In November 1997, after scoring 45 goals in 134 games for Chesterfield, he joined Preston North End as part of the deal that involved David Reeves going in the opposite direction. However, despite a goal on his debut at Luton and a brace at Southend, he was never able to repeat his Chesterfield goalscoring exploits at Deepdale and was loaned to Notts County. Unlucky not to score in his time at Meadow Lane, Lormor headed back to Deepdale but did not make any further appearances before being transferred to Mansfield Town for £20,000. After a difficult start at Field Mill, he began to find the net and win over the fans but in the summer of 2000 he was surprisingly allowed to join Hartlepool United. Injuries hampered his progress at the Victoria Ground and after a loan spell with Shrewsbury Town, he moved into non-League football with Telford United. He went on to become a Class 1 referee.

LOWE, Henry

Left-back

Born: Skelmersdale, 19 February 1907.
Died: 1975.
Career: Skelmersdale Mission. Southport, 1927. Everton, 1930. PRESTON NORTH END, 1932. Swindon Town, 1939. Skelmersdale United.

■ Harry Lowe played his early football with Southport in the Third Division North left-back before he joined Everton. Though he only managed a handful of first-team appearances in his time at Goodison, his debut was memorable for the fact that the Blues beat Oldham Athletic 6–4 and Dixie Deans netted four of the goals. Lowe joined Preston with 'keeper Harry Holdcroft in 1932 and went straight into the team for the game at Southampton which North End lost 1–0. He stayed in the side and played a notable part in the club's steady transformation of fortunes and outlook. Promotion was gained in his first full season, 1933–34, when he was ever present. Soon afterwards, North End made great efforts to achieve prominence in the First Division and figured in two successive FA Cup finals in 1937 and 1938. Due to the rapid advance of Andy Beattie, Lowe did not play in either. In fact, his first-class career was drawing to a close. Nevertheless, he had proved

himself a thoroughly dependable full-back: never a showy player, he did the simple things the easy and effective way.

LOWEY, John Anthony

Midfield

Born: Manchester, 7 March 1958.
Career: Manchester United, 1975. Chicago Stings (US). Blackburn Rovers, 1977. Port Vale, 1977. California (US). Sheffield Wednesday, 1978. Blackburn Rovers, 1980. Wigan Athletic, 1986. Chesterfield, 1986 (loan). York City, 1987 (loan). PRESTON NORTH END, 1987. Chester City, 1988.

■ Much-travelled midfielder John Lowey started out with Manchester United but, despite some impressive displays at youth-team and reserve-team level, could not force his way into the Reds' League side. He went to try his luck in the US before returning to the North West with Blackburn Rovers. Unable to

make much headway, he joined Port Vale, where he was laid low by injuries, and had another stint in the US before joining Sheffield Wednesday. He at last made his Football League debut and went on to help the Owls win promotion to the Second Division. In November 1980, Blackburn Rovers persuaded Lowey to return to Ewood Park and over the next five seasons he was one of their most consistent players as they challenged for a place in the top flight. Having scored 14 goals in 141 League games he signed for Wigan Athletic.

Unable to hold down a regular place, he had loan spells with Chesterfield and York before joining North End in the summer of 1987. He started the 1987–88 season wearing the number-nine shirt but, though he scored against Brentford, he failed to produce the form he had shown with Blackburn and moved on to end his career with Chester City.

LOWRIE, George

Centre-forward

Born: Rhondda, 19 December 1919.
Died: 1989.
Career: Tonypandy. Swansea City, 1937. PRESTON NORTH END, 1937. Coventry City, 1939. Newcastle United, 1948. Bristol City, 1949. Coventry City, 1952. Lovells Athletic.

■ George Lowrie played his early football with Swansea but moved to Preston North End after being unable to break into the Welsh club's side. Lowrie made his debut in a 1–1 draw at Stoke and appeared in a handful of games as North End finished the season in third

place in Division One, but he did not manage to find the net. After a season in the club's reserves, he joined Coventry City when manager Harry Storer paid £1,750 for his services. During the war years, Lowrie netted a headline-grabbing hat-trick for Wales against England at Wembley and scored regularly in his nine wartime international appearances. A prolific scorer during wartime football, he began the 1946–47 season in great style, scoring all Coventry's goals in a 4–1 win over Luton Town on the opening day of the season. He netted a hat-trick in the club's third game and later in the season scored another four goals in a 5–0 defeat of Bradford. Lowrie had scored 47 goals in 58 League games for Coventry when he left to play for Newcastle United for a club record fee of £18,500. Unable to settle in the North East, he joined Bristol City but broke a leg. After recovering he had another stint with Coventry before ending his career with Lovells Athletic.

LUCAS, David Anthony

Goalkeeper

Born: Preston, 23 November 1977.
Career: PRESTON NORTH END, 1994. Darlington, 1995 (loan). Darlington, 1996 (loan). Scunthorpe United, 1996 (loan). Sheffield Wednesday, 2003 (loan). Sheffield Wednesday, 2004.

■ England Youth international goalkeeper David Lucas made his North End debut in the title-clinching game at Hartlepool towards the end of the 1995–96 season and kept a clean sheet in a 2–0 win. He had earlier played six times in an impressive loan spell for Darlington. The following season he had another loan spell with the Quakers and at Scunthorpe to gain further experience before returning to Deepdale to keep clean sheets in the two final games of the campaign. In the summer of 1997 he was a member of the England Under-20 squad that played in Malaysia and during the course of the following season he was selected for the following squads: the Nationwide representative squad for the match against Italy's Serie 'B' side, the England Under-21 squad for the game against Switzerland and the England 'B' squad for the match against Portugal. He

finally got a run in the first team following an injury to Tepi Moilanen but he lost out to the Finn following a controversial sending-off in the home defeat by Wigan in 1999–2000. An excellent shot-stopper, he found himself sharing the goalkeeping duties for the next season or so, but when Moilanen left the club he lost out to new signing Jonathan Gould. In 2003–04 he made just two appearances as he slipped behind Andy Lonergan in the goalkeeping pecking order and opted for a loan move to Sheffield Wednesday. After some outstanding displays, he suffered medial ligament damage and this put paid to his campaign. He had made 150 first-team appearances for North End when he joined the Owls permanently in June 2004. He ended his first season by helping the club win promotion after defeating Hartlepool in the Play-offs at the Millennium Stadium.

LUCAS, Richard

Defender

Born: Chapeltown, 22 September 1970.
Career: Sheffield United, 1989. PRESTON NORTH END, 1992. Lincoln City, 1994 (loan). Scarborough, 1995. Hartlepool United, 1997. Halifax Town, 1998. Boston United.

■ Versatile defender Richard Lucas started his Football League career with Sheffield United before joining Preston for a fee of £40,000 in December 1992. He went straight into the North End side for the home game with Exeter City, which ended all square at 2–2. He missed very few games that season but the club lost their Second Division status after defeat in their last five games of the campaign. Lucas helped the club reach the Third Division Play-offs the following season but, due to competition for places, he went on loan to Lincoln before joining Scarborough. An uncompromising player, he turned in a series of solid-tackling displays for the Yorkshire club before a move to Hartlepool saw him score his first goals at League level. On his release from the North East club, he signed for Halifax Town but a series of niggling injuries hampered his efforts, though he never let anyone down when he did come into the side. He was subsequently released and left to play non-League football for Boston United.

LUCKETTI, Christopher James

Defender

Born: Rochdale, 28 September 1971.
Career: Rochdale, 1988. Stockport County, 1990. Halifax Town, 1991. Bury, 1993. Huddersfield Town, 1999. PRESTON NORTH END, 2001. Sheffield United (loan) 2006.

■ A commanding, powerful central defender, Chris Lucketti first impressed while playing for Halifax Town and it was his performances for the Shaymen that prompted Bury to pay £50,000 for his services in October 1993. He won the Player of the Season award in each of his first three seasons at Gigg Lane and demonstrated that he was destined to play at a higher grade of football. In 1996–97 he achieved that with the Shakers after helping them win the Second Division Championship. An ever present the following season, he was also appointed Bury's captain and continued to enhance his growing reputation with a string of consistent performances at the heart of the defence. Unable to prevent the Gigg Lane club's relegation the following season, Lucketti, who had made 277 appearances for Bury, left to play for Huddersfield Town after a fee of £750,000 was agreed. His performances were a major factor in Town's rise up the table until an innocuous challenge in the game against Bolton left him with a broken leg. On his return to action he was appointed the Terriers' captain but could do nothing to halt their slide into Division Two. Eventually the club's financial position led to Lucketti being sold to Preston North End for the same fee that had brought him to the McAlpine Stadium. A superb debut at Grimsby was followed by his first goal in the home defeat by Wolves and he remained a regular in the side during 2001–02 until suffering a gashed foot towards the end of the campaign. Lucketti was appointed Preston's captain and led by example throughout the 2002–03 season with his commanding presence in the air and in the tackle serving as an inspiration to those around him. Injuries hampered his progress the following season but he returned to form an effective partnership alongside Youl Mawene at the heart of the North End defence and help the club to the Play-offs. Lucketti started the 2005–06 season as the Preston captain and scored his side's goal when nine-man North End held Crystal Palace to a 1–1 draw, but in March 2006 he went on loan to Sheffield United where his displays helped the Blades win automatic promotion to the Premiership.

LUDDEN, Dominic James

Left-back

Born: Basildon, 30 March 1974.
Career: Billericay Town. Leyton Orient, 1992. Watford, 1994. PRESTON NORTH END, 1998. Halifax Town, 2001. Leigh RMI.

■ An England Schoolboy international, Dominic Ludden was spotted by Leyton Orient playing non-League football for Billericay Town and given his chance in the Football League. Particularly effective at going forward in support of his forwards, the tough-tackling left-back had made 66 appearances for the Brisbane Road club when Watford paid £100,000 for his

services in the summer of 1994. Ludden's early days at Vicarage Road were hampered by hamstring and back injuries that prevented him from confirming his first-team place and in 1997–98 he did not appear at all in the Watford side. In July 1998 he joined Preston on a free transfer and quickly became a huge favourite with the North End fans. Stunningly fast, he got forward well and could be relied upon to deliver a string of telling crosses from the left flank as well as being solid in defence. A groin strain and a niggling stomach injury restricted his appearances in 1999–2000 and he was released after only one substitute appearance the following season. He joined Halifax Town but continued to have a frustrating time with injuries and eventually left the Shay to play non-League football for Leigh RMI.

LUKE, William

Outside-right

Born: Acklington, 1890.
Died: January 1992.
Career: Bedlington United. PRESTON NORTH END, 1912. Hartlepool United.

■ Winger Billy Luke signed for Preston from Bedlington United and appeared in eight games for North End during the 1912–13 season, scoring a

couple of goals in the 2–1 win over Clapton Orient when he wore the number-nine shirt and in the 1–1 draw with Burnley. At the end of the season, in which North End won the Second Division Championship, he went on the club's continental tour to Holland, but by the time the following season got underway he had left Deepdale to continue his career with Hartlepool United. Unfortunately a leg injury sustained in World War One ended his career. When he died in January 1992, Billy Luke was the League's oldest former professional.

LYALL, George

Midfield

Born: Wick, 4 May 1947.
Career: Raith Rovers. PRESTON NORTH END, 1966. Nottingham Forest, 1972. Hull City, 1975.

■ Midfielder George Lyall began his career in his native Scotland with Raith Rovers, the club which produced former North Enders Alex James and David Morris in the 1920s. Lyall scored 32 goals

in his first season of senior football for the Starks' Park club and possessed a hard, dangerous shot. He was being chased by a number of clubs when he eventually signed for North End in March 1966. Initially he found it difficult to settle at Deepdale and most of his outstanding performances were at reserve-team level. In fact, after three seasons at Deepdale, he had only played in 23 first-team games. However, his obvious love of the game and zest shone through and he went on to blossom into a very good player. Lyall left North End to play for Nottingham Forest in May 1972 and over the next three seasons was a virtual ever present in their side, scoring 24 goals in 116 League games. He later ended his career with a couple of seasons at Hull City in the Second Division.

LYNCH, Simon George

Forward

Born: Montreal, Canada, 19 May 1982.
Career: Glasgow Celtic, 1999. PRESTON NORTH END, 2003. Stockport County, 2003 (loan). Blackpool, 2004 (loan).

■ Canadian-born striker Simon Lynch was only on the fringes of the Celtic side when he joined Preston North End in January 2003. After making his Football League debut as a substitute at Ipswich, he scored on his Deepdale debut the following week as North End drew 1–1 with Nottingham Forest. He remained in the squad for the rest of the season, alternating with Pawel Abbott between the bench and the starting line up. Despite being of slight build, he possesses surprising strength and quick feet. Lynch's first games of 2003–04 were for Stockport County, whom he joined on loan. Having scored three goals in successive games for the Hatters, he

returned to Deepdale where he featured regularly until the end of the season. In 2004–05 he struggled to win a place in the North End starting line up and had a three-month loan spell with neighbours Blackpool before rejoining his teammates.

LYNNE, Michael George Anthony

Goalkeeper

Born: Kettering, 20 March 1938.
Career: PRESTON NORTH END, 1956. Bournemouth, 1959.

■ Goalkeeper Michael Lynne spent most of his time in the club's reserve side but was called upon to play in five consecutive League and Cup games midway through the 1958–59 season following an injury to Fred Else. After playing on the winning side in two FA Cup victories – 4–2 against Derby County in round three and 3–2 against Bradford City in round four – Lynne was on the receiving end of two heavy League defeats: 4–2 at home to West Bromwich Albion and 5–1 at Birmingham City. He kept his place in the side for the FA Cup fifth-round tie against Bolton Wanderers, which ended all square at 2–2, before Else returned to the side that lost to the Trotters in a second replay. Lynne left Deepdale in the close season to play for Bournemouth, but after one season of Third Division football he parted company with the Cherries.

LYON, William John

Left-half

Born: Clachnacuddin, 1877.
Career: Walsall, 1899. Bristol Rovers. Manchester City, 1903. PRESTON NORTH END, 1903.

■ Left-half Billy Lyon arrived at Deepdale from Manchester City towards the end of the 1903–04 season and played in the final six games of the campaign, none of which were lost and with only one goal being conceded. This helped the club win the Second Division Championship. Lyon missed just a couple of games the following season as North End more than held their own in the top flight and was outstanding in 1905–06 as the club finished runners-up

to Liverpool. Appointed the club's captain, he continued to work tirelessly for the North End cause. In January 1910 he was suspended for an alleged offence in the home match against Aston Villa. Lyon apparently caught Harry Hampton above the thigh. It was reported that the Villa forward had two stud marks eight inches above the knee as well as skin torn below the knee, three inches long and one and a half inches wide. Though he claimed he could not have been the guilty player, having only one stud at the front of his boot, he was still suspended for a month. He continued to be a regular in the side until midway through the following season when he decided to retire after losing his place to Bill Wareing.

McATEER, Andrew William

Left-back

Born: Preston, 24 April 1961.
Career: PRESTON NORTH END, 1979. Blackpool, 1986. PRESTON NORTH END, 1988.

■ Local-born player Andy McAteer was signed by North End as a schoolboy and joined them straight from school as an apprentice. Working his way up through the youth and reserve teams, the

well-built player had always played in midfield until a Central League game at home to Burnley in September 1979. Steve Uzelac was sent off, Harry Wilson moved into the centre of defence and McAteer was switched into the left-back spot. He got his first-team chance when Harry Wilson reported injured on Boxing Day morning 1979 and, after a first-class display in North End's 3–0 win over Shrewsbury Town, he became a permanent fixture in the side. Over the next few seasons, McAteer played some cultured football but midway through the club's Fourth Division promotion-winning season, he left Deepdale to play for Blackpool. After a season and a half at Bloomfield Road, McAteer left the Seasiders to rejoin North End prior to the start of the 1988–89 campaign. He helped the club finish sixth in the Third Division, scoring his eighth and final League goal in a 3–2 defeat of Southend United before leaving the club in the close season.

MACAULEY, James Lowry

Inside-left

Born: Portarlington, 1889.
Died: 1945.
Career: Preston Rangers. Cliftonville Olympic. Brighton and Hove Albion. Huddersfield Town, 1910. PRESTON NORTH END, 1913. Leicester City, 1919. Grimsby Town, 1920. Lancaster Town. Morecambe.

■ Irish-born forward James Macauley made his Football League debut for Huddersfield Town as an unregistered

player after the Yorkshire club had signed him from Southern League Brighton and Hove Albion in 1910. Their ignorance of the transfer procedure resulted in them playing him without first confirming that his registration with Glasgow Rangers – for whom he had never played – had elapsed. The technicalities over, Macauley went on to give Huddersfield outstanding service. Having represented the Irish League while playing for Cliftonville, he became Town's joint-first full international as he and Charlie Morris of Wales opposed each other in Belfast. In 1913, after scoring 34 goals in 97 games, he joined Preston North End for £850 but Town were fined again, this time because the player was listed as a free agent and not subject to a fee. Macauley made his debut in a 1–0 home defeat at the hands of Liverpool and, though he scored seven goals in 22 games in that 1913–14 season, he was unable to prevent the club being relegated to Division Two. The following season he helped the club win immediate promotion, as he and Fred Osborn formed a potent strike partnership, with Macauley scoring 16 goals. After World War One he lent his experience to Leicester City before moving on to Grimsby Town. He later returned to the North West to play non-League football for Lancaster Town and Morecambe.

McBRIDE, Brian Robert

Forward

Born: Arlington Heights, US, 19 June 1972.
Career: St Louis University (US). VfL Wolfsburg (Germany). Columbus Crew (US). PRESTON NORTH END, 2000 (loan). Everton, 2003 (loan). Fulham, 2004.

■ A regular member of the US's national team, having played in 88 games, Brian McBride arrived at Deepdale in September 2000 on a six-month loan from Columbus Crew and made his debut against Stockport County just two days after putting pen to paper. The game, which ended all square at 1–1, was only a few minutes old when McBride smashed a shot against the bar from close range. After impressing the North End fans with his intelligent and

powerful play, he picked up a potentially fatal blood clot in his arm that required emergency surgery and he had to have complete rest for three months. McBride returned to Football League action over the Christmas period and in his first game back he scored his only goal for the club in a 5–0 rout of Queen's Park Rangers, a game that had been goalless at half-time. A firm favourite with the North End fans, he returned home in March 2001 and the following year represented his country in the World Cup, scoring goals against Portugal and Mexico as his side reached the quarter-finals before losing to Germany. Former

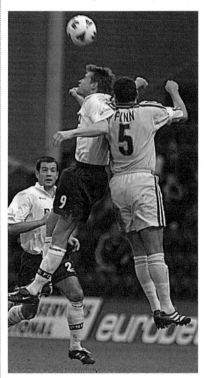

North End manager David Moyes brought him to Everton for a three-month loan spell in January 2003. McBride made an immediate impact, scoring after just 10 minutes of his debut against Spurs and netting twice against Sunderland in his first home game the following week. Although a permanent deal between the Blues and Major League Soccer – who owned his contract in the States – was mooted, failure to agree a fee resulted in him returning to the US. In January 2004, McBride returned to the Premiership as Fulham paid £600,000 for his services. He again made an immediate impact – also against Spurs –

as he netted after just four minutes of his debut. Though he often found himself on the bench, he became an important member of the Cottagers' squad.

McBRIDE, Peter

Goalkeeper

Born: Ayr, 15 September 1877.
Career: Ayr. PRESTON NORTH END, 1897.

■ After playing his early football with his home-town club, Ayr, Peter McBride was brought to Deepdale in the summer of 1896 as a replacement for North End's ageing 'Prince of Goalkeepers' James Trainer. However, he had to wait until the end of the 1897–98 season before making his first-team debut against Stoke. He went on to play consistently well until 1912 when failing eyesight forced him to step down. McBride was a huge man with a great reputation and a temper to match. He represented Scotland six times in full internationals and could be just as violent as the roughest opposing centre-forward. When North End played Blackburn Rovers at Ewood Park, Arnold Whittaker celebrated his Rovers' debut with a hat-trick. As the diminutive forward scored his third goal, McBride dashed out of his penalty area, caught him by the throat and shook him! On 20 March 1901, McBride played in a representative match for the Anglo Scots after impressing the Scottish selectors with a series of outstanding displays. Unfortunately for all concerned, he injured a shoulder and was forced to miss North End's last five games of the season. This resulted in the club conceding 15 goals in those games and being relegated to Division Two. When North End won the Second Division Championship in 1903–04, McBride had an outstanding season, keeping 14 clean sheets including five in successive games. McBride was also an expert penalty saver and the following season he saved spot-kicks in each of the encounters with high-flying Everton. One of McBride's best games for North End came in the local derby against Blackburn Rovers on New Year's Day 1909: he prevented Rovers from scoring on a number of occasions and saved a penalty after Holdsworth had upended Aitkenhead in the box. At the turn of the century, McBride's consistency was recognised by Tottenham Hotspur but he remained loyal to Preston North End. He went on to play a record 443 League games for the club – a record which stood until 1974 when it was broken by Alan Kelly.

McCALL, Joseph

Centre-half

Born: Kirkham, 6 July 1886.
Died: 1965.
Career: Kirkham. PRESTON NORTH END, 1906.

■ Joe McCall played his early football for Kirkham until he arrived at Deepdale in 1905 and made his debut in a 3–0 reversal against Woolwich Arsenal in September 1906. He was dropped for the next match and so started a career in a way familiar to many other famous players. It is safe to say that very few, if any, realised that he would go on to appear in 395 League and Cup games for North End, the last against Leeds United in January 1925. Despite standing just 5ft 8in, by the latter half of the 1908–09 season he had made the centre-half position his own. On 29 October 1909, Joe McCall was sent off in North End's 3–3 draw at Notts County after clashing with Cantrell, the scorer of County's third goal. McCall, usually such a good-tempered and fair player, was mortified by his dismissal. His actions in the fisticuffs suggest that the County player considerably provoked him. McCall was suspended for two weeks and Cantrell for four. On 24 November 1913, McCall was selected for the FA trial match between England and The South at Craven Cottage. Playing in his usual position of centre-half for the England team, he scored twice in a 3–1 win. This led to him making his full international debut against Wales, where again he scored in a 4–3 win. A regular in the England side until the hostilities broke out, he also appeared in two Victory Internationals for England. Joe McCall was one of Preston North End's greatest captains. He was a great leader who raised the flagging spirits of his players on many occasions. Accordingly, when it was known he was in dispute with the club shortly before Christmas 1919, there was a major crisis in the town. Acting with necessary urgency the directors summoned a board meeting for the same night and when that was adjourned in deadlock, it was reconvened the following morning. Happily the situation was resolved to the satisfaction of all parties: clearly there was no way in which the directors would allow the paths of club and player to diverge.

McCANN, James

Inside-right

Career: PRESTON NORTH END, 1893.

■ Inside-forward Jimmy McCann hailed from north of the border. He made six appearances for North End during the 1893–94 season, making a goalscoring debut in a 2–1 home defeat by Burnley. With the likes of Jimmy Ross, Frank Becton, John Cowan and Johnny Cunningham in the side, he did not get any further opportunities and left the club at the end of a season in which the club just hung on to its First Division status.

McCLELLAND, James

Inside-right, centre-forward

Born: Dysart, 11 May 1902.
Career: Rosslyn. Raith Rovers. Southend United, 1923. Middlesbrough, 1924. Bolton Wanderers, 1927. PRESTON NORTH END, 1929. Blackpool, 1930. Bradford Park Avenue, 1933. Manchester United, 1936.

■ After beginning his first-class career with Raith Rovers, Jimmy McClelland came south of the border to play for Southend United. In his first season with the club he led the scoring charts until Middlesbrough secured his services. In 1925–26, McClelland was Boro's top scorer with 38 goals in 40 games, including all five in a 5–1 FA Cup win over Leeds United and hat-tricks in wins over Wolves, Blackpool and Portsmouth. Though he was somewhat overshadowed by George Camsell's goalscoring exploits in 1926–27 he played his part in helping the club win the Second Division Championship. He had scored 48 goals in 85 games for Boro when he left to join Bolton Wanderers for £6,300. He immediately became a big hit, netting eight goals in the last 10 games of the 1927–28 season and helping the Wanderers win the 1929 FA Cup. In October 1929 he moved to Preston North End and made his debut in the 6–4 home defeat at the hands of Blackpool. Moving from centre-forward to inside-right, he went on to score 10 goals in 25 games. The following season his total of 12 goals included all four goals in a 4–1 win at Reading. In February 1931 he returned to the First Division with Blackpool before moving to Bradford Park Avenue three years later. In 1936, McClelland joined his last League club, Manchester United, who had just won promotion to Division One.

McCLUGGAGE, Andrew

Full-back

Born: Larne, 1 September 1900.
Died: 1954.
Career: Invervale. Cliftonville. Bradford Park Avenue, 1922. Burnley, 1925. Dundalk. PRESTON NORTH END, 1931. Morecambe. Larne.

■ Having impressed in his native Ireland with Cliftonville, full-back Andy McCluggage crossed the water to play in the Football League with Bradford Park Avenue. His early performances for the Yorkshire club led to him winning the first of 12 Irish caps when he played against England in 1923. He joined Burnley in the summer of 1925 and made his debut in the 10–0 defeat at Aston Villa on the opening day of the 1925–26 season. Despite this disastrous start to his Turf Moor career, McCluggage went on to be a regular first-team member for six seasons, missing very few games. Having scored 24 goals in 213 games for Burnley, he had a brief spell with Dundalk before joining North End in 1931. His first game for the Lilywhites was against Burnley at Turf Moor on Christmas Day 1931, when the teams shared four goals. He played in just three games for the Deepdale club before leaving to play non-League football for Morecambe before returning to Ireland to end his career with Larne.

McCLURE, William

Outside-left

Born: Shotts, 16 May 1921.

Career: Albion Rovers. PRESTON NORTH END, 1947. New Brighton, 1948. Carlisle United, 1949. Hartlepool United, 1950.

■ William McClure's displays for Albion Rovers in the Scottish 'B' Division in the first season and a half of competitive football after World War Two persuaded North End to secure his services midway through the 1947–48 season. Harry Anders made way for the flying Scot but after a disappointing display in a 1–0 defeat at Burnley, Anders returned to the side. McClure got a second chance later in the season, appearing in all but one of the last 11 games and scoring in the wins over Aston Villa and Manchester City. Even so, he was released at the end of the season and joined New Brighton. After a little over a season, he had a brief spell with Carlisle United before ending his career with Hartlepool United, for whom he scored 24 goals in 118 appearances in the Third Division North.

McCORMACK, Alan

Midfield

Born: Dublin, 10 January 1984.
Career: Stella Maris BC. PRESTON

NORTH END, 2002. Leyton Orient, 2003 (loan). Southend United, 2005 (loan). Motherwell (loan) 2005.

■ Republic of Ireland Youth international midfielder Alan McCormack joined North End from Stella Maris. Unable to break into the Preston side, he was loaned out to Leyton Orient, where he impressed as a hard-working player. On his return to Deepdale he gradually broke into the first-team squad and made his debut off the bench at Burnley during 2003–04 before starting the next game at Sunderland. An aggressive ball-winning midfielder, he had another loan spell the following season, this time at Southend United, helping their promotion challenge stay on track. Although he only made a couple of substitute appearances for Preston, his value was reflected when he was given an extended contract.

McDONALD, Neil Raymond

Right-back, midfield

Born: Wallsend, 2 November 1965.
Career: Newcastle United, 1983. Everton, 1988. Oldham Athletic, 1991. Bolton Wanderers, 1994. PRESTON NORTH END, 1995.

■ Capable of playing at full-back or in midfield, Neil McDonald began his career with Newcastle United, where at one stage he was the Magpies' youngest-

ever debutant at 16 years 326 days. His performances for the St James' Park club led to him winning Under-21 honours for England but in July 1988 he was transferred to Everton for £525,000 after scoring 28 goals in 208 League and Cup games. At the end of his first season on Merseyside he played in the FA Cup Final that saw local rivals Liverpool run out 3–2 winners after extra-time. In October 1991, McDonald joined Oldham Athletic in a £500,000 deal but appeared in only 24 League games for the Latics before signing for Bolton Wanderers on a free transfer. Injuries hampered his progress at Burnden Park, though he played in the Play-off semi-final against Wolves where he was shown the red card. McDonald also made a Wembley appearance in the Final against Reading but was substituted to make way for Fabian de Freitas. In November 1995, Preston paid £40,000 to take him to Deepdale and that season, after making his debut in an Auto Windscreens Shield match, he played his first League game in a 3–0 defeat of Hartlepool United. McDonald made 11 appearances that season as North End won the Third Division title. He remained an important member of the Preston side until retiring from the playing side to take up a coaching position on the North End staff. He later became the club's youth-team manager before taking up a coaching position with Bolton Wanderers. Neil McDonald moved on to become assistant manager to Ian Dowie at Crystal Palace.

McEACHRAN, David

Outside-left

Born: Clydebank, 1902.
Career: Clydebank. PRESTON NORTH END, 1925. Fall River Marksmen (US). Boston Wonder Workers (US). Boston Bears (US). New Bedford Whalers (US). Providence Gold Bugs (US). Carsteel (Canada). Clydebank. Beith.

■ Winger David McEachran helped his home-town team, Clydebank, win promotion to the Scottish First Division in 1924–25 before joining North End the following season. Signed mainly as an understudy to England international George Harrison, his only appearance in Preston colours came in a dismal goalless

home draw against Darlington. Released at the end of the season, he played for the next few years in North America for a number of clubs with great success before returning to Scotland to see out his career with Clydebank and Beith.

McFADYEN, Charles

Right-back

Born: Inellan, 1886.
Died: 1947.
Career: PRESTON NORTH END, 1907. Everton, 1914.

■ Full-back Charlie McFadyen made his first start for North End in a 3–1 win at Bristol City in February 1908. He went on to play in the remaining 13 games of the season in which the club finished mid-table in the First Division. McFadyen was the club's first-choice right-back for the next six seasons and missed very few games. It was during the 1911–12 relegation season that Charlie McFadyen scored his only goal for the club: it proved to be the winner in a 2–1 defeat of Manchester City. He was ever present the following season as Preston returned to the top flight at the first attempt as Second Division Champions, finishing three points clear of Burnley. However, North End were to go straight back down and McFadyen, who seemed to have lost the consistency he had always shown, moved to Everton but was unable to force his way into their League side.

McGEE, Paul Gerard

Forward

Born: Sligo, 19 June 1954.
Career: Sligo Rovers. Kidderminster Harriers. Hereford United. Finn Harps. Sligo Rovers. Toronto Mets and Montreal Castors (Canada). Queen's Park Rangers, 1977. PRESTON NORTH END, 1979. Burnley, 1981. Dundalk (loan). Shamrock Rovers. Waterford. Sligo Rovers. Galway. Haarlem (Holland). Derry City. Athlone Town.

■ A much-travelled and prolific scorer, Paul McGee started out with Sligo Rovers who introduced him to football when he was 16. In 1972 he joined Kidderminster Harriers and from there he signed for Hereford United. However, he failed to make the first team and

returned to Ireland to play for Finn Harps. After winning an FAI Cup-winners' medal, he rejoined Sligo Rovers and helped them win the League of Ireland Championship in 1976–77. During this period, he spent his summers in Canada initially with Toronto Mets and then Montreal Castors whom he helped win the Canadian League. In November 1977, McGee got his first taste of English League football when he joined Queen's Park Rangers. The Loftus Road club lost their top-flight status in 1979–80 and McGee was sold to Preston North End. After making his debut in a 1–1 home draw against Leicester City, he went on to score eight goals in 22 games, including five in consecutive games in March 1980, though four of those were drawn. Though McGee was not as prolific over the next couple of seasons, he still scored some vital goals. Following North End's relegation to the Third Division in 1980–81, he moved to Burnley early the following season. McGee helped the Clarets win the Third Division title in 1981–82 but a year later he was loaned to Dundalk prior to brief spells at Shamrock Rovers, Waterford, Sligo Rovers and Galway. He then joined Dutch club Haarlem before returning to his native Ireland for periods at both Derry City and Athlone Town.

McGIBBONS, Terence

Outside-right

Born: Irvine.

Career: Irvine Meadow. Ayr United. PRESTON NORTH END, 1938.

■ Having helped Ayr United win the Scottish Second Division Championship in 1936–37, flying winger Terry McGibbons came south of the border to play League football for Preston North End. He made his debut on the opening day of the 1938–39 season in a 2–1 defeat at Leeds United and played in the opening 20 games of the campaign, scoring in successive victories over Sunderland and Aston Villa. However, it was not enough and he lost his place to Frank White. He appeared in victories over Huddersfield and Bolton towards the end of the season but he was released and returned to Scotland.

McGREGOR, Paul Anthony

Midfield

Born: Liverpool, 17 December 1974.
Career: Nottingham Forest, 1991. Carlisle United, 1998 (loan). PRESTON NORTH END, 1999. Plymouth Argyle, 1999. Northampton Town, 2001.

■ Paul McGregor was a prolific scorer and record-breaker in Nottingham Forest's youth side. He hit the headlines with the winning goal in Forest's UEFA Cup victory over Lyon before being given his first full Premier League game a week

later – he celebrated by scoring in a 1–1 draw with Manchester United. An operation on a knee injury reduced his opportunities at first-team level and he had a couple of loan spells at Carlisle United before signing for North End in transfer deadline week in March 1999. He made his debut as a late substitute just two days later in a 3–0 win over Northampton Town. Used mainly off the bench, he was surprisingly released in the summer. McGregor joined Plymouth Argyle where he rediscovered his form of old, scoring hat-tricks against Barnet and Torquay United to finish the season as the club's leading scorer with 16 goals. Though he showed his goalscoring potential the following season, he left Home Park to join Northampton Town. He featured in a variety of roles in his first season with the Cobblers but thereafter suffered from injuries and was forced to retire.

McILMOYLE, Hugh

Centre-forward

Born: Port Glasgow, 29 January 1940.
Career: Port Glasgow. Leicester City, 1959. Rotherham United, 1962. Carlisle United, 1963. Wolverhampton Wanderers, 1964. Bristol City, 1967. Carlisle United, 1967. Middlesbrough, 1969. PRESTON NORTH END, 1971. Morton. Carlisle United, 1974.

■ Hugh McIlmoyle was one of the game's great goalscoring nomads, netting over 170 goals in more than 450 senior appearances for eight different clubs – one of which he served on three separate occasions. McIlmoyle was an instant hit when he broke into the Leicester City side during the 1960–61 campaign, scoring four goals in his first seven games. However, he failed to maintain that early momentum, despite wearing the number-nine shirt in the 1961 FA Cup Final against Spurs. He moved on to Rotherham United but just 12 games later he was on the move again. This time his destination was Carlisle United where he wrote his name into the record books as the country's top scorer in 1963–64, netting 39 goals in just 45 Fourth Division games. McIlmoyle moved on to Wolves where he was a consistent scorer for three seasons, including netting a hat-

trick in an FA Cup fifth-round second-replay win over Aston Villa at the Hawthorns in February 1965. After a short spell at Bristol City, he returned to Carlisle for more scoring exploits before he joined Middlesbrough in September 1969. After the North East club narrowly missed promotion in his first season at Ayresome Park and again in 1970–71 – despite a 15–goal contribution from McIlmoyle – he left to join Preston North End. He made his debut for the Deepdale club in a goalless draw at one of his former clubs, Carlisle United, and though the club spent the entire campaign struggling to avoid the drop into Division Three, McIlmoyle was the leading scorer with 13 goals. He failed to score in 25 League appearances in 1972–73 and left to continue his career north of the border with Morton before spending a third spell at Carlisle. On hanging up his boots, McIlmoyle worked as a warehouseman for Walkers Crisps.

McILROY, Samuel Baxter

Midfield

Born: Belfast, 2 August 1954.
Career: Manchester United, 1971. Stoke City, 1982. Manchester City, 1985. Orgryte (Sweden). Manchester City, 1986. Bury, 1987. VFB Modling (Austria). Bury, 1988. PRESTON NORTH END, 1990.

■ Sammy McIlroy announced his

arrival in Manchester United's senior side with a sizzling debut against Manchester City when he contributed a goal and two assists in the 3–3 draw at Maine Road. The fairytale soon turned sour and a motorcycle accident kept him sidelined for over half the 1972–73 season. Once restored to full fitness he claimed a regular place in the United side and won the first of 88 caps for Northern Ireland – McIlroy was awarded an MBE as the national side went on to World Cup glory in Spain in 1982 and Mexico in 1986. A midfielder full of energy and attacking purpose, his inspiration was important as United clinched the Second Division Championship. He played in the 1976 FA Cup Final and won a winners' medal the following year. He scored one of United's goals in the epic 1979 FA Cup Final which Arsenal won 3–2. Though he remained a permanent fixture in the Northern Ireland side, new United manager Ron Atkinson did not see him as part of the United set-up and he joined Stoke City for £350,000 in February 1982 after scoring 69 goals in 408 games. A free transfer saw him quit Stoke for the other half of Manchester but he played just a dozen games in blue. He tried his luck in Sweden with Orgryte before joining Bury. Another spell

abroad, this time in Austria with VFB Molding, was followed by his time with Preston North End. Making his debut in a 1–0 home defeat at the hands of Champions-elect Bristol Rovers, McIlroy played in the last 20 games of the 1989–90 season. North End were undefeated in half of those games and it was this form that prevented them from losing their Third Division status. After hanging up his boots he managed non-League Macclesfield, whom he led to two Conference titles and victory in the 1996 FA Trophy. After winning promotion to the Football League, he led the Silkmen into Division Two in their first season in the competition. He later managed the Northern Ireland side before taking over the reins of Stockport County, whom he has since parted company with.

McINTOSH, James McLaren

Centre-forward, outside-left

Born: Dumfries, 5 April 1918.
Career: Droylsden. Blackpool, 1935.
PRESTON NORTH END, 1937.
Blackpool, 1946. Everton, 1948. Distillery.

■ Jimmy McIntosh was discovered by Blackpool playing alongside future Seasiders' captain Harry Johnson for non-League Droylsden. A fast, strong, well-built player he was ideally suited to

step into the shoes of the prolific Jimmy Hampson. After just a handful of appearances over two seasons, he was part of the deal that saw Frank O'Donnell leave Deepdale and Watmough and McIntosh join the Lilywhites. He made his North End debut in a 2–0 defeat at Middlesbrough and appeared in three games towards the end of that 1937–38 season. While he found the net three times in 1938–39, he still could not be classed as a first-team regular and immediately after the war he rejoined Blackpool. He struck up a partnership with Stan Mortensen and during the course of the club's 1947–48 FA Cup campaign scored five goals prior to the Final. He was devastated when manager Joe Smith told him that due to loss of form he would not be playing against Manchester United. Blackpool lost the Final and a week later McIntosh was recalled to the side for the last game of the season, a rearranged match at Preston. McIntosh tore the North End defence apart scoring five goals in a remarkable 7–0 victory. Following the arrival of Willie McIntosh from Preston, he moved to Everton for a nominal fee, staying with the Blues until they lost their First Division status in 1950–51.

McINTOSH, William Dowling

Centre-forward

Born: Glasgow, 7 December 1919.
Died: 1990.
Career: St Johnstone. PRESTON NORTH END, 1946. Blackpool, 1949. Stoke City, 1951. Walsall, 1952.

■ Willie McIntosh joined North End from Scottish club St Johnstone for a fee of £6,000 in May 1946, having impressed during wartime football north of the border. He made his debut on the opening day of the 1946–47 season in a North End side fielding seven new players and scored one of the club's goals in a 3–2 win over Leeds United. The scourge of many opposition defences, he netted hat-tricks in successive games at the start of the season as Grimsby were beaten 3–2 and Charlton Athletic 5–1. During the course of that first season of peacetime football, McIntosh scored 32 League and Cup goals to top the club's scoring charts. The goals dried up slightly the following season, though he still netted 17 as North End finished seventh in the First Division. Having struck up a fine understanding it was a surprise when he was allowed to leave Deepdale in January 1949 to play for Blackpool. He was at Bloomfield Road for two and a half seasons and in 1950–51, his last season with the club, he was instrumental in them finishing third in the top flight. McIntosh had a season with Stoke City before he ended his playing career with Walsall.

McINTYRE, Peter

Centre-half, outside-right

Born: Glenbuck, 15 November 1875.
Career: PRESTON NORTH END, 1898. Sheffield United, 1901. Hamilton Academicals. Portsmouth.

■ Peter McIntyre played his first game for the club in a 3–2 home defeat by Sunderland on the opening day of the 1898–99 season. He gave the club three seasons of good service, playing in a variety of positions. He missed just one game in 1899–1900 but the club lost its top-flight status the following season after coming close in the previous two seasons. McIntyre was adamant that he wanted to stay in the First Division and so he left Deepdale to play for Sheffield United, a club that had finished just three places above relegated North End. Unable to make much impression at Bramall Lane, he had a spell back in Scotland with Hamilton Academicals before ending his career in the Southern League with Portsmouth.

McKELLAR, Charles

Centre-forward

Born: Preston, 1889.
Career: PRESTON NORTH END, 1911.

■ During the course of the 1911–12 season, when the club were relegated from the First Division, they used a total of 28 players. One of these was Charles McKellar whose goalscoring exploits in local football had attracted him to North End. He made a couple of appearances

but in both games he did not score and neither did the team, drawing 0–0 with Manchester United at Deepdale and losing 1–0 to Everton, the eventual runners-up in the First Division, at Goodison Park.

MACKEN, Jonathan Paul

Forward

Born: Manchester, 7 September 1977.
Career: Manchester United, 1996. PRESTON NORTH END, 1997. Manchester City, 2002. Crystal Palace, 2005.

■ Striker Jon Macken joined Preston North End from Manchester United for a fee of £250,000 in the summer of 1997. He soon became a great favourite of the North End fans with his commitment and bustling style. Modelling himself on his hero Mark Hughes, he demonstrated a good footballing brain. The 1999–2000 season saw Macken's emergence as a striker of some quality as he ended Preston's Second Division Championship campaign as the club's top scorer. The highlights of his season included six goals in six games during September and October. In his 100th game for North End, he scored the equaliser at Arsenal for the first FA Cup goal of his career. Not surprisingly he joined three teammates in the PFA's Second Division select side. Despite playing at a higher level in 2000–01, he was again the club's leading scorer, netting his first senior hat-trick in the Worthington Cup-tie against Shrewsbury Town. Other highlights included a goal after 19 seconds against Grimsby Town and his 50th strike for the club at Barnsley. Macken then became

unsettled at Deepdale and in March 2002 he joined Manchester City for a fee of £4 million. He immediately impressed, netting five times from eight appearances including the club's record-equalling 108th goal against Portsmouth. The following season saw him struggle with injuries, as he did in 2003–04, though he did head the Blues' winner in the epic FA Cup tie against Spurs. He had better fortune the following season as his club form won him a call up to the Republic of Ireland squad and he won his first cap against Bulgaria in August 2005. Macken left City in the close season to join Crystal Palace but since his arrival at Selhurst Park, much of his time Has been spent on the treatment table.

McKENNA, Paul Stephen

Midfield

Born: Chorley, 20 October 1977.
Career: PRESTON NORTH END, 1996.

■ Paul McKenna broke into the North End team during 1996–97 and marked his home debut against Wycombe Wanderers with a goal. A bustling all-action player, he became more of a regular the following season. In 1998–99 he featured both on the right and left of

midfield, although he preferred a more central role. Rebuked for not scoring enough goals, he netted his first goal of the following campaign with a 25–yard screamer against Brentford and claimed the winner in the FA Cup tie at Bristol Rovers. Unlucky to be kept out of action for three months due to a hernia operation, he returned for the run-in as North End clinched the Second Division Championship. He was a near ever present in the First Division season of 2000–01, showing great stamina and deceptive pace. A tireless box-to-box player, he contributed spectacular long-range goals against Crystal Palace, Sheffield Wednesday and Barnsley. Injuries hampered his progress the following season, notably a serious foot problem, but he returned to the side to net with a trademark rocket after only 20 seconds of the home game with Crewe and remained in the side until the end of the campaign. One of a number of players to benefit from playing alongside Brian O'Neil and one of the first names on the team sheet, he found his shooting boots towards the end of the 2003–04 season when he scored four goals in the last six games. A tigerish tackler, he had an outstanding season in 2004–05, as illustrated by his selection as the PFA Fans' Championship 'Player of the Season'. The club's longest-serving player, he remains very much the heartbeat of the North End side and was instrumental in the club reaching the Play-offs for the second successive season.

McKENNIE, William

Right-half, outside-right

Career: Royal Highlanders. PRESTON NORTH END, 1890. Chorley. Darwen, 1892.

■ William McKennie played his early football in his native Scotland with the Royal Highlanders. He made eight appearances during the 1890–91 season as North End finished runners-up to Everton in that season's First Division Championship. Playing across the forward line, he scored one of the goals in the 6–0 home win over Derby County and netted the only goal of the game at Aston Villa. Early the following season he lost his place

in the team and joined Darwen after a brief spell at Chorley. In his first season he helped Darwen win promotion to the First Division and went on to score 21 goals in 70 games before hanging up his boots.

McKNIGHT, James

Inside-forward

Career: Glentoran. PRESTON NORTH END, 1911. Glentoran. Nottingham Forest, 1913. Belfast Celtic.

■ It was the gate receipts of £1,130 from North End's match with rivals Blackburn Rovers on New Year's Day 1912 that allowed Preston to buy James McKnight from Glentoran. He had appeared in just two games for North End when he made his international debut against Scotland. Though the Irish lost 4–1 it was McKnight who scored his side's goal. On his return to Deepdale he scored in consecutive games as North End beat Liverpool 3–1 and Sheffield United 3–0. Though he held his place in the side for the last five games of the season he failed to hit the target again as North End were relegated along with Bury. The following season McKnight could not rediscover the understanding he had with John Morley that had been evident at the end of the club's relegation campaign. Although North End went on to win the Second Division Championship, McKnight had left midway through the campaign and returned to Glentoran. His stay with his former club was brief and in 1913 he returned to Football League action with Nottingham Forest. After a season at the City Ground, he returned to Ireland to see out his career with Belfast Celtic.

McLAREN, Andrew

Inside-forward

Born: Larkhall, 24 January 1922.
Died: 1996.
Career: Larkhall Thistle. PRESTON NORTH END, 1939. Burnley, 1948. Sheffield United, 1949. Barrow, 1951. Bradford Park Avenue, 1954. Southport, 1955. Rochdale, 1955.

■ Andy McLaren was one of football's nomads who perhaps never quite fulfilled his early promise. Although he

scored regularly throughout his career, most of his goals came in the lower Divisions. McLaren joined the groundstaff at Preston in 1939 just as war was about to break out and put his career on hold. He was a prolific scorer during wartime football. During the club's run to the second Wartime Cup Final against Arsenal, McLaren scored five of North End's goals in an incredibly one-sided third-round tie against Tranmere which Preston won 13–1 and a hat-trick in the second leg of the fourth-round tie against Manchester City. McLaren gave North End the lead in the Final but a Denis Compton equaliser meant the Final had to be replayed. North End won 2–1 thanks to two Bobby Beattie goals. A defeat at Blackpool left North End needing to win their last game of the season against Liverpool in order to clinch the Northern Regional League title. They did so, with McLaren scoring all six goals in a 6–1 rout of the Anfield club. Following his time in the forces it was December 1946 before McLaren returned to Deepdale, but after just 11 games in North End colours he won an unexpected place in Scotland's team for the game against England at Wembley. He scored their goal in a 1–1 draw. An intelligent player, he scored four goals in as many appearances at international level. In 1947–48 he was North End's leading scorer with 17 goals, including a double in the latter stages of the club's 7–4 win over top-of-the-table Derby County. After being injured in the early part of the following season, he was surprisingly exchanged for Burnley's

Jack Knight and months later North End were relegated. Things did not work out for McLaren at Turf Moor and he soon moved on to Sheffield United. After two seasons at Bramall Lane, he moved to Barrow, where he scored 52 goals in 155 League games. He later played for Bradford Park Avenue and Southport before ending his League career with Rochdale.

McLATCHIE, Colin

Outside-left

Born: New Cumnock, 2 November 1876.
Died: 1952.
Career: Lanemark. Kilmarnock Dean. New Cumnock United. PRESTON NORTH END, 1897. Sunderland, 1898. Grimsby Town, 1902. Lanemark.

■ Left-winger Colin McLatchie had played football for a number of Scottish junior clubs before he arrived at Deepdale for the start of the 1897–98 season. After playing in the opening three games of the campaign – none of which were won – he lost his place in the side and the number-11 shirt was worn by Eccleston, Becton, Whittle, Boyd and Halsall before he returned to the side. Towards the end of the season he netted his first goal for the club in a 3–1 win over Notts County. McLatchie scored on the opening day of the following season against Sunderland and within a matter of days was on his way to Roker Park – so much had he impressed the Wearsiders management team! McLatchie was a virtual ever present for the North East club and, having come close on a couple of occasions, they won the First Division Championship in 1901–02. McLatchie went on to score 33 goals in 129 games before seeing out his first-class career with Grimsby Town.

McLAUGHLIN, William John

Inside-forward

Born: Glasgow, 1882.
Career: Hamilton Academicals. Everton, 1904. Plymouth Argyle. PRESTON NORTH END, 1907.

■ Willie McLaughlin started out north of the border with local team Hamilton Academicals before attracting the attention of Everton. In 1904–05, his first season on Merseyside, he scored three goals in seven games as the Blues ended the campaign runners-up in Division One. He was in and out of the Everton side the following season and so decided to try his luck in the Southern League with Plymouth Argyle. His goalscoring exploits for the Devon club alerted North End and he was signed in 1907. Unable to get much of a look-in due to the fine form of John Carlin, he made just one appearance for the Lilywhites in a 5–1 defeat at Bury.

McLEAN, David Prophet

Centre-forward

Born: Forfar, 13 December 1887.
Died: 1967.
Career: Forfar West End. Forfar Celtic. Forfar Athletic. Glasgow Celtic. PRESTON NORTH END, 1909. Sheffield Wednesday, 1910. Forfar Athletic. Sheffield Wednesday, 1913. Dykehead. Third Lanark. Glasgow Rangers. Sheffield Wednesday, 1919. Bradford Park Avenue, 1919. Dundee. Forfar Athletic. Dykehead.

■ Davie McLean played his early football with Forfar, his home-town club, and Celtic before moving south of the border to play for Preston North End in 1909. After scoring on his debut in a 3–1 defeat at Notts County, he went on to become the club's top scorer in the 1909–10 season with a total of 19 goals. While McLean did not manage a hat-trick, he did net doubles against Woolwich Arsenal and in both games against high-flying Newcastle United. Though he was not as prolific the following season, scoring just seven goals, he was still joint-top scorer along with James Bannister. In February 1911 he joined Sheffield Wednesday for a fee of £1,000 and in his first full season with the club he topped Wednesday's scoring charts with 25 goals in 37 games. This total included four in an 8–0 Boxing Day win over Sunderland and a hat-trick on the final day of the season in a 5–1 win at West Bromwich Albion. The following season he won his only cap for Scotland when he played against England at Stamford Bridge. It was a good season for McLean, who set a club record with 30 goals in the League as well as eight in the FA Cup. His tally included four in a 5–1 first-round win over Grimsby and a hat-trick in a 6–0 defeat of Chelsea in a second-round replay. After disagreeing with the club over terms, he returned to play in Scottish football. He returned to Hillsborough for the 1914–15 season which he ended as the club's top scorer. During the hostilities he 'guested' for a number of Scottish clubs. McLean played in a few more games for the Owls, taking his tally of goals to 100 in 147 games, before playing for Bradford Park Avenue. After ending his playing days north of the border, he managed East Fife.

McLEAN, James

Right-half, outside-right

Born: Stoke-on-Trent, 1877.
Died: 1914.
Career: Eastville Rovers. Worcester Rovers. Walsall, 1899. West Bromwich Albion, 1901. PRESTON NORTH END, 1903.

■ Following Walsall's failure to gain re-election to the Football League, Jimmy McLean moved across the Midlands to join West Bromwich Albion in 1901. In his first season at the Hawthorns, he helped Albion win promotion to the top flight as Champions of Division Two. His impressive displays for Albion led to North End securing his services before the start of the 1903–04 season. He scored on his debut on the opening day of the campaign as Stockport County were beaten 5–1 but his only other goal came in a 2–2 draw at lowly Glossop as North End won that season's Second Division Championship. With the club back in the top flight, McLean continued to perform at the highest level, creating a number of goals for Percy Smith and Dickie Bond. He missed just one game in 1905–06 as Preston finished runners-up in Division One to Champions Liverpool. McLean was a regular in the North End side for the next five seasons of First Division football and after playing in 194 League and Cup games was deservedly awarded a benefit match against Blackburn Rovers in September 1910.

McLEAN, Lauchlan

Inside-left

Born: Inverness, 1888.

Career: PRESTON NORTH END, 1910.
St Mirren.

■ Spotted playing junior football in his native Scotland, Lauchlan McLean played in just one Football League game for the Lilywhites. This was in a 2–0 defeat at Nottingham Forest on the opening day of the 1910–11 season. After losing his place to Arthur Mountenay, he returned north of the border to play Scottish First Division football for St Mirren.

McMAHON, John

Full-back

Born: Clyde, 1878.
Died: 1933.
Career: Clyde. PRESTON NORTH END, 1900. Manchester City, 1902. Bury, 1906.

■ Full-back John McMahon began his career in the Scottish First Division with his home-town club, Clyde, before joining Preston midway through the 1900–01 season. He made his debut in a 2–1 reversal at Bury and kept his place in the side at left-back for the remainder of a campaign which saw North End lose their top-flight status. He missed just two games the following season as North End almost made an immediate return to the top flight but eventually had to settle for third place. Almost halfway through the 1902–03 season, McMahon left Deepdale to join Manchester City. In his first season with the club he helped them win the Second Division Championship – one of his first games was a 2–0 victory over North End. McMahon helped City finish runners-up in the First Division in 1903–04 and they were always in the top six while McMahon was in the side. He left City in 1906 to see out his career with Bury.

McMAHON, John

Right-back

Born: Manchester, 7 December 1949.
Career: PRESTON NORTH END, 1967. Southend United, 1970 (loan). Chesterfield, 1979 (loan). Crewe Alexandra, 1979. Wigan Athletic, 1981. Tranmere Rovers, 1983. Curzon Athletic. Irlam Town.

■ Though he was on schoolboy forms with Manchester United, it was Preston North End who secured John

McMahon's services once he had left school. However, when he made his League debut in September 1970 he was playing for Southend United because he had been loaned out to gain experience. On his return to Deepdale he was given his North End debut in a League Cup third-round tie at West Bromwich Albion before playing his first League game at Halifax two weeks later. McMahon made 11 appearances that season as North End won the Third Division Championship. He made great strides and at the end of the 1971–72 season was named as the club's Player of the Year. The following season he scored his first League goal for the Lilywhites when he netted after just 12 seconds in the 3–3 draw with Bristol City. His consistency did not go unnoticed and in 1976–77 his fellow professionals chose him for the PFA Third Division side. Twelve years after joining North End he led them to promotion from the Third Division and was awarded a testimonial, but shortly afterwards he left to play for Crewe Alexandra. After two seasons at Gresty Road, McMahon joined Wigan Athletic and in his first season at

Springfield Park he helped the club to their first promotion. He remained one of the Latics' better players, but in the summer of 1983 he left to play for Tranmere Rovers before playing non-League football for Curzon Athletic and Irlam Town.

McNAB, James

Wing-half

Born: Denny, 13 April 1940.
Career: Kilsyth Rangers. Sunderland, 1957. PRESTON NORTH END, 1967. Stockport County, 1974.

■ Jimmy McNab began his footballing career with his home-town team Denny Juniors. Recruited by Sunderland when he was 15 on the strength of a Scottish cap and promise shown with Kilsyth Rangers, he went on to make his debut for the Wearsiders against Ipswich Town in September 1958. Over the next eight seasons, McNab missed very few games and was ever present in 1961–62. In 1963–64 he played a major role in the North East club winning promotion to the First Division. From his position at wing-half, he went on to score 18 goals in 324 first-team games before signing for Preston North End in March 1967. Having made his debut in a 2–0 home win over Derby County, he soon began

to demonstrate that he was strong in the tackle and a good distributor of the ball. McNab worked hard in the North End cause but there was little he could do to prevent the club from being relegated in 1969–70. The following season McNab was in outstanding form as the club won promotion at the first attempt as Champions of Division Three. During the course of that campaign, McNab switched to left-back and scored his only goal of the season in a 1–1 draw with runners-up Fulham. He went on to give the club great service, appearing in 245 matches, but after the club were relegated in 1973–74 he left Deepdale to end his career with Stockport County.

McNEIL, Robert Muirhead

Right-back

Born: Bellshill, 1 November 1962.
Career: Hull City, 1980. Blackpool, 1985. Lincoln City, 1985. PRESTON NORTH END, 1985. Carlisle United, 1987.

■ Full-back Bob McNeil started out with Hull City. In five seasons with the Tigers he made 138 League appearances and helped them win promotion from the Fourth Division in 1982–83. On losing his place at Boothferry Park, he had brief non-contract spells with

Blackpool and Lincoln City before joining Preston North End in December 1985. After making his debut in a 3–1 defeat at the hands of Aldershot, McNeil missed very few games, but it was a most disappointing campaign as the club finished one off the bottom of the Fourth Division. He remained at Deepdale and in 1986–87 played in 24 games as the club won promotion to the Third Division as runners-up to Northampton. McNeil then parted company with the club, going to see out his career with a season playing for Carlisle United – they too ended in 23rd position in Division Four.

MAGEE, Kevin

Left-winger

Born: Bathgate, 10 April 1971.
Career: Partick Thistle. PRESTON NORTH END, 1993. Plymouth Argyle, 1995. Scarborough, 1995.

■ Winger Kevin Magee joined North End from Partick Thistle in the summer of 1993. After some impressive performances in the club's reserve side, he made his senior debut in a 1–1 draw at Doncaster Rovers towards the end of the 1993–94 season. After a handful of League appearances that season, and having recovered from three broken legs, he appeared in 14 games the following campaign as the club once again reached the Play-offs. Magee also scored his only goal for the club in a 4–2 home win over Hereford United. A player whose speed and acceleration were often rewarded by some heavy marking, he left Deepdale after his monthly contract was not renewed to join Plymouth Argyle. His stay in Devon was brief and he moved on to Scarborough where, despite some good performances, he was one of a number players released in a mass clear out in the summer.

MAGUIRE, Hugh

Full-back

Born: Preston, 1871.
Career: PRESTON NORTH END, 1892.

■ Able to play in either of the full-back positions, Hugh Maguire understudied Bob Holmes and Nick Ross for a couple of seasons in the early 1890s. In 1892–93,

when North End finished runners-up to Sunderland in the First Division, he replaced Holmes for three games but was never on the winning side. The following season, when Preston struggled to avoid relegation to Division Two, Maguire's only game came at Sunderland when the Wearsiders won 6–3.

MAHER, David

Outside-right, inside-right

Born: London, 1880.
Career: Brentford. PRESTON NORTH END, 1903. Carlisle United.

■ Versatile forward Davie Maher played his early football for Brentford where his goalscoring feats attracted North End. He arrived at Deepdale midway through the 1903–04 season and made his debut in a 2–0 home win over Gainsborough Trinity. That season he made 14 appearances, scoring against Stockport County and Bradford City, as North End went on to win the Second Division Championship. Unable to win a regular place in the side in the higher grade of football, Maher left Deepdale in the summer of 1905 to continue his career with Carlisle United.

MAIN, William

Outside-right

Born: Preston, 1886.
Career: PRESTON NORTH END, 1908.

■ Winger William Main played his first games for the Lilywhites during the 1908–09 season, but he only appeared in the team when England international Dickie Bond was injured. He made half a dozen appearances both in that campaign and in 1909–10. In each season, North End finished mid-table in the First Division.

MARQUIS, Frederick

Inside-right, centre-forward

Born: Kirkham, 15 June 1899.
Died: 1957.
Career: Rushden Town. Lancaster Town. PRESTON NORTH END, 1920. Tranmere Rovers, 1925. Lancaster Town.

■ Signed from Lancaster Town, Fred Marquis made a couple of appearances in Lancashire derby matches during the

1920–21 season against Manchester City and Bolton Wanderers, but both games ended in defeat. Over the next couple of seasons he made just a handful of appearances, but in the latter of those campaigns, 1922–23, he did net a hat-trick for North End as Aston Villa were beaten '3–2. He appeared on a more regular basis over the next couple of seasons, but in the 1925 close season he left Deepdale to continue his career with Tranmere Rovers. In his first season at Prenton Park he was Rovers' leading scorer with 22 goals as they finished seventh in the Third Division North. He continued to find the net the following season and had scored 32 goals in 70 League games when he left to rejoin non-League Lancaster Town.

MARSHALL, John

Right-half, inside-right

Born: Stenhousemuir, 1892.
Career: PRESTON NORTH END, 1912. Burnley, 1913. Clyde.

■ John Marshall made his debut for North End on the opening day of Preston's Second Division Championship-winning season of 1912–13 in a 1–1 draw against Stockport County, but he found it difficult to hold down a regular pace. He made 16 appearances and scored a couple of goals including one on the final day of the season as bottom-of-the-table Blackpool were beaten 2–1. It was a similar story the following season but he did net three goals in the space of five League and Cup games. Even this failed to impress the management and in the close season he joined Burnley. After a season at Turf Moor, he returned to his native Scotland to see out his career with Clyde.

MARSHALL, John

Centre-half

Born: Southport, 31 July 1895.
Died: 1968.
Career: St Paul's. Rochdale. Shelbourne. Southport. PRESTON NORTH END, 1919. Wigan Borough, 1924. Southport, 1925. Wigan Borough, 1925.

■ Centre-half Jack Marshall replaced the injured Joe McCall for four games towards the end of the 1919–20 season.

This was a role he fulfilled for the next couple of seasons until 1922–23 when he appeared in 28 games as McCall struggled with advancing years. However, the England international won back his place in 1923–24 and Marshall was forced to move in an effort to find regular first-team football. He remained in the North West and had brief spells with Third Division North clubs Wigan Borough and Southport.

MARSTON, James Edward

Centre-half

Born: Australia, 7 January 1926.
Career: Leichardt (Australia). PRESTON NORTH END, 1950.

■ Australian-born centre-half Joe Marston was the third and final piece in Preston's half-back line which included the tough-tackling Tommy Docherty and Willie Forbes. Joe Marston arrived at Deepdale on the recommendation of a man called Percy Sewell, who had emigrated to Australia a number of years earlier. Percy had spotted Marston playing for Leichardt FC in Sydney and contacted Blackpool boss Joe Smith, recommending the central defender came across for a trial. The Seasiders

ignored his advice and so Marston arrived at Deepdale. After impressing the coaching staff he made his North End debut at right-back in a 4–1 defeat at Barnsley. Initially he failed to impress some of the North End supporters, but after he was switched to centre-half he went on to become one of the most influential lynchpins in the club's post-war history. His chance of regular first-team football arrived after Harry Mattinson broke his leg in a fourth-round FA Cup tie at Huddersfield in January 1951. Having helped Preston win the Second Division Championship in 1950–51, Marston was ever present for the next three seasons and became the first Australian-born player to be selected for the Football League representative XI. His last appearance for Preston was as a member of the side that lost 3–2 to West Bromwich Albion in the 1954 FA Cup Final. On leaving Deepdale he returned to live in Australia, where he resettled with his wife and family.

MARTIN, Michael Paul

Midfield

Born: Dublin, 9 July 1951.
Career: Home Farm. Bohemians. Manchester United, 1973. West Bromwich Albion, 1975. Newcastle United, 1978. Vancouver Whitecaps (Canada). Cardiff City, 1984. Peterborough United, 1985. Rotherham United, 1985. PRESTON NORTH END, 1985.

■ The son of Con Martin, who won 30 caps for the Republic of Ireland and six for Northern Ireland playing as a goalkeeper, defender and midfielder, Mick Martin was also a versatile player. He began his career in Ireland with Home Farm and Bohemians and had already made his full international debut for the Republic of Ireland when Tommy Docherty, the newly appointed manager of Manchester United, paid £20,000 to bring him to Old Trafford. At the time this was a record receipt for a League of Ireland club. After difficulties in holding down a regular place at Old Trafford, he left to join West Bromwich Albion. In his first season at the Hawthorns, he helped the Baggies win promotion to the First Division. However, when Ron Atkinson

replaced Johnny Giles as manager, Martin found himself out of the side and moved to Newcastle United for £100,000. Appointed the Magpies' captain, he spent six seasons in the North East where he was one of the club's most consistent players. Just as Arthur Cox's side embarked on an entertaining season which ended in promotion, Martin was left to wander around England and Wales – even North America – to continue his football career. Capped 52 times by the Republic of Ireland, his last Football League club were Preston North End whom he joined in September 1985, initially on a month's contract. After making his debut in a 2–0 home win over Hereford United, he went on to appear in 35 League games in a campaign in which the club finished one off the bottom of the Fourth Division. After later coaching Celtic, he went into business on Tyneside, running a sports shop.

MASEFIELD, Paul

Right-back

Born: Lichfield, 21 October 1970.
Career: Birmingham City, 1989. Cheltenham Town. Exeter City, 1992. Bromsgrove Rovers. Stockport County, 1992. Doncaster Rovers, 1993. PRESTON NORTH END, 1993.

■ Unable to make the grade at Birmingham, right-back Paul Masefield

drifted into non-League football with Cheltenham Town where his impressive displays prompted Exeter City to give him another chance. He had made just one appearance for the Grecians when he was again shown the door and left to play for Bromsgrove Rovers. Again his displays for a non-League club alerted teams in the lower Divisions and he had spells with both Stockport County and Doncaster Rovers before arriving at Deepdale for the start of the 1993–94 season. Masefield's first game in North End colours was in the 4–3 victory at Scarborough and each of his six League appearances ended in victory – including a 6–1 mauling of Shrewsbury and a 4–1 defeat of Chesterfield. This was his last appearance for the club as he lost out to new signing Andy Fensome.

MATHIE, Alexander

Forward

Born: Bathgate, 20 December 1968.
Career: Glasgow Celtic, 1987. Morton, 1991. Port Vale, 1993 (loan). Newcastle United, 1993. Ipswich Town, 1995. Dundee United, 1998. PRESTON NORTH END, 1999 (loan). York City, 2000. Pickering Town.

■ Alex Mathie appeared only rarely in senior football for Celtic before moving to Morton. There he became a prolific goalscorer, topping the scoring charts in his two seasons at Cappielow Park. He moved to Newcastle United as Andy Cole's deputy but after being unable to force his way into the Magpies side, left to join Ipswich Town for a fee of £500,000. An attacking player with tremendous ball skills, he had an outstanding first full season at Portman Road, forming a formidable strike force with Ian Marshall. Mathie scored in each of Town's first four games and netted a hat-trick against the eventual Champions, Sunderland. Once Marshall had left the club, Mathie bore the burden of being the club's main goalscorer well until he was told that he needed surgery on both shoulders. Unfortunately, this had to be carried out individually, thus doubling the time of his absence. In February 1998 he ensured that he had a place in Ipswich Town folklore when he netted a first-half hat-trick in the East

Anglian derby against Norwich City. Finding himself on the bench more and more, he left Portman Road to seek first-team football with Dundee United. In September 1999 he went on loan to Preston as cover for injured strikers Steve Basham and Kurt Nogan. He made his debut in a win at Gillingham and netted twice on his home debut against Sheffield United in the Worthington Cup. His goal against Bristol City was the 100th of his senior career and though he later returned to Tannadice, he had played in enough games to warrant a Second Division Championship medal. Mathie returned to the Football League with York City in 2000. Injuries limited his appearances at Bootham Crescent and he left to link up with Northern Counties East outfit Pickering Town.

MATTHEW, Henry

Left-half

Born: Bolton, 1871.
Career: Bolton Wanderers, 1892. PRESTON NORTH END, 1897.

■ Henry Matthew started out with his home town club but in five seasons at Burnden Park, he made just eight League appearances. These were all in 1892–93 when the club finished fifth in the First Division. A regular reserve, he jumped at the opportunity of first-team football with Preston North End in 1897. He had a good season, playing in 18 games and helping to create a number of goals for Sandy Brown and James Stevenson, but he did not appear in North End colours after that campaign.

MATTHEWSON, Trevor

Centre-half

Born: Sheffield, 12 February 1963.
Career: Sheffield Wednesday, 1981. Newport County, 1983. Stockport County, 1985. Lincoln City, 1987. Birmingham City, 1989. PRESTON NORTH END, 1993. Bury, 1994. Witton Albion. Hereford United, 1996.

■ Defender Trevor Matthewson began his League career with home-town team Sheffield Wednesday. However, after only a handful of appearances he was given a free transfer and joined Newport County. He made 90 appearances for the Somerton Park club before joining Stockport County and later Lincoln City. He skippered the Imps back into the Football League and they were somewhat put out when an independent tribunal fixed his transfer fee to Birmingham City at just £45,000. In 1989–90 he was the Blues' only ever present as they finished seventh in Division Three. He was ever present again in 1990–91 and also played his part in the club winning the Leyland Daf Cup Final at Wembley. He spent four seasons at St Andrew's and had scored 13 goals in 203 games before leaving to join Preston North End in the summer of 1993. After playing in a League Cup defeat at Burnley, he made his League debut three days later as North End thrashed Shrewsbury Town 6–1. Matthewson had played in 12 games when he left to join Bury. He later had a spell with non-League Witton Albion before returning to League action with Hereford United.

MATTINSON, Harry

Centre-half

Born: Wigton, 20 July 1925.
Died: 8 June 2001.
Career: Middlesbrough, 1945. PRESTON NORTH END, 1949. Queen of the South.

■ Harry Mattinson arrived at Deepdale from Middlesbrough in March 1949 and soon filled a variety of roles in North End's back four. There were times when he deputised for Willie Cunningham at right-back and at wing-half for either Tommy Docherty or Willie Forbes. He was even asked to play at centre-forward in an FA Cup tie against Sunderland but

asked not to be considered for the position in case he let everybody down. Mattinson played in a couple of games in North End's relegation season of 1948–49 before establishing a regular place in the Preston side. He had reverted to his normal position of centre-half for a FA Cup tie against Huddersfield Town at Deepdale in January 1951 but sadly he broke his leg. Australian-born Joe Marston replaced him and after his recovery Mattinson was forced to spend two whole seasons languishing in Preston's reserve side, much to his disappointment and frustration. His absence from the Preston side also meant that he missed out on the club's promotion to the top flight in 1950–51 season as the club finished the campaign as Second Division Champions. Eventually, Mattinson sought pastures new and in June 1960 he left Deepdale to play Scottish League football for Queen of the South.

MAWENE, Youl

Defender

Born: Caen, France, 16 July 1979.
Career: RC Lens (France). Derby County, 2000. PRESTON NORTH END, 2004.

■ Derby County signed Youl Mawene from French club RC Lens in the

Youl Mawene

summer of 2000. He spent the first half of the campaign settling in with the reserves before making an accomplished debut on a frozen pitch at Southampton. A promising young defender blessed with pace and good vision, he did not play senior football at all in 2002–03 due to a cartilage operation. When he did try to return he suffered a knee ligament injury. Mawene finally returned to action in November 2003 to make his first senior appearance for 21 months. After helping the Rams successfully avoid relegation he was voted Player of the Year by Derby supporters. In August 2004 he joined North End on a free transfer and was simply magnificent in the Preston defence throughout the entire 2004–05 season – whether playing at right-back or in his preferred central position. Mawene quickly established himself as the fans' favourite, winning plaudits for his work in the community and making a clean sweep of the Player of the Year awards at Deepdale. The French defender's only goal of last season came in injury-time in the match against Queen's Park Rangers at Deepdale – the shock equaliser earning North End a point.

MAXWELL, James Morton

Centre-forward

Born: Kilmarnock, 15 January 1913.
Died: 1990.
Career: Kilmarnock. PRESTON NORTH END, 1934. Barnsley, 1939. Kilmarnock. Shrewsbury Town.

■ Known as 'Bud', a nickname he had acquired in his Kilmarnock days, Jimmy Maxwell joined North End for £4,000 from the Scottish club in the summer of 1934. Just before coming to Deepdale, he played for the Scottish League representative side and soon afterwards was in an Anglo Scots XI that played in a Jubilee game at Highbury. After making his Preston debut in a 1–0 home win over Grimsby Town on the opening day of the 1934–35 season, Maxwell went on to become the club's leading scorer with 26 League and Cup goals. This total included hat-tricks in a 4–3 win at Huddersfield Town and a 5–2 home defeat of Stoke and during that season he scored some magnificent goals. Fast, nippy and packing a terrific shot with his

left foot, he was the club's top scorer again in 1935–36 with a total of 19 goals in all competitions. Maxwell's left foot was so much to the fore that when he scored one with his right foot Jim Taylor, who was in the pottery trade, had a dozen flower vases made as a joke to commemorate the event! This became known as the Maxwell vase, so marked on its base, and Jimmy good-humouredly accepted one in the spirit in which Taylor had given it. Maxwell continued to find the net and the following season he netted another hat-trick in a 3–2 defeat of West Bromwich Albion, though he lost out as leading scorer to Frank O'Donnell. Maxwell was nearing the end of his service at Deepdale and had been discarded when Jimmy Dougal broke down with cartilage trouble in the FA Cup semi-final of 1938. Maxwell stepped in and won a FA Cup-winners' medal as North End beat Huddersfield Town. However, within 12 months he had been put on the transfer list and eventually joined Barnsley.

MAY, James

Outside-right

Born: Cambusnethan, 1873.
Career: St Mirren. PRESTON NORTH END, 1897.

■ Winger James May was recruited from Scottish League club St Mirren, with whom he was always challenging for First Division honours. He played in three games during North End's 1897–98 season when they were struggling to avoid relegation. Though the club did not win any of the three games in which May appeared, they drew two and May did create Sandy Brown's goal for the 1–1 draw at Everton.

MAYERS, Derek

Outside-right

Born: Liverpool, 24 January 1935.
Career: Everton, 1952. PRESTON NORTH END, 1957. Leeds United, 1961. Bury, 1962. Wrexham, 1963.

■ Winger Derek Mayers started his career with Everton. However, for much of his time at Goodison he was playing reserve-team football and so when the opportunity of a move to Preston North

End arose in the summer of 1957 he jumped at it. Mayers made a goalscoring debut for North End in a 3–1 home win over Spurs and soon slotted into the side, making the number-seven shirt his own. In that 1957–58 season, North End finished as runners-up to Wolves in the race for the First Division Championship. Mayers continued to be a regular in the Preston side for four seasons until he left to play for Leeds United after the Deepdale club lost their top-flight status in 1960–61. After a season at Elland Road, he moved on to Bury before playing for Wrexham. After the Robins were relegated to the Fourth Division at the end of his first season at the Racecourse Ground, he decided it was time to hang up his boots.

MEARS, Tyrone

Defender
Born Stockport, 18 February 1983.
Career Manchester City 2000; PRESTON NORTH END 2002;

■ Tyrone Mears' only appearance for his first club, Manchester City, was when he came off the bench to replace Stuart Pearce for the final six minutes of the home game against Nottingham Forest in 2001–02. He arrived at Deepdale in

the close season but an injury sustained before the start of the campaign ruled him out until October. One of the fastest players at Preston in recent memory, Mears made an impressive start to his North End career, demonstrating his versatility by playing in both full-back positions, wide midfield and even up front as a substitute, scoring his only goal at Reading. Injuries, notably a stress fracture, hampered his progress in 2003–04 and he missed most of the following campaign with a serious shin injury. When North End beat Luton Town 5–1 last season, it was Tyrone Mears who deflected the ball into his own net after Brkovic's rocket came off the bar – the only goal Preston conceded in 9 hours 31 minutes! He had, though, scored at the other end. Mears also forced the ball over the line in the Play-off semi-final second leg but after discussion with his assistant, the referee disallowed the effort.

MEIJER, Erik

Forward

Born: Meerssem, Holland, 2 August 1969.
Career: Meerssem (Holland). PSV Eindhoven (Holland). VV Fortuna Sittard (Holland). Bayer Leverkusen (Germany). Liverpool, 1999. PRESTON NORTH END, 2000 (loan). SV Hamburg (Germany).

■ Giant Dutch striker Erik Meijer arrived at Anfield from Bundesliga side

Bayer Leverkusen in the summer of 1999. He showed during his first season with the Reds that he was excellent on the floor, but even better with his head. Possessing an excellent professional attitude, he commanded respect with his demeanour. A valuable addition to the Anfield squad, he never shirked a challenge and excited the Liverpool fans with his wholehearted attitude. In 2000–01 he found himself on the fringes of the Liverpool team and in October 2000 was loaned out to Preston North End. On his debut against Norwich City, he set up an injury-time winner but after nine League appearances without a goal he opted for a return to the Bundesliga by joining SV Hamburg on a free transfer.

MELIA, James

Full-back
Born: Darlington, 2 April 1874
Died: February 1905
Career: Sheffield Wednesday. Tottenham Hotspur 1898. PRESTON NORTH END 1901.

■ After two years as a Sheffield Wednesday reserve, full-back James Melia joined Spurs as cover for the big Scot, Harry Erentz. He certainly provided him with stiff opposition, frequently winning a first-team spot on merit. After being selected for the Southern League against the Southern Amateurs in a War Fund match, he left White Hart Lane and signed for Preston North End. He made his debut on the opening day of the 1901–02 season in a 3–1 defeat at West Bromwich Albion and then made his second and final appearance in a 2–0 loss at Chesterfield later in the campaign. Sadly, he later fell ill and died in February 1905, aged only 30.

MERCER, William

Wing-half
Born: Preston, 14 March 1896.
Died: 1975.
Career: PRESTON NORTH END, 1919. Blackpool, 1925. Lancaster Town. Boston Town.

■ Wing-half Billy Mercer played in two Lancashire derbies during the first season of League football after World War One: both games, against Bolton

and Burnley, ended in 1–1 draws. By the end of the following season he had become an established member of the North End side. All of Billy Mercer's football for North End was played in a struggling First Division side. In his six seasons with the club, their best position in the top flight was 16th in three successive seasons. Mercer left Deepdale following the club's relegation in 1924–25 but after just one game for Blackpool he moved into non-League football with Lancaster Town and Boston.

METCALF, Thomas

Outside-right
Born: Preston, 1868.
Career: PRESTON NORTH END, 1890.

■ Winger Thomas Metcalf's only first-team outing for North End brought him a goal in a 4–1 home win over Aston Villa in January 1891. Replacing the injured Jack Gordon, he also provided the cross for Bernard Crossan to sweep home his second goal of the game. Despite this promising debut, he played out the season in the reserves and then parted company with the club.

METCALFE, James Alfred

Wing-half, centre-half
Born: Sunderland, 10 December 1898.
Died: 1975.
Career: Sunderland Royal Rovers. Southwick. South Shields, 1920. PRESTON NORTH END, 1927. Nelson, 1928.

■ James Metcalfe was able to play in any of the half-back line positions. He began his first-class career with Second Division South Shields, whose best position in his time with the club was sixth in 1921–22. He moved to Preston in 1927 and made his debut on the opening day of the 1927–28 season in a 2–2 draw at Fulham. Metcalfe played in 16 games that season but, though he starred in a 3–2 win at his former club South Shields early in the campaign, he had lost his place in the side by the time North End won the return 7–2 at Deepdale. Metcalfe left Deepdale after just one season and joined Nelson who were playing in the Third Division North.

MILLAR, Alexander

Centre-half

Born: Mossend, 21 October 1911.
Died: 28 January 1978.
Career: Mossend Celtic. Parkhead Juniors.
Shawfield Juniors. Glasgow Celtic.
PRESTON NORTH END, 1938.
Motherwell. Dundee United. Morton.
Glasgow Celtic. Inverness Caledonian.
Stranraer.

■ Alex Millar was of Lithuanian parentage. A big, fair-haired centre-half, he helped Celtic reserves win the Alliance League and the 2nd XI Cup in 1935–36. He played in both legs of the Champions' Match against Sunderland in September 1936 and made his Old Firm debut at Parkhead in between the two matches. Desperate to play first-team football on a regular basis, he joined Tommy Muirhead's Preston side in October 1938. Millar had a disastrous debut as North End went down 4–1 at Liverpool and he made only one more appearance before returning to Scotland to 'guest' for a number of clubs in the war years. After spells with Motherwell and Dundee United, he joined Morton and figured prominently in the two finals against Rangers in 1948. He was secretary of the Scottish Players' Union until November 1950. While playing for Preston, Millar married a Motherwell girl and was the father of 10 children.

MILLER, David Brian

Defender, midfield

Born: Burnley, 8 January 1964.
Career: Burnley, 1982. Crewe Alexandra, 1983 (loan). Tranmere Rovers, 1985.
Colne Dynamoes. PRESTON NORTH END, 1986. Burnley, 1989 (loan). Carlisle United, 1989. Stockport County, 1992.
Wigan Athletic, 1994.

■ David Miller, the son of Burnley legend Brian Miller, was a Clarets fanatic as a youngster and set his heart on playing for the Turf Moor club. In fact, his father Brian was the Clarets' manager when he first made his breakthrough into League football as a substitute on New Year's Day 1983. However, competition for places at Turf Moor was fierce and he was released. After a season at Tranmere, Miller joined Colne

Dynamos but he was soon back in League football, signing for Preston North End in December 1986. He helped Preston to a 3–0 win over Lincoln City on debut and by the end of the season was an important member of the club's Fourth Division promotion-winning side. He played for much of the following season but after a short spell on loan with former club Burnley, he joined Carlisle United. At Brunton Park, Miller enjoyed regular first-team football for the first time in his career. His consistency attracted Stockport County and he helped the Hatters reach the Play-offs in two consecutive seasons before joining Wigan Athletic in November 1994. Sadly, injuries and a loss of form hampered his time at Springfield Park and in May 1996 he was released.

MILLER, Harry James

Inside-forward

Born: Preston, 1895.
Career: Fleetwood. Leyland. Everton, 1922. PRESTON NORTH END, 1924.
Lancaster Town.

■ Inside-forward Harry Miller made a couple of appearances for Everton after some impressive displays for Leyland, but he could not force his way into the

Blues' side on a regular basis. In 1924 he moved to Preston North End and made his debut in a 1–0 defeat at West Ham United on the opening day of the 1924–25 season. However, he managed just a handful of first-team outings without finding the net before being released in the summer. After leaving Deepdale he returned to the non-League scene with Lancaster Town.

MILLER, Henry

Centre-forward

Born: Paisley, 1874.
Career: PRESTON NORTH END, 1893.
Bury, 1894. Reading. Sheffield Wednesday, 1899. Queen's Park Rangers.

■ Henry Miller played in a couple of games for North End towards the end of the 1893–94 season – a campaign when the Lilywhites just avoided relegation to Division Two. There was a big clear-out in the close season and Miller moved to Bury where he rediscovered the form that he had shown while playing junior football in Scotland. In his first season with the Shakers, he helped them win the Second Division Championship. For the rest of his time at Gigg Lane, he helped them consolidate their position as a First Division club. Miller had scored 38 goals in 109 games when a brief sojourn into the Southern League with Reading was followed by a return to League action with Sheffield Wednesday. He scored 16 goals in 32 games as the Owls won the Second Division title. He later ended his career back in the Southern League with Queen's Park Rangers.

MILLER, James

Outside-right

Born: Tynemouth, 10 May 1889.
Career: Wallsend Park Villa. Newcastle United, 1912. Grimsby Town, 1913.
Everton, 1919. Coventry City, 1919.
PRESTON NORTH END, 1919.
Pontypridd. Darlington, 1921.
Chesterfield, 1922. Bournemouth, 1923.
Swansea Town, 1924. Luton Town, 1925.

■ Much-travelled winger Jimmy Miller failed to make the grade with his local club, Newcastle United. After playing for Grimsby Town in the seasons prior to World War One, he played for both Everton and Coventry in the early part of the 1919–20 season. Preston North End were his third club during that first season of League football after the hostilities. Miller made his debut in a 3–1 home win over Middlesbrough and played in 15 games that season, scoring his only goal in the 1–0 defeat of relegation rivals Sheffield Wednesday. He helped Chesterfield finish fourth in the Third Division North in 1922–23 and then moved to Bournemouth for their first season in the Football League. This was by spells with Swansea, whom he helped win the Third Division South Championship, and Luton where he ended his career.

MILLS-ROBERTS, Dr Robert Herbert

Goalkeeper

Born: Penmachno, 5 August 1862.
Died: 1935.
Career: Barnes. St Thomas' Hospital. Casuals. PRESTON NORTH END, 1888. Warwick County. Birmingham St George's. Llanberis.

■ Robert Mills-Roberts, who won eight caps for Wales, played both football and rugby at Aberystwyth University before entering the teaching hospital at St Thomas' in 1882. In London he gave up the idea of playing rugby and took up

goalkeeping for the hospital team. He appeared for the Corinthians against North End at the Jubilee football festival of 1887 at the Oval in front of the Prince of Wales. This led to an invitation to join the Deepdale club, despite Preston winning 4–3. Regular goalkeeper James Trainer had to serve a two-year qualification period to be eligible for FA Cup matches whereas the amateur Mills-Roberts only had to register for a month. In 1887, North End lost 2–1 to West Bromwich Albion in the Final but won the Cup in 1888–89 with Mills-Roberts between the posts. They did so without conceding a goal in any of their five matches. Mills-Roberts qualified as a doctor in July 1887 and very often had to travel from his Stroud home by horse and carriage to catch a train from Gloucester to wherever North End were playing. He became house surgeon at Birmingham General Hospital in February 1888 and appeared in the occasional game for Warwick County and Birmingham St George's when he was not playing for Preston. After retiring from football in 1890, he was appointed surgeon for the hospital at Dinorwic Slate Quarry in North Wales. He held the post for 24 years which was interrupted only by service in the Boer War.

MILNE, Gordon

Wing-half

Born: Preston, 29 March 1937.
Career: Morecambe. PRESTON NORTH END, 1956. Liverpool, 1960. Blackpool, 1967. Wigan Athletic, 1970.

■ Gordon Milne was capped 14 times by England and was included in the 1966 World Cup squad. The son of former Preston North End manager Jimmy Milne, he began his career with non-League Morecambe before joining his home-town team, Preston North End. A strong, constructive wing-half, he made his debut in a 2–2 draw at Portsmouth in September 1956. Over the next couple of seasons he appeared in a handful of games before replacing Tommy Docherty in the North End side in 1958–59. A regular in the Preston side for a couple of seasons, he was then made a scapegoat after a poor start to what proved to be the club's relegation

season of 1960–61. Three days after being dropped, he was transferred to Liverpool, where he enjoyed his greatest success. Although he missed the 1965 FA Cup Final through injury, he played in two League Championship-winning sides and a Second Division title side as well as a European Cup-winners' Cup Final. Milne left Anfield in 1967 and joined Blackpool, making his Seasiders debut on his old hunting ground of Deepdale. Blackpool just missed out on promotion to the First Division in Milne's first season at Bloomfield Road, but thereafter injuries and a loss of form curtailed his appearances. In January 1970 he joined Wigan Athletic as player-manager. He then held managerial posts with Coventry City and Leicester City, whom he helped into the First Division. Milne also managed the England Youth side before moving to Turkey where he had great success managing Besiktas.

MILNE, James Low

Left-half

Born: Dundee, 24 January 1911.
Died: 13 December 1997.
Career: Dundee Arnot. Dundee Violet. Dundee United. PRESTON NORTH END, 1932. Wigan Athletic. Morecambe.

■ One of the best uncapped wing-halves of the inter-war period, Jimmy

Milne was initially with his home-town team, Dundee United, but spent just a year at Tannadice before moving to North End in 1932. He made his debut in a 2–1 reversal at Lincoln and it was not long before he was an established member of the North End side. In 1933–34 his only goal of the campaign helped Preston beat Burnley 3–2 and by the end of the season the club were celebrating a return to the top flight as runners-up in the Second Division to Champions Grimsby Town. Over the next few seasons Milne missed very few games and in 1937 he was playing at Wembley in the FA Cup Final. The following season of 1937–38 saw North End finish third in Division One as well as reaching the FA Cup Final for the second year in succession. On the losing side against Sunderland in 1937, Milne was unlucky again a year later as he missed the Final through injury. In a vital home match against Arsenal a week earlier, he had broken his collarbone in a collision with Kirchen. North End lost 3–1 with 10 men and Arsenal became Champions. During the war Milne played for Preston and Bury before joining Wigan as player-manager in the 1946–47 season. He subsequently held a similar post at Morecambe and then became trainer with Doncaster Rovers. He returned to Preston in 1949, first as trainer and then as manager in the early 1960s, a position he occupied until 1968.

MIMMS, Robert Andrew

Goalkeeper

Born: York, 12 October 1963.
Career: Halifax Town, 1981. Rotherham United, 1981. Everton, 1985. Notts County, 1986 (loan). Sunderland, 1986 (loan). Blackburn Rovers, 1987 (loan). Manchester City, 1987 (loan). Tottenham Hotspur, 1988. Aberdeen, 1990 (loan). Blackburn Rovers, 1990. Crystal Palace, 1996. PRESTON NORTH END, 1996. Rotherham United, 1997. York City, 1998. Mansfield Town, 2000.

■ Bobby Mimms began his career with Halifax Town but moved on to Rotherham United without making the first team. He soon came under scrutiny from the bigger clubs, particularly after he had appeared as a substitute for the

England Under-21 side. He moved to Everton as cover for Neville Southall and, with the Welsh international injured, finished the season with an FA Cup runners'-up medal after Everton lost to rivals Liverpool. He also won further Under-21 honours. With Southall fully recovered, Mimms went on loan to Sunderland, Blackburn and Manchester City before Spurs' boss Terry Venables signed him for a fee of £375,000. Though he started as the White Hart Lane club's first-choice 'keeper, he lost his place to Erik Thorsvedt and, after a loan spell with Aberdeen, moved to Blackburn Rovers for £250,000. In 1991–92 he helped Rovers gain promotion back to the top flight via a Wembley Play-off Final. He kept his place in the Blackburn side until the signing of Tim Flowers, but after appearing in 156 games he moved to Crystal Palace before joining North End in September 1996. At Deepdale, the experienced 'keeper continued to demonstrate the talent which saw him play in the Premiership and he rescued

his defenders on many occasions. Despite losing his place in mid-season, it was short-lived and he returned strongly. Allowed to return to the club where he made his League debut, Mimms proved to the Rotherham fans that he was still a fine shot-stopper, but after just one season back at Millmoor he moved to his home-town club, York City. A player-coach at Bootham Crescent, he later joined Mansfield Town, whom he also helped as a goalkeeping coach.

MITCHELL, Barrie

Forward

Born: Aberdeen, 15 March 1947.
Career: Aberdeen. Tranmere Rovers, 1974. PRESTON NORTH END, 1976. York City, 1977.

■ Barrie Mitchell came south to play for Tranmere Rovers after helping his home-town team, Aberdeen, finish runners-up in the Scottish First Division in successive seasons in the early 1970s. He was a regular in the Wirral club's side for a couple of seasons, scoring 10 goals in 83 League outings, and in 1975–76 he helped them win promotion to the Third Division. He joined Preston North End in the summer of 1976 and, though he only made seven starts as the club challenged for promotion to Division Two, he did find the net in the games

against Brighton and Peterborough United. Released after a season, he joined York City where he played in a handful of games before returning north of the border.

MITCHELL, James Frederick

Goalkeeper

Born: Manchester, 18 November 1897.
Died: 30 May 1975.
Career: Blackpool, 1914. Northern Nomads. Manchester University. PRESTON NORTH END, 1920. Manchester City, 1922. Leicester City, 1926.

■ The son of a famous billiards player, Fred Mitchell began his Football League career with Blackpool but his impressive start was halted by World War One. After the hostilities, Mitchell left Bloomfield Road and joined Preston North End. Still an amateur, his move to Deepdale was one of the few times when he was not the centre of attraction, for few players were as conspicuous. A wartime graduate of Manchester University, Mitchell warranted more attention than most since high academic qualifications were rare amongst footballers at that time. Mitchell's methods were unorthodox to say the least, for he used his feet as much as his hands. The feature that preserved him in North End folklore, and that of every club he played for, was that he sported spectacles on the field of play. He represented England in the 1920 Olympic Games in the high jump. Mitchell was a teacher at Arnold School, Blackpool, and his duties resulted in him missing a number of games. Though his appearances were both sporadic and erratic, he was in goal when North End played Huddersfield Town in the 1922 FA Cup Final. The game at Stamford Bridge was one of the worst ever finals and was goalless until Hamilton brought down Town's Billy Smith. The referee pointed to the spot and, after a series of protests and tantrums from the North End players were waved away, Smith took the kick. As he ran up to the ball, Mitchell started to jump up and down gesticulate wildly in an astonishing display of gamesmanship. However,

Smith was completely unruffled and stroked home the winner. It was Mitchell's last game for Preston as he joined Manchester City in the summer. While with City he won full international honours for England when he played in the 3–1 win over Ireland at Anfield in October 1924. On leaving Maine Road he took up an appointment just outside Leicester with Stead and Simpson, the footwear chain, and ended his distinguished football career by playing for a season with Leicester City.

MITTON, Gilbert Keith

Goalkeeper

Born: Leyland, 30 December 1928.
Died: 1995.
Career: Leyland Motors. PRESTON NORTH END, 1950. Carlisle United, 1954.

■ Goalkeeper Keith Mitton arrived at Deepdale from local club Leyland Motors. He understudied a number of North End 'keepers including Newlands, Gooch and Thompson before making a couple of appearances during the 1953–54 season when George Thompson was injured. Mitton was in goal in two big wins for North End – a 4–1 victory over Manchester City at Maine Road and a 6–2 home defeat of Sunderland when Charlie Wayman netted a hat-trick. Even so, he returned to the reserves before being allowed to join Carlisle United in the 1954 close season. He spent two seasons at Brunton Park, making 47 League appearances, but the Cumbrian side struggled near the foot of the Third Division North in both campaigns.

MOILANEN, Teuvo Johannes

Goalkeeper

Born: Oulu, Finland, 12 December 1973.
Career: Ilves (Finland). FF Jaro (Finland). PRESTON NORTH END, 1995. Scarborough, 1996 (loan). Darlington, 1996 (loan). Heart of Midlothian, 2003.

■ Finnish international goalkeeper Teuvo Moilanen joined North End from FF Jaro in December 1995 and his debut in a goalless draw at Lincoln City made him the tallest 'keeper in the club's

history. He started the 1996–97 season as the club's first-choice 'keeper but some indifferent form led to him being replaced by Bobby Mimms. His confidence was restored with loan spells at Scarborough and Darlington and after winning back his place he won the first of three international caps for Finland. His second appearance for his country came against Hungary in the 1998 World Cup qualifiers – the Finns were knocked out due to a bizarre last-minute goal when the ball hit Moilanen's backside and went in! A fractured breastbone cost him his place in 1998–99 but even on recovering he could not oust David Lucas. However, when North End won the Second Division Championship in 1999–2000, Moilanen set new seasonal club records for clean sheets in the Football League with 24 and in all matches with 28. Despite being lobbed from the halfway line straight from the restart after a North End goal at Brentford, he became a model of consistency and won his third cap against Wales. Back in the First Division, he was again hampered by injuries, though when he did play he showed his value in the club's tremendous return to the higher grade of football. He was sorely missed during the Play-off run-in. After again sharing the goalkeeping duties with David Lucas, he started the 2002–03 season as the club's first choice and was recalled to the Finland squad for the Euro 2004 qualifiers. However, after suffering a dip in form he went on loan to Heart of Midlothian, with the move later becoming a permanent one.

MONTGOMERY, Gerald

Centre-half

Born: Liverpool, 1879.
Career: PRESTON NORTH END, 1900. Tottenham Hotspur. PRESTON NORTH END, 1902.

■ Towering centre-half Gerald Montgomery made four appearances for North End during the 1900–01 season. The first was in a 3–1 defeat at local rivals Blackburn Rovers. After playing in two 1–1 draws, his last appearance in North End colours came in a 6–1 hammering at Notts County. He left Deepdale in the summer to join Tottenham Hotspur, but played in only one competitive match for the North London club – against Woolwich Arsenal in the London League in September 1901. He then sustained a serious injury which put him out of action for the remainder of the season. Though he later tried to make a comeback with Preston, he decided to retire from football and pursue a business career.

MOONEY, Brian John

Winger

Born: Dublin, 2 February 1966.
Career: Home Farm. Liverpool, 1983. Wrexham, 1985 (loan). PRESTON NORTH END, 1987. Sunderland, 1991. Burnley, 1992 (loan).

■ Republic of Ireland Under-23 international Brian Mooney joined Liverpool from the famous nursery club Home Farm in 1983, but in two years at Anfield he was unable to break into the Reds' League side. Mooney's first experience of League football was a loan spell in the Fourth Division with Wrexham during 1985–86. In October 1987, Mooney joined Preston North End and made his debut in a 3–2 home win

over Port Vale. In 1988–89, his first full season, Mooney was outstanding, showing some incredible dribbling skills and becoming a huge favourite with the Preston fans. The skilful Irishman's best season in terms of goals scored was 1989–90 when he netted 10 in the League, including a hat-trick in a 5–0 home win over Chester City. Midway through the following season, Sunderland paid £25,000 for his services. Mooney was very much on the fringe of first-team action at Roker Park and had to watch from the sidelines during Sunderland's run to the FA Cup Final in 1992 where Liverpool beat them 2–0. In September 1992 he joined Burley on loan but returned to Wearside after a month. He forced his way back into first-team reckoning, only to be released at the end of the season.

MORLEY, Jonathan Bell

Outside-right, inside-right

Born: Carlisle, 29 January 1884.
Died: 1957.
Career: Workington. Sunderland, 1907. Burnley, 1908. PRESTON NORTH END, 1911.

■ Having started out with Workington, John Morley made a handful of appearances for Sunderland before joining Second Division Burnley at the start of the 1908–09 season. He had scored 15 goals in 96 games for the Clarets when he stepped up to the First

Division with Preston North End in 1911–12. Morley's first game in the higher grade of football was in a goalless draw at Manchester City. Though North End were relegated at the end of that campaign, Morley netted his first goal for the club in a surprise 4–1 defeat of high-flying Aston Villa. He was an important member of the Preston side the following season as the club returned to the top flight as Champions of the Second Division some three points ahead of runners-up Burnley. Though not a prolific scorer, the winger netted the club's only hat-trick in that campaign in a 3–2 win at Glossop on New Year's Day 1913. This result put them on top of the League for the first time that season. Morley found himself in and out of the Preston side in 1913–14 as the club once again lost their First Division status, but he had a better campaign as the club again won promotion from Division Two.

MORLEY, William Anthony

Left-winger

Born: Ormskirk, 26 August 1954.
Career: PRESTON NORTH END, 1972. Burnley, 1976. Aston Villa, 1979. West Bromwich Albion, 1983. Birmingham City, 1984 (loan). Den Haag (Holland). West Bromwich Albion, 1987. Burnley, 1988 (loan). Tampa Bay Rowdies (US). Hamrun (Malta). Bromsgrove Rovers. Stratford.

■ On his day Tony Morley was an exceptionally fine winger – fast, comfortable on the ball, able to take on the best of defenders and deliver accurate crosses. Morley signed for Preston North End as an apprentice in the summer of 1970 and turned professional a couple of years later. He made his League debut for the Lilywhites as a substitute for David Wilson at Queen's Park Rangers in January 1973. North End were relegated at the end of the 1973–74 season, a campaign in which Morley made just 10 appearances. He was a first-team regular in 1974–75, scoring his first goal for the club on the opening day of the season against Plymouth Argyle. Already an England Youth international, Morley's outstanding performances in the Third Division brought him to the attention of

the Under-23 selectors and he won his only cap at that level against Wales at Wrexham in January 1975. In February 1976 an offer of £100,000 was too much for Preston to resist and he was on his way to Turf Moor to help Burnley's fight to retain their top-flight status. It was a lost cause but even then the shaven-headed Morley was still unable to create much of an impact in three mediocre seasons of Second Division football. He joined Aston Villa in the summer of 1979 for £200,000 and in 1980–81 was one of their stars as they took the First Division by storm. He continued to perform with pace and style the following season and scored four goals in Villa's triumphant European Cup campaign. Earlier that season he had arrived on the England scene, collecting the first of his six caps against Hungary. He joined West Brom in 1983 and later played in Holland

before returning to the Hawthorns in 1987. He had a spell on loan with Burnley before playing in the US for Tampa Bay Rowdies and Maltese side Hamrun. Morley went on to play non-League football for Bromsgrove Rovers and finally Stratford.

MORRIS, David

Centre-half

Born: Leith, 21 August 1899.
Died: 1971.
Career: Newtongrange. Arniston Rangers. Raith Rovers. PRESTON NORTH END, 1925. Chester. Dundee United. Leith Athletic.

■ Scottish international centre-half David Morris won six caps for the national side. He arrived at Deepdale midway through the 1925–26 season after playing in the Scottish First Division for Raith Rovers. He did not enjoy the best of debuts as North End were beaten 4–0 at South Shields, but he kept his place in the side for the rest of the season, scoring his first goal for the club in a 1–1 draw at Stockport County. Morris was appointed captain for the 1926–27 season and led by example, missing just one game as the club rose to sixth in Division Two. Bringing a much-needed stability to the Preston defence, Morris was ever present the following season as North End came close to returning to the top flight, finishing fourth. He spent another couple of seasons at Deepdale before a spell with Chester was followed by a return north of the border to play for Dundee United and finally his home-town team, Leith Athletic.

MORRISON, Angus Cameron

Outside-left

Born: Dingwall, 26 April 1924.
Died: 18 December 2002.
Career: Ross County. Derby County, 1944. PRESTON NORTH END, 1948. Millwall, 1957. Nuneaton Borough. Belper Town.

■ Angus Morrison was signed by Derby County for a box of cigars, the gift the Rams sent in return for the recommendation. Morrison was in the RAF at the time and proved an extremely

talented forward, either in the centre or at outside-left, and had an excellent scoring record. He played for Derby in the first six Cup-ties in 1945–46 and was unfortunate not to make the team for Wembley. He was one of those unsettled by the arrival at the Baseball Ground of Scottish international Billy Steel and in November 1948 he proved a fine £8,000 buy for the Lilywhites. He was already well known to North End fans as he had netted a hat-trick for Derby in the game at Deepdale in 1947 when the Lilywhites came back from 4–3 down to win 7–4. Morrison made his Preston debut in a 1–1 home draw against Wolverhampton Wanderers. Playing his first games in the number-nine shirt, he scored doubles in the next two games against Bolton and Liverpool and then repeated the feat three games later against Charlton Athletic – unfortunately only one of those three matches was won. Six goals in his first six games were not enough to prevent Preston from losing their place in the top flight. Morrison was ever present in 1950–51 as the club won the Second Division Championship and he did not miss a game the following season. In the run-in, which saw North End finish seventh in Division One, Morrison scored seven goals in the last

ten games of the campaign – including one in each of the last four games. Morrison was ever present for a third consecutive season in 1952–53 as Preston finished runners-up to Arsenal in the First Division. He was a member of the North End side that lost 3–2 to West Bromwich Albion in the 1954 FA Cup Final. Morrison played for Scotland 'B' against England 'B' while he was with North End. A firm favourite with the Deepdale crowd because of his willingness to shoot on sight, he had a season playing for Millwall before spells as player-manager at both Nuneaton Borough and Belper Town.

MOSS, Frank

Goalkeeper

Born: Leyland, 5 November 1909.
Died: 7 February 1970.
Career: Leyland Motors. PRESTON NORTH END, 1927. Oldham Athletic, 1929. Arsenal, 1931.

■ With the exception of Birmingham's Harry Hibbs, Frank Moss was considered to be the most complete and confident goalkeeper of the 1930s. He was a brave, agile 'keeper with an uncanny sense of anticipation. He began his career at junior level with local teams Lostock Hall and Leyland Motors before joining Preston North End midway through the 1927–28 season. Replacing Tony Carr, he kept a clean sheet in a goalless draw at home to Clapton Orient and kept his place in the side for the remaining 13 games of that campaign. Though North End eventually finished fourth in Division Two, Moss was in goal when Notts County beat North End 6–2 and on the final day of the season he conceded four goals at Grimsby but the Lilywhites ran out 6–4 winners. The following season he lost out to Jock Ewart though he returned for an 11-game run midway through the campaign. In the close season he joined Oldham where he was used primarily as cover for England international Jack Hacking. In November 1931 he left Boundary Park for Arsenal for a fee of £3,000. He was in goal for the Gunners in that season's FA Cup Final against Newcastle United and won his first representative honours when selected for

the Football League XI. Over the next three seasons, in which Arsenal won a hat-trick of League Championships, Frank Moss missed just 15 of the club's 126 games. During this spell he won four full caps for England. In March 1935, Moss dislocated a shoulder in the match against Everton and was forced to play the rest of the game on the wing. He always thought he was good enough to be an outfield player and proved this by scoring the opening goal in a 2–0 win. Still troubled by the injury he was forced to retire at the age of 27 and left Highbury to later become manager of Heart of Midlothian. At the time of his death in February 1970, Moss, who had worked as a driller at Leyland Motors, was employed as a licensee in Chorley.

MOUNTENAY, Arthur

Inside-forward, outside-left

Born: Belgrave, 11 February 1883.
Died: 1 June 1933.
Career: Leicester Imperial. Leicester Fosse, 1903. Birmingham, 1905. PRESTON NORTH END, 1909. Grimsby Town, 1911. Portsmouth. Hinckley Athletic.

■ Arthur Mountenay, who had the nickname 'Pecker', joined Leicester Fosse when they were at their lowest ebb. He won a regular place in the side shortly after the start of the 1904–05 season and ended the campaign as the club's top scorer. It was, though, his FA Cup hat-trick against West Bromwich Albion that alerted top-flight clubs to his potential and in April 1905 he joined Birmingham. A big, burly forward – but not the battering ram one might expect – Mountenay was frequently criticised for not using his weight enough. Having scored 30 goals in 97 games for the Blues, he arrived at Deepdale in the summer of 1909 and made his debut in a 1–0 defeat at Nottingham Forest on the first day of the 1909–10 season. Though he had by now developed into a cool and precise all-round forward, in the early part of the following season he was summoned before Preston Court for being drunk in charge of a child under seven. However, the bench dismissed the case owing to a lack of corroborative evidence. Mountenay then played in the 2–1 win over Newcastle that afternoon! On

leaving Deepdale, he played for Grimsby and then in the Southern League for Portsmouth. Mountenay was also a first-class cricketer, playing in 144 matches for Leicestershire between 1911 and 1924.

MOYES, David William

Centre-half

Born: Glasgow, 25 April 1963.
Career: Drumchapel Amateurs. Glasgow Celtic, 1980. Cambridge United, 1983. Bristol City, 1985. Shrewsbury Town, 1987. Dunfermline Athletic, 1990. Hamilton Academicals, 1993. PRESTON NORTH END, 1993.

■ David Moyes began his career with Celtic, with whom he won a League Championship medal in 1981–82 and played in Europe. He left Parkhead and moved south of the border to Cambridge United. He spent two seasons at the Abbey Stadium, appearing in 79 League games, before Bristol City manager Terry Cooper paid £10,000 for his services in October 1985. Appointed the Robins' captain, he figured prominently as Bristol City contested two successive Freight Rover Trophy finals and was a Wembley winner in 1986. In October 1987 he left Ashton Gate to follow Brian Williams to Shrewsbury Town for a fee of £25,000. Moyes was ever present and the club's second top scorer in 1989–90 before leaving Gay Meadow to return to Scotland with Dunfermline Athletic. He was their top scorer in 1991–92 before having a brief spell with Hamilton Academicals prior to joining North End in September 1993. He made his Preston debut in a 2–2 draw at Mansfield Town and appeared in 29 games as North End reached the Play-offs, only to lose 4–2 to Wycombe Wanderers in the Final at Wembley. Moyes was in great form again the following season as the club once more reached the Play-offs and in 1995–96 he was instrumental when North End gained promotion as Third Division Champions. He played on for another couple of seasons but an interest in management soon came to the fore. When Gary Peters left Deepdale in 1998, Moyes was promoted from the coaching staff to become the club's player-manager. After hanging up his boots he led North End to the Second Division

Championship in 1999–2000, later turning down the opportunity to become Sir Alex Ferguson's number-two at Old Trafford. However, it was only a matter of time before he left Deepdale and in 2002, after being linked to various vacancies, he was appointed manager of Premiership Everton.

MOYLON, Craig

Defender

Born: Germany, 16 October 1972.
Career: PRESTON NORTH END, 1991.

■ German-born defender Craig Moylon's only taste of League football came during the club's relegation season of 1992–93 when he came off the bench to replace John Tinkler in a 3–1 defeat at Leyton Orient. He had been on the bench for the opening game of that season at Bournemouth but he parted company with the club in the close season.

MULLEN, James

Centre-half

Born: Jarrow, 8 November 1952.
Career: Sheffield Wednesday, 1970. Rotherham United, 1980. PRESTON NORTH END, 1981 (loan). Cardiff City, 1982. Newport County, 1986.

■ Jimmy Mullen began his career with Sheffield Wednesday and stayed with the Owls for 10 years during which they suffered relegation a couple of times. Mullen though did captain them to promotion from the Third Division in 1979–80. Having appeared in over 250 first-team games, he joined Rotherham United and skippered the Millers to the Third Division Championship in 1980–81. While at Millmoor, he spent a loan period with Preston North End. He made his only appearance for the club in the number-six shirt in a 3–0 defeat at Oxford United in November 1981. The following year Mullen joined Cardiff City and in 1982–83 he completed a unique treble by captaining his third club to promotion from the Third Division. After becoming Cardiff's manager on a temporary basis, he failed to secure the job permanently and joined Newport County as player-manager. After a spell as Ian Porterfield's assistant

at Aberdeen, he took over the reins at Blackpool but his only season at Bloomfield Road ended in relegation. Mullen moved on to manage Burnley, leading the Clarets to the Fourth Division Championship in 1991–92 and to promotion from the new Second Division two years later, but he left Turf Moor after the club lost their First Division status.

MULLIN, John Michael

Midfield

Born: Bury, 11 August 1975.
Career: Burnley, 1992. Sunderland, 1995. PRESTON NORTH END, 1998 (loan). Burnley, 1998 (loan). Burnley, 1999. Rotherham United, 2001.

■ After impressing as a goalscorer in Burnley's Central League side, John Mullin began to appear in the Clarets' League side during their Second Division promotion-winning season of 1993–94. His first goal in League football was a spectacular strike against Port Vale. After Burnley's relegation back to Division Two he was transferred to Sunderland for £40,000 in August 1995 but as Peter Reid's side swept to the First Division title, he found himself on the fringes of the Black Cats team. Enduring a frustrating time at the Stadium of Light, Mullin joined North End on loan in February 1998. He first game in North

End colours was a goalless draw against Brentford. During his seven-game League spell, Mullin's pace and strength in the air were not fully exploited by his teammates as North End tried to improve their poor scoring rate. After a loan spell with Burnley he rejoined the Clarets on a permanent basis and began to play in a much deeper role. Having lost his place in the Burnley side, he was sold to Rotherham United where he impressed with his ability at dead-ball situations.

MURDOCK, Colin James

Centre-half

Born: Ballymena, 2 July 1975.
Career: Manchester United, 1992. PRESTON NORTH END, 1997. Hibernian, 2003. Crewe Alexandra, 2005.

■ Colin Murdock was one of a trio of Manchester United players that joined Preston North End in the summer of 1997. He certainly benefited from regular first-team football and his partnership at the heart of the North End defence with Michael Jackson blossomed. Murdock, who has won 30 full caps for Northern Ireland, made his international debut in February 2000 when he came off the bench in the match against Luxembourg. During the course of the 1999–2000 season, when North End won the Second Division Championship, Murdock's dominance in the air and his timely tackles were seen to good effect. At the end of the campaign David Moyes gave him a new contract, which was just reward for his contribution to the club's success. In the higher grade of football, Murdock displayed his growing skill and confidence but, after receiving his marching orders in the game at Nottingham Forest, he took a while to win back his place. When he returned he scored his first goal for 18 months, and the club's opening goal of the 2001–02 campaign against Walsall, before following this with another in the next game. For much of the following season he had to share the central defensive duties with Marlon Broomes; this was after the club dispensed with playing three centre-halfs and reverted to two. Murdock was made captain in the absence of Chris Lucketti for the game at Ipswich, but in January 2003 he was injured in the match against Nottingham Forest and forced to sit out the rest of the season. After refusing to sign a new contract, he was placed on the transfer list. Murdock joined Hibernian where he scored a number of vital goals from set pieces in his first season. He returned to Football League action with Crewe Alexandra and his displays at the heart of the Railwaymen's defence was paramount in them keeping their place in the Championship in 2004–05.

MURPHY, Andrew Colin

Midfield

Born: Preston, 18 October 1966.
Career: PRESTON NORTH END, 1984.

Midfielder Andy Murphy was on a youth training scheme at Deepdale when he was given his chance in the Football League. He made his debut in a 3–1 home win over Orient while only 17. He started four games towards the end of that 1983–84 season and was only on the losing side on his last appearance when he was substituted in a 2–1 defeat at Exeter City. The following season, which saw North End relegated to the Fourth Division, Murphy played in a handful of games but was released at the end of a very disappointing campaign.

MURRAY, Patrick

Outside-right, inside-right

Born: Currie, 13 March 1874.
Died: 1925.
Career: Royal Albert. Hibernian. Darwen, 1896. East Stirlingshire. PRESTON NORTH END, 1898. East Stirlingshire. Wishaw Thistle. Royal Albert. Nottingham Forest, 1900. Glasgow Celtic. Portsmouth. East Stirlingshire. Royal Albert.

Having won Scottish international honours while with Hibernian, Paddy Murray tried his luck in the Football League with Darwen. He then played for East Stirlingshire before joining Preston before the start of the 1898–99 season. He made his debut in a goalless draw at Wolverhampton Wanderers and made 31 appearances that season, scoring seven goals, as North End just avoided relegation to Division Two. It was a similar story the following season, but it was his goal – the only goal of the game – that gave North End victory in the relegation six-pointer at Burnley. On leaving Deepdale he had spells with a number of clubs back in Scotland before spending a season with Nottingham Forest. The much-travelled forward then played Scottish League football for Celtic and in the Southern League with Portsmouth before winding down his career with his third spells at both East Stirlingshire and Royal Albert.

MUSTARD, John

Outside-right, inside-right

Born: Boldon, 1905.
Career: Bolden Colliery Welfare. Crawcrook Albion. Queen's Park Rangers, 1926. South Shields, 1929. Wrexham, 1930. PRESTON NORTH END, 1932. Burnley, 1932. Southend United, 1933. Crewe Alexandra, 1934. Wrexham, 1935. New Brighton, 1936.

Jack Mustard had played football for a couple of local sides before signing for Queen's Park Rangers in October 1926. He spent three seasons with Rangers before joining South Shields of the Third Division North in September 1929. Mustard was soon on the move again, this time to Wrexham. At the Racecourse Ground, Mustard won a Welsh Cup-winners' medal in 1931 after the 7–0 thrashing of Shrewsbury Town

and a runners'-up medal the following season. He was a very fast winger and regarded as a 'sprinter of some repute' in local athletics. He left Wrexham in 1932 to sample First Division football with Preston North End. Mustard made his debut in the second game of the 1932–33 season when he created three of Ted Harper's four goals in a 6–1 mauling of Burnley. He went on to score five goals in 15 games, including a spell of four in five games; one of these came in the 5–5 draw at Grimsby Town. He left Deepdale in the summer to join Burnley before spells at Third Division clubs Southend United and Crewe Alexandra. Mustard then rejoined Wrexham but struggled to keep his place and was transferred to New Brighton where he ended his career.

MUTCH, George

Inside-right

Born: Ferryhill, Aberdeenshire, 21 September 1912.
Died: 2001.
Career: Avondale. Hawthorn. Banks o'Dee. Arbroath. Manchester United, 1934. PRESTON NORTH END, 1937. Bury, 1946. Southport, 1947. Banks o'Dee.

George Mutch joined Manchester United from Arbroath in the summer of 1934. He soon adapted to English football and was an instant success at Old Trafford. Mutch was bought as a goal-scoring forward who could perhaps revive United's flagging fortunes – the previous season had seen them narrowly avoid relegation to the Third Division. Mutch was the Reds' leading scorer in his first season and again a year later when United won the Second Division title. In September 1937, high-flying North End secured his goalscoring prowess with a £5,000 bid. Following the introduction of the Scotsman, there was a big improvement in North End's form and the following month the resurgence was confirmed. Preston were 3–1 down at Goodison Park but staged an astonishing recovery that shocked Everton. New hero Mutch converted two penalties, a rare luxury for a club where successful spot-kicks were so seldom seen! In the third round of that season's FA Cup, Mutch scored a hat-trick inside 11 minutes as North End beat West Ham United 3–0.

He scored with a powerful header in a 2–0 fourth-round win over Leicester City and created the goal that beat Cup favourites Arsenal at Highbury in the next round. He also scored in the semi-final as North End beat Aston Villa 2–1 at Bramall Lane. North End had reached the Final for the second year in succession – their opponents were Huddersfield Town. The game was goalless after 90 minutes and extra-time brought high drama. With only a minute remaining, Mutch was clean through on goal when Town defender Alf Young brought him down just inside the box. The referee had no hesitation in pointing to the spot. Mutch, the delegated penalty-taker, had to receive treatment from the trainer before he could continue. His shot rebounded off the underside of the bar and over the line for the only goal of the game. Mutch's only international cap came against England in April 1938, when along with fellow North Enders Andy Beattie, Bill Shankly and skipper Tom Smith, he helped Scotland to a 1–0 win. On leaving Deepdale, Mutch joined Bury before ending his playing career at Southport. Later he managed Banks o'Dee, the Scottish junior club he played for as a youngster.

NAPIER, Christopher Robin Anthony

Centre-forward

Born: Dunblane, 26 September 1943.
Career: Blackpool, 1960. PRESTON NORTH END, 1963. Workington, 1964. Newcastle United, 1965. Brighton and Hove Albion. 1966. Blackburn Rovers, 1972.

■ After failing to make much of an impression with his first club, Blackpool, Kit Napier joined North End in the summer of 1963. However, in his only season at Deepdale he made just one League appearance, replacing David Wilson in a 3–0 defeat at Charlton Athletic during the early part of the 1963–64 season. Leaving to join Workington, he was a prolific scorer in the lower Divisions – 25 in 58 games for the Cumbrian club – until Newcastle United's Joe Harvey signed him in November 1965. Sadly, he was not quick enough for top-flight football and he joined Brighton and Hove Albion. Napier had a tremendous season for the Seagulls in 1967–68, netting 28 League and Cup goals. The following campaign he netted his first hat-trick in a 3–1 home win over Bristol Rovers. Injuries then began to hamper his progress, although he continued to score with great regularity, netting another treble against Mansfield in August 1971. At the end of that promotion-winning season Napier, who had scored 99 goals in 291 games for the South Coast club, remained in the Third Division by signing for Blackburn Rovers where he ended his career.

NASH, Carlo James

Goalkeeper

Born: Bolton, 13 September 1973.
Career: Clitheroe. Crystal Palace, 1996. Stockport County, 1998. Manchester City, 2001. Middlesbrough, 2003. PRESTON NORTH END, 2005.

■ Carlo Nash was spotted keeping goal for Clitheroe against Brigg Town in the 1996 FA Vase Final and signed by Crystal Palace. A part-time model, he helped the Eagles win promotion to the Premiership via the Play-offs in his first season at Selhurst Park. However, following the signing of Kevin Miller, Nash did not appear at all for Palace in 1997–98 and in the close season he moved to Stockport County. Arriving at Edgeley Park under the Bosman rule, he had a great first couple of seasons, including a magnificent display against North End in an FA Cup third-round tie. Due to be out of contract in the summer of 2001, the club cashed in by selling him to Manchester City for £100,000. Nash had to bide his time at Maine Road. He eventually made his debut against Arsenal but found himself picking the ball out of the net four times before he

had the chance to make a save. Following City's relegation from the top flight, he lost his place to Peter Schmeichel and joined Middlesbrough as cover for Mark Schwarzer. With his first-team opportunities at the Riverside limited, he joined Preston in March 2005. He took over the goalkeeper's jersey from Andy Lonergan and made some telling contributions to North End's Play-off effort. Nash showed his form with some terrific saves in the Play-off Final against West Ham United including a brilliant double effort. Ever-present in 2005–06, Carlo Nash had an outstanding season and after making some fine saves on the final day of the season in a 2–0 win over Leeds United, broke Teuvo Moilanen's clean sheet record.

NAUGHTON, William Balloch Stirling

Left-winger

Born: Catrine, Ayrshire 20 March 1962.
Career: PRESTON NORTH END, 1980. Walsall, 1985. Shrewsbury Town, 1989. Walsall, 1991.

■ After some impressive displays for the club's reserve side, Willie Naughton

progressed to the senior side, making his debut as a substitute for Paul McGee in a 2–0 defeat at Wrexham on New Year's Day 1980. The following season he appeared a little more frequently and bagged his first goals for the club, scoring twice in a 3–2 home win over Queen's Park Rangers. He missed very few games over the next three seasons but in each campaign North End were a mid-table Third Division side. In March 1985, with the club heading towards the Fourth Division, Naughton left Deepdale to join Walsall. He was an important member of the Saddlers' side and helped them win promotion to the Second Division in 1987–88. In August 1989 he joined Shrewsbury Town but after a season and a half at Gay Meadow he rejoined Walsall, taking his tally of goals to 17 in 167 League games.

N'DUMBU-NSUNGU, Guylain

Forward

Born: Kinshasa, DR Congo, 26 December 1982.
Career: Amiens (France). Sheffield Wednesday, 2003. PRESTON NORTH END, 2004 (loan). Colchester United, 2005.

■ A pacy, exciting striker, Guy N'Dumbu-Nsungu originally arrived at Sheffield Wednesday from French club Amiens on loan but was quickly signed up on a permanent contract. Registering goals in all competitions, he went on to finish the 2003–04 season as the Owls' leading scorer with 10 goals. He struggled to match his form of the previous campaign in 2004–05 and joined Preston on loan. He made six appearances and provided extra attacking options for the Deepdale club. However, he failed to find the net during his time with North End and returned to Hillsborough before signing for Colchester United.

NEAL, Christopher Michael

Goalkeeper

Born: St Albans, 23 October 1985.
Career: PRESTON NORTH END, 2004.

■ An injury crisis at Deepdale saw goalkeeper Chris Neal promoted to the

bench for North End in the local derby against Burnley in December 2004. Three months later he was called up again and this time he made his Football League debut as a late substitute for the injured Gavin Ward in the televised clash with Ipswich Town. In a match that North End drew 1–1, Neal produced an excellent point-blank save to thwart Town's Shefki Kuqi. He is a 'keeper for whom great things are expected in the future.

NEAL, Lewis Ryan

Midfield

Born: Leicester, 14 July 1981
Career: Stoke City 1998; PRESTON NORTH END 2005;

■ Left-sided midfielder Lewis Neal broke into the Stoke City first-team squad in 2000–01 and the following season began to appear on a regular basis until he was hampered by an ankle injury. Though his performances were appreciated by the fans, Neal didn't seem to figure in new manager Tony Pulis's plans. However, as the fight for First Division survival in 2002–03 intensified, the manager was made to think again. On his return to the side, Neal provided the immaculate cross for Ade Akinbiyi's

winner against Reading to clinch the Potters' First Division status. Blessed with two good feet, the Stoke management offered to extend his contract at the club, but even then he couldn't win a regular place in the City side. Having appeared in 82 League and Cup games, Neal joined North End in the summer of 2005 and, though almost half his first-team appearances were made from the bench, he did score goals in the victories over Luton Town and Wolverhampton Wanderers.

NEBELLING, Gavin Mark

Centre-half

Born: South Africa, 15 May 1963.
Career: Arcadia Shepherds (South Africa). Crystal Palace, 1981. Northampton Town, 1985 (loan). Fulham, 1989. Hereford United, 1991 (loan). PRESTON NORTH END, 1993.

■ Signed by Crystal Palace from South African side Arcadia Shepherds, Gavin Nebelling was an integral member of the Eagles side for seven seasons, appearing

in 151 League games. In 1988–89, his last season at Selhurst Park, he helped Palace win promotion to the First Division, but by the time the club played in the higher grade he had signed for Fulham. During his time at Craven Cottage, the club were struggling in the lower reaches of the Third Division and in the summer of 1993 he opted for a move to Deepdale. His first game in North End colours came on the opening day of the season as the Lilywhites went down 2–0 at home to Crewe Alexandra. Nevertheless, he settled in well in the heart of the Preston defence and scored useful goals in the victories over Shrewsbury, Bury and Darlington. Injuries cost him his place in the side but he later returned to help the club reach that season's Play-offs.

NELSON, John Henry

Centre-half

Born: Chorley, 15 March 1906.
Died: 1984.
Career: Chorley All Saints. Chorley. PRESTON NORTH END, 1928. Wolverhampton Wanderers, 1932. Luton Town, 1935.

■ Chorley-born defender Jack Nelson started out with his home-town club before North End manager Alex Gibson signed him in 1928. Nelson played his first game for North End as a replacement for the injured David Morris in a 3–2 win at Middlesbrough during the early part of the 1928–29 season. Over the next couple of seasons, he began to appear more frequently but it was 1931–32 before he established himself as a first-team regular. That season he scored a couple of goals, the first curiously enough against the club he was to make his name with, Wolverhampton Wanderers. Nelson left Preston for Molineux early the following season as cover for Hollingworth. The Midlands club had just returned to the top flight. However, he soon won a place and after the club avoided immediate relegation he was a regular in the Wolves' side for three seasons. He was then allowed to join Luton Town and he helped the Hatters win the 1936–37 Third Division South Championship. Nelson later returned to Molineux as Wolves' trainer.

NEWLANDS, Malcolm

Goalkeeper

Born: Wishaw, 28 March 1925.
Died: 1996.
Career: St Mirren. PRESTON NORTH END, 1948. Workington, 1952.

■ Signed from Scottish League St Mirren, goalkeeper Malcolm Newlands made his North End debut in a 5–2 win at Newcastle United in the third game of the 1948–49 season. He went on to share the goalkeeping duties that campaign with Jimmy Gooch. Though he had his good days, he also had bad days – conceding six goals at home to Manchester United and five at Bolton. Not surprisingly with such a leaky defence, North End were relegated at the end of the campaign. He continued to share the number-one jersey with Gooch over the next three seasons, one of which – 1950–51 – saw the club win the Second Division Championship. Newlands started the 1952–53 season as the club's first-choice 'keeper, but following the signing of George Thompson he left Deepdale to play for Workington. He spent seven seasons with the Cumbrian club, making 251 League appearances before injury curtailed his career.

NEWTON, Sydney

Goalkeeper

Born: Tyldesley, 1888.
Career: Bolton Wanderers, 1910. PRESTON NORTH END, 1914.

■ Sydney Newton's first Football League club was Bolton Wanderers. Although he never let the Trotters down in the 15 games that he played during four seasons at Burnden Park, he could never oust regular 'keeper John Edmondson from between the posts. He joined Preston before the start of the 1914–15 season but after making his debut on the opening day of the campaign in 2–2 draw at Grimsby, he lost out to Billy Hayes. He returned to the side midway through the campaign for a run of seven games and on his last appearance made a couple of outstanding saves in a goalless draw at Bury. He was one of three 'keepers used by the club as they won promotion to Division One.

NIDD, George Frederick

Full-back

Born: Boston, 1869.
Died: 1956.
Career: PRESTON NORTH END, 1893. Everton, 1893. Southport Central. Stalybridge Rovers. Halliwell Rovers. Lincoln City, 1897. Grimsby Town, 1898. Watford. Brentford. Fulham. Grays United. Clapton Orient, 1905. Watford.

■ A talented athlete and a tenor of repute, George Nidd began his footballing career with Preston North End. He made three appearances in the 1893–94 season, the first in a 3–1 home win over West Bromwich Albion. One of six players to wear the number-three shirt in that 30–match season, Nidd left Deepdale and played for several clubs before settling at Grimsby Town for the start of the 1898–99 season. He was a regular in the Mariners side for a couple of seasons but had played in just a handful of games in their Second Division Championship-winning season when he left to play for Watford. He later played for a number of other Southern League clubs before rejoining Watford for a second spell. Having had a brief experience as a goalkeeper with Grimsby, he was persuaded at the age of 47 to play in goal for the Hornets, but they lost 8–2.

NISBET, Gavin

Right-half

Born: Hamilton, 11 October 1904.
Career: Coalburn Juniors. Blantyre Victoria. PRESTON NORTH END, 1927. Burnley, 1935. Accrington Stanley, 1936. Stalybridge Celtic.

■ Gavin Nisbet's first two games for North End were quite remarkable – and not only for the fact that he was played out of position at inside-right. In the first game against Wolverhampton Wanderers, Tommy Roberts netted a hat-trick in a 5–4 win and in the next game Nisbet scored one of the goals in a 7–2 defeat of South Shields. Over the next couple of seasons he began to appear on a more regular basis, until in 1930–31 he was an established member of the North End side. He helped the Lilywhites win promotion to the First Division in 1933–34 but played in just two games in the top flight before switching to Burnley. His stay at Turf Moor was brief and he ended his League career with Accrington Stanley in the Third Division North before playing non-League football for Stalybridge Celtic.

NOGAN, Kurt

Forward

Born: Cardiff, 9 September 1970.
Career: Luton Town, 1989. Peterborough United, 1992. Brighton and Hove Albion, 1992. Burnley, 1995. PRESTON NORTH END, 1997. Cardiff City, 2000.

■ At the end of his first season with Luton Town, Kurt Nogan's potential was recognised by his country when he was awarded a Wales Under-21 cap against Poland in May 1990. He did his cause no harm with a goal in a 2–0 victory. However, he struggled to hold down a regular place at Kenilworth Road and was released at the end of the club's relegation season of 1991–92. Following a trial with Peterborough, Nogan joined Brighton and soon the goals began to flow, as he ended the 1992–93 season as top scorer with 20 goals in 30 games. He was also the Seagulls' leading scorer again in 1993–94, his total of 26 League and

Cup goals including a hat-trick against Cambridge United. After a bright start the following season, the goals dried up. After a shoulder injury ruled him out, he left the Goldstone Ground for a fee of £300,000 to play for Burnley. Though not as prolific as his time with Brighton, the goals started to flow again and in March 1997, following a much-publicised contractual dispute and problems off the field, he joined Preston for £150,000. Nogan quickly impressed with his skill on the ball, pace and awareness and was unlucky not to find the net on his debut against Blackpool. He eventually broke his duck in 1997–98 with a brace against Watford and a typical goal against his former club, Burnley. In his second full season, he finally refound his goalscoring touch, netting on the opening day and going on to grab the winner at Turf Moor. Other highlights included two goals against Arsenal in the televised FA Cup third-round tie and his 100th League goal against his first club, Luton. In what was a good season for club and player, he also played for the Wales 'B' side. Nogan was in and out of the North End side in 1999–2000 and, although he had made sufficient appearances to earn a Second Division Championship medal, he was transferred to his home-town club, Cardiff City. Unfortunately, he had injury problems from the outset and was forced to retire after failing to start a match in the club's promotion-winning season of 2000–01.

NORBURY, Michael Shaun

Forward

Born: Hemsworth, 22 January 1969.
Career: Ossett Town. Scarborough, 1989. Bridlington Town. Cambridge United, 1992. PRESTON NORTH END, 1992. Doncaster Rovers, 1994.

■ Mickey Norbury's goalscoring feats for non-League Ossett Town attracted the attention of Scarborough, but he failed to make the grade and returned to the non-League scene with Bridlington Town. Again he found the net with great regularity and was given another chance at League level by Cambridge United. Most of his games for United were from the bench and in December 1992 he moved to Preston. Norbury scored on his

debut in a 2–2 draw at home to Exeter City and netted four in his first six senior outings. He netted eight goals in 21 League games, but will be remembered for his part in an incident that sealed the club's relegation to the Third Division. In the game against Mansfield, North End were 1–0 up courtesy of a Tony Ellis goal when they were awarded a penalty. Norbury missed it and the Stags stormed back into the game and won 5–1. Half of his appearances the following season were off the bench and he later left to end his first-class career with Doncaster Rovers.

NORRIS, Frank

Left-back

Born: Preston, 1870.
Career: PRESTON NORTH END, 1891.

■ In 1891–92, a season in which North End finished as runners-up in the First Division to Sunderland, left-back Frank Norris appeared in three games – two of them against Wolverhampton Wanderers. The number-three shirt was worn by four different players over the course of the season and Norris was not retained.

NOWLAND Adam Christopher

Midfield

Born: Preston, 6 July 1981.
Career: Blackpool 1999; Wimbledon 2001; West Ham United 2004; Gillingham (loan) 2004; Nottingham Forest 2004; PRESTON NORTH END 2005;

■ Adam Nowland was just 16 years old when he came off the bench for Blackpool for the last six minutes of the 1997–98 campaign against Chesterfield. Highly rated at Bloomfield Road, he top scored for the juniors and appeared on a regular basis, although mostly as a substitute, for the Seasiders until he was replaced by Brett Ormerod. He continued to net regularly for the reserves until the summer of 2001 when he left Blackpool to join Wimbledon. He spent most of his first season with the Dons in the reserves, scoring a 40-yard cracker in the game against Arsenal. Much of his time at Wimbledon was spent either on the bench or watching from the stands,

as they employed a formation not suited to Nowland's talents. Switched into a midfield role, he soon began attracting the scouts and it didn't take too long for the Wimbedon administrators to ship him off to West Ham United for a bargain fee. Used mainly as a substitute during his time at Upton Park, he was loaned to Gillingham prior to being sold to Nottingham Forest. His time at the City Ground saw him hampered by hamstring problems and he later moved on to Preston North End. Though he was unable to win a regular place in the side, he did score three goals in the wins over Crewe Alexandra, Coventry and Norwich City.

NUGENT, David James

Forward

Born: Liverpool, 2 May 1985.
Career: Bury, 2001. PRESTON NORTH END, 2005.

■ The 2001–02 season was very much a fairytale campaign for Bury striker David Nugent, who started the season as a first-year scholar and ended it by forcing his way into the Shakers League side at the age of 16. His debut came as a late substitute in the game against Port Vale and he made three more appearances from the bench before making his first start at Peterborough on the final day of the season. He netted a hat-trick for the reserves in their final game to help them clinch promotion in the Avon Insurance League. Bury manager Andy Preece gave him more of a run out the following season and he scored his first goal with a superb header in the match against Darlington. Nugent continued to flourish at Gigg Lane, his work rate and pace continually unsettling defenders, and in the first half of the 2004–05 season he just could not stop scoring. After adding physical strength to his game, he left Bury to join North End in

January 2005. He was quickly promoted to start alongside Richard Cresswell and soon the goals began to flow. He netted his first against Queen's Park Rangers and his total of eight League goals in 18 games included a brace in the 3–0 defeat of Cardiff City. Last season he was troubled by a virus but still looked the club's most dangerous striker when not fully fit! He added to his increasing value by scoring a number of wonder goals in his overall total of 11, with his stunning volley at Burnley and vital goal in the Play-off semi-final at Leeds, the pick of the bunch. Nugent also netted twice in both games against Ipswich and North End fans will hope that the club's failure to reach the Premiership will not hasten the departure of this outstanding prospect.

NUTTALL, William

Full-back

Born: Preston, 7 December 1920.
Career: PRESTON NORTH END, 1946. Barrow, 1948.

■ Full-back Willie Nuttall played in a couple of games during the first season of peacetime football after World War Two. In both the games he played, North End failed to score and lost. Nuttall's second and final appearance for the club was in a 5–0 defeat at Stoke. He left Deepdale to continue his career with Barrow, playing in 65 League games for the Third Division North club.

O'DONNELL, Francis

Centre-forward

Born: Buckhaven, 31 August 1911.
Died: 4 September 1952.
Career: Glasgow Celtic. PRESTON NORTH END, 1935. Blackpool, 1937. Aston Villa, 1938. Nottingham Forest, 1946.

■ The signing of the O'Donnell brothers, Frank and Hugh, from Celtic in the summer of 1935 was greeted with delight by the North End fans. Frank O'Donnell was probably the better known of the two, a forceful bustling player with a record of 50 goals in 75 games for the Parkhead club. After a successful first season, he had an outstanding campaign in 1936–37,

achieving the rare distinction of scoring in every round of the FA Cup without gaining the winners' medal he had earned. This included a hat-trick in a 5–3 defeat of lowly Exeter City and two goals in the semi-final defeat of West Bromwich Albion. The Lilywhites dominated the first half of the final against Sunderland and the big Scot coolly drove past the helpless Mapson shortly before half-time. Unfortunately, Sunderland came out a different side after the break and Raich Carter's prompting led to the Wearsiders winning 3–1. O'Donnell scored on his international debut as Scotland beat England 3–1 at Hampden Park on 17 April 1937. By November 1937, he had scored 48 goals in 101 games for North End but then left the club to join Blackpool in exchange for Dicky Watmough and Jimmy McIntosh. His transfer from Deepdale was a bold, highly controversial decision which split supporters into two camps, even though events proved the far-sighted wisdom behind it. One section regarded it as madness to part with a star credited with 11 Cup goals in one season. Others

realised that Frank's deliberate, orthodox methods would not fit in with the more fluid style envisaged when it was decided to convert Jimmy Dougal into a roving centre-forward. During his short spell with Blackpool he scored 17 goals in 29 games before playing for Aston Villa and Nottingham Forest. Sadly, big Frank, who was one of 15 children, died prematurely at the age of 40.

O'DONNELL, Hugh

Outside-left

Born: Buckhaven, 15 February 1913.
Died: 9 May 1965.
Career: Glasgow Celtic. PRESTON NORTH END, 1935. Blackpool, 1939. Rochdale, 1947. Halifax Town, 1948.

■ The younger brother of Frank, Hugh O'Donnell made his English League debut alongside his brother in a 1–0 defeat at Huddersfield Town on the opening day of the 1935–36 season. He netted 15 goals in his 39 League appearances that season including braces against Manchester City and Wolverhampton Wanderers. The 12th set of brothers to play for North End, they both played at Wembley a year later as North End lost to Sunderland in the FA Cup

Final. In 1938, O'Donnell had the satisfaction of repeating Jimmy Delaney's achievement of adding a FA Cup-winners' medal to his memento of success in the Final of the Scottish Cup. Having lost his place to Jimmy McIntosh, who had been signed in exchange for his brother in November 1937, O'Donnell followed his brother to Bloomfield Road. In the early war years he returned to Deepdale as a 'guest' player and helped the club achieve a minor League and Cup double. After the hostilities he had spells with Rochdale and Halifax Town.

O'FARRELL, Francis

Wing-half

Born: Cork, 9 October 1927.
Career: Cork United. West Ham United, 1948. PRESTON NORTH END, 1956. Weymouth.

■ Frank O'Farrell will probably be remembered more for his achievements as a manager than for his prowess as a player. Having played his early football for Cork United, he joined West Ham United in January 1948. O'Farrell was drilled in the Upton Park football philosophy in the Football Combination where he made 50 appearances before making his League debut in December 1950. A competent, polished wing-half, he kept his place in the Hammers side for six years, making 197 League appearances. It was during his time in West Ham's reserves that he came under the international spotlight for the first time, winning the first of nine caps for the Republic of Ireland in May 1952 against Austria. In November 1956, O'Farrell became Preston manager Cliff Britton's first signing; he was ready-made to replace the departed Willie Forbes at left-half. He made his League debut for North End against Manchester City and scored in a 3–1 win. He went on to play in 17 League games for the Lilywhites before he was on the losing side. In 1957–58, O'Farrell was an important member of the Preston side that finished runners-up in the First Division with 59 points, five behind League Champions Wolverhampton Wanderers. In four seasons at Deepdale, O'Farrell made 118 League appearances before joining Southern

League Weymouth as player-manager. His League management career began at Torquay United in 1965 before he took over at Leicester City three years later. He took the Filbert Street club to the FA Cup Final in 1969 and the Second Division Championship in 1970–71. He later managed Manchester United, followed by a spell as coach to the Iranian national side and Cardiff City before ending his managerial career back at Torquay.

O'HANLON, Kelham Gerard

Goalkeeper

Born: Saltburn, 16 May 1962.
Career: Middlesbrough, 1980. Rotherham United, 1985. Carlisle United, 1991. PRESTON NORTH END, 1993. Dundee United. PRESTON NORTH END, 1996.

■ Goalkeeper Kelham O'Hanlon had trials with Aston Villa and Derby County before joining Middlesbrough where he succeeded Northern Ireland international Jim Platt. When he later lost his place in the Boro side to former Manchester United 'keeper Stephen Pears, he was allowed to leave Ayresome Park and join Rotherham United. His displays for the Millers led to him winning full international honours for the Republic of Ireland against Israel in November 1987. Unable to displace Gerry Peyton as Paddy Bonner's understudy, he continued to serve Rotherham well. In 1988–89 he helped the Yorkshire club to the Fourth Division Championship. In the summer of 1991, after making 304 appearances for the

Millers, he was transferred to Carlisle United. At the end of his first season at Brunton Park, the PFA voted him the Fourth Division's best 'keeper. In the summer of 1993 he moved on to Preston North End and made his debut against Crewe on the opening day of the 1993–94 season. After some good displays, he lost out to Steve Woods and decided to move north of the border to continue his career with Dundee United. He later rejoined North End as the club's assistant manager, although he was forced back into action following an injury to the club's Finnish international Teuvo Moilanen.

OLIVEIRA, Filipe

Midfield

Born: Braga, Portugal, 27 May 1984.
Career: FC Porto (Portugal). Chelsea, 2001. PRESTON NORTH END, 2004 (loan).

■ Portuguese Under-21 international Filipe Oliveira joined Chelsea from FC Porto in September 2001 when the previous regime scoured Europe to develop the best of the continent's young talent. Over the next few seasons he made a handful of League appearances as a substitute but the creative midfielder, who is also comfortable in the space behind the front players, was in danger of becoming lost in Chelsea's star-studded midfield. In December 2004 he went on loan to promotion-chasing North End to gain some urgently needed first-team experience. He acquitted himself very well at Deepdale, showing great pace on the ball and excellent vision. On his return to Stamford Bridge, his only involvement with the Blues was confined to the last five minutes of the 2004–05 Premiership season when he again came off the bench.

O'NEIL, Brian

Midfield

Born: Paisley, 6 September 1972.
Career: Glasgow Celtic. Porirua Viard United (New Zealand, loan). Glasgow Celtic. Nottingham Forest, 1997 (loan). Aberdeen, 1997. Wolfsburg (Germany), 1998. Derby County, 2000. PRESTON NORTH END, 2003.

■ Brian O'Neil represented Scotland in the World Youth Cup in 1989 and scored the goal against Portugal that put Young Scotland into the Final. On the big day itself, he had a penalty saved by the Saudi 'keeper in normal time and missed another in the shoot-out. After joining Celtic, despite possessing talent in abundance, he showed a tendency to play off the pace of the game so in his early days at Parkhead he was largely a fringe player. After a loan spell in New Zealand,

he rejoined the Bhoys but, though his displays earned him selection for the Scotland Under-21 side, domestic honours eluded him. In March 1997, O'Neil was loaned to Nottingham Forest before leaving Celtic to join Aberdeen. He spent just one season at Pittodrie before trying his luck in German football with Wolfsburg. He enjoyed two successful seasons on the continent before he joined Derby County in the summer of 2000. Just two minutes into his County debut against Manchester United, O'Neil suffered a serious knee injury that led to a long lay-off. After a trial period with Preston North End, he secured a long-term contract, demonstrating a simple but effective passing game that improved the play of many of those around him, most notably Nigerian Dickson Etuhu. The following season he demonstrated his versatility by playing at centre-half during an injury crisis at the club before his experience and composure on the ball were missed following an injury that forced him to miss the last couple of months of the campaign. O'Neil had an excellent 2004–05 season and his effort during games gave little indication that the years were taking their toll. Indeed, he earned a surprise recall to the Scotland squad as fitting reward for his consistency. The experienced midfielder continued to impress for North End whenever selected and was in the starting line-ups for both legs of the Play-off semi-final against Leeds United.

O'NEILL, John

Defender

Born: Dublin, 9 September 1935.
Career: Drumcondra. PRESTON NORTH END, 1958. Barrow, 1963. Waterford 1965.

■ John O'Neill joined Preston North End from League of Ireland Champions Drumcondra in April 1958. He had played regularly at centre-half for Drumcondra and represented the League of Ireland in that position. However, upon his arrival at Deepdale he was immediately switched to full-back. Though he made a good debut in a 2–1 win over Arsenal at Highbury, the following week he was back in the

reserves and did not return to first-team action until 1960–61. Despite North End's relegation to Division Two, O'Neill's performances won him full international honours for the Republic of Ireland. A spate of niggling injuries and a loss of form saw O'Neill in and out of the North End side for the next couple of seasons before he left Preston for Barrow. After one season at Holker Street in which he was a virtual ever present, he returned to Drumcondra and in his first season back helped them win the League Championship. In 1965 he joined Waterford and immediately set about putting together one of the most impressive arrays of medals of any player in the Irish game: six League Championship medals, a League Cup-winners' medal and two FAI Cup runners'-up medals.

O'NEILL, Joseph

Forward

Born: Blackburn, 28 October 1982.
Career: PRESTON NORTH END, 2002. Bury, 2003 (loan). Mansfield Town, 2004 (loan). Chester City, 2005 (loan).

■ Joseph O'Neill joined Bury on a season long loan from Preston, but he

was disappointed to be sidelined for much of the second half of the 2003–04 season. Earlier in that season he had netted three goals for the Shakers, his first a diving header against York City. He gained more experience with a loan spell at Mansfield. On his return to Deepdale he featured as a substitute in the match against Reading before going on to make his full debut in the FA Cup against West Bromwich Albion. Towards the end of the 2004–05 season, he had another loan spell, this time with Chester City.

O'RAWE, Frank

Centre-half, inside-right

Born: Uphall, 20 December 1900.
Career: Bathgate. PRESTON NORTH END, 1923. Southend United, 1924. Brighton and Hove Albion, 1926. Vernon Athletic. Whittaker Ellis Works (London).

■ Frank O'Rawe played in four games for North End during the 1923–24 season; two at inside-right and two at centre-half. He was more successful in the latter position as Preston played out a goalless draw at Notts County and then beat the Meadow Lane club 2–1 at home in the return match. Due to the

consistency of Joe McCall, there were few opportunities for O'Rawe and he left in the close season to join Southend United. After two seasons of regular football in the Third Division South for the Shrimpers, he signed for Brighton and Hove Albion but was only there briefly before drifting into non-League football.

O'RIORDAN, Donald Joseph

Centre-half, midfield

Born: Dublin, 14 May 1957.
Career: Derby County, 1975. Doncaster Rovers, 1978 (loan). Tulsa Roughnecks (US). PRESTON NORTH END, 1978. Carlisle United, 1983. Middlesbrough, 1985. Grimsby Town, 1986. Notts County, 1988. Mansfield Town, 1989 (loan). Torquay United, 1993. Scarborough, 1995. Gloucester City. Dorchester Town.

■ Don O'Riordan began his career with Derby County and, though he showed plenty of promise, he had a spell on loan with Doncaster Rovers before being allowed to cross the Atlantic to play for Tulsa Roughnecks. This was one of the American deals that came under review when the police investigated Derby County's affairs in 1979. O'Riordan returned from America in October 1978 to have a long and successful career. His first game for North End was in a 3–2 home defeat at the hands of Crystal Palace and he played in every game except the final game of the season as the club finished seventh in Division Two. He was in and out of the Preston side over the next couple of seasons before being ever present in 1981–82, a season in which he had his best return in terms of goals; he netted four times including three in five games. He was an important member of the Preston side in 1982–83 before being transferred to Carlisle United. After two seasons with the Cumbrian outfit, he switched to Middlesbrough but they were relegated to the Third Division in his only season at Ayresome Park. It did not get much better at his next club, Grimsby, as they suffered relegation in 1986–87 and 1987–88 to enter the League's basement. With Notts County he combined playing with coaching but was injured

after helping them win promotion to the First Division in 1990–91.

ORMEROD Brett Ryan

Forward

Born: Blackburn, 18 October 1976.
Career: Accrington Stanley; Blackpool 1997; Southampton 2001; Leeds United, (loan) 2004; Wigan Athletic (loan) 2005; PRESTON NORTH END 2006;

■ Having scored prolifically for then non-League Accrington Stanley, Brett Ormerod was snapped up by Blackpool for a fee of £50,000. Despite scoring regularly for the club's reserve side, he was used sparingly at first-team level until 1999–2000 when he won a regular place. The season was going really well for him until he suffered a broken leg at Wycombe and was forced to sit out the rest of the campaign. Restored to full fitness, he forged an excellent striking partnership with John Murphy and finished the 2000–01 season by scoring five goals in the Play-offs as the Seasiders went on to win promotion. The following season he netted 20 goals for the Bloomfield Road club including two hat-tricks before being sold to Southampton for £1.75 million. A medial ligament injury, sustained in a reserve game for the Saints, sidelined him for a month before he scored on his full debut at Ipswich Town. His work rate and commitment at St Mary's could not be faulted, and after netting a League Cup hat-trick against Tranmere Rovers, he netted the opener in the 2–1 FA Cup semi-final win over Watford. In the Cup Final, he was Southampton's best player, looking the most likely to make the breakthrough. In fact, it was his strike with eight minutes remaining that brought an outstanding save from Arsenal's David Seaman. An unashamed grafter rather than a classic striker, Ormerod later found his first-team opportunities at St Mary's limited and had spells on loan with both Leeds and Wigan before returning to the south coast club as they lost their top-flight status. Ormerod joined North End midway through the 2005–06 season and scored on his debut as the Lilywhites beat promotion rivals Crystal Palace 2–0. He also netted in wins over Crewe and Wolves before finding the net on the final day of the season in a 2–0 win over Leeds United, North End's opponents in the Play-off semi-finals. Substituted in the first-leg of the Play-offs, he then suffered

a fractured fibia of the right leg in the second leg at Deepdale.

ORR, William

Left-half

Born: Shotts, 20 June 1873.
Died: 26 February 1946.
Career: Airdrieonians. PRESTON NORTH END, 1894. Glasgow Celtic.

■ Signed from Scottish League side Airdrie, left-half Willie Orr made his Preston debut in October 1894 in a 1–0 win at Sheffield United. However, it was only towards the end of the 1894–95 season that he established himself and scored in successive home victories over West Bromwich Albion and Nottingham Forest. The following season he missed just a couple of games as North End finished in mid-table in the First Division and in 1896–97 he was instrumental in the club finishing fourth in the top flight. Orr moved back to Scotland to play for Celtic and captained the Bhoys to success in a 3–2 defeat of Rangers in the first Scottish Cup Final to be played at Hampden Park. He led Celtic to the Championship in 1905 and 1906, the first two of six in a row. He later managed Airdrieonians to a Scottish Cup triumph before taking over the reins of both Leicester City and Falkirk.

ORRELL, Richard

Full-back

Born: Preston 1878.
Died: 1919.
Career: PRESTON NORTH END, 1899.

■ Richard Orrell was able to play in either of the full-back positions. He replaced Bob Holmes in the North End side midway through the 1899–1900 season, playing in 18 consecutive League and Cup games. He had made his debut earlier in the campaign in a 4–3 home win over Notts County. Following Preston's relegation the following season, Orrell played in 32 games in 1901–02 as the club almost returned to the top flight at the first time of asking, finishing third in Division Two. Orrell continued to be a regular in the North End side and in 1903–04 was a member of the side that won the Second Division Championship. In and out of the side for the next couple

of seasons, he played the last of his 140 League games on the final day of the 1905–06 season as North End finished runners-up to Liverpool in the First Division.

OSBORN, Frederick

Centre-forward, inside-forward

Born: Leicester, 10 November 1889.
Died: 11 October 1954.
Career: Avondale. Hinckley United. Leicester Fosse, 1910. PRESTON NORTH END, 1913. Nuneaton Town.

■ Freddie Osborn joined local side Leicester Fosse after developing a fine reputation for marksmanship, scoring 45 goals for Hinckley in 1909–10. Osborn, who also played county cricket for Leicestershire, went on to score 30 goals in 71 games for Fosse and soon after was snapped up by First Division Preston. Though North End were relegated in his first season at Deepdale, Osborn had a tremendous season, netting 26 League and Cup goals. This total included three hat-tricks, against Middlesbrough and Sheffield Wednesday in the League and Bristol Rovers in the FA Cup. The following season he was again the club's leading scorer with 17 goals as the club returned to the top flight as runners-up to Derby County. Osborn attempted to play on in the First Division after the war despite receiving a bullet through the thigh while on active service as a driver with the RAF in November 1918. Ironically, it was the form of Leicester Fosse's wartime discovery Tommy Roberts which was largely responsible for Osborn losing his place in the North End side. Roberts was transferred to Preston in the 1919 close season and was destined to become an England international. Osborn later played non-League football for Nuneaton Town.

OWENS, Edward

Right-back, centre-forward

Born: Trimdon Grange, 1913.
Career: Stockport County, 1929. PRESTON NORTH END, 1930. Crystal Palace, 1934. Bath City.

■ Edward Owens was unable to make the grade with Stockport County and moved to Preston in the summer of 1930.

He spent almost four seasons with the Deepdale club but made just 19 appearances in that time, scoring seven goals. The majority of his goals came in 1930–31, his first season with the club, and included three in a five-game spell. Owens lost out to Ted Harper and his total of first-team appearances dwindled until in 1934 he left for Crystal Palace. After switching to full-back, Owens spent five successful seasons at Selhurst Park, helping the London club finish runners-up in the Third Division South in 1938–39. He continued his career playing non-League football for Bath City.

PALETHORPE, John Thomas

Centre-forward, inside-left

Born: Leicester, 23 November 1909.
Died: 1984.
Career: Maidenhead United. Crystal Palace, 1929. Reading, 1930. Stoke City, 1932. PRESTON NORTH END, 1933. Sheffield Wednesday, 1934. Aston Villa, 1935. Crystal Palace, 1936. Chelmsford City. Shorts Sports. Colchester United.

■ Jack Palethorpe started his career with Maidenhead in the Spartan League and was on Crystal Palace's books for one season as an amateur. He was introduced to League football by Reading and scored 23 goals in 1931–32, when the club were runners-up in the Third Division South, and 29 the following season before signing for Stoke. He helped the Potters win promotion before moving to Preston North End in January 1934. After making his debut in a 2–1 home defeat by Grimsby, Palethorpe scored nine goals in his next six games including a hat-trick in a 4–0 FA Cup win over Northampton Town. His goals – 11 in 18 League games – helped North End win promotion to the First Division as runners-up in Division Two to Grimsby Town. In 1934–35, Palethorpe lost out to Bud Maxwell but returned to score four goals in his six League appearances before joining Sheffield Wednesday. He arrived at Hillsborough in December 1934 and netted a hat-trick in the Owls' 4–0 win at Birmingham on Boxing Day. That season he played in all five games in the club's run to the FA Cup Final. In the Final, his early goal settled Wednesday's

nerves and they went on to beat West Bromwich Albion 4–2. Palethorpe had scored five goals in the opening eight games of 1935–36 when he left to join Aston Villa. Unable to prevent their relegation, he had a second spell with Crystal Palace before playing non-League football.

PARKER, Harold

Full-back

Born: Preston, 1878.
Career: PRESTON NORTH END, 1899.

■ Though he was able to play in either full-back berth, Harold Parker made just three appearances in his two seasons at Deepdale due to the fine form of Dunn, Holmes and Orrell. The first of these came in a 2–0 defeat against Manchester City in April 1900 as North End just avoided the drop to Division Two. In 1900–01, when the club did lose their top-flight status, Parker's final appearance in a North End shirt saw him wear number seven in a 1–1 draw against eventual runners-up Sunderland.

PARKINSON, Gary Anthony

Right-back

Born: Thornaby, 10 January 1968.
Career: Middlesbrough, 1986. Southend United, 1992 (loan). Bolton Wanderers, 1993. Burnley, 1994. PRESTON NORTH END, 1997. Blackpool, 2001.

■ Gary Parkinson starting out with Middlesbrough after a short apprenticeship with Everton was terminated because of homesickness. He was an ever present in 1986–87, his first season of League football. Playing alongside the likes of Gary Pallister, he helped Boro win promotion from the Third Division as runners-up to Bournemouth. He was still a regular the following season as Boro stormed straight through the Second Division to the top flight via a two-legged Play-off Final victory over Chelsea. It was at the end of that campaign that he was switched from the centre of defence to right-back. After the club were relegated, Parkinson helped them win promotion once more in 1991–92. After a loan period at Southend, he joined Bolton Wanderers but things did not work out for him at

Burden Park and he moved to Burnley. In his first season with the Clarets, he scored the winning goal in the Wembley Play-off Final against Stockport County and was a regular in the side until he moved to North End in May 1997. Parkinson provided the solution to the club's long-standing right-back problem and also scored a number of spectacular long-range goals. His performances were rewarded by selection for the PFA divisional award-winning side. During the course of the following season he played his 500th senior game at Wycombe before sustaining a serious knee injury at Chesterfield in his 56th consecutive game since his debut. He tried to make a comeback but it was too soon and the recurrence he suffered led to an operation. Though he made a full recovery and signed a new one-year contract at Deepdale he was never a regular and in March 2001 he joined Lancashire neighbours Blackpool. He appeared regularly for the Seasiders before announcing his retirement.

PARNELL, Gresham Frederick

Outside-right

Born: Sutton-in-Ashfield, 1886.
Career: Skegby. Pinxton. Derby County, 1903. Leeds City, 1905. Exeter City.

PRESTON NORTH END, 1909. Exeter City. Sutton Junction. Mansfield Town.

■ Fred Parnell joined Leeds City after being given nine games at outside-right with Derby County when the Rams were struggling to fill the position. He spent four seasons with the Yorkshire club, making 104 League appearances. Parnell joined Preston North End after a spell in the Southern League with Exeter City. He appeared in 15 games for the Deepdale club in 1909–10, scoring his only goal in a 2–1 reversal at Tottenham Hotspur. Unable to hold down a regular place, he rejoined Exeter before returning to the East Midlands to play for a number of local teams.

PARRY, George

Inside-left

Born: Ibstock, 1906.
Career: PRESTON NORTH END, 1928.

■ George Parry made a disappointing debut when he missed a number of chances in a 4–1 defeat at Nottingham Forest. He was recalled to the side for the final game of the 1928–29 season as North End drew 2–2 at home to Stoke. His only appearance the following season came when he replaced George Harrison

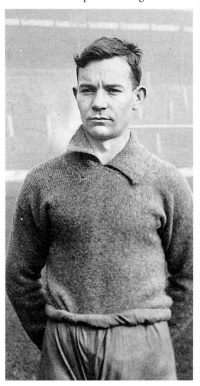

for the home game against Cardiff City but, though he created Alex Reid's goal, the Welsh club won 3–2. Parry was not offered a contract and he left to play local non-League football.

PATERSON, John William

Centre-forward, inside-forward

Born: Dundee, 14 December 1896.
Career: Fort Hill. Dundee North End. Leicester City, 1919. Sunderland, 1921. PRESTON NORTH END, 1924. Mid-Rhondda United. Mansfield Town. Airdrieonians. Cowdenbeath. Montrose.

■ John Paterson proved his fitness at Dundee after being wounded five times while serving with the Black Watch in France. He signed for Leicester City and claimed the reconstructed club's first League hat-trick against Lincoln in March 1920. A week later he scored for the Anglo-Scots in the international trial and was chosen to face England for his full international debut. After finishing top scorer in each of his three seasons at Filbert Street, he attracted an irresistible bid of £3,790 from Sunderland. He subsequently led the Wearsiders to second and third positions in the First Division with 37 goals in 74 games. He joined Preston in October 1924 and made his debut in a 1–0 home defeat at the hands of Notts County. Paterson played in 17 games that season but failed to find the net: at the end of the campaign the Lilywhites were relegated. On parting company with North End he played for a number of clubs, ending his career back in Scotland with spells at Airdrie, Cowdenbeath and Montrose.

PATRICK, Bert

Full-back

Born: Kilsyth, 26 April 1946.
Career: PRESTON NORTH END, 1963. Barrow, 1971.

■ Tough-tackling full-back Bert Patrick worked his way up through the ranks at Preston and played his first game in the senior side as a replacement for the injured George Ross in a 1–0 defeat at Crystal Palace. He made just one appearance over the next two seasons before establishing himself in 1967–68, a season in which the club just avoided

relegation from Division Two. Thereafter Patrick lost out to Ross. His only goal in 50 League appearances for North End came on the final day of the club's relegation season of 1969–70, when he netted in a 2–1 home defeat by Cardiff City. He remained at Deepdale until July 1971 when he left to join Barrow. He played in the Holker Street club's last season of League football before leaving the first-class game.

PATTERSON, Darren James

Centre-half

Born: Belfast, 15 October 1969.
Career: West Bromwich Albion, 1988. Wigan Athletic, 1989. Crystal Palace, 1992. Luton Town, 1995. PRESTON NORTH END, 1996 (loan). Dundee United, 1998. York City, 2000. Oxford United, 2001.

■ Northern Ireland international Darren Patterson began his career with West Bromwich Albion. In April 1989 he left the Hawthorns to join Wigan Athletic on a free transfer after being unable to make the grade with the Baggies. Patterson's appearances in his first couple of seasons at Springfield Park were mainly off the bench but in 1991–92 the versatile player established himself as a first-team regular. His form was so good that at the end of the season Crystal Palace paid £225,000 for his services. After two seasons in the Eagles' reserves he was given his chance in the League but was then sold to Luton Town. The strong-tackling defender was later hampered by injuries. He had a two-match loan spell at Preston North End, but both matches ended in defeat. The first was a 4–3 loss at Peterborough United. On leaving Kenilworth Road he went north of the border to try his luck with Dundee United, but much of his time at Tannadice was spent on the treatment table. He had brief spells with York and Oxford before deciding to retire. He later returned to Oxford as the club's manager.

PATTERSON, Mark Andrew

Midfield

Born: Darwen, 24 May 1965.
Career: Blackburn Rovers, 1983. PRESTON NORTH END, 1988. Bury, 1990. Bolton Wanderers, 1990. Sheffield United, 1995. Southend United, 1997 (loan). Bury, 1997. Blackpool, 1998 (loan). Southend United, 1999. Leigh RMI.

■ Mark Patterson made his name as a left-winger with his local club, Blackburn Rovers, netting his first hat-trick in a 6–1 defeat of Sheffield United at Ewood Park in April 1986. He made a Wembley appearance in the Full Members' Cup Final, coming off the bench in a 1–0 win over Charlton Athletic. In June 1988, after scoring 20 goals in 101 League games, he joined Preston North End for a fee of £20,000. Patterson made his debut on the opening day of the 1988–89 season when Preston went down 3–1 at home to Port Vale. He was a regular in the side that season as they reached the Play-offs only to lose in the semi-final against Port Vale. Patterson scored 15 goals including five penalties. Midway through the following season, Bury paid £80,000 for him and the diminutive midfielder helped the Shakers into the Third Division Play-offs where they went down to Tranmere Rovers. In January 1991, Patterson joined Bury's local rivals

Bolton Wanderers and, though injuries hampered his early games with the club, he played a major part in the club's promotion success in 1992–93 when he also captained the side on a number of occasions. He was a regular in the Bolton side for the next three seasons, having his first taste of top-flight football, but in the last of his 215 games for the Wanderers he missed in a League Cup quarter-final penalty shoot-out against Norwich City. He left to join Sheffield United and helped them away from the First Division relegation zone to Play-off contenders. Following a loan spell with Southend, he rejoined Bury but failed to settle under new boss Neil Warnock. A brief loan spell with Blackpool was followed with another stint at Southend prior to leaving to play non-League football with Leigh RMI.

PAULS, Charles

Outside-left

Born: Preston, 1868.
Career: PRESTON NORTH END, 1889.

■ Winger Charles Pauls played three games for North End in 1889–90, the club's second season of League football.

Though the club retained the League title, Pauls could not force his way into the Preston side with Drummond and Thomson sharing the left-winger's duties. He did get on the score sheet in the FA Cup second round, heading home Gordon's immaculate cross, but it did not prevent Bolton Wanderers from running out 3–2 winners.

PEARS, John

Outside-left

Born: Ormskirk, 23 February 1907.
Career: Skelmersdale United. Burscough Rangers. Liverpool, 1927. Rotherham United, 1928. Accrington Stanley, 1929. Oldham Athletic, 1930. PRESTON NORTH END, 1933. Sheffield United, 1934. Swansea Town, 1935. Hull City, 1937. Rochdale, 1938. Mossley.

■ Much-travelled winger John Pears failed to make the League side at Liverpool and left Anfield to join Rotherham United. After a season at Millmoor he returned over the Pennines to play for Accrington Stanley prior to playing for Oldham Athletic. With the Latics he had his best seasons, scoring 34 goals in 92 games. It was this form that prompted Preston North End to bring him to Deepdale and he played his first game for the club in a 2–0 defeat of Notts County. A week later he scored the winning goal in a 2–1 success at Swansea

and his performances in the seven games in which he played went a long way in helping the club win promotion to the First Division. In 1934–35, Pears missed two penalties in the games against Grimsby Town and Everton: while the first was not too costly as the Mariners were beaten 1–0, Everton ran out 4–1 winners in the second. Pears left Deepdale shortly afterwards to join Sheffield United and later Swansea Town. He then had a successful spell with Hull City, helping them finish the 1937–38 season in third place in the Third Division North.

PEARSON, Frank

Centre-forward, inside-left

Born: Manchester, 18 May 1884.
Career: PRESTON NORTH END, 1901. Manchester City, 1903. Chelsea, 1905. Hull City, 1906. Luton Town. Rochdale. Eccles Borough.

■ Frank Pearson played for Preston in the last five games of the 1901–02 season, scoring in the 3–1 defeat of Burnley and netting North End's goal on the final day of the season in a 2–1 loss at Lincoln City. The following season, Pearson was the club's leading scorer with 18 League and Cup goals and this led to newly promoted Manchester City securing his services. He failed to make much impact with City and left to play for Chelsea where he was appointed captain. He was the club's first real centre-forward and scored twice on his debut against Lincoln City. On leaving Stamford Bridge he played for Hull City. He went on to appear for a number of other clubs before hanging up his boots.

PEEL, Nathan James

Forward

Born: Blackburn, 17 May 1972.
Career: PRESTON NORTH END, 1990. Sheffield United, 1991. Halifax Town, 1992 (loan). Burnley, 1993. Rotherham United, 1995 (loan). Mansfield Town, 1995 (loan). Doncaster Rovers, 1996 (loan). Rotherham United, 1996. Macclesfield Town, 1997. Winsford United.

■ After starring for Lancashire schoolboys, Nathan Peel, who was a big

Burnley fan, escaped the Clarets' scouting net and joined Preston North End. In the 1990–91 season, Peel came off the bench nine times. In his only start for the club, he scored in a 3–3 draw at Reading. Unable to win a regular place, he was transferred to Sheffield United for £50,000. He made the briefest of impressions on the Premier League and then signed for Burnley following a loan spell with Halifax. While at Turf Moor he came off the bench to fire two goals in four minutes past Plymouth 'keeper Peter Shilton. However, he was unable to capitalise on his goalscoring start at Turf Moor and had loan spells with Rotherham, Mansfield and Doncaster before signing for the Millers on a permanent basis. Unable to force his way into the Rotherham side, he left for Macclesfield Town who were starting their first season in the Football League. Following the arrival of new faces, he left to play non-League football for Winsford United.

PEGG, Ernest Richard

Centre-forward

Born: Leicester, 1878.
Died: 1916.
Career: Leicester Fosse, 1896. Loughborough Town, 1897. Kettering Town. Reading. PRESTON NORTH END, 1901. Manchester United, 1902. Fulham. Barnsley, 1905.

■ Bustling centre-forward Dick Pegg failed to make much headway with his home-town team, Leicester Fosse, so he joined Loughborough Town where he netted 15 goals in 56 League games. This was followed by spells in the Southern League with Kettering and Reading before he returned to League action with North End. Pegg only played in 15 League games, but scored nine goals including a hat-trick in an 8–0 mauling of Lincoln City. In games either side of that win, he netted a further three goals but despite this good scoring rate he was allowed to join Manchester United. He continued to find the net for the Reds with 13 goals in 41 first-team outings as the club challenged for promotion to the First Division. After another spell in the Southern League with Fulham, Pegg ended his first-class career with Barnsley.

PHILLISKIRK, Anthony

Forward

Born: Sunderland, 10 February 1965.
Career: Sheffield United, 1983. Rotherham United, 1986 (loan). Oldham Athletic, 1988. PRESTON NORTH END, 1989. Bolton Wanderers, 1989. Peterborough United, 1992. Burnley, 1994. Carlisle United, 1995 (loan). Cardiff City, 1995. Macclesfield Town, 1997 (loan).

■ A former England Schoolboy international, Tony Philliskirk started out with Sheffield United. Eight goals in his first season, 1983–84, helped the Blades win promotion from the Third Division. He could not hold down a regular place in the Bramall Lane club's side and had a loan spell with Rotherham. After scoring 20 goals in 80 games for the Blades, he joined Oldham Athletic. Philliskirk had made only 10 appearances for the Latics when in February 1989 he signed for Preston North End. His stay at Deepdale was also

short, as he appeared in just 14 games. However, he did score six goals including two in the 6–0 rout of Chesterfield. In the summer of 1989 he joined Bolton Wanderers for £50,000 and formed a partnership with David Reeves that would give him the most prolific period of his career. In his first season at Burnden Park, Philliskirk topped the club's scoring charts with 25 goals and he led the way again in 1990–91, with his goals getting Bolton to Wembley in the Play-off semi-finals. Voted that season's Player of the Year, he later lost his place to John McGinlay and moved on to Peterborough United where he scored 11 goals in their First Division campaign. He returned to the North West in January 1994 to play for Burnley prior to a loan spell with Carlisle and a transfer to Cardiff City. At Ninian Park he was switched to a sweeper role and, though he later ended his playing career with Macclesfield, he also looked to his future in the game by taking refereeing examinations.

PHIZACKLEA, James Robert

Full-back

Born: Barrow, 29 September 1898.
Died: 1971.
Career: Barrow Submarine Engine Athletic. Barrow, 1921. Nelson, 1924. PRESTON NORTH END, 1924. South Shields, 1926. Thames.

■ Full-back James Phizacklea started his career with his home-town team of Barrow and played in the Holker Street club's first three seasons in the Football League, scoring 3 goals in 71 appearances before a brief spell with Nelson. He then joined Preston and, after making his debut in a 2–1 home defeat by high-flying West Bromwich Albion, played in the remaining 15 games of the season. Despite some solid performances, he was unable to prevent the Deepdale club losing their top-flight status. After playing in just seven games in 1925–26 he moved to North End's fellow Second Division side South Shields. He spent two seasons in the North East but his return to Deepdale ended in a 4–0 win for the Lilywhites.

PICKERING, Francis

Outside-right

Born: Preston, 1903.
Career: PRESTON NORTH END, 1924.

■ In 1924–25, a season in which North End were relegated from the First

Division after finishing seven points adrift of next-placed club Arsenal, Francis Pickering made just one appearance. The winger played his only game as a replacement for Willie Aitken in a 3–1 home defeat by Cardiff City.

PIERCE, Jack

Inside-forward

Born: Blackburn, 1872.
Career: PRESTON NORTH END, 1894. Bristol Rovers.

■ Jackie Pierce made his debut on the final day of the 1894–95 First Division season, scoring twice in a 5–2 win over already-relegated Liverpool. The following season he appeared in 19 games but still finished the campaign as North End's leading scorer with eight goals. The signing of Sandy Brown limited his appearances over the next few seasons but in 1899–1900, Pierce netted a hat-trick for the club in a 4–3 home win over Notts County. However, he still could not win a regular place and he left to continue his career with Bristol Rovers after scored 16 goals in 74 League games for North End.

PILKINGTON, William

Outside-right

Born: Chorley, 1904.
Career: PRESTON NORTH END, 1927. Chorley.

■ Winger William Pilkington's only appearance for Preston North End came in the fifth game of the 1927–28 season

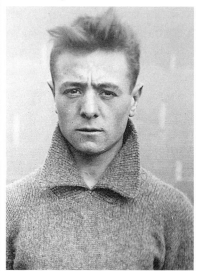

when both Alex Reid and his understudy Bert Smith were injured. He had a fine game and laid on goals for both Robson and Harrison in a 3–2 win over Wolverhampton Wanderers. On leaving Deepdale he played non-League football for Chorley.

PILLING, Andrew James

Midfield

Born: Wigan, 30 June 1969.
Career: PRESTON NORTH END, 1985. Wigan Athletic, 1987. Leigh RMI.

■ Though he was born in Wigan, Andy Pilling began his career with Preston North End where he joined as a trainee in 1985. However, in a little over two years on the Deepdale staff his only League appearance for the Lilywhites came in a 4–0 defeat at Aldershot on the final day of the 1985–86 season when North End finished one off the bottom of the Fourth Division. After another season of Central League football, Pilling joined his home-town club and made a goalscoring debut, albeit in a 2–1 defeat against Brentford. Pilling was an important member of the Wigan side for the next five seasons, scoring some vital goals and showing his versatility by appearing in eight different outfield positions. Following the club's relegation to the Third Division in 1992–93, he left Springfield Park to play non-League football for Leigh RMI.

PINCH, Charles Edward

Left-half

Born: Preston, 1891.
Career: PRESTON NORTH END, 1913. Scunthorpe and Lindsey United. Swansea Town.

■ Left-half Charlie Pinch played three games for North End when they lost

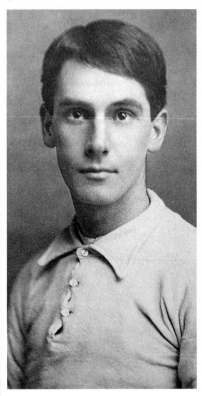

their First Division status in 1913–14. On his final appearance for the club on the last day of the season, he wore the number-five shirt as Preston drew 2–2 with Manchester City. When he was not retained, Pinch moved on to play for non-League Scunthorpe before ending his playing days with Swansea Town.

PINNELL, Archibald

Goalkeeper, outside-right

Born: Liverpool, 1871.
Career: Everton, 1892. PRESTON NORTH END, 1893. Chorley. Burnley, 1898. New Brompton. Argyle.

■ Archie Pinnell kept goal for Everton in three games during the 1892–93 season, including a 6–0 defeat of Newton Heath, before he was transferred to Preston North End. His first appearance in Preston colours came in the number-

seven shirt against Sheffield Wednesday but his next and last was back in goal for the test match against Notts County. Needing to win to avoid the drop, Preston won convincingly with Pinnell keeping a clean sheet in a 4–0 win. After a spell playing non-League football for Chorley, he appeared in a handful of games for Burnley before signing for Southern League New Brompton.

PLATT, Jack

Inside-forward

Born: Preston, 1880.
Career: Portsmouth. Northampton Town. PRESTON NORTH END, 1908.

■ Inside-forward Jack Platt impressed with his goalscoring exploits in the Southern League and was given his chance at Football League level when North End signed him prior to the start of the 1908–09 season. In his first campaign in North End's colours he impressed with four goals in 12 games but, though he remained at Deepdale for a further two seasons, he never really established himself as a regular in the side. He scored seven goals in 30 League games.

PLATT, John Roger

Goalkeeper

Born: Ashton-under-Lyne, 22 August 1954.
Career: Ashton United. Oldham Athletic, 1972. Bury, 1981. Bolton Wanderers, 1983. Tranmere Rovers, 1984 (loan). PRESTON NORTH END, 1985.

■ John Platt's performances for his local side Ashton United alerted a number of League clubs, but it was Oldham Athletic who secured his signature in the summer of 1972. Platt had to bide his time in the club's reserves before breaking into the Latics side midway through the 1975–76 season. With the exception of the 1978–79, season when he suffered a serious injury, Platt was the club's first-choice 'keeper for four seasons. He made 109 League appearances before switching to Bury. His performances for the Shakers saw them constantly around the Fourth Division promotion pack, but after a period with Bolton and a loan spell with

Tranmere Rovers, he moved to Preston North End in February 1984. He made a good debut in a 3–1 win over Cambridge United but was on the winning side just once more in his seven appearances as the club were relegated to the Fourth Division. Platt was the club's 'keeper in the disastrous 1985–86 season when they finished 91st in the Football League and was also between the posts when North End lost 7–3 at Walsall in the first round of the FA Cup.

POOLE, Frederick

Centre-forward, inside-right

Born: Preston, 1871.
Career: PRESTON NORTH END, 1893. Rotherham Town, 1895.

■ Fred Poole made a couple of appearances for North End in the 1893–94 season, but the side failed to score in either of them. He featured in a goalless draw with Wolverhampton Wanderers and a 2–0 defeat to West Bromwich Albion. After a season in North End's reserves, Poole moved to Rotherham Town but he again failed to hit the target and the club failed to win re-election to the League at the end of the season.

POTTS, Eric Thomas

Winger

Born: Liverpool, 16 March 1950.
Career: Oswestry Town. Sheffield Wednesday, 1969. Brighton and Hove Albion, 1977. PRESTON NORTH END, 1978. Burnley, 1980. Bury, 1982. Witton Albion. Clitheroe.

■ Winger Eric Potts was spotted by Sheffield Wednesday playing for Oswestry Town in the Cheshire League and they thought highly enough of his potential to offer a fee of £5,000 in December 1969. The flame-haired Potts made his League debut in October 1975 as Wednesday were coming to terms with life after relegation from the top flight. Potts became a regular in the Owls side but could not prevent them from being relegated to the Third Division for the first time in their history. Potts left to join Brighton, who were newly promoted from Division Three, and helped the Seagulls to within a point of promotion to the top flight. In August 1978 he was transferred to Preston for £37,000 and made his League debut off the bench in a 3–1 defeat by Sunderland. Potts played in the majority of North End's games that season with his best performance coming in the 6–1 demolition of Charlton Athletic when he scored two of his side's goals. After another season at Deepdale, Potts joined Burnley and, though he eventually lost out to a young Trevor Steven, he played his part in the Clarets' Third Division Championship campaign of 1981–82. He then spent two seasons playing Fourth Division football with Bury before he was released to play non-League football for Witton Albion and Clitheroe.

PRATT, Thomas Peet

Centre-forward

Born: Fleetwood, 28 August 1873.
Died: August 1935.
Career: Fleetwood Rangers. Grimsby Town, 1895. PRESTON NORTH END, 1896. Tottenham Hotspur. PRESTON NORTH END, 1900. Fleetwood. Woolwich Arsenal, 1903. Fulham. Blackpool, 1904.

■ Tom Pratt was a big, brawny and tough centre-forward who began his career in junior football with his home-town club, Fleetwood Rangers. He came to prominence with Grimsby Town where he scored 16 goals in 29 League games. This prompted Preston North End to sign him in the summer of 1896 and he lost no time in showing his prowess and no little skill. Pratt's first game in North End colours was on the opening day of the 1896–97 season when they played out a goalless draw at Bury. In the main, Pratt's first two seasons with the club saw him in and out of the side, but in 1898–99 he was the club's top scorer with 17 goals. This total included four goals in a 7–0 win over his former club Grimsby in the first round of the FA Cup. At the end of that season, Pratt signed for Spurs, which caused quite a stir. He scored the goals that took the London club to their only Southern League Championship but could not settle in the south and returned to his former club. In his second spell at Deepdale he was a regular in the North End side and, though the club were relegated in 1900–01, Pratt almost helped them return at the first attempt. He netted a hat-trick in a 4–0 defeat of Stockport County. Pratt left Preston a second time in August 1903, joining Woolwich Arsenal, whom he helped to promotion to Division One for the first time in their history. He later spent a season with Fulham before ending his career in the North West with Blackpool. After hanging up his boots, he worked as a motor mechanic.

PRITCHARD, Thomas Francis

Centre-half

Born: Wellington, 18 June 1904.
Died: 1980.
Career: Wolverhampton Wanderers, 1924. Sunbeam Motors. Stockport County, 1925. Newport County, 1926. Wolverhampton Wanderers, 1927. Charlton Athletic, 1929. Thames, 1931. Marseille (France). PRESTON NORTH END, 1933. Lancaster Town. Mansfield Town, 1935. Lancaster Town.

■ Thomas Pritchard began his career with the Great Western Railway while working as a boiler maker. He left to work successfully in a cycle factory and

play for Sunbeam Motors at the weekends. After a spell as an amateur with Stockport County, he moved to Newport and on to First Division Wolves. Pritchard was certainly the right size and build for a defender and he put these qualities to good use during his two seasons at Molineux. Following the arrival of Reg Hollingsworth, he was transferred to Charlton Athletic but in a game against his former club he had the misfortune to break a leg. He recovered from that mishap and joined Thames FC in November 1931. He had 27 outings for the now defunct London club prior to a spell in France with Marseille. Pritchard rounded off his League career with a single appearance for Preston North End as the Lilywhites, who went on to win promotion, beat Manchester United 3–2. After a spell with Lancaster Town he became trainer of Mansfield Town.

PROUT, George William

Goalkeeper

Born: Dalton-in-Furness, 3 November 1902.
Career: Dalton Casuals. PRESTON NORTH END, 1923. Grimsby Town, 1926. Carlisle United, 1928. Bath City.

■ Goalkeeper George Prout impressed with his home-town team, Dalton

Casuals, and this prompted North End manager Jimmy Lawrence to bring him to Deepdale before the start of the 1923–24 season. Prout replaced Jimmy Branston midway through the season, keeping a clean sheet in a goalless draw at Notts County, and he kept his place for the remainder of a campaign in which Preston just avoided relegation to Division Two. Prout shared the goalkeeping duties with Branston in 1924–25 but this time was powerless to prevent the club from losing their top-flight status. At the end of the following season he joined Grimsby Town after appearing in 46 League games for North End. He could not establish himself at Blundell Park and moved on to Carlisle United, where he was the regular 'keeper in their first two seasons in the Football League.

QUANTRILL, Albert Edward

Winger

Born: Punjab, India, 22 January 1897.
Died: 19 April 1968.
Career: Boston Swifts. Derby County, 1914. PRESTON NORTH END, 1921. Chorley. Bradford Park Avenue, 1924. Nottingham Forest, 1930.

■ Alf Quantrill was born in India but was playing in a Lincolnshire Cup match for Boston Swifts when Derby County spotted him. Quantrill signed a week after the outbreak of World War One and played in three games for the Rams' 1914–15 promotion-winning side. After service with the Derbyshire Yeomanry, he contracted malaria in Salonika. Quantrill resumed his career in 1919 and was called up to play for England within six months of his First Division debut. He played in the surprise 2–1 defeat by Wales and was the only forward to retain his place for the game against Scotland at Hillsborough, where he scored in England's 5–4 victory. A son-in-law of Steve Bloomer, Quantrill had tremendous speed. After four appearances for England and following Derby's relegation to Division Two, he moved to Preston North End. He made his Preston debut in a 2–2 draw at Bolton on the opening day of the 1921–22 season, but injuries and the form of Peter Quinn meant that he made just five appear-

ances. Following Quinn's transfer to Bury, Quantrill got more of a look in over the next two seasons. Having scored seven goals in 64 League games, he left for a brief spell with Chorley before returning to League action with Bradford Park Avenue. Quantrill rediscovered his best form at the Yorkshire club and, after they finished in the top four for three seasons, he helped them win the Third Division North Championship in 1927–28. Park Avenue almost won immediate promotion to the top flight, finishing third in Division Two. Quantrill went on to score 58 goals in 191 League games before ending his playing days with Nottingham Forest.

QUIGLEY, Edward

Inside-forward

Born: Bury, 13 July 1921.
Died: April 1997.
Career: Bury, 1941. Sheffield Wednesday, 1947. PRESTON NORTH END, 1949. Blackburn Rovers, 1951. Bury, 1956.

■ In December 1949, Eddie Quigley became the most expensive footballer in Britain when he joined Preston North End from Sheffield Wednesday for £26,000. He had started out with his

home-town team, Bury, before he signed for the Owls in October 1947. He was capable of playing both inside-forward or centre-forward, though he preferred to play much deeper than most of his contemporaries. Quigley scored four of Wednesday's goals on Boxing Day 1947 as they beat West Ham United 5–3. He ended his first season at Hillsborough as the club's top scorer with 22 goals in 30 League appearances. He top scored again in 1948–49 and had netted 10 goals the following campaign when he was transferred to North End. After making his debut in a 2–1 defeat of Swansea Town, Quigley scored five goals in 20 games. He appeared in a similar number of games in 1950–51 as the club won the Second Division Championship. In November 1951 he joined Blackburn Rovers and scored the only goal of the game on his debut against Birmingham. His best season for Rovers in terms of goals scored was 1954–55 when his total of 28 included hat-tricks against Middlesbrough and Notts County. Quigley had scored 95 goals in 166 League and Cup games when he left Ewood Park to rejoin Bury. On hanging up his boots, he managed non-League Mossley and Stockport County before becoming assistant manager to Jack Marshall at Blackburn. When Marshall was sacked, Quigley replaced him but with the club languishing near the foot of Division Two, he exchanged duties with Johnny Carey before leaving for good following the club's relegation to the Third Division. He later found employment with Blackburn for a third time as Howard Kendall's chief scout.

QUINN, Peter

Outside-left

Born: Sunderland, 3 December 1892.
Died: 1976.
Career: Spennymoor United. Blackpool, 1910. PRESTON NORTH END, 1919. Fleetwood. Bury, 1922. New Brighton, 1923.

■ Peter Quinn's impressive form for non-League Spennymoor United led to him joining Blackpool in 1910. He soon worked his way up through the ranks and by 1911–12 he had become an important member of the Seasiders' team. During his time at Bloomfield Road, Blackpool were struggling near the foot of the Second Division. When League football resumed in 1919–20, Quinn produced his best football for them before joining North End in March 1920. He made his debut in a 2–0 defeat at Derby and later scored his first goal for the club in a 5–2 win over his home-town side, Sunderland. Quinn was a regular over the next couple of seasons and played for Preston in the FA Cup Final of 1922. He left Deepdale early the following season and, after a few games for non-League Fleetwood, he played for both Bury and New Brighton before deciding to retire.

RAESIDE, Harry

Centre-forward

Born: Glasgow, 1869.
Career: PRESTON NORTH END, 1890.

■ Harry Raeside was a bustling centre-forward who appeared in the final two games of Preston's 1890–91 season, when they finished runners-up in the Football League to Everton. He played his part in McKenna scoring the only goal of the game at Aston Villa and was in the side that lost 3–0 to Sunderland on the final day of the season.

RAMSCAR, Frederick Thomas

Inside-forward

Born: Salford, 24 January 1919.
Career: Stockport County. Wolverhampton Wanderers, 1945. Queen's Park Rangers, 1947. PRESTON NORTH END, 1949. Northampton Town, 1951. Millwall, 1954. Peterborough United.

■ Fred Ramscar served in France and Germany during World War Two and gained plenty of experience on the soccer pitch while in the armed forces. He developed into an efficient, well-groomed and exceedingly useful inside-forward with Wolves before switching to Queen's Park Rangers in October 1947. In his first season at Loftus Road, he helped the club win the Third Division South Championship. Ramscar joined North End in November 1949 and made his debut in a goalless home draw against Chesterfield, but he was unable to hold down a regular place. His best performance was when he scored both goals against Cardiff City in a 3–2 defeat by the Bluebirds. He left Deepdale to join Northampton Town in 1951. Ramscar helped the Cobblers challenge for promotion from the Third Division South for three seasons, scoring 55 goals in 139 games. He left to end his first-class career with Millwall before he had a spell with non-League Peterborough United.

RANKINE, Simon Mark

Midfield

Born: Doncaster, 30 September 1969.
Career: Doncaster Rovers, 1988. Wolverhampton Wanderers, 1992. PRESTON NORTH END, 1996. Sheffield United, 2003. Tranmere Rovers, 2004.

■ A hardworking player, Simon Rankine started out with his home-town club, Doncaster Rovers, and made 195 appearances for them before Wolverhampton Wanderers paid £70,000 for his services in January 1992. He proved himself a utility player at Molineux, playing at right-back, in attack alongside Steve Bull and in his more favoured role on the right side of midfield. Having

won a regular place in the Wolves side, he went on to play in 167 games before Gary Peters splashed out £100,000 to bring him to Deepdale. Rankine made his debut in a League Cup-tie against Spurs and his first League outing followed four days later at Wrexham. Unfortunately, after making a promising start, a hamstring injury meant that his participation in the starting line up was more sporadic and he seemed to suffer from a lack of confidence. His form in 1997–98 was a revelation until an injury sustained in a freak DIY accident in December almost resulted in the loss of a finger and restricted his first-team appearances. The following season Rankine marked the 450th senior appearance of his career with a goal against Burnley before suffering a bad facial injury. Forming a strong central midfield partnership with Sean Gregan, he helped North End win the Second Division Championship in 1999–2000. The only blot on his season was the failure to convert one of the many chances that fell to him. He had a good first season in the higher grade of football and continued to be a regular in the North End side under David Moyes. Loss of form and a broken foot cost him his place in 2001–02. Suspension cost him his place the following season after being sent off against Sheffield United. He was then allowed to join the Blades on loan and helped them to the Play-offs. Rankine later joined the Yorkshire club on a permanent basis. After a season at Bramall Lane, he moved to Tranmere Rovers and in his first season at Prenton Park he was voted the club's Player of the Year.

RATHBONE, Michael John

Left-back

Born: Birmingham, 6 November 1958.
Career: Birmingham City, 1976.
Blackburn Rovers, 1979. PRESTON NORTH END, 1987.

■ Michael Rathbone, popularly known as 'Basil', joined Blackburn Rovers from his home-town club Birmingham City in February 1979. The move was initially on loan until Rovers decided to sign him on a permanent basis for a fee of £40,000. Although Rathbone was a

right-back, he had to switch positions to the opposite flank to win a regular place in Howard Kendall's side. Despite helping Rovers win the Second Division Championship in 1979–80 he was dropped and did not win a regular place again until the appointment of Bob Saxton as manager. He had just re-established himself in the side when he broke a leg against Sheffield Wednesday. Injury also cost him his place in the Full Members' Cup Final at Wembley and, while he was out of action, Rovers signed Chris Sulley from Dundee United as his replacement. Rathbone had scored 2 goals in 302 League and Cup games when he left Ewood Park to join North End for a fee of £20,000. He made his debut on the opening day of the 1987–88 season in a 1–0 home defeat by Chesterfield and appeared in 36 games as North End ended the season in mid-table in the Third Division. He had a good season in 1988–89 as the club finished sixth to reach the Play-offs, but then injuries and the emergence of players like Gary Swann limited his appearances. During this time, Rathbone combined playing for North End with organising the commercial activities of North West Counties League side Darwen. He later became North End's physiotherapist.

RAWLINGS, Archibald

Outside-right

Born: Leicester, 2 October 1891.
Died: 1952.
Career: Wombwell. Shirebrook. Northampton Town. Barnsley, 1911. Rochdale. Shirebrook. Dundee. PRESTON NORTH END, 1920. Liverpool, 1923. Walsall, 1926. Bradford Park Avenue, 1926. Southport, 1928. Dick Kerr's XI. Burton Town.

■ Archie Rawlings arrived at Deepdale from Dundee in the summer of 1920. A much-travelled player, he had previously seen service with Barnsley, Rochdale and Northampton Town. A well-built, long-legged winger, Rawlings was an ever present in 1920–21. His form for Preston led to him winning full international honours for England when he played against the Olympic Champions Belgium in Brussels. Though England won 2–0, Rawlings did not have the best of debuts. Rawlings was instrumental in the club reaching the FA Cup Final in 1922. In the semi-final against Spurs at Hillsborough, he had raced onto an immaculate through ball from Jefferies to sweep home the equaliser and then created the chance for Tommy Roberts to net the winner. Following the game, Rawlings was one of two Preston players found guilty of breaches of discipline. Although the other player apologised, Archie Rawlings refused and was suspended *sine die* (indefinitely). The term obviously had a different interpretation at Deepdale, for the player

only missed a couple of games before his name reappeared on the team sheet. He lined up in the Final but Huddersfield ran out 1–0 winners. Rawlings left North End after four seasons in which he scored 22 goals in 64 League and Cup games. He joined Liverpool and had two good seasons at Anfield before leaving to play for Walsall. He later appeared for Bradford Park Avenue before ending his first-class career with Southport. On hanging up his boots, Rawlings returned to Deepdale as North End's assistant-trainer.

RAWLINGS, James Sydney Dean

Outside-right

Born: Wombwell, 5 May 1913.
Died: 1956.
Career: Dick Kerr's XI. PRESTON NORTH END, 1933. Huddersfield Town, 1933. West Bromwich Albion, 1934. Northampton Town, 1936. Millwall, 1937. Everton, 1945. Plymouth Argyle, 1946.

■ When Syd Rawlings, the son of Archie Rawlings, made his debut for

North End in a goalless home draw against Port Vale in October 1933 it was the first case of a father and son playing for the club. Rawlings played in 12 games that season as North End went on to win promotion to the First Division as runners-up to Grimsby Town. His pinpoint crosses created numerous goalscoring chances, most of which were taken by the likes of George Stephenson and Bob Kelly. On leaving Deepdale he spent brief spells with Huddersfield Town and West Bromwich Albion before signing for Northampton Town. After two good seasons with the Cobblers, he moved on to Millwall and in his first season with the Lions he helped them win the Third Division South Championship. After the hostilities, Rawlings ended his career with a couple of seasons playing for Plymouth Argyle.

RAYNOR, Paul James

Forward, midfield

Born: Nottingham, 29 April 1966.
Career: Nottingham Forest, 1984. Bristol Rovers, 1985 (loan). Huddersfield Town, 1985. Swansea City, 1987. Wrexham, 1988 (loan). Cambridge United, 1992. PRESTON NORTH END, 1993. Cambridge United, 1995. Guang Deong (China). Leyton Orient, 1998. Kettering Town.

■ Much-travelled Paul Raynor began his League career with his home-town team, Nottingham Forest. A loan spell with Bristol Rovers followed before he joined Huddersfield Town on a free transfer. Injuries hampered his progress with the Yorkshire club and in March 1987 he teamed up with Swansea. He went on to serve the Vetch Field club for five years, appearing in 228 games and scoring 34 goals – many of them valuable ones – before signing for Cambridge United. In the summer of 1993, Preston manager John Beck paid £36,000 to bring Raynor to Deepdale and he made his debut on the opening day of the 1993–94 season, a 2–0 defeat at home to Crewe. Things got better and Raynor played in most of the games that season as the club reached the Play-off Final, only to lose to Wycombe Wanderers. Raynor continued to be a virtual ever present in 1994–95 as the club once

again reached the Play-offs, but during the early stages of the following season he rejoined Cambridge in a straight swap deal for Dean Barrick. Excellent at dead-ball situations, Raynor left Cambridge in the summer of 1997 after playing in 142 games in his two spells with the club to play on a non-contract basis for Chinese club Guang Deong. He later returned to League action with Leyton Orient before ending his career playing non-League football for Kettering Town.

REAY, Harold

Outside-left

Born: Sunderland, 1896.
Died: 1959.
Career: Margate. Sunderland, 1922. PRESTON NORTH END, 1923. Grimsby Town, 1924.

■ Harold Reay was playing non-League football for Margate when his home-town Sunderland gave him the opportunity to play League football. Unable to break into the North East club's side, he joined Preston North End. However, his only appearance in Preston colours came when Alf Quantrill was injured and he wore the number-11 shirt in a 3–1 defeat at Liverpool. Reay moved on to Grimsby but again just made a solitary appearance for the Mariners before leaving the club.

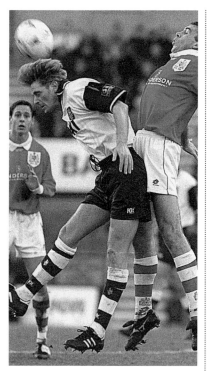

REEVES, David Edward

Forward

Born: Birkenhead, 19 November 1967.
Career: Heswall. Sheffield Wednesday, 1986. Scunthorpe United, 1987 (loan). Burnley, 1987 (loan). Bolton Wanderers, 1989. Notts County, 1993. Carlisle United, 1993. PRESTON NORTH END, 1996. Chesterfield, 1997. Oldham Athletic, 2001. Chesterfield, 2002. Ards.

■ Though he started out with Sheffield Wednesday, David Reeves made his League debut while on loan at Scunthorpe United, netting twice in the Irons' 3–1 defeat of Exeter City. He had a second loan spell with Scunthorpe, this time hitting a hat-trick in a 3–2 win for his side at Hereford United. In November 1987 he joined Burnley on loan before eventually making his League debut for Sheffield Wednesday. In August 1989 he joined Bolton Wanderers for a tribunal-set fee of £80,000. Although Reeves was a regular at Burnden Park for four seasons, his only hat-trick for the club came in a 4–1 Autoglass Trophy win over Rochdale in front of just 1,507 spectators. He found his starting appearances limited due to the signing of Scottish inter-national Andy Walker and, after scoring 42 goals in 173 games, the fans' favourite made a £100,000 move to Notts County.

His stay at Meadow Lane was brief and, in October 1993, Carlisle United paid a club record £121,000 for his services. Reeves was their leading scorer as they reached the Play-offs, only to lose to Wycombe. He hit 33 goals in 1994–95 as Carlisle won the Third Division Championship and reached the Auto Windscreens Shield Final. Once again he was their leading scorer in 1995–96 as they suffered relegation and in October 1996 he joined Preston North End. Bought to replace Andy Saville, he had a fairly successful start to his career at Deepdale. Reeves' hit list included a FA Cup hat-trick against Altrincham and his 100th League goal in the 5–1 thrashing of Luton Town. Despite notching four goals at the start of the 1997–98 season, he hit a barren spell and in November 1997 he was exchanged for Chesterfield's Tony Lormor. Reeves was an immediate hit at Saltergate, scoring winners in his first two games and ending his first full season as the Spireites' leading scorer. In 1999–2000 he scored four goals against Cambridge United and, though the club were relegated, he was again top scorer and voted Player of the Year. He later left Chesterfield to play for Oldham Athletic but after losing his place he rejoined the Saltergate club and netted a hat-trick against Grimsby Town. Reeves had scored 68 goals in 273 games in his two spells when he was released and left to play for Ards.

REID, Alexander

Outside-right

Born: West Calder, 1899.
Career: Aberdeen. Airdrieonians. PRESTON NORTH END, 1927. Blackpool, 1932. Chorley.

■ One of the trickiest wingers ever to play for North End, Alex Reid played his early football in his native Scotland for Aberdeen and Airdrie before joining the Lilywhites before the start of the 1927–28 season. He made his debut on the opening day of that campaign in a 2–2 draw at Fulham and went on to score 13 goals in 33 games as North End finished fourth in Division Two. Reid missed just a single game the following season and he again netted 13 goals. This total included four in a 7–1 defeat of Port Vale.

A versatile player, he was seen in every forward berth and in both wing-half positions. In 1930–31, Reid's last season with the club, he again netted 13 goals. The North End supporters dubbed him 'Daddy' Reid due to his sparse locks, but he was popular because of his fondness for cutting in and shooting hard; assets which made him a potential match winner. In five seasons, he scored 50 goals in 193 League outings. Will Scott, North End's trainer, told the story of how he once dashed out to attend Reid and was told, 'Dinna fash mon, I'm only having a breather'. On leaving Deepdale, Reid had a brief spell with Blackpool before ending his playing days with Chorley.

REID, Paul Mark

Defender, midfield

Born: Carlisle, 18 February 1982.
Career: Carlisle United, 1999. Glasgow Rangers, 2000. PRESTON NORTH END, 2002 (loan). Northampton Town, 2002 (loan). Northampton Town, 2003. Barnsley, 2004.

■ Paul Reid was one of a number of highly-rated players to emerge from the youth ranks at Carlisle United and he soon established himself as a first-choice defender for the Cumbrian club. At the

end of his first season at Brunton Park, he was invited to join Leeds United for a seven-a-side tournament in Singapore, but shortly after that he signed for Glasgow Rangers. Although Reid was capped by England at Under-20 level in 2001–02, he was unable to win a place in the Glasgow giants' first-team squad and joined North End on loan in January 2002. His only appearance for North End was when he came off the bench and scored in the 4–2 home win over Sheffield Wednesday. Even in that briefest of moments, he showed great determination. After a loan spell with Northampton, Reid joined the Cobblers on a permanent basis. Despite his tender years, he was appointed Northampton captain, but later left the Sixfields Stadium to sign for Barnsley where he matured into a most accomplished performer.

REID, Shaun

Midfield

Born: Huyton, 13 October 1965.
Career: Rochdale, 1983. PRESTON NORTH END, 1985 (loan). York City, 1988. Rochdale, 1992. Bury, 1995. Chester City, 1996.

■ Shaun Reid, the brother of England international Peter Reid, began his career with Rochdale. Although the club were always struggling in the lower reaches of the Fourth Division, Reid stood out as the club's most consistent player. Midway through his time at Spotland, Reid joined North End on loan and appeared in three games in December 1985. Unfortunately, he was never on the winning side in a season in which the club finished one off the bottom of the Fourth Division. On leaving Rochdale in December 1988 he joined York City for a fee of £32,500. After three-and-a-half seasons at Bootham Crescent, Reid rejoined Rochdale where he certainly lived up to his nickname of 'The Terminator' – even playing with two cracked ribs. Reid went on to make 288 appearances for Rochdale before joining Bury. After being sent off in only his second game for the Shakers, Reid failed to win a regular place and moved on to Chester City where he proved to be the catalyst behind the club's push for the

Play-offs in 1996–97. After recovering from a career-threatening knee injury, he was later appointed to the club's youth coaching staff.

RICHARDSON, Barry

Goalkeeper

Born: Wallsend, 5 August 1969.
Career: Sunderland, 1988. Scunthorpe United, 1989. Scarborough, 1989. Stockport County, 1990. Northampton Town, 1991. PRESTON NORTH END, 1994. Lincoln City, 1995. Mansfield Town, 1999 (loan). Doncaster Rovers.

■ Goalkeeper Barry Richardson was unable to make the grade with either of his first two League clubs, Sunderland and Scunthorpe United. He joined Scarborough in 1989 and played in 30 games. This was followed by a spell as a non-contract player with Stockport County before he signed for Northampton Town. Richardson was the Cobblers' first-choice 'keeper for three seasons, appearing in over 100 League and Cup games before he moved to Preston in the summer of 1994. After keeping a clean sheet on his debut in a goalless draw at Darlington on the opening day of the 1994–95 season, Richardson lost his place midway through the campaign to John Vaughan, but he reclaimed it after the turn of the year. His displays helped North End reach the Play-offs. After appearing in just three games in the early stages of the 1995–96 Third Division Championship-winning season, he moved to Lincoln City. Richardson was a big favourite with the fans at Sincil Bank but not the management. After he had made 150 appearances and had a spell on loan at Mansfield Town, he left to end his career with Doncaster Rovers.

RICHARDSON, Garbutt

Centre-half

Born: Newcastle, 24 October 1938.
Career: Huddersfield Town, 1955. PRESTON NORTH END, 1957. Accrington Stanley, 1961. Halifax Town, 1962. Barrow, 1964.

■ Unable to win a place in the Huddersfield Town League side, centre-half Garbutt Richardson joined Preston

North End in the summer of 1957. He spent a couple of seasons in the club's reserve side before making his senior bow in a 4–3 home win over eventual First Division runners-up Wolverhampton Wanderers. Deputising for the injured Joe Dunn, he made 13 appearances that season but lost out to the up-and-coming Tony Singleton in 1960–61. Richardson's last appearance for North End was in the number-nine shirt in the penultimate game of that campaign when he scored in a 4–2 home defeat at the hands of Manchester United. After a brief stay with Accrington Stanley, where he failed to make a first-team appearance, he was in the Halifax side that were relegated to the Fourth Division in 1962–63. Richardson ended his career with Barrow.

RIMMER, Stuart Alan

Forward

Born: Southport, 12 October 1964.
Career: Everton, 1982. Chester City, 1985. Watford, 1988. Notts County, 1988. Walsall, 1989. Barnsley, 1991. Chester City, 1991. Rochdale, 1994. PRESTON NORTH END, 1994.

■ Much-travelled forward Stuart Rimmer was a nippy striker who started his career with First Division Everton. The former England Youth international could not hold down a regular place and joined Chester City in January 1985. In his first full season with the Cestrians, he helped them win promotion to the Third Division and on his 21st birthday he scored four goals away from home. Rimmer had brief spells with Watford and Notts County before he signed for Walsall. In his first two games for the Saddlers he missed a penalty at home in a 7–0 defeat by Chelsea and then scored a hat-trick at Sunderland to end Walsall's run of 15 League defeats. After a short stay at his next club, Barnsley, Rimmer rejoined Chester City and took his total of League goals to 134 in 351 games, making him the only player to have scored more than 100 League goals for the Cestrians. Towards the end of his career with Chester he had a loan spell with Rochdale, followed by one with Preston in December 1994. Rimmer came off the bench twice in wins over Hereford United and Barnet but failed to impress and returned to Chester.

RITCHIE, John

Full-back

Born: Ashington, 10 April 1944.
Career: Whitley Bay. Port Vale, 1965. PRESTON NORTH END, 1967. Bradford City, 1972. Stafford Rangers.

■ John Ritchie was a quick full-back and occasional striker who became an England amateur international with Whitley Bay before joining Port Vale in December 1965. He made his League debut against Torquay United the following month and became a regular in the Vale team. In a FA Cup first-round tie in November 1966, he scored a goal from fully 40 yards in a 2–1 win at Bradford City. After making 54 appearances for the Valiants he joined North End in April 1967 and played his first game as a replacement for Jimmy Smith in a 2–2 home draw against Bristol City. In 1967–68, Ritchie made the number-three shirt his own as the club just avoided relegation to Division Three. Injuries hampered his progress the following season and, though he was back to his best in 1969–70, he could not prevent the club dropping into the Third Division. Ritchie did not play a single game during North End's Third Division Championship-

winning season of 1970–71. He later played for Bradford City before ending his playing days in non-League football with Stafford Rangers.

ROBERTS, John William

Inside-left

Born: Liverpool, 1880.
Career: White Star Wanderers. Tottenham Hotspur. Stockport County, 1901. Grays United. Brighton and Hove Albion. Queen's Park Rangers. PRESTON NORTH END, 1906. Leicester Fosse, 1907.

■ Inside-left Billy Roberts played for a number of clubs, but his only League appearances were for Preston North End. He failed to make the grade at both Stockport County and Leicester Fosse while Spurs, Brighton and Queen's Park Rangers were all playing in the Southern League during his time with them. Roberts made just two appearances for North End in the 1906–07 season: a 3–0 defeat at Bolton and a 2–0 success over Sunderland.

ROBERTS, Robert

Left-half, centre-half

Born: Penycae, July 1864.
Died: 1932.
Career: Druids. Bolton Wanderers, 1888. PRESTON NORTH END, 1891. Lincoln City, 1892.

■ Welsh international Bob Roberts was an ever present for his first club, Bolton Wanderers, during the inaugural season of League football in 1888–89. He missed very few games over the next couple of seasons before signing for Preston North End in March 1892. Roberts made his Preston debut in a 4–1 defeat at Sunderland and played in the last five games of the 1891–92 season. In the other games Preston beat Accrington 4–1 and Darwen 4–0 but went down 3–0 to Wolves and 3–1 to Aston Villa. Roberts left Deepdale in the close season to spend a season playing for Lincoln City.

ROBERTS, William Thomas

Centre-forward

Born: Handsworth, 29 November 1898.
Died: 13 October 1965.

Career: Soho Villa. Leicester Fosse, 1914. PRESTON NORTH END, 1919. Burnley, 1924. PRESTON NORTH END, 1926. Tottenham Hotspur, 1928. Dick Kerr's XI. Chorley.

■ Having hit the goal trail with Leicester Fosse, Tommy Roberts' war work in late 1918 enforced a change of residence to the North West. Southport Vulcan used his playing services for much of the final World War One season while North End leapt in for his professional signature in the following close season. After making his League debut in a goalless draw against local rivals Blackburn Rovers, he went on to top the club's scoring charts with 29 League and Cup goals, including eight doubles. Roberts continued to find the net with great regularity in 1920–21, despite difficulties with the management off the field. During the course of the season he notched up three hat-tricks – against Watford and Luton Town in the FA Cup and in a 3–0 League win at West Bromwich Albion. In 1921–22, Roberts topped North End's scoring charts for a third successive season, netting another treble in the victory over Bolton Wanderers. In October 1922, Roberts played for the Football League against the Irish League at Burnden Park and scored two goals. That season he equalled his best tally with another 29–goal haul; 28 of these were in the League, including a hat-trick in a 4–2 defeat of Stoke. Roberts' first England cap came in November 1923 against Belgium and he won a second against Wales the following March. Although Roberts failed to finish on the winning side, he scored in both games. During the early part of the 1924–25 season, Roberts left Deepdale to join Burnley but with his departure the goals dried up. He was only away from Deepdale for two seasons before he rejoined the Lilywhites in the summer of 1926. In 1926–27, Roberts again enjoyed some prolific goalscoring. He topped the club's charts with 30 goals including all four in a 4–2 FA Cup victory at Lincoln City. Midway through the following season, Roberts was injured in a car crash and missed eight games due to a broken arm. He had scored 179 goals when he left Deepdale a second time to join Tottenham Hotspur. Suffering from recurring injury problems, he soon returned to the North West to play for Dick Kerr's XI and later Chorley before settling back in Preston, where he worked as a publican for 30 years.

ROBERTSON, Alexander

Wing-half

Born: Edinburgh, December 1860.
Died: 1927.
Career: PRESTON NORTH END, 1888.

■ Sandy Robertson played in all but one of Preston North End's 22 League matches in their inaugural season in the Football League and, as the Lilywhites did not lose a game, he was never on the losing side. Robertson scored goals in wins over Bolton Wanderers, Derby County and Stoke. However, he was injured in the FA Cup win at Bootle and missed the last League game of the season and the ensuing Cup matches, which saw North End go on and complete the double with a 3–0 win over Wolverhampton Wanderers. The following season, Robertson could not hold down a regular place in the side. North End retained the title and felt they could manage without the Scotsman so he was released.

ROBERTSON, William

Outside-left

Born: Glasgow, 1889.
Died: 1960.
Career: PRESTON NORTH END, 1910. St Mirren.

■ It was during North End's 1910–11 season that outside-left William Robertson played his two games for the club. He made his debut on the opening day of the season in a 2–0 defeat at home to Nottingham Forest and played in another reversal at Deepdale against Sheffield Wednesday, before returning to Scotland to play for First Division side St Mirren.

ROBERTSON, William James Taverndale

Wing-half

Born: Montrose, 9 November 1923.
Career: Montrose Roselea. PRESTON NORTH END, 1942. Southport, 1955.

■ Wing-half Willie Robertson, who joined Preston from his home-town team Montrose Roselea during World War Two, eventually made his League debut for the club in October 1946. He wore the number-two shirt in a 3–1 win over Aston Villa, but that was his only appearance of the season. Although he played more games with each passing season, with a best of 24 games in 1949–50, Robertson never really established himself. After two seasons out of the first-team scene, he made his last appearance in 1952–53 as North End finished runners-up to Arsenal in Division One. He left Deepdale to join Southport. In his only season at Haig Avenue, he helped the Sandgrounders finish fifth in the Third Division North, their highest position since World War Two.

ROBINSON, Michael John

Forward

Born: Leicester, 12 July 1958.
Career: PRESTON NORTH END, 1976. Manchester City, 1979. Brighton and Hove Albion, 1980. Liverpool, 1983. Queen's Park Rangers. Osasuna (Spain).

■ After showing great promise in Preston North End's youth and reserve teams, Michael Robinson quickly

established himself in the Deepdale club's first team, following his debut against Cardiff City in April 1976. However, he did not play at all the following season and made just 10 appearances when North End won promotion from Division Three in 1977–78. The following season though he was outstanding, scoring 14 League and Cup goals including a spell of five in four games at the beginning of the campaign. With every appearance that

season, Robinson attracted a posse of scouts from other clubs. Their interest developed to the point where Manchester City offered £750,000 for his services. North End agreed to let him leave, though his time at Maine Road was limited as he struggled to make an impact at that relatively early stage of his career. A little over 12 months after joining City, he was transferred to Brighton and Hove Albion for less than half the amount he had cost in the first place. Not long after his arrival at the Goldstone Ground, he won the first of 24 caps for the Republic of Ireland. He won the right to wear the green shirt through an Irish-born grandmother and his call-up to Eoin Hand's side brought the Football Association of Ireland criticism from both the football authorities and the media. Robinson hit a rich vein of form on the South Coast, which ultimately led to Liverpool paying £200,000 to take him to Anfield. He won a League Championship medal as the Reds clinched their third successive title, a European Cup-winners' medal as a substitute for Kenny Dalglish in the victory over AS Roma on penalties and a League Cup-winners' medal, again as a substitute. Robinson's last League club were Queen's Park Rangers before he tried his luck in Spain with Osasuna. Injury forced his retirement two years later, but he remained in Spain where he now enjoys celebrity status as a leading television football anchorman.

ROBINSON, Raymond

Inside-forward

Born: Durham, 2 December 1950.
Career: PRESTON NORTH END, 1968.

■ Inside-forward Ray Robinson was given a couple of run-outs in the Second Division season of 1968–69 after the club had pulled away from the relegation zone. Robinson played in games against already-promoted Crystal Palace and neighbours Bolton Wanderers. Both games ended goalless.

ROBINSON, Stephen

Midfield

Born: Lisburn, 10 December 1974.
Career: Tottenham Hotspur, 1993. Bournemouth, 1994. PRESTON NORTH

END, 2000. Bristol City, 2002 (loan). Luton Town, 2002.

■ Steve Robinson won five full caps for Northern Ireland. He began his career with Spurs and made a couple of appearances in the Premiership before he joined Bournemouth on a free transfer. His early displays for the Cherries, whether in midfield or up front, were impressive. In 1997–98, he was Bournemouth's leading scorer with 13 goals, while the following season he was the second highest scorer with 17. Robinson helped the Cherries stay in contention with the promotion pack right until the end of the season and was rewarded with selection for the PFA award-winning Second Division side. He continued to find the net the following season but in May 2000, after scoring 60 goals in 286 games, he signed for Preston North End for a fee of £375,000. Robinson made his debut for North End as a substitute on the opening day of the 2000–01 season at Grimsby when he came on as a makeshift striker. He showed his versatility by playing in a number of positions for North End, but knee and ankle injuries forced an early end to his season. Lack of first-team opportunities the following season led to him going out on loan to Bristol City, prior to a move in the close season to Luton Town. Injuries hampered Robinson's progress in his first season at

Kenilworth Road, but in 2003–04 he was back to his best. His strike at Blackpool won the Hatters' Goal of the Season award. In 2004–05, he helped Luton to win the Division One Championship.

ROBSON, Norman

Centre-forward, inside-right

Born: Ryton-on-Tyne, 1908.
Career: West Stanley. PRESTON NORTH END, 1926. Derby County, 1930. Bradford City, 1932. Wigan Athletic, 1934.

■ Norman Robson joined Preston from non-League West Stanley in the summer of 1926. After impressing in the club's reserve side, he played in the last nine games of the 1926–27 season and scored five goals. The following season he was in fine form, scoring 19 goals in just 22 League appearances. This total included a hat-trick in a 4–0 win over Notts County and a spell of eight goals in five consecutive outings. However, due to the fine form of Sandy Hair and George Harrison, Robson only figured in a handful of games over the next two seasons and he left to continue his career with Derby County. Much of his time at the Baseball Ground was spent as cover for Bobby Barclay and Peter Ramage and he moved on to Bradford City. After one season of Second Division football with the Valley Parade club, he ended his career with non-League Wigan Athletic.

ROCHE, George

Left-half

Born: Birkenhead, 1889.
Career: Northern Nomads. PRESTON NORTH END, 1909. Liverpool University. Stoke. Lancaster Town.

■ Signed from Northern Nomads, left-half George Roche made his Football League debut for Preston North End for the injured Billy Lyon midway through the 1909–10 season. He played in three consecutive games, helping Preston to 1–0 wins over Manchester United and Sheffield Wednesday, but after a 2–0 defeat at Bristol City he lost out to the fully-recovered Lyon. Roche went on to play for Liverpool University and Stoke before returning to the North West to end his playing days at Lancaster Town.

RODGER, Thomas

Winger, inside-left

Born: Dundee, 9 June 1882.
Career: Dundee. Manchester United, 1903. PRESTON NORTH END, 1904. Grimsby Town, 1906. Reading. Brighton and Hove Albion. Leeds City, 1908.

■ Tom Rodger played his early football with his home-town club, Dundee, until he signed for Manchester United. After being unable to force his way into United's side, he moved to Preston. Fast and with an eye for goal, Rodger made his debut as a replacement for the injured Dickie Bond at Newcastle but then returned to the reserves. He appeared on the opposite flank for the last four games of the season and his only goal proved to be the winner in a 2–1 defeat of Stoke. Robson moved on to Grimsby Town, where he scored 13 goals in 34 games, prior to spells in the Southern League with Reading and Brighton. He returned to League action with Leeds City before hanging up his boots.

RODGERS, Mark

Midfield

Born: Broxburn, 20 September 1967.
Career: PRESTON NORTH END, 1985.

■ Midfielder Mark Rodgers had impressed in the club's reserves before he was given what turned out to be his only appearance in the Football League during the disastrous 1985–86 season. Wearing the number-eight shirt, he played in the 1–0 home defeat by Scunthorpe United but was replaced by substitute Mel Tottoh.

RODWAY, Thomas

Left-back

Born: Cannock Chase, 1879.
Career: Wellingborough. PRESTON NORTH END, 1903.

■ Left-back Tommy Rodway was 24 years old when he joined North End in the summer of 1903 from Southern League Wellingborough. He had previously had a trial with Aston Villa before joining the Southern League club. He made his North End debut on the final day of the Second Division Championship-winning season of 1903–04 in a 1–0 win over Blackpool. He soon began to display the remarkable positional sense and determined tackling that were to see him through 335 League games in his time at Deepdale. During the course of the 1904–05 season, one of Rodway's 27 appearances was in the 6–1 defeat at Manchester City. At one stage in the game, North End were down to nine men as Percy Smith had a head injury and Rodway had a broken collarbone. Rodway helped Preston to the runners'-up spot in the First Division in 1905–06 and his form won him selection for a number of England trial games, though he never won full international honours. When North End played Everton in January 1907, the Merseyside outfit were awarded a penalty. McBride flung himself to his left to make a superb save but as two Everton players rushed in and kicked him, fighting broke out among all the players. After two minutes of trying to restore order, the referee found Rodway and Everton's Taylor still rolling around the floor, throwing punches. Needless to say, both were dismissed. After Preston's relegation in 1911–12, Rodway played his part in ensuring the club returned to the top flight the following season as Champions of Division Two. Unfortunately, Preston went straight back down again in 1913–14, but the club again won promotion at the first time of asking, though Rodway made just eight appearances.

ROGERS, Joseph James

Outside-right

Born: Coventry, 5 May 1876.
Died: 1955.
Career: Stoke United. Macclesfield. Southampton. Grimsby Town, 1896. Newcastle United, 1898. PRESTON NORTH END, 1900. Tivoli, Grimsby.

■ Joe Rogers arrived at Southampton from Macclesfield and caused a sensation by scoring 10 goals in a friendly against the Wiltshire Regiment. Despite this feat, he was not considered to be a forward, but a full-back. He never really settled on the South Coast and joined Grimsby Town where he bagged 23 goals in 53 League games. He then joined Newcastle United for their first season in the top flight and soon became a hugely popular player. Rogers was effective when he had a sight of goal and was good enough to become the Magpies' first international player when he was chosen to represent the FA XI to tour Germany at the turn of the century – an international appearance in all but name. He had a field day on the continent, netting seven goals including five in one fixture. Rogers joined Preston in January 1901 but, though he netted in a 5–3 defeat of his former club Newcastle and scored twice in the last two games of the season, he could not prevent North End's relegation to Division Two. He had a good 1901–02 season but then left Deepdale to spend some time coaching in Germany. He returned to England to see out his career with the Tivoli club in Grimsby.

ROSS, George

Full-back

Born: Inverness, 15 April 1943.
Career: PRESTON NORTH END, 1960. Southport, 1972. Washington Diplomats (US). Morecambe. Telford United.

■ George Ross played his early football for Scottish junior side Hilton Athletic and was a wing-half when he arrived at Deepdale in September 1958. He was a member of the successful North End youth side which reached the FA Youth Cup Final against Chelsea. Such was Ross' progress that he made his League debut on Boxing Day 1960 in a 1–0 defeat at home to Nottingham Forest. Within a year he had become a regular in the Preston side, playing alongside North End legend Willie Cunningham. He was an ever present in 1963–64, a season which culminated in him playing in the FA Cup Final against West Ham United. A tough-tackling, no-nonsense defender, Ross also had the ability to turn defence into attack with a swift and incisive pass to a colleague. During his time at Deepdale, he won a Third Division Championship medal in 1970–71 and accolades from both friends and foes alike. Ross played the last of his 386 League games in April 1973 when he came off the bench in the derby at Blackpool. He left to join Southport, who had just won promotion, and spent a season at Haig Avenue before playing for a season in the NASL for Washington Diplomats. On his return, he played non-League football for both Morecambe and Telford United.

ROSS, James

Inside-right, centre-forward

Born: Edinburgh, 28 March 1866.
Died: 12 June 1902.
Career: St Bernard's. PRESTON NORTH END, 1883. Liverpool, 1894. Burnley, 1896. Manchester City, 1898.

■ Jimmy Ross came south to Preston to join his famous elder brother Nick. His debut for North End happened by chance – he had gone to Padiham on 24 November 1883 as a spectator to watch his brother play but, as the team were a couple of men short, he was invited to play. He scored two goals in North End's 4–0 win. Nicknamed 'The Little Demon', Ross was a phenomenal goalscorer: in the four seasons up to the formation of the Football League in 1888, he scored over 250 goals in only 220 appearances. He also had the distinction of scoring goals for North End in both the FA Cup and

Lancashire Cup finals. Born in Edinburgh, he was unlucky not to have been chosen for his country but the selectors only chose from players at clubs north of the border. Ross formed a highly successful partnership up front for North End with England international John Goodall. He scored seven goals against Hyde in a 26–0 win and six against Reading when North End won 18–0. In the inaugural season of the Football League, he scored four goals in a 7–0 win over Stoke to help the club win the League Championship. He also netted one of the goals in the 3–0 FA Cup Final defeat of Wolves to help the club achieve the double. He netted 21 goals in 1888–89 and repeated the feat the following season, netting another treble. In 1892–93 he scored hat-tricks in successive wins over Sheffield Wednesday and FA Cup opponents Burton Swifts. After one more season, in which Ross hit hat-tricks in the games against Darwen and West Bromwich Albion, he was transferred to Liverpool. Although he had agreed to sign for the club, he almost never arrived at Anfield. His brother Nick, who had been taken seriously ill and was on his deathbed, pleaded with Jimmy to remain with Preston. Jimmy was torn but in the end decided that he had to keep his agreement with Liverpool. He played in 78 League games for the Reds and even skippered the side for some of the time. In 1894 he joined Burnley, helping them into the First Division, before joining Manchester City where he played alongside the great Billy Meredith. His last first-class game was for Manchester City against Preston North End in the FA Cup on 25 January 1902. Five months later, on 12 June 1902 – exactly nineteen years after he had arrived at Deepdale – Jimmy Ross died aged just 36.

ROSS, Nicholas John

Left-back, centre-forward

Born: Edinburgh, 1863.
Died: 1894.
Career: Heart of Midlothian. PRESTON NORTH END. Everton, 1888. Linfield. PRESTON NORTH END, 1889.

■ Nick Ross, one of the game's greatest defenders, was the 20-year-old captain of Hearts when he was given

work as a slater in Preston and signed for North End in the summer of 1883. He was the subject of a furious debate over professionalism but, undaunted, Preston made him their captain, converting him from a forward to one of the best backs of any generation. In many ways, though, he was an unlucky footballer. Ross was on the losing side when Preston were defeated by West Bromwich Albion in the 1888 FA Cup Final and he missed the famous Preston double-winning season of 1888–89 because by then he had joined Everton. Within two weeks of his arrival on Merseyside, he had been made Everton captain. His wage was reported to be £10 a month, nearly twice that of most players. Ross stayed with the Blues for just one season and then rejoined Preston, at last tasting success when they won the League Championship again in 1889–90. In April 1891 he played in the first-ever Football League representative side against the Football Alliance. Sadly, Ross died of consumption aged only 31.

ROWLEY, Richard William Morris

Inside-forward, centre-forward

Born: Enniskillen, 13 January 1904.
Died: 18 April 1984.
Career: Andover. Swindon Town, 1925. London Casuals. Southampton, 1926. Tottenham Hotspur, 1929. PRESTON NORTH END, 1931.

■ Dick Rowley was a Northern Ireland international with a good goalscoring record. The son of an Army officer, he first played football with the Fulwood Barracks team but on going to Taunton Grammar School he was forced to give up football in favour of rugby. Once his schooldays were over, Rowley took up football again and had spells with Andover, London Casuals and Swindon Town before joining Southampton. It was at The Dell that his career took off. He scored five goals in the club's 1926–27 FA Cup run and netted 25 goals in 25 games in the 1929–30 season. This total included hat-tricks in successive games against Chelsea and Nottingham Forest as well as four goals in a 5–2 win over Bradford City. This form prompted Spurs to pay £3,750 for his services but, even though

Rowley continued to play for Northern Ireland, he found himself confined to the reserves for much of his time at White Hart Lane. In December 1931 he signed for Preston and made his debut in a 2–1 reversal at Plymouth Argyle. The following season he laid on a number of Ted Harper's 37 goals but the following season, when North End won promotion, injuries restricted his appearances and in the close season he decided to retire.

ROY, James

Centre-forward

Born: Preston, 1872.
Career: PRESTON NORTH END, 1893.

■ James Roy was discovered playing in local junior football. The bustling centre-forward's only Football League game came in March 1894 when he played in the game at Deepdale against West Bromwich Albion. Though he did not get on the score sheet, he did lay on one of Jimmy Ross' hat-trick of goals in a 3–1 win.

RUDGE, Dale Anthony

Midfield

Born: Wolverhampton, 9 September 1963.
Career: Wolverhampton Wanderers, 1981. PRESTON NORTH END, 1984. Djvre 1919 (Norway). Hednesford Town.

■ Midfielder Dale Rudge began his career with his home-town team,

Wolves, and played reasonably well for the Molineux side when he was called into action. He was part of the side that won promotion from Division Three in 1982–83, but only made 29 appearances in his three years with the club. Rudge joined Preston in the summer of 1984 and played his first game in the 2–0 home win over Doncaster Rovers on the opening day of the 1984–85 season. He made 23 appearances during that season, but North End were relegated to the Fourth Division for the first time in their history. He appeared in a similar number of games the following season as the club dropped to just one place from the bottom of Division Four. Rudge was released and went to Norway where he played for three seasons before drifting into non-League football with Hednesford Town.

RUSSELL, David

Centre-half, centre-forward

Born: Airdrie, 6 April 1868.
Career: Broxburn. Heart of Midlothian. PRESTON NORTH END, 1892. Heart of Midlothian. Glasgow Celtic. PRESTON NORTH END, 1898. Glasgow Celtic.

■ Davie Russell joined North End for the 1892–93 season after impressing north of the border with Broxburn and Hearts, for whom he scored the only goal of the 1891 Scottish Cup Final. He soon repaid the faith shown by the Preston management, scoring 17 goals including a hat-trick in a 4–1 defeat of Aston Villa. His goals, along with those of Frank Becton, helped the club finish runners-up to Sunderland in the First Division. Russell then returned north of the border and, after a spell with Hearts, he signed for Celtic. Having helped the Bhoys to League Championship success in 1898, he returned to Deepdale for a second spell. By now he was playing as a centre-half and struggled alongside his teammates as they just avoided the drop into Division Two. Russell rejoined Celtic and won another Scottish Cup-winners' medal in 1900, but he was on the losing side the following season. After football he worked full-time down the Greenrigg Pit in Fauldhouse and was severely crushed in a roof fall in October 1906.

RUSSELL, David Kennedy

Centre-half

Born: Beith, 1862.
Died: 1918.
Career: Stewart Cunningham. PRESTON NORTH END, 1888. Nottingham Forest.

■ Centre-half David Russell joined North End in their pre-League days and soon gained a reputation as a strong-tackling defender. He was certainly not a player to cross, as he showed in the match against Blackburn Olympic in 1886. Russell chased an opponent down the pitch and kicked him in the back – a novel defensive technique! He was still the club's first-choice centre-half when the first Football League season got underway. He played in 18 of the 22 League games and the successful FA Cup Final, having scored the only goal of the semi-final to defeat West Bromwich Albion. He played in all but one of the games the following season as Preston retained their title and then informed the management team that he no longer wished to play for the club and moved on to Nottingham Forest.

RUSSELL, William Fraser

Inside-right, right-half

Born: Falkirk, 6 December 1901.
Career: Glasgow Benburb. Airdrieonians. PRESTON NORTH END, 1925.

■ Scottish international Willie Russell was sold to Preston to fund ground repairs at Airdrie. In fact, one of the newly erected stands became known as the Willie Russell Stand. He made his debut for Preston in a 3–0 defeat at Wolverhampton Wanderers on the opening day of the 1925–26 season. As the campaign wore on, he formed a good understanding with Alex James and the two of them terrorised Second Division defences, with Russell netting 13 goals. The following season Russell missed just two games – one of these was the match against Middlesbrough when he got married. He continued his fine form throughout the next season, when once again the club were challenging for promotion to Division One. Russell started the 1928–29 season on fire. After netting two of his side's goals in a 3–1 home win over Blackpool on the

of the 1963–64 season, but is best remembered for netting a hat-trick that season in the second leg of the FA Youth Cup Final win over Swindon Town. However, shortly afterwards he was converted into a centre-half. Tall and well-built, Sadler's style was unspectacular but effective. He helped United win the League Championship in 1966–67 and a year later was a member of the side that beat Benfica 4–1 at Wembley in the European Cup Final. After playing in 333 League and Cup games, he left Old Trafford and spent a summer playing in the US. On his return he signed for North End. He made his debut in a 2–2 draw against Luton Town but, though he gave some solid displays in whatever position he was selected, he could not prevent the club's relegation to the Third Division. He continued to be a regular in the Preston side until he lost his place to an up-and-coming Mick Baxter.

SALE, Mark David

Forward

Born: Burton, 27 February 1972.
Career: Stoke City, 1990. Cambridge United, 1991. Birmingham City, 1992. Torquay United, 1993. PRESTON NORTH END, 1994. Mansfield Town, 1995. Colchester United, 1997. Plymouth Argyle, 1999 (loan). Rushden and Diamonds.

■ At 6ft 5in, Mark Sale was one of the tallest players in the Football League when he started out with his local club, Stoke City. He had made just a couple of appearances from the bench when he was released and joined Cambridge United. Unable to make the grade at the Abbey Stadium, he joined Birmingham City. Though he scored goals for the Blues in both the FA Cup and League Cup, he did not find the net in 21 League games for the St Andrew's club. Moving on to Torquay United, he was given more of a run in the side and responded with eight goals in 44 League games. In July 1994, Sale joined Preston after boss John Beck paid £20,000 to bring him to Deepdale. After playing his first game in a League Cup-tie against Stockport County, Sale scored on his League debut in a 2–0 win at Hereford United. He found the back of the net six times during the first few

weeks of the season but was then forced to miss four months of the campaign through hernia and toe injuries. He was allowed to leave the club in the close season and joined Mansfield Town, where he played in the second half of the season with a broken nose. Sale moved on to Colchester United and the man known as 'Carboot' scored three goals in the last four games as the team missed the Play-offs by a point. During his time at Layer Road, Sale was often the unsung hero of the team. After scoring 13 goals in 96 games, he left the club to play non-League football for Rushden and Diamonds.

SANDERS, Moses

Centre-half, left-back

Born: Preston, 26 September 1873.
Died: 1941.
Career: Crewe Alexandra. Accrington, 1890. PRESTON NORTH END, 1891. Woolwich Arsenal, 1899. Dartford.

■ Moses Sanders' playing career began on the Marsh with a side known as the Black Knights. Major Sudell spotted his potential and tried to persuade him to join North End. However, he had no success and Sanders joined Fishwick Ramblers. Later he signed for Crewe where his outstanding performances led to him signing for First Division Accrington. After impressing with the East Lancashire club, he eventually joined his home-town team. Sanders made his debut for North End in a 2–0 defeat at Notts County on the opening day of the 1891–92 season and went on to be ever present as the club finished runners-up to Sunderland in the First Division. Sanders remained an important member of the Preston side for eight seasons. During that time he helped the club to the runners'-up spot again in 1892–93 as well as to the FA Cup semi-final in the same campaign. The Deepdale crowd idolised him and no game in which he played was ever dull. Sanders was a robust player who took many knocks, but he usually returned them with interest. He left Deepdale to play for Woolwich Arsenal but injuries meant that he made just a handful of appearances for the Gunners. Sanders later played in the Southern League with Dartford.

opening day of the campaign, he went on to score five goals in the first five fixtures before a serious injury ruled him out of action until the closing stages of the season. The injury resurfaced and he decided to retire after his first-team opportunities dwindled.

SADLER, David

Centre-half

Born: Yalding, 5 February 1946.
Career: Maidstone United. Manchester United, 1963. PRESTON NORTH END, 1973.

■ Manchester United won the race to sign David Sadler, Maidstone United's England amateur international inside-forward, in November 1962. He made his United debut as a replacement for the injured David Herd in a 3–3 draw at Sheffield Wednesday on the opening day

SANDERSON, Benjamin Salisbury

Right-half

Born: Preston, 1878.
Career: PRESTON NORTH END, 1899.

■ Ben Sanderson's first League game for the Lilywhites came towards the end of the 1899–1900 season when North End visited Champions-elect Aston Villa. Not surprisingly the home side won 3–1 and Sanderson went back to the reserves. He appeared in just one game the following season with the same 3–1 result, this time against Blackburn Rovers. He did not appear at all in 1901–02 but after playing four games at the start of the following season, he lost out to Rabbi Howell.

SANDERSON, William

Outside-left

Born: Walbottle, 1885.
Career: PRESTON NORTH END, 1906.

■ After appearing in the last game of the 1906–07 season, a 2–2 draw against Stoke, outside-left Willie Sanderson appeared on a more regular basis the following season and scored his first goal for the club at Sunderland. During the course of the 1908–09 season Sanderson, who had established himself in the number-11 shirt, came close to netting a hat-trick. After scoring both his side's goals in a 2–1 defeat of Bristol City he shot against the woodwork when put clear. He shared the outside-left duties with Danson and Winterhalder in 1909–10 but left the club in the close season.

SAPSFORD, George Douglas

Inside-left

Born: Higher Broughton, 10 March 1896.
Died: 1970.
Career: Clarendon. Manchester United, 1919. PRESTON NORTH END, 1921. Southport, 1925.

■ George Sapsford spent a couple of seasons playing for Manchester United, where he scored 16 goals in 52 League games, before signing for North End towards the end of the 1921–22 season – a campaign in which United lost their top-flight status. His first game in North

End colours came on the final day of that season when he scored both his side's goals in a 2–0 win at Birmingham. Even more remarkable than Sapsford netting twice on debut was the fact that, prior to that game, Preston had gone 13 away games without scoring a goal. During the next three seasons, Sapsford was never an automatic choice and when he left Deepdale to play for Southport in the Third Division North he had made just 36 League appearances.

SAVILLE, Andrew Victor

Forward

Born: Hull, 12 December 1964.
Career: Hull City, 1983. Walsall, 1989. Barnsley, 1990. Hartlepool United, 1992. Birmingham City, 1993. Burnley, 1994 (loan). PRESTON NORTH END, 1995. Wigan Athletic, 1996. Cardiff City, 1997. Hull City, 1998 (loan). Scarborough, 1999. Gainsborough Trinity.

■ After signing for his home-town team, Hull City, Andy Saville first began to appear regularly in the Tigers' Second Division side during 1986–87 when he was the club's top scorer. He joined Walsall for £100,000 in March 1989 and scored twice on his debut for the Saddlers. After just a year at Fellows Park, he moved to Barnsley and in March 1992 he was transferred to Hartlepool

United for a club record fee of £60,000. Following a £155,000 move to Birmingham City in March 1993, he scored two goals on his debut for the Blues. In 1994–95 he helped the St Andrew's club win the Second Division Championship and triumph in the Auto Windscreens Shield against Carlisle at Wembley. During that season, Saville had a loan spell at Burnley but it was Preston North End who secured his services in the summer of 1995. After scoring against Lincoln on the opening day of the 1995–96 season, he was an immediate hit at Deepdale, scoring goals for fun. Saville netted 29 League goals, including hat-tricks in the wins over Leyton Orient and Mansfield Town, to guide the club to the Third Division Championship. In fact, only Alan Shearer (with 31) scored more goals in English football during that 1995–96 season. Unable to rediscover his goalscoring form the following season, he moved to Wigan Athletic for £125,000. Though injuries then began to hinder his progress, he had played in enough games to qualify for another Third Division Championship medal, this time with the Latics. With stiff competition for places, Saville moved to Cardiff City but, even after netting a hat-trick against Scunthorpe United, he did not figure in Frank Burrows' plans. He had a brief spell on loan at Hull and then played for Scarborough but following the club's relegation to the Conference, he was not retained and went to play for Gainsborough Trinity.

SAYER, Peter Anthony

Winger

Born: Cardiff, 2 May 1955.
Career: Cardiff City, 1973. Brighton and Hove Albion, 1978. PRESTON NORTH END, 1980. Cardiff City, 1981 (loan). Chester City, 1984. Northwich Victoria.

■ Peter Sayer worked his way up through the ranks of his home-town club, Cardiff City, before making his debut for the Bluebirds against Hull City in September 1974. By the following season he had won a regular place in the Cardiff side, but then he broke his ankle in a match at Southampton. He did not return to action until the 1975–76 season

when he helped the club win promotion to the Second Division. His form for Cardiff led to him winning the first of seven international caps for Wales. Though not a prolific scorer, on his return to Ninian Park he found the net six times in six games. Midway through the 1977–78 season he joined Brighton and Hove Albion for £100,000. In his first full season at the Goldstone Ground, he helped the Seagulls win promotion to the First Division before later moving to Preston North End. Sayer made his debut for the Deepdale club in a 3–0 defeat at Sheffield Wednesday. Injuries and a loss of form then hampered his progress and it was 1982–83 before he played in a decent run of games. He rejoined Cardiff on loan, taking his tally of goals to 20 in 98 first-team outings, before ending his League career with Chester. He later appeared in non-League football for Northwich Victoria.

SCOTT, Leslie

Goalkeeper

Born: Sunderland, 1895.
Career: Fulwell. Sunderland, 1913. Stoke, 1922. PRESTON NORTH END, 1923.

■ Goalkeeper Leslie Scott played in the First Division for his home-town team, Sunderland, either side of World War One. He made 95 appearances before joining Stoke. The Potters had just won promotion to the top flight but Scott's career at the Victoria Ground was ill-fated and he sustained a very badly cut finger which delayed the start of his season for a week. One problem after another seemed to affect him and with relegation beckoning the directors signed two other 'keepers and released Scott. He joined Preston North End for the 1923–24 season but only appeared twice – in a 3–1 defeat by Newcastle United and a 1–1 draw against Chelsea – before returning to the reserves to allow the fit-again Jimmy Branston to resume his goalkeeping duties.

SCOTT, Thomas

Inside-forward

Born: Newcastle-upon-Tyne, 6 April 1904. Died: 24 December 1979.
Career: Newcastle Swifts. Pandon Temperance. Sunderland, 1923. Darlington, 1924. Liverpool, 1924. Bristol City, 1928. PRESTON NORTH END, 1930. Norwich City, 1932. Exeter City, 1934. Bangor City.

■ Much-travelled inside-forward Tommy Scott developed with Pandon Temperance in his native North East before joining Sunderland midway through the 1922–23 season. Unable to break into their League side, he moved to Darlington and in 1924–25 was a member of their Third Division North Championship-winning squad. His next club were Liverpool but most of his time at Anfield was spent in the reserves. After a spell with Bristol City, Scott arrived at Deepdale in readiness for the 1930–31 season. He scored twice on his debut on the opening day of the campaign as Southampton were crushed 5–0. Scott ended the season as joint-top scorer with George Bargh and his total of 14 goals included a hat-trick in the 7–5 win at Millwall. He was in and out of the side the following season but did score in each of the club's last three games to lead the Lilywhites away from the foot of Division Two. Scott then joined Norwich City, helping them win the Third Division South title in 1933–34, before playing for Exeter City and finally non-League Bangor City.

SCOTT, William John

Full-back

Born: Preston, 14 June 1921.
Career: PRESTON NORTH END, 1939.

■ Full-back Bill Scott joined North End just before World War Two but, though he played in a number of the club's wartime games, he had to wait until the resumption of peacetime football before he made his Football League debut. After playing in the club's first game following the hostilities, a 3–2 win over Leeds United, Bill Scott was the club's only ever present as they finished seventh in Division One. Unable to prevent the club from dropping into Division Two in 1948–49, Scott shared the full-back duties with legends like Willie Cunningham and Joe Walton. However, in 1950–51, when the club won the Second Division Championship, he appeared in 32 games. Scott was outstanding during the club's 1952–53 season when they finished runners-up to Arsenal. He went on to play for another season before deciding to retire.

SCULLY, Patrick Joseph

Centre-half

Born: Dublin, 23 June 1970.
Career: Arsenal, 1987. PRESTON

NORTH END, 1989 (loan). Northampton Town, 1990 (loan). Southend United, 1991. Huddersfield Town, 1994.

■ Centre-half Pat Scully was sent to Highbury as a youngster by Arsenal's celebrated Irish scout Bill Darby and, at 18 years old, a bright future seemed assured. Indeed, in October 1988 while still a member of the Gunners' Football Combination side, he won full international honours for the Republic of Ireland in a 4–0 win over Tunisia. At Highbury he was unable to displace the likes of Tony Adams, David O'Leary and Steve Bould so he went on loan to Preston North End. Scully appeared in 13 games for Preston but while he was pleased to score his first League goal, it did come in a 4–1 defeat by Bolton Wanderers. He later had a spell on loan at Northampton before signing for Southend United. He made an immediate impact at the heart of the Shrimpers' defence, helping them win promotion to Division Two in 1990–91. In March 1994, having appeared in 127 games for the Roots Hall club, he was transferred to Huddersfield. The following month he appeared in the Autoglass Trophy Final at Wembley, while the following season he helped Town win promotion to the First

Division via the Play-offs. A loss of form then hampered his progress and he decided to return to Ireland.

SEDGWICK, Christopher Edward

Midfield, winger

Born: Sheffield, 28 April 1980.
Career: Rotherham United, 1997. PRESTON NORTH END, 2004.

■ In his early days at Millmoor, winger Chris Sedgwick showed outstanding promise, with his ability to run at defences and supply good crosses. In 1999–2000, after establishing himself as a regular member of the Rotherham side, he helped the Millers win promotion, scoring some vital goals. One of these was a spectacular individual effort in front of a live television audience against Mansfield. After breaking down in pre-season training, Sedgwick missed the first half of the following season and had to undergo a knee operation. His appearances were disrupted by a series of other injuries before he played on a more regular basis in 2003–04. In November 2004, after scoring 21 goals in 272 first-team games, he joined Preston North End for a fee of £300,000. He played his first game for the club in a 3–0 win over Derby County. A

tireless worker, he went on to help Preston reach the Play-offs by weighing in with some useful goals including one on his return to Millmoor. When Sedgwick was replaced shortly before the final whistle he was given a standing ovation from all four sides of the ground. A tireless worker, Chris Sedgwick scored four goals last term, perhaps none more important than the sensational late winner against Crewe Alexandra, which stretched North End's unbeaten run to 17 games.

SENIOR, Stephen

Right-back

Born: Sheffield, 15 May 1963.
Career: York City, 1981. Darlington, 1984 (loan). Northampton Town, 1987. Wigan Athletic, 1987. PRESTON NORTH END, 1990. Witton Albion. Bamber Bridge.

■ Steve Senior began his career with York City and had six seasons at Bootham Crescent. In 1983–84 he helped the Minstermen win the Fourth

Division Championship. Despite being one of the club's better players in that promotion-winning campaign, he found it difficult to adjust to a higher grade of football and went on loan to Darlington. Senior later joined Third Division Northampton Town but injuries and a loss of form restricted his appearances at the County Ground. In October 1987 he moved to Wigan and over the next few seasons he proved himself to be a solid if unspectacular performer. With the Latics he turned out in nine different outfield positions before eventually settling at

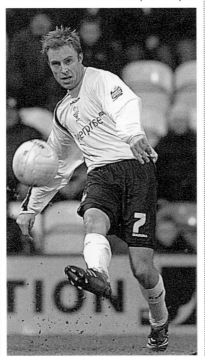

right-back. Senior was surprisingly allowed to join Preston North End in the summer of 1990 and he made his debut in a 3–1 home defeat by Grimsby on the opening day of the 1990–91 season. He missed very few games in two seasons with the club before injury forced his release. He had a brief spell with Witton Albion before helping Bamber Bridge win the Unibond League Championship.

SHANKLY, William

Wing-half

Born: Glenbuck, 2 September 1913.
Died: 29 September 1981.
Career: Glenbuck Cherries. Carlisle United, 1932. PRESTON NORTH END, 1933.

■ Bill Shankly was a deeply philosophical man who was much quoted for his witticisms. He always believed that football belonged to the fans and during 15 magnificent years as manager of Liverpool he carried out his theories to the letter. His death at the age of 68 on 29 September 1981 in the intensive care unit of the city's Broadgreen Hospital was mourned worldwide, illustrating the esteem in which he was held. In commemoration of his achievements, the 'Shankly Gates' were erected at his beloved Anfield and adorned with the title words from the club's adopted anthem 'You'll never walk alone'. Soon after starting his playing career with Carlisle United, Shankly's blossoming talents were transferred to Preston North End. At Deepdale his skills were honed to perfection among a growing contingent of Scotsmen. Always fiercely enthusiastic, Shankly's brash, competitive nature made him a key figure in helping his new club to promotion from Division Two at the end of his first season. A teetotaller, non-smoker and fitness fanatic, he was instrumental in helping North End reach two successive FA Cup finals, picking up a winners' medal in 1938. In his first eight seasons at Deepdale, Shankly missed only 28 out of a maximum 319 games and stood down only once through injury. By now he was a highly respected wing-half and his displays earned him five Scotland caps between April 1938 and April 1939. Although the outbreak of World War Two interrupted

his First Division career, his country further honoured him with the award of seven unofficial caps. A boxer of some repute during his military service, Shankly helped North End to the North Regional title and a Wartime Cup Final success against Arsenal – his two penalty goals against Newcastle United ensured their place in the Wembley Final. He

played for North End until 1949 and played in 296 League games and a record 43 successive FA Cup-ties for the club. He was quickly appointed player-coach for the club's reserve team before being offered his first chance in management with Carlisle United. Grimsby tempted him with another managerial post, but two years later he surprisingly quit to join struggling Workington Town. A year later he was on the move again as assistant to Andy Beattie at Huddersfield Town. Within a year Beattie had been sacked and Shankly appointed manager, a post that lasted for three years before Liverpool stepped in. Shankly's first success came in 1961–62 as Liverpool lifted the Second Division Championship. Two years later the Anfield team were League Champions and they followed that up in 1965 by winning the FA Cup for the first time in their history. Over the next nine years, Shankly ruled supreme as Liverpool lifted two more League titles as well as

the UEFA Cup and the FA Cup for a second time. In 1974, following the Reds' FA Cup victory, Bill Shankly shocked the football world by resigning.

SHANLEY, Frank

Goalkeeper

Born: Preston, 1891.
Career: PRESTON NORTH END, 1913.

■ Goalkeeper Frank Shanley joined North End from local junior football before the start of the 1913–14 season as cover for the club's regular 'keeper Bert Taylor. Shanley made just one appearance for North End in that relegation season when he kept a clean sheet in a 2–0 win over fellow relegation side Derby County.

SHARKEY, Bernard John

Inside-right

Born: Middlesbrough, 25 March 1894.
Career: Grangetown. PRESTON NORTH END, 1920. Barrow, 1921. Tranmere Rovers, 1922.

■ Inside-right Bernard Sharkey made just a single Football League appearance for Preston in the 1920–21 season when he replaced Frank Jefferies for the local derby against Bolton Wanderers at Deepdale. The Trotters were challenging for the title and ran out 2–1 winners against a Preston side that were perilously close to the foot of the table. Sharkey left Deepdale to play for Barrow in what was the inaugural season in the Football League and scored 14 goals in 36 games. He then joined Tranmere Rovers where he finished his first-class career.

SHARP, James

Right-half

Born: Jamestown, 1869.
Career: PRESTON NORTH END, 1891. Darwen, 1896. Reading.

■ James Sharp played his first game for North End against Notts County on the opening day of the 1891–92 season. He was an important member of the Preston side for five seasons and helped the club finish as runners-up in the First Division in his first two seasons at Deepdale. At the start of the 1895–96 season, Sharp's last with the club, he was part of the Preston side invited by neighbours Bolton to play a friendly to mark the opening of their new Burnden Park ground. North End spoiled the party by winning 1–0, with Sharp scoring the goal. Sharp later had a season playing for Darwen before joining Reading in the Southern League.

SHARP, Raymond

Left-back

Born: Stirling, 16 November 1969.
Career: Gairdoch United. Dunfermline Athletic. Stenhousemuir (loan). PRESTON NORTH END, 1994. Dunfermline Athletic.

■ Ray Sharp had made 161 appearances for Dunfermline Athletic when he arrived at Deepdale in October 1994. He did not have the best of debuts as North End lost 3–1 to Hartlepool United. Nevertheless, he held his place in the side, making 21 appearances and helping the club reach the Play-offs. Calm and assured in possession, he overlapped well and set up a number of goals for the club's strike force of Conroy and Smart. Quick in recovery and a strong and determined tackler, the former Scotland Under-21 international later rejoined Dunfermline Athletic and continued to give the Pars excellent service.

SHAW, George Rickerby

Winger

Born: Withnell Mill, 7 April 1904.
Died: 1987.
Career: Withnell St Josephs. Horwich RMI. Brinscall. Accrington Stanley, 1925. PRESTON NORTH END, 1926. Wigan Borough, 1927. Southport, 1927. Darwen.

■ After playing local junior football for a number of teams, winger George Shaw joined Accrington Stanley. Although he found the net in his first game for them, he was released at the end of his only season with the club. Shaw then joined Preston for the 1926–27 campaign but figured in only three matches; the first was a 2–0 defeat of Wolves. Recalled to the side for the final two games of the season, Shaw and his teammates were on the receiving end of two heavy defeats: 3–0 at Reading and 5–1 at Portsmouth. On leaving Preston, he had brief spells with Wigan Borough and Southport before ending his career with Darwen.

SHAW, Graham Paul

Forward

Born: Stoke, 7 June 1967.
Career: Stoke City, 1985. PRESTON NORTH END, 1989. Stoke City, 1992. Plymouth Argyle, 1994 (loan). Rochdale, 1995.

■ Graham Shaw began his career with his home-town club, Stoke City, after joining them as an apprentice. He soon showed that as well as creating goalscoring chances for others, he could also find the net himself with great regularity. In the summer of 1989, Preston manager John McGrath paid £70,000 to bring Shaw to Deepdale and he made a goalscoring debut on the opening day of the 1989–90 season in a 3–1 defeat by Rotherham. On his home debut in a League Cup-tie against Tranmere Rovers, he netted a hat-trick but the Wirral-based club won 4–3. Niggling injuries hampered his progress throughout the season, but in 1990–91 he was the club's leading scorer with 15 goals. The following season, Shaw was North End's most consistent player and it came as a surprise when he was allowed to rejoin Stoke. He helped the

Potters win the Second Division Championship in 1992–93 and had scored 29 goals in 165 games in his two spells when, following a loan spell with Plymouth Argyle, he signed for Rochdale. Injuries again marred his progress at Spotland and he was eventually released.

SHEARS, Albert Edward

Centre-half, centre-forward

Born: Newcastle-upon-Tyne, 12 May 1900.
Died: 1954.
Career: Spen Black and White. PRESTON NORTH END, 1921. Doncaster Rovers, 1923. Aberaman. Liverpool, 1925. Tranmere Rovers, 1930. Wigan Borough, 1931. Barnsley, 1931. Aldershot, 1932. Morecambe.

■ Preston North End were Bert Shears' first Football League club in a career that saw him play for seven different League teams. He made his North End debut in a 1–1 draw against Cardiff City, but made just one more appearance before moving on to Doncaster Rovers. Unable to make much of an impression at Belle Vue, he drifted into non-League football before signing for Liverpool. He was at Anfield for four seasons before he crossed the Mersey to join Tranmere Rovers. Tranmere were the club that Shears made most appearances for (27), as they finished fourth in the Third Division North in 1930–31. He continued to move from club to club before ending his playing days back in the North West with Morecambe.

SHERRY, Alexander

Left-back

Born: Bonnybridge, 1904.
Career: Denny Hibernian. PRESTON NORTH END, 1929. Marseille (France).

■ Signed from Scottish junior club Denny Hibernian, Alex Sherry played his first game for North End in a 2–2 draw at Bristol City during the early part of the 1929–30 season. He had a run of four games in the League side but, once Kerr had recovered from his injury, he was back in the reserves. Sherry doubled his number of appearances the following season, but after playing in the opening two games of the 1931–32 season he left to try his luck on the Continent with Marseille.

SHORROCK, James

Outside-left

Born: Preston, 1881.
Career: PRESTON NORTH END, 1902.

■ Winger James Shorrock made just one appearance for Preston North End. During the 1902–03 season he replaced Fred Fenton, the club's regular outside-left, in a 2–1 defeat at Bristol City. It was Shorrock's cross that set up North End's goal for Percy Smith, but even so he never appeared again.

SIDDALL, Barry Alfred

Goalkeeper

Born: Ellesmere Port, 12 September 1954.
Career: Bolton Wanderers, 1972. Sunderland, 1976. Darlington, 1980 (loan). Port Vale, 1982. Blackpool, 1983 (loan). Stoke City, 1985. Tranmere Rovers, 1985 (loan). Manchester City, 1986 (loan). Blackpool, 1986. Stockport County, 1989. Hartlepool United, 1990. West Bromwich Albion, 1990. Mossley. Carlisle United, 1990. Chester City, 1991. Northwich Victoria. PRESTON NORTH END, 1992.

■ Barry Siddall began his long career with Bolton Wanderers where he was a member of the club's successful youth team. He won England Youth honours before displacing Charlie Wright as the club's first-choice 'keeper towards the end of the 1972–73 season. Siddall made a great impact on the club's return to the Second Division and played in 133 consecutive games before Sunderland paid £80,000 for his services in September 1976. He went on to make 167 League appearances for the Wearsiders, helping them win promotion to the top flight in 1979–80. After a loan spell at Darlington, Siddall joined Port Vale. Loan spells at Blackpool and Stoke followed before he joined the Potters on a permanent basis. Following a mistake in the televised game against Spurs, when he miskicked and allowed Crooks to score, he went on loan to Tranmere and Manchester City before moving around a number of clubs. Siddall had just turned 38 when he played his one and only game for North End in December 1992. He replaced Simon Farnworth, another former Bolton 'keeper, in a game against Port Vale, but had a disastrous time as the Valiants won 5–2 at Deepdale.

SIMMONS, Henry Richard

Inside-right, centre-forward

Born: Sunderland, 1910.
Career: Bankhead Albion. West Ham United, 1928. Sunderland, 1928. Bankhead Albion. Hartlepool United, 1930. PRESTON NORTH END, 1931. Chorley. Oxford City. Aldershot, 1933.

■ After failing to make the grade with both West Ham United and Sunderland, versatile forward Harry Simmons joined Hartlepool United. Although they had a poor season in the Third Division North, Simmons was impressive and scored 17 goals in 31 games. This prompted North End to offer him terms before the start of the 1931–32 season. He played the first of his eight games for the club on the opening day of the season in a 2–2 draw against Oldham Athletic. Simmons scored three goals in his eight appearances including the winner against Southampton and both goals in a 4–2 defeat at Barnsley. After being replaced by Ted Harper, he played non-League football for Chorley and Oxford City before returning to League action with Aldershot who were embarking on their second season in the Football League.

SIMPSON, Reginald

Defender

Born: Blackburn, 14 June 1923.
Career: PRESTON NORTH END, 1943. Carlisle United, 1948.

■ Reginald Simpson, a Blackburn-born defender, joined North End during World War Two. He played in four of the club's First Division games following the resumption of League football in 1946–47. All of the games in which Simpson appeared produced a flurry of goals: after North End beat Brentford 5–2 on his debut, they thrashed Huddersfield 6–2 and lost to Arsenal and Wolves by the same 4–1 scoreline. Simpson spent the following season in the reserves before moving to play for Carlisle United in the Third Division North.

SINGLETON, Anthony Joseph

Centre-half

Born: Preston, 30 March 1936.
Career: PRESTON NORTH END, 1955.

■ Tony Singleton made his Preston debut alongside other North End legends Alan Spavin and Peter Thompson in a 2–0 defeat of Arsenal in August 1960. However, a rib injury sustained in the first half curtailed his contribution for the rest of the game. Nevertheless, after missing the following game, he returned and went on to play in 37 games that season. Unfortunately, the end of his first season in the side ended with North End relegated to Division Two. Singleton was a solid and totally reliable defender. He played in a total of 287 League games for the club without ever getting on the score sheet. However, it was Singleton's goal in the FA Cup semi-final against Swansea in 1964 that helped the club reach their first FA Cup Final in 10 years. He missed very few games in his time at Deepdale and played his final game in North End colours in a 4–1 defeat at Blackpool in December 1967.

SISSOKO, Habib

Forward

Born: Juvisy Orge, France, 24 May 1971.
Career: Louhans (France). PRESTON NORTH END, 1998.

■ Habib Sissoko was completely unknown to Preston North End fans

when he arrived at Deepdale in February 1998 on a free transfer from French club Louhans. He was signed on the strength of just one reserve game. Sissoko made his debut as a substitute in a 1–1 home draw with Wycombe Wanderers and won over the fans with his obvious talent and commitment. Good in the air and displaying strength and skill on the ground, he was released after just seven weeks at the club following a much publicised off-field incident.

SKORA, Eric

Midfield

Born: Metz, France, 20 August 1981.
Career: Nancy (France). PRESTON NORTH END, 2001. Kilmarnock, 2004 (loan). Walsall, 2005 (loan). Kilmarnock, 2006.

■ Having failed to break into the first team with French club Nancy, Eric Skora signed a short-term contract for Preston following a successful trial period. After an impressive debut at Walsall, he scored on his FA Cup debut at Brighton in only his second start. He also rattled the post with a header against Gillingham before being forced out of contention with a foot injury in the next match. In the early part of the 2002–03 season, Skora

produced some excellent displays on the right-side of midfield: he tackled tenaciously and always looked comfortable on the ball. He only scored one goal that season, in the League Cup, but was the First Division player with the highest number of shots without scoring in the League. The following season Skora went on loan to Kilmarnock and, though he had not scored in 42 League outings for Preston, he netted a goal for Kilmarnock against Celtic. He returned to Deepdale but, following a change of management, his first-team opportunities dwindled. Skora later had a spell on loan with Walsall before returning north of the border to sign for Kilmarnock on a permanent basis.

SMART, Allan Andrew Colin

Forward

Born: Perth, 8 July 1974.
Career: Caledonian Thistle. PRESTON NORTH END, 1994. Carlisle United, 1995 (loan). Northampton Town, 1996 (loan). Carlisle United, 1996. Watford, 1998. Hibernian, 2001 (loan). Stoke City, 2001 (loan). Oldham Athletic, 2002. Dundee United.

■ Allan Smart was signed by Preston for £15,000 from Caledonian Thistle in November 1994. He made his debut in a 1–0 defeat at Chesterfield before scoring in his first game at Deepdale in an FA Cup tie with Walsall. Smart scored six League goals as North End reached the Play-offs, including five in a nine-game spell midway through the campaign. A strong, aggressive and determined centre-forward, he established an instant rapport with the North End faithful. The following season Smart lost out due to the form of Andy Saville and he went on loan to both Carlisle United and Northampton Town. He signed for Carlisle on a permanent basis as part of the deal that took David Reeves to Preston. In his first season at Brunton Park, he topped United's scoring charts and helped them win the Auto Windscreens Shield Final at Wembley. Despite being hampered by injuries in 1997–98, he did score one of Carlisle's goals in their 3–0 defeat of North End at Deepdale. Smart then signed for Watford for a fee of just £75,000 and soon

impressed. Though hampered by injuries, he scored a memorable goal in Watford's Play-off victory over Bolton. In the Premiership, Smart scored a number of vital goals and perfected his goal celebration – mimicking the shot-putter on the Scott's Porridge Oats packet – and was rewarded with a year's supply of the breakfast cereal. Unfortunately, he began to endure a frustrating time with injuries and, after loan spells with Hibs and Stoke, he signed for Oldham Athletic. However, following two breaches of the club's disciplinary code, his contract was cancelled and he returned north of the border to play for Dundee United.

SMITH, Albert Charles

Outside-right, centre-forward

Born: Glasgow, 1900.
Career: Petershill. Manchester United, 1926. PRESTON NORTH END, 1927. Dolphin. Carlisle United, 1932. Ayr United.

■ Following a handful of games for Manchester United, versatile forward Albert Smith joined Preston for the 1927–28 season. After playing in a goalless draw against Hull City, Smith played in a total of eight games that campaign without finding the net. He made amends early the following season, netting two of Preston's goals in a 5–2 win over Wolves. Although he never really got an extended run in the side, he

did score in three successive outings towards the end of the 1929–30 season. He started the 1930–31 campaign in fine form but an injury curtailed his appearances. Smith later played for Carlisle United before returning home to Scotland to play for Ayr United.

SMITH, Alexander

Goalkeeper

Born: Lancaster, 29 October 1938.
Career: Weymouth. Accrington Stanley, 1961. Bolton Wanderers, 1962. Halifax Town, 1968. PRESTON NORTH END, 1976.

■ After Accrington Stanley lost their Football League status at the end of the 1960–61 season, goalkeeper Alex Smith joined Bolton Wanderers where he was understudy to England international Eddie Hopkinson for five seasons. In January 1968, Smith joined Halifax Town and was the Shaymen's first-choice 'keeper for the next eight seasons. In his first full season with the club he helped them win promotion from the Fourth Division. Smith went on to appear in 341 League games for the Yorkshire side before joining North End in the summer of 1976. He was approaching 38 years of age when he made his debut as a replacement for Roy Tunks in a 3–1 defeat at Mansfield. He later had a run of seven successive games when he generally acquitted himself well.

SMITH, Andrew William

Forward

Born: Lisburn, 25 September 1980.
Career: Ballyclare Comrades. Sheffield United, 1999. Bury, 2000 (loan). Glentoran. PRESTON NORTH END, 2004. Stockport County, 2004 (loan).

■ Northern Ireland international Andy Smith started out with Sheffield United, but in his early days at Bramall Lane he was loaned out to Bury to gain more first-team experience. On returning to United he contributed to the reserve side's double success, featuring in the Avon Insurance League Cup. victory over Stoke when he scored the last goal in a 3–1 win. Despite his promise, he was released in February 2002 and returned to Ireland to play for Glentoran. National

team manager Sammy McIlroy selected the free-scoring Smith for the full Northern Ireland side and, though he has yet to hit the target at this level, he has won 18 caps. In July 2004, Preston North End came calling and Smith moved to Deepdale for a fee of £150,000. He took time to settle in – a process not helped by his lack of goals. Smith was loaned out to Stockport but returned to Deepdale where he made several appearances from the bench. A change of boss soon after his arrival did not help his cause and neither did a patella tendonitis knee injury.

SMITH, E. David

Centre-forward, inside-left

Born: Preston, 1872.
Career: PRESTON NORTH END, 1893.

■ A player whose first name cannot be traced in any of the records, Smith made his North End debut in a 4–2 defeat by Nottingham Forest in March 1894. He scored his side's first goal after less than a minute. The following season he was the club's leading scorer in the League with 12 goals including five in his last four appearances of a campaign in which the club finished fourth in Division One. After a promising start to the 1895–96 season, Smith left Deepdale to continue his career in local football.

SMITH, George

Inside-right

Born: Preston, 28 July 1879.
Died: 1908.
Career: St Christopher's. Leyland.
PRESTON NORTH END, 1899. Aston
Villa, 1901. New Brompton. Blackburn
Rovers, 1903. Plymouth Argyle.
Southampton.

■ George Smith played for local side Leyland before he joined Preston North End for the start of the 1899–1900 season. He appeared in eight games as Preston struggled near the foot of the First Division. He appeared much more regularly in 1900–01 and scored his only goal for the club against Nottingham Forest, but he could not prevent the club from losing their top-flight status. Smith moved on to Aston Villa for a brief spell and then on to Blackburn. He played in 58 games for the Ewood Park club before he joined Southern League Plymouth Argyle. His last club, Southampton, were also in the Southern League at the time but Smith, who looked a promising acquisition, tragically died suddenly in the close season of 1908.

SMITH, James

Inside-left

Born: Preston, 1874.
Career: PRESTON NORTH END, 1895.

■ Inside-forward James Smith made five League appearances for North End during the course of the 1895–96 season. His first game in Preston colours was a seven-goal thriller against Wolves – a match North End won 4–3. Smith's last game for the Lilywhites came against Champions-elect Aston Villa: Preston lost 1–0.

SMITH, James Alexander Grant

Defender

Born: Arbroath, 16 October 1937.
Career: Arbroath Lads. PRESTON
NORTH END, 1955. Stockport County,
1969.

■ A cultured defender, Jimmy Smith made his debut for North End in a 4–3 defeat to Manchester United at Deepdale in December 1958. In Smith's first full season with the club he represented the Army at right-half, centre-half and left-half in games against the FA at Newcastle, The Navy at Aldershot and the Belgian Army in Brussels. When Preston lost their First Division place in 1960–61, Smith even played a few games at centre-forward and got his name on the score sheet three times. Smith, who was a member of the Preston side beaten 3–2 in the 1964 FA Cup Final, went on to appear in a total of 314 League games before he left Deepdale in the summer of 1969 to sign for Stockport County. Unable to prevent County's relegation to the Fourth Division, Smith – one of North End's most popular players – decided to retire.

SMITH, John

Forward

Born: Coatbridge, 27 November 1956.
Career: PRESTON NORTH END, 1974.
LA Skyhawks (US). Halifax Town, 1979.

■ Having worked his way up through the ranks, John Smith made his debut in a 4–2 defeat at Luton during Preston's Second Division relegation season of 1973–74. He again figured in only a handful of games the following season but managed to net his first goal for the club in a 2–2 draw at Colchester United. Smith then began to appear on a more regular basis and in 1977–78 he helped the club win promotion to the Second Division. After making just one start in Division Two, Smith left to play in the NASL for Los Angeles Skyhawks. On his return to these shores, he spent a season with Halifax Town.

SMITH, Percy James

Centre-forward, centre-half

Born: Burbage Spring, 16 February 1880.
Died: 1959.
Career: Hinckley Town. PRESTON
NORTH END, 1902. Blackburn Rovers,
1910. Fleetwood. Barrow, 1921.

■ Percy Smith joined North End for the 1902–03 season following his impressive goalscoring feats with non-League Hinckley Town. Smith was the club's leading scorer in the League with 16 goals, including a hat-trick in a 5–1 defeat of Burslem Port Vale. Smith's best season at Deepdale was 1903–04, when he scored 26 goals, including another treble in a 4–1 win at Leicester Fosse. It was Smith's goals in the main that led to Preston winning that season's Second Division Championship. Smith continued to find the net in the top flight and, indeed, netted two hat-tricks over the course of the campaign in wins over Sunderland and Notts County. He reached double figures again the following season and, after a season in which he found the net eight times, he was back as leading scorer in 1907–08 with 12 goals. In 1909–10, Smith played the last of his 240 League games – in which he scored 94 goals – and left to join rivals Blackburn Rovers. The Preston supporters were upset at seeing him go and he proved it was a mistake for the North End board to let him go by winning two Championship medals with the East Lancashire club in 1911–12 and 1913–14. After World War One, Smith played non-League football for Fleetwood before returning to the League with Barrow for whom he made a handful of appearances.

SMITH, Richard

Centre-forward

Born: Preston, 1887.
Career: PRESTON NORTH END, 1908.

■ Local-born centre-forward Richard Smith played in six First Division games during the course of the 1908–09 season when North End finished the campaign in mid-table. Replacing the injured Percy Smith, his only goal for the club came in a 2–0 home win over Blackburn Rovers. However, with Percy Smith restored to full fitness, he went back into the reserves before leaving the club in the close season.

SMITH, Thomas

Outside-right

Born: Maryport, 26 November 1876.
Died: 1937.
Career: PRESTON NORTH END, 1895.
Tottenham Hotspur. PRESTON NORTH
END, 1903. Carlisle United. Maryport
Tradesmen.

■ Winger Tom Smith scored on his Preston debut as they drew 1–1 at home to Blackburn Rovers in November 1895. He played in most of the remaining games of the season and scored some vital goals towards the end of he campaign to help keep the club in the First Division. He was in fine form in 1896–97 and helped North End finish fourth in Division One. The following season saw two Tom Smiths in the Preston line up, but not for long because this Tom Smith joined Tottenham Hotspur in May 1898. He proved to be one of the North London club's most influential players, helping them win the Southern League title in 1899–1900 and the FA Cup in 1901. Though he never won full international honours, Smith did play for an England XI against a Scotland XI in a match to raise funds for the fledgling Players' Union. A vital cog in the Spurs team, the club were most surprised and upset when Smith announced his retirement at the end of the 1901–02 season and returned to his native Cumberland. In March 1904, Preston persuaded him out of retirement and he scored three goals in eight games to help them take the Second Division Championship. He later appeared for Carlisle United in the early years of their existence and was still playing in 1909 for Maryport Tradesmen in the West Cumberland League.

SMITH, Thomas

Outside-right

Born: Ashton-in-Makerfield, 1876.
Career: Ashton Athletic. Ashton Town.
PRESTON NORTH END, 1897.
Southampton. Queen's Park Rangers.
PRESTON NORTH END, 1900.

■ Tom Smith played for local clubs Ashton Athletic and Ashton Town before signing for Preston North End in 1897. At the time there were two Tom Smiths, both outside-rights, playing for the club – one was a star, the other was a most average player. When Southampton and Spurs signed T Smith, both clubs were under the impression that they had acquired the star. Smith played Southern League football for the Saints and Queen's Park Rangers before returning to Deepdale for a brief second spell.

SMITH, Thomas McCall

Centre-half

Born: Fenwick, 4 October 1909.
Died: 21 June 1998.
Career: Sinclair Celtic. Cumnock Juveniles. Kilmarnock. Galston (loan). PRESTON NORTH END, 1936.

■ Tom Smith was a dominating centre-half north of the border with Kilmarnock, whom he joined at the end of the 1920s and played for with distinction until December 1936. During that period he won a Scottish Cup runners'-up medal in 1932 after Killie were beaten by Rangers in the replayed

Final. Smith also made his full international debut against England in 1934 and in October 1936 he represented the Scottish League against the Football League. Two months later he was on his way to Preston North End, making his debut in a 1–1 home draw against Portsmouth. After that he shared the number-five shirt with Bill Tremelling but lost out when the line up for the 1937 FA Cup Final against Sunderland was announced. It was a different story the following season as he not only lined up at centre-half in the 1938 FA Cup Final but also captained the side to a 1–0 win over Huddersfield Town. That same year he won his second cap for Scotland as they beat England at Wembley. He continued to play for Preston during the war years and also 'guested' for Burnley, Rochdale and Manchester United. Following the hostilities, he rejoined Kilmarnock to become the Rugby Park club's secretary-manager before returning to live in Lancashire.

SMITHIES, George Herbert

Centre-forward

Born: Ribchester, 1907.
Career: Northern Nomads. PRESTON NORTH END, 1929. Birmingham, 1931. Darley Dale. Measham Motors.

■ George Smithies was a late arrival into the League game after a successful amateur career with Northern Nomads while he was busy completing his teaching studies. Despite being somewhat undersized for a striker, he met with early success after joining Preston North End. Smithies scored on his debut in a 4–1 defeat of Bradford Park Avenue and went on to net nine times in his first nine games. He finished the season with 10 goals in 18 games. After a couple of appearances in 1930–31, his career went into decline and he left Deepdale to play for Birmingham, but after just one appearance he returned to non-League action.

SNEDDON, David

Inside-forward

Born: Kilwinning, 24 April 1936.
Career: Dundee. PRESTON NORTH END, 1959.

Signed from Scottish First Division side Dundee, Dave Sneddon made his League debut for North End in a 2–2 home draw against Spurs on the final day of the 1958–59 season. The following season he missed just two games and scored six goals, which were often spectacular; this included four in five games. He helped the club finish ninth in the First Division. However, Sneddon was unable to prevent the club from being relegated in 1960–61. The Scotland Under-23 international stayed with the club for one more season, taking his tally of League goals to 17 in 91 appearances, before he returned to Scotland.

SNOOKES, Eric

Left-back

Born: Birmingham, 6 March 1955.
Career: PRESTON NORTH END, 1973. Crewe Alexandra, 1974. Southport, 1975. Rochdale, 1978. Bolton Wanderers, 1983.

Tough-tackling left-back Eric Snookes started out with Preston North End, making his debut in a 2–0 defeat at Brighton towards the end of the 1972–73 season. He appeared in the last seven games of the season and helped Preston draw their last game at home to Burnley. This result ensured that they would be playing Second Division football the

following season. Snookes had a run of 13 games midway through the 1973–74 campaign, but this was a season when the club were relegated to Division Three. After a spell with Crewe, he spent three seasons playing for Southport and in each of those campaigns they finished in the same position: one place off the foot of Division Four. He then joined Rochdale, making 183 League appearances for the Spotland club, before ending his career with Bolton Wanderers.

SNOW, Simon Gordon

Forward

Born: Sheffield, 3 April 1966.
Career: Scunthorpe United, 1983. Sutton Town. PRESTON NORTH END, 1989.

Simon Snow worked his way up through the ranks at Scunthorpe, but

after a couple of first-team appearances he left the Irons to play non-League football for a number of clubs. The last of these was Sutton Town before he joined Preston in the summer of 1989. Snow made his League debut in a 3–2 home defeat by Bury and, though Steve Harper replaced him in the second half, he kept his place in the side for the League Cup visit to Tranmere Rovers. These were, however, his only games for the club.

SPARK, Alexander McAlpine

Centre-half

Born: Stenhousemuir, 16 October 1949.
Died: August 1993.
Career: PRESTON NORTH END, 1966. Motherwell. Bradford City, 1976.

Defender Alex Spark played junior football in his native Stenhousemuir. He was tracked by a number of clubs from both north and south of the border but,

on the advice of his father, he left Scotland to sign for Preston in the mid-1960s. Spark made his first-team debut from the bench, replacing Jim McNab in a 1–0 defeat at Rotherham in December 1967. A player with a determined but cool style of play, he soon found favour with the Preston fans. However, these were awkward times for Preston and Spark, along with young players like Ricky Heppolette, was learning his trade in difficult circumstances. Though his main forte was as a cultured defender, he liked nothing better than to help out in attack and he was extremely dangerous at set pieces. He missed very few games in North End's Third Division Championship-winning season of 1970–71 and was an important member of the side over the next couple of seasons as the club struggled to retain its Second Division status. They were eventually relegated again in 1973–74 and Spark, who had played in 225 League games, had a brief spell with Motherwell before ending his first-class career with Bradford City. In his first season at Valley Parade he helped City win promotion from the Fourth Division. Sadly, the popular Scot contracted a rare illness called Bueghar's Disease and had to have both legs amputated. This failed to save his life and he died aged only 43.

SPARROW, Paul

Right-back

Born: Wandsworth, 24 March 1975.
Career: Crystal Palace, 1993. PRESTON NORTH END, 1996. Rochdale, 1998. Lancaster City.

■ Right-back Paul Sparrow was languishing in the reserves at Crystal Palace when he was signed by Preston boss Gary Peters towards the end of the club's 1995–96 Third Division Championship-winning season. Calm

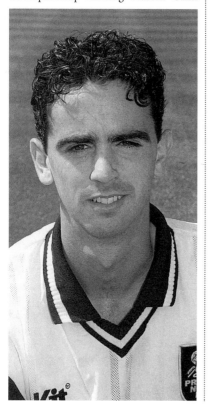

and steady with a good turn of speed and accurate distribution, he went on to play in 13 games and so win a Third Division Championship medal. Injured on the first day of pre-season training, he made few appearances the following season. Sparrow was appointed captain of the club's reserve team and played all across the back four before he appeared in the penultimate game of the 1997–98 season against Wrexham. He was released in the close season and joined Rochdale. Sparrow suffered a torrid start to his Spotland career but, following the club's decision to change to a wing-back system, he seemed to flourish. Even so, he was released after just one season and moved into non-League football with Lancaster City.

SPAVIN, Alan

Midfield

Born: Lancaster, 20 February 1942.
Career: PRESTON NORTH END, 1959. Washington Diplomats (US). PRESTON NORTH END, 1977.

■ Lancaster-born midfielder Alan Spavin was spotted playing in local junior football for Carnforth Rangers and taken to Deepdale in the summer of 1959. Spavin made a goalscoring League debut in a 2–0 win over Arsenal in August 1960 and later starred in North End's youth team which made it to the FA Youth Cup Final in 1960, only to lose out to Chelsea. He appeared in nine first-team games in that 1960–61 season but could not prevent the club from being relegated to Division Two. Spavin soon found himself a regular in Preston's first team and quickly established a reputation as a midfield dynamo. The midfielder was always willing to help out in both defence and attack and, though not a prolific scorer, it was his tenacity and perseverance that kept the team going. He played in the 1964 FA Cup Final defeat by West Ham United and was the club's most consistent player throughout the decade. Spavin did score two goals on the final day of the 1970–71 season as North End beat Rotherham United 3–0 to clinch the Third Division Championship. In 1973, Spavin left Deepdale for a new life across the Atlantic with NASL side Washington

Diplomats. His career in the US went quite well but he rejoined North End before the start of the 1977–78 season. He went on to take his total of Football League appearances for the club to 424 before hanging up his boots.

SPEAK, George

Left-back

Born: Blackburn, 7 November 1890.
Died: 10 March 1953.
Career: Clitheroe Central. Darwen. Liverpool, 1910. Grimsby Town, 1911. Gainsborough Trinity. West Ham United. PRESTON NORTH END, 1919. Leeds United, 1923.

■ Left-back George Speak was a rugged and fearless character who was noted for his powerful clearance kicking. He played for Clitheroe Central and Darwen before having trials with Liverpool. Unable to make the grade at Anfield, he joined Grimsby Town in the summer of 1911 and won his League spurs with them before joining Gainsborough Trinity. Speak later played for Southern League West Ham United before 'guesting' for North End during World War One. When the hostilities ended, he signed for North End and made his League debut in the 4–0 defeat at Blackburn on the opening day of the 1919–20 season. Speak found himself in and out of the side over the next four seasons as the Lilywhites struggled near the foot of Division One. On leaving Deepdale, he finished his career with Leeds United by helping them win the 1923–24 Second Division Championship.

SPENCE, George

Inside-forward

Born: Rothesay, 1876.
Career: St Mirren. Derby County, 1897. Reading. PRESTON NORTH END, 1901. Reading. Southampton. Hull City, 1905. Clyde.

■ George Spence began his career with St Mirren before coming south to sign for Derby County. He could not force his way into the Rams' League side and went to play Southern League football for Reading before joining North End in 1901. He made his debut on the opening day of the 1901–02 season in a

3–1 defeat at the hands of eventual Champions West Bromwich Albion. Spence went on to score seven goals in 19 games to help the club finish third in Division Two. After another brief spell with Reading he had a season each with Southampton and Hull City before returning north of the border to see out his career with Clyde.

SPENCE, William Edward

Inside-forward

Born: Preston, 1887.
Career: PRESTON NORTH END, 1909.

William Spence made a goalscoring debut for North End on the final day of the 1909–10 season, netting the only goal of the game against local rivals Bolton Wanderers. However, he failed to establish himself in the Preston side the following season and made just one more appearance before being released by the Deepdale club.

SQUIRES, James Alexander

Centre-half

Born: Preston, 15 November 1975.
Career: PRESTON NORTH END, 1994. Stafford Rangers (loan). Mansfield Town, 1997 (loan). Dunfermline Athletic.

Jamie Squires was potentially a big star of the future when he made his

debut for North End in a 2–0 home win over Walsall towards the end of the 1993–94 season. He went on to play in the last four games and help the club reach the Play-offs. The following season he went on loan to Stafford Rangers and the experience he gained showed on his return to the North End side. Injuries hampered Squires' progress in 1995–96, though when he did turn out he continued to display coolness under pressure and strong defensive qualities. The following campaign he was never a first choice for Preston at full-back or in his preferred central-defensive role, though he did captain the club's Championship-winning reserve side. Following a loan spell with Mansfield, Squires left North End to continue his career north of the border with Dunfermline Athletic.

STALLARD, Mark

Forward

Born: Derby, 24 October 1974.
Career: Derby County, 1991. Fulham, 1994 (loan). Bradford City, 1996. PRESTON NORTH END, 1997 (loan). Wycombe Wanderers, 1997. Notts County, 1999. Barnsley, 2004. Chesterfield, 2004 (loan). Notts County, 2005 (loan).

Mark Stallard began his career with his home-town club and was just 16 when he made his Derby County debut as a substitute against Oxford United in September 1991. However, he did not fit into Jim Smith's plans and after a loan spell with Fulham he joined Bradford City. The bustling striker was instrumental in the Bantams reaching the 1995–96 Play-offs. He scored the deciding goal that took them to Wembley and the second in a 2–0 win over Notts County that confirmed First Division football for the Valley Parade club. A drop in form in 1996–97 saw Stallard join North End on loan and he impressed in his four appearances for the club. Stallard scored against Bury before leaving the club abruptly to sign for Wycombe Wanderers. He was the Chairboys' leading scorer in his first season and his 18 goals included a hat-trick against Walsall. Troubled by a medial ligament injury, he later signed for Notts County. He rediscovered his

shooting boots at Meadow Lane and was the club's top scorer for most of his time there, with a best of 24 in 2002–03. The club's financial situation led to Stallard joining Barnsley. Later finding himself surplus to requirements, he went on loan to Chesterfield before returning to Notts County in a similar role.

STANSFIELD, Harold

Outside-right

Born: Manchester, 21 July 1878.
Career: Berry's. PRESTON NORTH END, 1899. Stockport County, 1900. Tottenham Hotspur. Luton Town. Bristol Rovers.

Harry Stansfield played four games for North End during the 1899–1900 season as the club just avoided the drop into Division Two, finishing a point ahead of Burnley after a 2–0 defeat of rivals Blackburn on the final day of the campaign. This was Harry Stansfield's last appearance in North End colours but he signed off with a goal in the victory. He joined Stockport County and went on to score 11 goals in 88 games before joining Spurs when County failed to gain re-election. Able to play in any of the forward positions, Stansfield was a regular in his first season at White Hart Lane but then lost out. He stayed with Spurs for four years before moving to Luton Town and finally Bristol Rovers where he finished his career shortly after World War One.

STEELE, David Morton

Wing-half

Born: Carluke, 26 July 1894.
Died: May 1964.
Career: Armadale. St Mirren. Douglas Water Thistle. Bristol Rovers, 1920. Huddersfield Town, 1922. PRESTON NORTH END, 1929. Bury, 1930. Ashton National.

■ David Steele mixed his job as a miner with that of footballer with Armadale and St Mirren. After World War One, he joined Scottish junior club Douglas Water Thistle before he was transferred to Southern League Bristol Rovers in November 1919. The following season he made his bow in the newly formed Third Division. A tireless wing-half, he moved to Huddersfield Town in May 1922. Towards the end of his first season, after recovering from pneumonia, Steele became the club's first Scottish international. With Town, he gained a hat-trick of League Championship medals and an FA Cup runners'-up medal. Steele had made 203 appearances for the Yorkshire club when he joined North End on a free transfer in the summer of 1929. Steele made his Preston debut in a 2–0 defeat at Reading on the first day of the 1929–30 season and went on to make 29 appearances. His two goals came in the 6–4 defeat by Blackpool and on the final day of the season against Bristol City. On leaving Preston, he became Bury's player-coach before joining Cheshire League side Ashton National. After coaching in Denmark, he was appointed coach to Sheffield United, prior to managing Bradford Park Avenue. He later took charge of his beloved Huddersfield before taking over the reins at Bradford City. In doing so he become one of the rare breed to have been in charge of both Bradford clubs.

STEPHENSON, George Ternent

Inside-forward

Born: New Delaval, 3 September 1900.
Died: 18 August 1971.
Career: New Delaval Villa. Leeds City, 1919. Aston Villa, 1919. Stourbridge (loan). Aston Villa, 1921. Derby County, 1927. Sheffield Wednesday, 1930. PRESTON NORTH END, 1933. Charlton Athletic, 1934.

■ When Leeds City were expelled from the Football League in 1919, their players were put up for auction at the Metropole Hotel in Leeds in October of that year. George Stephenson was sold to Aston Villa, where he joined his brother Clem. He was soon loaned to Stourbridge but on his return to Villa Park he developed into a thoughtful and cultured schemer, scoring 22 goals in 95 games during seven seasons with Villa. He moved to Derby County in November 1927 for a fee of £2,000 and, after making his debut against Everton, he scored 13 goals in the next 11 League games. That same season he won full international honours for England and scored four in a 5–4 defeat of Grimsby Town. Stephenson was an integral member of the Rams' side until he was sold to Sheffield Wednesday with Tommy Davison. Stephenson spent less than two years at Hillsborough before switching to Preston North End. His first game in North End colours was in the 2–1 defeat of Blackpool on the opening day of the 1933–34 season. Though he only spent one season at Deepdale, he was the club's leading scorer with 16 goals, including a hat-trick in a 3–1 win over Southampton. Having helped North End win promotion to the First Division, Stephenson moved to Charlton Athletic where he helped the London club win promotion from the Third Division South to the First Division in successive seasons. On hanging up his boots, he joined the coaching staff at The Valley before later ending his involvement with the game following a spell as manager of Huddersfield Town.

STEVENS, Ian David

Forward

Born: Malta, 21 October 1966.
Career: PRESTON NORTH END, 1984. Lancaster City. Stockport County, 1986. Lancaster City. Bolton Wanderers, 1987. Bury, 1991. Shrewsbury Town, 1994. Carlisle United, 1997. Wrexham, 1999. Cheltenham Town, 2000 (loan). Carlisle United, 2000. Shrewsbury Town, 2002. Gretna.

■ Born in Malta, striker Ian Stevens started his long Football League career with Preston North End, making his debut off the bench against Lincoln City in March 1985. He appeared in a handful of games towards the end of the season and scored his first goal on the final day of the campaign in a 1–0 win at York City, when the club were already relegated to the Fourth Division. Unable to make much headway the following season, he played non-League football for Lancaster City either side of a brief spell with Stockport before joining Bolton Wanderers. Though Stevens scored freely for the club's reserves – 63 in 97 games – he struggled in the first team and joined Bury. He was the Gigg Lane club's leading scorer over the next couple of seasons before moving to Shrewsbury Town. It took him a little time to find his feet at Gay Meadow but he did so eventually and scored the goals that took the club to Wembley for the Final of the Auto Windscreens Shield. In 1997, Carlisle United paid £100,000 to take Stevens to Brunton Park. His hat-trick against Bristol Rovers was the first at Brunton Park for over a decade but, even though he was the Cumbrian club's top scorer in his two seasons with the club, he left to play for Wrexham before making a surprise return to Carlisle. A first-half hat-trick against Leyton Orient helped Stevens take his tally of goals for United to 54 in 160 games. Following a second stint at Shrewsbury, he moved north to play for Gretna.

STEVENSON, James

Centre-half, centre-forward

Born: Bonhill, August 1875.
Died: 1925.
Career: Dumbarton Fereday. Dumbarton.
PRESTON NORTH END, 1895. Bristol St
George. PRESTON NORTH END, 1899.
West Bromwich Albion, 1900.
Dumbarton.

■ Signed from Scottish club Dumbarton, James Stevenson scored on his Preston debut on New Year's Day 1896 as the club played out a 1–1 draw at Sheffield Wednesday. Stevenson continued to find the net with great regularity during his time at Deepdale and in 1896–97 he scored 12 goals. This included five in the club's FA Cup run. After reaching double figures again the following season, he left to spend a season playing for Bristol St George before returning to Deepdale. Early the following campaign Stevenson, who had scored 26 goals in 82 League games for Preston, left to continue his career with West Bromwich Albion. Stevenson helped Albion win the Second Division Championship in 1901–02 and went on to appear in 120 League games for them before his career went full circle as he returned north of the border to play for Dumbarton.

STEWART, Gerald

Goalkeeper

Born: Dundee, 2 September 1946.
Career: PRESTON NORTH END, 1963.
Barnsley, 1971.

■ Goalkeeper Gerry Stewart spent eight years at Deepdale as understudy to Republic of Ireland international and North End legend Alan Kelly. During that time he made just four League appearances. The first was in a 3–2 defeat at Wolverhampton Wanderers during the 1966–67 season when the Molineux club went on to win promotion to the top flight. His next appearance was a final-day defeat at Crystal Palace in 1967–68, followed by another last-day game the next season when he kept a clean sheet in a 1–0 win at Charlton Athletic. His last appearance came in the club's relegation season of 1969–70 at Cardiff. On joining Barnsley, Stewart suffered another

relegation as the Oakwell club dropped into the Fourth Division. However, he was their first-choice 'keeper for four seasons and went on to play in 138 League games for the club.

STEWART, William Marcus Paul

Forward

Born: Bristol, 7 November 1972
Career: Bristol Rovers 1991; Huddersfield
Town 1996; Ipswich Town 2000;
Sunderland 2002; Bristol City 2005;
PRESTON NORTH END (loan)

■ Beginning his career with his home-town team Bristol Rovers, he broke a 39-year club record in 1994–95 by scoring in nine consecutive matches. Also that season he produced an excellent performance at Wembley in the Play-off Final against Huddersfield, culminating in a superb goal, which took his tally for the campaign to 23. In 1995–96 his total of 30 goals for the Pirates included the club's quickest League goal in just 28 seconds in the match against Hull City. He also netted a League Cup hat-trick against Gillingham and was selected by his colleagues for the PFA award-winning Second Division team. In the summer of 1996 he joined Huddersfield Town for a fee of £1.2 million as a replacement for Andy Booth. In just his second outing for the Yorkshire club he netted a hat-trick in the Coca-Cola Cup win over Wrexham. His fortunes at the McAlpine Stadium increased when he was partnered up front with Wayne Allison and in 1998–99 he netted his first League hat-trick against Crystal Palace. He continued to find the net and had scored 68 goals in 160 games for Huddersfield when in February 2000 he became Ipswich Town's record signing when the Suffolk club paid £2.5 million for his services. He scored for Town in the Play-off semi-final and final and was selected in the PFA award-winning First Division select. In 2000–01 he scored in seven consecutive games for Ipswich and was the Premiership's leading scorer right up to the last game of the season! He made the short-list of six for the PFA's Player of the Season and was voted Player of the Year by Ipswich fans. A broken jaw the following season seemed to knock his

confidence. In August 2002, Sunderland paid £3.25 million to take Stewart to the Stadium of Light and it was his goals that helped the club reach the Play-offs. The following season he topped the club's scoring charts as they won the Championship title. His 16 goals included hat-tricks against Gillingham and Watford. Surprisingly not offered a new contract, he joined Bristol City from where he moved to Preston on loan. Although he didn't find the net during his time at Deepdale, his experience and unselfish play helped North End record important victories towards the end of the season as they once more made the Play-offs.

STEWART, William S.

Left-half

Born: Arbroath, 1864.
Career: Strathmore. Arbroath. Black
Watch. Belfast Distillery. PRESTON
NORTH END, 1890. Everton, 1893.
Bristol City.

■ Billy Stewart first made his reputation with the Black Watch team which won the Army Cup. While stationed with the Royal Scots Greys in Ireland, he helped Belfast Distillery win the Irish Cup. Preston North End bought him out of the Army and he made his debut in a 3–0 home win over West Bromwich Albion on the first day of the 1890–91 season. He helped the club finish runners-up to Everton. One of the key features of Stewart's play was his exceptionally long throw-in, although his running and jumping technique was eventually outlawed. The following season, Stewart received his marching orders in the 5–1 home win over Burnley. He helped the club to runners'-up spot again in 1892–93 before leaving to play for Everton. He formed part of a famous Everton half-back line with Holt and Campbell and played in the 1897 FA Cup Final. Once, when the Everton team were training at Hoylake, he was the victim of a practical joke. As he slept, string was attached to every piece of the bedroom furniture. Out in the hotel corridor the rest of the team pulled on the strings as hard as they could. Stewart woke up with the biggest fright of his life! He later signed for Bristol City and was appointed captain as they established themselves as a professional club.

STILES, Norbert Peter

Wing-half

Born: Manchester, 18 May 1942.
Career: Manchester United, 1959. Middlesbrough, 1971. PRESTON NORTH END, 1973.

■ Nobby Stiles wore the number-four shirt throughout England's triumphant World Cup campaign in 1966, making his mark as a world-class player with his brilliant covering, especially against Portugal's Eusebio in the semi-final. No one will forget Nobby's antics after England had won the World Cup, putting the trophy on his head and dancing with delight. One of the hard men of British football, Stiles made his Manchester United debut against Bolton Wanderers in October 1960. He stayed in the side for the rest of the season and shared in United's successful 1963 FA Cup run, though he did not win a place in the Final. Having helped the Reds win the League Championship in 1964–65, he hardly missed a match as the club repeated the feat in 1966–67 and then won the European Cup in 1968. It has been said that many of Nobby's awkward-looking tackles in the early days were the result of him not wearing his spectacles – his tackling seemed to improve after he was fitted with contact lenses. Whatever the case, the fans abroad certainly did not like him. He was called an assassin in South America, spat at in Italy and hit on the head by a bottle in Madrid. Playing without his false teeth made him look like Dracula and, according to the French, who met him in the 1966 World Cup tournament, he was twice as dangerous. In May 1971, after

two cartilage operations, Stiles was transferred to Middlesbrough but after two seasons in the North East he joined Preston North End. Stiles made his League debut in a 1–0 defeat at Hull after playing in a League Cup-tie against Bolton. Even with all his experience though, he was powerless to prevent the club dropping into the Third Division and after one more season he hung up his boots. He spent the next seven years at Deepdale as the club's coach and then manager. On leaving Preston, he teamed up with his brother-in-law Johnny Giles as coach of Vancouver Whitecaps before following him in a similar capacity to West Bromwich Albion. Stiles later coached the juniors at Old Trafford.

STOCK, Brian Benjamin

Midfield

Born: Winchester, 24 December 1981
Career: Bournemouth, 2000. PRESTON NORTH END, 2006.

■ One of the many youngsters to graduate through Bournemouth's successful youth system in recent seasons, Brian Stock struggled to make an impact in his first few games in the side. However, in 2001–02, he started to

live up to his promise and the free-kick specialist wrote his name into the club's history books by scoring the first-ever goal at the new Fitness First Stadium. Despite undergoing an appendix operation midway through the following season, it didn't stop him from winning international recognition when being selected for Wales at Under-21 level. He continued to make progress with the Cherries, for whom his fine passing and distribution skills stood out. He had made over 160 appearances for Bournemouth when in January 2006 he became North End's second signing of the transfer window. The midfielder was flown up from the south coast town to sign on loan so that he could play in the game against Millwall before the move was made permanent shortly afterwards. He was allowed space to flash a superb volley inches wide of the target and was named man-of-the-match as North End extended their unbeaten run to 18 games. Though he still has a lot to learn, he netted his first goal for the club on the final day of the season in a 2–0 defeat of fellow Play-off side, Leeds United.

STOREY, John

Left-back

Born: Marley Hill, 14 February 1901.
Career: Chopwell Institute. PRESTON NORTH END, 1922. Hartlepool United, 1923. Grimsby Town, 1924.

■ Full-back John Storey made just one appearance for North End during the 1922–23 season when he deputised for Wilf Yates in a 3–2 home defeat by Sheffield United. He remained at the club until the close season and then joined Hartlepool United, who were then playing in the Third Division North. After one season at the Victoria Ground, he signed for Grimsby Town but failed to make it into the Mariners' League side.

STORMONT, Robert

Centre-forward, inside-forward

Born: Dundee, 1872.
Career: PRESTON NORTH END, 1893. Dundee. Tottenham Hotspur. Brentford. Maidstone United.

■ Bob Stormont was a rough, tough Scottish forward who played in nine games for Preston during the course of the 1893–94 season. Although he did not find the net, his unselfish play led to goals for players like Jimmy Ross and Frank Becton. Stormont returned north of the border to play for his home-town team, Dundee, before joining Spurs. He was a member of the side that won the Southern League in 1899–1900 but, though he was a great favourite with Spurs' fans in his four years with the club, he was not chosen for the 1901 FA Cup Final side. Stormont then spent a year playing for Brentford and when he was released he took up refereeing. He returned to the playing side of the game with Maidstone before an injury forced his retirement.

STOWELL, Michael

Goalkeeper

Born: Preston, 19 April 1965.
Career: Leyland Motors. PRESTON NORTH END, 1985. Everton, 1985. Chester City, 1987 (loan). York City, 1987 (loan). Manchester City, 1988 (loan). Port Vale, 1988 (loan). Wolverhampton Wanderers, 1988. PRESTON NORTH END, 1990 (loan). Wolverhampton Wanderers, 1990. Bristol City, 2001.

■ Mike Stowell was signed from local

club Leyland Motors, but he could not force his way into the North End side due to the fine form of Platt, Kelly and Brown. In December 1985 he left Deepdale to join Everton without appearing in Preston's League side. Signed as understudy to Welsh international Neville Southall, he had loan spells with a number of clubs. The last was Preston North End in February 1990. Stowell was on the losing side in both of his games for the Deepdale club as North End went down at Deepdale 1–0 to Bristol Rovers and 3–0 to Leyton Orient. He had previously been on loan at Wolves and when the Molineux club offered him the chance of regular first-team football he jumped at the chance. His early appearances led to him being selected in the England 'B' squad. Stowell was a fine shot-stopper who missed very few games in his time at Molineux. He eventually beat the total of 420 appearances made by legendary England international 'keeper Bert Williams. After 10 years at Molineux, he was awarded a thoroughly deserved testimonial against Aston Villa. He went on to play in 448 games for Wolves before leaving to end his career with Bristol City.

STRINGFELLOW, Harry

Centre-half, right-half

Born: Burscough, 1877.
Career: Southport Central. Everton, 1898. Portsmouth. Swindon Town. Leeds City, 1905. Wigan Town. PRESTON NORTH END. 1906. Wigan Town.

■ After he was unable to make much of an impression with Everton, Harry Stringfellow played Southern League football for Portsmouth and Swindon Town before signing for Leeds City. He had just left the Yorkshire club to play for Wigan Town when his services were secured by Preston as an emergency signing. The club's regular centre-half Billy Lyon was suspended and his replacement Percy Hartley was injured. As a result, Preston had to pay Leeds £40 for his registration. Stringfellow made his debut in a 1–0 defeat at one of his former clubs, Everton, and went on to make 19 appearances in that 1906–07 season. He scored his first goal in a 4–2

defeat of Middlesbrough. He continued to play for North End the following season before leaving to end his career with Wigan Town.

SULLEY, Christopher Stephen

Left-back

Born: Camberwell, 3 December 1959.
Career: Chelsea, 1978. Bournemouth, 1981. Dundee United. Blackburn Rovers, 1987. Port Vale, 1992. PRESTON NORTH END, 1993.

■ Unable to make the grade at Stamford Bridge, left-back Chris Sulley joined Bournemouth. In his five seasons at Dean Court he made 206 League appearances for the Cherries, helping them win promotion to the Third Division in 1981–82. On leaving Bournemouth, he tried his luck in Scottish football with Dundee United before returning to the Football League with Blackburn Rovers. Sulley was an important member of the Rovers side, playing in 134 games in the Second Division as the club continually challenged for promotion to the top flight. After a season with Port Vale, whom he helped finish third in Division Two, he joined Preston North End. Sulley's first game for the Deepdale club came on the opening day of the 1993–94 season when North End lost 2–0 to Crewe. Sulley played in 21 games that season as the club reached the Play-offs. He scored his only goal for the club in a 3–1 defeat of Torquay United. Though he remained at Deepdale for a couple more seasons, he never played in the club's League side again.

SUMMERBEE, George Michael

Full-back

Born: Winchester, 22 October 1914.
Died: 1955.
Career: Winchester City. Aldershot, 1934. PRESTON NORTH END, 1935. Chester City, 1946. Barrow, 1947.

■ George Summerbee, the father of England international Mike Summerbee, started his League career with Aldershot before moving to Preston in January

1935. He had to bide his time in the reserves before making his North End debut in a 4–1 home win over Derby County in April 1938. Summerbee's only other appearance came on the final day of the following season against Charlton Athletic. When League football resumed in 1946, Summerbee turned out for Chester City but played his best football for his last club, Barrow of the Third Division North, for whom he made 122 League appearances.

SWANN, Gary

Midfield, full-back

Born: York, 11 April 1962.
Career: Hull City, 1980. PRESTON NORTH END, 1986. York City, 1992. Scarborough, 1994.

■ Versatile performer Gary Swann began his career with Hull City, helping the Tigers win promotion from the Fourth Division in 1982–83. Swann had appeared in 186 League games for Hull when North End manager John McGrath brought him to Deepdale in November 1986. Following his debut off the bench against Peterborough United, Swann played in all the remaining games, scoring some vital goals as Preston won promotion from the Fourth Division as

runners-up to Northampton Town. The following season, Swann did not miss a game and was second-top scorer with 12 goals including a couple of doubles in the games against Brighton and Doncaster. Swann continued to be a regular in the Preston side and was ever present in 1989–90. He had scored 37 goals in 199 League outings when he parted company with the club and signed for his home-town club, York City. In his first season at Booth Crescent, he helped the Minstermen win promotion to the Third Division. He later left to see out his first-class career with Scarborough.

SWARBRICK, William

Outside-left

Born: Preston 1890.
Career: PRESTON NORTH END, 1912.

■ When Preston won the Second Division Championship in 1912–13, local-born winger William Swarbrick made his debut in a 1–0 win over Leicester Fosse. Though North End were relegated after just one season back in the First Division, Swarbrick made three appearances, scoring two goals in the 3–2 defeat of Manchester United. Despite this he was not retained by the Deepdale club.

TAIT, Alexander Gilchrist

Full-back

Born: Glenbuck, 1873.
Died: 6 April 1949.
Career: Glenbuck Athletic. Ayr. Royal Albert. Glasgow Rangers (loan). Motherwell. PRESTON NORTH END, 1894. Tottenham Hotspur. Leyton. Croydon Common.

■ One of 13 children, Sandy Tait worked as a pitboy leading the ponies and in his free time he played for Glenbuck Athletic. After a brief spell with Ayr he had three years with Royal Albert, part of which were spent on loan to Rangers. After turning professional with Motherwell, he soon caught the eye and in 1894 he joined North End. Tait made his Preston debut in a 3–1 win over Nottingham Forest towards the end of the 1894–95 season and he became an important member of the Preston side. He showed his versatility in November 1925 when he went in goal to replace the

injured John Wright in a game against Small Heath. His last game in North End colours came on the final day of the 1898–99 season against Bolton. Even though he was known as 'Terrible Tait' for his ferocious tackling, he took his football very seriously and, despite his intimidating nickname, was not a dirty player. He always played the game to the rules and was never booked. On leaving Deepdale, he joined Spurs and was a member of the team that won the Southern League Championship in 1899–1900 and the FA Cup the following year. Tait appeared in 422 games in all competitions for the London club before he joined Leyton, first as a player and then as manager. He also had a season in charge of the short-lived Croydon Common, for whom he also played in a few games.

TARBUCK, Alan David

Winger

Born: Chester, 10 October 1948.
Career: Everton, 1966. Crewe Alexandra, 1967. Chester City, 1969. PRESTON NORTH END, 1971. Shrewsbury Town, 1973. Rochdale, 1976.

■ Alan Tarbuck was not given much of a look-in at Everton so he joined Crewe Alexandra. In his first season at Gresty Road he helped the club finish fourth in Division Four and win promotion to the Third Division. Tarbuck was one of the Railwaymen's most consistent performers and the fans were disappointed when he left to join

rivals Chester City after a couple of years. He had scored 24 goals in 69 games for the Cestrians when North End brought him to Deepdale in September 1971. Even though the club struggled near the foot of the Second Division for most of the 1971–72 season, Tarbuck formed a good understanding up front with Hugh McIlmoyle and ended the season with 10 goals. He continued to play well the following season but with the club again languishing at the bottom of Division Two he was allowed to join Shrewsbury. In 1974–75 he helped them win promotion from Division Four but, having scored 17 goals in 124 League games, he returned to the North West with Rochdale with whom he ended his career.

TATTON, John Henry

Outside-right

Born: Dunston-on-Tyne, 23 November 1894.
Died: 1973.
Career: Dunston Atlas Villa. Newcastle United, 1911. Gillingham. PRESTON NORTH END, 1919. Oldham Athletic, 1919.

■ Winger John Tatton failed to win a place in the Newcastle United side and, after a spell playing Southern League football with Gillingham, he arrived at Deepdale for the first season of League football after World War One. With North End finding life hard in the top flight, Tatton made 18 appearances, creating a number of chances for the prolific Tommy Roberts and scoring one himself in a 3–0 win over Aston Villa. At the end of that season, he joined Oldham Athletic and spent three seasons with the Latics, who also struggled near the foot of Division One.

TAYLOR, Brian John

Full-back, winger

Born: Gateshead, 2 July 1949.
Died: 1993.
Career: Durham City. Coventry City, 1968. Walsall, 1971. Plymouth Argyle, 1977. PRESTON NORTH END, 1978. Wigan Athletic, 1982 (loan).

■ Brian Taylor began his career with Durham City in his native North East before joining Coventry City. Unable to

make much progress with the Sky Blues, he left Highfield Road to sign for Walsall. He stayed at Fellows Park until 1977, scoring 25 goals in 216 League appearances for the Saddlers. During his stay with Walsall, the West Midlands club came close to winning promotion to Division Two a number of times. Then came a move to Plymouth but after a year in Devon he joined Preston North End. His first game for the Deepdale club saw him come off the bench to replace Don O'Riordan in a 5–3 defeat at Fulham. Taylor was a virtual ever present after that, helping the club to seventh place in Division Two. The following season Taylor scored his only League goal for the club in a 2–0 defeat of Notts County. He remained a regular but, following the club's relegation, he went on loan to Wigan and his eight appearances helped them seal promotion from Division Four. Despite his success at Springfield Park he returned to Deepdale and in the close season he retired just a single League game short of 100. Sadly, Brian Taylor died of motor neurone disease in 1993 aged just 44.

TAYLOR, Colin David

Forward

Born: Liverpool, 25 December 1971.
Career: Wolverhampton Wanderers, 1990. Wigan Athletic, 1992 (loan). PRESTON NORTH END, 1992 (loan). Doncaster Rovers, 1993 (loan).

■ England Youth international Colin Taylor began his career with Wolverhampton Wanderers. After making his debut as a substitute in a goalless League Cup-tie at Hull City, the youngster was given an extended run in the Molineux side. He scored twice in the 4–1 home win over Millwall but an injury against Watford three games later brought his season to a premature end. In January 1992 he joined Wigan Athletic on loan and scored on his debut in a 1–1 draw at Fulham. He netted another at Leyton Orient, as the Latics played four away games on the trot in the space of 23 days. He then had a loan spell with Preston North End, playing the first of four games in a 2–2 draw with Bolton Wanderers. Unfortunately for North End, Taylor did not find the net in his

stay at Deepdale. After returning to Molineux he spent a final loan spell with Doncaster Rovers before parting company with Wolves.

TAYLOR, Herbert

Goalkeeper

Born: Burbage, 1881.
Career: Hinckley Town. PRESTON NORTH END, 1903.

■ Goalkeeper Herbert Taylor joined Preston North End from non-League Hinckley Town in the summer of 1903 as cover for the Scottish international 'keeper Peter McBride. Taylor was at Deepdale for 10 years and made a total of 108 Football League appearances during that time. His first game was in a 1–0 defeat at Barnsley in December 1903 and, though he never let the side down when he replaced the injured McBride, he had to wait until the great man's retirement in the 1911–12 season before establishing himself as the club's first-choice 'keeper. Unfortunately his first full season in the side coincided with the club's relegation to Division Two. However, he did play in 28 of the 38 games the following season as the club bounced straight back as Second Division Champions. Taylor's first-class career came to an end at the close of the following season. He missed just four games that season but North End were once again relegated.

TAYLOR, John S

Inside-left

Born: Preston, 1870.
Career: PRESTON NORTH END, 1891.

■ In a season when North End finished runners-up to Sunderland, John Taylor replaced the injured Towie for the home game with Derby County in March 1892. Despite scoring a goal in a 3–0 win, Taylor was not given another opportunity as more experienced players returned to the side.

TAYLOR, Royston

Midfield

Born: Blackpool, 28 September 1956.
Career: PRESTON NORTH END, 1974. Sunderland, 1975. Blackburn Rovers, 1978.

■ Midfielder Royston Taylor played in three games during the 1975–76 season and was on the winning side twice. Unable to force himself into the side on a more regular basis, he spent a season in the club's reserves. Following a spell as a non-contract player with Sunderland, he joined North End's rivals, Blackburn Rovers. It was a similar story at Ewood Park and, though he got on the score sheet in his three games for Rovers, he drifted into the local non-League scene.

TAYLOR, Samuel McGregor

Winger

Born: Glasgow, 23 September 1933.
Career: Falkirk. PRESTON NORTH END, 1955. Carlisle United, 1961. Southport, 1964.

■ Sammy Taylor arrived at Deepdale from Falkirk in the summer of 1955 for a fee of £8,500 plus a curious proviso added to his newly signed contract that North End would lay on a floodlit game at Deepdale for the Scottish League side. Taylor made his Preston debut in a 4–3 home win over Newcastle United in August 1955, though his first season with the club was primarily as understudy to both Finney and Morrison. Taylor eventually made the left-wing berth his own, even though he preferred the other flank occupied by the 'Preston Plumber'. When Finney switched to centre-forward, Taylor got his wish and switched wings. In his second season with the club, Taylor scored 15 goals including a hat-trick in a 7–1 thrashing of Portsmouth. In 1957–58, when North End finished runners-up to Wolves in the First Division, Taylor scored 14 goals with trebles in the 5–2 win over Chelsea and the 8–0 beating of Birmingham City. Following Preston's relegation to the Second Division at the end of the 1960–61 season, Taylor joined Carlisle United, who paid £2,5000 for his services. He went on to play in almost 100 games for the Cumbrian club, helping them win promotion to the Third Division in his first season at Brunton Park. He later ended his playing days with Southport where North End legend Willie Cunningham was manager.

TAYLOR, Steven Jeffrey

Forward

Born: Royton, 18 October 1955.
Career: Bolton Wanderers, 1973. Port Vale, 1975 (loan). Oldham Athletic, 1977. Luton Town, 1979. Mansfield Town, 1979. Burnley, 1980. Wigan Athletic, 1983. Stockport County, 1984. Rochdale, 1984. PRESTON NORTH END, 1986. Burnley, 1987. Rochdale, 1989.

■ Steve Taylor began his Football League career with Bolton Wanderers, learning his goalscoring trade at Burnden Park, before making the first of many career moves. He joined Oldham Athletic in October 1977 and netted twice on his debut and top scored in his first season at Boundary Park. Two big money transfers involving Luton and Mansfield in a six-month spell during 1979 did not work out for him and in the summer of 1980 he joined Burnley for a fee of £35,000. After helping them win the Third Division Championship, Taylor left to join Wigan Athletic in the summer of 1983. He had scored 10 goals in 37 games for Wigan when in March 1984 he moved on to Stockport County. He did not stay for long and joined Rochdale eight months later. In 1985–86

he hit the best goalscoring form of his career, hitting 25 of Dale's 57 League goals that season. He had a five-game spell with North End in the club's promotion-winning season of 1986–87, scoring goals against former club Stockport County and Northampton. He then rejoined Burnley and appeared for the Clarets in the Sherpa Van Trophy Final before ending his League career with another spell at Rochdale. On hanging up his boots, he became manager of non-League Mossley.

TEALE, Shaun

Centre-half

Born: Southport, 10 March 1964.
Career: Southport. Northwich Victoria. Weymouth. Bournemouth, 1989. Aston Villa, 1991. Tranmere Rovers, 1995. PRESTON NORTH END, 1997 (loan). Happy Valley (Hong Kong). Motherwell, 1998. Carlisle United, 2000. Northwich Victoria. Southport. Burscough. Northwich Victoria. Chorley.

■ A late starter in football, Shaun Teale began in non-League circles. He served Southport, Northwich Victoria and Weymouth, where he was selected for England in a semi-professional international before making his debut for Bournemouth at the age of 24. Recognised as one of the most accomplished defenders in the lower Divisions, Teale was then transferred to Aston Villa for a fee of £300,000. In 1991–92, his first season with the club, he was an ever present and formed an excellent central-defensive partnership with Paul McGrath. With Villa he won a Football League Cup-winners' medal but after appearing in 181 games he moved to Tranmere Rovers for a club record fee of £450,000 in the summer of 1995. The tough, combative defender, who was a natural leader on the field, was dogged by a long-standing injury while at Prenton Park and in January 1997 he went to Preston on loan. Teale made his debut for North End in a 1–0 win at Rotherham United but towards the end of his stay he was at the heart of the defence in a 5–1 hammering at Luton. On his return to Prenton Park, he was made available for transfer and joined Motherwell. Playing with vigour and passion, he was a huge

favourite at Fir Park, but later returned to Football League action with Carlisle United. He gave some commanding performances in the relegation battles but after being overlooked for the vacant manager's position, he re-entered the non-League scene. He went on to become player-manager of Chorley.

TELFER, George Andrew

Winger

Born: Liverpool, 6 July 1955.
Career: Everton, 1972. San Diego (US). Scunthorpe United, 1981. Altrincham. PRESTON NORTH END, 1983. Runcorn. Barrow.

■ George Telfer was a speedy winger who scored some spectacular goals during his time with Everton. After making his debut for the Blues in 1973, his form was so impressive that he was being talked about as a future England international. Things were going well for him until the arrival of Duncan McKenzie cost him his place. Telfer decided to stay at Goodison and fight for a recall despite offers from other clubs. Having scored 22 goals in 113 games, he eventually grew tired of Central League football and signed for NASL club San

Diego. He returned to England to play for Scunthorpe United – where England cricket legend Ian Botham cleaned his boots – and then as a non-contract player at Preston. Telfer made appearances from the bench in two home games: a 3–3 draw against Brentford and a 4–1 win over Southend United. After spells in non-League football with Runcorn and Barrow, he was appointed Football Development Officer for the Merseyside Youth Association.

TEMPLE, Derek William

Outside-left

Born: Liverpool, 13 November 1938.
Career: Everton, 1956. PRESTON NORTH END, 1967. Wigan Athletic.

■ A former England Schoolboy international, Derek Temple's form with the Everton Colts was amazing – in one season alone he scored 70 goals. This included six in one match and five on a number of occasions. His form was such that he made his first-team debut for the Toffees in a 2–1 win over Newcastle United in March 1957. An important member of the Everton side, Temple missed the majority of the club's League Championship-winning season of 1962–63 through injury. However, he bounced back to win full international

honours in 1965 in England's 1–0 win over West Germany in Nuremburg. The following season he won a place in Everton's 'Hall of Fame' when he scored the winning goal in the Blues' marvellous 3–2 win over Sheffield Wednesday in the FA Cup Final at Wembley. Temple went on to score 82 goals in 273 League and Cup games including a hat-trick in a 5–2 defeat of Ipswich Town in September 1961. In September 1967 he joined Preston North End and in a season in which the club just avoided the drop into the Third Division, he was Preston's leading scorer with eight goals. Temple played in a variety of roles during his time at Deepdale and it was his crosses that provided Willie Irvine with most of his goalscoring opportunities. Following North End's relegation to Division Three in 1969–70, Temple left to see out his career with Wigan Athletic.

THOMAS, John William

Forward

Born: Wednesbury, 5 August 1958.
Career: Everton, 1977. Tranmere Rovers, 1979 (loan). Halifax Town, 1979 (loan). Bolton Wanderers, 1980. Chester City, 1982. Lincoln City, 1983. PRESTON NORTH END, 1985. Bolton Wanderers, 1987. West Bromwich Albion, 1989. PRESTON NORTH END, 1990. Hartlepool United, 1992. Halifax Town, 1992. Bamber Bridge.

■ A carpenter by trade, John Thomas failed to make the first team at Everton. After loan spells with Tranmere and Halifax, he joined Bolton Wanderers. Though he was hampered by injuries while with the Trotters, he did net the club's 5000th goal in the League, against Grimsby. He then joined Chester City and top scored for them in 1982–83 with 21 goals. Lincoln City paid £22,000 to take him to Sincil Bank and he hit 21 goals in 71 games before returning to the North West with Preston North End. After scoring on his debut in a 4–2 home defeat by Peterborough United on the opening day of the 1985–86 season, Thomas went on to top the club's scoring charts with 18 goals. However, the club had to apply for re-election for the first time. In 1986–87, when the club won promotion from the Fourth Division,

Thomas again led the way with a total of 28 goals in all competitions. His total included three hat-tricks – in the 3–2 League win over Halifax Town and in the FA Cup victories against Bury (5–1) and Chorley (5–0). In July 1987, Bolton paid £30,000 to take 'JT' back to Burnden Park and his goals, which included another two hat-tricks, gave him a personal feat of two successive promotions with different clubs. He went on to appear for the Wanderers in their 4–1 win over Torquay United in the Sherpa Van Trophy Final at Wembley. Following a brief spell with West Bromwich Albion, Thomas rejoined North End. After taking his tally of League goals to 44 in 105 games, he had a spell with Hartlepool United before ending his League career with Halifax in 1993. He moved into non-League football with Bamber Bridge.

THOMPSON, Charles Henry

Left-half

Born: Preston, 1900.
Career: Wolseley Motors. PRESTON NORTH END, 1924.

■ Signed from Wolseley Motors, left-half Charles Thompson made just one appearance for the Lilywhites. This was during the 1924–25 season, a campaign in which North End lost their First Division status. Replacing the legendary Bobby Crawford, Thompson and the team did not have the best of games as they were beaten 4–0 by Arsenal. The Gunners finished the season just one place ahead of the relegated North End.

THOMPSON, David Stephen

Right-winger

Born: Manchester, 27 May 1962.
Career: North Withington. Rochdale, 1981. Notts County, 1986. Wigan Athletic, 1987. PRESTON NORTH END, 1990. Chester City, 1992. Rochdale, 1994.

■ Winger David Thompson started out with North Withington before Rochdale gave him the chance to play in the Football League. He made his debut for the Spotland club in September 1981 and over the next five seasons he terrorised full-backs in the lower Divisions. He left Rochdale in the summer of 1986 and spent just over a season with Notts County before making a £35,000 move to Wigan in October 1987. During his time with the Latics, Thompson missed very few games and scored some vital goals, including a hat-trick against Shrewsbury Town. However in the summer of 1990 he joined Preston North End where, after being hampered by injury, he made his debut in a 2–1 defeat by Bolton. The Lilywhites had paid £77,500 to take him to Deepdale but he never really delivered the goods and left to play for Chester City. In the summer of 1994 the much-travelled winger rejoined his first club, Rochdale, and took his tally of goals for the Spotland club to 24 in 307 games before deciding to retire.

THOMPSON, George Herbert

Goalkeeper

Born: Maltby, 15 September 1926.
Career: Chesterfield, 1947. Scunthorpe United, 1950. PRESTON NORTH END, 1952. Manchester City, 1956. Carlisle United, 1957.

■ Goalkeeper George Thompson was on the books of Chesterfield before switching to Scunthorpe United prior to the start of the 1950–51 season, the club's first in the Football League. He had played in 92 League games for the Irons when North End manager Will Scott brought him to Deepdale. Thompson understudied Malcolm Newlands for the first half of the 1952–53 season before making his debut in a 5–2 win at Portsmouth. He kept his place for the rest of the season, making 30 appearances and keeping 10 clean sheets, as the club finished runners-up to Arsenal. Thompson had another good season in 1953–54 and was between the posts in the 1954 FA Cup Final when West Bromwich Albion beat Preston 3–2. He continued to be the club's first-choice

'keeper for the next couple of seasons but, with Fred Else showing fine form in the club's reserve side, Thompson was allowed to leave Deepdale to join Manchester City. Understudy to Bert Trautmann, he made just two appearances in a season at Maine Road before moving on to Carlisle United where he made 206 League appearances before retiring.

THOMPSON, John William

Outside-right

Born: Alnwick, 1885.
Career: North Shields Athletic. Sunderland, 1907. PRESTON NORTH END, 1910.

■ Having impressed with local club North Shields Athletic, winger John Thompson joined Sunderland. In three seasons with the Wearsiders, he scored 13 goals in 34 games and helped them to finish third in the 1908–09 First Division campaign. He left Roker Park in the summer of 1910 to join Preston and made his debut in a 2–0 reversal against Nottingham Forest on the opening day of the 1910–11 season. During the early stages of the campaign, the flying winger scored in three successive games but he could not raise the club to more than a mid-table placing. Thompson was again the club's first-choice right-winger the following season but, though he scored some spectacular goals, the club were relegated and he left Deepdale.

THOMPSON, Peter

Left-winger

Born: Carlisle, 27 November 1942.
Career: PRESTON NORTH END, 1959. Liverpool, 1963. Bolton Wanderers, 1973.

 Peter Thompson started his long and illustrious career with Preston North End, turning professional the year that the legendary Tom Finney retired. He made his debut in a 2–0 win over Arsenal in August 1960 and went on to play in the remaining 38 games, ending the season as the club's leading scorer in all competitions with 12 goals. However, he could not prevent the team's relegation from the First Division. Thompson was ever present the following season and scored 15 goals including a couple in North End's run to the sixth round of the FA Cup. The winger was again ever present in 1962–63 but in the close season, in the face of opposition from Everton, Wolves and Juventus, Liverpool manager Bill Shankly paid £40,000 to take him to Anfield. Thompson soon became a great favourite with Reds' supporters. At the end of his first full season, Liverpool won the League Championship and Thompson gave his best display in a 5–0 rout of Arsenal, scoring twice as the Reds made certain of the title. The accuracy of Thompson's crosses played an important part in establishing Roger Hunt as one of the most feared goalscorers of the time. In 1965–66 it was no coincidence that Thompson played in 40 games and that Hunt scored 27 goals. Thompson was a regular in the England side, although he was a victim of Alf Ramsey's decision to play the 1966 World Cup without wingers. A fantastic winger who could take on defenders in tight situations and go past them with ease, he collected two League Championship medals and an FA Cup-winners' medal with Liverpool. He became plagued by knee trouble and was languishing in the reserves and considering retirement when Bolton Wanderers signed him in November 1973. His displays for the Trotters helped the club through one of their most exciting periods and to promotion to Division One. He retired in 1978 and, after running a caravan park, became a hotelier in Harrogate.

THOMPSON, Robert

Centre-forward

Born: Trimdon Grange, 1886.
Career: Wingate Albion. Chester. PRESTON NORTH END, 1910. Durham City.

 Signed from Chester towards the end of the 1910–11 season, centre-forward Robert Thompson made his debut for North End on the final day of the campaign in a 2–0 win over Bradford City. The following season, when Preston lost their top-flight status, Thompson was one of five players tried in the number-nine shirt. Thompson played in 11 games, scoring against Bolton and Notts County, before he moved on to end his career with Durham City in the years before they entered the Football League.

THOMPSON, Thomas

Inside-forward

Born: Houghton-le-Spring, 10 November 1928.
Career: Lumley YMCA. Newcastle United, 1946. Aston Villa, 1950. PRESTON NORTH END, 1955. Stoke City, 1961. Barrow, 1963.

 Tommy Thompson was one of the top inside-forwards in the 1950s. He

possessed delicate touches and speed off the mark that eventually saw him turn into a potent schemer and attacker who was always able to score goals. He began his career with Newcastle United where he was blooded in the Magpies' promotion-winning season of 1947–48. Unable to win a regular place, Thompson moved to Aston Villa in September 1950. At Villa Park he blossomed as a free-scoring inside-forward and was good enough to earn recognition for England. In 1951 he scored four goals for the Football League. Nicknamed 'Topper', he scored 76 goals for Villa in 165 games before moving to Deepdale. It cost North End £27,000 to lure Thompson to Deepdale but, after scoring in the second minute of his debut in a 4–0 win at Everton on the opening day of the 1955–56 season, there was little doubt the club had got themselves a bargain. Thompson's popularity soared even higher as he scored five times in the opening six games of the campaign. He ended the season as North End's leading scorer with 24 goals. Thompson continued to score freely in 1956–57, again topping the club's scoring charts with 29 goals including his first hat-trick

in a 6–0 hammering of Sunderland. His best season in terms of goals scored was 1957–58, the season North End finished runners-up to Wolves in the First Division. Thompson got his name on the score sheet 34 times that season, netting another treble as Birmingham City were beaten 8–0. Thompson's form led to him winning his second English cap against Scotland at Wembley in 1957, but his North End teammate Tommy Docherty had one of his finest games, restricting Thompson to a couple of shots. Following North End's relegation in 1960–61, the club had to let certain players go and Thompson found himself surplus to requirements. He joined Stoke City, helping them win promotion to Division One, before leaving to end his playing career with Barrow. He later returned to Deepdale to coach the club's 'B' team under Bobby Charlton but, after becoming disenchanted with modern attitudes, he left to concentrate on his family joinery business.

THOMSON, Richard Blair

Forward

Born: Edinburgh, 26 June 1957.
Career: PRESTON NORTH END, 1975.

■ Ricky Thomson made his Preston debut in a goalless draw at Chesterfield

towards the end of the 1974–75 season, but over the next few seasons he appeared in just a handful of games. He only really established himself in 1977–78 when the club won promotion to Division Two. That season he scored six goals in 26 League games including a brace in a 3–2 defeat of Oxford United. He certainly did not look out of place in the higher grade of football but after one more season at Deepdale he parted company with the club.

THOMSON, Samuel

Centre-forward, inside-forward

Born: Lugar, 14 February 1862.
Died: 23 December 1943.
Career: Lugar Boswell. Glasgow Rangers. PRESTON NORTH END, 1888. Wolverhampton Wanderers, 1890. Everton, 1891. Accrington, 1891.

■ Samuel Thomson was a stylish forward and a member of the Preston 'Invincibles'. He won two caps for Scotland while with Rangers, prior to arriving at Deepdale. Thomson made his Football League debut in North End's second game of the 1888–89 season as North End won 4–0 at Wolverhampton Wanderers. Thomson played in 16 games during that inaugural campaign, but it was his performances in the club's run to the FA Cup Final that endeared him to Preston fans. Thomson netted one of the goals in the 3–0 defeat of Wolves in the Final. He was an important member of the

side that retained the title in 1889–90 but in the close season he was persuaded to join Wolves without the Deepdale club's permission. The incident went before the committee and Wolves were fined £50 for their misconduct. After scoring nine goals in 24 games for Wolves, Thomson moved to Everton but after just a handful of games he was on the move again, this time to Accrington where he ended his playing days. He later became a railway clerk based in Preston.

THORNBOROUGH, Elijah Holden

Wing-half

Born: Bolton, 17 January 1903.
Career: Halliwell United. Bolton Wanderers, 1925. PRESTON NORTH END, 1930. Horwich RMI. Chorley.

■ Ernie Thornborough joined Bolton Wanderers in the summer of 1922 but did not play for the first team until November 1926. For the remainder of that season he became a regular at left-half, but he missed the FA Cup semi-final and Final when Billy Jennings was preferred. The remainder of Thornborough's career at Burnden Park was spent as understudy to any of the half-back positions. He understudied such famous players as Nuttall, Seddon and Haworth without ever winning a regular spot. The arrival of Fred Kean further restricted his chances of first-team football and in August 1930 he moved to Preston North End. Thornborough played his first game for the Lilywhites in a 4–2 home defeat by Nottingham Forest, but players of the calibre of Nisbet and Crawford restricted his chances at Deepdale. He did make 19 appearances in 1931–32 before leaving to play non-League football for Horwich RMI and later Chorley.

THRELFALL, Thomas

Left-back

Born: Preston, 1898.
Career: PRESTON NORTH END, 1919.

■ Strong-tackling full-back Thomas Threlfall made a couple of appearances for Preston in 1919–20, the first season of League football following World War Two. He played in the games at Sheffield United and Middlesbrough in the space of three days after the turn of the year – both of which were lost by the Lilywhites. Threlfall saw out the season in the reserves before leaving the club in the close season.

TICKLE, Bert

Wing-half

Born: Preston, 1880.
Career: PRESTON NORTH END, 1901.

■ Bert Tickle replaced Joe Elliott for a couple of games in the 1901–02 season. He made his debut in a 1–0 win over Burton United and helped the side keep another clean sheet on his next appearance in a goalless draw against Bristol City. His only appearance the following season was in a 3–0 defeat of Barnsley. Preston won two and drew one of the games in which Tickle played during 1903–04. Despite never being on the losing side, Tickle was released after the club won promotion to Division One.

TINKLER, John

Midfield

Born: Trimdon, 24 August 1968.
Career: Hartlepool United, 1986. PRESTON NORTH END, 1992. Walsall, 1993.

■ Midfielder John Tinkler began his career with Hartlepool United. In a little over five seasons at the Victoria Ground, he made 170 League appearances and helped United win promotion to the Third Division in 1990–91. In July 1992 he joined Preston North End and made his debut in a 1–1 home draw against Bournemouth on the opening day of the 1992–93 season. Tinkler appeared in 24 games that season and scored goals against Burnley and Bournemouth. Following the club's relegation to the Third Division, he left to play for Walsall where he ended his first-class career.

TINSLEY, Alan

Midfield

Born: Fleetwood, 1 January 1951.
Career: PRESTON NORTH END, 1969. Bury, 1970.

■ Alan Tinsley played for North End in nine games during the 1969–70 relegation season. His only goal secured a point in a 1–1 draw against Middlesbrough. Despite never letting the side down when selected, he was allowed to leave Deepdale and join Bury where he gave five seasons of loyal service. In 1973–74, he helped them win promotion to the Third Division. Tinsley, who had scored 15 goals in 94 League outings for the Shakers, was forced into premature retirement following an injury.

TOD, George

Left-half, right-back

Born: Preston, 1879.
Career: Linthouse. PRESTON NORTH END, 1900. Grimsby Town, 1907.

■ A versatile player, George Tod's first season with Preston was the 1900–01 relegation campaign when the club lost their top-flight status for the first time. Even so, he was one of North End's better players and made 26 appearances. In 1902–03, when the club were unlucky not to make an immediate return, Tod was an ever present. He missed just three games of the club's promotion-winning 1903–04 season. In the top-flight seasons that followed, Tod found himself on the fringes of the first team and at the end of the 1906–07 campaign he left to join Grimsby Town. However, he was unable to force his way into the side.

TOONE, Percy Edward

Goalkeeper

Born: Colchester, 27 July 1883.
Died: 1955.
Career: Woolwich Arsenal, 1907. Leyton. Southend United. PRESTON NORTH END, 1911. Barrow. Southend United. Bolton Wanderers, 1914. Plymouth Argyle. Newport County, 1920.

■ Unable to make the grade with Woolwich Arsenal, Percy Toone had spells in the Southern League with Leyton and Southend before joining Preston before the start of the 1911–12 season. This was Peter McBride's last season with the club and Toone and Herbert Taylor were left to share the goalkeeping duties in a campaign that saw the club lose its First Division status. Toone made just four appearances. After conceding four on his debut against Sheffield United, he kept a clean sheet in the 1–0 win over Bury, the other club to drop into the Second Division. He started the 1912–13 season as the club's first-choice 'keeper, but only played in 10 games as the club returned to the top flight as Division two Champions. With little chance of playing on a more regular basis, Toone had brief spells with Barrow and Southend before signing for Bolton. He made just three appearances for the Trotters before he had a spell with Plymouth Argyle. He ended his career after the war with Newport County.

TORBET, John

Outside-left

Born: Benwhat, 1907.
Career: Cumnock Juniors. Partick Thistle. PRESTON NORTH END, 1933. Burton Town. Stockport County, 1935. Ayr United.

■ John Torbet was a member of the Partick Thistle side that were continually challenging near the top of the Scottish First Division in the late 1920s and early 1930s. He was a fleet-footed winger who signed for North End in the summer of 1933. Torbet scored from the penalty spot on his debut in a 2–1 win at Blackpool on the opening day of the 1933–34 season and, though he only played in 11 games as the club won promotion to Division

One, he did score four goals. This total included two in the 4–0 defeat of Nottingham Forest, but three games later he had given way to Arthur Fitton. Torbet had a brief spell in the Third Division North with Stockport County before returning north of the border to end his career with Ayr United.

TOTTOH, Melvyn

Winger

Born: Manchester, 26 July 1956.
Career: Lytham. PRESTON NORTH END, 1985.

■ Injuries at Deepdale were so bad during the calamitous 1985–86 season that local park footballer Mel Tottoh was drafted into the side. His only Football League action was as a substitute for Mark Rodgers in a 1–0 home defeat at the hands of Scunthorpe United.

TOWARD, Alfred Vickers

Centre-forward, centre-half

Born: Castleside, 1882.
Died: 1962.
Career: Leadgate Park. Hull City, 1908. Oldham Athletic, 1909. PRESTON NORTH END, 1913. Darlington.

■ Alf Toward was one of several brothers in the Leadgate Park team of the mid-1900s. He began his Football League career with Hull City but he moved to Oldham Athletic after being unable to cement a regular place in the side. In his first season with Oldham, it was the speedy centre-forward's goal against his former club that helped the Latics win promotion to the First Division on goal average – the Tigers finished third. Toward went on to score 30 goals in 72 games for Oldham before he was transferred to Preston prior to the 1913–14 season. His first game in Preston colours was against Oldham, but it was the Latics who ran out 1–0 winners. He scored fout goals in 18 games that season as the club were relegated from the First Division. He was in and out of the side in 1914–15 but his four goals in 18 games helped the club return to the top flight at the first attempt. Toward later ended his career with Darlington.

TOWIE, Thomas

Inside-left, outside-left

Born: Glasgow.
Career: Dumbarton United. PRESTON NORTH END, 1891. Renton. Glasgow Celtic (loan). Derby County, 1893. Renton. Rossendale.

■ Tom Towie was signed from Dumbarton United and made his Preston debut in the number-nine shirt on the opening day of the 1891–92 season as North End went down 2–0 at Notts County. He went on to appear in 22 games that season, scoring nine goals and another in the 6–0 FA Cup defeat of Middlesbrough Ironopolis. There is no doubt that his performances in various forward positions helped the club finish as runners-up to Sunderland. He then returned north of the border to play for Renton. The Scottish club were seldom out of dispute with the Scottish Football Association as Celtic were able to borrow Tom Towie for Cup matches only. He later returned to the Football League with Derby County where he played on both wings. Another spell with Renton was followed by a few games back in the North West with Rossendale.

TRAINER, James

Goalkeeper

Born: Wrexham, 7 January 1863.
Died: 1915.
Career: Wrexham Victoria. Wrexham Grosvenor. Wrexham. Great Lever. Bolton Wanderers. PRESTON NORTH END, 1888.

■ James Trainer, a time-served coachbuilder, played his first senior match for Wrexham and before long had established a reputation as an excellent goalkeeper. He left the Robins under a cloud, following a particularly rough FA Cup tie against Oswestry in December 1883. He was alleged to have insulted the referee and the FA banned Wrexham from the competition and reported Trainer's offence to the Football Association of Wales. After a spell with Great Lever, he joined Bolton Wanderers. He went on to appear in a number of pre-League games for the Wanderers and his form earned him international recognition when he played for Wales against Scotland in 1887. Trainer enjoyed his greatest success at Preston North End as a member of the 'Invincibles'. Curiously he had impressed North End while playing for Bolton at Deepdale in a match in which he let in 12 goals! He first appeared for North End in August 1887 on a short tour of Scotland. Although he was on the losing side against Hibernian, it was another eight months before he tasted defeat again. Trainer sharpened up his catching ability by playing for the club's baseball team and in North End's pre-League days was known to 'wear a mackintosh' and 'shelter under an umbrella' during a game. In May 1893 in the Lancashire Cup Final against Bolton, Trainer dived to save a shot by Weir and the ball burst! It was at the end of this season that Trainer became landlord of the Lamb Hotel on Church Street. In 1893–94 he played in every game of a gruelling League campaign but was injured for the test-match encounter with Notts County which Preston lost 4–0. By now, Trainer had become a director of the club but he later resigned to become involved with an indoor exhibition soccer scheme at London Olympia. The venture failed, the FA banned the participants and the one-time 'Prince of Goalkeepers' was out of work. Trainer, who was separated from his wife and 10 children, died in poverty in 1915. He had received some financial help in his later years from fellow Welsh international Leigh-Roose.

TREACY, Raymond Christopher Patrick

Forward

Born: Dublin, 18 June 1946.
Career: Home Farm. West Bromwich Albion, 1964. Charlton Athletic, 1968. Swindon Town, 1972. PRESTON NORTH END, 1973. Oldham Athletic, 1975 (loan). West Bromwich Albion, 1976. Shamrock Rovers. Drogheda United.

■ After learning his trade with Home Farm, Ray Treacy had a brief spell with West Bromwich Albion before he joined Charlton Athletic in February 1968. He fitted in well at The Valley and scored 44 goals in 149 League games in just over four seasons. After the Addicks were relegated in 1971–72, Treacy moved on

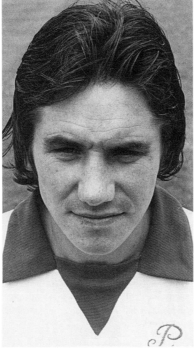

to Swindon Town and it was from there that he joined Preston North End for £30,000 in December 1973. He was put straight into the first team and made his debut in a 3–0 reversal at Middlesbrough. Unfortunately, he was asked to play in midfield for the remainder of the season, a campaign in which North End lost their Second Division status. Injuries hampered his progress in 1974–75 but the following season he started with a bang. Playing as a forward – his preferred position – he scored 11 goals in 27 League games. This included seven in his first nine games of the season. However, Treacy fell out with manager Harry Catterick. He had a loan spell with Oldham Athletic but in the summer of 1976 he returned to the club where he started his Football League career, West Bromwich Albion. He later returned to Dublin to join Shamrock Rovers and was the Hoops' leading scorer in two of his three seasons with the club. He later played for Drogheda United and managed Home Farm before taking charge at Shamrock Rovers.

TREBBLE, David Neil

Forward

Born: Hitchin, 16 February 1969.
Career: Stevenage Borough. Scunthorpe

United, 1993. PRESTON NORTH END, 1994. Scarborough, 1995. Stevenage Borough.

■ A big, strong striker with good heading ability, David Trebble was discovered playing non-League football for Stevenage Borough and joined Scunthorpe United in the summer of 1993. He struggled to hold down a regular place and after just a season at Glanford Park he moved to Preston North End on a free transfer. Trebble made his Preston debut on the opening day of the 1994–95 season as they played out a goalless draw at Darlington. In a season in which North End reached the Play-offs, Trebble scored four goals in 19 League appearances – more than half of which were made from the bench. In fact, three of his four strikes came when he appeared as a substitute. He left Deepdale with a couple of months of the 1994–95 season remaining and joined Scarborough. Trebble was influential in helping the Yorkshire club to climb away from the bottom of the Third Division but he suffered from poor service the following season and found goals hard to come by. The upshot was that Scarborough released him and he rejoined Stevenage Borough.

TREMELLING, William Reuben

Centre-half, centre-forward

Born: Newhill, May 1904.
Career: Kirkby Colliery. Mansfield Town. Welbeck Colliery. Worksop Town. Retford Town. Blackpool, 1924. PRESTON NORTH END, 1930.

■ Bill Tremelling joined Blackpool as a promising 21-year-old centre-forward from Retford Town. He made his League debut in a goalless draw at Manchester United in March 1925 but played in just one more game that season. The following campaign he broke his leg at Swansea and it was not until midway through the 1926–27 season that he regained his place. He ended the season – in which the Seasiders finished ninth in Division Two – as the club's leading scorer with 30 goals in 26 games including hat-tricks against Port Vale and Clapton Orient. Unbelievably, at the start of the next season Blackpool manager Sydney Beaumont switched Tremelling to centre-half. However, it proved to be an inspirational move with Tremelling feeding Jimmy Hampson. It was a tactical switch that paid dividends as Hampson scored 45 goals and Blackpool won the Second Division Championship. Tremelling had scored 44 goals in 119

games when in December 1930 he joined Preston North End. The Lilywhites were badly in need of a centre-forward and that was the position in which he made his North End debut in the 7–0 defeat of Cardiff City. He scored two of his side's goals. With the signing of Ted Harper and Jack Nelson's move to Wolves, Tremelling moved to centre-half. He missed just one game in 1933–34 as North End won promotion to the First Division and was ever present in 1935–36. The following season he captained Preston in the 1937 FA Cup Final, which they lost 3–1 to Sunderland. Tremelling had scored 12 goals in 230 League and Cup games for North End when he hung up his boots. He returned to Bloomfield Road where he became a much-respected coach.

TUNKS, Roy William

Goalkeeper

Born: Worthing, 21 January 1951.
Career: Rotherham United, 1968. York City, 1969. PRESTON NORTH END, 1974. Wigan Athletic, 1981. Hartlepool United, 1988. PRESTON NORTH END, 1988.

■ Roy Tunks began his career as a centre-forward, captaining Worthing Boys. He was invited for a trial for the county team and, when the goalkeeper failed to turn up, he volunteered to take his place. He began his Football League career with Rotherham United and made the first of 138 appearances for the Millmoor club just a few days after his 17th birthday. During his time with the Yorkshire club, he became dissatisfied and had trials with Newcastle United, Ipswich Town and York City. Eventually, in November 1974 he joined Preston North End for the knock down price of £7,000. Replacing John Brown, he made his debut in a 3–1 defeat at Tranmere but kept his place for the rest of the season. In fact, Tunks missed very few games for North End and was ever present in 1977–78 when the club won promotion to Division Two. He played in every game over the following two seasons but in November 1981, following Preston's relegation to the Third Division, he left to play for Wigan Athletic. During his time at Springfield Park, Tunks missed

very few games and in his first season he kept 12 clean sheets in 31 games to help the Latics win promotion. After a brief spell with Hartlepool United, Tunks rejoined Preston and took his total appearances in his two spells to 342. After a playing career which lasted for well over 20 years, Roy Tunks went on to work as a coach for the Lancashire FA.

TURNBULL, James McLachlan

Centre-forward

Born: Bannockburn, 23 May 1884.
Career: Falkirk. East Stirlingshire. Falkirk. Dundee. Glasgow Rangers. PRESTON NORTH END, 1904. Leyton. Manchester United, 1907. Bradford Park Avenue, 1910. Chelsea, 1912. Hurst FC.

■ Jimmy Turnbull was the star of Scottish football in the early 1900s. He bagged five goals for Falkirk against Aberdeen in the semi-final of the Dewar Cup in 1903 and netted eight times in 34 games for Rangers before joining Preston North End in January 1905. He made his debut in a 3–0 win over Woolwich Arsenal but failed to find the net in his eight games during that 1904–05 season. The following campaign North End finished as runners-up to Liverpool in the First Division but Turnbull only played in five games and again did not score. On leaving Deepdale, he joined Leyton and claimed 15 of their 38 goals in a season of Southern League football. He then signed for Manchester United and nipped in with 42 goals in 76 games for the Red Devils as well as helping them win the League Championship in 1908 and the FA Cup a year later. A well-built forward, aggressive with an appetite for hard work, he later played for Chelsea before returning to Manchester where he ran his own business.

TURNER, Robert Frewen

Outside-left

Born: Leicester, 15 July 1885.
Died: 15 February 1959.
Career: Leicester Imperial. Leicester Fosse, 1906. Everton, 1908. PRESTON NORTH END, 1911. Darlington. Coventry City.

■ Bob Turner was the younger and more successful of the Turner brothers. 'Leggy', as he was usually known, was a speedy outside-left and a cricketing all-rounder for Leicestershire. His transfer to Everton following Fosse's relegation fate was a truly controversial affair with his new club reporting him to the FA for demanding an illicit £100 signing-on fee. The player suddenly found himself somewhat worse off after a £50 fine. Undaunted, however, he made a scoring Goodison debut in the Merseyside derby and set about marking his final preparations for his impending marriage – the notoriously celebrated affair attended by most of the Fosse team on the eve of the 12–0 defeat at Nottingham Forest. On leaving Everton, Turner joined Preston and played the first of eight games in a 1–0 win at Sheffield Wednesday on the opening day of the 1911–12 season. He lost his place to Bert Danson and, though he came back to play in the last four games of the season, he could not prevent the club from being relegated. He then played for North Eastern League Champions Darlington and for Coventry City in the Southern League's Second Division but his efforts since leaving Everton seem somewhat mundane!

TWENTYMAN, Geoffrey

Centre-half

Born: Liverpool, 10 March 1959.
Career: Chorley. PRESTON NORTH END, 1983. Bristol Rovers, 1986.

■ Signed form Chorley, Geoff Twentyman replaced Tommy Booth at the heart of the Preston defence midway

through the 1983–84 season. He played his first game in a 2–1 win over Exeter City. The following season North End were relegated to the Fourth Division for the first time in their history with Twentyman playing in all but two of that campaign's League games. He was also at Deepdale in 1985–86 when the club finished one off the bottom of Division Four, but in the close season he left to join Bristol Rovers. He was a regular in the Rovers' side for the next six seasons, appearing in 252 League games, and in 1989–90 he helped the club win the Third Division Championship.

TWIST, Richard

Goalkeeper

Born: Burnley, 1910.
Career: Burnley, 1931. PRESTON NORTH END, 1932.

■ Goalkeeper Richard Twist played his early football for his home-town team, Burnley, and made 10 appearances for the Clarets as they just avoided relegation from the Second Division in 1931–32. He moved to Preston in the close season and replaced George Wolf for three games midway through the 1932–33 season. Unfortunately all the games were lost and Twist conceded nine goals in the process. He was replaced by fellow new signing Harry Holdcroft and after playing a handful of reserves games he left the club.

UZELAC, Steven

Centre-half

Born: Doncaster, 12 March 1953.

Career: Doncaster Rovers, 1971. Mansfield Town, 1976 (loan). PRESTON NORTH END, 1977. Stockport County, 1980.

■ Steve Uzelac started out with his home-town team, Doncaster Rovers, and made 185 League appearances in five seasons of Fourth Division football for the Belle Vue club. Towards the end of his stay at Doncaster, he had a spell on loan at Mansfield Town before joining Preston North End in May 1977. After making his debut in a goalless draw at Port Vale, he made just one more appearance that season as the club won promotion to the Second Division. Injuries hampered his progress the following season and in March 1980 he moved on to Stockport County where he later ended his career.

VAUGHAN, John

Goalkeeper

Born: Isleworth, 26 June 1964.
Career: West Ham United, 1982. Charlton Athletic, 1985 (loan). Bristol Rovers, 1985 (loan). Wrexham, 1985 (loan). Bristol City, 1986 (loan). Fulham, 1986. Bristol City, 1988 (loan). Cambridge United, 1988. Charlton Athletic, 1993. PRESTON NORTH END, 1994. Lincoln City, 1996. Colchester United, 1997 (loan). Colchester United, 1999 (loan). Chesterfield, 2000 (loan).

■ Unable to make the grade with his first club, West Ham United, goalkeeper John Vaughan went on loan to a number of clubs before signing for Fulham in the summer of 1986. After a couple of

seasons at Craven Cottage, where he appeared in 55 games, he had a loan spell with Bristol City before signing on a permanent basis for Cambridge United. He was a virtual ever present at the Abbey Stadium, appearing in 231 games and helping United win the Third Division Championship in 1990–91 and promotion to the First Division the following season. Following a season with Charlton Athletic, Vaughan joined Preston, making his debut in a 3–1 defeat at Hartlepool United. His first season at Deepdale was spent sharing the goalkeeping duties with Barry Richardson as North End reached the Play-offs. His lack of inches did not prove to be a handicap as he pulled off some remarkable reflex saves. In 1995–96, having seen off Richardson's challenge, he kept 19 clean sheets as North End swept to the Third Division Championship. However, Vaughan was out of contract at the end of that successful campaign and both club and player decided it was time for a change. Vaughan joined John Beck for a third time when he signed for Lincoln City. At Sincil Bank, he again found himself competing for the number-one jersey with Barry Richardson, but he played in the majority of games as the club won automatic promotion from Division Three. Vaughan was then hampered by injuries and he retired after loan spells with Colchester and Chesterfield.

VEALL, Raymond Joseph

Outside-left

Born: Skegness, 16 March 1943.
Career: Skegness. Doncaster Rovers, 1961. Everton, 1961. PRESTON NORTH END, 1965. Huddersfield Town, 1965.

■ Despite Doncaster Rovers struggling near the foot of the Fourth Division, the form of winger Ray Veall was attracting attention from a number of top-flight clubs. Known as 'Pork Chop', he signed for Everton after just 19 appearances for the Belle Vue club. However, most of the four seasons he spent at Goodison were as understudy to Johnny Morrissey. All of Veall's 11 League appearances for Everton came in the League Championship-winning season of 1962–63 when his only goal

was the winner in a 4–3 win at Nottingham Forest. However, the diminutive winger needed three more appearances to win a medal. After two more seasons in the club's reserves, he joined Preston. Although he made his debut on the opening day of the 1965–66 season in a 1–0 defeat at Ipswich, Veall could not win a regular place in the team and at the turn of the year he joined Huddersfield Town where he ended his first-class playing career.

VERNON, Joseph Leslie

Inside-forward

Born: Sheffield, 27 December 1905.
Died: 1979.
Career: Worksop Town. Bury, 1927. PRESTON NORTH END, 1934. Swansea Town, 1937.

■ Les Vernon joined Bury from non-League Worksop Town where he had proved himself a prolific goalscorer. He spent seven seasons at Gigg Lane and, though there were occasions when serious injuries ruled him out of contention, he went on to score 50 goals in 127 League appearances for the Shakers. After helping the club to fifth place in Division One in his first season with the Shakers, he could do little to prevent their relegation to the Second Division the following season. North End had just returned to the top flight

and saw Les Vernon as just the type of experienced forward they would need in the First Division. He made his debut in a 2–1 defeat at Sheffield Wednesday but, because of the calibre of players such as Dougal, Kelly, Palethorpe, Maxwell and Bargh, he did not get much of a look in. He stayed at Deepdale for three seasons before leaving to end his career with Swansea.

VICKERS, Simeon

Goalkeeper

Born: Preston, 1892.
Career: PRESTON NORTH END, 1913.

■ Goalkeeper Simeon Vickers made just one appearance for the Lilywhites, in the First Division relegation season of 1913–14. Replacing Herbert Taylor, he certainly did not let the side down as North End beat high-flying Middlesbrough 4–1.

WADDELL, George Barr

Wing-half

Born: Lesmahagow, 13 July 1889.
Died: 17 September 1966.
Career: Dalziel Rovers. Burnbank Athletic. Larkhall United. Glasgow Rangers. Kilmarnock (loan). Bradford City, 1914. PRESTON NORTH END, 1920. Oldham Athletic, 1922. Birmingham, 1922. Hamilton Academicals. New Brighton, 1923. Wolverhampton Wanderers, 1923. Aberaman Athletic. Chorley. Fraserburgh. Dick Kerr's XI. Ribble Motors.

■ George Waddell had a varied career and kicked his last ball at the age of 43. A man of many clubs, but principally a reserve with most of them, he was a heavily built wing-half with a powerful if not always accurate shot. Waddell played First Division football either side of World War One for Bradford City. He left Valley Parade to join North End in the summer of 1920. After making his debut in a 3–2 home win over Newcastle United, Waddell became an important member of the Preston side and, in fact, it was with the Deepdale club that he made the highest number of appearances. Having played with numerous clubs, he ended his playing days back in the North West with Dick Kerr's XI and finally Ribble Motors.

WADE, William Alexander

Right-back

Born: Jarrow, 22 March 1901.
Died: 1958.
Career: Jarrow. PRESTON NORTH END, 1923. West Ham United, 1929. Wigan Borough, 1931.

■ After solid displays for his home-town team, Jarrow, North End acquired the services of tough-tackling full-back Bill Wade in readiness for the 1923–24 season. Initially he found himself understudy to Tommy Hamilton and did not make his debut until October 1923 in a 1–1 draw with Sheffield United. He won a regular place in the side the following season but, despite some sound performances in the number-two shirt, he could not prevent North End from being relegated. One of the club's most consistent players at this time, he missed just one game in 1926–27 as North End challenged for promotion to Division One. Having appeared in 139 League games he left Deepdale to play for West Ham United before later returning to the North West to see out his career with Wigan Borough.

WALSH, Charles

Wing-half

Born: Glossop, 1 November 1898.
Career: Glossop. Stalybridge Celtic, 1921.

Birmingham, 1923. Halifax Town, 1924. PRESTON NORTH END, 1925. Barnsley, 1926.

■ Charlie Walsh's displays for his home-town club Glossop led to him being given a chance in the Football League with Stalybridge Celtic. But after just one appearance, and a fruitless trial with Birmingham, he signed for Halifax Town. He made 19 appearances as the Shaymen finished ninth in the Third Division North before signing for Preston. After making his debut in a 5–2 defeat at Portsmouth, he played in three consecutive League games later in the season including a 4–0 win over Hull City and a 5–0 defeat at Chelsea. This last reversal was Walsh's last appearance for the club. He joined Barnsley where he ended his League career.

WALSH, Mark

Midfield

Born: Preston, 7 October 1962.
Career: PRESTON NORTH END, 1980. New Zealand. Exeter City, 1985.

■ Midfielder Mark Walsh scored on his North End debut on the opening day of the 1981–82 season in a 2–1 defeat at Millwall. However, more than half of his 10 League appearances that season were made from the bench. He was more of a regular the following season when his only goal proved the winner in a 3–2 win over Southend United. During the 1984 close season, Walsh parted company with the Deepdale club and went to play in New Zealand. He later returned to the UK and made a single substitute appearance as a non-contract player for Exeter City.

WALTON, Joseph

Full-back

Born: Manchester, 5 June 1925.
Career: Manchester United, 1943. PRESTON NORTH END, 1948. Accrington Stanley, 1960.

■ Joe Walton arrived at Deepdale from Manchester United in March 1948 having already made a name for himself at Old Trafford as a steady, if unspectacular full-back. He made his debut in a 2–0 win at Sunderland and soon settled into life in his new surroundings. In his 11 appearances at the end of the 1947–48 season, he netted a couple of penalties. Preston were relegated the following season but in 1950–51 they returned to the top flight as Champions of Division Two. However, this was the season when Walton hit a bad patch and lost his place

to Billy Scott, albeit temporarily. His perseverance and hard work during his spell in the reserves paid off and he was soon reinstated. Walton was a member of the Preston side beaten 3–2 by West Bromwich Albion in the 1954 FA Cup Final. After that, he missed very few matches and was ever present in 1956–57 and 1957–58 when North End finished third and second respectively in the top flight. Walton played in every game in the 1959–60 season but in February 1961, after becoming the first full-back in the club's history to make 400 appearances, he was allowed to join Accrington Stanley for the last few games of their last season in the Football League.

WALTON, Joseph

Outside-right/Inside-right

Born: Lunes, 8 January 1881.
Career: PRESTON NORTH END, 1901. Tottenham Hotspur, 1903. Sheffield United, 1909. Stalybridge Celtic.

■ Joe Walton first played for Preston North End towards the end of the 1901–02 season, scoring twice in seven games as the club finished third in Division Two. A nifty, mobile winger, he played on a more regular basis the

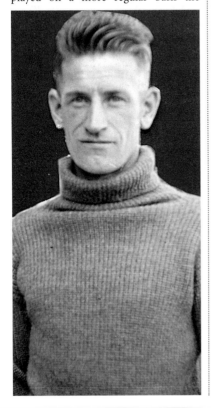

following season but left the club in the close season to play Southern League football for Tottenham Hotspur. Walton was at White Hart Lane for two years before he could lay claim to the outside-right position. He started to attract the attention of the international selectors but, although he played in three trial games while with Spurs, he did not manage to win international recognition. After refusing the maximum wage to re-sign, he joined Sheffield United where he played for two years before moving to Stalybridge Celtic for their first year as a professional club in the Lancashire Combination.

WARD, Frank

Right-back, half-back

Born: Leigh, 21 January 1903.
Career: Walshaw United. Bury, 1923. PRESTON NORTH END, 1927. Southampton, 1933. Worcester City. Folkestone.

■ Frank Ward was a versatile player who began his first-class career with Bury and, in his first season with the club, helped them win promotion to the First Division. Although he was at Gigg Lane for three years and made 44 appearances, he was never a fully established member of the side. He left Bury in 1927 to join Preston and made his debut in a 3–3 home draw against West Bromwich Albion. After that, Ward was a virtual ever present, missing very few games in five seasons at Deepdale. A sound tackler and a good distributor of the ball, Ward had made 208 League appearances for North End before being allowed to join Southampton. He spent two seasons at The Dell but was never an automatic choice. After leaving the South Coast club, Ward played non-League football for Worcester City and later Folkestone.

WARD, Gavin John

Goalkeeper

Born: Sutton Coldfield, 30 June 1970.
Career: Aston Villa. Shrewsbury Town, 1988. West Bromwich Albion, 1989. Cardiff City, 1989. Leicester City, 1993. Bradford City, 1995. Bolton Wanderers, 1996. Burnley, 1998 (loan). Stoke City, 1999. Walsall, 2002. Coventry City, 2003.

Barnsley, 2004 (loan). PRESTON NORTH END, 2004.

■ After being released by Aston Villa, goalkeeper Gavin Ward had spells with Shrewsbury Town and West Bromwich Albion without making either club's League side. He joined Cardiff City in October 1989, but in his first two seasons at Ninian Park he found himself understudy to Roger Hansbury before winning a regular place in 1991–92. He was the club's first-choice 'keeper in 1992–93 when the Bluebirds won the Third Division Championship, but at the end of that campaign Leicester City paid £175,000 for his services. During his time at Filbert Street, he found it hard to displace the in-form Kevin Poole and moved on to Bradford City were he proved a huge hit. His next club were Bolton Wanderers but again he found himself in the shadows as understudy to Keith Branagan. He went on loan to Burnley where lack of funds ruled out a permanent signing. In February 1999 he moved to Stoke City and helped the Potters win the Auto Windscreens Shield Final at Wembley. While with Stoke he suffered a bad back injury that kept him out of action for six months. Further long absences followed and in the summer of 2002 he moved to Walsall prior to playing for Coventry and going on loan to Barnsley. Ward arrived at Deepdale in the summer of 2004 as back up for Andy Lonergan. He made his North End debut in October when Lonergan broke his hand in the game against Queen's Park Rangers. He enjoyed a brief run of four matches before stepping in for a second time when his rival was again injured. Ward then suffered an eye injury in the televised clash with Ipswich and this kept him out for three weeks, after which he returned to the bench.

WAREING, William

Centre-half, left-half

Born: Southport, 1887.
Career: Southport. Chorley. PRESTON NORTH END, 1910. Everton, 1912. Swindon Town, 1920.

■ Billy Wareing played his early football with his home-town team, Southport, and then Chorley, before

being given a chance at League level with Preston North End. After making his debut in a 1–1 home draw against Manchester City in the second game of the 1910–11 season, Wareing established himself as a regular member of the Preston side for about two seasons. During the early part of the club's Second Division promotion-winning season of 1912–13, Wareing left to play for Everton. His debut for the Toffees was a disaster as they were beaten 6–0 by Newcastle United. However, he did go on to make 69 appearances, helping them win the League Championship in 1914–15. He continued to play for Everton throughout World War One, but he signed for Swindon Town when the hostilities ended. His first game for the Wiltshire club was in their 9–1 defeat of Luton Town on the opening day of the 1920–21 season. He missed very few games during his stay at the County Ground and played the last of 156 games at Aberdare Athletic in April 1925.

WARNER, John

Full-back

Born: Preston, 1883.
Career: St Michael's (Preston). PRESTON NORTH END, 1902. Southampton. Portsmouth.

■ Jack Warner signed for Preston from local side St Michael's and in

1902–03, his first season with the club, he featured in the 6–1 mauling of Stockport County and the 1–0 win over Manchester United. Understudy to Derbyshire and Orrell the following season, he made just nine appearances as North End won the Second Division Championship. Finding himself spending most of his time in the reserves, he later moved to Southampton. Although he never let the side down when playing for the Saints, the directors considered him suspect due to a nagging knee injury and he moved to Portsmouth. Proving the Saints' directors wrong, Warner remained at Pompey as a player until 1915 and later became their trainer.

WATERHOUSE, Kenneth

Wing-half, inside-forward

Born: Ormskirk, 23 January 1930.
Career: Burscough. PRESTON NORTH END, 1948. Rotherham United, 1958. Bristol City, 1963. Darlington, 1964.

■ Ken Waterhouse was on Preston's books for a number of years before making his debut on Christmas Day 1953 in a 2–1 defeat at Burnley. It was his only appearance that season. In 1954–55

he played in eight games, scoring a hat-trick on the final day of the season in a 4–0 win at Charlton Athletic. However, he still could not win a regular place in the North End first team and, after making a handful of appearances in each of the next two seasons, he moved to Rotherham United. Waterhouse was a regular in four seasons at Millmoor, making 123 League appearances and proving his versatility by playing in a number of different outfield positions. He then had a spell with Bristol City before ending his playing days in the North East with a single appearance for Darlington.

WATERS, Patrick

Centre-half

Born: Dublin, 31 January 1922.
Career: Glentoran. PRESTON NORTH END, 1947. Carlisle United, 1950.

■ Centre-half Paddy Waters had impressed in the Irish League with Glentoran before North End signed him in June 1947. Unable to displace Emlyn Williams, Waters had to wait until the following February before he made his debut in a 1–1 draw at Manchester United. He appeared on a more regular basis in 1948–49, making 21 appearances, but he could do nothing to

prevent the club's slide into the Second Division. He was the club's first-choice centre-half in 1949–50 until he lost his place to Harry Mattinson. On leaving Deepdale he joined Carlisle United. Waters made 261 League appearances for United in seven seasons of Third Division North football at Brunton Park, as the Cumbrian club almost won promotion on a number of occasions.

WATMOUGH, Richard

Outside-right

Born: Idle, 1912.
Died: 1962.
Career: Calverley. Thackley. Greengates United. Idle. Bradford City, 1931. Blackpool, 1934. PRESTON NORTH END, 1937.

■ Dickie Watmough was a fast, tricky winger who joined Blackpool from Bradford City in October 1934 after scoring 25 goals in 94 games for the Yorkshire club. He scored on his debut for the Seasiders against Norwich City and became a regular in the Blackpool side. In 1935–36, he netted 10 goals in 25 games and many of his pinpoint crosses were converted by Bobby Finan who became the Second Division's leading scorer with 34 strikes. The following

season, the Seasiders won promotion to the First Division as runners-up to Leicester City with Watmough in outstanding form, netting 12 goals in 31 games. He found it difficult to adapt to First Division football and joined North End in an £8,000 exchange deal that took Frank O'Donnell to Blackpool and also took Jim McIntosh to Deepdale. Watmough resurrected his career with North End, scoring both his side's goals on debut in a 3–2 defeat by Portsmouth. He went on to help Preston finish third in the top flight and won an FA Cup-winners' medal after North End beat Huddersfield Town 1–0 in the Wembley Final. Sadly, injuries forced him to miss the entire 1938–39 season and at the end of that campaign he decided to retire. Watmough, who acted as 12th man for Yorkshire in a County Championship cricket match, later scouted for Bradford Park Avenue.

WATSON, Liam

Forward

Born: Liverpool, 21 May 1970.
Career: Warrington Town. PRESTON NORTH END, 1993.

■ Signed from non-League Warrington Town, Liam Watson made a sensational start to his Preston career. Replacing the injured Mickey Norbury, he scored in a 5–2 win over Rotherham United and then netted in each of his

next two appearances against Port Vale and Huddersfield Town. He made a couple of appearances from the bench either side of playing in a 5–1 home defeat by Mansfield Town. Watson played in the emotional defeat at Bolton on the last day of the season but made just one appearance the following season before leaving the club.

WATSON, William Thomas

Full-back

Born: Swansea, 11 June 1918.
Died: 1978.
Career: PRESTON NORTH END, 1946. Cardiff City, 1947.

■ Bill Watson was a no-nonsense full-back who played wartime football for Preston North End. When League football resumed in 1946–47, he was still on North End's books. After making his first-team debut in the number-six shirt in the 3–2 defeat of Leeds United on the opening day of the campaign, Watson went on to make 15 appearances for North End before returning to his native South Wales with Cardiff City. Despite some impressive displays at youth team level he made just one League appearance for the Bluebirds before being released.

WATT, William Douglas

Outside-left

Born: Aberdeen, 6 June 1946.
Career: PRESTON NORTH END, 1963.

■ Willie Watt spent most of his time at Deepdale in the club's reserves, making just eight League appearances in four seasons. His first senior game in North End colours came towards the end of the 1964–65 season as a replacement for Doug Holden in a 2–2 draw with Bury. He played in three more games that season and was never on the losing side. In addition, his crosses enabled Alex Dawson to score twice on the final day of the season in a 3–1 defeat of Norwich City. Unable to make much headway with competition from Lee and Veall, he parted company with the club.

WAYMAN, Charles

Centre-forward

Born: Bishop Auckland, 16 May 1922.
Died: 27 March 2006.

Career: *Spennymoor United. Newcastle United, 1941. Southampton, 1947. PRESTON NORTH END, 1950. Middlesbrough, 1954. Darlington, 1956.*

◼ Born in Bishop Auckland, Charlie Wayman started his working life in the coalmines. After playing for Spennymoor United, he joined Newcastle United for whom he proved to be a prolific scorer in the war leagues. When League football resumed in 1946–47, Wayman was a regular in the Magpies' forward line. In that season he topped the Second Division scoring charts with 30 goals as well as netting a hat-trick to knock Southampton out of the FA Cup. Surprisingly he was allowed to leave St James' Park and in October 1947 he joined Southampton for £10,000. He settled in immediately and scored 17 goals in 27 games as Saints ended the season third in Division Two. The following season he scored five goals in a 6–0 home win over Leicester City – a club record that still stands today. In 1949–50, Wayman scored 24 goals in 36 League games, including a hat-trick against Hull City, but the Saints ended the season on 52 points, the same as both Sheffield clubs. Tottenham Hotspur were the Champions and Sheffield Wednesday

were promoted with them on goal average. Wayman's wife had never really settled in the South and after scoring 81 goals in 107 games he moved to Preston North End. He was instrumental in the club winning the Second Division Championship in his first season with the club, as he netted 27 goals in the League. He scored four goals in the first-half against Queen's Park Rangers at Loftus Road on Christmas Day and a hat-trick against Grimsby Town. The following season, Wayman still scored on a regular basis, his total of 24 goals including a scintillating treble against Arsenal at Highbury. In 1952–53 he netted two hat-tricks in his total of 26 League and Cup goals – against Middlesbrough and Wolverhampton Wanderers. In 1954, the courageous Wayman netted another League hat-trick against Sunderland and scored in every round of the FA Cup, including the Final against West Bromwich Albion. That season made Charlie Wayman the only player in the entire 92 League clubs to have scored 20 or more goals in each of his last six League seasons. He hit a hat-trick on the opening day of the 1954–55 season against Manchester City and scored two in the 7–1 rout of Cardiff City. After scoring 116 goals in 171 games, he left Deepdale to play for Middlesbrough and later Darlington.

WEALANDS, Jeffrey Andrew

Goalkeeper

Born: *Darlington, 26 August 1951.*
Career: *Wolverhampton Wanderers, 1968. Darlington, 1970. Hull City, 1972. Birmingham City, 1979. Manchester United, 1983. Oldham Athletic, 1984 (loan). PRESTON NORTH END, 1984 (loan). Altrincham.*

◼ Though he turned professional with Wolverhampton Wanderers, Jeffrey Wealands never made their League side. He was transferred to his home-town team, Darlington, who had offered him terms in 1966. After appearing in 31 games for the Quakers he joined Hull City. In 7? years at Boothferry Park he played in 270 League and Cup games before joining Birmingham City for a fee of £30,000 in the summer of 1979. In his first season at St Andrew's, he kept 16

clean sheets in 40 games and helped the Blues win promotion to the First Division. Wealands was the club's first-choice 'keeper for the next couple of seasons but after 117 appearances he joined Manchester United as cover for Gary Bailey. Following a loan spell with Oldham, Wealands joined North End on a similar basis midway through the 1984–85 season and made his debut in a 2–1 defeat at Walsall. With Preston struggling in Division Three, Wealands was never on the winning side. On leaving Old Trafford, he played non-League football for Altrincham.

WEARMOUTH, Michael

Centre-half

Born: *Barrow, 16 May 1944.*
Career: *Barrow, 1962. PRESTON NORTH END, 1964.*

◼ Mick Wearmouth began his career with his home-town club, Barrow, but after two seasons in which they challenged for promotion to the Third Division, the 1962–63 campaign saw them finish at the foot of the Fourth Division. Wearmouth, who made 33 appearances in his time at Holker Street, joined Preston and made his North End debut in place of the injured Tony Singleton at Newcastle. It was not the best of debuts as the Magpies ran out 5–2 winners. He never really established himself in the Preston side and played the last of his 11 League outings in a 4–0 defeat at Cardiff in April 1967.

WELSH, Paul William

Centre-half

Born: Liverpool, 10 May 1966.
Career: Formby. PRESTON NORTH END, 1984.

■ Central defender Paul Welsh was discovered playing for Formby and joined Preston in May 1984. After impressing in the reserves, he made his first-team debut in a 3–2 home win over

Bristol City the following November. He kept his place for the next game but after North End went down 4–0 at Gillingham he lost out to Geoff Twentyman. The following season, the club's first in Division Four, Welsh appeared a little more regularly but could not prevent the club finishing one off the bottom. He did score his only goal for the club when he came off the bench in the 6–3 home defeat by Chester City but, like a number of players, this was his last season with the club.

WESTWELL, Simon

Full-back

Born: Clitheroe, 12 November 1961.
Career: PRESTON NORTH END, 1979.

■ Full-back Simon Westwell worked his way up through the ranks at

Deepdale to make his first-team debut in a 1–1 draw at Chelsea in September 1980. He went on to make 20 appearances in that 1980–81 season but was helpless to avoid the club being relegated to the Third Division. Westwell found himself in and out of the side the following season but in 1982–83 he appeared on a more regular basis. He scored his only goal for the club in a 3–0 home win over Brentford. After ending the campaign in mid-table, Preston decided they no longer needed Westwell's services.

WHALEY, Simon

Midfield

Born: Bolton, 7 June 1985.
Career: Bury, 2002. PRESTON NORTH END, 2006.

■ A product of Bury's youth side, this attacking midfielder made his League debut from the bench in the game against Torquay United in November 2002, after having appeared in the LDV Vans Trophy. Stretchered off while playing for the reserves, he was offered an extension to his existing contract at Gigg Lane prior to picking up another knee injury in training. He had just returned to first-team action when he suffered medial ligament damage and yet another lay-off. The 2004–05 season was Simon Whaley's first full campaign of senior football and as the season wore on he continued to improve and grow in confidence. Signed by Preston North End, more than half his first-team appearances in the Championship were from the bench, but as the season drew to

a close, he netted three vital goals. His first for an injury-hit Preston team came at Coventry. It not only ended the Sky Blues' 130–match unbeaten home record, but virtually sealed his team a Play-off spot. After netting at Leicester, his next goal at Hull was his third in the last three away games and the first strike by a visiting team at the KC Stadium for six hours!

WHALLEY, David Neil

Midfield

Born: Prescot, 29 October 1965.
Career: Warrington Town. PRESTON NORTH END, 1993.

■ After joining Preston from Warrington Town, Neil Whalley did not have the best of League debuts as he was in the side that lost 4–0 at Plymouth in March 1983. He appeared in all but one of the remaining 15 games of that 1992–93 season but could not prevent the club from being relegated to the Third Division. He appeared in slightly more games the following season as the club reached the Play-offs and again in 1994–95 as North End repeated the achievement. During the course of this latter season, his final one at Deepdale,

Whalley scored his only goal for the club in a 2–1 home defeat at the hands of eventual runners-up, Walsall.

WHALLEY, Frederick Harold

Goalkeeper

Born: Salford, 9 October 1898.
Died: 1976.
Career: PRESTON NORTH END, 1919. Grimsby Town, 1920. Leeds United, 1921. Fulham, 1923.

■ A product of the Preston schools and Army football, Frederick Whalley enlisted in the North Lancashire Regiment at the age of 15 and saw active service in France before signing for Preston North End in June 1919. Whalley was one of four goalkeepers used in the 1919–20 season and appeared in eight successive games following an injury to Arthur Causer. He was on the winning side on his debut as Preston beat Oldham Athletic 2–1 but, though he proved himself dependable, in his last game North End were beaten 4–0 at Chelsea. He left Deepdale in the close season and spent the 1920–21 campaign with Grimsby before signing for Leeds United in the summer of 1921. Whalley thought nothing of chatting to the fans behind his goal when the action was at the other end of the pitch. His antics made him extremely popular at all the clubs he played for, but beneath the comic exterior was a dedicated professional who excelled at his job.

WHARTON, Clarence Norman

Goalkeeper

Born: Askam-in-Furness, 28 July 1903.
Died: 13 July 1961.
Career: Askam. Barrow, 1922. PRESTON NORTH END, 1925. Barrow, 1927. Sheffield United, 1928. Norwich City, 1931. Doncaster Rovers, 1935. York City, 1936. Leeds United, 1939.

■ Norman Wharton was not the most agile of goalkeepers, but he was one of the bravest and most consistent. An electrician by trade, he joined his local club Barrow and his displays between the posts for the Holker Street club alerted North End, who secured his services in 1925. He made his Preston debut in the game against Darlington in April 1926, keeping a clean sheet in a goalless draw against Darlington. He played in the last seven games of that season and was only on the losing side once. Surprisingly, Jimmy Branston started the 1926–27 season as the club's first-choice 'keeper but after three games he gave way to Wharton. He played in the next six games, again only finishing on the losing side once, before Carr replaced him. Wharton then had a season back with Barrow before being transferred to Sheffield United. His next club were Norwich City and in 1933–34, when he was ever present, he won a Third Division South Championship medal with the Canaries. He went on to have spells with Doncaster and York before joining Leeds United at the age of 36. A keen pianist, Wharton died in his home town where his seven brothers had all been good rugby players.

WHARTON, John Edwin

Winger

Born: Bolton, 18 June 1920.
Died: May 1997.
*Career: Plymouth Argyle, 1937. PRESTON NORTH END, 1939. Man-*chester City, 1947. Blackburn Rovers, 1948. Newport County, 1952.

■ Jack Wharton, the father of Terry Wharton who played for Wolves, Bolton, Crystal Palace and Walsall, was an outside-right who played for Plymouth Argyle in the late 1930s and scored twice on his League debut. After just 10 appearances for the Pilgrims, he was snapped up by Preston North End but had to resume his career after World War Two. He made his Preston debut wearing the number-11 shirt in the 3–2 defeat of Leeds United on the opening day of the 1946–47 season. A great crosser of the ball, he provided plenty of goalscoring opportunities for Willie McIntosh. Although he only scored seven himself in his 25 appearances, his total included two in the 3–1 win over Aston Villa. He almost claimed a hat-trick but the other goal was deemed an own goal by Villa's Lowe. On leaving Preston, he spent a little over a season with Manchester City before signing for Blackburn Rovers. He enjoyed almost five years at Ewood Park, playing in 129 League matches and finding the net 14 times. In February 1953 he joined Newport County and ended his career with the Welsh club.

WHITE, Frank Robert Harvey

Winger

Born: Winecote, 14 November 1911.
Died: 1985.

Career: Tamworth Juniors. Stoneware Limited (Tamworth). Birmingham, 1932. PRESTON NORTH END, 1938. Redditch Town.

■ Frank White was a marvellous goalscoring winger. Fast, a good dribbler and with a telling shot, he was recommended to Birmingham by the club's international goalkeeper Harry Hibbs. White had been a prolific marksman in junior circles before moving to St Andrew's but, surprisingly, his early days with the Blues were spent in the wing-half berth. The Birmingham management soon realised their mistake and thereafter White obliged with some sparkling performances and match-winning goals. His best season with Birmingham in terms of goals scored was 1934–35 when his total of 16 included a hat-trick in a 3–0 home win over Preston North End. White had scored 50 goals in 156 games for Birmingham when he joined the Deepdale club in December 1938. After starring on his debut in a 2–0 win over Leeds United, White scored six goals in his next four games including successive doubles in the Cup game against Aston Villa and the League match with Middlesbrough. He had scored 12 goals in 22 games before League football came to a halt following the outbreak of war. During the hostilities, he 'guested' for Aldershot, Mansfield, Sheffield United and Wrexham but when football resumed in 1946–47, White played non-League football for Redditch.

WHITEHEAD, William Thomas

Centre-forward

Born: Saffron Walden, 11 September 1897.
Career: Swansea Town, 1923. Queen's Park Rangers, 1925. PRESTON NORTH END, 1926. Manchester City, 1927. Boston United. Yeovil & Petters United.

■ Unable to make much progress with his first club, Swansea Town, Bill Whitehead joined Queen's Park Rangers where he appeared on a more regular basis. In 1925–26, he scored four goals in 25 games but Rangers still ended the campaign at the foot of the Third Division South. He left Rangers to join Preston as understudy to Tommy Roberts. Though Whitehead made only

three appearances, he did find the net on his debut as Preston beat Grimsby Town 3–2. He moved to Manchester City but left Maine Road without appearing in their League side to play non-League football for Boston and later Yeovil.

WHITTLE, Daniel

Forward

Born: Preston, 1876.
Career: PRESTON NORTH END, 1897.

■ A most versatile forward, Daniel Whittle made 10 League appearances for North End spread over three seasons as he understudied the likes of Sandy Brown, Tom Pratt and Adam Gara. His first game for the Deepdale club came in a goalless draw against Bolton in October 1897 and his last against Liverpool in April 1900. Although he never got on the score sheet for the first team, he was quite a prolific scorer for the reserves.

WHITTLE, Richard

Right-back

Born: Preston, 1867.
Career: PRESTON NORTH END, 1888.

■ Right-back Richard Whittle's only League appearance for the Lilywhites came in the fifth game of 1888–89, the inaugural season of the competition. The strong-tackling defender actually scored for North End as they annihilated Stoke 7–0, with Jimmy Ross netting four of the goals.

WHITWORTH, Neil Anthony

Centre-half

Born: Wigan, 12 April 1972.
Career: Wigan Athletic, 1988. Manchester United, 1990. PRESTON NORTH END, 1992 (loan). Barnsley, 1992 (loan). Rotherham United, 1993 (loan). Blackpool, 1993 (loan). Kilmarnock, 1994. Wigan Athletic, 1998 (loan). Hull City, 1998. Exeter City, 2000. Southport.

■ Neil Whitworth had made just a couple of appearances for Wigan Athletic when he was transferred to Manchester United for £45,000 before he had signed a professional contract for the Latics. After making his United debut at right-back against Southampton in March 1991, Whitworth was loaned out to

Preston North End. He played the first of his six games for the Deepdale club in a 3–1 home defeat by Exeter and was only on the winning side twice in that spell before returning to Old Trafford. He had further spells on loan with Barnsley, Rotherham and Blackpool before a £265,000 transfer took him north of the border to Kilmarnock. After four seasons in the Scottish Premier League he was released and joined Wigan on a short-term contract. Whitworth later joined Hull City but after just a handful of games, he picked up a troublesome Achilles tendon injury. Following surgery, the ankle joint became infected and this led to another operation and rehabilitation at the National Sports Centre before the Tigers released him. He then joined Exeter City but with his cause not being helped by the various changes in managers, he left to play for Southport.

WIJNHARD, Clyde

Forward

Born: Paramaribo, Surinam, 9 November 1973.
Career: Ajax (Holland). Groningen (Holland). RKC Waalwijk (Holland). Willem II Tilburg (Holland). Leeds United, 1998. Huddersfield Town, 1999. PRESTON NORTH END, 2002. Oldham Athletic, 2002. Vitoria Guimaraes (Portugal). Darlington.

■ Signed from Willem II as Leeds United prepared for the 1998–99 season, Clyde Wijnhard was a direct replacement for Rangers-bound Rod Wallace. He

began brightly but then found it difficult to settle into English football. His arrival also coincided with the emergence of Harry Kewell and Alan Smith and he spent a lot of his time on the bench. Signed by Huddersfield Town for a fee of £750,000 – half what Leeds paid for him – Wijnhard proved to be a bargain purchase. He struck up a fearsome partnership with Marcus Stewart and netted his first senior hat-trick in a 7–1 demolition of Crystal Palace. After just five appearances the following season, he was involved in a road accident from which he considered himself lucky to be alive at all. Wijnhard suffered a broken arm but his injuries kept him out of action for the entire season. On recovering he was sold to Preston North End to ease the Yorkshire club's financial burden. At Deepdale he showed he had lost none of his former power with a Man of the Match display – scoring one, winning a penalty and hitting the post in a 2–0 win over Portsmouth. He formed a tremendous partnership with Richard Cresswell and had scored three goals in six games when he was surprisingly allowed to join Oldham. Wijnhard scored 11 times in 16 games for his new club before being released. He joined Portuguese side Vitoria Guimaraes but injuries hampered his progress. He returned to the Football League with Darlington and ended his first season as the Quakers' leading scorer.

WILCOCK, George Harrie

Goalkeeper

Born: Edinburgh, 24 January 1890.
Died: 1962.
Career: Bradford Park Avenue, 1909. Barnsley, 1911. Goole Town. Brighton and Hove Albion. Southampton. PRESTON NORTH END, 1920. Caerphilly. Southampton Docks & Marine.

■ Having originally been on the books of Bradford Park Avenue, George Wilcock played a handful of League games for Barnsley before dropping into non-League football with Goole Town. He served in World War One and was wounded at Loos before being signed by Brighton in 1918. He moved to Southampton the following year before Preston gave him the opportunity to

resurrect his League career. Wilcock started the 1920–21 season as the club's first-choice 'keeper and made his debut in a 1–0 home defeat by Huddersfield on the opening day of the 1920–21 season. He later lost out to Arthur Causer after he had let in six goals against Liverpool. He dropped out of League football and played for Caerphilly before returning to the South Coast to end his playing days.

WILCOX, Harry Melbourne

Forward

Born: Dalston, London, 7 January 1878.
Died: 21 July 1937.
Career: Eastville Rovers. Selly Oak St Mary's. Small Heath, 1898. Watford. PRESTON NORTH END, 1901. Plymouth Argyle. Leicester Fosse, 1906. West Bromwich Albion, 1907. Plymouth Argyle.

■ After starting out with Small Heath, Harry Wilcox joined Watford of the Southern League. After one season in which he was ever present Wilcox, who possessed a rather flamboyant moustache, moved to Preston North End. On his debut against Leicester Fosse, he scored twice from the penalty spot in a 5–0 win. He went on to top the goalscoring charts in 1901–02 with 14 goals as Preston finished third in Division Two. Wilcox was ever present the following season, netting five penalties in his total of 14 goals, while his total of 15 in 1903–04 went a long way in helping the Lilywhites win the Second Division Championship. After a brief spell with Plymouth, Wilcox signed for Leicester Fosse. He missed out on a further promotion when Fosse and West Bromwich Albion agreed to exchange attackers, with Albion's Fred Shinton going in the opposite direction. Wilcox later made his final move back to Plymouth where he earned a formidable reputation as a centre-half and captain. He represented the Southern League on a couple of occasions and also led the Pilgrims to the Southern League Championship in 1912–13.

WILCOX, Russell

Centre-half

Born: Hemsworth, 25 March 1964.
Career: Doncaster Rovers, 1980. Frickley

Athletic. Northampton Town, 1986. Hull City, 1990. Doncaster Rovers, 1993. PRESTON NORTH END, 1995. Scunthorpe United, 1997.

■ Russ Wilcox made his Football League debut as an apprentice with his local club, Doncaster Rovers, but was not retained by the Belle Vue club and drifted into non-League football with Frickley Colliery. While with Frickley, he won England semi-professional international honours before joining Northampton Town in the summer of 1986. In his first season with the Cobblers he won a Fourth Division Championship medal and he went on to play in 162 games before Hull City paid £120,000 for his services in August 1990. The Tigers were relegated in Wilcox's first season at the club and, though he was a regular at the heart of the Hull defence, he rejoined Doncaster Rovers after 116 appearances for Hull. Shortly after his arrival, he was appointed captain and for the two seasons he played at the club, he won the supporters' Player of the Year award. In 1994–95, Wilcox was elected into the PFA's Third Division team by his fellow professionals. Much to the disgust of Doncaster fans, he was allowed to join Preston and he made his North End debut in a 2–2 draw at Fulham. He

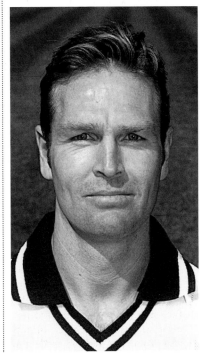

brought a wealth of experience to the Preston back four and also contributed one of the goals of the season with a match-winning chip over the Carlisle 'keeper in injury time of the first-round FA Cup tie. Always one to lead by example, he was again selected to the PFA divisional team and also won a Third Division Championship medal as North End swept to the title. Though Wilcox was not always first choice the following season, his wholehearted approach helped to steady the younger players around him when he did play. He was allowed to join Scunthorpe United in the summer of 1997, but he suffered more than his fair share of injuries at Glanford Park. In 1999–2000, he combined a playing role with that of the club's assistant manager before eventually hanging up his boots to concentrate on the management side.

WILKES, Stephen Brian

Midfield

Born: Preston, 30 June 1967.
Career: Wigan Athletic, 1985. PRESTON NORTH END, 1986.

■ Though he was born in Preston, midfielder Steve Wilkes joined Wigan

Athletic as an apprentice. However, on being unable to make the grade with the Latics he joined his home-town team. During North End's promotion-winning season of 1986–87, he appeared in a Freight Rover Trophy game against Crewe Alexandra which Preston won 1–0 but he had to wait until the following season before making his League debut. He came off the bench in a 3–0 defeat at Blackpool and made another substitute appearance before starting his only game, against Gillingham; a match North End lost 4–0.

WILKIE, Thomas

Goalkeeper

Born: Preston, 1879.
Career: PRESTON NORTH END, 1900.

■ During the club's relegation season of 1900–01, goalkeeper Tom Wilkie made three appearances for the North End side at the end of the season following injuries to Peter McBride and his replacement Sidney Woodhouse. His first two games brought victories over Bury and Sheffield Wednesday, leaving North End needing to beat bottom-of-the-table West Bromwich Albion to stay up. While Preston were losing 3–2, their nearest rivals Stoke were pulling off a shock win at Notts County. North End were relegated and Wilkie did not play for the club again.

WILKINS, Paul

Forward

Born: Hackney, 20 March 1964.
Career: Tottenham Hotspur. Crystal Palace, 1982. PRESTON NORTH END, 1984.

■ Paul Wilkins started out as an apprentice with Tottenham Hotspur, but made the switch to Crystal Palace in January 1982. Although he proved a prolific scorer in the Eagles' reserve side, he was not given much of a chance at League level. In the summer of 1984, Wilkins joined Preston North End and started his Deepdale career with a bang, scoring one of the goals on the opening day of the season in a 2–0 defeat of Doncaster Rovers. He also found the net in the League Cup-tie with Tranmere and then netted another League goal from

the bench in a 3–0 win over Cambridge United. Despite this promising start, he lost out to players such as Peter Houghton and Nigel Greenwood and left the club.

WILKINSON, Stephen John

Forward

Born: Lincoln, 1 September 1968.
Career: Leicester City, 1986. Crewe Alexandra, 1988 (loan). Mansfield Town, 1989. PRESTON NORTH END, 1995. Chesterfield, 1997. Kettering Town.

■ After working his way through the ranks at Leicester City, where he was a prolific teenage goalscorer, Steve Wilkinson made just a handful of appearances for the Foxes before going on loan to Crewe Alexandra. In September 1989 he was allowed to join Mansfield Town for a fee of £80,000. There, in a lowly Stags side, he equalled the Third Division scoring record by scoring all his side's goals in a 5–2 defeat of Birmingham City. Relegation for Mansfield followed in 1990–91 and, despite Wilkinson forming a twin spearhead with the veteran Trevor Christie, the Stags' divisional yo-yoing continued over the next couple of seasons. He helped Mansfield reach the Play-offs in 1994–95, scoring a hat-trick against Chesterfield, and was voted the club's Player of the Year. He had taken his tally of goals to 90 in 273 games before Preston manager Gary Peters paid £80,000 for his services. Instead of scoring goals for North End from Andy Saville's knockdowns, Wilkinson performed more of a linking role between midfield and attack. Much of his running off the ball went unnoticed

but the space he created benefited the team's attacking moves. Without doubt his personal highlight – apart from winning a Third Division Championship medal – was his hat-trick (along with Saville also scoring a treble) in a 6–0 win over his former club. After starting the 1996–97 season on fire with seven goals in five games, including a hat-trick in a League Cup-tie at Wigan, his season was effectively ruined by a knee injury which required surgery. Wilkinson obviously returned too soon because a second operation was required. While his constructive forward play was missed he became the club's programme editor. He later signed for Chesterfield where, in his second full appearance for the Spireites, he recorded his 100th League goal. Sadly, he began to suffer from a spate of injuries and had to watch from the sidelines as the club were relegated in 1999–2000. He then left Saltergate to continue his career with non-League Kettering Town.

WILLACY, David L.

Outside-right

Born: Dumfries, 1912.
Died: 1944.
Career: Queen of the South. PRESTON NORTH END, 1938.

■ Winger David Willacy began his football career with Queen of the South where his displays led to scouts from a number of leading clubs north and south of the border visiting Palmerston Park to watch him. Preston North End were the quickest off the mark and signed Willacy. With the exception of the final game of the 1938–39 season, in which Willacy played his only game for the club in a 3–1 defeat at Charlton, the number-seven shirt was worn by McGibbons and White.

WILLIAMS, Emlyn

Centre-half

Born: Maesteg, 15 January 1912.
Died: 1989.
Career: Buxton Town. Barnsley, 1936. PRESTON NORTH END, 1939. Barnsley, 1948. Accrington Stanley, 1948.

■ Emlyn Williams, an uncompromising centre-half, played non-League football for Buxton Town before being signed by Barnsley in October 1936. During the first of two stints at Oakwell, Williams helped the club win the Third Division North Championship in 1938–39 before leaving to play for Preston North End. Because of the hostilities, he did not appear in his first League game for the Deepdale club until September 1946 in a 2–1 home defeat by Sheffield United. He went on to play in 33 games that season as North End finished seventh in the top flight. Williams was a regular member of the side the following season as North End again finished seventh, but in the close season he rejoined Barnsley, taking his total number of League appearances for the Tykes to 105. In December 1948 he moved on to Accrington Stanley where he ended his career.

WILLIAMS, Frank H.

Winger

Born: Cefn-y-bedd, 1903.
Career: Wrexham, 1924. PRESTON NORTH END, 1926. Port Vale, 1928. Oswestry Town. Northern Nomads. Ashton National Gas. Altrincham. Shrewsbury Town. Buxton.

■ Frank Williams was a flying winger who became a Wales amateur international while with his first club, Wrexham. However, he failed to win a regular place in the Robins' side over two seasons at the Racecourse Ground and moved to Preston. He made his debut in a 3–1 win over Reading and laid on a goal apiece for Chandler and Roberts. Selected for the Lilywhites on both flanks, he had made just eight appearances when he left Deepdale to play for Port Vale. After a single appearance for the Valiants, Williams moved into non-League, playing for a number of clubs, the last being Buxton.

WILLIAMS, Gary Peter

Left-back

Born: Liverpool, 8 March 1954.
Career: Marine. PRESTON NORTH END, 1972. Brighton and Hove Albion, 1977. Crystal Palace, 1982.

■ Gary Williams arrived at Deepdale from non-League club Marine and made his League debut for Preston in the final game of the 1971–72 season, a 2–2 draw with Swindon Town. In his first few seasons with the club, when he struggled to win a regular place in the side, Williams was played at outside-left and it was only when manager Nobby Stiles decided to try him at left-back that his career began to take off. In 1975–76 he missed just two of North End's games and was voted the club's Player of the Year by the fans. The following campaign even eclipsed the previous season for Williams as his outstanding form continued. Suddenly, he was hot property with a host of top clubs vying for his signature. Brighton and Hove Albion put in an offer of £100,000 as they sought to take both Williams and Mark Lawrenson to the Goldstone Ground. But, even though the club were suffering financial difficulties, the North End board rejected the offer. In hindsight it was a good decision because a few months later the Seagulls came back with improved offers for both players: £100,000 for Lawrenson and £45,000 for Williams. This time the board accepted the offer. Williams did very well on the South Coast, helping the club win promotion to the First Division in 1978–79. He certainly did not look out of place in the top flight and appeared in 158 League games for the Seagulls. In the summer of 1982 he moved to Crystal Palace but, after just 10 appearances, he sadly suffered a terrible knee injury which prematurely curtailed his first-class career.

WILLIAMS, Neil John Frederick

Winger, full-back

Born: Waltham Abbey, 23 October 1964.
Career: Watford, 1982. Hull City, 1984. PRESTON NORTH END, 1988. Carlisle United, 1992.

■ Unable to make the grade with Watford, Neil Williams joined Hull City. In 1984–85, his first season with the club, he helped the Tigers win promotion to the Second Division. He went on to make 91 appearances for Hull before signing for North End in the summer of 1988. He made a goalscoring debut on the opening day of the season but the visitors Port Vale won 3–1. Williams missed very few games that season as North End reached the Play-offs, only to lose at the semi-final stage to Port Vale. He remained an important member of the Preston side for the next season or so but then broke his leg. After recovering he took his tally of League appearances to 121 before leaving to spend a season playing for Carlisle United.

WILLIAMS, Oshor Joseph

Winger

Born: Stockton, 21 April 1958.
Career: Middlesbrough. Manchester United, 1976. Gateshead. Southampton, 1978. Exeter City, 1978 (loan). Stockport County, 1979. Port Vale, 1984. PRESTON NORTH END, 1986.

■ Oshor Williams began his career as an apprentice with his local League club, Middlesbrough, before joining Manchester United in 1976. Although he was elevated to the first-team squad, he failed to make an appearance. Williams was released by United and returned to

the North East to play for Northern Premier League side Gateshead. As he considered a move to Fort Lauderdale in the US, a £5,000 move to Southampton materialised. While at The Dell, he had a brief loan spell with Exeter but Stockport County paid £10,000 to take Williams to Edgeley Park in August 1979. While County failed to achieve more than a mid-table place during his five years with the club, Williams enjoyed a fine understanding with Mick Quinn. He also stood in as captain when Tommy Sword was injured but, following a dispute over his salary, he played on a weekly contract until Port Vale paid £8,000 to take him to the Potteries. Williams had scored 31 goals in 216 games for County. At the

end of his second season with Vale he helped them win promotion, but in the summer of 1986 he moved back to the North West with Preston North End. His first game for the Deepdale club came on the opening day of the 1986–87 season in a 1–1 draw at Tranmere. Williams scored 10 goals in 29 League outings that season to help the club win promotion from the Fourth Division. Unfortunately, injury ended Williams' playing career at the age of 29, although he remained at Deepdale for three years as Preston's Community Development Officer. After coaching spells at Halifax and Winsford United, he moved to Witton Albion.

WILLIAMS, Paul Andrew

Centre-half, forward

Born: Sheffield, 5 September 1963.
Career: Nuneaton Borough. PRESTON NORTH END, 1986. Newport County, 1987. Sheffield United, 1988. Hartlepool United, 1989. Stockport County, 1990. West Bromwich Albion, 1991. Coventry City, 1992 (loan). Stockport County, 1993. Rochdale, 1993. Doncaster Rovers, 1996 (loan).

■ Northern Ireland international Paul Williams joined Preston from non-League Nuneaton Borough in December 1986. He made just one appearance at League level for North End in a 2–0 defeat at Cambridge United. He joined Newport County and played in their last ever season of League football. After a brief spell with Hartlepool he joined Stockport County and, in his only season at Edgeley Park, helped the Hatters win promotion to Division Three. While with his next club, West Bromwich Albion, Williams made a full international appearance for Northern Ireland against the Faroe Islands. He had a second spell with Stockport before ending his career with Rochdale.

WILLIAMSON, Charles W.

Outside-right

Born: Preston, 1885.
Career: Preston Winckley. PRESTON NORTH END, 1907.

■ Signed from local junior football, Charles Williamson made just a single appearance for North End during the course of the 1907–08 season. Replacing Charlie Dawson, he played in a 4–2 home defeat by Chelsea but did have the satisfaction of providing Percy Smith with the pass from which he scored one of his side's goals.

WILLIAMSON, John

Wing-half

Born: Fauldhouse, 16 October 1896.
Career: Armadale. PRESTON NORTH END, 1921. Grimsby Town, 1926. Lancaster Town. Darwen.

■ Tough-tackling wing-half Johnny Williamson played the first of his 63 League games for Preston in a 2–0 home win over Newcastle United in October 1921. Though he found himself in and out of the side that season, he wore the number-six shirt in the FA Cup Final which North End lost 1–0 to Huddersfield Town. Over the next couple of seasons, he appeared only spasmodically and it was not until 1924–25 that he played on a more regular basis. At the end of that campaign, however, Preston lost their First Division status and towards the end of the following campaign, Williamson left to play for Grimsby Town. A single appearance for the Mariners was followed by a return to the North West and spells with non-League clubs Lancaster Town and Darwen.

WILSON, Albert

Centre-forward

Born: Lochee, 1905.
Career: Dundee Violet. PRESTON NORTH END, 1929.

■ Albert Wilson showed impressive form north of the border playing for Dundee Violet and this prompted North End manager Alex Gibson to bring him to Deepdale in the summer of 1929. He scored a hat-trick in his first game at Deepdale in a pre-season practice match and a few weeks later he netted six goals for the club's reserve side in a 9–4 win over Everton reserves. Wilson made his League debut in a 2–2 draw with Bradford City and kept his place for the following game, but these were his only appearances in the 1929–30 season. The following campaign he did score his first

goal for the senior team in a 2–1 defeat of Plymouth Argyle, but he could not hold down a regular place in the side and moved on.

WILSON, David Charles

Winger

Born: Nelson, 24 December 1942.
Career: PRESTON NORTH END, 1960. Liverpool, 1967. PRESTON NORTH END, 1968. Bradford City, 1972 (loan). Southport, 1973 (loan).

■ Winger Dave Wilson arrived at Deepdale as a raw youngster but quickly established himself in North End's junior sides. He starred in a famous FA Youth Cup-tie against Wigan Athletic when he was 16 years old and continued

to do so right through to the Final against Chelsea, which Preston unfortunately lost. Soon afterwards, Wilson was called up for first-team duty, making his debut in a 1–0 defeat at Nottingham Forest on Boxing Day 1960. He also appeared in the final game of that 1960–61 season, scoring Preston's goal in a 1–1 draw at Bolton Wanderers. North End were relegated but over the next few seasons Wilson established himself as one of the best wingers outside the top flight. In addition to creating numerous goalscoring chances for the likes of Alex Dawson, Alec

Ashworth and Brian Godfrey, he too could find the net. During the course of the 1963–64 season he netted a hat-trick in a 4–0 win at Cardiff City. Though he seemed happy at Preston, when former Deepdale legend Bill Shankly offered to take him to Anfield he jumped at the chance. Shankly was looking for cover in his squad but Wilson struggled to stake a claim in the Reds' first team and in the summer of 1968 he rejoined North End. He quickly found favour with his new manager Bobby Seith and, though he later had spells on loan with Bradford City and Southport, he took his total of League appearances for Preston to 281, with 40 goals, before hanging up his boots.

WILSON, Francis

Outside-right

Born: Motherwell, 1906.
Career: Mid Annadale. Motherwell. Hamilton Academicals. PRESTON NORTH END, 1933. Alloa Athletic. Rochdale, 1937.

■ Francis Wilson's displays north of the border for Motherwell and Hamilton Academicals led to him being offered the chance to play League football for Preston North End. Wilson played in six games during the club's promotion-winning season of 1933–34 and scored on his second appearance in a 4–1 win at Burnley. He was released at the end of the season and went back to Scotland to play for Alloa Athletic. He later returned to the North West to spend a season playing for Rochdale.

WILSON, Harry

Left-back

Born: Hetton-le-Hole, 29 November 1953.
Career: Burnley, 1970. Brighton and Hove Albion, 1973. PRESTON NORTH END, 1977. Darlington, 1980. Hartlepool United, 1983.

■ The son of a miner, Harry Wilson played for England Schoolboys before going on to win an England Youth cap in 1971. He joined Burnley as an apprentice and was only 17 when he made his First Division debut for the Clarets at Chelsea in April 1971. Though Burnley won that game, relegation was already a certainty.

Wilson found himself in and out of the Clarets side before being transferred to Brighton for £30,000 in December 1973. At the Goldstone Ground he soon became a first-team regular and helped the Seagulls win promotion to the Second Division in 1976–77. He then joined Preston and made his League debut in a goalless draw at Plymouth, having previously played in a couple of League Cup games against Port Vale. Wilson was a regular for the first half of the season until he lost out to Danny Cameron as the club won promotion from the Third Division. After that he found his first-team opportunities limited and in 1980 moved to Darlington. Wilson later ended his career in the North East with Hartlepool United. After a spell in the US, he worked for 'Football in the Community' before returning to Turf Moor as a member of the coaching staff.

WILSON, James

Inside-forward

Born: Glasgow, 1880.
Career: St Mirren. PRESTON NORTH END, 1903. Oldham Athletic, 1911.

■ As part of the transfer deal that brought inside-forward Jimmy Wilson to Preston in 1903, the Deepdale club had to visit St Mirren to play a friendly. It was a game North End won 1–0 with Wilson

scoring his new side's goal. He played in a handful of games towards the end of the club's Second Division Championship-winning season of 1903–04 before establishing himself as a first-team regular the following season. Although he did not score too many goals himself in 1905–06, Wilson created goals for Bond, Bell and Smith as Preston ended the campaign as runners-up in the First Division to Liverpool. His best season in terms of goals scored was 1908–09 when he top scored with 11 goals. After that injuries limited his first-team appearances and he left Deepdale to join Oldham Athletic, where further injuries meant he never played in the Latics' League side.

WILSON, John G. (Ian)

Outside-left

Born: Kennoway, 11 February 1923.
Career: Forfar Athletic. PRESTON NORTH END, 1946. Burnley, 1948. Leicester City, 1950. Chesterfield, 1951. Rotherham United, 1953. Boston United.

■ A direct, powerful and speedy winger, Ian Wilson was spotted by Preston playing for Forfar Athletic. He came to Deepdale in 1946 faced with the inevitable comparison to the man on the opposite flank, a certain Tom Finney. He scored on his debut in a 5–2 defeat of Brentford and in fact netted in each of his first three games for the club. The other two games brought mixed results: a 4–1 defeat at Arsenal and a 6–2 win over Huddersfield Town. Wilson also scored in his only appearance in 1947–48 but then left to join Burnley. Unable to hold down a regular place at Turf Moor, he spent much of his time there in the reserves, helping them win the Central League Championship in 1948–49. He joined Leicester City but again was not a regular. Then, after two seasons in the Third Division North with Chesterfield, he signed for Rotherham United. Wilson enjoyed the best spell of his career at Millmoor and in 1954–55, as the club just missed out on promotion to the First Division on goal average, he scored four goals in a 6–1 win over Liverpool. After a spell with Boston United, he emigrated to Canada and played an active part in the development of football across the Atlantic.

WILSON, John Robert

Right-back

Born: Liverpool, 8 September 1928.
Career: Burscough. PRESTON NORTH END, 1950. Tranmere Rovers, 1962.

■ Signed from non-League Burscough, right-back Bob Wilson forced his way into the Preston side following a series of good displays for the Deepdale club's reserve side. He made his debut as a replacement for the injured Willie Cunningham in a 4–0 win over Portsmouth in March 1953. After making a handful of appearances the following season, he played on a more

regular basis in 1954–55 and 1955–56 but then his appearances became few and far between. The last of Wilson's 91 League appearances came in a 7–1 defeat at Plymouth in August 1962 and he left Deepdale to play for Tranmere Rovers. He was a regular for the Prenton Park club for the next two seasons as they challenged for promotion from the Fourth Division.

WILSON Kelvin James

Defender

Born: Nottingham, 3 September 1985
Career: Notts County 2004; PRESTON NORTH END (loan) 2006;

■ A versatile defender who can play either at right-back or in the centre of defence, he was a member of the Notts County youth team that won the

Midland Youth Cup in 2003–04. He made his Football League debut as a substitute at Hartlepool in April 2003 and went on to feature in the starting line-ups of the final two games of the campaign. He firmly established himself in the Meadow Lane club's side the following season and he continued to impress in 2005–06. He had appeared in 86 games for County when he joined Preston on loan for the run-in to the Championship. Never letting the side down in the six games in which he featured, it remains to be seen whether Billy Davies attempts to make the move a permanent one.

WINCHESTER, John

Right-back

Born: Kirkham, 1885.
Died: 1960.
Career: PRESTON NORTH END, 1906. Eccles Borough.

■ A schoolteacher on the Fylde coast, John Winchester was therefore an amateur when he first turned out for North End in a 1–0 home win over Derby County in March 1907. It was his only appearance that season. After playing in a handful of games in 1907–08, he appeared on a more regular basis thereafter. Facing severe competition for the number-two shirt from Charlie McFadyen, Winchester left to play for Eccles Borough.

WINTERHALDER, Arthur

Winger

Born: Oxford, 1885.
Career: West Ham United. Everton, 1907. PRESTON NORTH END, 1908.

■ Having played Southern League football for West Ham United, Arthur Winterhalder joined Everton for the start of the 1907–08 season. However, he failed to make much impression with the Merseyside club and left to join Preston North End after just one season with the club. He made his debut for the Lilywhites in a 6–0 mauling of Chelsea, his pinpoint crosses helping Percy Smith net a hat-trick and John Platt a brace. Even so, he made only seven appearances, although he was more of a regular the following season. He was the club's

first-choice number-11 in 1910–11 but faded from the scene at the start of the following campaign.

WOLF, George

Goalkeeper

Born: Newcastle-upon-Tyne, 23 April 1903.
Career: Walker Celtic. Blackpool, 1929. PRESTON NORTH END, 1931. Carlisle United, 1933. Blyth Spartans.

■ Goalkeeper George Wolf's first League club were Blackpool and in his first season at Bloomfield Road he kept goal in 26 games as the Seasiders won the Second Division Championship. After just a couple of appearances in the top flight, Wolf parted company with Blackpool and joined rivals Preston North End. He made his debut for the Lilywhites as a replacement for Des Fawcett in a 2–1 win over Southampton. An injury in a game at Bury cost him his place but on his return he was the club's first-choice 'keeper until Harry Holdcroft arrived at Deepdale. Wolf left and spent two seasons playing in the Third Division North for Carlisle United before leaving to finish his career in his native North East with Blyth Spartans.

WOODHOUSE, Rowland Thomas

Inside-forward

Born: Leyland, 15 January 1897.
Died: 1969.
Career: Lancaster Town. PRESTON NORTH END, 1919. Everton, 1926. Wrexham, 1927. Halifax Town, 1930. Chorley.

■ Signed from Lancaster Town, Rowland Woodhouse was one of the smallest players ever to turn out for Preston. He scored on his debut in September 1919 in a 2–2 draw with Bradford City and soon struck up a good understanding with Tommy Roberts. During the course of the 1920–21 season, Woodhouse suffered a couple of unusual accidents. In October he cut his ankle on a broken bottle in the Villa Park dressing rooms. On his return to action for the reserves at Stockport, he received a blow to the mouth and had to walk from the ground to Stockport Hospital

to have three stitches. However, it did not prevent him from scoring 16 goals including a hat-trick in a 4–2 defeat of Blackburn Rovers. Woodhouse continued to find the net the following season and also gained an FA Cup runners'-up medal after Preston were beaten 1–0 by Huddersfield Town. Woodhouse was then moved into a deeper midfield role, but in 1924–25 he still topped the club's scoring charts with nine goals in all competitions. This total included another hat-trick in the first-round FA Cup tie against Manchester City, which Preston won 4–1. In May 1926 he joined Everton but after just one season at Goodison he signed for Wrexham. A regular for the Robins, he scored 16 goals including a treble against Nelson in his first season at the Racecourse Ground. He later played for Halifax Town before going into non-League football with Chorley. He spent three years at Victory Park before hanging up his boots. Woodhouse took up the job of trainer with the Magpies and remained until 1953 when he retired from football altogether.

WOODHOUSE, Sidney H.

Goalkeeper

Born: Leyland, 1879.
Career: PRESTON NORTH END, 1900.

■ Discovered in local League football, goalkeeper Sidney Woodhouse played in a couple of games for Preston North End during the 1900–01 season. Replacing the injured Peter McBride, he conceded three goals on his debut at home to Bolton Wanderers. On his second and final appearance for the club four days later, he was part of the Preston side beaten 6–1 by Notts County. To make matters worse, North End were relegated.

WOODS, Stephen Gerard

Goalkeeper

Born: Glasgow, 23 February 1970.
Career: Hibernian. Clydebank. PRESTON NORTH END, 1993. Motherwell.

■ Stevie Woods, a bright, young goalkeeper, started out with Hibernian but he failed to play for their first team. Woods made his breakthrough with

Clydebank and excelled for the club. From the Bankies he moved south of the border to play for Preston North End. Woods got his chance in the Deepdale club's side when he came off the bench to replace the injured Kelham O'Hanlon during the 3–2 home defeat by Wycombe. Thereafter he shared the goalkeeping duties with O'Hanlon but was between the posts when North End participated in the Play-offs. In the summer of 1994, Motherwell paid £75,000 for his services. Although Woods initially had to compete with Scott Howie, he won the day and was the Fir Park club's regular 'keeper until the arrival of Andy Goram. Even then, Goram was in the veteran stages of his career so Stevie Woods had ample opportunity to stand in.

WOODWARD, Thomas George

Right-half

Born: Troedyrhiw, 8 December 1917.
Died: 1981.
Career: Merthyr Town, 1921. Chesterfield, 1922. Llanelly. PRESTON NORTH END, 1924. Swansea Town, 1926. Merthyr Town, 1929. Taunton Town.

■ Unable to establish a regular first-team place at either of his first two League clubs, Tom Woodward moved into non-League football with Welsh club Llanelly. His displays led to him being given another chance by Preston North End. Woodward made his debut in a 2–1 home defeat at the hands of West Bromwich Albion during the 1924–25 season and went on to appear in the last 15 games of a campaign which saw North End relegated to Division Two. The following season he played centre-forward in an emergency and scored his first goal for the club in a 2–0 win over Stoke. Released during the following close season, he joined Swansea Town and spent three seasons at the Vetch Field before remaining in his native Wales to see out his first-class career with his first club Merthyr Town.

WORTHINGTON, Frank Stewart

Forward

Born: Halifax, 23 November 1948.
Career: Huddersfield Town, 1966. Leicester City, 1972. Bolton Wanderers, 1977. Birmingham City, 1979. Leeds United, 1982. Sunderland, 1982. Southampton, 1983. Brighton & Hove Albion, 1984. Tranmere Rovers, 1985. PRESTON NORTH END, 1987. Stockport County, 1987.

■ A talented footballer and an extrovert character, Frank Worthington was an England international but his elegant and effective centre-forward play should have brought him many more than the eight caps he won. Worthington began his career with Huddersfield Town. After helping them win the Second Division Championship in 1970, the chance came for him to join Liverpool. A fee of £150,000 had been agreed but a medical examination revealed that he had high blood pressure. Leicester City seized their chance and a cut-price Worthington moved to Filbert Street for £80,000. He went on to score 72 goals in 210 games for the Foxes before he joined Bolton Wanderers on loan. Their manager, Ian Greaves, was searching for some extra quality to lift the Wanderers into the First Division after two near misses. Soon signed on a permanent basis, Worthington became a footballing hero at Burnden Park in what was a relatively short career there. He swiftly redis-

covered the style that had made him one of the best strikers in the game and in 1977–78 he helped the Trotters win the Second Division title. The following season he proved his class as a target man and a finisher, topping the First Division scoring charts with 24 goals. His televised goal against Ipswich Town won him the Goal of the Season competition. On leaving Bolton, he joined Birmingham City and later had spells with Leeds United, Sunderland, Southampton, Brighton and Tranmere before arriving at Deepdale in February 1987. Worthington made his debut in a 2–0 win over Torquay United. He gave some virtuoso performances and scored some vital goals as the club won promotion from the Fourth Division. Most of his appearances the following season were off the bench so he moved on to Stockport County. One of the game's most gifted and colourful strikers, Worthington made 757 League appearances in a career that saw him approaching his 40th birthday before he left the first-class game.

WRIGHT, John

Goalkeeper

Born: Preston, 1874.
Career: PRESTON NORTH END, 1895. Fleetwood Rangers.

■ Better known as 'Nanny' Wright, the local-born goalkeeper was understudy to

Welsh international James Trainer. Wright made his debut in a 2–1 win at West Bromwich Albion in the third game of the 1895–96 season. His second appearance for the Lilywhites came in November that season but he sustained a broken wrist in the game against Small Heath. Tait went in goal to replace him and 10-men Preston lost 5–2. Wright never played for the senior side again.

WRIGHT, Mark Stephen

Forward

Born: Chorley, 4 September 1981.
Career: PRESTON NORTH END, 1999.

■ Mark Wright, a left-sided striker, made his North End debut as a substitute in an FA Cup second-round tie against Walsall and also appeared off the bench against Burnley in the Auto Windscreens Shield three days later. North End's injury problems saw him make his League debut against Oldham Athletic, when he almost netted twice in Preston's 2–1 win. After being on the bench for the club's two opening League games of 1999–2000, he returned to the reserves

where his form was such that he made further appearances for the senior side. The exciting progress was then sadly hampered by a hip injury that required an operation and on medical advice he was forced to retire.

WRIGHTSON, Jeffrey George

Centre-half, midfield

Born: Newcastle-upon-Tyne, 18 May 1968.
Career: Newcastle United, 1986. PRESTON NORTH END, 1987. Gateshead.

■ As a junior, Jeff Wrightson helped his home-town team Newcastle United lift the FA Youth Cup alongside Paul Gascoigne in 1985. With the Magpies near the foot of the First Division in 1986–87, the young Wrightson was thrown into the cauldron during the Christmas and New Year programme. Stepping into David McCreery's anchor role in midfield, he was up against it and saw Everton inflict a hefty defeat on his Football League baptism. In the summer of 1987, Wrightson left St James' Park and joined Preston North End. Wrightson came off the bench in a 3–1

defeat at Bristol City to make his Preston debut and appeared in 25 games that season. In 1988–89 he was an important member of the North End side that reached the Play-offs, only to lose to Port Vale at the semi-final stage. He missed very few games over the next few seasons and had appeared in 166 League games when in August 1992, after trials with Darlington and Blackpool, he joined Gateshead, where he became a commanding player in the Vauxhall Conference.

WYLIE, John Edward

Wing-half

Born: Newcastle-upon-Tyne, 25 September 1936.
Career: Huddersfield Town, 1954. PRESTON NORTH END, 1957. Stockport County, 1962. Doncaster Rovers, 1964.

■ Having spent three seasons at Huddersfield Town, where he failed to figure in the Yorkshire club's first team,

John Wylie left for Preston North End in the summer of 1957. After a season of reserve-team football, he replaced Frank O'Farrell in a 2–1 defeat by Leeds United in the fifth game of the 1958–59 season. He did not play at all the following season but missed just three games in 1960–61 as North End were relegated to Division Two. It was during the course of this season that Wylie scored his only League goal for the club against Manchester City. He had previously scored in the League Cup against Aston Villa. Wylie was a virtual ever present again in 1961–62 but in November 1962 he left to play for Stockport County. After two seasons at Edgeley Park he signed for Doncaster Rovers and in 1965–66 he played his part in helping the club win the Fourth Division Championship.

YATES, Wilfred James

Full-back

Born: Southport, 1898.
Career: Southport. PRESTON NORTH END, 1921. Crewe Alexandra, 1925. Tranmere Rovers, 1926. Mansfield Town. PRESTON NORTH END, 1930.

■ Wilf Yates did not have the best of debuts as Preston went down 3–0 at Cardiff City midway through the 1921–22 season. After another season of being in and out of the side, he established himself as a regular first-team player in 1923–24, missing just two of his side's games. Surprisingly, during the early part of the following season he was allowed to leave Deepdale to join Crewe Alexandra of the Third Division North. Within a year he had moved to Tranmere Rovers and made 92 appearances for the Wirral-based club before having a stint with Mansfield Town. Yates returned to Deepdale but he did not make any further League appearances for the club.

YOUNG, Matthew Spratt

Outside-right

Born: Cambois, 1901.
Career: Preston Colliery. Hartlepool United, 1923. Reading, 1924. Workington. PRESTON NORTH END, 1926. Aldershot.

■ Winger Matty Young started his Football League career with Hartlepool United and he made 29 League appearances in 1923–24 before joining Reading. He only managed a handful of appearances for the Royals before playing non-League football for Workington. His displays led to Preston manager Frank Richards bringing him to Deepdale and in December 1926 he started a run of six League games that saw him find the back of the net in a 4–0 defeat of South Shields. These were to be his only appearances for Preston and he left to see out his career in the Southern League with Aldershot.

YOUNG, Neil James

Forward

Born: Manchester, 17 February 1944.
Career: Manchester City, 1961. PRESTON NORTH END, 1972. Rochdale, 1974.

■ One of Manchester City's first-ever apprentice professionals, Neil Young signed for the Maine Road club in the summer of 1960. He made his League debut in November 1961 against Aston Villa and, though City lost, he had the distinction of setting up Peter Dobing for the City goal. In his early days with the club, Young was switched around the

forward line but when Mercer and Allison moved him permanently to the number-10 spot he flourished. They gave him a free-roving commission and he repaid their faith by scoring 17 goals, including a hat-trick against Leyton Orient, to end the 1965–66 season as the club's top scorer. He top scored again in City's Championship-winning season of 1967–68 with 22 goals and crowned a great season by scoring twice in the club's 4–3 win at Newcastle United. It was Young's splendid left-foot shot that won the Blues the FA Cup in 1969. The following year he scored one of the goals in Vienna which brought victory over Gornik Zabrze in the European Cup-winners' Cup. In January 1972, Young moved to Preston North End for a fee of £48,000 and made his debut in a goalless draw against Birmingham City. His experience and vital goals went a long way in ensuring the club kept its Second Division status. It was a similar struggle the following season but, in 1973–74, North End were relegated to the Third Division. Young never really reproduced his best form while at Deepdale and left to end his career with Rochdale.

ZELEM, Peter Richard

Centre-half

Born: Manchester, 13 February 1962.
Career: Chester City, 1980. Wolverhampton Wanderers, 1985. PRESTON NORTH END, 1987. Burnley, 1987.

■ Central-defender Peter Zelem was a regular with his first club Chester City, playing in the lower reaches of the Football League until Tommy Docherty signed him for Wolves in January 1985. His inclusion in the Wolves side could not stop their slide out of Division Two at the end of that 1984–85 season, which continued on to Division Four the following campaign. During Preston's promotion-winning season of 1986–87, manager John McGrath brought in Peter Zelem and he started a six-game run with a 2–1 defeat of Burnley. Zelem also got his name on the score sheet in a 2–0 win at Rochdale but, despite never being on the losing side, he was allowed to leave and join Burnley. Injuries hampered his progress at Turf Moor and he was released in May 1989.

Managers

Charlie Parker: 1906 to 1915

North End record:

P	W	D	L
357	134	86	137

Honours:
Division Two Champions: 1912–13
Division Two promotion: 1914–15

Charlie Parker was the club's secretary-manager from 1906 until the outbreak of World War One, and during that time North End suffered relegation from the First Division on two occasions. Relegation in 1911–12 seemed inevitable throughout the season as the threat of Division Two football loomed for a second successive season. Despite a poor start to the following campaign, North End went on to lose just four games and win the Second Division Championship. Following relegation after just one season back in the top flight, Preston began to acquire a reputation as a yo-yo side, especially when they won promotion in 1914–15 as runners-up to Derby County. During the war years, Parker worked for the civil service as an accountant. Though Vincent Hayes had taken over the manager's role at the end of the hostilities, Parker remained at Deepdale until May 1926 when he took over as manager of Southport. Though the Sandgrounders finished in mid-table in each of his three seasons in charge, they did have an excellent FA Cup run in 1926–27, knocking out First Division Blackburn Rovers on their way to round four. They also reached this stage of the competition the following season. On leaving Haig Avenue, Parker became secretary-manager of Manchester Central.

Vincent Hayes: 1919 to 1923

North End record:

P	W	D	L
166	59	41	66

Honours:
FA Cup runners-up: 1921–22

Vince Hayes made 114 appearances for Manchester United in his two spells with the club and also won an FA Cup-winners' medal when the Reds beat Bristol City 1–0 at Crystal Palace in the 1909 Final. After coaching abroad and holding the managerial reins at Rochdale, he arrived at Deepdale as manager in 1919. Hayes and the club's directors were certainly very busy on the transfer market in the close season, but his signings did not signal an upturn in the club's fortunes, although they did reach the FA Cup semi-finals in 1921 before losing to Spurs. Hayes had little power during his time at Deepdale, for a couple of the directors ran the club. They selected the team, worked out the tactics and bought the players. Hayes's primary role was to organise and motivate the players. From 1922 he devoted more time to coaching and preparing the players and he left the secretarial and financial side of the game in the hands of the chartered accountants. Preston reached the FA Cup Final in 1922 but lost 1–0 to Huddersfield Town.

Jim Lawrence: 1923 to 1925

North End record:

P	W	D	L
107	31	19	57

Jim Lawrence was probably the finest goalkeeper ever to play for Newcastle United, where he holds the appearance record of 432 games. He was a fine, consistent 'keeper who occasionally received criticism for the way he handled high crosses. Even so, Lawrence did not miss a single game for six seasons until he was temporarily dropped in November 1910. With the Magpies, he gained three League Championship medals and five FA Cup medals with one FA Cup-winners' medal against Barnsley in 1910. He was capped by Scotland against England in a 1–1 draw at Anfield in April 1911. Lawrence had not even completed a season as manager of South Shields when he was appointed Preston boss in 1923. When he arrived at Deepdale, he encountered a financial crisis at the club and in 1924 he was forced to sell North End's leading goalscorer Tommy Roberts to Burnley. Preston were relegated to the Second Division in 1924–25 after gaining a meagre 26 points. Lawrence resigned shortly afterwards.

Frank Richards 1925 to 1927

North End record:

P	W	D	L
89	39	18	32

Although Frank Richards was officially in charge of team affairs in his two spells with Birmingham, he was mainly regarded as the club's administrative secretary. He left most of the day-to-day running of the team to his trainers and had very little say in who was bought or sold. Birmingham won the Second Division Championship in 1920–21 but, prior to the start of the following season, Richards forgot to enter the St Andrew's club for the 1921–22 FA Cup competition – an oversight that would no doubt have meant the sack in today's game. In May 1925, Richards took over the reins at Preston after the Lilywhites had just been relegated. In an attempt to return to the top flight at the first time of asking, he brought in former Aston Villa and England international Harry Hampson as coach but, despite an impressive home record, the club's performances on their travels were dire.

There is no doubt that Richards' best piece of business was to bring the mercurial Alex James to Deepdale. Though the club performed better in 1926–27, Richards decided to resign after two years in the post. After a brief spell back at St Andrew's, he spent two seasons as secretary-manager to Bournemouth.

Alex Gibson: 1927 to 1931

North End record:

P	W	D	L
165	65	36	64

Alex Gibson's best season as manager of Preston North End was undoubtedly his first when the club finished fourth in Division Two, scoring 100 goals in the process. The Lilywhites had been determined to build on the previous campaign but blew their chances of promotion over Easter with two defeats, including a 6–2 reversal at Notts County. This was followed by three seasons of mediocrity and limited success in the FA Cup competition. Gibson's actions over the use of Alex James led to the Scottish international's discontent with the club: he decided to play James in a League match rather than release him to play for the national side. James was soon sold to Arsenal for a record fee of £8,000 in the summer of 1929. If Gibson had been a little shrewder, there is no doubt he would have got more money for the Scottish player. Gibson left Deepdale with the club feeling gloomy about their prolonged stay in Division Two.

Lincoln Hyde: 1931 to 1932

North End record:

P	W	D	L
35	10	12	13

Lincoln Hyde moved from secretary to secretary-manager at Stockport County in 1926 and immediately appointed Fred Westgarth as his trainer. During his time at Edgeley Park he often had to sell players in order to pay his way, but he did have the happy knack of finding capable men to fill the gaps. Hyde was desperately unlucky not to get the Hatters promoted. They finished third in 1927–28 and were runners-up in the next two seasons in the Third Division North, but in those days only the Champions went up. In each of his last two seasons with County, they scored over 100 goals and gained over 60 points. In April 1931, he accepted the offer of the manager's job at Preston North End. Hyde did not see out the 1931–32 campaign as North End failed to challenge for promotion and he believed that he had too little control over the buying and selling of players. After leaving football he ran a successful business in Belfast.

Tommy Muirhead: 1936 to 1937

North End record:

P	W	D	L
56	22	15	19

Honours:
FA Cup runners-up: 1936–37

A fine utility player, Tommy Muirhead was at his best at wing-half. He was a fine passer of the ball and a keen tackler who went on to score 49 goals in 352 appearances for Rangers in 13 years with the club. While at Ibrox he gained eight Scottish League Championship medals, but his only Scottish Cup-winners' medal was awarded to him in 1928 even though he did not play in the Final. Muirhead later took St Johnstone into the First Division as runners-up in 1931–32 when he became the club's manager. They also held their own in the higher grade of football and reached the Scottish Cup semi-finals in 1933–34. Tommy Muirhead took charge at Preston in April 1936 and, in what turned out to be his only full season in charge, led North End to third place in Division One and to the FA Cup Final where they lost 3–1 to Sunderland. Surprisingly, Muirhead resigned at the end of this most successful season to become a sports journalist.

Will Scott: 1949 to 1953

North End record:

P	W	D	L
163	78	36	49

Honours:
Division Two Champions: 1950–51

Will Scott started his career with South Shields before World War One but in 1914 he joined the Navy. After he had 'guested' for Crystal Palace during the hostilities, they tried to sign him as a professional in 1919 but he preferred to return to South Shields. He continued to appear at centre-half and was also the club's assistant-trainer and masseur. In January 1923 he moved to Preston as the club's trainer and arrived at Deepdale with the man who had been his boss at Horsley Hill, Jim Lawrence. Scott spent the next 24 years at Deepdale as trainer, coach and often in charge of team affairs. He was appointed the club's secretary in 1941 and remained in that post until April 1947 when he became the manager of Blackburn Rovers. Scott stayed just

eight months at Ewood Park before ill health forced his resignation, though he remained at the club as a scout. Once Scott recovered, he returned to Preston in June 1949 as manager. The first player he bought was Willie Cunningham, quickly followed by Tommy Docherty. In December 1949 the club broke the British transfer record when Eddie Quigley was signed from Sheffield Wednesday for £26,500. The 1950–51 season was an excellent one for the club as they walked away with the Second Division Championship, finishing five points clear of Manchester City. They were unbeaten from November until April, going 20 games without defeat. They also achieved 14 consecutive League victories, equalling the record set by Burnley in 1946–47. Scott left Deepdale in March 1953 just as they were in hot pursuit of Arsenal and Wolves at the top of the First Division. They eventually finished runners-up on goal average behind the Gunners. He later held the post of assistant manager to Allan Brown at Sunderland.

Scott Symon: 1953 to 1954

North End record:

P	W	D	L
63	30	11	22

Honours:
Division One runners-up: 1952–53
FA Cup runners-up: 1953–54

Scott Symon made his name as a wing-half with Dundee in the 1930s before moving south to join Portsmouth, who paid £7,000 for him plus Lewis Morgan. Symon gained a Scottish League Championship medal with Rangers in 1938–39 and then steered East Fife into Division One when he became their manager in 1947. They also reached the semi-finals of the Scottish Cup in 1948–49 and lost 3–0 in the Final to Rangers the following season. East Fife also finished third in Division One in 1951–52 and 1952–53. After replacing Will Scott as Preston manager in March 1953, Symon guided the club to runners'-up spot in the First Division. In his only full season in charge he took

North End to an FA Cup Final where they lost 3–2 to West Bromwich Albion. After that he moved to Rangers and took them to six League titles, five Scottish Cups and four League Cup victories. They also reached two European Cup-winners' Cup finals, losing to Fiorentina in 1961 and Bayern Munich in 1967. He came in for a lot of criticism after this and parted company with the club.

Frank Hill: 1954 to 1956

North End record:

P	W	D	L
88	31	17	40

In his playing days, Scottish international Frank Hill was a combative wing-half who was tenacious, tough and uncompromising. Nicknamed 'The Tiger', he managed to keep playing until he was 41 years old. He started out in 1924 with Forfar Athletic, his home-town club, before being transferred to Aberdeen in 1928. While at Pittodrie he won three Scottish caps and played for the Scottish League before a move to Highbury in 1932. Hill won three League Championship medals with Arsenal, although he was never a regular in their side. After four years with the Gunners the success continued as Hill captained Blackpool to promotion from Division Two in 1936–37. After spells at Southampton and as trainer at Preston he was appointed player-manager of Crewe. In 1948 he was appointed manager of Burnley where he was responsible for bringing to Turf Moor many of the players who would go on to become household names, including the great Jimmy McIlroy. On the eve of the 1954–55 season, Hill accepted an invitation to return to Preston as manager. At Deepdale he produced entertaining sides rather than successful ones and left after two seasons to take up a coaching position in Iraq. Returning to England to take over from Tommy Lawton as manager of Notts County, he took the club to promotion as runners-up in the Fourth Division in 1959–60. Hill later managed Charlton Athletic but had little success at The Valley.

Cliff Britton: 1956 to 1961

North End record:

P	W	D	L
230	102	54	74

Honours:
Division One runners-up: 1957–58

After playing his early football for Bristol Rovers, Cliff Britton was transferred to Everton in 1930 for a substantial fee, but he took some time to establish himself in the League side at Goodison Park. When he did, he was in the team to stay. At the end of 1932–33, his first season as a regular, he won an FA Cup-winners' medal as Everton beat Manchester City 3–0 at Wembley. Britton's cultured and stylish play at wing-half brought him his first England cap in 1934 against Wales and he won nine altogether in the years leading up to World War Two. He had a reputation as a dour man with a strict disciplinary code. After being appointed manager of Burnley, he led them to promotion to the First Division in 1946–46. After one more season at Turf Moor, when he guided the Clarets to a respectable third place in the top flight, he returned to Everton. The Mersey-siders were relegated to Division Two in 1951 but regained their top-flight status in 1954. After a series of disagreements

with the club's directors Britton resigned, but six months later Preston managed to persuade him back into football as their new manager. During his five-year stay at Deepdale, Preston went close to the League Championship twice, in 1956–57 and 1957–58. With the retirement of Tom Finney in April 1960, however, the club went into decline. Although there was reason for some optimism with the youth side reaching the FA Youth Cup Final in 1960, sadly they had not developed in time for Preston to avoid relegation to Division Two and Britton resigned in April 1961. He became Hull City's manager later that year and steered the Tigers to the Third Division Championship in 1965–66.

Jimmy Milne: 1961 to 1968

North End record:

P	W	D	L
350	126	96	128

Honours:
FA Cup runners-up: 1963–64

Jimmy Milne was one of the best uncapped wing-halves of the inter-war period. Signed from Dundee United, Milne was a regular in the Preston side until the outbreak of World War Two and made a total of 256 appearances for the club. A very consistent player who attacked well and was reliable in defence, he played in the 1937 FA Cup Final defeat by Sunderland but missed the club's winning Final the following year due to injury. He returned to Deepdale as trainer in the 1950s and was appointed manager in 1961. When he was boss at Deepdale, North End surprised everybody when they reached the FA Cup Final in 1964, losing 3–2 to West Ham United at Wembley. They also went close to winning promotion to the First Division that season. He became general manager after he was replaced by Bobby Seith and was appointed chief scout at the end of the season. While with Preston he sold on his son Gordon to Liverpool's Bill Shankly, a former teammate of his at Deepdale.

Bobby Seith: 1968 to 1970

North End record:

P	W	D	L
70	15	21	34

The son of a former Scottish League player, wing-half Bobby Seith enjoyed a distinguished playing career at Burnley. He was a regular in the Clarets' side from 1953–54 until the club's League Championship-winning season of 1959–60, appearing in 238 games for the club. Despite playing 27 games during that successful campaign, he was denied a Championship medal after a row with chairman Bob Lord. Seith requested a transfer and moved to Dundee where he gained a Scottish League Championship medal in 1961–62. After his playing days were over, he joined the Dundee coaching staff before moving to Rangers in a similar capacity. In 1968 he left Ibrox to become manager of Preston North End. However, he did not gain full control at Deepdale until the departure of Jimmy Milne. Seith left the club after they had finished bottom of Division Two in 1969–70. In 1970 he returned north of the border as the manager of Scotland's Youth team, while in the early

part of that decade he managed Hearts. A qualified chiropodist, he also worked as a radio sports commentator.

Alan Ball senior: 1970 to 1973

North End record:

P	W	D	L
118	44	36	38

Honours:
Division Three Champions: 1970–71

Alan Ball senior was a hardworking linkman with good ball control. He was effective, despite his light build, and appeared for a number of clubs just after the war. Ball was still in his 20s when he took up management with Oswestry Town. He gained Birmingham League honours and also lifted the Shropshire Senior Cup for the club. Ball won a reputation for his coaching skills and secured a job in League management with Halifax Town. At the end of his first season at The Shay, Halifax won promotion for the first time in their history as runners-up to Doncaster Rovers in the Fourth Division. A most outspoken manager, he moved to take over the reins at Preston in 1970. Ball took North End to the Third Division Championship in 1970–71, his first season with the club. Following the sale of Archie Gemmill, Ball used the money to bring in Bobby Ham, who formed an

excellent strike partnership with Gerry Ingram. Ball managed to keep North End in the higher Division until he lost his job in February 1973. After a season at Southport, Ball returned to Halifax but things did not go as well the second time round and the Yorkshire club had to seek re-election at the end of the 1976–77 season. Ball died in a motoring accident in Cyprus where he had accepted a short-term coaching post prior to resuming with Vester Haringer of Sweden.

Bobby Charlton: 1973 to 1975

North End record:

P	W	D	L
89	29	25	35

A survivor of the Munich air disaster, Manchester United's Bobby Charlton went on to break Billy Wright's record for England caps and still holds the record for goalscoring for his country with 49 goals. Charlton was admired and respected all over the world. Alongside his brother Jack, he was a member of the 1966 World Cup-winning side. When he retired in 1973, Charlton had played in more than 750 games for United and scored 198 goals in 606 League matches – both club records. Though Charlton was

one of the finest players in the world, he was not such a successful manager. He took over the reins at Deepdale in the summer of 1973 and his appointment created a great deal of national interest in the club. North End were relegated to Division Three at the end of Charlton's first season in charge. The club were struggling again when Charlton resigned in August 1975 after a dispute with the directors over a deal involving John Bird's transfer to Newcastle, which was made without the manager's knowledge. Charlton later took over briefly as caretaker manager of Wigan Athletic after the sacking of Larry Lloyd.

Harry Catterick: 1975 to 1977

North End record:

P	W	D	L
90	38	22	30

Harry Catterick transformed Everton into a great footballing side. He was appointed manager in 1961 and was given a simple brief by chairman John Moores: get the club back to the top by means of good entertaining football. Catterick proved very adept in the transfer market, bringing some top-class players to Goodison. In only his second season at the club, he led the Blues to their sixth League Championship title. In 1966, Everton reached the FA Cup Final and Catterick's huge gamble – the inclusion of Mike Trebilcock – paid off. Trebilcock scored twice in a 3–2 defeat of Sheffield Wednesday. In 1968 he took the club back to Wembley, only for them to lose to West Bromwich Albion. The Blues swept to another League title in 1969–70 as Ball, Harvey and Kendall ran the midfield but within a year the club had slumped to 14th place with the Everton manager unable to explain why his side had run out of confidence. In January 1972, Catterick had a heart attack while driving home from Sheffield and the club moved him sideways into a senior executive role. In 1975 he made a comeback as team manager of Preston North End. In each of his two seasons in charge, North End finished just outside the promotion places in the Third Division. Just as Catterick

made a determined bid to bring former Preston favourite Howard Kendall back to Deepdale, he stepped down to allow Nobby Stiles to take over as manager. Harry Catterick collapsed and died after watching an Everton versus Ipswich FA Cup tie at his beloved Goodison Park in March 1985.

Nobby Stiles: 1977 to 1981

North End record:

P	W	D	L
174	56	67	51

Honours:
Division Three promotion: 1977–78

A great competitor, Nobby Stiles became famous throughout the football world for his toothless grin after England won the World Cup in 1966. He made almost 400 appearances for Manchester United in which he gained two League Championship medals and also played in the club's European Cup Final triumph over Benfica at Wembley in 1968. On leaving Old Trafford to join Middlesbrough, Stiles was made captain but he was affected by injuries and a loss of form. After a couple of seasons playing for North End, Stiles became coach prior to being appointed manager in 1977. In his first season at the helm he took the club to promotion from the Third Division. Following two seasons when the club finished in the top half of

Division Two, they were relegated in 1980–81. Unfortunately, Stiles was unable to put across his burning desire to win to his players and, on losing his job, joined his brother-in-law Johnny Giles at The Hawthorns. Stiles succeeded Giles when he left but was unable to prevent the Baggies' relegation in 1985–86.

Tommy Docherty: 1981

North End record:

P	W	D	L
17	3	6	8

Scottish international wing-half Tommy Docherty made over 350 appearances as a player for North End before joining Arsenal, where his career was almost brought to a premature end following a broken leg in a game against Preston. In his first managerial job with Chelsea he helped them return to the top flight following a relegation he could do little about. He also led them to a win in the League Cup in 1965 and an appearance in their first Wembley FA Cup Final. Though there was talk of Docherty managing Greek side Panathinaikos, he had spells in charge of Rotherham United, Queen's Park Rangers and Aston

Villa before leaving the UK to manage Porto. In September 1971 he was appointed Scotland's national team manager but a little over a year later he took over the reins at Manchester United. Certainly the United job seemed to suit him and, though the Reds lost their top-flight status in his first season at Old Trafford, they bounced back as Second Division Champions in 1974–75. While at Old Trafford, Docherty helped United win the FA Cup in 1977 but lost his job for well-documented reasons. He took over at Derby County and managed to keep them in the First Division. This was followed by another spell with Queen's Park Rangers before he took charge of Australian side Sydney Olympic. In June 1981, Docherty returned to the North West to manage Preston North End. Docherty was at Deepdale for just six months and in that time Preston never scored more than one goal in a home League game, but never conceded more than one either. Though he made a number of new signings, Preston continually struggled to win games. After being in charge for just 17 games, Docherty was sacked. He then managed Wolves but again lost his job after the Molineux club were relegated.

Gordon Lee: 1981 to 1983

North End record:

P	W	D	L
93	32	25	36

Gordon Lee had a reputation as one of football's troubleshooters. His first managerial post was with Port Vale whom he led to promotion from the Fourth Division. He also won promotion for Blackburn Rovers during their centenary season of 1974–75. As manager of Newcastle United, he steered the Magpies to the League Cup and into Europe. He was appointed manager of Everton when the Blues were struggling near the foot of the First Division. By the end of his first season, they had finished ninth in the top flight, reached the FA Cup semi-final and lost the League Cup Final after two replays. Lee went on to build a side of considerable ability and one worth watching. He was later charged with bringing the game into disrepute when he criticised a referee for allowing a game to go ahead on a treacherous pitch at Southampton (though he was later cleared by an FA disciplinary committee) and then things really started to go wrong. Everton fans became disillusioned by his team permutations and he lost his job in 1981. In December 1981, following the dismissal of Tommy Docherty, the Preston board appointed Gordon Lee as the club's new manager. Despite making an impressive start to his managerial

reign, the club made little progress in 1982–83 and, after some desperate away performances the following season, Lee lost his job. He later coached abroad before returning to England to coach Leicester City, with whom he also had a brief spell as caretaker manager.

Alan Kelly:
1983 to 1985

North End record:

P	W	D	L
71	23	13	35

Alan Kelly was a tall and commanding goalkeeper who won an Irish Cup-winners' medal with Drumcondra before joining Preston North End. At Deepdale he took over from Fred Else and developed into a highly reliable 'keeper. Kelly made 447 League appearances before retiring to become coach at

Deepdale in 1974. He was the Republic of Ireland team manager but this interfered with his duties at Preston, so he resigned after a short spell in charge of the national side. Appointed manager of Preston in December 1983, he managed to steer the club clear of relegation in his first season in charge, but they went down to the Fourth Division the following year. Poor results continued and he ended his association with the club in April 1985 after 27 years.

Tommy Booth:
1985 to 1986

North End record:

P	W	D	L
42	11	10	21

Tommy Booth had a meteoric rise to fame with Manchester City, scoring the wining goal in an FA Cup semi-final victory over Everton in 1969, five months after his debut for the club. He went on to gain a winners' medal as well as two League Cup-winners' medals and a European Cup-winners' Cup medal. Booth had appeared in 478 games for City when he joined North End as a player. He was appointed North End manager in April 1985 but unfortunately he was not a success as the club entered one of the worst spells in their history.

They were heading for relegation to Division Four but the end came after a 4–1 FA Cup defeat at home to non-League Telford United.

Brian Kidd:
1986

North End record:

P	W	D	L
4	0	1	3

On his 19th birthday in 1968, Brian Kidd lined up alongside such greats as Bobby Charlton and George Best to score a goal in Manchester United's famous European Cup Final victory over Benfica at Wembley. While with the Reds, Kidd won full international honours for England. He left Old Trafford for Arsenal where he was top scorer in his two seasons at Highbury. Anxious to return north, he signed for Manchester City, later playing for Everton and finally Bolton Wanderers. On leaving the first-class game in this country, he went to play in the NASL with Fort Lauderdale, Atlanta Chiefs and Minnesota Strikers. After a spell as player-manager of non-

League Barrow, Kidd joined Preston as Tommy Booth's assistant. He took over the reins when Booth left but, with the club failing to win a game, he was sacked. After a period as Alex Ferguson's assistant, he became manager of Blackburn Rovers and was subsequently assistant to Terry Venables at Leeds United.

John McGrath:
1986 to 1990

North End record:

P	W	D	L
192	74	53	65

Honours:
Division Four promotion: 1986–87
Division Three Play-offs: 1988–89

John McGrath was a tough, muscular centre-half who never shirked a challenge. He moved to Newcastle United in a deal which took Bob Stokoe the other way and left Bury just before they clinched the Third Division

Championship. McGrath made 489 League appearances during his career, including over 150 at both Newcastle and Southampton. When he hung up his boots, McGrath concentrated on coaching the youth team at The Dell. He took his first managerial post at Port Vale and was fortunate to retain his job after a poor season in 1980–81. At the end of

1982–83, Vale won promotion to Division Three but McGrath was sacked the following season with the club at the bottom of the table. Chester finished bottom of the League when he moved to Sealand Road but the damage had been done before his arrival. McGrath was appointed Preston boss in May 1986 and completely transformed the club as they won promotion to the Third Division as runners-up to Northampton Town. After a season of consolidation and just missing out on a visit to Wembley in the Sherpa Van Trophy, North End reached the Play-offs in 1988–89 where they lost over two legs to McGrath's former club, Port Vale. During the first half of the following season, Preston lost an FA Cup tie to Whitley Bay and then lost four consecutive games in January, results which led to McGrath losing his job. He later had a spell managing Halifax Town.

Les Chapman: 1990 to 1992

North End record:

P	W	D	L
91	32	19	40

A durable player, Les Chapman made over 700 appearances in 22 seasons for

his various clubs. By January 1988, he was the second-longest serving player in action after Frank Worthington, another North Ender. When Oldham Athletic signed him, Chapman was a trainee accountant. Chapman moved to Huddersfield Town and played in their Second Division Championship side but missed out on a medal as he had not made enough appearances. He appeared in all four Divisions of the Football League as well as the NASL with San Jose Earthquakes. Chapman had a terrible season as player-manager with Stockport County, who finished 91st in the League during his season in control. Replacing John McGrath as Preston manager, initially in a caretaker role, Chapman steered the Lilywhites away from relegation in 1989–90 before being appointed on a permanent basis in the close season. The club continued to struggle at the wrong end of Division Three and the directors' patience eventually ran out and Chapman was sacked.

Sam Allardyce: 1992

North End record:

P	W	D	L
10	3	3	4

Sam Allardyce spent the first 11 years of his playing career with Bolton Wanderers, helping the club win the Second Division Championship in

1977–78. He left to play for Sunderland, after which he became something of a journeyman, representing Millwall, Coventry City and Huddersfield Town, as well as a spell in the US with Tampa Bay Rowdies, all within four years. He rejoined Bolton in 1985 but was soon on his way to Preston. A brief spell at West Bromwich Albion followed, where Allardyce was coach, and he continued his coaching apprenticeship on his return to Deepdale in 1992. Allardyce was later appointed caretaker manager following the sacking of Les Chapman and one of his games in charge saw Tony

Ellis net a hat-trick in a 3–2 win at Blackpool. His first permanent appointment as manager was with Limerick, but Blackpool were the first English club to spot his potential. His next club was Notts County and in 1997–98 he led them to promotion as they won the Third Division title with 99 points. After resigning his post in October 1999, Allardyce returned to Bolton and, within a year, the Trotters were FA Cup and League Cup semi-finalists. Bolton were back in the Premiership in 2001 and, two years later, were finalists in the Carling Cup. Allardyce then took the Wanderers to sixth place in the Premiership and a UEFA Cup spot.

John Beck: 1992 to 1994

North End record:

P	W	D	L
99	36	20	43

Honours:
Third Division Play-offs: 1993–94

John Beck gained a reputation as a dead-ball specialist and was also a fine crosser of the ball. In 1988 he took over as assistant manager at Cambridge United under Chris Turner. When Turner resigned in January 1990, Beck became the club's caretaker manager and became the first caretaker boss to win the divisional Manager of the Month award twice in succession. After taking full control at the Abbey Stadium, he led the club to the FA Cup quarter-finals and promotion to Division Three via the

Play-offs at Wembley. Beck's initial impact as a manager can only be described as stunning as United then won the Third Division Championship in 1990–91. In December 1992, Beck was appointed manager of Preston – but it was a season in which he was in charge of two clubs that were eventually relegated. Cambridge lost their place in the First Division, while he could do nothing to prevent North End slipping into the Third Division when they lost their last game of the season at Bolton. As a manager he was renowned for a 'direct style' – which was not often appreciated by the football purists. In 1993–94, North End finished fifth in Division Three but missed out on promotion in the Play-offs when they lost to Wycombe Wanderers. In December 1994, Beck resigned rather than change his long-ball game and took over at Lincoln City. In

1997–98 he led the Imps to promotion from the Third Division but parted company with the Sincil Bank club the following season. Beck later managed Cambridge United for a second spell.

Gary Peters: 1994 to 1998

North End record:

P	W	D	L
166	72	42	52

Honours:
Third Division Play-offs: 1994–95
Third Division Champions: 1995–96

After he was rejected as a trainee at non-League Aldershot, Gary Peters began his career with Reading and helped them win promotion to Division Three in his first season with the club. After failing to agree terms on a contract extension he joined Fulham, having made 156 appearances for Reading. His next club were Wimbledon and in 1982–83, his first season with the Dons, he helped the club win promotion as Fourth Division Champions. The following year, Wimbledon won promotion again to reach Division Two. Peters then rejoined Aldershot and later Reading, helping the Royals clinch promotion to Division Two. Following his retirement, Peters took on roles as assistant manager at Fulham and Cambridge before arriving at Deepdale as John Beck's assistant. In December 1994, Peters was promoted to

manager and immediately changed the club's style of play to a more attractive passing game. He changed the club's fortunes too as North End won the Third Division Championship in 1995–96. During his time at Preston, Peters brought in players like David Beckham (on loan) and Jon Macken. In 1997 he sold Kevin Kilbane for a club record £1.2 million while Macken would eventually be sold for another record – £5 million. In January 1998, with the club sinking back towards Division Three, Peters resigned but a month later he returned to Deepdale as the club's Centre of Excellence manager. But with the Centre of Excellence ticking over, Preston chose to make Peters redundant. He later managed Exeter City and scouted for David Moyes at Everton but in November 2004 he took over the reins at Shrewsbury Town after the club had been promoted out of the Football Conference.

David Moyes: 1998 to 2002

North End record:

P	W	D	L
234	113	58	63

Honours:
Division Two Play-offs: 1998–99
Division Two Champions: 1999–2000
Division One Play-offs: 2000–01

David Moyes began his playing career with Celtic but after winning a Championship and playing in Europe he moved south of the border to play for Cambridge United. He had further spells at Bristol City and Shrewsbury Town followed by Dunfermline Athletic, Hamilton Academicals and Preston North End. His playing days ended at Deepdale and, when Gary Peters left the club in 1998, Moyes was promoted from the coaching staff to become player-manager. After narrowly avoiding relegation to the Third Division, Moyes retired from playing and concentrated on bringing his own brand of passing football to the club. Preston improved season by season and initial Play-off disappointment in 1999 was cast aside the following season when North End

were Champions and promoted to the First Division. They qualified for the Play-offs at the first time of asking and, although they fell short of the Premiership, Moyes' talents had been noticed and he received an offer to become Alex Ferguson's number two at Old Trafford, but the ambitious Scot turned it down. It was, however, only a matter of time before Moyes left Preston and, in 2002, after being linked to numerous vacancies, he became manager of Everton. Moyes reinstalled the talismanic Duncan Ferguson as captain, a move that endeared him to the Goodison faithful. After helping the club avoid relegation, he unleashed Wayne Rooney on an unsuspecting Premiership and the Blues ended the season in seventh place. The following year was a dramatic anti-climax and Everton finished fourth off the bottom. Rooney was eventually sold to Manchester United for £27 million and, though the Merseyside club struggled at the start of the 2005–06 season, Moyes turned things around. Everton's greatest challenge is now to cling on to the former Preston boss.

Kelham O'Hanlon: 2002

North End record:

P	W	D	L
8	4	1	3

The former Republic of Ireland international goalkeeper Kelham O'Hanlon was appointed first-team coach at Deepdale, although the club continued to register him as a player just in case of an emergency situation arising.

When Moyes left Preston in March 2002, O'Hanlon, who was also the club's assistant manager, took over as caretaker manager for the last eight games of the 2001–02 campaign. In the summer of 2003, after one season working alongside Craig Brown, O'Hanlon was released as the Deepdale club, forced on the back foot by the prevailing economic climate in football, sought to cut costs in preparation for meeting rising expenses during another season in the First Division.

Craig Brown: 2002 to 2004

North End record:

P	W	D	L
106	36	30	40

As a player with Rangers, Craig Brown was unable to find a regular first-team place and moved on to Dundee where in 1961–62 he won a League Championship medal. He stayed at Dundee for six years before moving to Falkirk where he eventually called time on his playing career in 1971 after five operations on his knee. He became assistant manager of Motherwell in 1974 and got his first managerial job as part-time manager of Clyde in 1977. He spent 10 seasons there, winning the Second Division Championship in 1982–83 while working as a primary school headteacher. He returned to football full time in 1986 when Scotland manager Andy Roxburgh appointed him as

assistant manager. In 1989 he coached Scotland's Under-16s to the Final of the World Championship. Brown was appointed manager of Scotland in December 1993. He failed to take Scotland to the World Cup in 1994 but soon made up for this by taking them to Euro 96. He also took Scotland to France 98 but resigned in 2001 after failing to take Scotland to Euro 2000 and the 2002

World Cup. Brown was appointed manager of Preston North End in April 2002 but after two seasons of mid-table placings in the First Division and a poor start to the 2004–05 season, he left the club by mutual consent. Disappointed that he was unable to mount a promotion challenge, Brown became Fulham's international representative.

Billy Davies: 2004 to 2006

North End record:

P	W	D	L
96	44	33	19

Honours:
Division One Play-offs: 2004–05
Division One Play-offs: 2005–06

Billy Davies started his playing career at Rangers where he spent six years. He then had a brief spell with Swedish team IF Elsborg and later played for St Mirren,

Leicester City and Dunfermline Athletic before finishing his playing career with Motherwell. He later went on to manage Motherwell, where he took them to the brink of European football. However, he was sacked after poor form. Having been Craig Brown's assistant, Davies was appointed manager of Preston in August 2004. His first season in charge at Deepdale was a great success as he took them to the brink of the Premiership via the Play-offs in May 2005. Despite a difficult start to the 2005–06 season, Preston went on an unbeaten run from September until February, which saw them go 22 games unbeaten – equalling the record set in 1888 by the double-winning 'Invincibles' side. Although a number of players suffered injuries, Billy Davies kept North End in the hunt for promotion to the Premiership and, as the season drew to a close, the club had once again qualified for the Play-offs. Their opponents in the two-legged semi-final were Leeds United and, after a 1–1 draw in the first leg at Elland Road, Davies must have had high hopes for a place in the Play-off Final. But it wasn't to be – the Yorkshire club ran out 2–0 winners at Deepdale. Davies left in the summer of 2006 to manage Derby County, after being considered by Charlton Athletic.

Progressive Scoring Records

John Goodall set the first target in Preston North End's opening League season, scoring 20 goals and adding another two in the FA Cup. This table shows how individual scoring records have been equalled and beaten since then.

	League			All Matches	
1888–89	John Goodall	20		John Goodall	22
1889–90	Nick Ross	22		Nick Ross	24
1893–94	-			Jimmy Ross	24
1903–04	Percy Smith	26		Percy Smith	26
1913–14	-			Fred Osborn	26
1919–20	Tommy Roberts	26		Tommy Roberts	29
1922–23	Tommy Roberts	28		Tommy Roberts	29
1926–27	-			Tommy Roberts	30
1932–33	Ted Harper	37		Ted Harper	37

100+ Consecutive Appearances

League				All Matches		
187	Bobby Crawford	February 1928 to September 1932		194	Bobby Crawford	February 1928 to September 1932
176	Jimmy Marston	February 1951 to April 1955		190	Jimmy Marston	February 1951 to April 1955
164	Roy Tunks	April 1977 to February 1981		172	Harry Holdcroft	December 1932 to October 1936
162	James Trainer	September 1889 to September 1895		157	Harry Lowe	April 1933 to November 1936
158	Harry Holdcroft	December 1932 to October 1936		147	Willie Cunningham	November 1956 to December 1959
144	Harry Lowe	April 1933 to November 1936		143	Peter Thompson	September 1960 to May 1963
134	Willie Cunningham	November 1956 to December 1959		142	Joe Walton	October 1955 to December 1958
134	Joe Walton	October 1955 to December 1958		139	Tommy Docherty	March 1950 to April 1953
133	Tommy Docherty	March 1950 to April 1953		136	Angus Morrison	August 1950 to August 1953
130	Angus Morrison	August 1950 to August 1953		109	James Trainer	September 1889 to February 1893
119	Peter Thompson	September 1960 to May 1963				

Individual Scoring Feats

Six goals in a game

J. Ross	v Reading (h) 18–0	FA Cup	27 January 1894

Four goals in a game

J. Ross	v Stoke (h) 7–0	Football League	6 October 1888
N. Ross	v Derby County (h) 5–0	Football League	
G. Drummond	v Notts County (h) 6–0	Football League	12 December 1891
F. Becton	v Notts County (h) 4–0	First Division	31 March 1893
J. Cowan	v Reading (h) 18–0	FA Cup	27 January 1894
F. Becton	v Reading (h) 18–0	FA Cup	27 January 1894
T. Pratt	v Grimsby Town (h) 7–0	FA Cup	28 January 1899
T. Roberts	v Lincoln City (a) 4–2	Second Division	8 January 1927
G. Harrison	v Grimsby Town (h) 5–2	Second Division	3 November 1928
A. Reid	v Port Vale (h) 7–1	Second Division	23 February 1929

B. Crawford	v Stoke (h) 5–1	Second Division	21 September 1929
J. McClelland	v Reading (a) 4–1	Second Division	6 September 1930
D. Rowley	v Plymouth Argyle (a) 5–2	Second Division	23 April 1932
T. Harper	v Burnley (h) 6–1	Second Division	29 August 1932
T. Harper	v Lincoln City (h) 5–0	Second Division	11 March 1933
C. Wayman	v Queen's Park Rangers (a) 4–1	Second Division	25 December 1950
A. Bruce	v Colchester United (h) 4–0	Third Division	28 February 1978

Three goals in a game

7 times	T. Harper; T. Roberts; J. Ross; C. Wayman.
6	F. Becton.
5	A. Dawson; N. Ross.
4	T. Ellis; B. Maxwell; P. Smith.
3	S. Elliott; F. Osborn; S. Taylor; J. Thomas; T. Thompson.
2	G. Bargh; A. Biggs; A. Bruce; G. Drummond; B. Godfrey; J. Goodall; G. Harrison; W. McIntosh; F. O'Donnell; T. Pratt; N. Robson; A. Saville; S. Wilkinson; R. Woodhouse; L. Ashcroft; A. Ashworth; J. Barton; J. Baxter; B. Beattie; D. Bond; G. Brazil; K. Cameron; M. Conroy; J. Cowan; B. Crawford; C. Dawson; V. Farrell; J. Ferris; R. Foster; R. Fuller; A. Gara; J. Gordon; B. Greenhalgh; A. Hair; E. Hannigan; D. Hatsell; D. Healy; A. Henderson; P. Higham; M. Holden; J. Horton; G. Ingram; W. Irvine; W. Jackson; R. Jepson; J. McClelland; J. Macken; F. Marquis; B. Mooney; J. Morley; G. Mutch; J. Palethorpe; R. Pegg; J. Pierce; D. Reeves; A. Reid; D. Rowley; D. Russell; T. Scott; G. Shaw; G. Stephenson; K. Waterhouse; D. Wilson.

Ever-Present in a Football League Season

	Games	
1888–89	22	J. Graham; B. Holmes.
1889–90	22	J. Gordon; J. Trainer.
1890–91	22	B. Holmes; J. Trainer.
1891–92	26	H. Gallacher; J. Ross; M. Sanders; J. Trainer.
1892–93	30	J. Trainer.
1893–94	30	B. Greer; J. Trainer.
1894–95	30	J. Trainer.
1895–96	30	R. Blyth; B. Holmes.
1896–97	30	R. Blyth; J. Trainer.
1898–99	34	P. McBride.
1899–1900	34	H. Dunn; P. McBride.
1902–03	34	P. McBride; G. Tod; H. Wilcox.
1903–04	34	J. Derbyshire.
1904–05	34	P. McBride.
1911–12	38	W. Kirby.
1912–13	38	E. Holdsworth; C. McFadyen.
1920–21	42	A. Rawlings.
1921–22	42	T. Roberts.
1922–23	42	J. Branston.
1923–24	42	B. Crawford; T. Roberts.
1926–27	42	B. Crawford.
1927–28	42	T. Hamilton; D. Morris.
1928–29	42	B. Crawford.
1929–30	42	B. Crawford.
1930–31	42	B. Crawford.
1931–32	42	B. Crawford.
1932–33	42	F. Gallimore.
1933–34	42	H. Holdcroft; H. Lowe.
1934–35	42	H. Holdcroft; H. Lowe; B. Shankly.
1935–36	42	F. Gallimore; H. Holdcroft; H. Lowe; B. Tremelling.
1938–39	42	F. Gallimore; H. Holdcroft; R. Beattie; G. Mutch.
1946–47	42	B. Scott.
1950–51	42	T. Docherty; W. Forbes; A. Morrison.
1951–52	42	W. Cunningham; T. Docherty; J. Marston; A. Morrison.
1952–53	42	J. Marston; A. Morrison; C. Wayman.
1953–54	42	J. Baxter; J. Marston.
1955–56	42	T. Thompson.
1956–57	42	F. Else; J. Walton.
1957–58	42	W. Cunningham; J. Walton.
1958–59	42	W. Cunningham.
1959–60	42	F. Else; J. Walton.
1961–62	42	P. Thompson.
1962–63	42	P. Thompson.
1963–64	42	G. Ross; T. Singleton.
1964–65	42	A. Spavin.
1965–66	42	G. Ross.
1966–67	42	E. Hannigan.
1968–69	42	K. Knighton.
1970–71	46	A. Kelly; G. Hawkins.
1971–72	42	J. Bird.
1973–74	42	F. Burns; J. McMahon.
1974–75	46	J. Bird.
1975–76	46	M. Elwiss.
1976–77	46	A. Bruce; M. Lawrenson.
1977–78	46	M. Elwiss; R. Tunks.
1978–79	42	R. Tunks.
1979–80	42	S. Elliott; R. Tunks.
1980–81	42	M. Baxter.
1981–82	46	A. Bruce; D. O'Riordan.
1986–87	46	A. Jones.
1989–90	46	G. Swann.
1994–95	42	A. Fensome.
1999–2000	46	G. Alexander; M. Jackson.

Most Ever-Present Seasons

6	J. Trainer.
5	B. Crawford.
4	H. Holdcroft; P. McBride.
3	W. Cunningham; F. Gallimore; B. Holmes; H. Lowe; A. Morrison; R. Tunks; J. Walton.
2	J. Bird; A. Bruce; T. Docherty; F. Else; M. Elwiss; J. Marston; T. Roberts; G. Ross; P. Thompson.

Leading Scorers 1888–89 to 2004–05

	League		All Matches	
1888–89	John Goodall	20	John Goodall	22
1889–90	Nick Ross	22	Nick Ross	24
1890–91	Hugh Gallacher	6	Hugh Gallacher	6
1891–92	Jimmy Ross	16	Jimmy Ross	18
1892–93	Frank Becton	15	Frank Becton	23
1893–94	Jimmy Ross	18	Jimmy Ross	24
1894–95	David Smith	12	David Smith	12
			Adam Henderson	12
1895–96	Jackie Pierce	8	Jackie Pierce	8
1896–97	David Boyd	13	David Boyd	14
1897–98	Alexander Brown	11	Alexander Brown	11
1898–99	Tom Pratt	13	Tom Pratt	17
1899–1900	Adam Henderson	12	Adam Henderson	13
1900–01	Adam Gara	11	Adam Gara	11
1901–02	Harry Wilcox	14	Harry Wilcox	14
1902–03	Percy Smith	16	Frank Pearson	18
1903–04	Percy Smith	26	Percy Smith	26
1904–05	Percy Smith	14	Percy Smith	14
1905–06	Dickie Bond	17	Dickie Bond	17
1906–07	Charlie Dawson	11	Charlie Dawson	11
1907–08	Percy Smith	12	Percy Smith	12
1908–09	James Wilson	11	James Wilson	11
1909–10	David McLean	18	David McLean	19
1910–11	David McLean	7	David McLean	7
	James Bannister	7	James Bannister	7
1911–12	William Kirby	14	William Kirby	14
1912–13	Ben Green	13	Ben Green	13
1913–14	Fred Osborn	22	Fred Osborn	26
1914–15	Fred Osborn	17	Fred Osborn	17
1919–20	Tommy Roberts	26	Tommy Roberts	29
1920–21	Tommy Roberts	18	Tommy Roberts	25
1921–22	Tommy Roberts	18	Tommy Roberts	25
1922–23	Tommy Roberts	28	Tommy Roberts	29
1923–24	Tommy Roberts	26	Tommy Roberts	26
1924–25	George Harrison	8	Rowland Woodhouse	9
	Horace Barnes	8		
1925–26	Alex James	14	Alex James	14
1926–27	Tommy Roberts	26	Tommy Roberts	30
1927–28	Norman Robson	19	Norman Robson	19
1928–29	Alex Hair	19	Alex Hair	19
1929–30	James McClelland	10	James McClelland	10
	George Smithies	10	George Smithies	10
1930–31	George Bargh	14	George Bargh	14
	Tom Scott	14	Tom Scott	14
1931–32	Ted Harper	24	Ted Harper	26
1932–33	Ted Harper	37	Ted Harper	37
1933–34	George Stephenson	16	George Stephenson	16
1934–35	Bud Maxwell	23	Bud Maxwell	26
1935–36	Bud Maxwell	17	Bud Maxwell	19
1936–37	Frank O'Donnell	16	Frank O'Donnell	27
1937–38	Jimmy Dougal	14	George Mutch	18
1938–39	Jimmy Dougal	19	Jimmy Dougal	19
1946–47	Willie McIntosh	27	Willie McIntosh	32
1947–48	Andy McLaren	17	Andy McLaren	18
1948–49	Bobby Langton	12	Bobby Langton	12
1949–50	Eddy Brown	12	Eddy Brown	13
1950–51	Charlie Wayman	27	Charlie Wayman	29

	League		All Matches	
1951–52	Charlie Wayman	24	Charlie Wayman	24
1952–53	Charlie Wayman	23	Charlie Wayman	26
1953–54	Charlie Wayman	25	Charlie Wayman	32
1954–55	Jimmy Baxter	17	Jimmy Baxter	17
1955–56	Tommy Thompson	23	Tommy Thompson	24
1956–57	Tommy Thompson	26	Tommy Thompson	29
1957–58	Tommy Thompson	34	Tommy Thompson	34
1958–59	Tommy Thompson	19	Tommy Thompson	21
1959–60	Tom Finney	17	Tom Finney	21
1960–61	Alec Alston	9	Peter Thompson	12
1961–62	Alfie Biggs	21	Alfie Biggs	22
1962–63	Alex Dawson	22	Alex Dawson	27
1963–64	Alex Dawson	30	Alex Dawson	36
1964–65	Alex Dawson	26	Alex Dawson	27
1965–66	Brian Godfrey	17	Brian Godfrey	20
1966–67	Alex Dawson	13	Alex Dawson	13
1967–68	Derek Temple	8	Derek Temple	8
1968–69	Willie Irvine	15	Willie Irvine	20
1969–70	Archie Gemmill	6	Archie Gemmill	6
1970–71	Gerry Ingram	22	Gerry Ingram	24
1971–72	Hugh McIlmoyle	10	Hugh McIlmoyle	13
	Alan Tarbuck	10		
1972–73	Alex Bruce	13	Alex Bruce	13
1973–74	Alex Bruce	9	Alex Bruce	9
1974–75	Mel Holden	17	Mel Holden	22
1975–76	Mike Elwiss	15	Mike Elwiss	16
	Alex Bruce	15		
1976–77	Alex Bruce	24	Alex Bruce	26
1977–78	Alex Bruce	27	Alex Bruce	30
1978–79	Alex Bruce	21	Alex Bruce	26
1979–80	Steve Elliott	16	Steve Elliott	23
1980–81	Alex Bruce	13	Alex Bruce	15
1981–82	Alex Bruce	18	Alex Bruce	19
1982–83	Steve Elliott	19	Steve Elliott	23
1983–84	Steve Elliott	16	Steve Elliott	20
1984–85	John Kelly	7	Peter Houghton	9
1985–86	John Thomas	17	John Thomas	18
			Gary Brazil	18
1986–87	John Thomas	21	John Thomas	28
1987–88	Gary Brazil	14	Gary Brazil	20
1988–89	Tony Ellis	20	Tony Ellis	20
1989–90	Warren Joyce	11	Warren Joyce	13
1990–91	Graham Shaw	10	Graham Shaw	15
1991–92	Graham Shaw	14	Graham Shaw	17
1992–93	Tony Ellis	22	Tony Ellis	25
1993–94	Tony Ellis	26	Tony Ellis	31
1994–95	Mike Conroy	10	Mike Conroy	11
1995–96	Andy Saville	29	Andy Saville	30
1996–97	David Reeves	11	David Reeves	14
1997–98	Lee Ashcroft	14	Lee Ashcroft	16
1998–99	Kurt Nogan	18	Kurt Nogan	21
1999–2000	Jonathan Macken	22	Jonathan Macken	25
2000–01	Jonathan Macken	19	Jonathan Macken	22
2001–02	Richard Cresswell	13	Richard Cresswell	16
2002–03	Richard Cresswell	16	Richard Cresswell	16
2003–04	Ricardo Fuller	17	Ricardo Fuller	19
2004–05	Richard Cresswell	16	Richard Cresswell	21
2005–06	David Nugent	10	David Nugent	11

Top 20 Scorers

	All Matches				League Matches	
1	Tom Finney	210		1	Tom Finney	187
2	Tommy Roberts	179		2=	Alex Bruce	157
3	Alex Bruce	171			Tommy Roberts	157
4	Alex Dawson	132		4	Tommy Thompson	117
5	Tommy Thompson	129		5	Alex Dawson	114
6	Charlie Wayman	116		6	Charlie Wayman	104
7	Jimmy Ross	101		7	Percy Smith	94
8	Percy Smith	94		8	Jimmy Ross	85
9	Tony Ellis	85		9	Tony Ellis	75
10	Steve Elliott	78		10	George Harrison	72
11=	George Harrison	75		11=	Steve Elliott	70
	Angus Morrison	75			Angus Morrison	70
13	Jonathan Macken	74		13	Ted Harper	67
14=	Gary Brazil	72		14	Jimmy Baxter	65
	Mike Elwiss	72		15=	Mike Elwiss	63
16	Jimmy Baxter	71			Jonathan Macken	63
17	Ted Harper	69		17	Bud Maxwell	60
18	Bud Maxwell	65		18	Gary Brazil	58
19	Frank Becton	62		19	Denis Hatsell	54
20	Rowland Woodhouse	61		20	Alex James	53

Top 20 Appearances

	All Matches				League Matches	
1	Alan Kelly	512		1	Alan Kelly	447
2	Willie Cunningham	487		2	Peter McBride	442
3	Lee Cartwright	367/100		3	Willie Cunningham	440
4=	Tom Finney	473		4	Tom Finney	433
	Peter McBride	473		5	Alan Spavin	411/6
	Alan Spavin	465/8		6	Joe Walton	401
7	George Ross	439/2		7	Lee Cartwright	312/85
8	Joe Walton	435		8	Bobby Crawford	392
9	Bobby Crawford	407		9	George Ross	384/2
10	Alex Bruce	382/22		10	Joe McCall	370
11	Joe McCall	395		11	Alex Bruce	343/20
12	Tom Rodway	351		12	Tom Rodway	335
13	Tommy Docherty	350		13	Tommy Docherty	324
14	Jimmy Smith	345		14	Jimmy Smith	314
15	Bill Shankly	337		15	Graham Alexander	305/2
16	Graham Alexander	334/3		16=	Bill Shankly	300
17	Tony Singleton	332/1			Bob Holmes	300
18	Bob Holmes	332		18	Tony Singleton	286/1
19	Dave Wilson	308/15		19	Dave Wilson	267/14
20	Roy Tunks	313		20	Roy Tunks	277

Notes:
1. Substitute appearances are given to the right of full appearances, eg 382/22.
2. Up to end of the 2004–05 season.

North End Career Records

Below are the career records of every North End player to have played League football for the club since the inaugural season of 1888–89. The years given are the first years of the seasons: for example, 1927 means 1927–28. The others list includes all the competitions not accounted for in the rest of the table: test matches, Associate Members Cup, Freight Rover Trophy, Sherpa Van Trophy, Leyland Daf Cup, Autoglass Trophy, Auto Windscreens Shield and League Play-offs. Substitute appearances are given to the right of full appearances, eg 13/2.

Player	Played	LEAGUE A	LEAGUE G	FA CUP A	FA CUP G	FL CUP A	FL CUP G	OTHERS A	OTHERS G	TOTAL A	TOTAL G
Abbott, P.T.	2000–03	8/17	6	1/3	0	0/1	0	0	0	9/21	6
Agyemang, P.	2004	34/35	10	5	0	1	0	0/5	0	40/40	10
Ainsworth, G.	1992–95 and 2002	81/11	13	3/1	0	3/2	0	9/1	1	96/15	14
Aitken, W.J.	1924–25	56	11	2	0	0	0	0	0	58	11
Akers, G.	1932	1	0	0	0	0	0	0	0	1	0
Alexander, G.	1998–2005	305/2	46	16	5	19/1	6	8/1	0	348/4	57
Allan, R.	1894	2	1	0	0	0	0	0	0	2	1
Allardyce, C.S.	1992	0/1	0	0	0	0	0	0	0	0/1	0
Allardyce, S.	1986–88 and 1992	89/4	2	11	0	8	2	8/1	0	116/5	4
Allatt, V.	1985	17/2	3	1	0	0	0	1/1	1	19/3	4
Allpress, T.J.	1991	7/2	0	2	0	0	0	1	0	10/2	0
Alstead, A.	1914–19	14	0	0	0	0	0	0	0	14	0
Alston, A.G.	1957–62	102	26	6	1	9	3	0	0	117	30
Anders, H.	1947–52	69	4	4	1	0	0	0	0	73	5
Anderson, D.R.	1910–11	9	3	0	0	0	0	0	0	9	3
Anderson, I.	1999–2002	46/36	13	3/1	1	5	0	1/2	0	55/39	14
Anderson, J.C.P.	1979–81	47/4	0	1	0	2	0	0	0	50/4	0
Anderton, S.D.	1989	0/1	0	0	0	0	0	0	0	0/1	0
Angell, B.A.M.	1999	9/6	8	0	0	0	0	0	0	9/6	8
Anyinsah, J.	2006	0/3	0	0/1	0	0	0	0	0	0/4	0
Appleton, M.A.	1997–2000	90/25	12	9/1	1	7/1	1	6/1	1	112/28	15
Arnold, J.A.	1982	6	0	0	0	0	0	0	0	6	0
Arthurs, C.H.	1909	8	1	0	0	0	0	0	0	8	1
Ashcroft, L.	1991–92 and 1996–97	141/14	35	10	5	7	0	8/3	1	166/17	41
Ashton, H.	1905–06	4	0	0	0	0	0	0	0	4	0
Ashworth, A.	1963–65	42/1	14	4	0	2	1	0	0	48/1	15
Atherton, J.	1899	13	0	0	0	0	0	0	0	13	0
Atherton, J.J.	1936	4	1	0	0	0	0	0	0	4	1
Atkins, R.G.	1984–89	198/2	5	12	2	14	0	16	2	240/2	9
Atkinson, G.	1994–97	63/16	6	2/1	0	5	1	5	2	75/17	9
Bailey, J.A.K.	2001	0/1	0	0	0	0	0	0	0	0/1	0
Bainbridge, S.	1919	14	1	3	1	0	0	0	0	17	2
Baird, S.	1954	15	2	0	0	0	0	0	0	15	2
Baker, G.	1909–12	24	0	0	0	0	0	0	0	24	0
Ball, A.	1893	5	0	0	0	0	0	0	0	5	0
Bamber, L.	1993	0/1	0	0	0	0	0	0	0	0/1	0
Banks, R.	1899	4	0	0	0	0	0	0	0	4	0
Bannister, J.	1909–11	65	12	3	0	0	0	0	0	68	12
Barber, D.E.	1961–63	38	2	1	0	5	0	0	0	44	2
Barbour, J.	1914	12	2	0	0	0	0	0	0	12	2
Bargh, G.W.	1928–34	142	42	8	1	0	0	0	0	150	43
Barlow, G.H.	1906–07 and 1912–14	89	7	5	1	0	0	0	0	94	8
Barnes, H.	1924–25	39	16	2	0	0	0	0	0	41	16
Barr, R.	1894–95	29	9	2	0	0	0	0	0	31	9
Barrick, D.	1995–98	98/11	1	5	0	7/1	1	6	0	116/12	2
Barry-Murphy, B.	1999–2002	6/15	0	1/1	0	1/3	0	1	0	9/19	0
Barton, J.	1893	2	0	1	3	0	0	0	0	3	3
Barton, J.B.	1958–65	48	0	3	0	3	0	0	0	54	0
Basham, S.B.	1998–2001	37/31	15	1/2	0	5/2	1	0	0	43/35	16
Batey, R.	1934–39	93	0	1	0	0	0	0	0	104	0
Batey, J.C.	1936	9	0	0	0	0	0	0	0	9	0
Baxter, J.C.	1952–58	245	65	22	6	0	0	0	0	267	71
Baxter, M.J.	1974–80	209/1	17	6	0	16	1	0	0	231/1	18
Baxter, S.W.	1972–75	34/7	1	1	0	5	0	0	0	40/7	1
Beattie, A.	1934–46	125	4	15	0	0	0	0	0	140	4

Player	Played	LEAGUE		FA CUP		FL CUP		OTHERS		TOTAL	
		A	G	A	G	A	G	A	G	A	G
Beattie, R.	1937–53	267	57	22	5	0	0	0	0	289	62
Beaumont, S.	1911	1	0	0	0	0	0	0	0	1	0
Beaver, J.	1900–02	21	2	2	0	0	0	0	0	23	2
Beckford, D.R.L.	1996	0/2	0	0	0	0	0	1	0	1/2	0
Beckham, D.R.	1994	4/1	2	0	0	0	0	0	0	4/1	2
Becton, F.	1891–94 and 1900	113	46	16	19	0	0	0	0	129	65
Becton, M.	1906–07	23	3	0	0	0	0	0	0	23	3
Becton, T.	1897	4	0	0	0	0	0	0	0	4	0
Beesley, M.	1999	0/1	0	0	0	0	0	0/1	0	0/2	0
Bell, G.T.	1979–82	140/3	9	1/1	0	11/1	1	0	0	152/5	10
Bell, J.	1903–07	109	25	10	2	0	0	0	0	119	27
Bell, J.G.	1933–34	20	5	7	0	0	0	0	0	27	5
Bennett, G.M.	1995–96	15/9	4	0	0	0	0	1	1	16/9	5
Bennett, M.	1986–89	85/1	1	7	0	2	0	10	0	104/1	1
Beresford, D.	1998	1/3	0	0/1	0	0	0	1	0	2/4	0
Beresford, F.E.	1933–34	36	4	0	0	0	0	0	0	36	4
Beresford, J.	1935–37	76	10	9	2	0	0	0	0	85	12
Berry, G.F.	1991	4	0	0	0	1/1	0	0	0	5/1	0
Best, H.O.	1910	4	0	0	0	0	0	0	0	4	0
Biggs, A.G.	1961–62	49	22	7	1	4	1	0	0	60	24
Birch, P.	1995	11	2	0	0	0	0	0	0	11	1
Bird, J.C.	1970–75	166	9	8/1	0	10	0	0	0	184/1	9
Bishop, C.D.	1995	4	0	0	0	0	0	0	0	4	0
Blackley, J.H.	1979–81	51/2	0	0	0	5	0	0	0	56/2	0
Bleasdale, D.G.	1983	4/1	0	0	0	1	0	1	0	6/1	0
Blessington, J.	1897–98	15	1	0	0	0	0	0	0	15	1
Blyth, J.A.	1971	1	0	0	0	0	0	0	0	1	0
Blyth, R.	1894–98	114	8	10	0	0	0	0	0	124	8
Blyth, W.J.	1905	1	0	0	0	0	0	0	0	1	0
Bogan, T.	1948	11	0	0	0	0	0	0	0	11	0
Bogie, I.	1988–90	67/12	12	3	0	3/1	0	4/1	0	77/14	12
Bond, J.	1913	1	1	0	0	0	0	0	0	1	1
Bond, R.	1902–08	148	34	17	3	0	0	0	0	165	37
Booth, T.A.	1981–84	84	2	2	0	9	0	1	0	96	2
Bosbury, C.E.	1925	2	0	1	0	0	0	0	0	3	0
Bourne, R.A.	1902–04	62	6	8	1	0	0	0	0	70	7
Boyd, D.	1896–97	37	14	5	1	0	0	0	0	42	15
Bradford, J.W.	1925	1	0	0	0	0	0	0	0	1	0
Bradley, H.	1911	2	0	0	0	0	0	0	0	2	0
Brain, J.	1933	7	2	0	0	0	0	0	0	7	2
Branagan, J.P.S.	1987	3	0	0	0	2	0	0	0	5	0
Brandon, J.	1890	8	3	0	0	0	0	0	0	8	3
Branston, J.H.	1921–26	129	0	7	0	0	0	0	0	136	0
Brazil, G.N.	1984–88	163/3	58	10	3	13	6	13	5	199/3	72
Bright, D.	1968	1	0	0	0	0	0	0	0	1	0
Briscoe, J.E.	1936	5	0	0	0	0	0	0	0	5	0
Briscoe, L.S.	2003	2	0	0	0	0	0	0	0	2	0
Broadbent, W.H.	1932	2	0	0	0	0	0	0	0	2	0
Broadhurst, F.	1910 and 1911–21	107	3	8	0	0	0	0	0	115	3
Broome, T.A.	1913–19	65	2	2	0	0	0	0	0	67	2
Broomes, M.C.	2002–05	59/10	0	2	0	4	0	0/2	0	65/12	0
Brown, A.	1896–98	63	25	4	4	0	0	0	0	67	29
Brown, A.F.	1904–05	22	7	1	0	0	0	0	0	23	7
Brown, D.J.	1986–88	74	0	6	0	9	0	6	0	95	0
Brown, E.	1948–50	36	6	2	1	0	0	0	0	38	7
Brown, J.C.	1966–74	67	0	1	0	4	0	0	0	72	0
Brown, J.K.	1975–77	64	3	3	1	5	1	0	0	72	5
Brown, M.A.	1995–96	11/5	1	0	0	0/1	0	1	0	12/6	1
Brown, W.	1895	1	0	0	0	0	0	0	0	1	0
Brown, W.F.	1946–49	40	0	2	0	0	0	0	0	42	0
Bruce, A.R.	1971–73 and 1975–82	343/20	157	16	6	23/2	8	0	0	382/22	171
Brunton, M.	1899	8	2	0	0	0	0	0	0	8	2
Bryson, J.I.C.	1993–96	141/10	19	7/2	0	6/1	1	7	0	161/13	20
Buckley, G.	1981–82	27/7	2	1	0	2	0	0	0	30/7	2
Bulmer, P.	1986	4	0	0	0	3	0	0	0	7	0

Player	Played	LEAGUE		FA CUP		FL CUP		OTHERS		TOTAL	
		A	G	A	G	A	G	A	G	A	G
Burley, C.W.	2003	1/3	0	0	0	0	0	0	0	1/3	0
Burns, F.	1973–80	271/2	9	16	0	17/1	0	0	0	304/3	9
Burns, M.T.	1936–37	12	0	4	0	0	0	0	0	16	0
Burton, S.	1992–93	19/5	3	0	0	0/1	0	1/1	0	20/7	3
Butler, W.	1906	3	0	0	0	0	0	0	0	3	0
Butterworth, A.	1934–35	14	4	0	0	0	0	0	0	14	4
Byfield, D.	1995	3/2	1	0	0	0	0	1	0	4/2	1
Callaghan, A.J.	1992–93	34/2	2	2	1	3	0	3	0	42/2	3
Calverley, A.	1947	13	0	0	0	0	0	0	0	13	0
Cameron, D.	1975–80	120/2	0	6	0	5/1	0	0	0	131/3	0
Cameron, K.	1926–28	24	5	0	0	0	0	0	0	24	5
Cameron, S.J.	1983	1	0	0	0	0	0	0	0	1	0
Campbell, A.G.	1982–84	18	0	0	0	0	0	2	0	20	0
Campbell, L.	1953–59	64	6	6	1	0	0	0	0	70	7
Campbell, W.C.	1890	4	4	1	0	0	0	0	0	5	4
Carlin, J.	1907–08	32	5	1	0	0	0	0	0	33	5
Carmichael, M.	1994	7/3	3	0	0	0	0	0	0	7/3	3
Carr, A.G.	1926–27	59	0	3	0	0	0	0	0	62	0
Carrick, M.D.	1973	0/2	0	0	0	0	0	0	0	0/2	0
Cartwright, L.	1990–2003	312/85	22	18/6	1	19/4	2	20/5	1	369/100	26
Catterall, J.	1904–09	6	1	0	0	0	0	0	0	6	1
Causer, A.H.	1919–21	46	0	6	0	0	0	0	0	52	0
Chadwick, T.	1908	9	0	0	0	0	0	0	0	9	0
Challender, G.L.	1993	5/5	2	1	0	0	0	1	0	7/5	2
Chalmers, J.	1898	10	2	3	1	0	0	0	0	13	3
Chandler, S.E.	1926–28	65	12	2	0	0	0	0	0	67	12
Chapman, L.	1986–87	50/3	1	2	0	4	0	6/1	0	62/4	1
Charlton, R.	1974	38	8	4	1	3	1	0	0	45	10
Charnley, R.O.	1967	23	4	2	3	0	0	0	0	25	7
Chester, A.	1910	2	1	0	0	0	0	0	0	2	1
Chippendale, B.A.	1985	5/1	0	0	0	0	0	0	0	5/1	0
Christie, D.	1991–92	1/3	0	0	0	0	0	0	0	1/3	0
Clark, C.	1969–72	71/1	9	3	2	6/1	0	0	0	80/2	11
Clark, J.	1981–86	107/3	10	6	0	16	1	3	0	132/3	11
Clarke, T.	1975	3	0	0	0	0	0	0	0	3	0
Clement, N.	1998	4	0	0	0	0	0	0	0	4	0
Clifton, W.	1914–19	4	0	0	0	0	0	0	0	4	0
Cochrane, J.	1976–78	3/2	2	0	0	1	0	0	0	4/2	2
Coleman, A.G.	1964	5	1	0	0	0	0	0	0	5	1
Coleman, G.M.	1973–82	248/21	25	12	3	20	2	0	0	280/21	30
Common, A.	1912–13	35	9	1	0	0	0	0	0	36	9
Common, E.W.	1933	1	0	0	0	0	0	0	0	1	0
Connor, D.R.	1971–72	29	0	2	0	0/1	0	0	0	31/1	0
Connor, E.A.	1893	1	0	0	0	0	0	0	0	1	0
Conroy, M.K.	1993–94	50/7	22	7	2	2/1	0	2	0	61/8	24
Cook, G.	1924–25	23	0	2	0	0	0	0	0	25	0
Cook, L.	1905–06	4	0	0	0	0	0	0	0	4	0
Corbett, W.	1948	19	0	0	0	0	0	0	0	19	0
Corr, P.J.	1946	3	0	0	0	0	0	0	0	3	0
Cowan, J.	1892–93	55	8	8	8	0	0	0	0	63	16
Cox, J.	1938	5	1	0	0	0	0	0	0	5	1
Cranston, W.	1964–69	89/7	1	7	0	5/1	1	0	0	92/8	1
Craven, J.G.	1925–30	65	1	2	0	0	0	0	0	67	1
Crawford, R.	1921–32	392	17	15	1	0	0	0	0	407	18
Crawley, T.	1935	2	0	0	0	0	0	0	0	2	0
Cresswell, R.	2000–04	164/23	49	2/1	3	8/2	5	4/2	1	178/28	58
Critchley, E.	1934	11	1	0	0	0	0	0	0	11	1
Croft, H.	1920–21	2	0	0	0	0	0	0	0	2	0
Cross, G.F.	1977–78	45	1	0	0	8	0	0	0	53	1
Cross, P.	1991	5	0	0	0	0	0	1	0	6	0
Crossan, B.	1890	7	3	0	0	0	0	0	0	7	3
Crossley, P.	1966–67	3	0	0	0	1	0	0	0	4	0
Cunningham, J.	1893–96	51	8	3	1	0	0	0	0	54	9
Cunningham, W.C.	1949–62	440	3	39	0	8	0	0	0	487	3
Curtis, J.C.K.	2004	12	0	0	0	0	0	0	0	12	0

Player	Played	LEAGUE A	G	FA CUP A	G	FL CUP A	G	OTHERS A	G	TOTAL A	G
Dagger, J.L.	1956–60	61	8	10	2	1	0	0	0	72	10
Dainty, A.	1946	1	1	0	0	0	0	0	0	1	1
Daley, O.	2004	1/13	0	0	0	1/2	1	0	0	2/14	1
Daniel, D.	1925	1	0	0	0	0	0	0	0	1	0
Daniels, G.	1919	12	1	1	0	0	0	0	0	13	1
Danson, H.	1902–11	156	23	8	0	0	0	0	0	164	23
Daby, J.T.	1997	18/14	1	2/2	1	1/1	0	2/2	1	23/19	3
Davey, S.	1994–97	97/9	21	2/1	0	4	1	7	0	110/10	22
Davidson, C.I.	2004–	42/4	5	3	0	1/1	0	0	0	46/5	5
Davidson, I.	1962–64	67	1	10	0	1	0	0	0	78	1
Davidson, J.S.	1992	18/3	1	2	1	2	0	2	0	24/3	2
Davie, J.G.	1948–49	28	0	0	0	0	0	0	0	28	0
Davies, R.	1972	2	0	0	0	0	0	0	0	2	0
Davies, S.C.	1919–20	24	11	2	0	0	0	0	0	26	1
Davis, C.	2003	75/20	4	5	0	4	0	5	0	89/20	4
Dawson, A.D.	1961–66	197	114	24	13	14	5	0	0	235	132
Dawson, C.	1906–09	67	23	3	0	0	0	0	0	70	23
Dawson, G.	1912–20	123	3	8	0	0	0	0	0	131	3
Day, C.N.	2004	6	0	0	0	0	0	0	0	6	0
Derbyshire, J.E.	1902–08	126	8	11	0	0	0	0	0	137	8
Devlin, J.T.	1925–26	8	1	0	0	0	0	0	0	8	1
Dewhurst, F.	1888 and 1889–90	24	13	5	1	0	0	0	0	29	14
Dexter, G.	1914	1	0	0	0	0	0	0	0	1	0
Diaf, F.	1999	1/2	0	0/1	0	0	0	2	0	3/3	0
Dickie, G.J.	1925	3	1	0	0	0	0	0	0	3	1
Dickinson, T.J.	1910	1	0	0	0	0	0	0	0	1	0
Dickson, C.	1893	3	1	0	0	0	0	0	0	3	1
Dichio, D.	2006	19/15	0	1/3	2	1/1	1	2	0	23/19	3
Dobson, S.	1890	8	5	0	0	0	0	0	0	8	5
Docherty, T.H.	1949–57	324	5	26	0	0	0	0	0	350	5
Donaldson, J.	1907	1	0	0	0	0	0	0	0	1	0
Donnelly, J.	1962–66	56/1	1	3	0	9	0	0	0	68/1	1
Doolan, A.	1920–22	77	0	15	0	0	0	0	0	92	0
Dougall, J.	1933–46	170	51	25	6	0	0	0	0	195	57
Dougal, W.	1947–48	22	2	0	0	0	0	0	0	22	2
Doyle, S.C.	1974–81	178/19	8	11/1	1	16/1	0	0	0	205/21	9
Drummond, G.	1888–98	139	36	19	4	0	0	0	0	158	40
Drummond, J.	1890	11	4	1	0	0	0	0	0	12	4
Duggins, A.E.	1923	2	0	0	0	0	0	0	0	2	0
Dunn, B.	1981	8	1	1	0	2	0	0	0	11	0
Dunn, H.	1893–1900	164	0	15	0	0	0	0	0	179	0
Dunn, J.	1951–60	223	2	15	0	0	0	0	0	238	2
Duxbury, T.	1920–23	51	1	8	0	0	0	0	0	59	1
Easter, G.P.	1990	1	0	0/1	0	0	0	1/1	0	2/2	0
Eastwood, C.M.	1925	20	2	2	0	0	0	0	0	22	1
Eaton, A.P.	1999–2002	7/7	0	1	0	2	0	0/1	0	10/8	0
Eaves, D.M.C.	1990–92	2/5	0	0	0	0/1	0	1/1	0	3/7	0
Eccleston, T.	1895–1900	26	2	1	0	0	0	0	0	27	2
Eccleston, W.	1895–99	72	6	6	0	0	0	0	0	78	6
Edwards, J.	1888	4	3	0	0	0	0	0	0	4	3
Edwards, R.W.	1999–2003	156/13	4	10	0	13	0	5	1	184/13	5
Elliott, J.W.	1920–21	12	0	0	0	0	0	0	0	12	0
Elliott, J.	1898–1901	80	4	8	0	0	0	0	0	88	4
Elliott, S.B.	1978–83	202/6	70	6	3	16/1	5	0	0	224/7	78
Ellis, A.J.	1987–89 and 1992–93	150/8	75	11	3	7	2	12/1	7	180/9	87
Else, F.	1953–60	215	0	18	0	5	0	0	0	238	0
Elwiss, M.W.	1973–77 and 1979	199/3	63	12	6	13	3	0	0	224/3	72
Emerson, D.	1994	1/1	0	0/2	0	0	0	0	0	1/3	0
English, J.C.	1910–11	6	0	0	0	0	0	0	0	6	0
Etuhu, D.P.	2002–05	94/27	15	4	1	8	0	0/3	0	106/30	16
Evans, R.	1953–56	33	2	1	0	0	0	0	0	34	2
Ewart, J.	1928–29	35	0	0	0	0	0	0	0	35	0
Eyres, D.	1997–2000	85/23	19	10	3	3/4	0	5	3	103/27	25
Fagan, W.	1936–37	35	6	6	0	0	0	0	0	41	6
Fairbrother, J.	1946	41	0	4	0	0	0	0	0	45	0

Player	Played	LEAGUE		FA CUP		FL CUP		OTHERS		TOTAL	
		A	G	A	G	A	G	A	G	A	G
Farnworth, S.	1990–92	81	0	3	0	6	0	7	0	97	0
Farrall, A.	1957–59	27	9	3	3	0	0	0	0	30	12
Farrell, V.	1930–32	16	5	0	0	0	0	0	0	16	5
Farrelly, M.	1981–84	77/5	4	1	0	7/1	1	3	0	88/6	5
Farrington, G.	1906	2	0	0	0	0	0	0	0	2	0
Fawcett, D.H.	1929–31	44	0	1	0	0	0	0	0	45	0
Fee, G.P.	1990	15	0	0	0	0	0	2	0	17	0
Fensome, A.B.	1993–95	93	1	9	0	3	0	6	1	111	2
Fenton, F.	1901–02	20	0	0	0	0	0	0	0	20	0
Ferris, J.	1921–23	53	11	3	0	0	0	0	0	56	11
Fielding, M.J.	1974	9	0	4	0	0	0	0	0	13	0
Findlay, A.	1896	2	1	0	0	0	0	0	0	2	1
Finney, S.K.	1991–92	1/5	1	0/1	0	0	0	1/1	0	2/7	1
Finney, T.	1946–59	433	187	40	23	0	0	0	0	473	210
Fitton, G.A.	1932–34	62	18	8	2	0	0	0	0	70	20
Fitzpatrick, P.J.	1988	2	0	0	0	0	0	0	0	2	0
Fleming, T.M.	1994–95	25/7	2	0/1	0	4	0	1/2	0	30/10	2
Flitcroft, D.J.	1992	4/4	2	0	0	0/1	0	0/1	0	4/6	2
Flynn, M.A.	1989–92	134/2	7	6/1	1	6	0	13	0	159/3	8
Folly, Y.	2004	0/2	0	0	0	0	0	0	0	0/2	0
Foot, G.	1919	5	0	0	0	0	0	0	0	5	0
Forbes, W.	1949–55	192	7	20	1	0	0	0	0	212	8
Ford, J.	1913–14	43	4	5	0	0	0	0	0	48	4
Forrest, J.	1923–25	51	0	2	0	0	0	0	0	53	0
Forrest, J.	1966–67	24/2	3	0	0	1	1	0	0	25/2	4
Forshaw, E.	1901	2	0	0	0	0	0	0	0	2	0
Foster, J.	1929	1	0	0	0	0	0	0	0	1	0
Foster, R.J.	1951–56	99	40	10	1	0	0	0	0	109	41
Foster, W.P.	1985	25/6	3	1	0	3	1	1/1	0	30/7	4
Fowler, J.A.	1992	5/1	0	0	0	0	0	0	0	5/1	0
Fowler, L.E.	1992	29/3	2	2	1	2	0	0	0	33/3	3
Fox, F.S.	1921	3	0	0	0	0	0	0	0	3	0
Friar, J.	1934–35	26	8	6	1	0	0	0	0	32	9
Fullam, J.R.	1959–60	49	6	2	0	5	0	0	0	56	6
Fuller, R.D.	2002–04	57/1	27	2	2	2/1	2	0	0	61/2	31
Gage, K.W.	1995–96	20/3	0	1	0	0	0	0	0	21/3	0
Galbraith, D.	1909–10	4	0	0	0	0	0	0	0	4	0
Gallacher, HM.	1890–92	55	12	4	1	0	0	0	0	59	13
Gallacher, KW.	2001	1/4	1	0	0	0/1	1	0	0	1/5	2
Gallimore, F.	1931–39	244	0	30	0	0	0	0	0	274	0
Gallimore, L.	1933–36	9	0	0	0	0	0	0	0	9	0
Galloway, D.W.	1932–33	31	1	0	0	0	0	0	0	31	1
Galloway, T.	1911–12	24	0	1	0	0	0	0	0	25	0
Gara, A.	1898–1901	66	27	7	1	0	0	0	0	73	28
Garrett, A.C.	1937	2	2	0	0	0	0	0	0	2	2
Garth, J.R.	1946–47	23	7	1	0	0	0	0	0	24	7
Garvie, J.	1949	5	0	0	0	0	0	0	0	5	0
Gemmill, A.	1967–70	93/6	13	5	1	5	0	0	0	103/6	14
Gerrard, E.D.	1925	10	0	0	0	0	0	0	0	10	0
Gerrish, W.W.W.	1912	3	0	0	0	0	0	0	0	3	0
Gibson, D.	1925	13	0	2	0	0	0	0	0	15	0
Gibson, S.J.	1984–85	42	5	1	0	3	0	3	1	49	6
Gilchrist, J.W.	1922–23	19	0	0	0	0	0	0	0	19	0
Gillespie, T.B.	1925	19	2	0	0	0	0	0	0	19	2
Gillibrand, C.S.	1907	3	2	1	0	0	0	0	0	4	2
Gillow, W.B.	1914–19	7	1	0	0	0	0	0	0	7	1
Godfrey, B.C.	1963–67	121/1	52	13	4	7	1	0	0	141/1	57
Gooch, J.A.G.	1946–51	135	0	6	0	0	0	0	0	141	0
Good, M.H.S.	1901	24	2	3	0	0	0	0	0	27	2
Goodall, A.L.	1888	2	1	0	0	0	0	0	0	2	1
Goodall, J.	1888	21	20	5	2	0	0	0	0	26	22
Goodburn, H.	1906	2	0	0	0	0	0	0	0	2	0
Goodwin, R.	1919	7	0	0	0	0	0	0	0	7	0
Gordon, J.B.	1888–94	113	27	20	7	0	0	0	0	133	34
Gornall, J.	1961–62	4	0	0	0	0	0	0	0	4	0

Player	Played	LEAGUE		FA CUP		FL CUP		OTHERS		TOTAL	
		A	G	A	G	A	G	A	G	A	G
Gould, J.A.	2002–04	54/1	0	3	0	1	0	0	0	58/1	0
Gowling, A.E.	1982	37/3	5	3	0	3	0	0	0	43/3	5
Graham, D.W.T.	1992	8	0	2	1	0	0	1	0	11	1
Graham, J.	1888–89	39	0	5	0	0	0	0	0	44	0
Graham, W.	1888	5	0	0	0	0	0	0	0	5	0
Grant, A.	1995	0/1	0	0	0	0	0	0	0	0/1	0
Grant, D.C.	1914	9	3	0	0	0	0	0	0	9	3
Gray, A.D.	1998	5	0	0	0	0	0	0	0	5	0
Gray, D.	1947	36	0	4	0	0	0	0	0	40	0
Gray, F.J.S.	1889	1	1	1	0	0	0	0	0	2	1
Gray, T.I.	1984–85	40	1	2	1	2	0	1	0	45	2
Greatorex, W.H.A.	1919–20	24	0	3	0	0	0	0	0	27	0
Greaves, S.R.	1990	2	0	0	0	0	0	0	0	2	0
Green, B.H.	1911–13	73	23	2	0	0	0	0	0	75	23
Green, E.	1900–01	27	8	2	0	0	0	0	0	29	8
Green, J.	1898–99	6	0	0	0	0	0	0	0	6	0
Green, J.	1919–20	7	0	1	0	0	0	0	0	8	0
Green, T.	1920	1	0	0	0	0	0	0	0	1	0
Greenall, C.A.	1991–92	29	1	0	0	0	0	0	0	29	1
Greenhalgh, B.A.	1965–67	19	9	1	0	0	0	0	0	20	9
Greenwood, N.P.	1984–85 and 1989–91	60/15	18	1/2	1	2/3	0	2/2	1	65/22	20
Greer, W.H.	1891–96	107	7	11	0	0	0	0	0	118	7
Gregan, S.M.	1996–2001	206/6	12	15	1	14	0	10	0	245/6	13
Grierson, G.	1926–29	5	0	0	0	0	0	0	0	5	0
Griffiths, F.J.	1901	10	0	0	0	0	0	0	0	10	0
Gudjonsson, T.	2001	4/3	0	0/1	0	0	0	0	0	4/4	0
Gunnlaugsson, B.B.	1999–2001	17/28	2	3/3	1	0/1	0	2	4	22/32	7
Hair, A.	1928–29	45	22	1	0	0	0	0	0	46	22
Hales, H.	1931–32	57	10	4	0	0	0	0	0	61	10
Hall, J.E.	1910–11	18	3	0	0	0	0	0	0	18	3
Hall, W.F.	1947	7	0	0	0	0	0	0	0	7	0
Halligan, W.	1919	16	2	0	0	0	0	0	0	16	2
Halliwell, J.A.	1912–13	26	10	0	0	0	0	0	0	26	10
Halsall, L.	1897–99	54	6	4	1	0	0	0	0	58	7
Ham, R.S.	1970–71	43	14	2	0	4	1	0	0	49	15
Hamilton, H.H.	1927–30	24	0	10	0	0	0	0	0	25	0
Hamilton, T.	1920–28	267	0	14	0	0	0	0	0	281	0
Hamilton, W.	1946	37	0	4	1	0	0	0	0	41	1
Hampton, J.W.	1930	37	0	1	0	0	0	0	0	38	0
Hannah, W.K.	1947–49	15	4	0	0	0	0	0	0	15	4
Hannigan, E.	1964–67	97	29	7	3	4	0	0	0	108	32
Hargreaves, R.	1897–98	11	0	0	0	0	0	0	0	11	0
Harper, E.J.	1931–33	75	67	5	2	0	0	0	0	80	69
Harper, S.J.	1988–90	57/20	10	1/2	0	1/1	0	6/1	1	65/24	11
Harrington, P.	1985	2	0	0	0	0	0	0	0	2	0
Harris, J.A.S.	1998	9/25	6	2/1	1	0	0	2/2	0	13/28	7
Harrison, C.	1999	6	0	0	0	0	0	1	0	7	0
Harrison, G.	1923–30	274	72	10	0	0	0	0	0	284	72
Hartley, P.	1905–06	3	0	0	0	0	0	0	0	3	0
Haselgrave, S.M.	1977–80	111/2	2	5	0	4	0	0	0	120/2	2
Hatsell, D.	1953–59	115	54	7	4	0	0	0	0	122	58
Hawkins, G.N.	1967–73	241/4	3	8	1	16	0	0	0	265/4	4
Hayes, W.E.	1914	10	0	0	0	0	0	0	0	10	0
Healey, R.	1973	6	0	0	0	0	0	0	0	6	0
Healy, D.J.	2000–04	104/35	44	7/1	0	7/1	0	3	1	121/37	45
Heaton, C.	1889	2	1	0	0	0	0	0	0	2	1
Heaton, F.	1929–31	13	1	0	0	0	0	0	0	13	1
Henderson, A.	1893–96	77	28	8	2	0	0	0	0	85	30
Henderson, G.	1897	2	0	0	0	0	0	0	0	2	0
Henderson, J.T.	1908	7	0	0	0	0	0	0	0	7	0
Henderson, W.	1924	9	1	0	0	0	0	0	0	9	1
Henderson, W.M.	1913–19	11	1	0	0	0	0	0	0	11	1
Hendry, E.C.J.	2001	2	0	0	0	0	0	0	0	2	0
Hendry, W.H.	1889–90	15	0	1	0	0	0	0	0	16	0
Heppolette, R.A.W.	1967–72	149/5	13	9	1	11	0	0	0	169/5	14

Player	Played	LEAGUE		FA CUP		FL CUP		OTHERS		TOTAL	
		A	G	A	G	A	G	A	G	A	G
Hetherington, J.	1924	5	0	0	0	0	0	0	0	5	0
Hetherington, J.A.	1934–35	15	3	3	1	0	0	0	0	18	4
Heyes, K.	1959	3	0	0	0	0	0	0	0	3	0
Hibbert, D.	2006	0/9	0	1/2	0	0	0	0	0	1/11	0
Hicks, S.J.	1993–94	11/1	0	0	0	2	0	0	0	13/1	0
Hicks, T.G.	1924–26	9	0	1	0	0	0	0	0	10	0
Higham, P.	1953–54	15	10	0	0	0	0	0	0	15	10
Hildersley, R.	1986–87	54/4	3	7	1	5	1	4	0	70/4	5
Hill, M.C.	2004	11/3	0	0	0	0	0	3	0	14/3	0
Hindle, J.	1947	1	0	1	0	0	0	0	0	2	0
Hinnigan, J.P.	1982–83	51/1	8	1	0	3	2	3	0	58/1	10
Hirst, H.	1924	2	0	0	0	0	0	0	0	2	0
Hodge, M.J.	1981 and 1982	44	0	0	0	0	0	0	0	44	0
Hodgson, T.	1899–1900	4	0	0	0	0	0	0	0	4	0
Hidgson, W.H.	1908–09	3	0	0	0	0	0	0	0	3	0
Holbem, W.	1913–14	37	0	4	0	0	0	0	0	41	0
Holdcroft, G.H.	1932–39	266	0	26	0	0	0	0	0	292	0
Holden, A.D.	1962–64	89	13	11	2	2	0	0	0	102	15
Holden, M.G.	1972–74	69/3	22	4/1	4	5	1	0	0	78/4	27
Holdsworth, E.	1907–19	222	3	1	0	0	0	0	0	233	3
Holland, C.J.	1993	0/1	0	0	0	0	0	1	0	1/1	0
Holland, J.	1920–21	6	0	2	0	0	0	0	0	8	0
Holmes, J.	1891–93	20	0	1	0	0	0	0	0	21	0
Holmes, R.	1888–1902	300	1	26	1	0	0	0	0	326	1
Holmes, S.P.	1994–95	13	1	3	0	0	0	1	0	17	1
Holt, M.A.	1996–98	12/24	5	1/3	0	2/2	1	0/1	0	15/30	6
Horne, A.	1929–31	40	5	0	0	0	0	0	0	40	5
Horton, J.K.	1946–52	166	36	11	1	0	0	0	0	177	37
Hosker, J.	1919–20	12	2	0	0	0	0	0	0	12	2
Hough, W.A.	1931–36	69	0	2	0	0	0	0	0	71	0
Houghton, P.	1983–84	52/9	16	1	0	2/2	3	2/1	0	57/7	19
Houston, G.R.	1979–84	90/38	11	7	1	12/1	0	1/1	1	110/40	13
Howarth, R.H.	1888–91 and 1894–98	50	0	8	0	0	0	0	0	58	0
Howell, R.	1901–03	60	1	5	0	0	0	0	0	65	1
Hudson, G.	1973	1	0	0	0	0	0	0	0	1	0
Hughes, A.F.	1987–91	91/9	3	4	0	2/1	0	11	1	108/10	4
Hughes, D.R.	1966–71	22/9	0	1	0	2	0	0	0	25/9	0
Hughes, G.	1931	11	0	0	0	0	0	0	0	11	0
Humes, J.	1959–61	18	1	0	0	3	0	0	0	21	1
Hunter, C.P.	1982 and 1984	3/4	0	0/1	1	0	0	0	0	3/5	1
Hunter, J.	1897–98	16	0	0	0	0	0	0	0	16	0
Hunter, J.	1902–07	186	5	13	1	0	0	0	0	199	6
Ibbotson, D.	1985	1	0	0	0	0	0	0	0	1	0
Inglis, J.	1888–89	3	2	0	0	0	0	0	0	3	2
Ingram, G.	1968–71	107/3	40	7	2	7/1	2	0	0	121/4	44
Irvine, W.J.	1967–70	77/4	27	2	2	7	4	0	0	86/4	33
Irving, J.	1921	15	0	1	0	0	0	0	0	16	0
Jack, R.	1901	22	6	3	0	0	0	0	0	25	6
Jackson, H.	1947–48	18	5	0	0	0	0	0	0	18	5
Jackson, M.A.	1990–91	3/1	0	0	0	0	0	1	0	4/1	0
Jackson, M.J.	1996–2003	237/8	17	14	0	16	2	8	0	275/8	19
Jackson, M.P.	2004	0/3	0	0/1	0	1/2	0	0	0	1/6	0
Jackson, W.E.	1925–26	45	13	2	2	0	0	0	0	47	15
James, A.W.	1925–28	147	53	6	0	0	0	0	0	153	53
James, J.C.	1991	6	0	0	0	0	0	0	0	6	0
James, M.J.	1990–92	92/6	11	4	0	6	0	8/1	0	110/7	11
James, R.	1900	3	0	0	0	0	0	0	0	3	0
Jarrett, J.	2006	8/2	1	0	0	1	0	1	0	10/2	1
Jeffels, S.	1987	1	0	0	0	0	0	0	0	1	0
Jefferies, F.	1919–22	79	12	15	4	0	0	0	0	94	16
Jemson, N.B.	1985–87 and 1989	34/7	10	2	0	0	0	5/1	0	41/8	10
Jennings, J.	1936	19	1	1	0	0	0	0	0	20	1
Jepson, R.F.	1990–91	36/2	8	0	0	2	0	3	4	41/2	12
Jessop, W.	1946	4	0	0	0	0	0	0	0	4	0
Johnrose, L.	1991	1/2	1	0	0	0	0	0	0	1/2	1

Player	Played	LEAGUE A	LEAGUE G	FA CUP A	FA CUP G	FL CUP A	FL CUP G	OTHERS A	OTHERS G	TOTAL A	TOTAL G
Johnson, A.K.	1995	2	0	0	0	0	0	0	0	2	0
Johnson, D.E.	1984	20/4	3	2	2	0	0	2	0	24/4	5
Johnston, J.	1911–13	10	0	1	0	0	0	0	0	11	0
Johnson, J.	2006	1/2	1	0	0	0	0	0	0	1/2	1
Johnstone, G.P.	1992	10	0	0	0	0	0	0	0	10	0
Johnstone, W.	1889	2	0	0	0	0	0	0	0	2	0
Jones, A.	1986–89	100/1	3	7	0	10/1	0	11/1	0	128/3	3
Jones, C.E.	1913–19	34	0	0	0	0	0	0	0	34	0
Jones, D.R.	1983–84	50	1	2	0	6	0	4	0	62	1
Jones, D.		21/1	3	0	0	0	0	0	0	21/1	3
Jones, E.	1953–54	13	0	0	0	0	0	0	0	13	0
Jones, H.J.	1932	1	1	0	0	0	0	0	0	1	1
Jones, M.T.	1983–85	76	3	3	0	7	0	2	0	88	3
Joy, W.J.	1895	9	0	1	0	0	0	0	0	10	0
Joyce, W.G.	1987–91	170/7	34	6	1	8	2	17	7	201/7	44
Kaile, G.W.	1951–53	7	1	1	0	0	0	0	0	8	1
Kane, L.R.	1948–49	5	0	0	0	0	0	0	0	5	0
Kay, J.	1996	7	0	0	0	3	0	0	0	10	0
Keane, M.T.J.	2000–03	39/18	3	5	0	2/1	0	0	0	46/19	3
Keen, N.	1985	24	0	0	0	3	1	1	0	28	1
Kelly, A.J.A.	1960–73	447	0	35	0	29	0	0	0	511	0
Kelly, A.T.	1985–91	142	0	8	0	1	0	13	0	164	0
Kelly, H.	1914	4	1	0	0	0	0	0	0	4	1
Kelly, J.	1981–84	120/10	27	4	2	11	1	3	0	138/10	30
Kelly, R.	1932–34	78	17	6	2	0	0	0	0	84	19
Kelso, R.R.	1889–90	38	0	3	0	0	0	0	0	41	0
Kendall, H.	1962–66	104	13	14	2	6	0	0	0	124	15
Kendall, J.W.	1927	2	0	0	0	0	0	0	0	2	0
Kennedy, J.	1913	3	1	0	0	0	0	0	0	3	1
Kerfoot, J.J.T.	1990–91	0/4	0	0/1	0	0	0	0	0	0/5	0
Kerr, E.J.	1919	2	0	0	0	0	0	0	0	2	0
Kerr, J.	1926–31	121	0	2	0	0	0	0	0	123	0
Kidd, R.A.	1992–2001	241/18	9	18	0	17/3	1	19/1	1	295/22	11
Kilbane, F.N.	1993	0/1	0	0	0	0	0	0	0	0/1	0
Kilbane, K.	1995–96	39/8	3	1	0	4	0	1	0	45/8	3
Kirby, W.	1911–12	55	22	1	0	0	0	0	0	56	22
Knight, J.	1948–49	39	7	4	0	0	0	0	0	43	7
Knight, J.H.	1919–20	3	0	1	0	0	0	0	0	4	0
Knighton, K.	1967–68	62	3	3	0	3	0	0	0	68	3
Knowles, J.	1957	2	0	0	0	0	0	0	0	2	0
Koumantarakis, G.	2002–04	11/6	4	2	1	0	0	0	0	13/6	5
Kozluk, R.	2004	0/1	0	1	0	0	0	0	0	1/1	0
Laird, A.	1922–23	28	4	2	0	0	0	0	0	30	4
Lamb, A.D.	1972–76	76/4	2	4	0	7/1	0	0	0	87/5	2
Lambert, J.G.	1958–60	226	4	0	2	0	0	0	0	28	6
Lambert, M.R.	1990–91	11/5	2	0	0	0	0	0/1	0	11/6	2
Lancashire, G.	1994–95	11/12	2	0	0	0/1	0	0/1	0	11/14	2
Langmead, K.S.	2003	0/1	0	0	0	0	0	0	0	0/1	0
Langton, R.	1948–49	56	14	2	0	0	0	0	0	58	14
Lapot, S.	1962–66	16/3	2	0	0	0	0	0	0	16/3	2
Latham, N.	1921	1	0	0	0	0	0	0	0	1	0
Lavery, W.	1906	14	0	1	0	0	0	0	0	15	0
Lawrenson, M.T.	1974–76	73	2	5	0	2	0	0	0	80	2
Lawrenson, T.	1954	1	0	0	0	0	0	0	0	1	0
Lawton, N.	1962–67	143	22	15	1	5	0	0	0	163	23
Lee, F.	1962–70	144/9	22	11	1	7/1	1	0	0	162/10	24
Lees, J.W.	1919–20	31	0	3	0	0	0	0	0	34	0
Leonard, M.A.	1992	19/3	1	0	0	2	0	0	0	21/3	1
Lewis, D.I.E.	1951–52	37	14	3	2	0	0	0	0	40	16
Lewis, E.	1955–56	12	1	0	0	0	0	0	0	13	2
Lewis, E.J.	2002–	97/14	15	4	0	5/1	1	3	0	109/15	16
Lindley, T.	1891	1	0	0	0	0	0	0	0	1	0
Litchfield, P.	1980–84	107	0	7	0	17	0	0	0	131	0
Lloyd, N.W.M.	1968–70	18/2	6	0/1	0	0	0	0	0	18/3	6
Lockett, A.H.	1905–07	64	5	2	0	0	0	0	0	66	5

Player	Played	LEAGUE		FA CUP		FL CUP		OTHERS		TOTAL	
		A	G	A	G	A	G	A	G	A	G
Lodge, P.	1982–83	36/2	0	1	0	5	0	0	0	42/2	0
Lonergan, A.	2000–	32	1	1	0	3	0	0	0	36	1
Lonsdale, G.	1895	2	1	0	0	0	0	0	0	2	1
Lormor, A.	1997	9/3	3	3	0	0	0	3	0	15/3	3
Lowe, H.	1932–38	182	0	18	0	0	0	0	0	200	0
Lowey, J.A.	1987	4	1	0	0	2	0	1	0	7	1
Lowrie, G.	1937	5	0	0	0	0	0	0	0	5	0
Lucas, D.A.	1994–2003	117/5	0	7	0	10	0	11	0	145/5	0
Lucas, R.	1992–93	47/3	0	4	0	0	0	3	0	54/3	0
Lucketti, C.J.	2001–	161	9	6	0	7	0	3	0	177	9
Ludden, D.J.	1998–2000	29/8	0	2	0	2	0	3	0	36/8	0
Luke, W.	1912	8	2	1	0	0	0	0	0	9	2
Lyall, G.	1965–71	90/15	16	6/2	2	6	1	0	0	102/17	19
Lynch, S.G.	2002–	14/31	2	0	0	0/1	1	0	0	14/32	3
Lynne, M.G.A.	1958	2	0	3	0	0	0	0	0	5	0
Lyon, W.J.	1903–10	210	8	12	1	0	0	0	0	222	9
McAteer, A.W.	1979–86	236/2	8	10	1	25	0	5	0	276/2	9
Macauley, J.L.	1913–14	59	23	5	0	0	0	0	0	64	23
McBride, B.R.	2000	8/1	1	1	0	1	0	0	0	10/1	1
McBride, P.	1897–1911	442	0	27	0	0	0	0	0	469	0
McCall, J.	1906–24	370	15	25	0	0	0	0	0	395	15
McCann, J.	1893	6	1	0	0	0	0	0	0	6	1
McClelland, J.	1929–30	53	22	2	0	0	0	0	0	55	22
McCluggage, A.	1931	3	0	0	0	0	0	0	0	3	0
McClure, W.	1947	12	2	0	0	0	0	0	0	12	2
McCormack, A.	2002–	2/6	0	0	0	0/1	0	0	0	2/7	0
McDonald, N.R.	1995–96	20/13	0	3	0	0/2	1	2	0	25/15	1
McEachran, D.	1925	1	0	0	0	0	0	0	0	1	0
McFadyen, C.	1907–13	164	1	6	0	0	0	0	0	170	1
McGee, P.G.	1979–81	62/4	13	1/1	1	7	2	0	0	70/5	16
McGibbons, T.	1938	22	2	0	0	0	0	0	0	22	2
McGregor, P.A.	1998	1/3	0	0	0	0	0	0	0	1/3	0
McIlmoyle, H.	1971–72	59/1	10	4	0	7	3	0	0	70/1	13
McIlroy, S.B.	1989	20	0	0	0	0	0	0	0	20	0
McIntosh, J.M.	1937–45	27	3	4	0	0	0	0	0	31	3
McIntosh, W.D.	1946–48	91	46	8	8	0	0	0	0	99	54
McIntyre, P.	1898–1900	87	5	6	0	0	0	0	0	93	5
McKellar, C.	1911	2	0	0	0	0	0	0	0	2	0
Macken, J.P.	1997–2002	155/29	63	10/5	2	12/2	8	9/3	1	186/39	74
McKenna, P.S.	1996	251/20	24	10/2	2	14	0	9/2	0	284/24	26
McKennie, W.	1890–91	11	2	1	0	0	0	0	0	12	2
McKnight, J.	1911–12	12	2	0	0	0	0	0	0	12	2
McLaren, A.	1946–48	69	29	8	2	0	0	0	0	77	31
McLatchie, C.	1897–98	9	2	0	0	0	0	0	0	9	2
McLaughlin, W.J.	1907	1	0	0	0	0	0	0	0	1	0
McLean, D.P.	1909–10	49	25	3	1	0	0	0	0	52	26
McLean, J.	1903–10	185	4	12	0	0	0	0	0	197	4
McLean, L.	1910	1	0	0	0	0	0	0	0	1	0
McMahon, J.	1900–02	65	0	5	1	0	0	0	0	70	1
McMahon, J.	1970–78	256/1	7	12	0	22	0	0	0	290/1	7
McNab, J.	1966–73	222/2	6	11	0	9/1	0	0	0	242/3	6
McNeil, R.M.	1985–86	43	0	2	0	1	0	4	0	50	0
Magee, K.	1993–95	23/3	1	0	0	1	0	0	0	24/3	1
Maguire, H.	1892–93	4	0	0	0	0	0	0	0	4	0
Maher, D.	1903–05	24	2	3	0	0	0	0	0	27	2
Main, W.	1908–09	12	0	0	0	0	0	0	0	12	0
Marquis, F	1920–24	35	9	0	0	0	0	0	0	35	9
Marshall, J.	1912–13	26	4	3	1	0	0	0	0	29	5
Marshall, J.	1919–23	52	0	5	0	0	0	0	0	57	0
Marston, J.E.	1950–54	185	`0	15	0	0	0	0	0	200	0
Martin, M.P.	1985	35	0	1	1	0	0	0	0	36	1
Masefield, P.	1993	6	0	1	0	1	0	1	0	9	0
Mathie, A.	1999	5/7	2	1/2	0	2	2	1	0	9/11	4
Matthew, H.	1897	18	0	1	0	0	0	0	0	19	0
Matthewson, T.	1993	12	1	0	0	1	0	0	0	13	1

Player	Played	LEAGUE A	G	FA CUP A	G	FL CUP A	G	OTHERS A	G	TOTAL A	G
Mattinson, H.	1948–58	124	0	7	0	0	0	0	0	131	0
Mawene, Y.	2004–	72/4	3	5	0	3	0	5	0	85/4	3
Maxwell, J.M.	1934–38	129	60	9	5	0	0	0	0	138	65
May, J.	1897	3	0	0	0	0	0	0	0	3	0
Mayers, D.	1957–60	118	25	12	3	2	0	0	0	132	28
Mears, T.	2002–	50/20	4	5/2	0	3/2	0	1	0	58/24	4
Meijer, E.	2000	9	0	0	0	0	0	0	0	9	0
Melia, J.	1901	2	0	0	0	0	0	0	0	2	0
Mercer, W.	1919–24	113	0	8	0	0	0	0	0	121	0
Metcalf, T.	1890	1	1	0	0	0	0	0	0	1	1
Metcalfe, J.A.	1927	16	0	0	0	0	0	0	0	16	0
Millar, A.	1938	2	0	0	0	0	0	0	0	2	0
Miller, D.B.	1986–89	50/8	2	0/2	0	6	0	7/2	0	63/12	2
Miller, H.	1893	2	0	0	0	0	0	0	0	2	0
Miller, H.J.	1924	5	0	0	0	0	0	0	0	5	0
Miller, J.	1919	15	1	2	0	0	0	0	0	17	1
Mills-Roberts, Dr R.H.	1888	2	0	5	0	0	0	0	0	7	0
Milne, G.	1956–60	81	3	9	0	0	0	0	0	890	3
Milne, J.	1932–39	233	9	23	2	0	0	0	0	256	11
Mimms, R.A.	1996	27	0	2	0	2	0	0	0	31	0
Mitchell, B.	1976	7/4	2	0/2	0	0/1	0	0	0	7/7	2
Mitchell, J.F.	1920–21	21	0	8	0	0	0	0	0	29	0
Mitton, G.K.	1953	2	0	0	0	0	0	0	0	2	0
Moilanen, T.J.	1995–2003	155/3	0	1	0	12/1	0	2	0	170/4	0
Montgomery, G.	1900	4	0	0	0	0	0	0	0	4	0
Mooney, B.J.	1987–90	125/3	20	6	0	4/1	0	11/1	5	146/5	25
Morley, J.B.	1911–14	94	15	2	0	0	0	0	0	96	15
Morley, W.A.	1972–75	78/6	15	6/1	2	8	3	0	0	92/7	20
Morris, D.	1925–29	146	7	6	0	0	0	0	0	152	7
Morrison, A.C.	1948–56	262	70	19	5	0	0	0	0	281	75
Moss, F.	1927–28	24	0	1	0	0	0	0	0	25	0
Mountenay, A.	1909–10	52	11	2	0	0	0	0	0	54	11
Moyes, D.W.	1993–98	142/1	15	11/1	2	5	1	13/1	1	171/3	19
Moylon, C.	1992	0/1	0	0	0	0	0	0	0	0/1	0
Mullen, J.	1981	1	0	0	0	0	0	0	0	1	0
Mullin, J.M.	1997	4/3	0	0	0	0	0	1	0	5/3	0
Murdock, C.J.	1997–2003	163/14	6	9/2	0	13/1	0	10	0	195/17	6
Murphy, A.C.	1983–84	9/1	0	0	0	1	0	1/1	0	11/2	0
Murray, P.	1898–99	51	9	7	0	0	0	0	0	58	9
Mustard, J.	1932	15	5	0	0	0	0	0	0	15	5
Mutch, G.	1937–46	83	24	10	8	0	0	0	0	93	32
Napier, C.R.A.	1963	1	0	0	0	0	0	0	0	1	0
Nash, C.J.	2004	53	0	4	0	1	0	5	0	63	0
Naughton, W.B.S.	1979–84	148/14	10	7	1	13	3	5	1	173/14	15
N'Dumbu-Nsungu, G.	2004	4/2	0	0	0	0	0	0	0	4/2	0
Neal, C.M.	2004	0/1	0	0	0	0	0	0	0	0/1	0
Nebelling, G.N.	1993	22	4	3	0	2	0	2	0	29	4
Neal, L.	2006	13/11	2	3/1	0	1	0	0	0	17/12	2
Nelson, J.H.	1928–32	71	2	4	0	0	0	0	0	75	2
Newlands, M.	1948–52	80	0	4	0	0	0	0	0	84	0
Newton, S.	1914	8	0	0	0	0	0	0	0	8	0
Nidd, G.F.	1893	3	0	0	0	0	0	0	0	3	0
Nisbet, G.	1927–34	139	6	6	0	0	0	0	0	145	6
Nogan, K.	1996–99	74/19	27	6/3	3	4/3	0	4/3	1	88/28	31
Norbury, M.S.	1992–94	32/10	13	0/3	0	1/1	0	3/1	1	36/15	14
Norris, F.	1891	3	0	0	0	0	0	0	0	3	0
Nowland, A.	2006	9/4	3	0	0	0	0	0	0	9/4	3
Nugent, D.J.	2004–	40/10	18	2/1	0	1	0	5	2	48/11	20
Nuttall, W.	1946	2	0	1	0	0	0	0	0	3	0
O'Donnell, F.	1935–37	92	36	9	12	0	0	0	0	101	48
O'Donnell, H.	1935–38	132	29	16	5	0	0	0	0	148	34
O'Farrell, F.	1956–60	118	3	11	2	0	0	0	0	129	5
O'Hanlon, KG.	1993 and 1996	36	0	2	0	2	0	3	0	43	0
Oliveira, F.	2004	1/4	0	0	0	0	0	0	0	1/4	0
O,Neil, B.	2002–	101/11	5	6	2	3/1	0	5	0	115/12	7

Player	Played	LEAGUE A	LEAGUE G	FA CUP A	FA CUP G	FL CUP A	FL CUP G	OTHERS A	OTHERS G	TOTAL A	TOTAL G
O'Neill, J.	1958–62	50	0	4	0	9	0	0	0	63	0
O'Neill, J.	2002–	0/2	0	1	0	0	0	0	0	1/2	0
O'Rawe, F.	1923	4	0	0	0	0	0	0	0	4	0
O'Riordan, D.J.	1978–82	153/5	8	8	1	10	0	0	0	171/5	9
Ormerod, B.	2006	13/2	4	0	0	0	0	2	0	15/2	4
Orr, W.	1894–96	62	3	7	2	0	0	0	0	69	5
Orrell, R.	1899–1905	140	0	13	0	0	0	0	0	153	0
Osborn, F.	1913–19	68	40	5	4	0	0	0	0	73	44
Owens, E.	1930–33	19	7	0	0	0	0	0	0	19	7
Palethorpe, J.T.	1933–34	24	15	2	3	0	0	0	0	26	18
Parker, H.	1899–1900	3	0	1	0	0	0	0	0	4	0
Parkinson, G.A.	1997–2000	82/2	6	8	1	6	0	6	1	102/2	8
Parnell, G.F.	1909	15	1	0	0	0	0	0	0	15	1
Parry, G.	1928–29	3	0	0	0	0	0	0	0	3	0
Paterson, J.W.	1924	17	0	2	1	0	0	0	0	19	1
Patrick, B.	1964–69	50	1	2	0	4	0	0	0	56	1
Patterson, D.J.	1996	2	0	0	0	0	0	0	0	2	0
Patterson, M.A.	1988–89	54/1	19	4	0	3	0	5	1	66/1	20
Pauls, C.	1889	3	0	1	0	0	0	0	0	4	0
Pears, J.	1933–34	18	4	0	0	0	0	0	0	18	4
Pearson, F.	1901–02	32	17	3	3	0	0	0	0	35	20
Peel, N.J.	1990	1/9	1	0	0	1	0	1/1	0	3/10	1
Pegg, E.R.	1901	15	9	2	0	0	0	0	0	17	9
Philliskirk, A.	1988	13/1	6	0	0	0	0	0	0	13/1	6
Phizacklea, J.R.	1924–25	22	0	0	0	0	0	0	0	22	0
Pickering, F.	1924	1	0	0	0	0	0	0	0	1	0
Pierce, J.	1894–1900	74	16	4	0	0	0	0	0	78	16
Pilkington, W.	1927	1	0	0	0	0	0	0	0	1	0
Pilling, A.J.	1985	1	0	0	0	0	0	0	0	1	0
Pinch, C.E.	1913	3	0	0	0	0	0	0	0	3	0
Pinnell, A.	1893	1	0	0	0	0	0	0	0	1	0
Platt, J.	1908–10	30	7	1	0	0	0	0	0	31	7
Platt, J.R.	1984–85	38	0	1	0	4	0	2	0	45	0
Poole, F.	1893	2	0	0	0	0	0	0	0	2	0
Potts, E.T.	1978–80	50/7	5	2	0	2/1	1	0	0	54/8	6
Pratt, T.P.	1896–98 and 1900–02	144	43	12	6	0	0	0	0	156	49
Pritchard, T.F.	1933	1	0	0	0	0	0	0	0	1	0
Prout, G.W.	1923–25	46	0	0	0	0	0	0	0	46	0
Quantrill, A.E.	1921–23	64	7	1	0	0	0	0	0	65	7
Quigley, E.	1949–51	52	17	2	0	0	0	0	0	54	17
Quinn, P.	1919–22	87	10	13	0	0	0	0	0	100	10
Raeside, H.	1890	2	0	0	0	0	0	0	0	2	0
Ramscar, F.T.	1949–50	19	4	2	0	0	0	0	0	21	4
Rankine, S.M.	1996–2002	217/16	12	13	1	16/4	1	6	1	252/20	15
Rathbone, M.J.	1987–90	82/9	4	4	0	7/1	0	5/33	0	98/13	4
Rawlings, A.	1920–23	147	17	17	6	0	0	0	0	164	23
Rawlings, J.S.D.	1933	12	0	1	0	0	0	0	0	13	0
Raynor, P.J.	1993–95	72/8	9	7	1	4/1	0	5	0	88/9	10
Reay, H.	1923	1	0	0	0	0	0	0	0	1	0
Reeves, D.E.	1996–97	45/2	12	2	3	3	3	1	0	51/2	18
Reid, A.	1927–32	193	50	8	0	0	0	0	0	201	50
Reid, P.M.	2001	0/1	1	0	0	0	0	0	0	0/1	1
Reid, S.	1985	3	0	0	0	0	0	0	0	3	0
Richardson, B.	1994–95	20	0	3	0	2	0	2	0	27	0
Richardson, G.	1959–60	15	1	1	0	0	0	0	0	16	1
Rimmer, S.A.	1994	0/2	0	0	0	0	0	0	0	0/2	0
Ritchie, J.	1966–71	93	5	4	0	9	0	0	0	106	5
Roberts, J.W.	1906	2	0	0	0	0	0	0	0	2	0
Roberts, R.	1891	5	0	0	0	0	0	0	0	5	0
Roberts, W.T.	1919–24 and 1926–27	254	157	23	22	0	0	0	0	277	179
Robertson, A.	1888–89	28	3	2	0	0	0	0	0	30	3
Robertson, W.	1910	2	0	0	0	0	0	0	0	2	0
Robertson, W.J.T.	1946–52	52	0	0	0	0	0	0	0	52	0
Robinson, M.J.	1975–78	45/3	15	2	0	4	1	0	0	51/3	16
Robinson, R.	1968	2	0	0	0	0	0	0	0	2	0

Player	Played	LEAGUE A	G	FA CUP A	G	FL CUP A	G	OTHERS A	G	TOTAL A	G
Robinson, S.	2000–01	6/18	1	0/1	0	3/1	0	0	0	9/20	1
Robson, N.	1926–29	41	24	1	0	0	0	0	0	42	24
Roche, G.	1909	3	0	0	0	0	0	0	0	3	0
Rodger, T.	1904	5	1	0	0	0	0	0	0	5	1
Rodgers, M.	1985	1	0	0	0	0	0	0	0	1	0
Rodway, T.	1903–14	335	9	16	0	0	0	0	0	351	9
Rogers, J.J.	1900–01	39	11	3	1	0	0	0	0	42	12
Ross, G.	1960–72	384/2	3	34	0	18	0	0	0	436/2	3
Ross, J.	1888–93	130	85	21	16	0	0	0	0	151	101
Ross, N.J.	1889–93	95	25	14	2	0	0	0	0	109	27
Rowley, R.W.M.	1931–33	51	14	7	2	0	0	0	0	58	16
Roy, J.	1893	1	0	0	0	0	0	0	0	1	0
Rudge, D.A.	1984–85	46/1	2	1	0	5	1	2	0	54/1	3
Russell, D.	1892 and 1898	44	17	9	3	0	0	0	0	53	20
Russell, D.K.	1888–89	39	4	7	1	0	0	0	0	46	5
Russell, W.F.	1925–30	133	35	5	0	0	0	0	0	138	35
Sadler, D.	1973–76	104/1	3	11	1	5	0	0	0	120/1	4
Sale, M.D.	1994	10/3	6	0/1	0	1/1	0	2	0	13/5	6
Sanders, M.	1891–98	210	20	19	3	0	0	0	0	229	23
Sanderson, B.S.	1899–1902	6	0	0	0	0	0	0	0	6	0
Sanderson, W.	1906–09	45	6	3	0	0	0	0	0	48	6
Sapsford, G.D.	1921–25	36	9	0	0	0	0	0	0	36	9
Saville, A.V.	1995–96	56	30	2	0	6	0	2	1	66	31
Sayer, P.A.	1980–83	42/3	6	2	0	3/2	0	1/1	0	48/6	6
Scott, L.	1923	2	0	0	0	0	0	0	0	2	0
Scott, T.	1930–31	41	23	0	0	0	0	0	0	41	23
Scott, W.J.	1946–53	208	0	14	0	0	0	0	0	222	0
Scully, P.J.	1989	13	1	0	0	0	0	1	0	14	1
Sedgwick, C.E.	2004–	63/7	7	5	1	1	0	3/1	0	72/8	8
Senior, S.	1990–91	73	3	4	1	4	0	8	0	89	4
Shankly, W.	1933–48	300	13	37	1	0	0	0	0	337	14
Shanley, F.	1913	1	0	0	0	0	0	0	0	1	0
Sharkey, B.J.	1920	1	0	0	0	0	0	0	0	1	0
Sharp, J.	1891–95	93	3	6	1	0	0	0	0	99	4
Sharp, R.	1994–95	22	0	3	0	2	0	2	0	29	0
Shaw, G.P.	1989–91	113/8	29	5	2	3	2	13	8	134/8	41
Shaw, G.R.	1926	3	0	0	0	0	0	0	0	3	0
Shears, A.E.	1921	2	0	0	0	0	0	0	0	2	0
Sherry, A.	1929–31	14	0	0	0	0	0	0	0	14	0
Shorrock, J.	1902	1	0	0	0	0	0	0	0	1	0
Siddall, B.A.	1992	1	0	0	0	0	0	0	0	1	0
Simmons, H.R.	1931	8	3	0	0	0	0	0	0	8	3
Simpson, R.	1946	4	0	1	0	0	0	0	0	5	0
Singleton, A.J.	1960–67	286/1	0	26	2	17	0	0	0	329/1	2
Sissoko, H.	1997	4/3	0	0	0	0	0	0	0	4/3	0
Skora, E.	2001–04	37/14	0	3	1	3/1	1	0	0	43/15	2
Smart, A.A.C.	1994–95	17/4	6	2	1	0	0	0/1	0	19/5	7
Smith, A.	1976	8	0	0	0	0	0	0	0	8	0
Smith, A.C.	1927–30	39	10	1	0	0	0	0	0	40	10
Smith, A.W.	2004–	3/11	0	0	0	2/1	0	0	0	5/12	0
Smith, E.D.	1893–95	33	14	2	0	0	0	0	0	35	14
Smith, G.	1899–1900	28	1	0	0	0	0	0	0	28	1
Smith, J.	1895	5	0	0	0	0	0	0	0	5	0
Smith, J.	1973–78	80/11	14	7/1	2	4	1	0	0	91/12	17
Smith, J.A.G.	1958–68	314	13	31	3	12	0	0	0	357	16
Smith, P.J.	1902–09	240	94	15	1	0	0	0	0	255	95
Smith, R.	1908	6	1	1	0	0	0	0	0	7	1
Smith, T.	1895–97 and 1903	61	11	7	1	0	0	0	0	68	12
Smith, T.	1897	4	0	1	0	0	0	0	0	5	0
Smith, T.M.	1936–38	44	0	6	0	0	0	0	0	50	0
Smithies, G.H.	1929–30	20	10	0	0	0	0	0	0	20	10
Sneddon, D.	1958–61	91	17	9	4	6	3	0	0	106	24
Snookes, E.	1972–73	20	0	1	0	0	0	0	0	21	0
Snow, S.G.	1989	1	0	0	0	1	0	0	0	2	0
Spark, A.M.	1967–75	207/18	6	11	0	12	0	0	0	230/18	6

Player	Played	LEAGUE		FA CUP		FL CUP		OTHERS		TOTAL	
		A	G	A	G	A	G	A	G	A	G
Sparrow, P.	1996–98	20	0	1	0	0	0	1	0	22	0
Spavin, A.	1960–73 and 1977–78	414/10	26	32/2	2	26	3	0	0	472/12	31
Speak, G.	1919–22	65	0	7	0	0	0	0	0	72	0
Spence, G.	1901	19	7	2	0	0	0	0	0	21	7
Spence, W.E.	1909–10	2	1	0	0	0	0	0	0	2	1
Squires, J.A.	1993–96	24/7	0	0/1	0	1	0	4/1	0	29/9	0
Stallard, M.	1996	4	1	0	0	0	0	0	0	4	1
Stansfield, H.	1899	4	1	0	0	0	0	0	0	4	1
Steele, D.M.	1929	29	2	1	0	0	0	0	0	30	2
Stephenson, G.T.	1933	25	16	3	0	0	0	0	0	28	16
Stewart, M.	2006	4	0	0	0	0	0	1	0	5	0
Stevens, I.D.	1984–85	9/2	2	0	0	0	0	1	0	10/2	2
Stevenson, J.	1895–97	51	21	7	5	0	0	0	0	58	26
Stewart, G.	1966–69	4	0	0	0	0	0	0	0	4	0
Stewart, W.S.	1890–92	69	4	10	1	0	0	0	0	79	5
Stiles, N.P.	1973–74	44/2	1	3	0	1	0	0	0	48/2	1
Stock, B.	2006	4/2	1	0	0	0	0	0	0	4/2	1
Storey, J.	1922	1	0	0	0	0	0	0	0	1	0
Stormont, R.	1893	9	0	0	0	0	0	0	0	9	0
Stowell, M.	1989	2	0	0	0	0	0	0	0	2	0
Stringfellow, H.	1906–07	39	2	2	0	0	0	0	0	41	2
Sulley, C.S.	1993	21	1	0	0	2	0	0	0	23	1
Summerbee, G.M.	1937–38	3	0	0	0	0	0	0	0	3	0
Swann, G.	1986–91	194/5	37	12	1	11	2	25	5	242/5	45
Swarbrick, W.	1912–13	4	2	0	0	0	0	0	0	4	2
Tait, A.G.	1894–98	76	0	3	0	0	0	0	0	79	0
Tarbuck, A.D.	1971–72	42/6	17	2	0	1	0	0	0	45/6	17
Tatton, J.H.	1919	18	1	0	0	0	0	0	0	18	1
Taylor, B.J.	1978–81	93/6	1	4	0	2/2	0	0	0	99/8	1
Taylor, C.D.	1992	4	0	0	0	0	0	0	0	4	0
Taylor, H.	1903–13	108	0	5	0	0	0	0	0	113	0
Taylor, J.S.	1891	1	1	0	0	0	0	0	0	1	1
Taylor, R.	1975	3	0	0	0	0	0	0	0	3	0
Taylor, S.J.	1986	5	2	0	0	0	0	0	0	5	2
Taylor, S.M.	1955–60	149	40	14	7	3	0	0	0	166	47
Teale, S.	1996	5	0	0	0	0	0	0	0	5	0
Telfer, G.A.	1983	0/2	0	0	0	0	0	0	0	0/2	0
Temple, D.W.	1967–69	75/1	14	7	1	2	0	0	0	84/1	15
Thomas, J.W.	1985–86 and 1989–91	93/12	44	8/1	7	10	0	6	3	117/13	54
Thompson, C.H.	1924	1	0	0	0	0	0	0	0	1	0
Thompson, D.S.	1990–91	39/7	4	0	0	1/1	0	3/1	0	43/9	4
Thompson, G.H.	1952–55	140	0	15	0	0	0	0	0	155	0
Thompson, J.W.	1910–11	58	9	3	0	0	0	0	0	61	9
Thompson, P.	1960–62	121	20	11	3	13	8	0	0	145	31
Thompson, R.	1910–12	17	0	0	0	0	0	0	0	17	0
Thompson, T.	1955–60	189	117	20	10	4	2	0	0	213	129
Thomson, R.B.	1974–79	60/11	20	0	0	7/1	1	0	0	67/12	21
Thomson, S.	1888–89	34	10	8	4	0	0	0	0	42	14
Thornborough, E.H.	1930–31	20	0	0	0	0	0	0	0	20	0
Threlfall, T.	1919	2	0	0	0	0	0	0	0	2	0
Tickle, B.	1901–03	6	0	0	0	0	0	0	0	6	0
Tinkler, J.	1992	22/2	2	0/1	0	2	0	1	1	25/3	3
Tinsley, A.	1969	8/1	1	0	0	0	0	0	0	8/1	1
Tod, G.	1900–06	131	4	9	0	0	0	0	0	140	4
Toone, P.E.	1911–12	14	0	0	0	0	0	0	0	14	0
Torbet, J.	1933	11	4	0	0	0	0	0	0	11	4
Tottoh, M.	1985	0/1	0	0	0	0	0	0	0	0/1	0
Toward, A.V.	1913–14	30	8	3	0	0	0	0	0	33	8
Towie, T.	1891	22	9	3	1	0	0	0	0	25	10
Trainer, J.	1888–97	253	0	22	0	0	0	0	0	275	0
Treacy, R.C.P.	1973–75	54/4	11	2	0	3	2	0	0	59/4	13
Trebble, D.N.	1994	8/11	4	2/1	0	1	0	2	0	13/12	4
Tremelling, W.R.	1930–37	209	11	21	1	0	0	0	0	230	12
Tunks, R.W.	1974–80 and 1988–89	302	0	16	0	21	0	3	0	342	0
Turnbull, J.M.	1904–05	13	0	0	0	0	0	0	0	13	0

Player	Played	LEAGUE		FA CUP		FL CUP		OTHERS		TOTAL	
		A	G	A	G	A	G	A	G	A	G
Turner, R.F.	191	8	0	0	0	0	0	0	0	8	0
Twentyman, G.	1983–85	95/3	4	3/1	0	11	3	4/1	0	113/5	7
Twist, R.	1932	3	0	0	0	0	0	0	0	3	0
Uzelac, S.	1977–78	9	0	0	0	0	0	0	0	9	0
Vaughan, J.	1994–95	65/1	0	2	0	2	0	3	0	72/1	0
Veall, R.J.	1965	11	0	0	0	1	0	0	0	12	0
Vernon, J.L.	1934–36	14	2	1	0	0	0	0	0	15	2
Vickers, S.	1913	1	0	0	0	0	0	0	0	1	0
Waddell, G.B.	1920–21	51	2	6	0	0	0	0	0	57	2
Wade, W.A.	1923–28	139	0	8	0	0	0	0	0	147	0
Walsh, C.	1925	4	0	0	0	0	0	0	0	4	0
Walsh, M.	1981–83	56/6	2	2	0	7/1	0	2	0	67/7	2
Walton, J.	1901–02	25	4	0	0	0	0	0	0	25	4
Walton, J.	1947–60	401	4	34	0	0	0	0	0	435	4
Ward, F.	1927–32	208	3	8	0	0	0	0	0	216	3
Ward, G.J.	2004–	6/1	0	0	0	1	0	0	0	7/1	0
Wareing, W.	1910–12	79	2	3	0	0	0	0	0	82	2
Warner, J.	1902–03	11	0	0	0	0	0	0	0	11	0
Waterhouse, K.	1953–56	30	8	3	0	0	0	0	0	33	8
Waters, P.	1947–49	64	0	5	0	0	0	0	0	69	0
Watmough, R.	1937	20	4	6	0	0	0	0	0	26	4
Watson, L.	1992–93	7/2	3	0	0	0	0	0	0	7/2	3
Watson, W.T.	1946	15	0	0	0	0	0	0	0	15	0
Watt, W.D.	1962–65	7/1	0	0	0	1	0	0	0	8/1	0
Wayman, C.	1950–54	157	104	14	12	0	0	0	0	171	116
Wealands, J.A.	1984	4	0	0	0	0	0	0	0	4	0
Wearmouth, M.	1964–66	11	0	0	0	1	0	0	0	12	0
Welsh, P.W.	1984–85	13/7	1	0	0	2	0	2	0	17/7	1
Westwell, S.	1980–82	63	1	2	0	11	0	0	0	76	1
Whaley, S.	2006	7/9	3	0	0	0	0	0/2	0	7/11	3
Whalley, D.N.	1992–94	45/5	1	2/2	0	4	0	4/1	0	55/8	1
Whalley, F.H.	1919	8	0	0	0	0	0	0	0	8	0
Wharton, C.N.	1925–26	13	0	0	0	0	0	0	0	13	0
Wharton, J.E.	1939–46	25	7	4	0	0	0	0	0	29	7
White, F.R.H.	1938–39	22	10	3	2	0	0	0	0	25	17
Whitehead, W.T.	1926	3	1	1	0	0	0	0	0	4	1
Whittle, D.	1897–99	10	0	0	0	0	0	0	0	10	0
Whittle, R.	1888	1	1	0	0	0	0	0	0	1	1
Whitworth, N.A.	1991	6	0	0	0	0	0	0	0	6	0
Wijnhard, C.	2001	6	3	0	0	0	0	0	0	6	3
Wilcock, G.H.	1920	7	0	0	0	0	0	0	0	7	0
Wilcox, H.M.	1901–04	99	42	13	3	0	0	0	0	112	45
Wilcox, R.	1995–96	62	1	3	1	4	0	2	0	71	2
Wilkes, S.B.	1987	1/2	0	0	0	0	0	0	0	1/2	0
Wilkie, T.	1900	3	0	0	0	0	0	0	0	3	0
Wilkins, P.	1984	3/3	2	0	0	2/1	2	0	0	5/4	4
Wilkinson, S.J.	1995–96	44/8	13	3	1	4	4	3	0	54/8	18
Willacy, D.L.	1938	1	0	0	0	0	0	0	0	1	0
Williams, E.	1939–47	65	0	7	0	0	0	0	0	72	0
Williams, F.H.	1926	8	0	1	0	0	0	0	0	9	0
Williams, G.P.	1971–76	107/5	2	4	0	6	0	0	0	117/5	2
Williams, N.J.F.	1988–91	109/12	6	4	0	4/1	0	6	0	123/13	6
Williams, O.J.	1986–88	38/1	12	3	2	5	2	1/1	0	47/2	16
Williams, P.A.	1986	1	0	0	0	0	0	1	0	2	0
Williamson, C.W.	1907	1	0	0	0	0	0	0	0	1	0
Williamson, J.	1921–25	63	2	9	0	0	0	0	0	72	2
Wilson, A.	1929–30	10	1	0	0	0	0	0	0	10	1
Wilson, D.C.	1960–66 and 1968–73	267/14	41	21/1	0	20	0	0	0	308/15	41
Wilson, F.	1933	6	1	0	0	0	0	0	0	6	1
Wilson, H.	1977–79	38/4	0	0	0	3	0	0	0	41/4	0
Wilson, J.	1903–10	162	32	7	0	0	0	0	0	169	32
Wilson, J.G.	1946–47	16	6	1	1	0	0	0	0	17	7
Wilson, J.R.	1952–62	91	0	7	0	1	0	0	0	99	0
Wilson, K.	2006	3/3	0	0	0	0	0	0	0	3/3	0
Winchester, J.	1906–09	37	0	3	1	0	0	0	0	40	1

Player	Played	LEAGUE		FA CUP		FL CUP		OTHERS		TOTAL	
		A	G	A	G	A	G	A	G	A	G
Winterhalder, A.	1908–11	56	6	3	0	0	0	0	0	59	6
Wolf, G.	1931–32	45	0	4	0	0	0	0	0	49	0
Woodhouse, R.T.	1919–25	206	52	19	6	0	0	0	0	225	58
Woodhouse, S.H.	1900	2	0	0	0	0	0	0	0	2	0
Woods, S.G.	1993	19/1	0	2	0	0	0	2	0	23/1	0
Woodward, T.G.	1924–25	24	1	1	0	0	0	0	0	25	1
Worthington, F.S.	1986–87	10/13	3	0	0	0/2	0	0/1	0	10/16	3
Wright, J.	1895	2	0	0	0	0	0	0	0	2	0
Wright, M.S.	1999	1/2	0	0/1	0	0	0	0/1	0	1/4	0
Wrightson, J.G.	1987–91	161/5	4	6	0	6/2	1	16/1	0	189/8	5
Wylie, J.E.	1958–62	91	1	10	0	9	1	0	0	110	2
Yates, W.J.	1921–24	63	0	1	0	0	0	0	0	64	0
Young, M.S.	1926	6	1	0	0	0	0	0	0	6	1
Young, N.J.	1971–73	67/1	16	0	0	2	1	0	0	69/1	17
Zelem, P.R.	1986	6	1	0	0	0	0	0	0	6	1

Roll of Honour

Eric P Abbott
Stephen Ainscough
Rod Alker
Philip Armstrong
Daniel Armstrong
Allan Armstrong
Brian Ashcroft
Peter Ashcroft
Rachel Aspinall
Michael J Bamber
John Barbarewicz
Joan Barnes
Alan Barnish
Jordan Louis Baron
Robert Edward Barratt
E A Barton
Mr S G Bennett
Ian David Bentham
Brian Berry
Brian Bibby
John Anthony Billington
Ken Birkinshaw
Jonathan Blackburn
Sharon & Nathan Blake
Lawrence Bland, Lancaster
Martin Boden
Michael Bontiff
George Edward Bowes
Andrew Bradshaw
Alan Bridson
Mr Fred Brome
Stephen Brown
John Brown
Mr Keith Buck
Kenneth Burns
Michael Burns
Peter Butler
Mr Harvey Butler, Morecambe
David Butters
Fiona Butters
Kieran Carroll
Daniel Thomas Carter
Paul Carter
Kenneth Clarke
Ken Clarke

Neil T Clarke
Richard Raymond Clegg
Ian John Clough
J.W.A Collins
Tim Conlon
Lee Cook
Jakob Cookson Jnr
Michael J Corbett
Stephen P Corbett
Ellen Cornall
Paul Counsell
John Coupe
Paul Crangle
Steve Critchley
Brian Crombleholme
Mick Crook (Chorley)
Jack Cross
Michael Cross
David Cross
Kevin Cross
Neil C Cruickshank
Leslie Cunliffe
Daniel Christian Dalby
Edward H Davis
Tony Davison
John Despard
Joe Dobson & Family
Steven Donaldson
William Dowbing
Christopher J Drazek
Peter Drummond-Scott
Stephen Drummond-Scott
Vernon Eastham
David Eccles
Dennis Esplin
Eddie Fairclough
Ashley Farber
John Fazackerley
Ian M Fenton
Michael H Fletcher
John Leslie Freeman
Bob Friend
Jennie Isabel Gammon
Kenneth E Garratt
Stephen Gaughan

Len Goodburn (Builder)
Hope Goodier
Michael Goodier
Robbie Goodier
James Goodier
Ben Hackett
Joyce-Margaret Haddon
Sandra Hall
John W Hall
John Halsall
John Hamer
Christine Handley
Mr Charles Hankinson
Mark Harford
John Gerald Harrison
Dean Harrison
Terry Hartley
Philip Michael Hartley
Ian Hendrick
Michael Hewitt
Harry Heys
David Higham
Matt, Jane & Jeannie Higham
T M A Hill
Thomas A Hilton
Stephen Hindle
Michael Hindle
Charlie Hird
Sean Hobson
Colin Hodson
Adam Holden
Anthony D Holden
Geoff Holderness
David Thomas Holmes
David James Holmes
Matthew Hopkins
Mark R Houghton
Claire Hull
Paul S Hutton
Mick Ingham
John Jackson
Kara Johnson
Linda Jolly
Andrew Jolly
Mark Jordan

Philip John Kay
Ian J Kerfoot
Robert Kidd
Philip Kirby
Christopher J Leach
Keith Leaver
John Michael Leeming
David Vincent Lewis
David Joseph Lewis
Mr James D Lofthouse
Nathan Lovatt
Lee McClay
Martin McDonagh
Glen McDonald
Lucy McDonough
David McDougall
Andrew McGrath
Bernard McGuill
John Francis Maguire
Jeff Major
Joe Mayor
Robert David Melling
Iain Mellis
Stephen Mellor
Jamie Messenger
Harold Metcalf
Peter Metcalf
Stephen Millan
Stuart R Milne
Jean C Molloy (née Howell)
Bernard Molyneux
Derek Moorby
Gary Mounsey
Michael Nash
Scott Newsham
Leslie Nicholson
Chris Noblet
Malcolm Norburn
Dave & Sheila Odlum
Stuart J Oliver
Edward Wesley Ormsby
James C Parker
Peter David Parkinson
Andrew Parkinson
Michael (Mike) Parkinson
Geoff Pearce
Michael J Phillips
Edward Wesley Pilling

Steven Pool
John Porter
Roy Raby
Malcolm Rae
Robert Rafferty
Joe Rainford
Helen L Reid
James C Reynolds
George Richardson
John R Richmond
Graham Riding
Gren Rigby
Brenda Riley
Howard Robinson
Justin Robinson
Carole Robinson
Andrew Robinson
SteveRobinson (Rhino)
Graham A Rogerson
Frank Rooney
David Rostron SNR
John M Rothwell
Peter Ruscoe
Ian Russell
Lee Salisbury
David Salisbury
Andrew Scott
Mr J K Seabrook
Matthew Shakeshaft
William Sharples
Richard Shepherd
Bill Shorrock
Trevor John Singleton
Malcolm George Singleton
David James Singleton
Gordon Small
Peter A Smith
Brendon Smith
Gareth Andrew Smith
S.P. Southworth
Jonathan A Squires (Fan of the Year 2006)
Derek Straker
Ian A Stuart
Peter Sutcliffe
Michael C Sutcliffe
Anthony Talbot
Roy Tallon

J G Tarrant
Ian Taylor
David Taylor
Joe Taylor
Bev Taylor
Geoffrey James Taylor
Trevor John Thompson
John C Thompson
Ian Christopher Threlfall
John Threlfall
Sal Tracey
University of Central Lancashire Library
M Vernon
Jordan Vickers
Kevin Wallace
Paul Walmsley
Bill Walton
Matthew Ward
Mick Ward
David G Ward
Tom Wareing
James Wareing
Edward Waring
Alan Watkinson
Keith Andrew Webster
Joan Wharton Jolly
David Whillis
Mr John Whiteside
Ms Heather Whittaker
Peter Wielgosz
David J Wiggins
Ken Wilding
Jeffrey Wilkins
John Wilkinson - Fulwood
Rowland Witts
Terry W Wood
Margaret M Woodhouse
Tony Worsick
Paul Worsley
Andy Wright (Kirkham)
Stuart Yardley
Charlie Yates
Polly Yates
Louis Yates

Edited and designed by
Ian Latham and Mark Swenarton

Cover design: Christopher Woodward

Copyright © 2002 Right Angle Publishing Ltd
All rights reserved. No part of this publication may be
reproduced in any manner whatsoever without prior
permission in writing from Right Angle Publishing.

First published by Right Angle Publishing,
161 Rosebery Avenue, London EC1R 4QX.
Printed in Singapore.

British Library Cataloguing in Publication Data.
A catalogue record for this book is available from
the British Library.

ISBN 0 9532848 2 4

Jeremy Dixon and Edward Jones

Buildings and Projects 1959-2002

Edited by Ian Latham and Mark Swenarton

Jeremy Dixon and Edward Jones: the adventure of architecture

Ian Latham and Mark Swenarton

This book documents the work of two of the UK's most respected architects, a story of shared concerns and differences, a story of architectural invention and evolution.

Having studied at the Architectural Association in London in the early 1960s and having worked together in the early 1970s, Jeremy Dixon and Edward Jones pursued successful independent careers until 1989 when circumstance and chance intervened. The idea of working together again had occured to both Dixon and Jones, and the timely coincidence of Jeremy Dixon in London trying to phone Edward Jones in Toronto who was himself trying to phone Dixon led in due course to their joint practice.

While working together at Milton Keynes with Christopher Cross and Michael Gold, Dixon and Jones collaborated in the development of Jeremy and Fenella Dixon's proposal for the Northamptonshire County Hall competition. By the mid-1970s however, they had taken different paths, setting out their respective positions with two iconic yet contrasting built works – Jones' Studio House in Chelsea and the Dixon's St Mark's Road housing in north Kensington. In articulating ideas about living in the city, both schemes went against the grain of most contemporary architectural production in Britain. Where Jones composed free-plan purist forms and spaces within the confines of an existing coach house in a spirited play of interior and exterior space, Dixon's project addressed popular and intellectual concerns regarding the character of urban social housing.

Major competition successes soon followed – for Jones with Mississauga City Hall in 1982 and for Dixon with the Royal Opera House in 1984. Both of these showpiece projects dealt with the urban condition, but they remain striking in their differences. Mississauga was to form the focus of a new (as yet unrealised) district outside Toronto, so Jones proposed a collage of monumental forms, at the same time prototypical and referential, intended to establish a sense of place and identity. Dixon, in contrast, inherited a building loaded with cultural meaning and memory, and proposed a substantive reworking of the Covent Garden complex with a robust yet flexible plan able to withstand the inevitable political, financial and planning machinations that ensued.

The first significant outcome of the new Dixon Jones partnership was the competition-winning proposal for Venice bus station.

The scheme deftly situates a huge circular arena within the historic grain of the city – not surprisingly was it singled out from some 277 anonymous entries by juror James Stirling. Although the bus station remained unrealised, the competition win acted as a spur to the joint practice, marking its arrival on the world scene.

Among the projects that followed, it is perhaps the Ondaatje Wing at the National Portrait Gallery in London that best epitomises their approach. Here a daunting series of problems, from access to identity to the need for more gallery space and public facilities, were solved with a deceptively simple yet decisive intervention. Dixon Jones suggested the inspired rights of light 'deal', making it possible for an under-used back yard to be filled with a new building. At the core of the scheme is a full-height circulation space with an escalator which effectively reverses the circulation route, taking visitors first to the (hitherto little visited) upper levels. It also allows for a rooftop cafe which affords (hitherto unseen) views across Trafalgar Square to Westminster and Parliament. It is an effective and intelligent intervention made all the more commendable for its self-effacing character – it is a building without facades.

Jeremy Dixon and Edward Jones refer to the process of design as an adventure – a path whose route is indefinite and whose destination is uncertain. They strive to avoid preconceptions, eagerly exploring options, at the same time acknowledging the importance of precedent and type. At times one such option will immediately suggest the obvious route; otherwise they will develop a number of alternatives in parallel before opting for a solution. It follows that they eschew a house-style – something which has at times counted against them in these days of signature architecture – and thereby set themselves apart from the high-tech orthodoxy of the British scene. Rather they represent an alternative tradition – informed by a critical reading of architectural history and a sympathy for humanitarian and cultural values.

Dixon and Jones' approach is to explore all the possibilities and potential of an idea, before carefully judging what to include and what to exclude as it evolves into a scheme – a kind of architectural editing guided equally by intuition and reason and driven by an extraordinary diligence – even now they will work through the night to complete a competition entry. Inspiration can emerge from any source, whether sought or by chance. This necessary unpredictability – 'straying off the route' – often arising from the contributions of other team members, brings a freshness and openness to the design process, an attitude that allows rules to be disregarded if need be in the interests of finding the best solution. The schemes that emerge can seem so well considered, so uncontrived, that it is difficult to imagine other, let alone better, solutions.

Such is the apparent variety of Dixon Jones' projects, it would be easy to conclude that the work is characterised more by difference than by similarity. In fact the common threads are there, but they are beneath the surface, as if woven into both the substance of the work as well as its method of creation.

First and (often) foremost of these themes is a continuing investigation into the nature of the city and landscape and the interface or 'edge' between them. Dixon and Jones take seriously the civic responsibilities of the architect – the significance of an architectural intervention to the greater whole, whether in remaking the piazza at Covent Garden or in the careful siting in the landscape of the residential towers at Robert Gordon University. Their sensibilities are perhaps most acute in the complex and unique city that is London, where both Dixon and Jones have lived and worked for most of their lives – and it is here that they have built some of their best work.

But the abstract disciplines of geometry are also a significant preoccupation – trace for instance the recurring circles, from Jeremy Dixon's 1959 measured drawing of the Great Laxey Wheel to Edward Jones' Schinkel Archives and Grand Buildings competition entries to the joint Venice bus station project of 1990. Here, typically, the character of the project derives from juxtaposing a pure form with the existing medieval street pattern and resolving the interface. Two dimensional geometries, in part derived from the English landscape tradition, play an important part in the masterplanning and large scale interventions, such as Stonehenge visitor centre, while the solid geometries of pyramids, cones, drums and octagons feature in many projects, from the Northampton pyramid to Mississauga. Alongside this, there is an intellectual enjoyment of the tangential line, the infinite trajectory contrasted with the self-contained regular forms – the play of the linear terraces in the early Netherfield housing against the undulating landscape and the distortion of the line as a curve when seen in perspective on the Bow Street elevation of the Royal Opera House.

Materials – the substance of architecture – offer Dixon Jones a means of giving expression, rather than a style, to the ideas embodied within the project. This too brings manifest differences to their work, whether in the restricted pallete of tectonic oak construction at Darwin College study centre, or in the rich collage that brings character to the Plymouth superstore.

Less noticed in Dixon Jones' work is an implicit socio-political agenda, an aspiration for egalitarian public space, whereby convention is subverted by design. It was no small feat, for example, to introduce escalators at the heart of such bastions of conservatism as the National Portrait Gallery and the Royal Opera House. And contrast the route up to the amphitheatre at the opera before and after the Dixon Jones project. Rather than a closed side staircase, those purchasing the cheaper seats now enjoy the promenade through the restored Floral Hall and up the escalator to the amphitheatre bar, with its double-aspect views out over the Covent Garden piazza and back over the Floral Hall.

Much like a Dixon Jones project this book has evolved from an initial concept, through exploration and investigation, to its final form. The result of a close collaboration between Jeremy Dixon, Edward and Margot Jones and the editors, each page has been drafted, worried over, revised, reconsidered, redesigned, reworked and refined. The book is organised in three main parts. Kenneth Powell's essay on the period up to 1989 introduces the first two parts, respectively on Jeremy Dixon's and Edward Jones' work to that date. Their subsequent joint work forms part three, introduced by Robert Maxwell's assessment of the key projects at the Royal Opera House and the National Portrait Gallery, with other joint projects following in chronological sequence. A full project list, together with credits, bibliographies, biographies and an index are found at the end. Within this structure are individual descriptions and comments by Dixon and Jones, plus accounts by their clients at the Royal Opera House and National Portrait Gallery – Jeremy Isaacs and Charles Saumarez Smith – and a critique by Alan Colquhoun of their recently completed project, the Saïd Business School in Oxford.

Jeremy Dixon and Edward Jones: the first 50 years – 1939-1989

Kenneth Powell

'Now that they are all dead', wrote Reyner Banham some 25 years ago of the great 'masters' of modern architecture, 'it is difficult not to feel liberation as well as loss'[1]. Both the positive legacy of the modern movement – more apparent today, perhaps, than it has been at any time in the last quarter century – and the sense of liberation from what had become a narrow and over-rigid orthodoxy find clear expression in the work of the architects Jeremy Dixon and Edward Jones. Schooled and trained at a time when classic modernism was already under fire from the adherents of Team X and the New Brutalism and from the neo-romantics of the 'townscape' school of design, Dixon and Jones started to practise architecture as the 'age of the masters' (Le Corbusier died in 1965 and Mies van der Rohe in 1969) drew to a close. Over more than 30 years, their work has exemplified the concerns of the postmodern age – for history, the sense of place, the identity of the city, particularism as against uniformity, nature and human diversity – without falling into any obvious 'school' or stylistic category.

Dixon and Jones' work illuminates issues which are central to architecture at the start of the twenty-first century. In its variety, resourcefulness, undogmatic expressiveness and commitment to the art of building, it is also immensely enjoyable. Beneath the wit and the polish however there is a seriousness, a sense of the gravity of the architect's task, which reflects a sound modernist upbringing. There is humour without flippancy, a decorative sense without a loss of discipline. Above all, Dixon and Jones are committed to the art of architecture – a social and a public art but one where the creation of appropriate beauty is a proper ambition and the architect himself is truly a creator and not just a facilitator. Sometimes depicted as the defenders of a 'middle ground' in British architecture – a depiction that neither recognises – they are both progressives and traditionalists. As schools and fashions dwindle, Dixon and Jones' stance seems all the more inevitable, even radical, a forward-looking retort to the late twentieth century taste for the arbitrary, the dissonant and the purely abstract. They care about the way buildings work and about the way they look.

Jeremy Dixon and Edward Jones met at the Architectural Association school in London in the late 1950s and became in turn friends and collaborators. Dixon had started at the AA in 1957. Born in 1939, he had been sent as a boarder to a traditional English public school but his academic career had suffered after he contracted polio. Strong backing from his family – his mother was an artist and the great critic Herbert Read a close family friend – helped him persevere with his ambition to train as an architect. The AA was 'a wonderful place, then as now… it offered a new landscape of opportunity and freedom', Dixon says. It was still largely a male world, populated by products of the public schools – 'an old-fashioned world, in a way, elitist but with a radical tinge', Dixon recalls. 'Ed and I were part of a particular generation: old enough to have been taken to the Festival of Britain as schoolboys but not old enough to have been called up for National Service'.

Edward Jones, born in St Albans in 1939 and schooled at Haileybury, went to the AA in 1958, completing his course there in 1963. Like Dixon, he came from a distinctly artistic background. His father had studied sculpture with Henry Moore at the Royal College of Art and went on to style cars for General Motors, while his mother was an accomplished portrait painter. Jones' continuing love affair with the USA began between his third and fourth years at the AA, when he worked for Eero Saarinen on the famous TWA terminal in New York, using his spare time to visit the offices of Mies and Louis Kahn. Dixon did not leave the AA until 1964, having taken an extra two years – 'I'm a late developer', he says. Dixon's closest friends at the AA (though they did not work on projects together) included Edward Jones, Christopher Cross and Mike Gold – already the makings of what was to become known as the 'Grunt Group'. Jeremy and Fenella Dixon and Edward Jones shared a house in Doughty Street, Bloomsbury, with Gold.

The mood of the AA in the late 50s and early 60s was confident, optimistic and determinedly modernist. 'Social' architecture was all. Students were encouraged to pursue projects for public buildings: commercial work was considered irresponsible, if not downright immoral. Peter Smithson, John Killick, Arthur Korn, Alan Colquhoun ('a vast influence'), Kenneth Frampton, Robert Maxwell and other tutors promoted the work of Dutch moderns like Rietveld, Duiker, and Oud alongside Corbusier, Mallet-Stevens and the French school. A cool minimalism was the growing fashion and the picturesque taste and predilection for 'townscape' then being promoted by the Architectural Review under H de Cronin Hastings was scorned as insular and reactionary – 'picturesque

turesque cobble-hobbling', as David Wild later described it[2]. The 'people's detailing' approach to public architecture influential at the LCC and elsewhere in the early 50s was equally loathed and the memory of the 1951 Festival of Britain was heartily excoriated for its Swedish-influenced eclecticism. 'Cool jazz was the natural corollary to the kind of architecture we admired', Jones recalls.

Colin Rowe's analysis of the links between the modern movement and the classical tradition (based on a reading of Wittkower) impressed Jones, who came to know his work through his AA tutor Alan Colquhoun (and later, while teaching in the USA, was to get to know Rowe well). A sense of history has always been central to the thinking of both Dixon and Jones. Taught at the AA by great critics of the orthodox modernist position, they learned to be sceptical. 'I can recall discovering the work of Terragni', says Jones. 'The urban decorum of the work had an immediate appeal – so different to Corb's Unité, which I'd admired so much!'. Le Corbusier, the presiding genius of the modern movement, was being subjected to a searching reappraisal. For Dixon and Jones, the 'white villas' of the 1920s and 30s were seminal – as they were some years later for the members of the 'New York Five' – but Le Corbusier's vision of urban high-rise in the 'ville radieuse' had little appeal. For them, as for others of their generation, the development of a new approach to the design of cities was to become a priority. The lectures delivered at the AA by John Summerson on the Georgian city and by Robert Furneaux Jordan on Victorian architecture encouraged them to look at the virtues of traditional streets and squares, but it was to be some years before their relevance to the contemporary scene became apparent.

The late 1950s saw a conscious rebirth in Britain of the idea that architecture was an art, not just a branch of the social sciences. The This is Tomorrow exhibition at the Whitechapel gallery in 1956 was a breakthrough, the source of the Independent Group and a landmark in the emergence of the New Brutalism. The prime movers were the Smithsons (for whom Dixon worked for a time), Reyner Banham and James Stirling (for whom Jones was to work briefly on a highly informal basis – 'moonlighting' as he describes it). The Institute of Contemporary Arts (then in Dover Street) became one of Dixon and Jones' London haunts, a place where architects communed with artists like Eduardo Paolozzi and

Richard Hamilton, although, Dixon insists, 'most of the action took place at the AA itself'.

Dixon met his future wife Fenella Clemens – they married in 1964 – in his first year at the AA. 'The boards were set out in alphabetical order, so, quite by chance, we got to sit next to each other', he recalls. The two collaborated on a number of projects. At the end of the second year, a measured drawing project was set. Fenella worked with Dixon and Christopher Woodward ('a great draughtsman') on a survey of the Great Laxey Wheel (the largest waterwheel ever built) in the Isle of Man. Working hard on the drawings, Dixon says, was 'an introduction to the obsessional quality which architectural projects tend to assume'. Their subject was interesting – an engineering structure rather than a conventional work of architecture. The pure forms of Laxey impressed Dixon – the great circle of the wheel and the tapering staircase of the tower were to reappear many times in his later work.

At the AA, housing was seen as the most vital concern and housing projects formed the core of the course. Jeremy Dixon recalls working on a housing project for London's South Bank in his fourth year – 'We set our faces against the typical mega-schemes of the day', he says. Edward Jones too pursued the issue of housing. His AA thesis was a scheme for a residential teacher training college, a city within a city, like the vast Park Hill estate in Sheffield ('very puritanical', he now calls it, 'and influenced by the social agenda of books like Richard Hoggart's The Uses of Literacy. You could, in fact, describe it as a mega-scheme'). After graduating, Jones spent a year (1963-64) working for Douglas Stephen, whose office was then a forcing-house of young talents, including Kenneth Frampton, Robert Maxwell, Birkin Haward, Elia Zenghelis and David Wild. At Stephen's office, Jones worked with David Wild on an office block at Watford – his first 'real' project. He moved on to the office of Colquhoun & Miller, working with Christopher Cross on buildings for Royal Holloway College. With Mike Gold, an old AA colleague who was perhaps the 'driest' of the 'Grunts', Jones entered the competition for a new housing development at Portsdown, Portsmouth. 'A Unité laid on its side', he describes it, 'low-rise, high-density, self-contained like a French bastide'. There is an interesting counterpoint perhaps between this project and Neave Brown's Alexandra Road estate in Camden

Above Celebrations at the respective 60th birthday parties of Jeremy Dixon and Edward Jones in 2000.

9

– although the latter was not completed until 1979.

'We had a horror of the arbitrary and picturesque then', Jones says, 'and any attempt at softness or popularism would have seemed like weakness'. Cool, cosmopolitan modernism with a hard edge seemed the only hope for a nation which actually admired so compromised a work as Basil Spence's Coventry Cathedral (opened in 1962). The pressure for architecture to be 'interesting' and 'original' was immense. As Mike Gold observes, 'in Britain, a nervously urgent desire to superimpose upon architecture the characteristics of an ebbing historical identity was accompanied by a resurgent nostalgia for the literal symbols of the past. Even that apparently progressive and certainly most poetic of movements, the New Brutalism, referred, in the end, to a nostalgic landscape already superseded and dethroned'.

Portsdown was not built, but Jones was soon to build on a considerable scale. In 1967, with Christopher Cross, he left Colquhoun & Miller to work for Frederick MacManus & Partners, which was well-established in London housing. The firm, run by senior partner Brian Smith ('a good friend over the years', says Dixon), was noted for its well-mannered, perhaps slightly cautious, approach and therefore represented something of a challenge. Dixon, having worked briefly for the Smithsons (assisting with the fit-out of the Economist tower) and then for Castle & Park after leaving the AA, subsequently joined MacManus and Mike Gold was soon recruited too. By now Cross, Dixon, Gold and Jones (who did not consciously see themselves as a group) had been dubbed the 'Grunt Group' by Peter Cook. The 'grunt', Cook wrote in 1977, was 'a grunt of seriousness and asceticism'[3].

Asceticism – the continuing 'horror of the wilful' – was a virtue to some. To Walter Segal, however, housing pioneer and humanist, the 'neo-purist school' was a disturbing phenomenon. 'This is not the time to seek purity in architecture', Segal argued. 'Our world wants complexity because it is complex itself'. The neo-purists were 'a sad anachronism… we shall never accept again the formal order of an austere architecture'[4]. Segal's attack (published by Monica Pidgeon in Architectural Design) appeared alongside a substantial feature on the various MacManus schemes designed by the team of Cross, Dixon, Gold and Jones. The residential building at the then Woolwich Polytechnic (1966-71) was designed by Jones

with, firstly, Cross and (subsequently) Brendan Woods. 'It's a very straight modern building', Jones admits. 'It intentionally makes no concessions to any ideas of social groupings or the picturesque'. Dixon describes the Plough Way housing in Rotherhithe as 'the product of analysis, a rationalisation of the needs of family life. It would have made very successful middle-class apartments in, say, St John's Wood, but as social housing it didn't accord with the lifestyles of the inhabitants'. According to Dixon (who sees it as disconnected from his later housing projects) the best aspect of the scheme is the approach to access – eliminating the pedestrian decks and corridors found in many large public housing schemes of the time in favour of direct access via lifts. Frameless windows slide back to open up the interiors to the open air, while movable partitions reflected the growing interest in tailoring mass housing to the needs and wishes of individuals. Mike Gold later explained the ethos of the Grunt Group as one of 'culture-free architecture', a return to the basics of modernism. But there was an element of nostalgia. Derek Walker wrote of Jones: 'his preoccupation with the 30s is still manifest… I think that Ed Jones is an extremely well preserved 65 year old'[5].

Purism was under attack, and not only for its apparently arrogant dismissal of human needs. Archigram – another movement with its roots in the AA and the foundation on which the high-tech school would grow during the 1970s – offered a flamboyant, expansive vision which seemed as progressive as the Grunt Group was nostalgic. For Dixon, Jones and friends, however, the battle was still against false picturesqueness. They all entered the Runcorn housing competition of 1968 – Jones working with Gold, Dixon with Cross – and the Dixon/Cross scheme was commended. Ruthlessly geometrical, the project nonetheless embodied a romantic view of the landscape, with the rigour of the grid highlighting the rich irregularity of the site. Dixon still finds the (unexecuted) project of some interest 'for its preoccupation with economy of means – which later became codified as minimalism'.

The Runcorn project undoubtedly influenced the design of the Netherfield housing in Milton Keynes (1971-73), the major fruit of the Grunt Group's work for Milton Keynes Development Corporation – Cross, Dixon, Gold and Jones were persuaded to leave MacManus in 1971 by Derek Walker, then chief architect to the MKDC. The development is vast – 1,000 homes in long, regular terraces. The roofline is constant, but because of the varying contours the height of the blocks ranges from one to four storeys. Everything about the scheme is highly repetitive, like Oud's Kiefhoek housing in Rotterdam (and also like Gower Street). The bloody-mindedness of the Netherfield housing extends to the neighbouring shopping centre, which deliberately rejects attempts at 'managing' the car in favour of a direct relationship between the parking area and the arcaded front of the shopping centre.

Dixon, in particular, was to react strongly against the Netherfield model in his later housing projects. How does he view it 25 years on? 'We tried to apply modernist principles to housing and it didn't happen easily', he says. Dixon still finds the formal, minimalist ideas behind Netherfield – like Runcorn, 'a landscape sculptural idea' – interesting. 'But it was badly built and detailed by other hands, and not really a success. In all, it was a horrible experience. We had to travel 50 miles up the M1 every day to work in a yellow tin box'. Jones is more measured: 'a matter of taking ideas to their absolute limits', he says. Netherfield, perhaps, represented the absolute limit of neo-purism. Housing, Dixon later noted, 'was always difficult'. Of Netherfield, he comments: 'we rather innocently tried to apply rational and modernist principles to this treacherous field of work. You have to deal with the tastes of residents as well as your own architectural ambitions'.

Dixon has never found architecture anything but a great challenge, something demanding enormous energy and commitment. Brought up in an artistic milieu, he also enjoys sculpting and making models. He derived enormous pleasure from working on the Art in Revolution exhibition of Soviet art and design at London's Hayward Gallery in 1971. 'It was one of my happiest times', he says. Working with Christoper Cross, Christopher Woodward and engineer Sven Rindl, Dixon secured the job of building a 12 metre high model – the original was intended to be 360 metres tall – of Tatlin's proposed monument to the Third International (1919-20). The project was something of a detective job – research into the geometry of the tower had to be carried out and the structure designed and built in a very short time. 'We worked through the night, sawing and drilling with loud rock music pounding away', Dixon remembers. The process, Dixon felt, revealed the dynamic

geometry behind the scheme. 'There was something of the pleasure a musician finds in interpreting someone else's creation'. Jones also worked on the exhibition, building with Mike Gold a model of the Vesnin brothers' Pravda tower (the model was subsequently acquired by the Sainsbury Centre in Norwich and even reappeared in 2001 at the Century City exhibition at the Tate Modern). Soviet revolutionary architecture was, at the time, something of a discovery – Kenneth Frampton's essay in the exhibition catalogue was significantly titled 'A Lost Avant-Garde'[6].

By this time both Dixon and Jones had families. Working at Milton Keynes paid the bills yet Dixon recalls feeling dissatisfied and more than a little bored. All this changed with success in the 1973 competition for a new county hall in Northampton which allowed the entire Grunt Group to quit the MKDC. 'We should never have gone there', Dixon says. Jones concurs: 'we felt trapped in an unsympathetic organisation'. Northampton was one stop up the M1 from Milton Keynes and the competition seemed the classic God-given opportunity. It was one of the most hotly contested competitions of the period and not only Jeremy and Fenella Dixon but Jones, Gold and Cross as well submitted their own entries. At the second stage of the competition, Jones joined the Dixon team, which was further reinforced by Cross, Gold, Birkin Haward and Adrian Sansom. Wearied by the constraints of housing work, they welcomed the chance to design in a more expansive manner. 'We wanted to make an enjoyable building that had an impact on the general public', Dixon says. 'Offices were generally sensible, boring places. We wanted to create a romantic building.'

The chosen form of the county hall was a pyramid, a form rich in meaning. The Egyptian pyramids had been built as tombs, the resting place of kings. There was a potential problem here, since the client was looking for a relatively informal and certainly democratic building, while the pyramid had hierarchical overtones. Dixon, however, was attracted to the idea of an 'object in the landscape', a twentieth-century version of the follies and monuments found in Georgian gardens, which seemed appropriate as the site was not in the centre, but on the edge, of Northampton. The drawings of Capability Brown and Charles Bridgeman were studied. 'The scheme started from a view of the landscape', says Dixon. 'We were re-evaluating the historic past, but we remained

Above Northamptonshire County Hall competition model; Edward Jones, Fenella and Jeremy Dixon in 1973.

committed to the modern'. Dixon speaks also of a new 'sensuality' in the Northampton scheme, a realisation of the appeal that architecture has to the emotions.

The assessors at Northampton were chaired by Richard Sheppard of Sheppard Robson, for whom Dixon had worked as a student (and got fired). Despite the implicit anti-democratic message of the pyramid, the jury was won over by the sheer force of the scheme. The appeal of a new landmark was strong and the architects' idea of providing parking not at ground level but on a raised spiral mound added to the potential drama of the site. The pyramid was an under-used but hugely symbolic form, with links to both neoclassicism and constructivism (for example, in the work of Vesnin); but there was to be nothing traditional or hierarchical about the interior plan of Northampton. True, the council chamber sat on top of the building, but beneath were floors of naturally-lit open-plan offices, flexible in arrangement and broken up by winter gardens, areas for relaxing in coffee breaks. Transparent inclined lifts at one corner would have provided marvellous views of the countryside. The project was a remarkable exploration of technical issues. There were ideas of natural ventilation and a sophisticated lighting system was intended to counter the generally bleak conditions endured by office workers (the services engineer Loren Butt was instrumental in developing this aspect of the project). Rationalism, the architects appeared to be conceding, was not enough. People deserved buildings with humanity and life. There were other approaches to designing in the landscape apart from the rigorous geometry of Netherfield.

Having won the competition, the Dixons and Jones looked forward to working up the scheme and seeing it built. But in the event it was cancelled by the incoming Labour administration in Northamptonshire. Dixon regrets the loss of the building to this day. 'It was advanced, inventive and ahead of its day', he says. It was not built but it ensured that the former Grunt Group (a name which Dixon has never warmed to) became, at last, an independent architectural practice – Cross Dixon Gold Jones Sansom.

For Dixon the elation of winning, in his early 30s, one of the most prestigious competitions of the day, faded when the project was abandoned, but he and Fenella became well established on the lecture circuit. 'We went all round the country giving lectures

to students and architects in towns we'd never visited before. Unfortunately, we found that most of these had been thoroughly wrecked – by modern architects from London. It almost made you hate your own profession and led to a lot of heart-searching'.

Dixon and Jones had never been attracted by the Corbusian view of the city. The arguments of Jane Jacobs' 1961 book The Death and Life of Great American Cities seemed to them as relevant to Britain as to the USA. 'We'd got to know Milton Keynes', Jones says, 'a place which seemed to be based on Los Angeles, all roads and roundabouts, about mobility and dispersal'. Dixon and Jones were increasingly concluding that the traditional street – an echo of it appeared in the Runcorn scheme – had many advantages. 'We felt shackled still by our modernist roots, torn between rationalist and romantic ambitions', says Dixon, 'but we decided to learn from surviving cities'.

With the abandonment of the Northampton project, the new partnership slowly began to split up, although it continued in formal existence until 1977. Gold, Cross and Sansom went their own ways. Cross, who later became head of the architecture school at Oxford Brookes University, practised with Sansom for a time, prior to the latter's tragically early death.

Jeremy and Fenella Dixon, working from their home in Highgate, were commissioned to design a house for a beautiful rural site near High Wycombe in the Chilterns. With its massive walls and great curved roof of untied rafters, the Weiss house took its cue from traditional barns, such as the one which stood just yards from the site. It would have been a virtuoso exercise in timber building and the lessons learned on the project were not wasted, but the project never went ahead. The mid-70s was a difficult time for young architects trying to establish a reputation. The oil crisis of 1973 precipitated a global recession, with public building projects being ruthlessly cut.

St Mark's Road, Notting Hill, was far removed, in every sense, from the Chilterns. London had suffered as badly as any city from ruthless clearances and intrusive new buildings. Housing formed the backbone of the capital but Georgian and Victorian terraces, many capable of being rehabilitated, had been torn down and replaced by modernist slabs and towers. A few of the latter had the heroic qualities of Erno Goldfinger's Trellick Tower, not far from

St Mark's Road, but most were architecturally banal and socially detrimental. Darbourne & Darke had experimented with one alternative at their Lillington Gardens development on Vauxhall Bridge Road, a brave but somewhat overworked design which Dixon and Jones found unappealing.

Lillington Gardens belonged within a reformed modernist tradition. But the Dixons' St Mark's Road was far more revolutionary – nothing less than a recantation of most of Dixon's work to date. It was based, Dixon says, on a very pragmatic, intuitive reaction to the increasingly obvious failure of modern housing design. 'In this case', he says, 'theory followed practice – but then you should always develop theory from practice'.

The essence of St Mark's Road (designed and built for the Kensington Housing Trust in 1975-79) lies in a deception. It appears to consist of 12 very large houses, but actually contains 24 houses and 12 flats (not unlike most of the surrounding streets – where the large Victorian houses have been subdivided into flats). Each 'house' contains two small, narrow maisonettes above a flat. In this way, the street elevation can have a generous scale and the informality of the garden elevation can give a contrast between front and back. The flats open only to the street. Drawing the elevations, Dixon says, 'meant abandoning everything you'd ever learned, putting your modern movement training behind you'. London was a city of streets and terraces, yet the terrace form had been completely neglected. Dixon decided to 'have a go' at terraced housing – and created a work of architecture which remains surprisingly undated today. He acknowledges the influence of the Victorian 'Queen Anne' style, which Mark Girouard expounded in a lecture at the AA, describing it as 'eclecticism with an artistic eye'[7]; but he insists that St Mark's Road is not an exercise in historicism but a fusion of history and modernity (with memories of Rietveld and Oud). 'Girouard gave me the idea that modern movement motifs could be incorporated into an otherwise historical and referential palette', says Dixon. Today it is the restraint and rigour of the development which impress and set it apart from the many housing schemes which it inspired in London and beyond.

The housing at Lanark Road (1981-83) was a clear progression from St Mark's Road. This time the model was not the London terrace but the classic nineteenth-century villa, adapted for a development of small, low-cost flats (seven to each 'house'). The scheme was promoted by Westminster council and the flats were to be sold at a price which allowed council tenants to buy them. The specific model was the development of linked villas of the 1820s on the Lloyd-Baker estate in Clerkenwell – perhaps Dixon remembered these from one of Summerson's lectures at the AA? Despite Dixon's reservations – 'more interesting as a social experiment than as a design', he comments – Lanark Road is another classic of postmodern housing. As at St Mark's Road, the scale is right, and the relationship to the street well considered – one of the failings of much low-rise housing of the 1960s and 70s had been its anti-urban layout (Darbourne & Darke's Lillington Gardens, for example, squats in a rather useless area of 'open space'). Dixon's villas are raised above the street in the manner of their Regency precursors. The doors are elevated and access, as far as possible, is external. There are proper back gardens. Dixon modestly describes the scheme as 'simple boxes with a decorated facade' and emphasises the economic imperative behind it – the flats were sold for £17,500. The frank historicism of the design now seems to worry him but his achievement in lending dignity, even nobility, to what could have been ordinary or mean is clear. Dixon recognised that street architecture has to be seen episodically, generally in perspective. Modernists tend to conceive of a building as a whole, to be perceived all at once. Dixon bravely cast off this obsession, along with the moralistic prohibition of 'facadism'. By 'sticking the architecture on the front', he did what every Georgian and Victorian house builder did – before housing design became part of ideology. In this sense Lanark Road was a landmark in social housing.

The housing at Ashmill Street, Marylebone, was a development of the earlier schemes. As at Lanark Road, it was built for sale at low cost and Jeremy and Fenella Dixon worked with the same developer. Again, economy was a prime objective. Perhaps the sense of adventure, of rebelling against an old order, had evaporated but the scheme is another appropriate contribution to the streetscape of inner London. The gap site abutted a surviving Georgian terrace. Dixon rendered and rusticated the ground floor of his block – raised, as at Lanark Road, over the typical London front 'area' – to match that of the Georgian houses and provide a base for the new work (the basic unit comprises two-storey houses

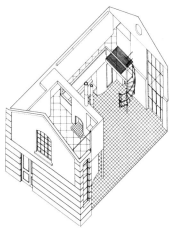

above basement flats). Above, he used a very un-Georgian brick, gently banded. The appearance of the new houses is anything but Georgian. The tall staircase windows which form a vigorous pattern along the facade are derived, perhaps, from Mackintosh. They perform a very practical function, directly lighting not only the stairs but also the open first-floor living rooms.

In a short period Jeremy Dixon made a substantial and positive contribution to the development of London housing, providing workable alternatives to the discredited (and generally detested) modernist approach. The collapse of Ronan Point and the growing recognition that many of the prestige developments of the 1950s and 60s had turned into desperate slums created the urgent need for new models for mass housing. Dixon offered these models but the 80s was a time when public housing as a whole was sacrificed to the new Thatcherite dogma and Dixon's other residential projects of the period were designed for the free market.

The riverside site at St George's Wharf was close to the Millbank site that had been the subject of a competition in 1977; the Dixons had submitted a scheme for this, rooted in St Mark's Road but also reflecting a close study of the Edwardian mansion blocks in the area. Similarly the (unbuilt) St George's Wharf development would have echoed the big Queen Anne and arts and crafts houses to be found a little further down the Thames at Chelsea – red brick, a steeply pitched roof covered in copper, projecting oriels and balconies, tall windows which might light artists' studios.

'St George's Wharf stretched the historicist approach', says Dixon. He is adamant, however, that the scheme is not – and neither were any of the other housing schemes of the period – post-modernist. Both Dixon and Jones have always resisted the 'PoMo' label. 'Our so-called 'postmodernist' work wasn't triggered by an interest simply in historical form or expressive shapes – like that of, say, Farrell or Graves', says Dixon; 'it had more to do with practical ways of achieving the repair of the city'. Dixon claimed in 1981 that stylistic issues were irrelevant to St Mark's Road. The message behind the scheme, he argued, was about 'the distinction between texture and monument in towns. Much modern housing had suffered by allowing schemes to become monuments to a social programme; and a monument, being concerned with the surprising and the original, nearly always makes bad housing. At a

time when virtually all new public housing was desperately unpopular, it seemed that the most original thing to do was to make housing that would actually be liked by its inhabitants'[8].

London's Docklands was the focus for a great deal of new housing development during the 1980s. Most of what was built was intended not for local people but for the newcomers working in the City or in new commercial developments like Canary Wharf. With very few exceptions, the new 'executive' housing was post-modern in style, brick-built with historicist details. It varied in quality; some was worse than banal. Dixon produced one of the most interesting schemes – for land at Cherry Garden Pier, Rotherhithe. A memory of Broom Water, on the Thames at Teddington, where a narrow canal allows boats to be moored in front of the houses, suggested the central idea. A 'water mews' would have led from the river, taking the place of the usual street. 'It could have been difficult to implement', Dixon allows. The scheme was not built.

Compass Point (otherwise Dudgeon's Wharf) on the Isle of Dogs was built in 1984-87. This was a large project – 160 units in all – but commissioned via an unusual (and not entirely satisfactory) route. Dixon was approached initially by the London Docklands Development Corporation, which asked him to produce 'guidelines' for the development of housing on the former industrial site. The site was then to be sold on to a developer, the expectation being that the latter would retain Dixon to design the scheme in detail and oversee its construction. In fact, Costain, which bought the land, agreed to implement the scheme but did not wish to engage the architect on those terms. The developer's chosen approach could have led to friction, but Dixon negotiated with Costain, worked up the scheme and handed over construction to a project manager. As a consequence, the detailing is sometimes less than perfect and the end-product certainly brought into question the apparently benevolent intentions of the LDDC. However, as Dixon says, Compass Point is 'a slice of city: it works as a place'. All the accumulated ideas of the previous London housing schemes were brought together – the riverside terrace of houses was inspired by St Mark's Road; the avenue which leads to it has echoes of Lanark Road; and a lesser street is based on Ashmill Street. Unity was provided by a common palette of materials – essentially, dark brick and white render. Reusing the ideas of the earlier projects was a very deliberate move – one, indeed, which a Georgian builder would naturally have made. Dixon had pioneered new London house-types; now he fitted them together to make an urban quarter. His 'experiment with the ground-rules of London housing design' worked. Compass Point, for all the blemishes of detail, is one of the few Docklands housing developments with a real sense of place.

After the cancellation of the Northampton county hall, Jeremy and Fenella Dixon and Edward Jones continued to teach at the AA. Dixon was there into the 1980s, though Jones soon transferred to the Royal College of Art and taught there (as senior tutor under John Miller) until his departure to Canada in 1982. Jones remembers the mid-70s as a time for 're-charging'. It was a time (as Jones noted in 1977) 'characterised by an orgy of professional doubt and self-questioning (both practically and theoretically), set against a general socio-economic climate indifferent to the making of architecture'[9]. A recession coincided with a crisis of confidence in modernism, especially regarding its impact on the city.

Like Dixon, Jones had come to realise how disastrous much postwar redevelopment had been. A series of competition projects dating from 1973-75 designed by Jones and Mike Gold (a regular collaborator in these years) addressed the issue of new housing in the fabric of London. The projects – for elderly people's housing in Haringey, Royal Mint Square in Tower Hamlets and rooftop housing in Covent Garden – decisively rejected the old agenda of 'watered down quotations from the Ville Radieuse, the freestanding object contextually disassociated from the existing urban forms' in favour of houses, streets and a proper delineation between private and public space. Like Dixon, Jones produced an entry for the 1977 Millbank competition. But in contrast to Dixon, he offered a monumental gesture, an inhabitable screen of housing 28 metres tall, clad in granite and punctuated by huge glazed openings. There is a touch of Rossi about the proposals, although Jones recalls he became acquainted with Rossi only when The Architecture of the City appeared in English translation in 1982.

None of these projects was built, but the Haringey design was developed for the sheltered housing at Cranford Lane, Hounslow, built in 1974-77 and designed with Gold and Christopher Cross. The single-storey houses look on to an enclosed courtyard. Private gardens are provided at the rear. The architecture remains impeccably 'modern', though friendly and human-scaled. Jones was worried, he admits, about the abandonment of the rational foundations of modern design. 'There was an anti-architecture movement – as we saw it – led by people like Walter Segal and Martin Pawley. Rigour seemed vital if architecture was to survive'. Typically, the Architectural Review complained of the 'blandness in detailing' in this humane and unpretentious work.

The Chelsea studio house (built in 1975-77, but since destroyed) occupied the site of an old stable block on a long, narrow plot. Externally, the house was unassuming – Jones liked the discontinuity between the plain brick exterior and cubist white interior. The centre of the new house was a double-height studio – the clients were a painter and a photographer – with other spaces concentrated in two blocks at either end. Jones' idea of 'a house within a house' gave the entrance block a fully-developed elevation to the central space. The strategy was one way of addressing a central problem of purist architecture – how do you keep the buildings looking clean and unsullied? The result was a purist microcosm, a beautifully layered series of spaces within an overall protective envelope. Bold use of colour and meticulous detailing made this a classic of the period.

Part of the process of 'recharging' for Jones at this time was an exploration of the potential of classicism. A fellow tutor at the RCA was Leon Krier, sometime assistant to Jones' friend and mentor Jim Stirling and now turning against the entire modernist programme. Krier, says Jones, 'had rejected modernism totally – he was even throwing out his monographs of modernist architects. I didn't want to go that far'. Krier's canonic classicism, with its espousal of the full apparatus of the orders, had no appeal for Jones. 'I've always seen my work as a journey, not a destination', he says. 'Strict classicism allows little scope for development – Asplund saw that'. Nonetheless, Jones, like Dixon, was steadily changing his position. For both, the issue of the city was paramount. When Jones went to teach alongside Colin Rowe at Cornell in the mid-1970s, he was already convinced that the ideas of Collage City were right (and many years later he was to be instrumental in securing Rowe's nomination for the Royal Gold Medal). But where was a new modern architecture which respected the lives of people and cities to be found?

In 1980 the two practices – Jeremy & Fenella Dixon and Edward Jones – were included in the British section of the Architecture Biennale in Venice. Dixon commented at the time on the importance of the particularity of place to his work, a concern (he conceded) that had not been central to the modern movement. 'But', he has written – drawing an analogy between St Mark's Road and the way that Queen Anne revival architects made a collage of any style they happened to like – 'it is possible to distinguish between a total rejection of the modern movement and its incorporation into one's list of references as one further historical style'[10]. Edward Jones recalled being 'carried along in the swell' of modernism but turning then to 'the inspiration of a broader view of history'.

Both architects had conceded that purism and minimalism offered an inadequate architectural language. But their views on the way forward diverged. Jones was seriously pursuing the possibilities of classicism. He was encouraged by the idea that classicism was not a specific style but a broader definition of a way of building. 'I was heartened by Demetri Porphyrios' statement that classicism is not a style' (the title of an issue of Architectural Design which Porphyrios guest-edited in 1982). Jones says that he has always been 'preoccupied with theory and the plan – less interested in the particular and the regional gestures, the romantic and the personal elements that Jeremy brings to the work'.

Jones' new interest in classicism emerged in two projects designed with Margot Griffin, whom he later married. Jones had tutored at University College, Dublin – as part of Ivor Smith's famous 'flying circus' – as early as 1970 and returned there on many occasions throughout the 70s, being appointed professor of housing in 1978. In 1979, he and Griffin submitted an entry to the competition for a new Taoiseach's (prime minister's) residence in Phoenix Park, Dublin. The scheme proposed a house in a humanistic classical mould, in effect a series of houses forming a whole but joined by gardens – a 'garden in the city'. Jones and Griffin's 1981 competition proposal for the Schinkel Archives Building in Berlin, for a site close to the Charlottenburg Palace, involved not just a building but a plan for reorganising the public spaces around it. The Archives Building itself 'floated' on the very edge of the river Spree (a memory of the church at Glienicke, on the

verge of a lake) and was conceived as an 'elemental' structure. The urban design exercise, however, rather than stylistic exploration, was the real point of the project. For Jones it was 'an awakening to the role of urban design and underlined how conventional prescriptions of modern architecture were totally inadequate in coming to terms with the complexities of the existing city'.

Jones' preoccupation with both urban form and a certain sort of classicism was demonstrated most spectacularly in the Mississauga City Hall, won in competition in 1982. Robert Maxwell said that the scheme 'projects a point of view that is as antipathetic to postmodern kitsch as it is to negative dialectic and other forms of protest'[11]. Jones is certainly unhappy about the building being lumped together with other postmodern classical work of the period. 'This is an inclusive architecture, but not about random applications. In a way this offers a sense of freedom and, dare one say, the introduction of the picturesque'. Unlike Northampton, Mississauga was built and built quickly – it was completed in 1987.

The background to the Mississauga project was Jones' work at the RCA in London, where he taught for a decade (1973-83) alongside John Miller, Su Rogers and Kenneth Frampton. Teaching and writing have always mattered a great deal for him; in 1982, the first edition of his (much reprinted) Guide to the Architecture of London, written with his old friend and collaborator Christopher Woodward, was published. Teaching, not only at the RCA but also, of course, at the AA, in Dublin and in the USA at Princeton, Cornell and Rice universities, was, says Jones, 'a very agreeable part of life, which I have come to miss greatly'. The stress in Jones' teaching had been urbanistic and involved a dialogue with anti-modern classicists like Krier and Porphyrios and continuing conversations with Colin Rowe. Appreciating the virtues of the traditional city wasn't hard but it did not necessarily lead to a total rejection of modern architecture. Jones envisaged not a complete break with the modern movement, 'but rather a counter-reformation, with an enquiry into how it might be enriched and in a sense made less restrictive'.

The site for the city hall was entirely suburban. Mississauga, a fast-growing city of some 300,000 people, has been described as 'the Croydon of Toronto' and a typical North American edge city. Close by was a big shopping centre, surrounded by car parking, a typical monument in the flat prairie landscape of Ontario. The city authorities were anxious to create an urban centre for the district. The new building had not so much to respond to a context as to make one. A real city, of sorts, it was hoped, would grow around it.

Jones had been approached by Michael Kirkland, an American architect (born in 1943) then practising and teaching architecture in Toronto, with a view to forming a partnership for the competition. With James Stirling as one of the jurors, Jones felt optimistic.

The competition scheme – selected unanimously by the judges from 246 entries – was praised by Stirling as 'of high quality by world standards' while Canadian critic Barry Byrne saw a connection with the Cornell school and the influence of Colin Rowe, who had taught Stirling[12]. Jones & Kirkland proposed a monumental group of buildings, expressive and rich in historical reference and thus outside the general run of projects at that time in Canada, where modernism was largely unchallenged. Helped by a brief which specified such provisions as an art gallery, chapel and public garden, Jones and Kirkland proposed not a single building, a monument like Michael Graves' municipal tower in Portland, Oregon, but a city in miniature, a piece of urban fabric which defied the ethos of 'edge city'. The influence of Krier has been detected in the form of the long, thin office slab – is it not a reworking of his St Quentin-en-Yvelines school project, with its eccentric device of a colonnade with an emphatic central column? The towering influence of Stirling is apparent and, further back into history, that of Asplund and Ledoux. But this city hall is a rational modern building, not a romantic historicist exercise, and a Canadian building, not a transplant from the European city. As Deyan Sudjic remarked, Jones 'plundered the imagery of the vernacular architecture of the prairies – water towers and silos – and reassembled them in monumental form to suggest a classical pedigree... Jones went well beyond the merely picturesque, employing a harsh, yellow industrial brick and an exposed steel frame for the clock tower, with the bleak melancholy of an Edward Hopper painting'[13].

Jones says that Mississauga was 'a fresh and spontaneous' project – the fact that it was built so quickly helped to retain these qualities. He likes to point out that the apparent formality of the building is challenged by 'the elements that just break through'. The client wanted a monument, a civic (in the true sense of the word) building, but the city hall is also a symbol of democracy. Breaking down the complex into a group of separate blocks – the council chamber, great public hall and offices – provides a sense of human scale and identity. The clock tower begins as solid brick but further up becomes a simple steel structure, a statement reflecting Jones' ambiguity about classicism. 'I remain... attached to and invigorated by the heroic period of modern architecture and am not prepared to wash it away', as he later declared.

Its forms may be evocative and rich in meaning, but the city hall has a noble austerity which justifies the perceived inspiration of rationalism and Nordic classicism – the great drum of the council chamber is clearly derived from Asplund's Stockholm Library. It is intensely memorable – never again will Mississauga lack an image. The mood changes as you progress through the interior – the council chamber, with its ingenious and striking decorative system, and the marble-lined great hall, have a distinctly civic look. Jones sees significance in the discontinuity between the 'quiet' exterior and solemn interior, a rebuttal of the modernist idea of interior and exterior space being integrated and overlapping.

Some Canadians felt that Jones & Kirkland's use of farm and prairie imagery was condescending. For others, the architecture seemed at odds with the function of the city hall. 'Some people there still felt that glass boxes were a symbol of freedom', says Jones. But he still praises the commitment and energy of the clients at Mississauga, firmly rejecting the idea that Canada was a creative backwater. The bold geometry of Mississauga was certainly to be echoed in many projects by the new practice of Dixon Jones after 1989. The idea of building projects as assemblages, visible typologies, still preoccupies Jones and underpins the passionate urbanism which has always run through his work.

There were other Canadian projects as well as Mississauga. The competition entry for Trinity Square in Toronto, a public garden planned for a waste site between the Victorian Trinity Church and the vast Eaton Square shopping centre, was related to the Schinkel Archive and Taoiseach's House projects and again Margot Griffin worked on the proposals. Jones discovered that Toronto, like the major British cities, had engaged in a massacre of fine nineteenth-century buildings during the 1960s. Four giant ionic capitals found on the competition site were believed to have formed part of a

Above Mississauga City Hall.

Victorian building demolished in 1964 to make way for the new Toronto City Hall. Jones identified other architectural fragments which could be used in what he saw as an 'architectural garden', a 'quiet and somewhat remote enclave' in the heart of the city, 'a memorial to our discarded past' which owed something to Schinkel's Schloss Glienicke. He envisaged the garden as a series of outside rooms, like an excavated Roman villa, defined by trees, hedges and trellises.

Another competition scheme was the Canadian Clay and Glass Museum at Waterloo, Ontario. This provided for a lakeside building as part of an overall urban programme (like the Schinkel Archives scheme) where landscape and architecture would be integrated. Jones & Kirkland came second (out of 292) in another near-miss for the new civic centre planned for a site in West Hollywood, close to Cesar Pelli's Pacific Design Center (the 'blue whale') on San Vicente Boulevard. Again, Jones broke down the constituent parts of the complex – fire station, theatre and library as well as a city hall – into a series of discreet buildings. Jones was 'preoccupied' with the idea of civic space at this time, a concern which was to resurface in later projects with Dixon, including the Royal Opera House and Venice bus station.

The SA Armstrong headquarters building in Scarborough, Ontario, saw Jones moving away from historicism, with a long curving wall of glazing fronting a lobby extending along the entire length of the building. Whereas the flank elevation recalls Gropius' Fagus factory, the symmetry of the frontage – applied to an existing 1950s factory – was, of course, not a modern movement motif. There were echoes of the 'modernistic' manner of the 1930s, equally detectable in the commercial development at Queen Street, Toronto, where the architecture was concentrated on the street facade with the rear of the building, facing a parking lot, left rigorously free of decoration but elegant and clear as a composition in its own right. There was a cool logic to this approach but it was also a rebuttal of dogmatic 'functionalism'.

In 1980s Britain, Jones says, 'a lot of this stuff would have been seen as scandalously reactionary and extreme', though he believes there was a 'subversive' element in his Canadian work. Jones' growing restlessness in Canada led him to enter several British competitions. For the ill-fated competition for Grand Buildings,

Trafalgar Square (1985), he tried to revive the strategy of Mississauga, breaking a large building down into a group of separate elements. The site was, of course, very different and a dense, tight composition resulted. The building centred on an internal court, lit by a striking conical dome expressed externally as a great drum. The scale of the scheme was bold, even arrogant. But the centre of London, at a time when the 'interventions' of the Prince of Wales carried enormous weight, was out of bounds for such a bold proposal. Jones' scheme was unplaced and the new Grand Buildings was built by Sidell Gibson to a rather weak historicist design akin to the pre-existing building on the site.

The Petershill competition (1989) saw Jones on a shortlist firstly of 11 practices (including Dixon), then of just four, for a major new office building close to St Paul's Cathedral (the winning scheme, by Edward Cullinan, was never built.) The Jones proposal was highly formal – and perhaps rather at odds with the informality of the City of London. It was also unequivocally classical (though a curious tower provided a focal point of rather baroque character). Temple-like rooftop pavilions recalled the rather stuffy 1930s commercial classical buildings of the City, though Jones' major inspiration was the Reuters building on Fleet Street by that unstuffy classicist, Edwin Lutyens. A rectangular court formed the centrepiece of the scheme, which reflected Jones' usual concern for rigorous planning. Eschewing the full apparatus of classical details, Jones favoured a more abstract and ironic approach. Nonetheless, he feels in retrospect that Petershill was a turning point in his work. 'I didn't share the ideology of classicists like John Simpson, Quinlan Terry and Demetri Porphyrios. I felt there was a dead hand at work in something like Paternoster Square. The classical language can only be stretched so far', he says, 'otherwise you end up with pure make-believe'.

Dixon's work during the 80s, always in collaboration with Fenella Dixon, was a good deal more eclectic, apparently confirming his attachment to a romantic particularism. The reconstruction of the coffee shop at the Tate Gallery in London was won in competition in 1981 and was followed by a similar commission for the restaurant. The director of the Tate at the time was Alan Bowness, later to prove (through his chairmanship of the Henry Moore Foundation) an important client. The Tate job was modest but intriguing. The restaurant already possessed a decorative scheme of significance, namely Rex Whistler's murals of the 1920s. Unfortunately, these were extremely badly lit, so that their impact was blunted, while the room was poorly furnished and generally dingy. The idea for the restaurant was to make the trompe l'oeil paintings seem as real as possible. The light is directed so that the room appears to be lit by the sky in the paintings. Dark furniture contrasts with the spot-lit food. The floor is conceived as a river and the edge of the ceiling appears to be blowing in the wind. Where the restaurant is about illusion, the coffee shop is an exercise in architectural furniture and composition.

The fascination with the arts and crafts aesthetic apparent in some of Dixon's housing schemes found expression in the garden shop at Clifton Nurseries in Maida Vale, a much-loved local institution that was part of the empire of Lord (Jacob) Rothschild (the commission came about through the critic Charles Jencks, who recommended Terry Farrell for other work for the company). The site is delightfully informal – 'extremely delicate', Dixon describes it. A new shop, linked to the street, was required. Dixon designed this as an addition to an existing greenhouse, using oak and copper, materials which would age well (and have done so). If there was an obvious inspiration for the delicate, almost spindly wooden pergola it was the garden at the Inverforth House in Hampstead – one of Dixon's favourite places – designed by the great Edwardian garden designer TH Mawson.

Jeremy and Fenella Dixon's success in the 1984 competition for the redevelopment of the Royal Opera House, Covent Garden, was an even greater coup than Northampton. Won in partnership with Bill Jack of Building Design Partnership – who had the unusual idea of combining two such dissimilar practices for the competition entry – the project was to preoccupy Dixon (and, from 1989, Jones too) for over a decade before work began on site, with the reconstructed ROH finally opening in December 1999.

A notional redevelopment scheme drawn up in 1981 formed the basis of the brief for the selection process which led to the appointment of Dixon and Jack. From 120 submissions, 21 leading international practices were selected; from these, eight were short-listed and four finalists eventually named including, as well as Dixon, Edward Cullinan Architects, Jack Diamond and the Richard Rogers Partnership. It was a very different process from the anonymous international competition for the new Bastille Opera in Paris, which led to the virtually unknown Carlos Ott gaining the commission for what became a very controversial project.

From the beginning, Dixon argued that the Covent Garden project had a twofold responsibility: first to the city and then to the theatre, with its practical requirements of accommodating audiences, performers and support staff in a theatre which met modern standards of comfort, safety and technical resources. In its first incarnation, the project was obliged to grapple with the challenge of combining a new opera house, with expanded facilities for its resident companies, with commercial development seen as a funding lifeline by the Thatcher government. The scheme submitted for planning consent in 1986 proposed offices on the area of land between Bow Street and Russell Street and on a subsidiary site off Long Acre. The commercial element was first reduced and later, with the award of Lottery funding in the mid 1990s, completely removed. The Long Acre site was sold off and the remaining land designated for ROH use.

During a decade of development, the scheme changed in many respects. But equally remarkable were the elements of continuity. These included the creation of separate blocks in different styles as a way of dealing with the fact that the project occupies a whole urban block as well as the arcaded frontages to the piazza which surrounds Covent Garden market. Dixon describes the approach to the design of the new arcades, which eschew any reproduction of the lost Inigo Jones originals (or of the rather approximate Victorian reinstatement), as 'a piece of necessary historicism'. In contrast, the elevations to Russell Street and Bow Street have always been conceived as modern in style and have gone through a number of permutations. The completed complex of buildings echoes the changes of mood and character seen in a city district developed over some considerable period of time, reflecting the changing brief and, indeed, the changing personalities involved in the project.

With the Royal Opera House in hand, Dixon was an obvious choice for the shortlist drawn up in 1985 for the National Gallery extension, subsequently known as the Sainsbury Wing. The background to the limited competition was the previous attempt,

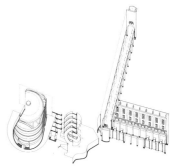

Above Royal Opera House, early model showing proposal incorporating office development and upview axonometric of the principal public spaces..

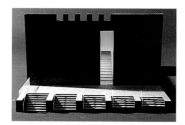

masterminded by environment secretary Michael Heseltine, to combine gallery and commercial office space on the Hampton's site, thus removing the need for public funding. The experiment generated much controversy and, in the end, great bitterness, after Ahrends Burton & Koralek's winning scheme was cancelled following derogatory remarks by the Prince of Wales. The Sainsbury family stepped in to save the situation by donating the necessary funds. Six architectural practices were invited to submit designs. Apart from Dixon (with BDP) and the winners, Venturi Rauch & Scott Brown, these were Henry Cobb of IM Pei & Partners, Colquhoun & Miller (with RMJM), CZWG and Stirling Wilford.

Predictably, after the debacle of the first competition, all the schemes were, to some degree, classical, though most freely rather than literally so. By decreeing that the new block should be a separate building, joined by only a narrow bridge to Wilkins' galleries, Dixon relinquished the opportunity for a grand enfilade along the entire length of the site, something realised very effectively in the otherwise rather weak Venturi building. Indeed, whereas Venturi's building is politely recessive (deferring to what has always been reckoned one of the least satisfactory public buildings in London) Dixon's would have been a monument in its own right. He argued that extending an already over-long frontage was a serious mistake. An octagonal 'tower of the winds', elevated on a high podium (a projection, in fact, of the level of Leicester Square), would have balanced the tower of St Martin-in-the-Fields at the north-west corner of the square, providing a new vertical element to counteract the flat horizontality of Wilkins's building.

There was an austere dignity about the National Gallery scheme which was not obviously postmodernist. In 1981 Dixon had been included – along with Jones and Terry Farrell, Piers Gough, James Gowan and John Outram – in an exhibition of Six British Postmodernists arranged by Architectural Design magazine. Reviewing the show, Peter Cook pictured Jeremy and Fenella Dixon 'in the late nineteenth or early twentieth century, discovering a local bricklayer, delighting in an awkward site, examining the technique of a local barn type and concocting a plan of immediate and necessary originality – just as they are doing now'[14]. Had the cancellation of Northampton driven them towards an eccentric, eclectic insularity?

There was no obvious turning back from historicism in the first project for a retirement village at Cliveden, Buckinghamshire, of 1986. The site contained an abandoned wartime hospital and was concealed in woodland some distance from the famous National Trust house. The 1980s saw many proposals for new 'villages' in green belt and open countryside, of which the most prominent was Poundbury Farm, near Dorchester, Dorset, promoted by the Prince of Wales and masterplanned by Leon Krier. At Poundbury – even now only partly developed – the aim was to give the impression of growth over the centuries, with a mix of styles and materials to suggest the accretive process which has produced the typical English village. Dixon rejected this 'fake' version of history, taking as his model the planned villages of the past described by Gillian Darley in her 1975 book Villages of Vision. He proposed a central rectangular green fronted by a formal range of villas, while scope for variety was provided in the small streets and paths behind. These join the larger grid of rides that make up the wooded Cliveden estate, with its extraordinary views over the vale of Oxford. The villas derive their form from those at Lanark Road but sit squarely on the ground in country fashion. The ground-floor windows look 'Gothick' but on closer inspection the tracery appears as more of an applied trellis. The site almost demands picturesqueness and charm but Dixon holds these firmly in check.

Jeremy and Fenella Dixon's contribution to the Chateau Bordeaux exhibition at the Pompidou Centre was a striking contrast to the understatement of Cliveden. Dixon was one of a number of architects invited to design an ideal twentieth-century chateau as a coda to a show which dealt with the historic architecture of the Bordelais. The focus of the scheme was a great rectangular lake, a frame for the buildings – chateau, cuvier, chais, cooperage and so on – conceived as a group of sculptural forms in the landscape. A pyramid, a cylinder, a Soanean dome, rectangles – 'a gentle intermingling of styles and building technology', as Dixon described it at the time[15].

Dixon's rejection of the expressive postmodernist language of this scheme led to a growing conviction that a return to minimalism could be the way to purge his architecture of the self-conscious charm which some critics identified in it. The Henry Moore Institute in Leeds was one of the products of this process of self-criticism. The project, completed in 1993, came to Dixon in 1988 as a direct commission; the client was Alan Bowness, the chairman of the Henry Moore Foundation. The foundation wanted to create a sculpture centre in Leeds in a listed terrace of former wool warehouses adjacent to the City Art Gallery. The terrace had been sawn off at its southern end when the Headrow ('the Regent Street of the North') had been constructed in the 1930s and its gable end, roughly rendered, presented a blank face to the square that was laid out at this time.

Fenella Dixon provided the spur to the development of the project when she suggested visiting Starlit Waters, an exhibition of minimalist art at the Liverpool Tate with work by (among others) Donald Judd, Sol Lewitt and Michael Craig Martin. In terms of the Leeds project, Dixon saw minimalism as a matter of 'extreme economy of means, extracting the maximum out of simple raw materials'. The sawn-off terrace gable was given a new sheer entrance facade and steps in plain black granite, with all the vertical surfaces polished and the horizontal surfaces matt. Elevation and steps reflected the practical needs of the interior and the need to form a new means of access to the building. There was no artifice, no attempt to cloak the abruptness of the slicing off of the terrace – the intention was, if anything, to leave evidence of this act of 'urban violence'.

Dixon's new modernist mood was expressed in a very different project, won in competition in 1989. This was the Study Centre at Darwin College, Cambridge, a small graduate college which occupied a narrow site along the millpool of the river Cam. There was only a sliver of land, with water on one side and a street on the other, to house the new library. There was no scope for the public radicalism of the Henry Moore Institute. But the interior has a strong geometrical idea based on the opposition of the straight and curved lines and pushes to an extreme the use of a single material, oak, in various degrees of refinement. Dixon feels that the Darwin project (completed in 1994) was part of the necessary process of 'shaking off the mood of the 1980s'.

Dixon and Jones' decision in 1989 to enter into a partnership was, for all their friendship over many years, a bold move. Both have forceful personalities and strong views on how any project should be approached. The partnership has not resulted – nor could it – in a fusion of their respective tastes and interests. The range and variety of the work which has emerged from the practice since 1989 reflects two vocal, sometimes contending, points of view. Back in the 1960s, both were critical of the preoccupations, social and aesthetic, of the modernist establishment in Britain. Initially as part of a loose alliance of like-minded souls, then pursuing their own careers, both sought to redefine what modern architecture was, what there was in the tradition of the modern movement that merited reassessment and what deserved to be repudiated. Both Dixon and Jones, from rather different directions, came to the conclusion that its urban formulae were irredeemably flawed and that its hostility to ornament and historical reference and its rigid anti-populism and prescriptiveness were no longer viable. During the 1970s, when the future of architecture seemed hard to predict, Dixon and Jones individually explored alternatives to modernism. They toyed with historic styles yet found the pursuit of style unfruitful. During the 1980s both Dixon and Jones worked the preoccupation with the past out of their systems. They came together at the end of the decade on the basis of a new agenda in which the spirit of modernism, purged of its social and functionalist baggage, was given a new sense of purpose. At the centre of their work is a vision of the natural and urban landscape which has a proper regard for the needs and tastes of people. It is this vision which has underpinned their unique position on the architectural scene at the beginning of a new century.

1   Reyner Banham, Age of the Masters (London 1975) p3.
2   David Wild, 'Theory into Practice', Architectural Design vol 47 no 9-10 (1977) p594.
3   Peter Cook, 'Unbuilt England', Architecture + Urbanism no 83 (October 1977) p13.
4   Walter Segal, 'The Neo-Purist School of Architecture', Architectural Design vol 42 no 6 (June 1972) p345.
5   Derek Walker, 'Pick of the Projects', Architectural Design vol 44 no 5 (1974) p286.
6   Kenneth Frampton, 'A Lost Avant-Garde', Art in Revolution – Soviet Art and Design since 1917 (Hayward Gallery, London 1971).
7   See Mark Girouard, Sweetness and Light: The 'Queen Anne' Movement 1860-1900 (Oxford 1977).
8   Project report.
9   Edward Jones, 'British Architecture', Architectural Design vol 47 no 9-10 (1977) p645.
10 Project report (1980 Venice Biennale catalogue).
11 Robert Maxwell, 'The New Classicism', Architectural Design vol 58 no 1-2 (1988) p43.
12 Barry Byrne, 'Mississauga City Hall', The Fifth Column vol 5 no 3-4 (1983), pp3-9.
13 Deyan Sudjic, The 100 Mile City (London 1992) p65.
14 Peter Cook, 'Current Projects', Architectural Design vol 51 no 12 (1981) p112.
15 Project report.

Jeremy Dixon

Buildings and Projects 1959-1989

generally in collaboration with Fenella Dixon

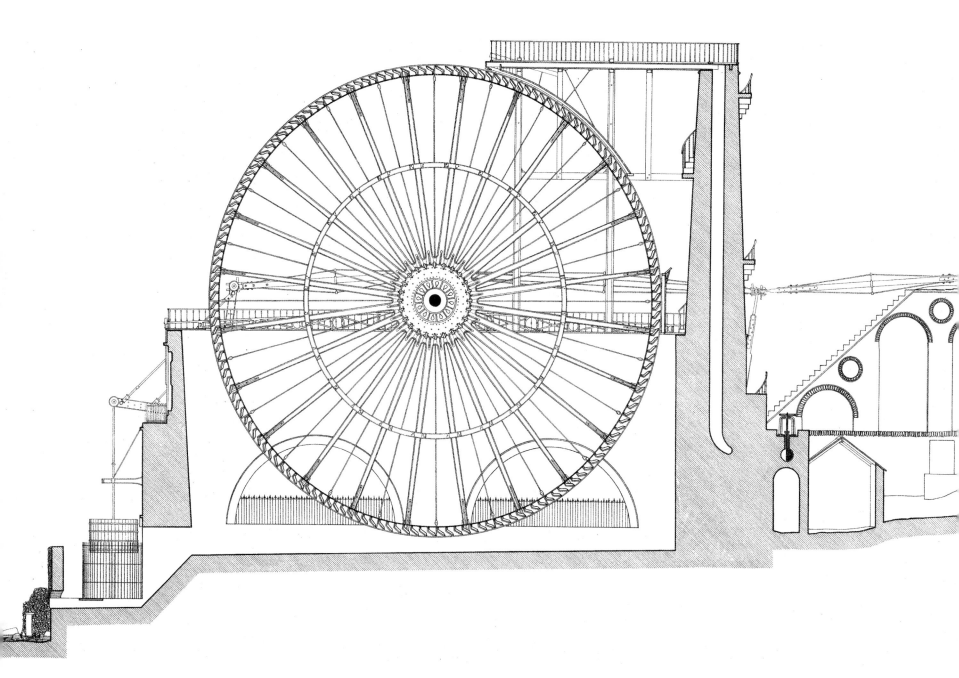

24

Great Laxey Wheel
Isle of Man

with Fenella Dixon
and Christopher Woodward

1959

'Measuring and drawing the Great Laxey Wheel was an extraordinary and memorable experience. It is an example of a piece of work, aside from one's own projects, that has remained in the mind and exerted a subtle influence over the years. The boldness of the shapes – the circle, the tapering spiral; the clarity of materials and construction – stone, cast iron, wood; and the overwhelming scale of the enterprise drove us (fellow second-year students Fenella Clemens, Christopher Woodward and myself) to an almost manic degree of care in making the drawings.

The wheel is situated at the bottom of Glen Moor in Laxey, Isle of Man. Designed in 1854 by local engineer Robert Casement, its function was to pump water out of the lead mines. The 21 metre diameter wheel, said to be the largest of its kind in the world, is driven by water collected from the surrounding high ground by a complex series of lades. The position of the shaft head in the valley required that the wheel should be built some 180 metres away from it. The wheel was connected to the shaft by a viaduct, along which ran a series of six metre rods. These were set in motion by a crank on the west end of the main axle and the horizontal motion was converted into vertical motion at the head of the 460 metre shaft. The speed of the wheel was 2.5rpm, each revolution representing 455 litres of water pumped.

Drawing techniques have changed so fundamentally with the introduction of computers that it is already difficult to remember how it was in 1959. Everything was drawn in Indian ink with Graphos pens, sharpened to give a finer line that cut into the tracing paper. My father, an antiques collector, gave us a set of Victorian compasses, enabling us to draw the microscopic circles'.

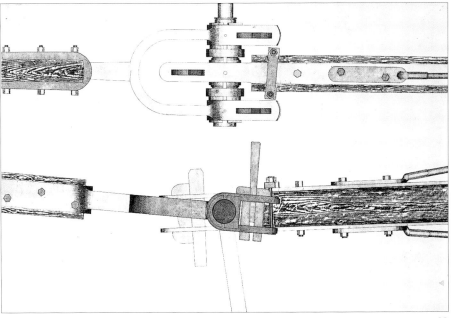

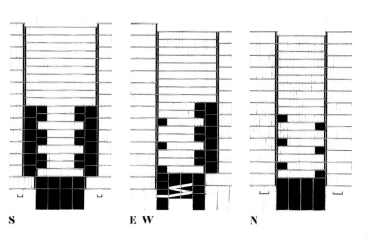

S E W N

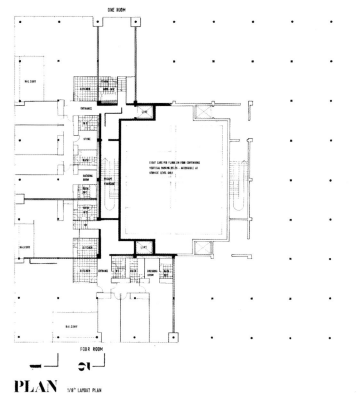

ONE ROOM

EIGHT CARS PER FLOOR IN FOUR CONTINUOUS VERTICAL PARKING DUCTS - ACCESSIBLE AT SERVICE LEVEL ONLY

FOUR ROOM

PLAN 1/8" LAYOUT PLAN

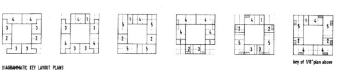

DIAGRAMMATIC KEY LAYOUT PLANS

key of 1/8" plan above

Housing project
South Bank, London

with Fenella Dixon

1962

'At a time when students were preoccupied with horizontal megastructures, we wanted to look at a different kind of model for high density housing. Flats are arranged around a giant core containing cars stacked vertically. The massive core supports a delicate outer structure into which are slotted horizontal flats of varying sizes. At the corners one-and-a-half height living rooms rotate in such a way as to keep level floors. One preoccupation was to make as simple and direct as possible the relationship between arriving by car and being inside the flat, avoiding walkways and extended horizontal journeys. The building has a fragile glazed exterior skin accentuated by cutting in balconies at the lower levels. The appearance of the building is of an eroded glazed cube that avoids any articulation based on flat size. The project was carried out during the fourth year at the Architectural Association'.

Left The models show respectively the light structure wrapping around the heavy tower storing cars and with the glass cladding.

Below Interlocking of flats at the corners give one-and-a-half height living rooms and level floors.

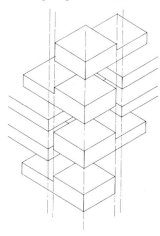

Plough Way housing Rotherhithe

1966-71

'The professional context within which this project was designed was a period of widespread activity in the construction of social housing – lots of big schemes and the beginnings of unease about the success and appropriateness of the results. The project, designed for the Sutton Dwellings Trust while I was working at Frederick MacManus & Partners, attempts to provide an analytical solution to the perceived shortcomings of high-density social housing. The flats are planned for maximum internal flexibility. All the family flats have direct staircase access to the garden while the living-rooms and kitchens overlook the garden. Cars are parked in a structure that supports a garden at first-floor level and a playgroup at one end. It was our idea of how a young family such as our own might organise its life. In reality the building was used in a very different way. The garden was shut off from residents virtually from day one. The open-plan flats were not used flexibly and sliding doors were closed off by furniture. In hindsight one can see a complete misunderstanding of the reality of the lifestyle of the residents in the way that furniture etc is drawn in the perspectives. The project raises the need to be accurate about what people value in housing. Rational analysis of function is not enough. Preconceptions, social habits, status and imagery are all part of the complex mélange that characterises peoples' feelings about housing'.

Above Three-track sliding windows open up the whole frontage of the living room.
Below Flats can be arranged as open-plan (left) or closed-plan (right)

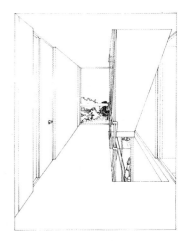

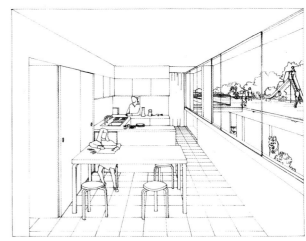

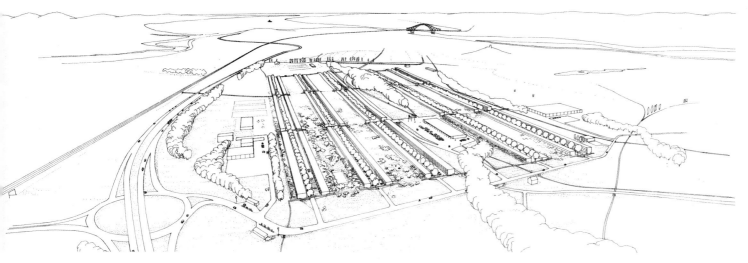

Runcorn housing competition

with Fenella Dixon, Christopher Cross
and Adrian Sansom

1968

'Large-scale low-density housing layouts
are a tricky subject. This project experiments with a rational grid that is subjected to the arbitrary forms of the landscape. Houses are laid out in streets and
the grid releases large areas of open
space between them. The manner of the
layout is in contrast to the wiggly lines of
houses and fake village forms that are
typical of most housing of this kind. The
use of the grid of paths and streets laid
over the curves of the landscape expresses a 'minimalist' taste for extracting complexity out of simple means. The shallow
curves, experienced in section, are exaggerated in perspective. This topic – the
extremely shallow curve as seen in the
foreshortened view – is a recurring theme
in the work. The shapes arise from the act
of laying down the grid and letting the
topography express itself'.

Above left Aerial perspective
Below Road and path grids distorted by landscape;
landscape curvature expressed by straight walls.

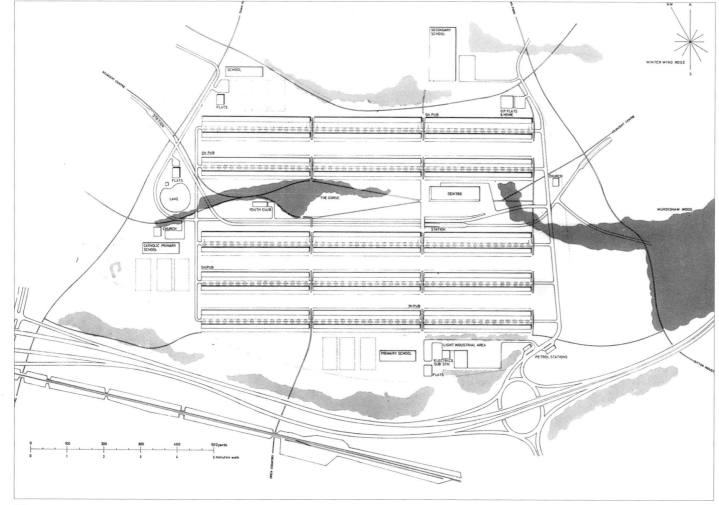

Netherfield housing
Milton Keynes

Cross Dixon Gold Jones

Left Landscape sculpture by Richard Serra; the play against the landscape of the horizontal tops of the housing blocks.

1971-73

'When the four of us – Christopher Cross, Edward Jones, Mike Gold and I – worked at Milton Keynes on one of the grid squares, the question of large-scale low-density housing layout came up again. The layout has similarities to Runcorn, but in this case the streets are on the outside of the double row of houses. The public spaces are part of the street system. The curvature of the land is emphasised by keeping a horizontal roof line that generates houses with varying numbers of floors.

In retrospect there is a strange coincidence with the work of the minimalist sculptor Richard Serra. At exactly the same time as we were working on this project, Serra was making his land sculpture (above right) and it is possible to see our work as close to a movement in the art world of which we were unaware. The Milton Keynes project falls down in its quality of detailing and the level of confidence to carry through the initial idea. It is interesting to speculate whether we would have had the confidence to realise the potential of this project if we had known more of the work of the contemporary minimalist movement'.

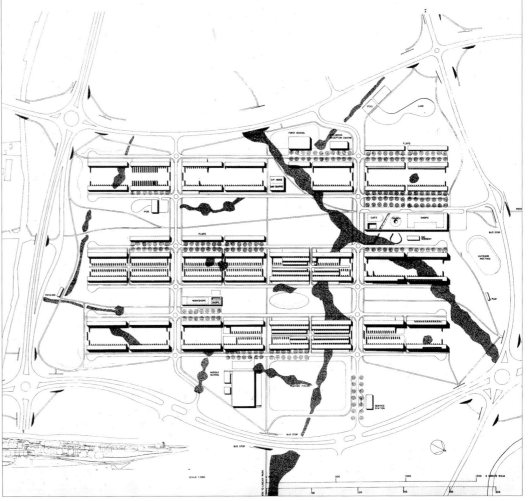

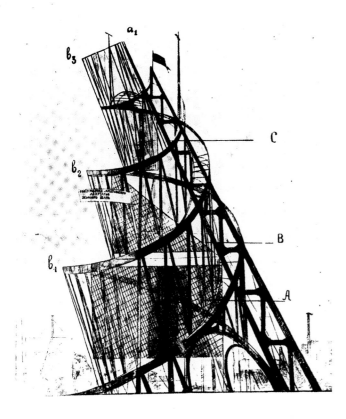

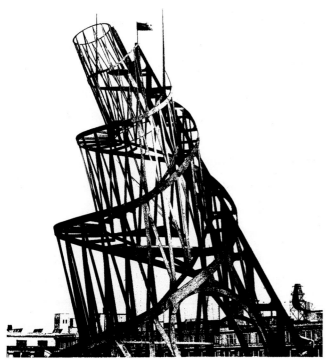

Tatlin Tower
Hayward Gallery

with Fenella Dixon, Christopher Cross,
Christopher Woodward and Sven Rindl

1971

'The reconstruction of the 1919 Tatlin Tower, like the measured drawing of the Laxey Wheel, was an influential and memorable experience that was not a conventional design project. The challenge was to make a 12 metre high model for the Art in Revolution exhibition at the Hayward Gallery in London. Vladimir Tatlin's drawings and model provide contradictory evidence as to the nature of the structure. We based our reconstruction on the best known drawing of the side elevation (left). After a lot of research and model making, it became clear that the key to the geometry lay in an invisible truncated inner cone made up of 24 lines. In order to construct the tower one had to first make the cone and then assemble the spirals before removing the cone members. The shapes in our small models were extrapolated into drawings from which the large model was constructed.

The construction process was a continual drama. We worked in the Hayward every day from 6pm until early in the morning. The tower was built in two halves inside the gallery, dismantled

and then reassembled on the terrace overlooking the Thames. The excitement of the detective work and the sheer physical pleasure of the construction process left an indelible memory. Shown here are some of engineer Sven Rindl's hundred-odd sketches, remarkable for their elegance and clarity even though they were often done on the spot'.

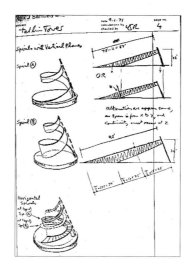

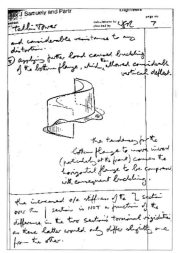

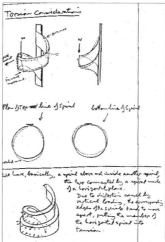

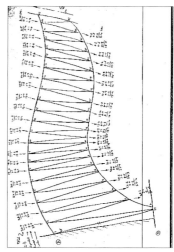

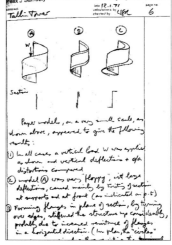

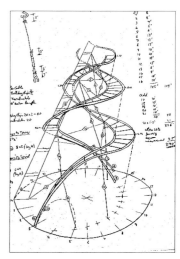

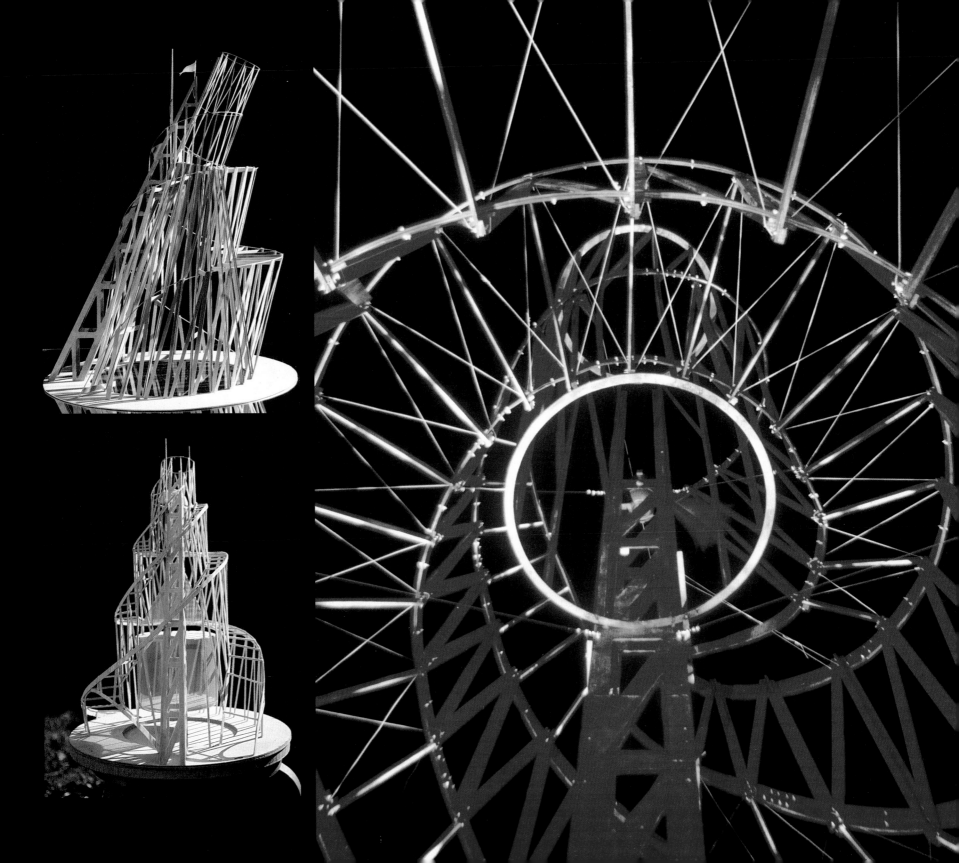

Northamptonshire County Hall competition

with Fenella Dixon and Edward Jones

1973

'Working on a competition can sometimes release a backlog of frustration. At the time we had been working in rather unsatisfactory circumstances at Milton Keynes, surrounded by the frustrations and limitations of social housing. The competition at Northampton, one motorway stop away from Milton Keynes, was a heaven-sent opportunity to explore new territory.

The circumstances were intriguing. The location of the site, on a small hill, lay between Northampton town and the M1 motorway. It was unusually suitable as the location for an object to be seen from a distance, a special shape that was a monument to the symbolic function of a county hall. It would be visible from a significant area of the county, all the traffic on the M1 and passengers on the main north-south railway line. The site itself comprised the remains of a landscape garden.

The proposition was to place a glass pyramid of offices on top of the hill set alongside a spiral mound of cars. The two objects are placed by eye in relation to the landscape rather than aligned with any site boundary. The pyramid contains references to the local authority hierarchy and has the council chamber symbolically placed at the apex. The site is organised around a series of landscape devices derived from looking at the drawings of Capability Brown and Charles Bridgeman. New axes cut existing bands of planting and these cuts are marked with short avenues of trees. The new axes are created in part by features such as the approach road to the spiral mound and in part by distant views such as that to the iron age hill fort on an adjacent hill. There were many experiments with alignments, including those associated with laylines.

The ceremonial route between the

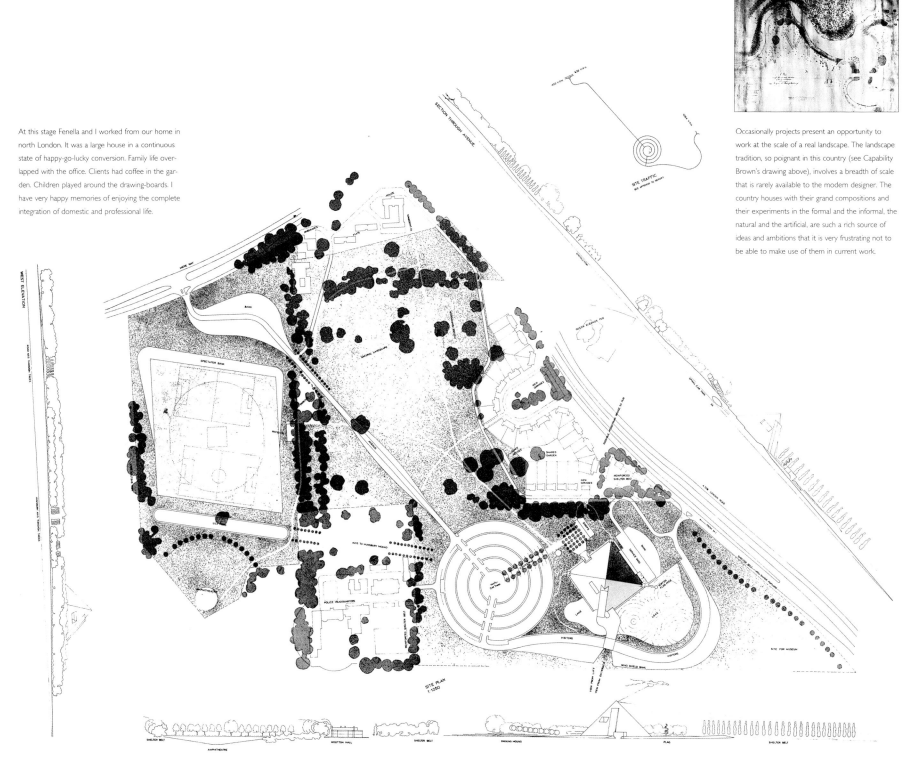

At this stage Fenella and I worked from our home in north London. It was a large house in a continuous state of happy-go-lucky conversion. Family life overlapped with the office. Clients had coffee in the garden. Children played around the drawing-boards. I have very happy memories of enjoying the complete integration of domestic and professional life.

Occasionally projects present an opportunity to work at the scale of a real landscape. The landscape tradition, so poignant in this country (see Capability Brown's drawing above), involves a breadth of scale that is rarely available to the modern designer. The country houses with their grand compositions and their experiments in the formal and the informal, the natural and the artificial, are such a rich source of ideas and ambitions that it is very frustrating not to be able to make use of them in current work.

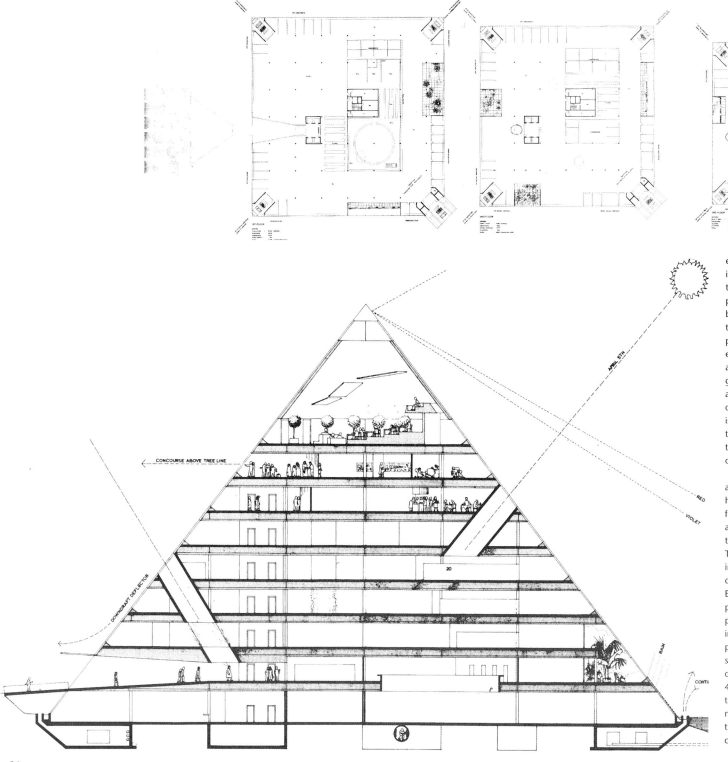

entrance and the council chamber is an inclined lift looking out across the country. The entrance itself is distorted in plan to accommodate the duality between the ceremonial entrance and the entrance to the county library. The pyramid is clad in solar reflective glass, except where the spaces behind are not air-conditioned; in these cases clear glass gives moments of transparency set against the general reflectivity of the outer skin. The very top of the pyramid is treated with prismatic lenses so that the top of the building appears to go through the colours of the spectrum as one approaches from a distance.

At the time the open-plan office was an emerging type. Generally these were horizontal buildings of two or three floors. The Northampton building was an opportunity to take a critical look at the quality of life in open-plan offices. The deep square floor plates were cut into by light shafts inspired by the drawings of the holes bored into Egyptian pyramids. These light shafts produce surprising areas of daylight and planting within the depth of the building. The sun comes down a shaft on a particular day of the year. One of the shafts was arranged to produce sunlight on the chief accountant's desk on the 4th April. This piece of levity was spotted by the assessors and apparently nearly lost us the competition. The theme of varying climatic and visual conditions was extended to the

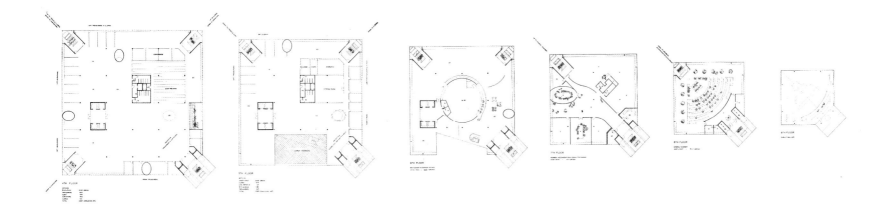

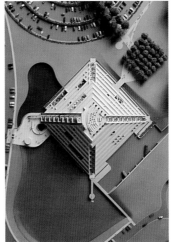

provision of winter gardens cut into the reflective surface of the pyramid. These would not be air conditioned and would have climatic conditions that reflected the orientation – temperate garden, Australian garden etc. The corner stair-cases which link departments together are also not air conditioned and have stepped planting in the manner of a hanging garden.

The structure was a rectilinear frame for the depth of the building, with a series of hangers to deal with the sloping edge condition. A lake, used as a heat sink for the air conditioning, wraps around the base of part of the pyramid and the entrance giving double reflections as one approaches the building.

This was a two-stage competition. The first stage entry was by myself and Fenella Dixon, assisted by Christopher Cross. For the second stage we were joined by Edward Jones and for the final drawing-up of the competition we were helped by Christopher Cross, Mike Gold, Adrian Sansom and Birkin Haward.

Like many grand competitions of its time, the project was never built. The local council changed from Conservative to Labour, the oil crisis produced the 'three-day week' and, understandably, money for building schools came before county halls. So we are left with Richard Davies' photographs of the model, which are so realistic as to give the illusion that it had been built after all'.

Right Diagram showing structure and services; section showing the variety of balcony and daylight conditions that enliven the open plan office areas. At this stage Fenella and I worked from our home in north London. It was a large house in a continuous state of happy-go-lucky conversion. Family life overlapped with the office. Clients had coffee in the garden. Children played around the drawing-boards. I have very happy memories of enjoying the complete integration of domestic and professional life.

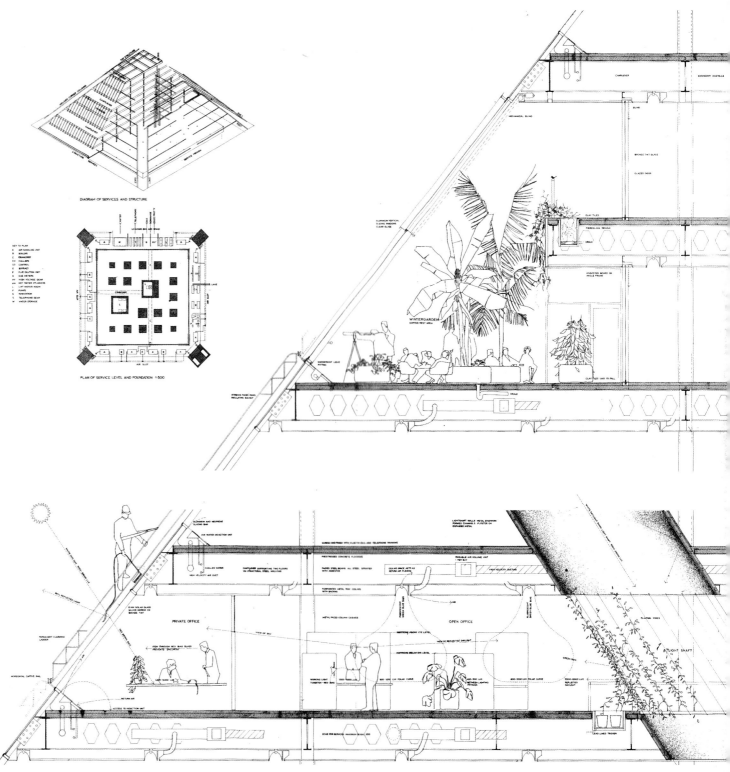

DIAGRAM OF SERVICES AND STRUCTURE

PLAN OF SERVICE LEVEL AND FOUNDATION 1:500

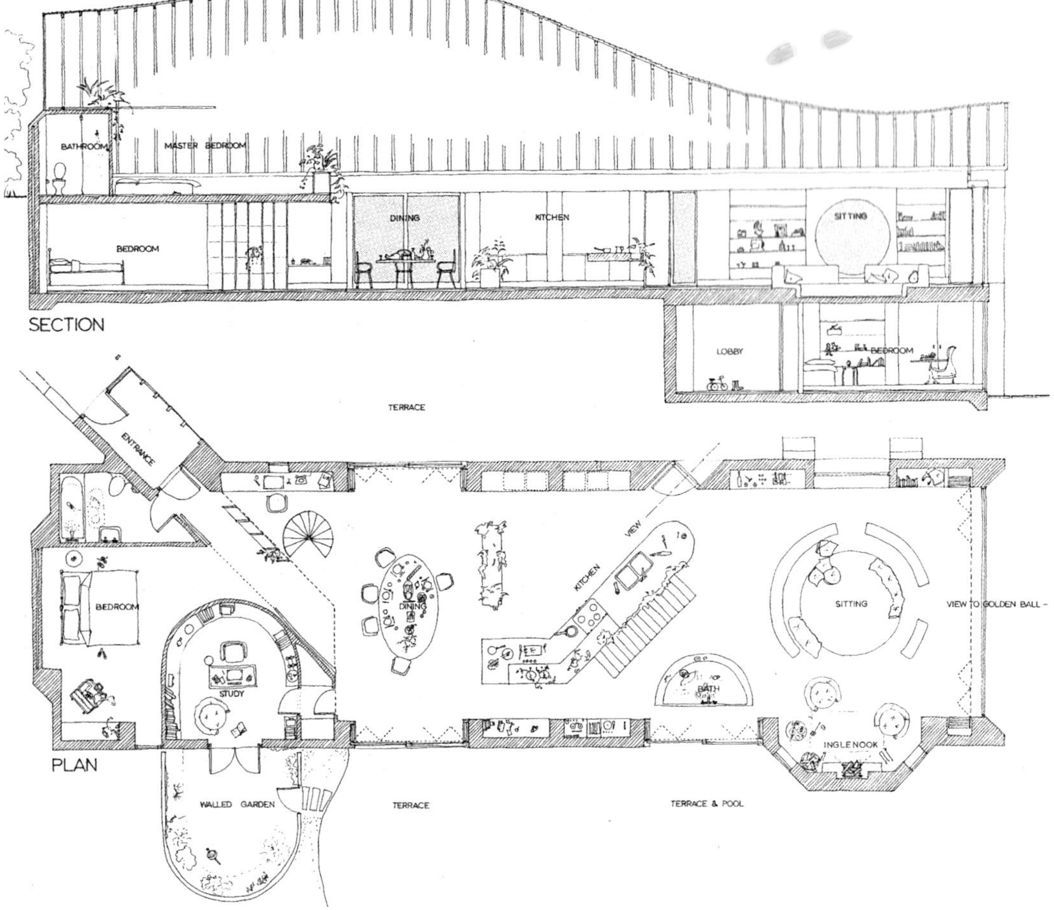
BATHROOM
MASTER BEDROOM
BEDROOM
DINING
KITCHEN
SITTING
LOBBY
BEDROOM
SECTION
TERRACE
ENTRANCE
BEDROOM
STUDY
DINING
KITCHEN
VIEW
SITTING
VIEW TO GOLDEN BALL
BATH
INGLENOOK
PLAN
WALLED GARDEN
TERRACE
TERRACE & POOL

Above The section shows how the varying height of the roof canopy defines a fomal dining area and an informal sitting area. Diagonal arrangements in the plan derive from the sloping ground.

Right Site plan showing alignment with the Golden Ball in the distance that sets up the diagonal relationship to the slope.

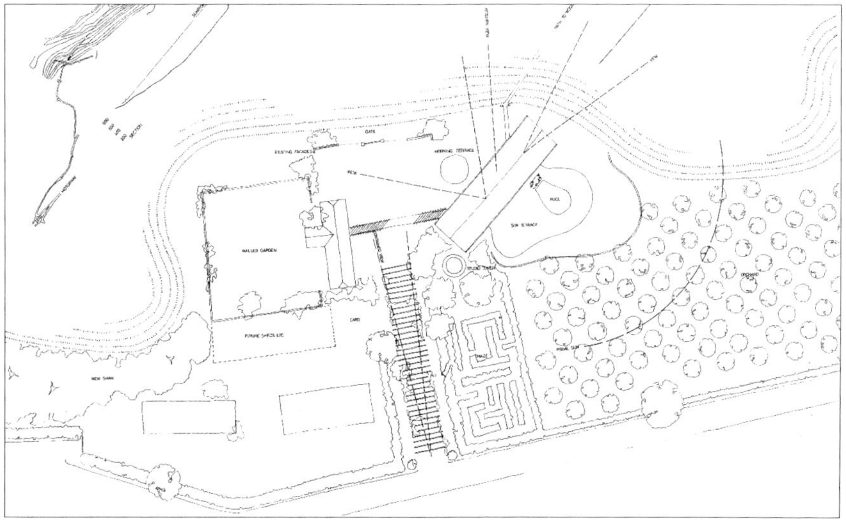

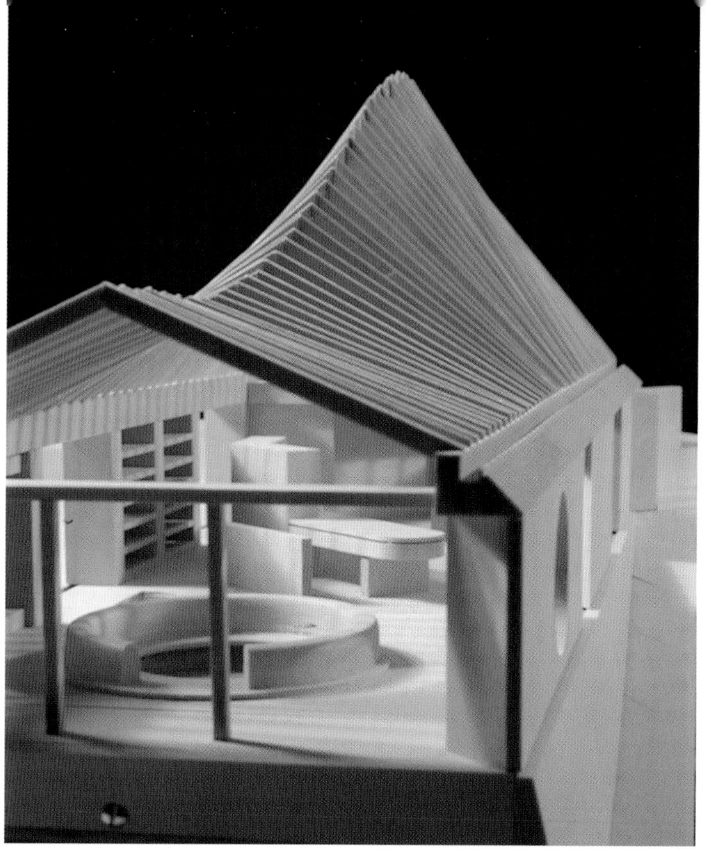

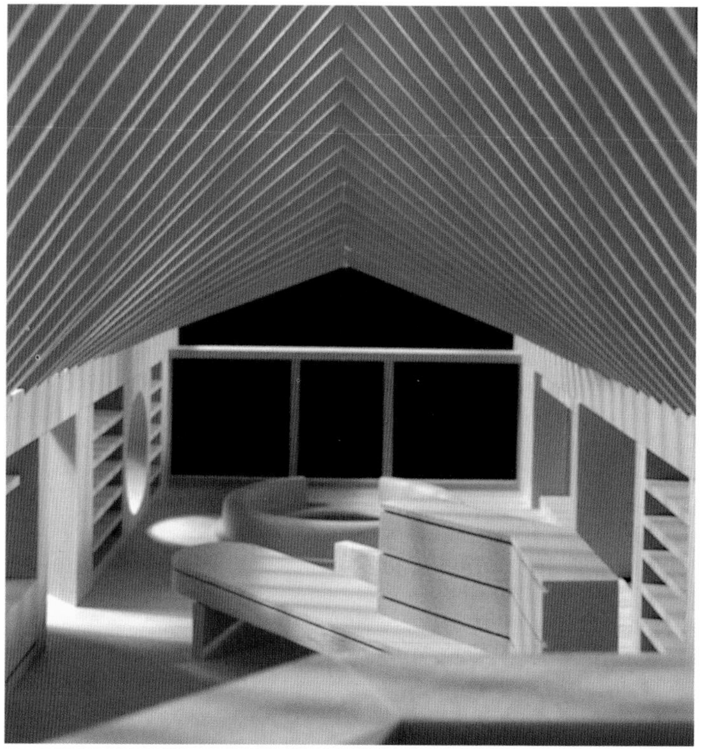

Weiss House
Buckinghamshire

with Fenella Dixon

1974

'This house was designed for a photographer and sculptress with an interest in astrology and the occult and a strongly-expressed dislike of cubic spaces. The site is at the head of a valley from which the Golden Ball at West Wycombe – an eighteenth-century folly – is visible in the distance. The two parallel massive walls, which contain storage and service equipment, buttress the curved roof of rafters that lean out on the walls without tie bars, giving the illusion of a roof that is a weightless curtain. The alignment to the Golden Ball twists the house at 45 degrees to the direction of the slope, so that horizontal entry sets up a 45 degree geometry in the plan. The interest is in the complex three-dimensional curved form created by the rafters as they connect the horizontal line of the wall to the curved line of the ridge. The design is influenced by a Japanese house seen in the magazines. It is an example of the process of imitation that, consciously or unconsciously, is a fundamental aspect of architectural design.

The house project was elaborated into a larger scale landscape idea. By taking the Golden Ball as the sun, the planets can be set out to correct scale, both in size and distance along an alignment that just reaches the ridge line of the Chilterns that forms the extent of the view of the Golden Ball. Each planet would become a small monument in the landscape connected by paths. The design of the monuments would incorporate references to the astronomical, mythological and astrological associations of each planet'.

Left The broken roof line of the adjacent barn provoked consideration of an undulating roof form.
Right View across the valley to the ridge-top site.

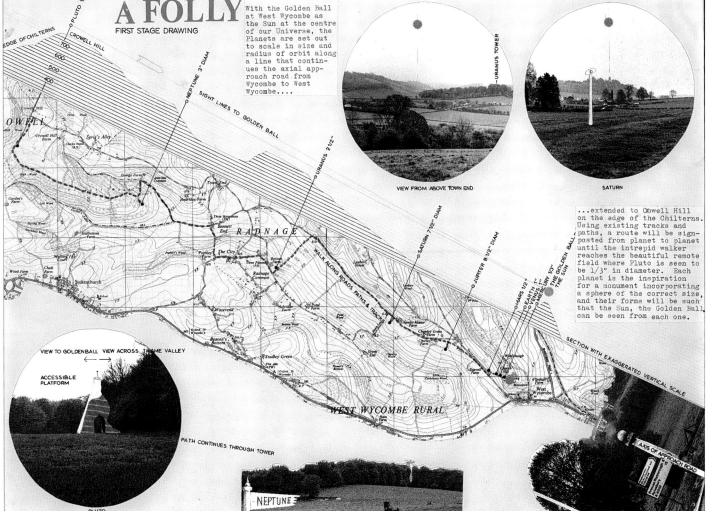

A FOLLY
FIRST STAGE DRAWING

With the Golden Ball at West Wycombe as the Sun at the centre of our Universe, the Planets are set out to scale in size and radius of orbit along a line that continues the axial approach road from Wycombe to West Wycombe....

...extended to Cowell Hill on the edge of the Chilterns. Using existing tracks and paths, a route will be signposted from planet to planet until the intrepid walker reaches the beautiful remote field where Pluto is seen to be 1/3" in diameter. Each planet is the inspiration for a monument incorporating a sphere of the correct size, and their forms will be such that the Sun, the Golden Ball, can be seen from each one.

VIEW FROM ABOVE TOWN END

SATURN

VIEW TO GOLDENBALL VIEW ACROSS THAME VALLEY

ACCESSIBLE PLATFORM

PATH CONTINUES THROUGH TOWER

SECTION WITH EXAGGERATED VERTICAL SCALE

AXIS OF APPROACH ROAD

NEPTUNE

St Mark's Road housing North Kensington

with Fenella Dixon

1975-79

'This project is the product of a moment of crisis in relation to design philosophies. There appeared at the time to be no way of reconciling 'modernism' with the need for an appropriate architectural language that protected what one valued about the city and provided local authority housing that would be liked by its occupants. Tower and maisonette blocks were still being built that would simply reinforce the widely-voiced dislike of public housing.

The project starts with a presumption that London is a city of streets of houses. The house has a powerful typology which permeates the suburban nature of London. The street, the pavement, the gate post, the front garden, the

Left/right The modelling of the facade gives a constantly changing perspective to the passer-by.
Above Surrounding domestic streets.
Model An architectural self-portrait was required by the 1982 Venice Biennale. Inspired by Charles Jencks' preoccupation with finding faces in facades, more importantly it reflected the idea that houses cast a benevolent and watchful eye on the street.

front door and the bay window are all part of the varying degrees of public experience. The back garden, balcony, garden shed etc make up the private zone. Removing the house in favour of a block of flats removes all these subtle zones of occupation.

The scheme appears to consist of 12 large houses. Each house is, in fact, two narrow houses over a flat. The houses have access to the garden at the rear. At the corner between the two terraces is a small block of flats with a major bay window. The plans of the houses are angled to the street to allow the corner to be turned, maintaining privacy between adjacent dwellings. This results in a maximum contrast in scale between the double-fronted street facades and the individual stepped form of the rear elevations.

The appearance of the scheme is derived, on the one hand, from the rather curious spiky Victorian terraces that surround the site and, on the other, from the desire to include historical and more recent references in the same elevational composition. The intention is summed up by a description used of the Queen Anne style as 'eclecticism with an artistic eye'.

Streets and houses are seen in perspective. The scheme emphasises those elements that protrude from the facade and form the rhythms and modelling typical of London's domestic streets.

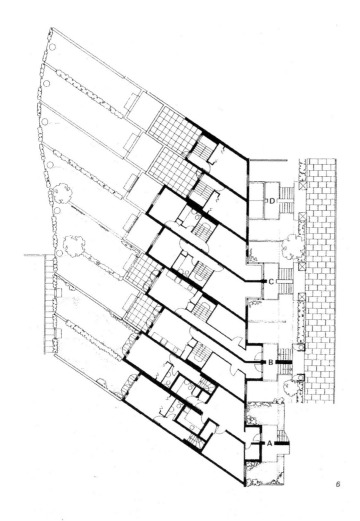

6

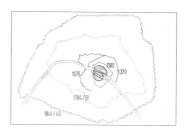

Working on the St Mark's Road project introduced a more general proposition about the special nature of London as a European city. The two plans (above, from 'History of Urban Form – Before the Industrial Revolutions' by AEJ Morris) compare the development of Paris as a pattern of concentric rings of fortification with that of London, an unconstrained urban spread incorporating the surrounding villages. The names of the villages in the Domesday Book correlate precisely with the present boroughs in London (below). Paris developed flats; London kept to houses. Paris emphasises public life in the street; London is characterised by the privacy of the house and garden. The urban quality of London is quite different from that of Paris and other European cities. For some reason, this very obvious quality has been ignored in almost all post-war public housing projects'.

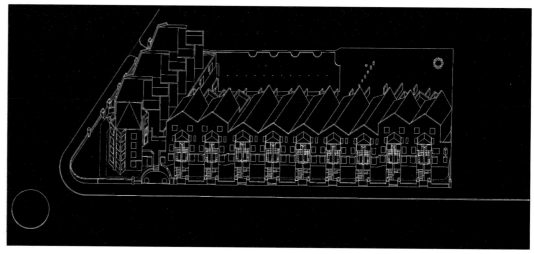

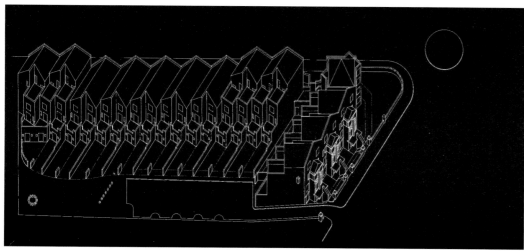

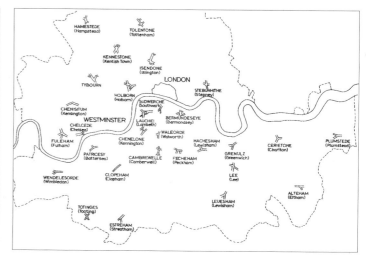

Lanark Road housing
Maida Vale

with Fenella Dixon

1981-83

'Although appearing to be villas, in fact these 'houses' each comprise seven starter flats. The elementary structure has external staircases and a bit of extra 'architecture' on the front. At this time all social housing had been stopped by the Thatcher government. Sheila Tribe, housing officer at Westminster council, decided to circumvent the moratorium. She offered the Lanark Road site free of charge to any developer who could build new housing that could be sold at a price equivalent to a local authority rent, allowing rent-payers to become first-time buyers. Michael Taylor, an enterprising young developer/builder, worked with us

to produce the villas to the stipulated cost, which was extraordinarily low – the flats were sold for £17,500. The individual units were left as unfinished shells with only a bathroom and kitchen sink installed. There was a four-year restriction on resale, after which time the flats were selling for £120,000. At first sight Tribe's idea looked like a way of solving the low-cost housing problem. However, it is evident that the enormous gains in value involved would lead to dubious speculation. The compact villa block of small flats is a type solution. The idea remains very tempting and it is surprising that no other authority has made use of it'.

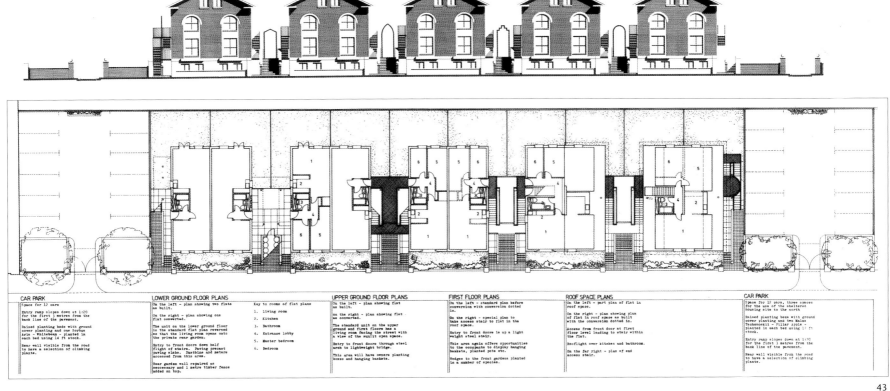

CAR PARK	LOWER GROUND FLOOR PLANS		UPPER GROUND FLOOR PLANS	FIRST FLOOR PLANS	ROOF SPACE PLANS	CAR PARK
Space for 12 cars. Entry ramp slopes down at 1:20 for the first 3 metres from the back line of the pavement. Raised planting beds with ground cover planting and one Sorbus Aria - Whitebeam - planted in each bed using 14 ft stock. Rear wall visible from the road to have a selection of climbing plants.	On the left - plan showing two flats as built. On the right - plan showing one flat converted. The unit on the lower ground floor is the standard flat plan reversed so that the living room opens onto the private rear garden. Entry to front doors down half flight of stairs. Paving precast paving slabs. Dustbins and metres accessed from this area. Rear garden wall repaired as neccessary and 1 metre timber fence added on top.	Key to rooms of flat plans 1. Living room 2. Kitchen 3. Bathroom 4. Entrance lobby 5. Master bedroom 6. Bedroom	On the left - plan showing flat as built. On the right - plan showing flat as converted. The standard unit on the upper ground and first floors has a living room facing the street with a view of the sunlit open space. Entry to front doors through steel arch to lightweight bridge. This area will have owners planting boxes and hanging baskets.	On the left - standard plan before conversion with conversion dotted in. On the right - special plan to take access stair to flat in the roof space. Entry to front doors is up a light weight steel stair. This area again offers opportunities to the occupants to display hanging baskets, planted pots etc. Hedges to the front gardens planted in a number of species.	On the left - part plan of flat in roof space. On the right - plan showing plan of flat in roof space as built with the conversion dotted in. Access from front door at first floor level leading to stair within the flat. Rooflight over kitchen and bathrooms. On the far right - plan of end access stair.	Space for 12 cars, three spaces for the use of the sheltered housing site to the north. Raised planting beds with ground cover planting and two Malus Tschonoskii - Pillar Apple - planted in each bed using 12 ft stock. Entry ramp slopes down at 1:20 for the first 3 metres from the back line of the pavement. Rear wall visible from the road to have a selection of climbing plants.

Compass Point
Isle of Dogs

with Fenella Dixon

1984-87

'Riverside housing that explores the typologies of domestic London, using elements from previous projects – terrace (St Mark's Road), square, villa (Lanark Road), mews (Ashmill Street) and crescent. Resolving the resulting collisions of style gives the kind of variety typical of a city. There is a common palette of materials but a diversity of forms'.

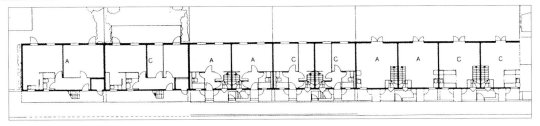

Ashmill Street housing
Maida Vale

with Fenella Dixon

1983-85

'A terrace consisting of mews houses over flats to be sold as starter units. The rendered plinth to the street elevation is cut through with tall staircase windows, providing dramatic lighting to the living spaces and clearly identifying the individual units. The tall windows are full of plants and objects that express the wish of occupants to embellish their homes'.

Coffee shop and restaurant Tate Gallery

with Fenella Dixon

1981-84

'The coffee shop and restaurant are contrasting spaces. Both are concerned with questions of illusion; both are significantly influenced by the work of John Soane; and both are in the basement of the Tate Gallery at Millbank (now Tate Britain), where there is an almost claustrophobic sense of interior. Where the coffee shop is an exercise in rescuing a thoroughly unprepossessing area, the restaurant is a homage to the romantic mural painted by the young Rex Whistler in the 1920s.

The coffee shop required the imposition of strong forms to overcome the existing sense of disorder. The layout consists of a large circular table, with its shape reflected in the ceiling. An unofficial social function of art galleries is the cultivation of spontaneous assignations and the communal table makes an ideal context in which this can happen. Mirrors are used in corner niches to emphasise the diagonals and in the ceiling as decorative elements, as in Soane's breakfast-room at Lincoln's Inn Fields.

Furniture is architectural in manner with tables, pilasters, central feature etc treated like small buildings. The adjacent small circular room is lined with faceted mirrors to expand and diffuse the perception of a pure cylindrical form.

The design of the restaurant sets out to foster the illusion of walking into the open landscape of the painting. In contrast to the coffee shop, the method here is to undermine the architectural references to a building's interior. Light is directed so as to appear to have come from the sky in the painting and the ceiling is treated as if it is unsupported, with a fragile edge 'blowing in the wind'. Mirrors suggest that the columns do not meet the ceiling and the design of the carpet evokes running water or blown grass. Light is directed either onto the painting or onto the food, with the furniture treated as a dark background'.

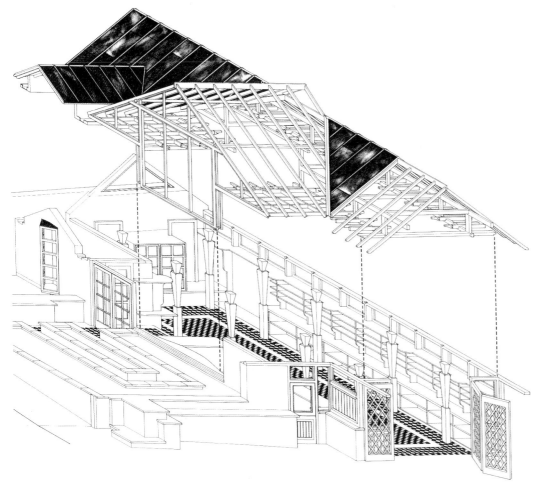

Clifton Nurseries shop Maida Vale

with Fenella Dixon

Below Pergola at The Hill Garden, designed by Thomas H Mawson at Inverforth House, London; summer house at Hidcote; site plan showing the nurseries as a hidden garden within a block of white villa houses.

1984-85

'Landlocked in the middle of a block of white neoclassical villas, Clifton Nurseries has a particular naive charm. To enter the garden centre, one has to pass between two of the villas down a narrow track, at the end of which is the delightful surprise of a mass of plants, garden furniture, greenhouse etc. The shop is treated as an addition to a cold greenhouse and takes the form of a roofed timber pergola. The materials – oak and copper – have the characteristic of becoming more interesting in appearance with the passage of time'.

Royal Opera House Covent Garden

with Fenella Dixon and Bill Jack of BDP

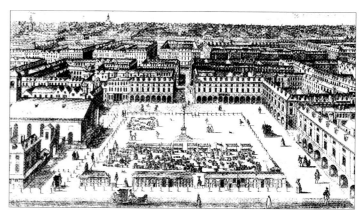

1984-89

'This period represents the first part of the 16 year saga of the Royal Opera House project – from the competition to the first planning application. The national Lottery was as yet but a gleam in the then prime minister John Major's eye. Money for the project had to be created out of the value of the site, in particular by a large office development.

From the first presentation the project has always been described as being as much about urban design as the theatre. The site occupies a whole block of Covent Garden, an area known for its diversity. The building is treated as an urban block in which the various facades are allowed to differ from one another according to location. The history of the

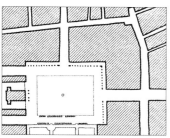

1640 St Paul's church and square with houses completed to the designs of Inigo Jones. Market stalls established on the south side c1650.

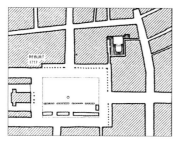

1732 First Covent Garden theatre built by Shepherd, with entrances from the corner of the square and Bow Street.

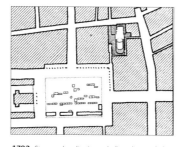

1782 Stage and auditorium rebuilt and extended, and again in 1792 with enlarged Bow Street entrance. Destroyed by fire in 1808.

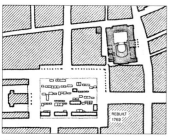

1809 New theatre built by Smirke. Fowler's central market building completed in 1830. Auditorium rebuilt as opera house in 1847.

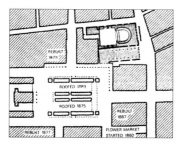

1858 After the fire of 1856, a new opera house is built by EM Barry. Floral Hall taken over by market in 1887. Extensive alterations 1899-1902.

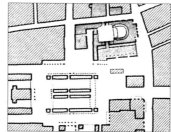

1986 Extensive reconstruction in 50s and 60s, including amphitheatre (1964). Market vacated in 1974, reopening with speciality shopping in 1980.

Left The new arcade (painting Carl Laubin); arcaded squares at Inigo Jones' Covent Garden and Livorno.
Right Preliminary sketch model dating from the first weeks of the competition; night view (Carl Laubin).
Below Part-built model illustrating the idea of developing the project as separate elements; long section showing the relationship between arcades, loggia and proposed double spiral staircase.

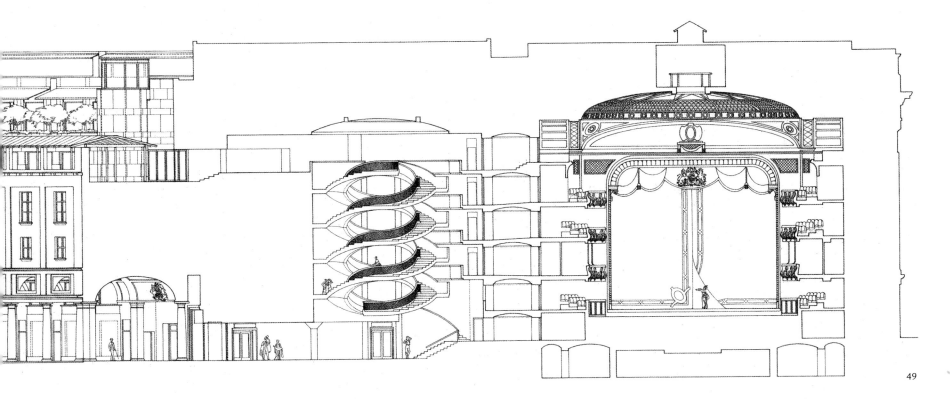

49

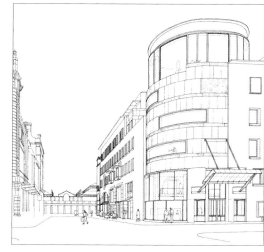

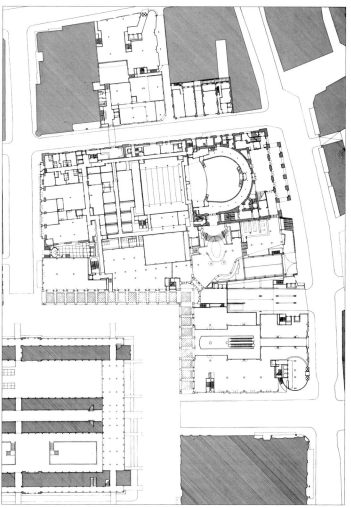

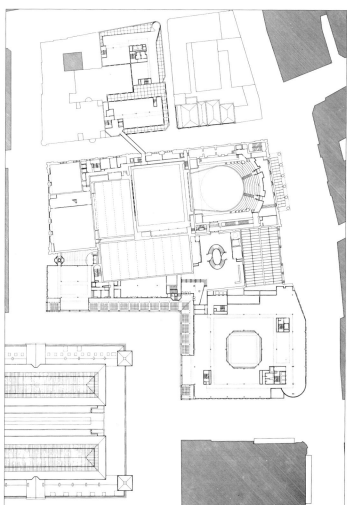

site is complex. Inigo Jones' upmarket residential square becomes a wholesale vegetable market. Fronts become backs and return to being fronts again with the re-establishment of the square as a popular meeting place.

From an early date the arcade corner served as the entrance to the theatre. In the project the arcade is recreated, using a style that has historical references but is not a direct copy of Inigo Jones. The obligation to history that exists in the square does not apply in the surrounding streets where the architectural style can be robustly contemporary. The project can thus be seen as a collection of separate buildings, a collage of styles that would be the normal contents of a Covent Garden block.

The technical heart of the project comprises the stage, flytower and surrounding areas that create a huge hidden volume in the middle of the block. The structure over these areas becomes a new 'ground level' on which are placed ballet studios and other facilities. These can have their own identity and become a 'village' of theatre activities.

New foyers were required. There was an opportunity to be part of the new popularity of Covent Garden square. A new entrance at the corner of the arcade connects the new foyers to the traditional main entrance in Bow Street. A double-spiral staircase linking all levels of the theatre removes the old social distinction between the amphitheatre and the rest

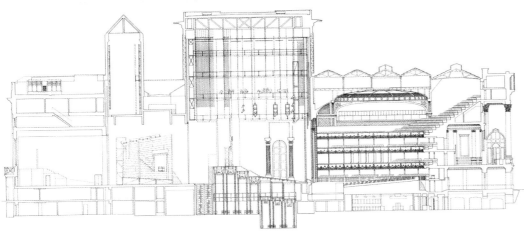

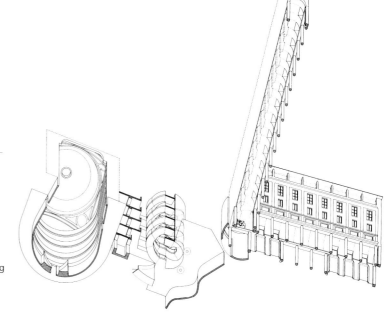

Above Section through auditorium and new stage areas; up-view axonometric of public areas.

Below King Street seen from the loggia and from the piazza (paintings Carl Laubin).

Left Ground and upper level plans; site model for first planning application; perspectives showing view down Bow Street with Floral Hall as scenery store and a major office entrance at the junction of Bow Street and Russell Street.

of the audience. At amphitheatre level there is an open loggia overlooking the square and it becomes as attractive to be in the amphitheatre as the stalls.

Money to rebuild the Opera House has always been a problem and at this stage a large office block on Russell Street and a shopping arcade were planned. It was only with the arrival of the Lottery that

the theatre gained the opportunity to occupy the whole site.

The competition was won in partnership with Bill Jack, chairman of Building Design Partnership and the first planning application was made just before the formation of Dixon Jones in 1989. This phase of the project was undertaken by Jeremy Dixon.BDP (see also p100).

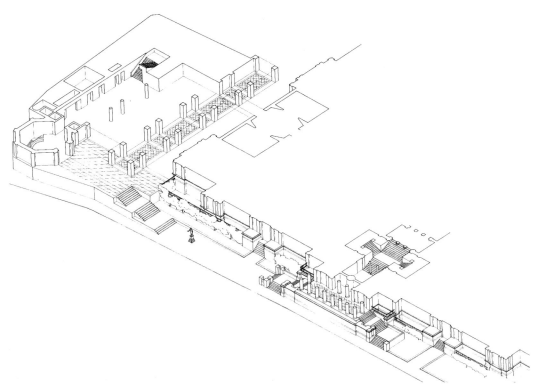

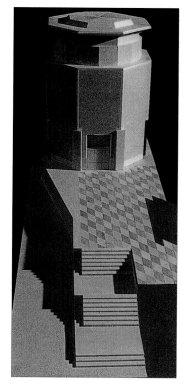

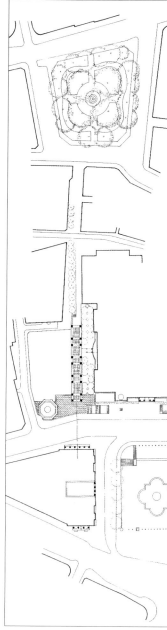

National Gallery extension competition

with Fenella Dixon

1984

'The elevation of Wilkins' National Gallery is often criticised for being too low for its length. The new wing should not extend the facade further but should be clearly identifiable as a separate building. The hitherto unexplored relationship between Leicester Square and Trafalgar Square (right) is exploited by striking a horizontal line against the slope of the land, producing a plinth and a grand flight of steps overlooking the square. The building, an octagonal 'tower of the winds' set on the plinth, acts as a counterpoint to the spire of St Martin-in-the-Fields. The National Gallery is best viewed in close perspective across the north side of Trafalgar Square and the new tower becomes part of that view'.

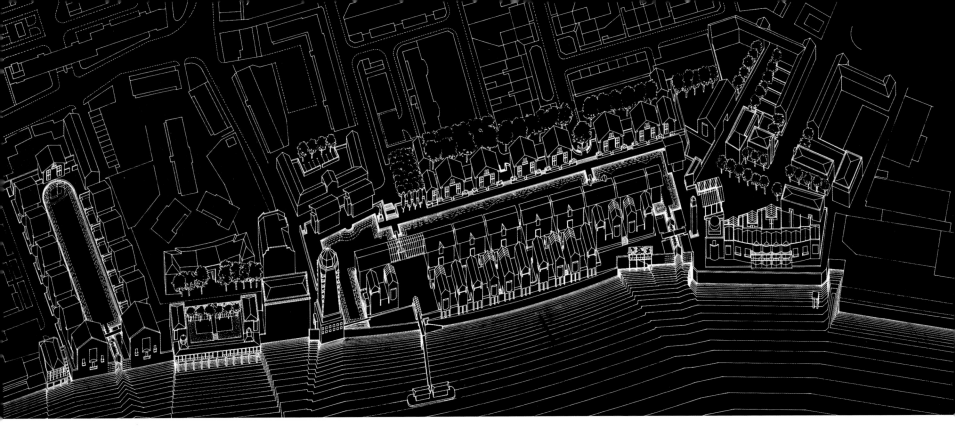

Cherry Garden Pier competition

with Fenella Dixon

1985

'The Thames Barrier can be used to stabilise the tidal movement of the river, giving adjacent sites a special relationship to the water. The project for Cherry Garden Pier in Southwark takes inspiration from the unique arrangement at Broom Water in Teddington, where two streets flank a mews that is a canal linking to the Thames. In the project houses, villas and blocks of flats exploit their relationship to the river. On the river front, exaggeratedly deep and narrow houses dramatise the relationship to the river's edge. The whole becomes a version of domestic London with the streets and squares consisting of water'.

Right Broom Water as a 'water mews'.

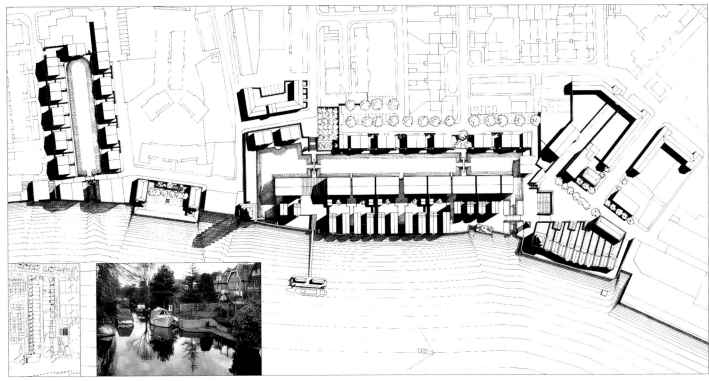

St George's Wharf
Pimlico

with Fenella Dixon

1985-87

'Domestic London is based on the house. Often large houses are divided into flats. These flats are all different from one another, reflecting the hierarchy of the levels in a house. There is variety, whereas in a normal block of flats there would be repetition. The project takes the model of a large house to create a complex interlocking set of flats that gives a wide range of character to the spaces created. The interlocking system has similarities to the early student housing project on the South Bank (see p26). The idea of a large 'house' as a block of flats was first proposed in an earlier competition scheme (1977) for the adjacent Millbank site. In both projects the relationship to the river is emphasised by building directly on top of the river wall, allowing bay windows and balconies to project dramatically over the water'.

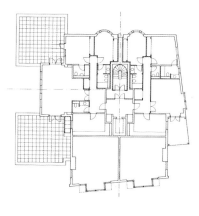

Below Diagram showing interlocking of the double-height spaces; the model shows the 1977 Millbank competition scheme.
Below left View from the river (painting Carl Laubin).

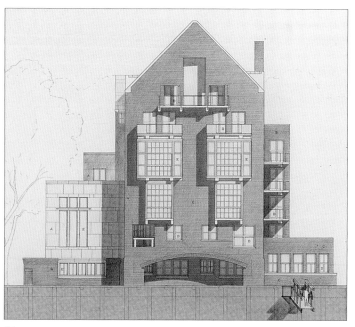

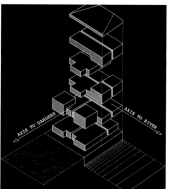

Cliveden planned village, Buckinghamshire

with Fenella Dixon

1986-91

'This site is a hidden clearing in the wonderful woods at Cliveden. A grid of green rides, like woodland 'streets', leads to one of the finest views in the country – an inland clifftop path that drops dramatically to the river Thames.

There is a long tradition of planned villages in the UK – the organic village is not the only prototype. The project uses the idea of an estate planned village as a basis for a geometrical layout of the central green, with informal secondary streets connecting back to the woodland grid of green rides. Residents are thus located by the routes to the unique moment of the special view.

The green is contained by a high wall that threads through the villas, as if they are built into the enclosure of a walled garden. In this kind of location houses have to be traditional in manner and materials – with the layout adding an unexpected quality and dimension'.

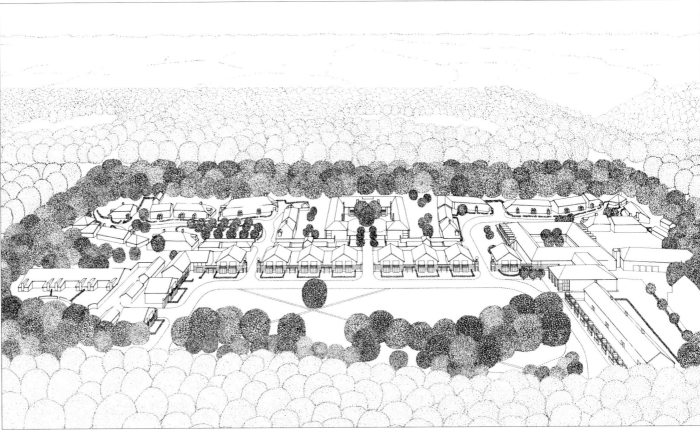

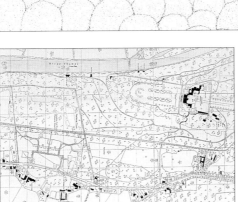

Postscript –
Henry Moore Institute
and Darwin study centre

Jeremy Dixon

'These two projects represent a moment at which the style and direction of the work changes. This is not for the first time and it might be said that the working manner is a 'style for the job' rather than a 'style for the practice'. However, I think there is another way of describing why this happens. It involves looking at how ideas come into the mind. My experience is that, rather than a linear development involving analysis and conclusions, a more mysterious and indefinable process takes place. After taking in information such as the brief and generally thinking around the topic, there is a significant and unpredictable moment, often prompted by visiting the site. At this point the brain works incredibly quickly, ranging back over previous ideas, fitting shapes to functions and projecting forward to fresh ideas. This happens in a flash, and the bones of the project both in shape and content are there as if by magic.

It represents the contribution of the intuitive aspect of the mind as a catalyst to the framework of logic. As a result the starting point for a project can have an unpredictable direction. This, allied with the wish to approach each project afresh, explains the shifts in position over time. In this world, theory follows practice; the larger theoretical idea develops from intuitive moves in the practical design process.

For example, a number of the projects are located in London, a city differently structured from other European cities. While starting with a presumption of an interest in the repair and continuity of city fabric, it was important to be finding a way of responding to this difference. The personal point of view developed – that London is a city of houses, domestic rather than monumental – came as a post-rationalisation to the process of completing the design for St Mark's Road (Rasmussen became

an obvious influence). The first moves in the design were intuitive and emotionally motivated. There was an anger about the extent of the architecturally created damage that had happened to London. At the same time the aesthetics of housing are always a problem. They inevitably become entangled with the taste and expectations of the inhabitants – there seemed to be no point in designing housing that would not be liked by its occupants. At the time of working on St Mark's, public housing had become almost universally unpopular; it was as if provocation and originality now lay in making housing likeable to its occupants. These thoughts led to re-valuing the ordinary street of semi-detached houses as the basis for the design of a project, and later to the more general understanding of the domestic typology of London.

After a number of years working on various London projects, which often involved making historical references, the Henry Moore Institute and Darwin College study centre represent the moment of a return to aspects of modernism. Here the emotional trigger was the break-up of the working relationship with Fenella, the trauma of which prompted a useful critical reassessment. She had taken me to see the minimalist exhibition at the Tate Liverpool. After all the contextual work this exhibition was like a breath of sharp cool air and profoundly influenced the approach to the Henry Moore Institute. Similarly, the Darwin project was a return to one of the classic modernist propositions, that of the direct expression of structure and materials. Over the years, the Royal Opera House project had resorted to many kinds of subterfuge in creating its elevational diversity. It seemed important to do a project, once more, in which there was a strict relationship between the concept for a building and the way in which it was to be built.

The two projects start in the individual practice and are developed and built in the joint practice. They span the change in partnership arrangements and, as a result, are both fully described later in the book (see p148 and p158).'

Edward Jones

Buildings and Projects 1963-1989

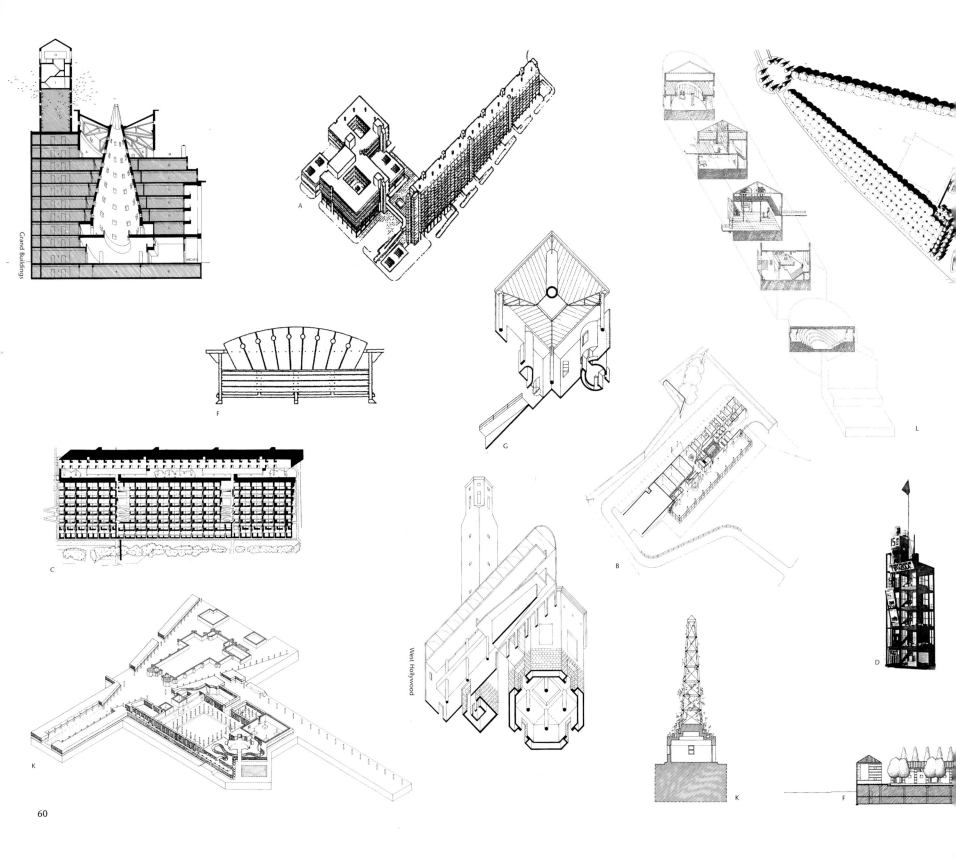

Grand Buildings

A

F

G

L

C

B

D

K

West Hollywood

K

F

60

The interior, the garden and the city – 1963-89

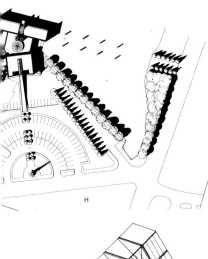

H

E

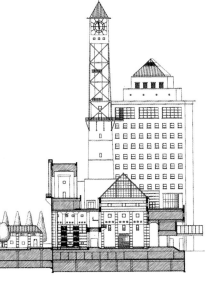

Edward Jones

For the first decade of my professional life I was an employed architect and, to make ends meet, a moonlighter draughtsman for Monica Pidgeon's Architectural Design magazine. After graduating from the Architectural Association [A] in 1963, I worked for one year for Douglas Stephen & Partners with David Wild (Watford offices), a year and a half for Alan Colquhoun and John Miller with Chris Cross (Royal Holloway College Chemistry Laboratories), five years for Frederick MacManus & Partners with Chris Cross, Mike Gold, Jeremy Dixon and Brendan Woods (Woolwich Polytechnic hostel [B]) and finally two and a half years for the Milton Keynes Development Corporation with Chris Cross, Mike Gold and Jeremy Dixon (Netherfield housing). The winning glass pyramid submission in the Northampton county offices competition of 1973 brought this ten-year period to an end. We all contributed in various ways to the second stage of Jeremy's first-stage shortlisted scheme. These could be described as the Grunt Group years – a title bestowed ambiguously, but I think affectionately, upon us by Peter Cook: 'The Grunt of the Grunt Group (generally assumed to have included Christopher Cross, Mike Gold, Jeremy and Fenella Dixon and Edward Jones at its core) was therefore giving a grunt of seriousness and aestheticism (though it had its origins in the actual throatal noise made by some of its members and their generally quiet English manner). Consistency and dedication to aims certainly did mark them off from the rest of the strip at this time'[1]. The grunt, I think, related to our continuing passion for drawing and its language and what David Wild described as 'a profound distrust of waffle to justify crumby building'[2].

This was a period of experiment, working in small groups on projects for the welfare state and often on competitions, such as the Portsdown housing [C] in 1965 with Mike Gold. Above all we could not see beyond the horizon of 'modern architecture', visiting buildings by Le Corbusier in France, Atelier 5 in Bern, Terragni in Como, and Bijvoet & Duiker in Holland. The reconstruction of the Pravda [D] and Tatlin Towers for the 1971 Hayward Gallery exhibition Art in Revolution were acts of homage.

In the course of teaching, other overlapping interests began to emerge. In 1968 I taught at the then Regent Street Polytechnic, followed by the AA (1970-72), University College Dublin (71-73) and the Royal College of Art (73-83) alongside various expeditions to Ivy League schools, particularly Cornell and the associated discovery of Colin Rowe. Within the various conversations there was a growing disquiet that modern architecture was antipathetic to the existing city and that cracks were beginning to appear in its impregnable confidence. Discussions included the reconstruction of the city within its own traditions and typologies, the architecture of the interior and its possible discontinuity from external appearances and the recovery of the garden as an extension of the built order of the plan. This was not a refutation of modern architecture but rather a counter-reformation, with an enquiry into how it might be enriched and in a sense made less restrictive. It was Michael Dennis and Klaus Herdeg who reminded us of the conundrum that 'modern architecture had produced some fine freestanding buildings but had been less successful in coming to terms with the traditional city'[3]. These topics broadly became the teaching agenda at the RCA. During this period the college was transformed from a school of interior design into a

school of architecture manqué and finally into an officially recognised graduate school of architecture, under the guidance of John Miller, Ken Frampton, Su Rogers and myself.

A number of projects predating the Canadian excursus of 1982-89 derived from teaching and can be seen in hindsight as focusing on topics of the *interior*, the *garden* and the *city*.

The Chelsea studio house [E] of 1975 encouraged thoughts about the interior as not necessarily being a logical outcome of the exterior. The modernist idea of the interpenetration of interior and exterior space was not universally useful. Here, the discontinuity between eighteenth-century residential street and the white cubist interior seemed quietly extreme and even radical. This idea of discontinuity of character was to re-emerge in Mississauga city hall.[F] Here, although there is a relatively close fit between external form and internal function, the quiet brick exterior in no way prepares you for the surprise of the civic dress inside. The Loosian interior might claim a place here. More recently our additions to the Royal Opera House and the National Portrait Gallery find a strategy of clear distinction between new and old, between consistency and collage. It is not the ambition of the one to cancel out the other; the aim is rather to enjoy the contrast between the two.

A parallel preoccupation has been the idea of the garden, or outside space, seen as an extension to the architecture rather than a foil to it. This is not to say that a strategy of contrast is unreasonable, but rather that it had become a cliché. The garden had become relegated to the roof! In our entry for the 1979 Taoiseach's House competition [G], a rather modest brief of accommodation was expanded by a series of garden rooms and promenades – Lutyens' Grey

Walls and Le Corbusier's League of Nations building were conscious references, both demonstrating how the 'field' of the house might be effectively extended. Two later Canadian competitions developed similar strategies. The Clay and Glass Museum in Waterloo, Ontario [H], established a reciprocal relationship between the gallery and a local park, between garden walks and the architectural promenade of the building. At Trinity Gardens in Toronto [J], the architectural ambitions of a small urban park are sustained exclusively by landscape elements – tree as column, hedge as wall, pergola as ceiling, and so on.

The 1981 Schinkel Archives project in Berlin [K] was an awakening to the role of urban design and underlined how conventional prescriptions of modern architecture were totally inadequate in coming to terms with the complexities of the existing city. In a sense, the 'garden' strategy found its urban equivalent here. Although the project was not large, the site and its boundaries were extensive – to the east, the Schinkel pavilion and the Charlottenburg Palace and gardens; to the south, the river Spree, marking the entrance into the nineteenth century city; and to the north, urban blocks unrepaired since wartime destruction. This ambitious setting raised many questions that were not answered either by a manipulation of the building programme or by the polemics of the modern city. We were being asked, indirectly, to comment on the form of the city and to provide for its continuity. These questions, I believe, have provided a basis for our work over the past two decades.

1 Peter Cook, 'Unbuilt England', Architecture + Urbanism no 83 (October 1977) p13.
2 David Wild, Architectural Design vol 43 no 1 (January 1973) p64.
3 Michael Dennis and Klaus Herdeg, Urban Precedents (Cornell University School of Architecture, 1974) p1.

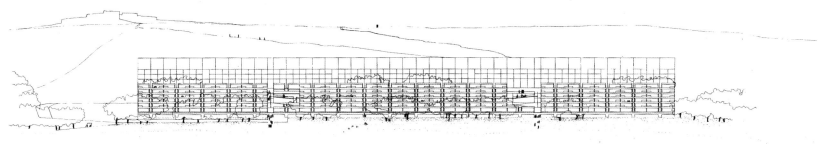

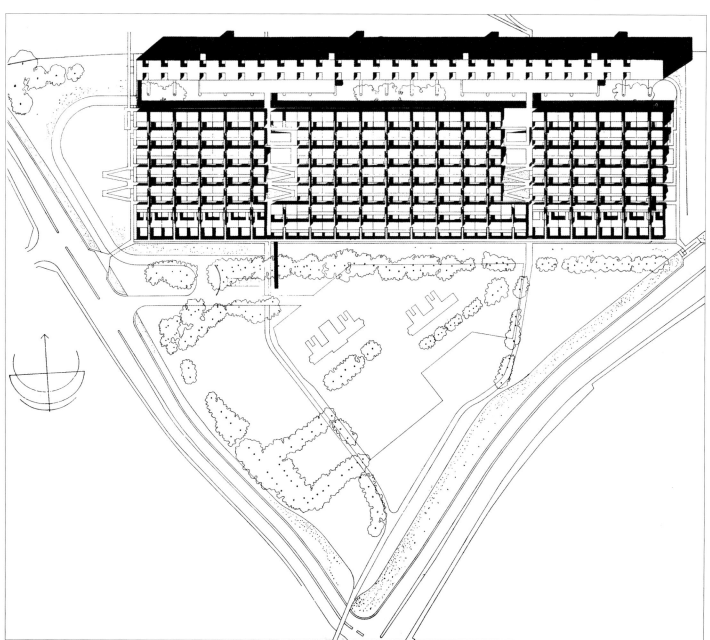

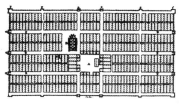

Gridded plan of the bastide town of Monpazier

Le Corbusier, Roq et Rob housing project, Cap Martin, 1948.

While teaching at Cornell in 1973, I was amused to see a very similar project built in 1970 by the late Werner Seligmann for UCD in Ithaca, New York.

Portsdown housing competition, Portsmouth

with Mike Gold

1965

This project comprises a unified group of 533 dwellings intended mainly for families. The scheme provides a direct and supervisable association with usable outdoor spaces which are protected from wind and which, with planting, would give a simple and direct movement system and ensure the continuity of the northern boundary of the town and the line of forts when seen from the coast.

There is a direct covered pedestrian link, separate from vehicular movement, between the car parking space and each front door. The vehicular system is a single, controlled cul de sac; the pedestrian system an even, non-hierarchical mesh.

Pedestrian movement up and down hill among the houses is by stairs and paths, which are covered by glazed roofs and links to the roof terraces; these lead to parking and public transport. Lateral movement is along level paths connected by ramps; these are used by parents with prams, delivery and collection trolleys, children on tricycles etc.

There is a sequence of public spaces coincident with the routes of movement and particularly the approaches to the building: paths, ramps between paths, walkways to the hill are all considered as usable outdoor areas and play spaces. Each house has a semi-private area at the lower level used mainly by children, with the possibility of easy contact between houses, and a private, shielded roof terrace with a view of the sea mainly used by adults.

All family houses have three zones: a communal area for cooking and eating; a children's area related to an outdoor space; and an adult area of living room and bedroom opening on to the second outdoor terrace.

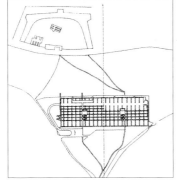

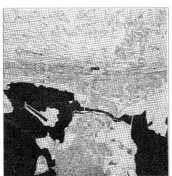

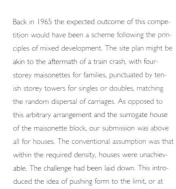

Back in 1965 the expected outcome of this competition would have been a scheme following the principles of mixed development. The site plan might be akin to the aftermath of a train crash, with four-storey maisonettes for families, punctuated by ten-ish storey towers for singles or doubles, matching the random dispersal of carriages. As opposed to this arbitrary arrangement and the surrogate house of the maisonette block, our submission was above all for houses. The conventional assumption was that within the required density, houses were unachievable. The challenge had been laid down. This introduced the idea of pushing form to the limit, or at least discovering what the limits might be. This endeavour was later to be termed 'low-rise high-density housing'. Taking an idea to near-absurdum has been a characteristic of our work, finding built expression in the housing at Netherfield, Milton Keynes. At Portsdown, the houses are formed by a tight grid of pedestrian routes, following the contours (or 'mat' as Team 10 would have it). Each house and its terrace, one behind the other, is given a view of Portsmouth harbour to the south. Le Corbusier's unbuilt housing projects at Roq et Rob in the south of France of 1948 and Atelier 5's Siedlung Halen of 1961 were obvious references for the project – a unité d'habitation laid on its side (coincidentally Le Corbusier died while we were working on this project). More distantly, the Bastide towns of fourteenth-century France might also be mentioned. The finite expression of these defended towns with their regular street grids, seemed to us at the time to be a useful antidote to the 'townscape' of the Architectural Review with its appetite for Welsh fishing villages or train derailments as inspiration for large scale housing projects.

Netherfield housing Milton Keynes

Cross Dixon Gold Jones

1971-73

Together with the 1968 Runcorn housing competition entry by Jeremy and Christopher Cross, Portsdown was an influential precursor to our joint project at Netherfield in Milton Keynes (see also p29). The finite geometry in plan, the constant roof set against the gently sloping ground, long terraces modified by the hedgerows of existing field boundaries, houses with fronts and backs, and abstraction and infinity were some of our preoccupations then.

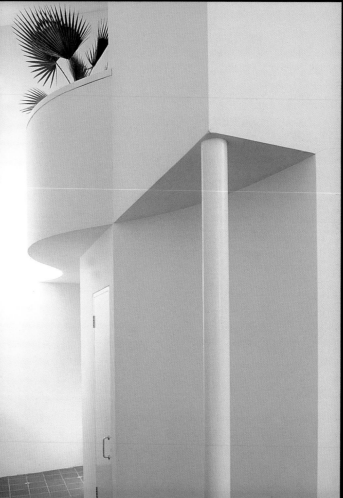

The traditional problem of weathering associated with the purist aesthetic is finally solved in Ed Jones' studio for a painter, by putting the buildings inside a gigantic roofed envelope, creating a purist microcosm, a building within a building, that is a perfect fit for this urbane and sophisticated function. The subtle layering of space, sensuous detail and controlled use of vibrant colour make this a genre masterpiece, demonstrating the luxury of simplicity promised by the purist ethos.

David Wild, 1977

Studio house
Chelsea

1975-77

'A dilapidated stables with a 50s rear extension was converted into a studio/house for a painter and a photographer. Apart from the rear extension and party walls the building was completely demolished and the street facade rebuilt with some revisions.

The clients' requirement for domestic and working spaces to co-exist while retaining their identity as rooms, together with the deep, enclosed site, contributed to the theme of a 'house within a house'. This was established spatially by transformations and layerings of the shell with new volumes and components, the latter acting as a visual code. The study, darkroom, picture store and sitting-room were formed into an entrance group on two floors, disassociated from the old shell on two sides, allowing the total volume to be read as an implied exterior space. The details to the old walls are traditional – a panelled front door, segmental brick arches, casement windows, and a double-height stained-glass south window. This window exploits the 'given' of a step in the street frontage and, with an enlarged vertical opening, allows an oblique view to the river. The details, windows, curved balcony and asymptotic junctions to the entrance building, on the other hand, use the language of modern architecture.

The studio is formed by this exterior space and uses components traditionally associated with a painter's studio, the details of which hopefully confirm the exterior allusion – north light, gallery, spiral stair, large Belfast sink, store and flue and the existing floor (a memory of the old stable) made of large exterior quality tiles. The existing rear wall to the studio contains the more private domestic functions (kitchen, bedroom/bathroom and gardens) and is connected by the gallery back to the

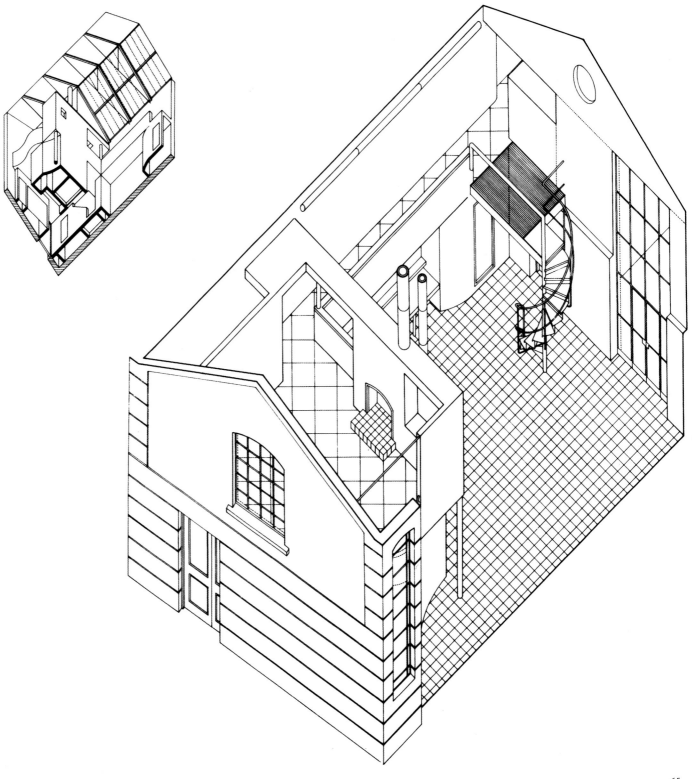

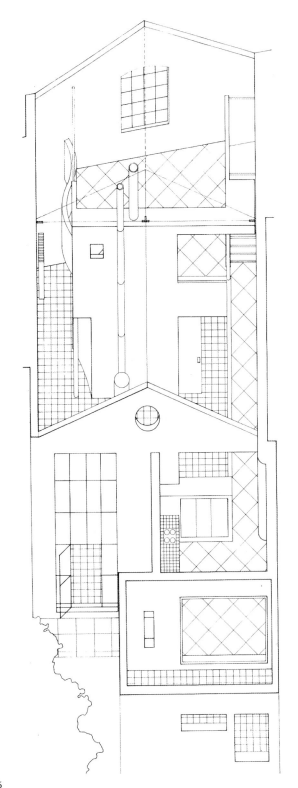

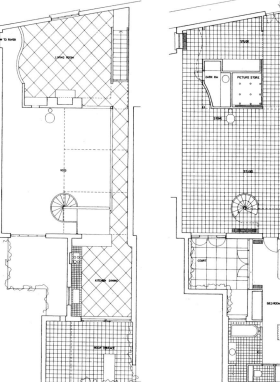

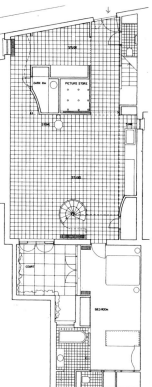

entrance group. A small garden was created adjacent to the kitchen at first floor level by removing the roof.

Whereas the ground floor is occupied by specific functions with definite physical limits, the first floor is less functionally prescribed. Spatially it explains the total site depth, with a slot of space projecting horizontally from the living-room through the higher volume of the studio to the kitchen and its courtyard and the quietude of the gardens beyond.

On the eve of my departure to Canada to build Mississauga city hall, the studio house was sold. The architect for the new owner telephoned to enquire whether I might provide drawings to facilitate its demolition. At that moment I mourned its passing and felt intensely the analogy between a building and a child. The house was demolished in 1983. As a result it has taken on a mildly dream-like status in my mind, as if it never existed.

Cranford Lane housing for the elderly, London

1974-77

'These 14 old persons' dwellings built to Parker Morris space standards for the London Borough of Hounslow are grouped around a south facing courtyard. The courtyard provides a focus for the residents in an otherwise continuous suburbia. The project was conceived at the height of the profession's enthusiasm for the random and the picturesque in local authority housing layouts (it also developed ideas from a competition entry, designed in 1971 with Mike Gold, for housing elderly people in Haringey.) It might be seen therefore as taking up a mildly polemical position. As an investigation into the courtyard and its livable qualities, it set out to demonstrate a series of elementary oppositions – public and private, front and back, stucco and brick, big room versus small rooms and so on. For some this was found to be too 'institutional' and for others maybe too nostalgic – Derek Walker described me as a 'well-preserved 65 year old' (following his assessment of the project for an AD award in 1974). I have occasionally mused on this comment (post-Netherfield) as to whether it was a joke at the architect's expense or a more serious comment on and about the character of the white architecture of the 1930s (and its reappearance here), a period for which I had and have much affection'.

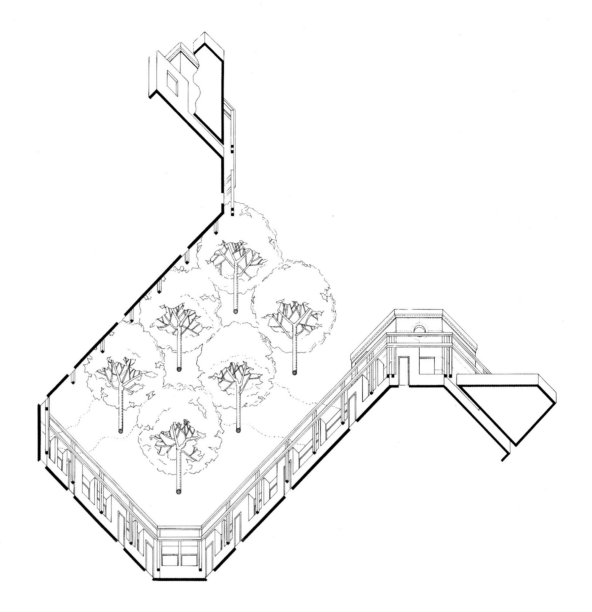

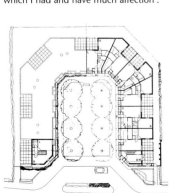

SWIMMING POOL   SECTION B-B   RECEPTION ROOMS   COMMEMORATIVE GARDEN

COMMEMORATIVE GARDEN   ENTRANCE TO RECEPTIONS   SECTION C-C   MAZE

Taoiseach's House competition, Dublin

with Margot Griffin and Russell Bevington

1979

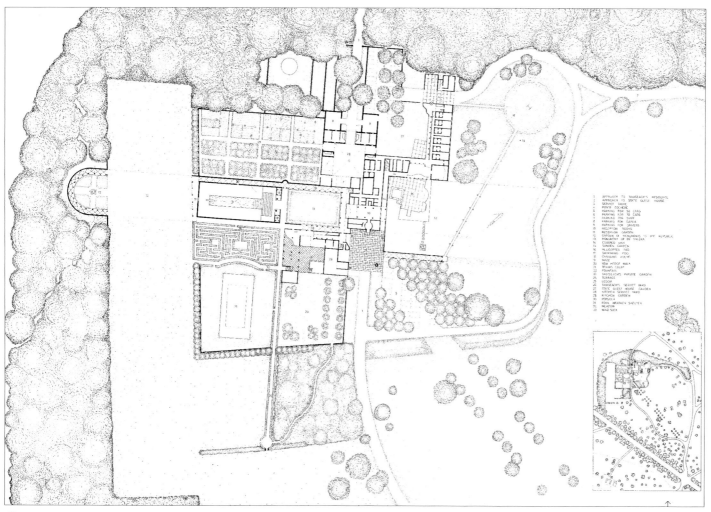

'The competition brief called for two independent buildings – a private residence for the Irish prime minister and a state guest house. These would replace the papal nunciate's residence in Phoenix Park and, with the existing residences for the Irish president and the American ambassador, would constitute three houses of national importance in the park.

Our proposal combines the separate structures required in the brief into the idea of a single symbolic 'house'. This involves a strategy of courts, walled gardens and pergolas, which draw together the private residence, banqueting house and guest house into a composite whole. The east facade of the banqueting hall expresses the public 'front' overlooking the lake, with its curved entablature representing the vaulted ceiling of the formal dining-room behind. The guest house wing is symmetrised by a grove of trees on the other side of the main axis.

The planning device of court and garden (seen for example in the Villa Giulia in Rome – opposite above) allows for a more generous expression and unfolding of the brief, introducing the ideas of the 'outside room' and the 'promenade architecturale'. Both these seemed highly appropriate to the 'walking and talking' and the realpolitik involved with visiting heads of state, with the maze providing the opportunity of losing unwanted guests!'

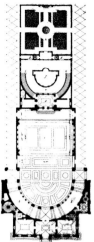

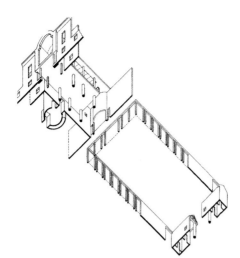

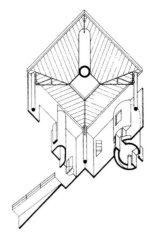

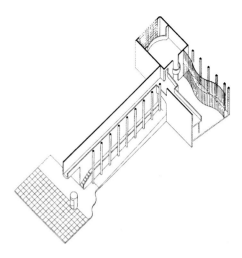

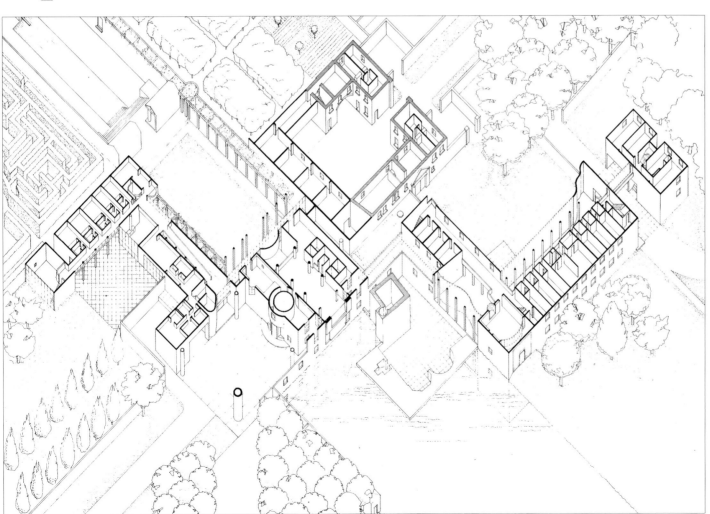

This was my first competition submission with Margot Griffin, who continued as a collaborator during the Canadian interlude. The competition confirmed the growing realisation that the jury, with its preferences and personal prejudices, was important to the outcome of a competition. We knew our submission would not find favour with Aldo van Eyck. The winning scheme by Eldred Evans and David Shalev was not built. The then prime minister, Charles Haughey, lived in a fine Palladian mansion and had no intention of moving to Phoenix Park! It would have been intriguing, in hindsight, if of all the entries, the project by Rem Koolhaas and Elia Zenghelis had been built.

I remember the relief on Jim Stirling's face when he was told that we had not won, which meant that Russell Bevington could remain in his office.

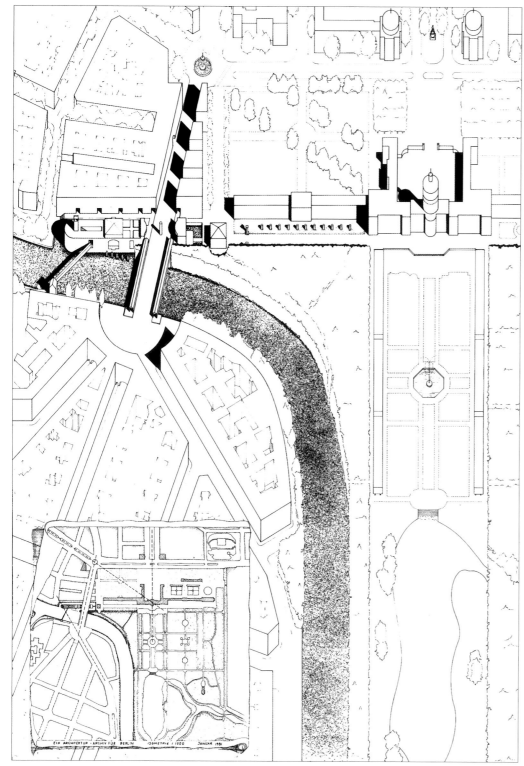

Schinkel Archives competition, Berlin

with Margot Griffin

1981

'In contrast to the monumental spaces of Rome and Paris, Berlin is a city of monumental objects. The site, adjacent to the Charlottenburg Palace and gardens, relates to a series of historic axes, prompting the perennial distinction between monument and city fabric. The brief required an architectural archive, gallery, theatre and an 'architectural' garden, to serve as a memorial to Schinkel and act as a live museum for Berlin. Influences on the design included the lakes and islands of Potsdam, the narrowness of the river Spree, the Berlin tradition of covered bridges and the church at Glienicke, apparently floating in the lake.

The building forms an island, a bridgehead, a 'floating' building and the termination of the Charlottenburg axis, bestowing significant urban design possibilities. The building is intentionally simple and elemental. Five obvious and interrelated architectural ideas are proposed along the axis: a portico (entrance to theatre and palace grounds); a circular theatre; a square pavilion (museum); a winter garden (cafe/exhibitions); and a linear and cellular building (archives). The building and the architectural garden are combined as: water garden (a space between the Schinkel pavilion and the archive); winter garden (forming the referential space between museum and archive); and roof garden, approached by a grand public staircase. The belvedere and roof garden give visual connections to the district. Our proposals included reconstruction of the adjacent city blocks, reworking the Berlin courtyard typology, and consolidation of the west side of Luisenplatz with four villas.

The new road is straightened as an arcaded civic space, cutting the frontal east-west space of the palace and thereby identifying the entrances to the archive and the palace grounds respectively. The covered bridge and crescent emphasise the civic nature of the road, giving it a point de vue. The archives building forms the southern bridgehead to the river, marking a rhetorical entrance to the nineteenth-century city'.

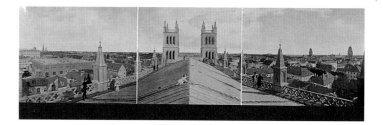

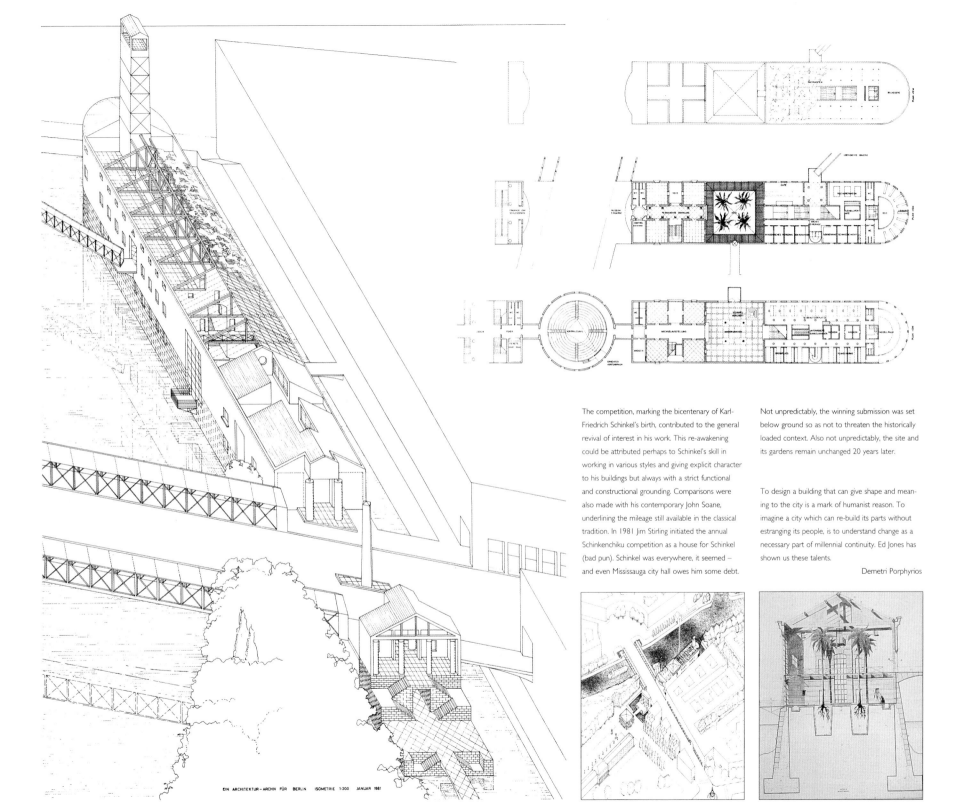

The competition, marking the bicentenary of Karl-Friedrich Schinkel's birth, contributed to the general revival of interest in his work. This re-awakening could be attributed perhaps to Schinkel's skill in working in various styles and giving explicit character to his buildings but always with a strict functional and constructional grounding. Comparisons were also made with his contemporary John Soane, underlining the mileage still available in the classical tradition. In 1981 Jim Stirling initiated the annual Schinkenchiku competition as a house for Schinkel (bad pun). Schinkel was everywhere, it seemed — and even Mississauga city hall owes him some debt.

Not unpredictably, the winning submission was set below ground so as not to threaten the historically loaded context. Also not unpredictably, the site and its gardens remain unchanged 20 years later.

To design a building that can give shape and meaning to the city is a mark of humanist reason. To imagine a city which can re-build its parts without estranging its people, is to understand change as a necessary part of millennial continuity. Ed Jones has shown us these talents.

Demetri Porphyrios

EIN ARCHITEKTUR – ARCHIV FÜR BERLIN   ISOMETRIE 1:200   JANUAR 1981

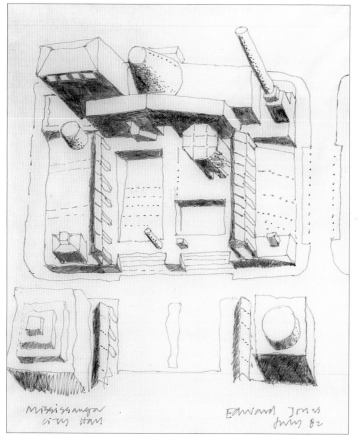

Mississauga
city hall

Edward Jones
July 82

Mississauga city hall
Ontario

1982-87

'Mississauga, a rapidly expanding suburb of Toronto, exemplifies Melvin Weber's characterisation of the north American suburb as the 'nowhere public realm'. The site for the new civic centre was, not untypically, on the edge of a large parking lot serving a very large regional shopping centre, which in turn was positioned in a superblock ringed by 12-storey office towers (the plan for the area was by Llewellyn Davies, the original planners of Milton Keynes!). The brief called for 37,820 square metres of detailed accommodation, including a parking garage for 1,000 cars. A set of common-sense urban design guidelines was included, the most particular of which was reference to the Toronto tradition of public buildings facing south to Lake Ontario and, by extension, to the world beyond.

The city hall is composed on a plinth 1.5 metres above the ground, thereby distinguishing it from the otherwise featureless and flat surrounding area. The civic square is formed by the south-facing facade and is defined on its east

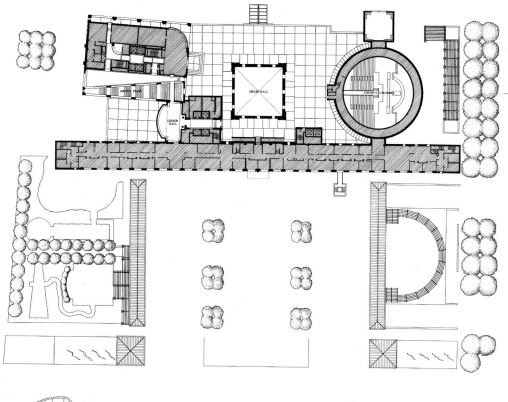

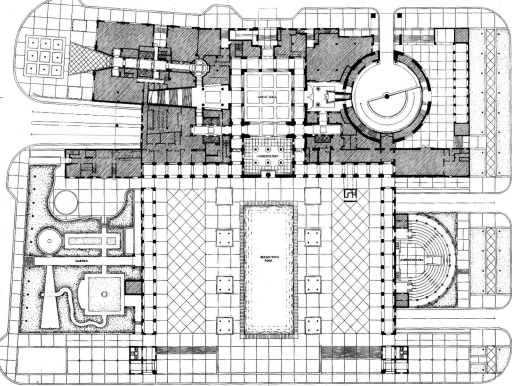

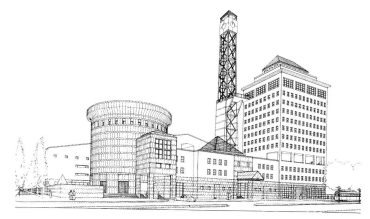

and west sides by open arcades. The arcades are terminated by pavilions and ramps which, with the plinth, represent the presence of the underground car park. The principal facade (a thin building 10 metres wide) is scaled to control a symmetrical and civic foreground with its gardens, amphitheatre and fountains. More informally, elements are grouped behind – the cylindrical council chamber, the pyramid of the great hall, the departmental office tower (staff canteen on the top floor) and the

clock tower. To the east the offices of the mayor and the elected officials are grouped around the council chamber and to the west are the offices of the city hall staff and their departments. Central to the composition is the great hall.

The building exterior is clad in brick with precast concrete bands and dressings, painted metal attachments and copper clad roofs. By way of contrast the public interiors use a strong polychromy of Uruguayan black granite and Verdi Alpi and Verona Rossa marble.

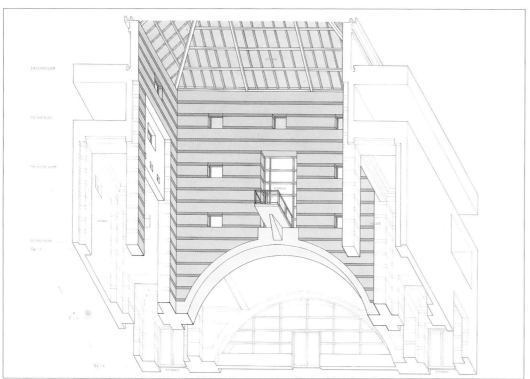

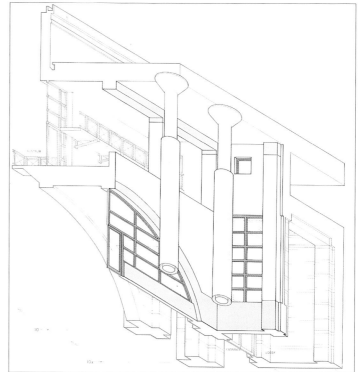

Dear Ed,

Thanks for your nice card. I hope your opening will not end there and that the queen mother will bring you back singing your praise. So do wear a tie and polish your shoes, that will as you know be more important to her than your glorious buildings

All the best

Leon

Above The model en route through Toronto.
Below Oliver, Jemima and Quentin Jones on the Mississauga Bench, 1987.
Left Philatelic wishes from Leon Krier.

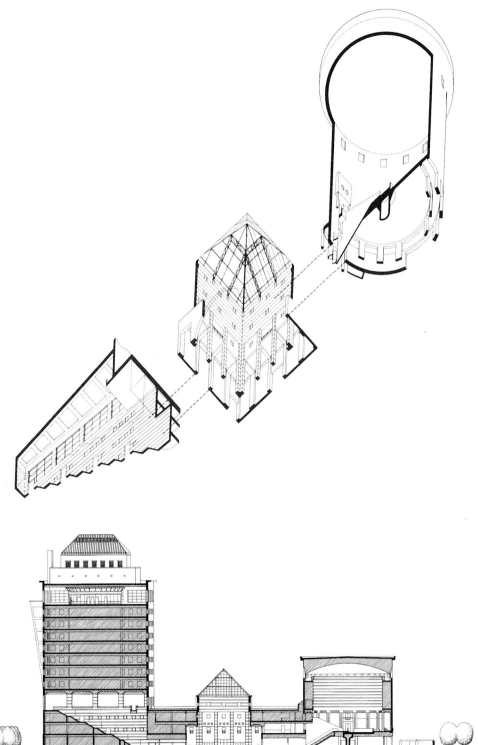

The principal organisation of the interior is bi-axial. The main entrances are arranged in a north-south direction and in the other direction either side of the great hall are the council chamber and great stair. These three public interiors establish the building's essential armature – a valley in section, anthropocentric in plan. The project was entitled 'a building for two seasons'. To this end the exterior civic square to the south and the interior great hall were understood as having seasonal equivalence – an outside room in summer and an interior piazzetta in winter.

Approached processionally by escalator from the great hall, the council chamber is the principal room of the city, 30 metres in diameter and 20 metres tall. The democratic circular form is naturally but invisibly lit from high clerestory windows. The saucer dome is painted to represent the universe with fibre optic lights representing the stars.

The great stair relates the lower three floors of the building to the ground. Within these floors are the departments most visited by the public and, not unlike the great hall, the staircase acts as a referential space giving identity to the occupants of the interior spaces. All three public voids allow daylight to penetrate and invigorate the otherwise deep floor plate'.

If Mississauga city hall received a mixed critical reception in Canada, the Hollywood film industry took it to its heart. Toronto became known as the Hollywood of the north and, because of advantageous tax arrangements, became an attractive venue for the production of American movies. The interiors of the city hall appeared in a number of films including Switching Channels (with Burt Reynolds and Kathleen Turner) but most memorably in Dead Ringers (Twentieth Century Fox), by the Canadian director David Cronenberg with Jeremy Irons. The interiors have formed sets as diverse as a hotel, a palais de justice and a headquarters for a learned society, confirming their character as civic and institutional. In this still from Dead Ringers, actor Jeremy Irons is falling drunkenly down the grand stair to join his twin brother for cocktails in the restaurant of the Grand Hotel – in reality, the city hall foyer.

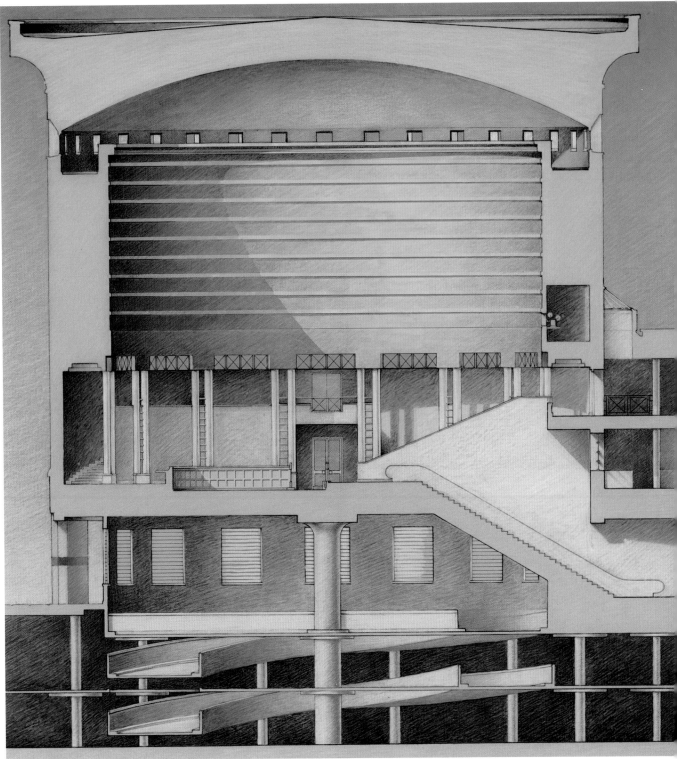

Trinity Gardens competition, Toronto

1983

'The scheme seeks to reverse the contemporary tendency for civic spaces to be ill-defined and vacuous. To this end Trinity Gardens is envisaged as a series of external 'rooms'. The central garden is like a grand salon, with the pergola as its long gallery and the circular garden its rotunda or entrance hall. The allusion to rooms is reinforced by an architectural code: hedge and trellis as wall; pergola and tree canopy as ceiling; lawn as floor or carpet. The 'greenhouse', of course, makes a more literal enclosure.

There are two spatial sequences. First, the principal visual axis. This runs north-south via the ramps from Trinity Church to the rotunda and is bisected by a minor east axis from James Street. The connections are clear although, in the words of Capability Brown, 'the feet may not follow the path the eye has travelled'. Second, there is a more secret and leisurely promenade connecting all the secondary spaces. This begins from Trinity Church, continues along the pergola, descends into the serpentine maze (with the head of the visitor disappearing unexpectedly into the verdure) and continues through to the Palm House.

Trinity Gardens offers an opportunity to make a memorial to our discarded past. The discovery of four giant Ionic capitals on the site provided our initial inspiration. These fragments probably originate from Charles Cobb's Registry of Deeds and Land Titles building, demolished in 1964 to make way for the new city hall. Together with other salvaged relics, these would be placed within the gardens, both as a memory of Toronto's architectural past and to confirm the classical composition of the Garden and its narrative'.

The plan underlines what our proposal is not, by a comparison with what exists (or what is proposed by the City of Toronto) and as a result we hope to clarify what it is. If we understand Nathan Phillips Square to be a square and St James Park to be a park, then the residual space around Trinity Church is certainly neither a square nor a park. Its more modest dimensions and its situation within the interior of the urban block characterise it as a garden. In opposition to the commercial bustle of Eaton's arcade, the civic agora of Nathan Phillips Square and the day of parades down University Avenue, Trinity Gardens suggests itself as a quiet and somewhat remote enclave. As the connection from Bay to Yonge Streets is a major pedestrian route, we propose that it should be distinct and separate from the Gardens.

Competition entry

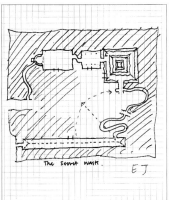

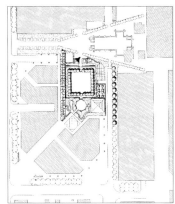

The original competition was entitled 'Trinity Park Square'. As this seemed to us to be a confusion of type, we included this rather didactic statement accompanied by a plan of the city in our submission. Apart from clarifying categories of public space, this became a way into the project.

EJ

Jones and Kirkland take an extreme exception to the disarray of the city by straightforwardly furnishing an explicit contrast with the discordant situation. Unabashedly critical of its surroundings, the garden appeals for a return to the design of civic spaces as opportunities for calm rather than chaos, intimacy rather than alienation, order rather than dissonance.

Michael Djordjevitch and Jim Saywell

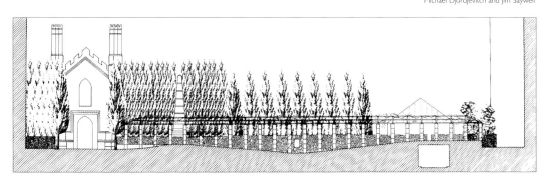

A. LOADING DOCK
B. SHOPS / STORAGE
C. CAR PARKING
D. SUBWAY TO TRAFALGAR SQ.
E. SHOPS
F. OFFICE SUITES
G. BANK
H. BANK STRONG ROOM
I. ESCALATOR
J. OFFICE LOBBY
K. KITCHEN
L. RESTAURANT
M. TERRACE
N. BOARD ROOM

Grand Buildings
competition, London

1985

'The upper floors of Grand Buildings happen to close Aston Webb's 'via triumphalis' from Buckingham Palace to Trafalgar Square. The scheme emphasises this alignment, proposing a crown to Admiralty Arch when seen in perspective from the midpoint of the Mall.

The principal entry facade to Grand Buildings addresses the Strand and Trafalgar Square. The loggia presents a face to the square (as do the porticos of

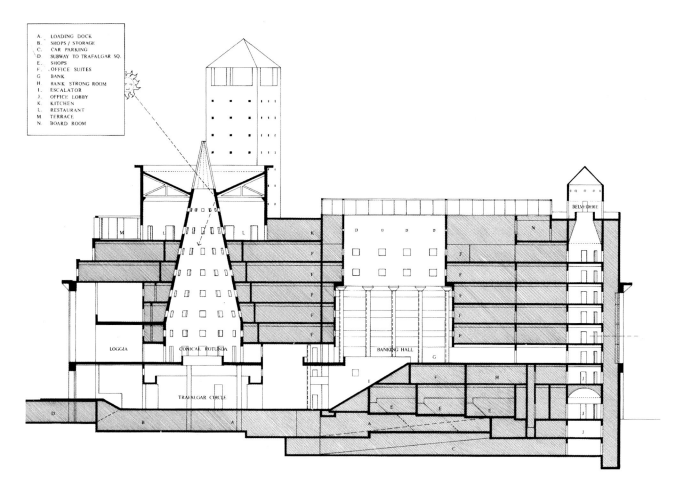

LOGGIA   CONICAL ROTUNDA   BANKING HALL

TRAFALGAR CIRCLE

BELVEDERE

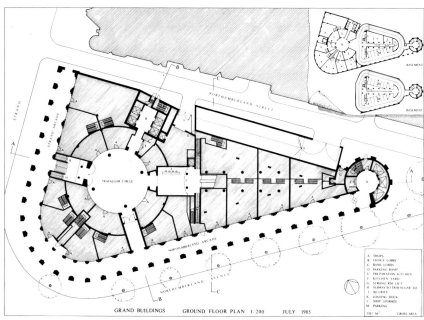

GRAND BUILDINGS   GROUND FLOOR PLAN 1:200   JULY 1985

A. SHOPS
B. OFFICE LOBBY
C. BANK LOBBY
D. PARKING RAMP
E. PREPARATION KITCHEN
F. KITCHEN YARD
G. STRONG RM LO. I
H. SUBWAY TO TRAFALGAR SQ.
I. SECURITY
K. LOADING DOCK
L. SHOP STORAGE
M. PARKING

2782 M² GROSS AREA

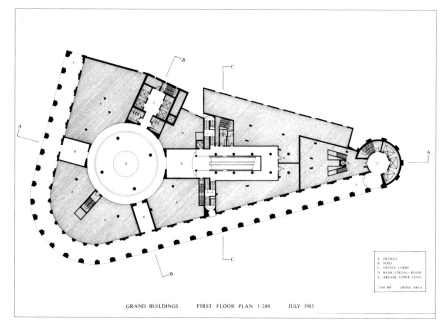

GRAND BUILDINGS   FIRST FLOOR PLAN 1:200   JULY 1985

A. OFFICES
B. VOID
C. OFFICE LOBBY
D. BANK STRONG ROOM
E. ARCADE UPPER LEVEL

2760 M² GROSS AREA

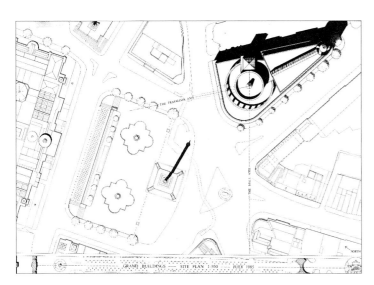

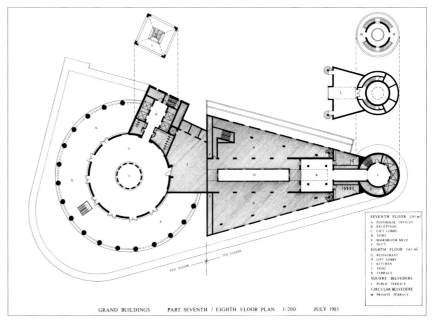

its neighbours) and honours the state route along the Strand. Its balconies form a collective place of assembly for spectators, its facade decorated with swags for such occasions.

The tower and rooftop restaurant allow a series of public terraces overlooking central London. The shaft of the tower incorporates a pigeon loft and from its belvedere it might be possible to have a conversation with the square's most celebrated resident.

The shopping circle is connected to the arcades and Underground system and forms the principal place of arrival from Trafalgar Square. The conical space of the office lobby rises above the shopping circle, presiding over it on the principal second floor.

The triangular banking hall, rising through four stories, gives further natural light to the deep building section as well as volumetric identity to the small office suites above. With a contemporary fashion for transforming bank interiors into European-style cafes, this space in the fullness of time might have had a similar future'.

This was an important competition for London, not least because it attracted the largest recorded entry for any UK competition. It was an opportunity to replace an urban block on Trafalgar Square and address the paradox of a modern yet background building. But to the dismay of competitors, a replica of the Victorian original was chosen as winner, and subsequently built. Either there was a loss of nerve by the assessors or, in the context of trouble across the square with the National Gallery extension, a new and pernicious orthodoxy was at large in the capital.

Many of London's most successful buildings are relatively quiet on the exterior and surprisingly dramatic inside. Soane's Bank of England and his house in Lincoln's Inn Fields come to mind. Here we have 'simple city, complex house' as against the 'complex city, simple house' of the European city. And so we had a go at a 'matter of fact' urban architecture – with a front and back, an arcaded base, a rooftop loggia, and above all, a dramatic and unexpected sequence of interior spaces. By good fortune, we were to return later to Trafalgar Square at the National Portrait Gallery, which also has an unexpected and dramatic interior, a roof-top loggia and an equally spectacular view of London.

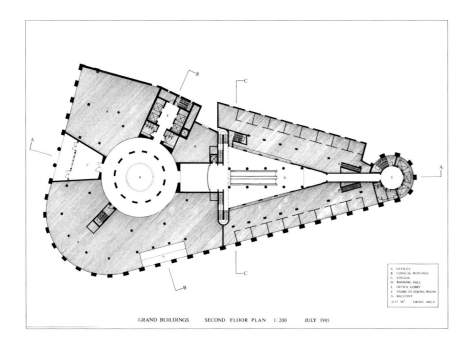

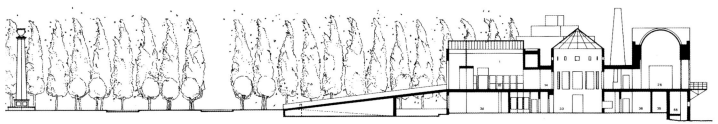

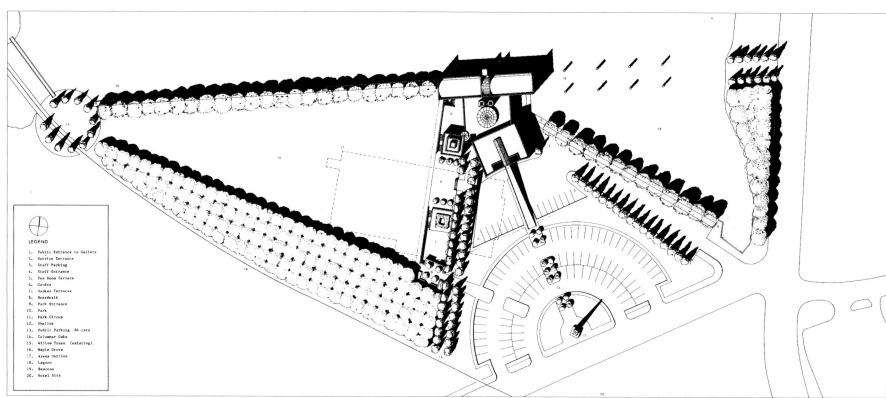

LEGEND

1. Public Entrance to Gallery
2. Service Entrance
3. Staff Parking
4. Staff Entrance
5. Tea Room Terrace
6. Garden
7. Sunken Terraces
8. Boardwalk
9. Park Entrance
10. Park
11. Park Circus
12. Obelisk
13. Public Parking 84 cars
14. Columnar Oaks
15. Willow Trees (existing)
16. Maple Grove
17. Arena Outline
18. Lagoon
19. Beacons
20. Hotel Site

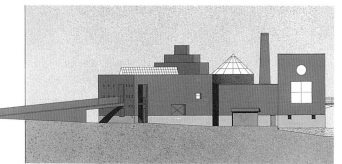

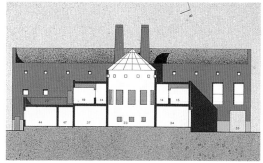

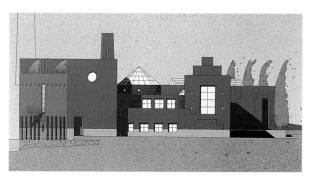

Clay and Glass Museum competition, Ontario

1986

'A small park opposite a museum dedicated to the memory of the early production of Seagram's whisky, in a city called Berlin before it was rechristened Kitchener Waterloo at the outbreak of the first world war: was the improbable site for this invited competition for the National Gallery of Clay and Glass.

The building acts as an entrance to Waterloo Park and forms a small part of the promenade through it. The crescent of cars accepts the inevitability and visibility of the parking lot as part of this sequence. The ramp and curved entrance screen form the entrance to the museum – lines of trees partially conceal the rest of the building, thereby emphasising the entrance. Although the volume of accommodation is small, the building with its entourage of landscape elements extends its influence into the park. For example the building alignment to the lakeshore is extended and reinforced by a boardwalk, an avenue of trees, beacons in the water and a cut in the landscape. In the opposite direction the cafe terrace looks to the triangular garden leading into Waterloo Park and beyond to the university campus.

The public galleries are at first-floor level, raised above a plinth of back-of-house areas. The perspective shows the 'theatre' of the glass-blowing studio, a technique which has not changed since Diderot's depiction in his eighteenth-century encyclopedia. The studio forms a focus to the plan and its circular form allows for the rotation of the galleries and the entrance pavilion to take up their respective orientations.

The initial response was to make a colourful pavilion in the park, its hard-glazed terracotta tiles and crystalline areas of glass reflecting in a literal way the building programme and dramatising the platonic forms of the architecture. The polychromy of the gallery would contrast vividly with the long and white Canadian winters and the reflective quality of Silver Lake.'

Jones and Kirkland's design is founded on the 'museum as a place of popular entertainment', to be experienced as a 'theatrical' place invoking memories of other studios and museum rooms. The sense of place and the role of art in the museum are framed in a collective experience.

Jury report

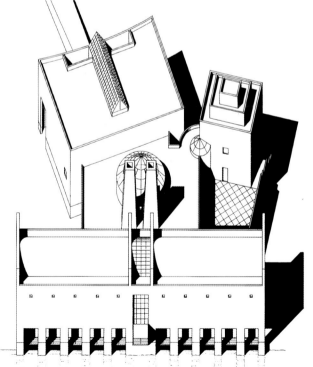

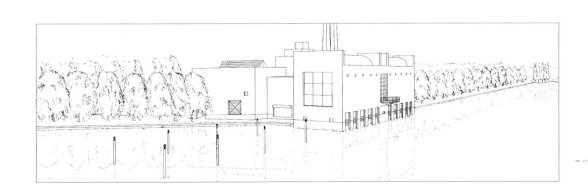

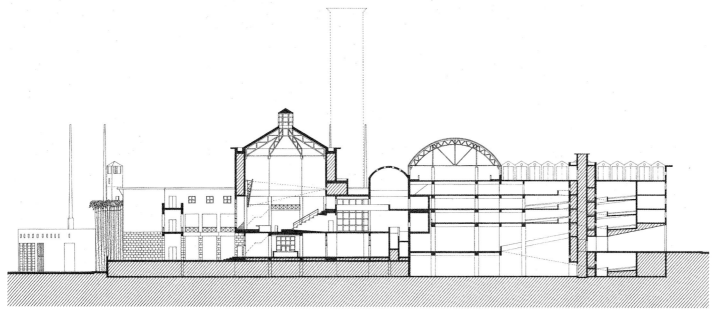

West Hollywood civic centre competition

1987

'The site is on San Vicente Boulevard in the city of West Hollywood, California, opposite Cesar Pelli's famous Blue Whale. The promoters sent a video of the site to all competitors and as a result this was the first project in which I did not visit the site before starting the design. The chairman of the jury was the late Charles Moore.

The competition brief called for a 5,300 square metre city hall, county library, 500-seat theatre, fire station and 1.6 hectare park. There was also a strict stipulation that basements should be avoided due to a high water table and so the public parking garage had to be situated above-grade.

The parking garage for 1,000 cars is a multi-storey stoa forming the informal boundary of the site – the most dominant building in the composition. Set against this wall are disposed the various elements of the brief, with independent and direct pedestrian access from San Vicente Boulevard and direct access from the parking garage behind. In the opposite direction a sequence of courts, gardens, passages and an arcade act as an entourage to the civic centre as a whole. Reflecting perhaps a northern European's preconception of California and the pursuit of the body beautiful, a 'promenade athlétique' is incorporated into the project – a netted tennis court enclosure is positioned on the roof of the garage defined by a running track. Above the circular parking ramp is a swimming pool (Le Corbusier's perspective of the Maison de Monsieur X in Brussels of 1929 comes to mind, with people diving apparently into nowhere!) and below, the sociability of sunbathing terraces, a baseball diamond and an outdoor cinema. It was a clear intention that the liberal and extrovert street life of West Hollywood would find a place in the project'.

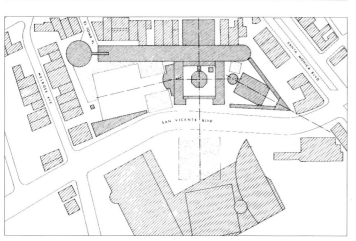

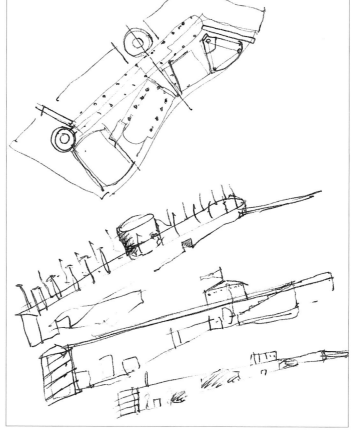

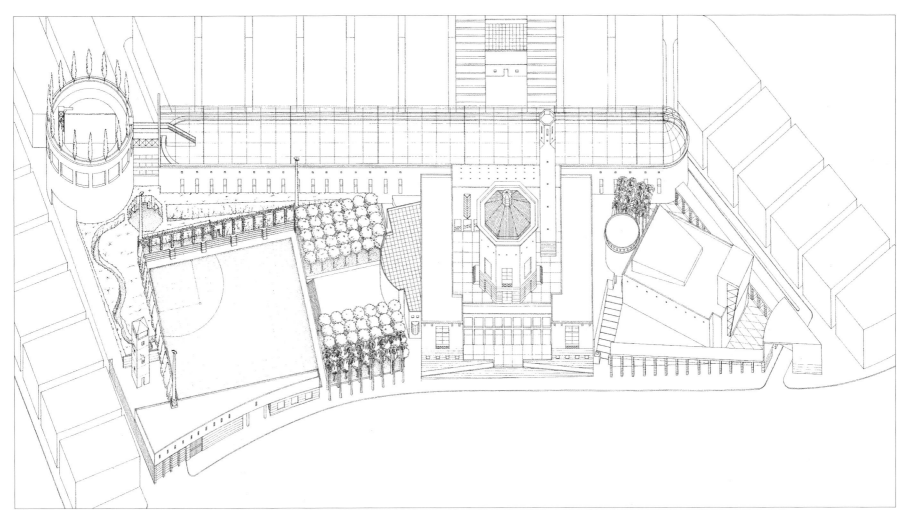

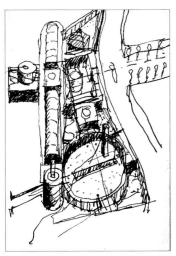

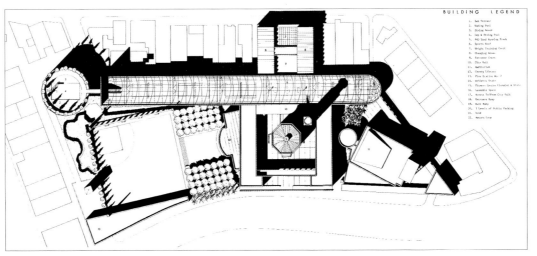

The role of chance or the accidental has a particular place in the Canadian works. These public projects employ, to a greater or lesser extent, what I think of as 'bumpy planning'. In the Clay and Glass Museum, the informal assemblage is generated by forces outside – the particular alignment of the lake, the angle of approach and so on. The elements that form these collages are either fragments or whole pieces of building with their own distinct typologies. The circular council chamber, the square atrium, and the trapezoidal staircase of Mississauga is an example: a composite whole is formed which avoids the spectre of the single and controlling geometry. Here again an overall geometric order is resisted in favour of an apparent informality. This is generated by the gentle curve of the street frontage and drawn together in a single composition by the large scale stoa of car parking behind.

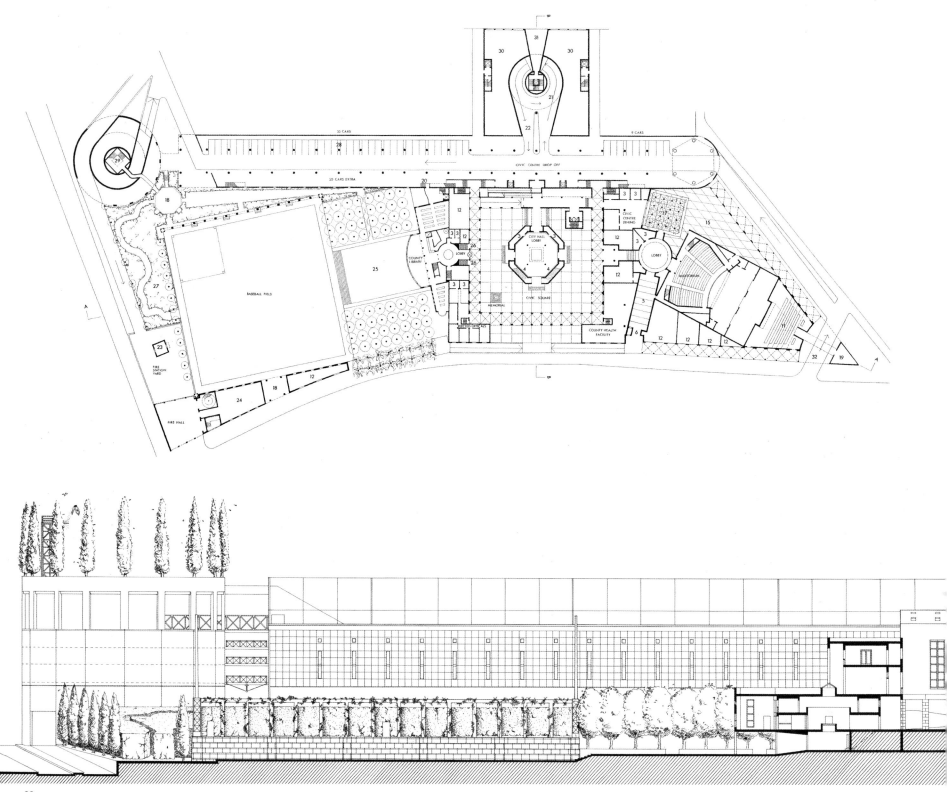

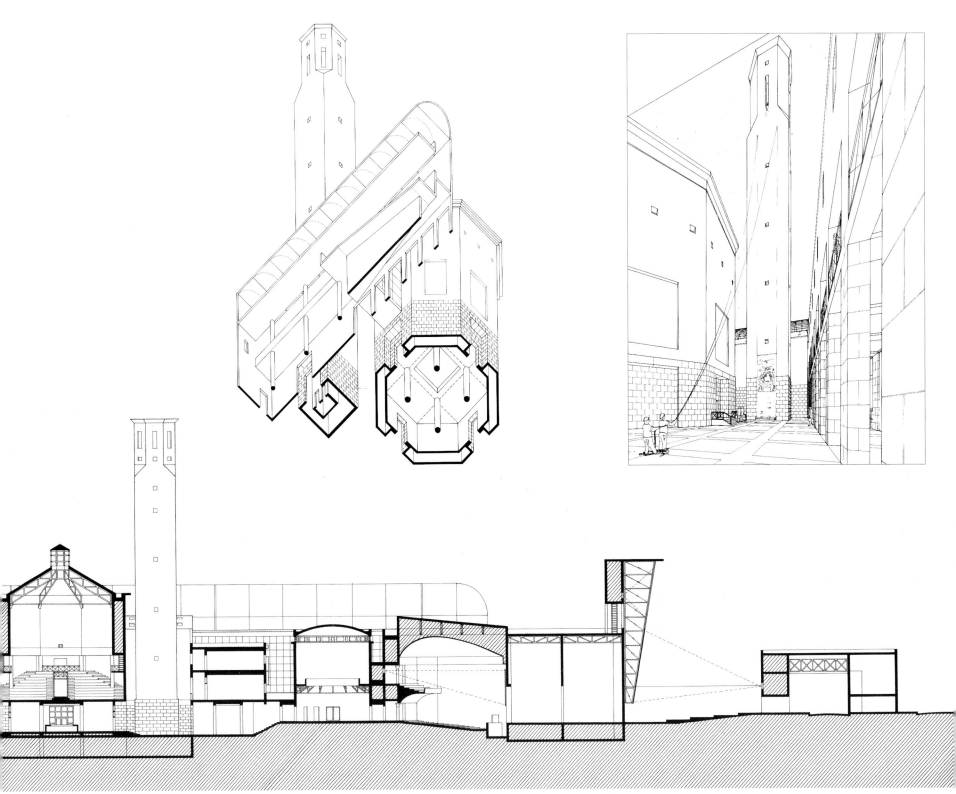

SA Armstrong
headquarters, Toronto

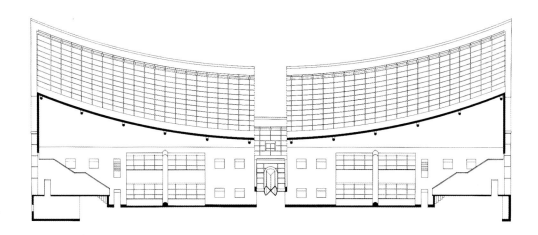

1987-89

'SA Armstrong is a family business that manufactures mechanical pumps and heat exchangers (they provided the pumps for Cesar Pelli's Canary Wharf tower in London). This headquarters building was part of the general relocation by the client Charles Armstrong, consolidating previously dispersed premises into a single corporate entity.

Located in Scarborough – known locally as Scarberia – in the manufacturing fringe of Toronto, this is as close as a site comes to the abstract! Hydro wires criss-cross above what appears to be an elevated ground plain, formed by the roofs of single-storey factories. But even then a clue presented itself within the extreme regularity of the concession grid. One atypical road focused on the site from the north. The significance of this marked the entrance and allowed the design to proceed. The curved glazed front elevation, not unlike a conventional crescent, received this road frontally from the north. In the other direction it forms a focus to the building's foreground when seen in steep perspective against the orthogonal world of the grid.

The project, a partial renovation and addition to an existing single-storey 1950s factory building, adopts the well-tried arrangement of offices fronting the manufacturing shed behind. The plan comprises large rooms on two floors reflecting the company's departmental structure – sales, engineering, administration and manufacture. On three sides smaller cellular offices form the boundaries to these departments. The fourth side is open to the double-height glazed hall and to the activity of arrival and departure and beyond to the industrial landscape of Scarborough. The double-height glazed space had two intentions: firstly the institutional idea of a generous place of arrival for both staff and visitors; and secondly the idea that externally this large screen might act as a representational device for the business as a whole – a Canadian portico.

The resemblance of the end elevations to Walter Gropius' Fagus factory is intentional. With the glazed front this gives the project a layered and technological appearance. It also fulfills a playful idea of not being able to see from one end of the space to the other'.

I have occasionally reflected on the expertise of north American mechanical systems and consultants. As the summer and winter climates there are so extreme, there is a real expectation for excellence – an expectation sadly missing in England.

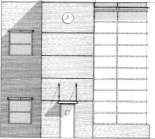

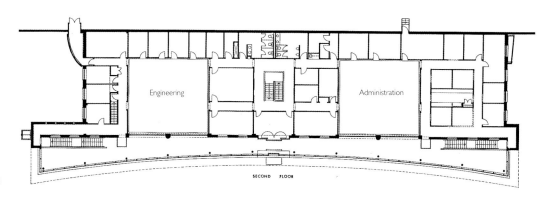

SECOND FLOOR

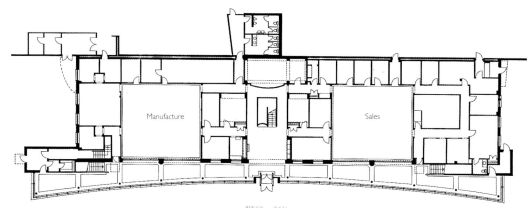

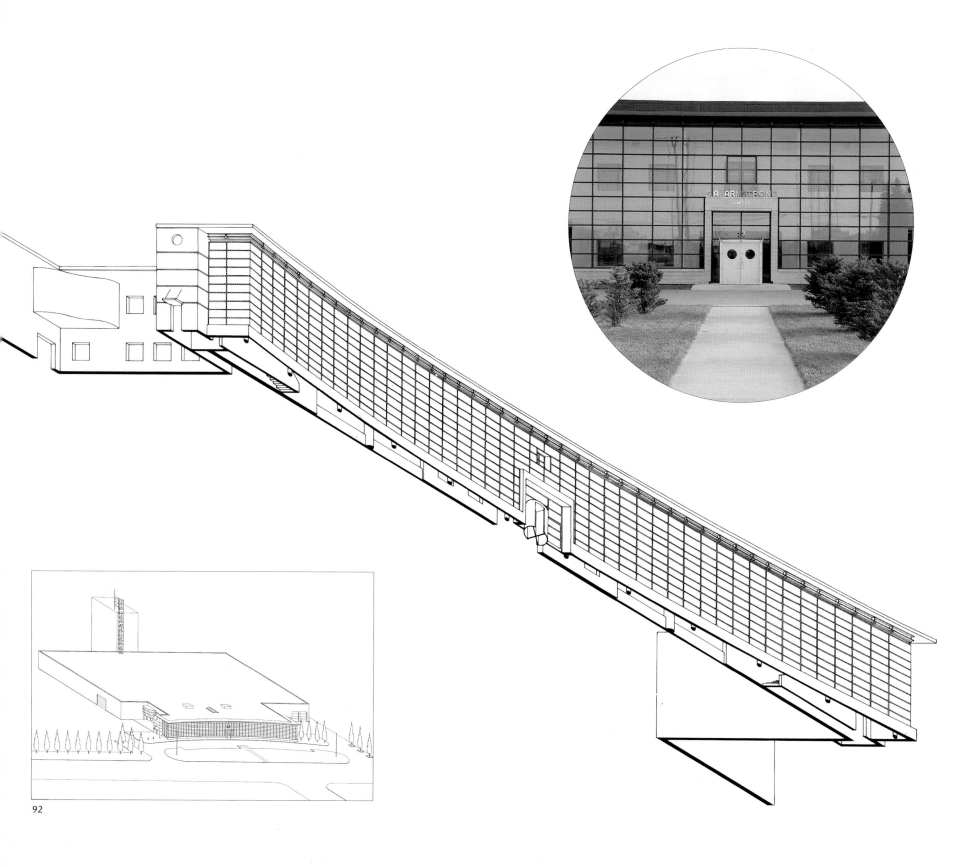

Jeremy Dixon and Edward Jones

Buildings and Projects 1989-2002

Millennium projects: the Royal Opera House and National Portrait Gallery

Robert Maxwell

No project associated with Jeremy Dixon and Edward Jones ever had such visibility as Dixon's winning design for Northamptonshire County Hall, the glass pyramid; and the design for the Royal Opera House is so set about by circumstance that it hardly restores that visibility. Both they, and architecture, have changed since that competition win of 1973. Since then they have worked together, apart and now again together. The conditions of practice are now more demanding. As their joint practice gains in cohesion, it also must accommodate an unprecedented complexity not only of the building, both in its internal organisation and in its interface with the city, but of the cultural conditions within which the building is to be judged. That is why there is a special interest to be found in the designs for the Royal Opera House and the National Portrait Gallery. In both cases the commissions were the result of a competition and so are based not only on circumstance but on a set of ideas. Yet in both cases the site is so embedded in previous acts of building and in the congestion of the city that the new architecture must look carefully around before taking the least step into space.

An opera house is a machine for spectacle. The longitudinal section of Charles Garnier's Paris Opéra, lavishly depicted in Bannister Fletcher, never failed to astonish me as a student. In spite of the grandeur of the auditorium with its staircase and foyer and the celebration of occasion that it implies, the importance of the social spaces is exceeded by the sheer size of the staging arrangements and fly tower. What it comprised was two vast interlocking systems in delicate equilibrium: theatre as enjoyment and theatre as effort – the mechanism of social display and the mechanism of thespian representation – both necessary, both acknowledged and voiced in the architecture. With the external volumes so completely echoing the disposition of necessary spaces, the dome of the auditorium virtually crashing into the fly tower, the whole thing was an example of functionalism avant la lettre. In this building Garnier, proficient in the social ideals of his time, created a masterpiece which is as dedicated to decorum as it is to performance. Big it is, but in proportion, and all on axis, since it occupies an isolated site.

The Royal Opera House of Covent Garden has an altogether more complicated history. On a site first occupied by a theatre in 1732, it took its present form with EM Barry's design of 1858 (beating Paris by three years) but greatly altered since. By now it is locked into the city fabric and, while the grip of the city is tighter, the demands of the programme are tougher. The fly tower was expanded in 1902 and is now greatly enlarged. Rehearsals have become always more demanding, as the schedule of performances becomes more complex, and staging itself is always increasing in complexity, so there are many more rehearsal spaces to be accommodated and the space needed for scenery is far more than just the fly tower. There was a moment in 1974 when the Floral Hall was taken over for scenery storage but this was an interim measure. Today the demands of the staging system for international opera have grown beyond what was necessary in 1902 (and far beyond what might have been contemplated when Garnier won his competition). An enormous additional area must now be found for the storage, preparation and manipulation of sets, in all about six times more than the area of the stage itself, and this is a huge stage.

In the new building this utilitarian zone is not confined to the area immediately behind the stage but extends sideways and forward almost all the way to the Bow Street and Russell Street frontages. It is high as well, the bulkiest element of the building volume. It is divided into adjacent sections, each bigger than a sea-going container, each capable of being raised or lowered on its own hydraulic supports to facilitate the handling of whole sets and each capable of being moved around. To wander through this area is to be astray in a vast industrial landscape, a shed for the construction of submarines or airships, maybe. As in the master criminal's control-centre in a James Bond movie, it seems to be the product of sheer fantasy, since it exists only to generate a fugitive enjoyment in an audience. It is astonishing to see yet if one didn't set out to find it, its presence would escape notice. This huge volume has been surreptitiously threaded through the core of the building, a necessary principle of its organisation, but it needn't trouble you on the night.

Almost as demanding were the requirements of the ballet company. The three practice rooms are arranged in a line directly behind the Floral Hall, at high level so that they can have rooflights, and there are three large studios tucked into the back-stage area on the west side. Add in capacious storage for the extensive wardrobe repertoire and you are almost back to the scale of industrial provision.

The long-running saga of the Opera House has been all too well ventilated in the press over the years and the waywardness of the committees must clearly have compounded problems for the architects; but even without that, one has to marvel at the intricacy of the functional requirements that had to be coordinated. The project was in one way constrained and simplified by the need to re-use existing facilities, in another way complicated by the impossibility of starting with a tabula rasa and an ideal layout. The result lacks the simplicity of Garnier's parti and succeeds on an entirely different level. We might say that it epitomises what Robert Venturi in Complexity and Contradiction in Architecture called the 'duty towards the difficult whole'. The whole that it suggests is not the finite balance of the work of art, more like the shifting complexity of the city to which its various parts are related. It is a solution for now.

The elements of this six-sided building which appear on the street are as follows. First there is the nearly symmetrical north elevation to Floral Street, beginning at the left with Barry's portico, incorporating at its centre the mass of the fly tower and then continuing to the right with the original rear addition, renovated with remarkable consistency of style by Gollins Melvin Ward in 1982. Next, rounding the corner, there is the projection of this volume onto James Street, corresponding satisfactorily to the fly tower behind and above, before we come to the transition to the new construction and the opening to the new colonnade. Next, there is the two-sided colonnade facing south and west on the market square; and then the administrative spaces facing south onto Russell Street. Finally comes the series of distinct pavilions facing Bow Street – new facilities incorporating first the truck entry (the only thing that gives a hint of the industrial scale of the scenery landscape), the restored and raised Floral Hall and finally the refurbished mass of Barry's porticoed temple. As you might expect, there is a main entry on axis beneath the portico but there is another main entry in the angle of the colonnade to the square, exactly where the entrance to the very first theatre stood. In terms of modern congestion, both are clearly necessary. From that

second entry, in summer, a glimpse of daylight towards the east indicates the direction of the social space and conversely it is towards that outlet from the square that the main approach from Bow Street eventually leads. There is no outright axis here; rather the system of public foyers has been threaded through the building with the same precision as that of the scenery.

The reconstruction of a quarter of Inigo Jones' piazza is itself a significant step. A single act of building thereby contributes towards the re-invention of an important city space, lending itself to field as much as to figure. The colonnades contain shops, reversing the tendency of large buildings to turn their backs on the street and obliterate street activities. The embrace of public space recurs at roof level, where a second colonnade provides terraces for strolling and taking coffee and for looking back at the city and its spires, Nelson's Column and all, vastly improving the enjoyment of the intervals. The form of the piazza thus provides something like the garden terrace of the classic country house, a destination to balance the formality of the main entrance, with the orientation to south and west reinforcing the idea of détente.

The entrance level is joined to this upper foyer by staircases but above all by escalator. The escalator provides the easy way up for those headed for 'the gods' and brings to an end the more or less shameful ascent via the back stairs that used to be the only access for impecunious youth. This is another case of a separate system being threaded through the whole; this time however the escalator is visible to the foyer and the two ideas offset each other. Now the privileged destined for the front stalls can survey the populace who will share the show, as they rise into prominence; and vice versa, the elite is under the scrutiny of the masses. The escalator defines the edge of the Floral Hall, from the closed volume of which however it escapes. The Floral Hall, while truncated by the demands of the secret scenery jungle behind it, is still a generous space and it has been scrupulously restored to provide the building with the foyer it deserves. A back wall of mirror glass retrieves some idea of its original appearance and creates a nice paradox, with the new amphitheatre bar penetrating as a balcony through the mirror wall and enabling the populace to survey the glitterati below. Used as we are to the hole-in-a-corner character of English theatre foyers, there is relief that here at last is an

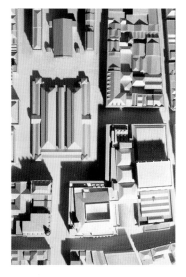

Above The Royal Opera House in the context of London's Covent Garden.
Below The National Portrait Gallery project centres on a five-storey intervention within a landlocked court between the NPG and the National Gallery.

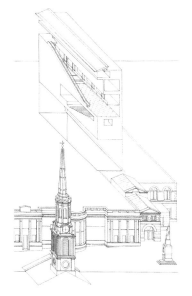

acknowledgement of the social enjoyment that expands beyond the confines of the auditorium, so elegantly demonstrated by Garnier.

The Bow Street frontage is dominated by the familiar forms of the Floral Hall and the Barry portico and so in a sense it is the colonnaded elevations that serve as the new 'front'. Here one may note the finesse with which the shopfronts are inserted, the windows rising high in the colonnade while the spaces drop down to fit under the heavy load of necessary accommodation just behind. At the same time, the first row of windows above the colonnade are in fact lunettes which illuminate the peak of the vault. The generous width of the closing opening to the colonnade is managed without excessive height by adopting a four-point arch. The facade above is cleverly handled so as to make an effortless transition from classical piers at ground level to the more basic structure of the roof terrace (although this critic would have preferred a more schematic treatment to come further down). Finally, the change in angle between the wall of the ballet studios and the frontage to the square is marked by a frank diminuendo in the lean-to roof to the ballet foyer, which to an architect's eye shows a consoling awareness of contemporary modes.

So we are offered a functionality that goes beyond the physical to include the social. The architects have bent their minds to creating not only the mechanism but also the amenity that is appropriate to the operatic tradition, so that London can continue to be classed with Paris and Milan. At least in this respect, we are firmly part of Europe. But, unlike the situation with Garnier, the result is not a single form unified in its expression, but a mixture of measures and a combination of languages.

It could hardly be otherwise with so much already occupying its space and in need of preservation and adaptation. The auditorium itself is retained, but improved and refurbished; the Floral Hall is truncated, but restored to its original appearance; some ancillary areas are renovated and vast new facilities have been added. So it is still possible to leave the stalls through the original entrance foyer and ascend into the grand salon via the original staircase to consume the traditional champagne in familiar surroundings, sheltered by the ancient portico. Or to cross the Floral Hall to the escalator landing and rise up to enjoy the interval in the more

modern decor of the new amphitheatre bar, with its views over the rooftops. Bars and fittings have been deliberately moulded to a curvaceous contemporary ideal of relaxation; these are indisputably modern spaces. This is a building that combines the traditional with the technological and atavistic pleasures with new ones. But not all in one place. The result is a delicate combination of different things.

It will be criticised by those who need above all to see a direct expression of the artistic unity that is thought to define an architectural statement. It was no problem for Garnier, active before planners as such existed and before opera houses became dedicated to special effects. With today's demand for specialisation, simplicity only comes with an overwhelming commitment to technological style. This is no problem with railway stations and airports, nor with any programme that can be interpreted as naturally implying the industrial forms that still approximate to our ideal of modernity. That applies up to a point also for art galleries and museums but it does not necessarily go with retrieving special nineteenth-century moments. Neither the auditorium nor the Floral Hall could be rejected, so the tabula rasa was not an option. Moreover the special conditions pertaining here have imposed a solution more responsive to the needs of the city block. What the architects have done is altogether more ingenious and civilised and also more sensitive to the place of architecture in the city.

With the National Portrait Gallery, the work envisaged was not visible from the street and did not involve ideas of preserving the urban block. It was a discreet and private adjustment that had no identifiable effect on the city at all. The strategy can afford to be more single-minded, but there is the same demand on the architects to integrate places of different character and provenance within an ensemble that has grown over time and to sew together diverse elements into a coherent experience for the visitor.

Here the whole design follows from the perception that simply extending into the lightwell separating the Portrait Gallery from the adjacent part of the National Gallery would produce little usable space, compared to what could be achieved by occupying the whole of the lightwell. A 'deal' followed, in which the National Gallery accepted their wall to the lightwell as a party wall (with no windows and no claims of light) in exchange for gaining from the

Portrait Gallery a band of rooms fronting Charing Cross Road that would complete the main spaces in the piano nobile behind Wilkins' facade. The exchange testifies to the enlightened approach of both directors and benefits both galleries. The light-well is now available not just as a means of bringing down daylight but as a principal foyer space leading up to the main suite of top-lit galleries on the top floor – a space that makes sense of the building as a whole. This solution was proposed, and indeed put forward as the preferred option, in Dixon Jones' winning presentation for the 1994 competition.

The escalator makes sense as an effortless way of taking the visitor to the heart of the collection. Charles Saumarez Smith, the director of the Portrait Gallery, notes that when the project was placed before the Royal Fine Arts Commission, there was a hesitation about this; an escalator, it was suggested, was something to do with airports and shopping malls, not with cultural institutions. Good sense prevailed: the general public do not think like that – and in any case flying, shopping and visiting art galleries are increasingly seen as leisure activities, based on convenience not on duty. Even more than at the Opera House, the escalator functions here in a purely architectural way, drawing together a vertically dispersed institution into a kind of vertical concourse and giving it coherence.

The volume in which the escalator rises is itself a triumph of imaginative design, in that the structure supporting the top floor has been condensed into a single column. This makes everything much clearer and maximises the light falling down through the space. At the top of the escalator is a new gallery of Tudor art, long, narrow and dark as Tudor spaces often were, its narrowness working for the mannerist intimacy of the paintings and its length working to distribute the circulation around the top floor. Here, top light has been restored to all the original spaces, giving the maximum amount of conventional display and making sense of the institution as a national storehouse.

Above the Tudor Gallery is a new restaurant, looking out over a roof landscape to take in a spectacular view of London's skyline to south and west. The way that this prospect has been combined in sectional design with the necessary windows for the vertical foyer space is typical of the finesse that the architects have shown throughout the project. They have preserved the best of the old and, where necessary, extended parts to improve its impact (as in the completion of the landing of the original staircase – even to the mosaic floor) and they have eliminated the wilder aberrations, such as the faux-medieval decor of the entrance lobby from Charing Cross Road; but they have modernised the amenity wherever that was possible, with the aim of bringing the visit together into a coherent experience.

There are certain similarities at a formal level between the Opera House and the Portrait Gallery: the seizing of social amenity and the space needed to create it; the careful handling of the old and venerable as being entitled to its own share of the action; the bold use of technology where it is helpful but not as an end in itself; the packing-in of all the technical requirements, with the space they need, so that the life of the building is extended as an up-to-date amenity. There is also a certain commonality of theme: in both cases an amenity space at upper level looks out across an urban roofscape towards the afternoon sun, reached by an empowering escalator that brings a sense of modern amusement to cultural events.

In both cases the result is a carefully balanced whole that does not display all its parts at the same level of noise. Boldness is balanced with discretion; directness of concept is balanced with a mature judgement. This is a conciliatory modern architecture, not a radically subversive one; an architecture that aims to serve client and users and promote the enhancement of life. In this it is in the tradition of modern architecture itself. The achievement in these two projects is tremendous. Together they offer exemplary instances of the way that well-loved amenities can be improved and modernised, indeed transformed, without losing their familiar character and their settled place in society.

Above Escalators at the National Portrait Gallery and the Royal Opera House.

Royal Opera House
Covent Garden

with BDP

1984-2000

The expanded and renovated Royal Opera House occupies an entire urban block; it also encloses and repairs London's first square. The significance of the project can thus be described first in terms of urban design and second as a theatre modernisation. It establishes a conventional urban hierarchy between the formal regularity of Covent Garden piazza and the greater particularity of the surrounding streets. Streets with shops are an important element of urban continuity. The location of the stage at first-floor level allows for almost continuous shopping frontages across the scheme, linking the surrounding streets to the new piazza arcades.

In addition a pedestrian mid-block connection between Bow Street and the piazza provides a second entrance to the theatre. This re-establishes an entrance that existed in the various theatres built on the site since 1732 and, more importantly, draws the theatre and its foyers into the life of the city. From this link the pedestrian is made aware of the Floral Hall and escalators above as a series of connected vertical foyers. Not unlike the nineteenth-century arcade, it is an ambiguous space; the public can pass through the block, buy tickets and enter the theatre, but during certain hours they are excluded.

The inspiration for Inigo Jones' original arcade came from Livorno, where the arcade acts as a framing device to the piazza, its six metre depth allowing for discontinuity between the form of the arcade and the buildings behind. Today, all that remains of Jones' arcade design is a nineteenth-century copy by Clutton, which adds an additional floor and thereby distorts the original. The

Left The Floral Hall on the occasion of the royal opening, December 1999.

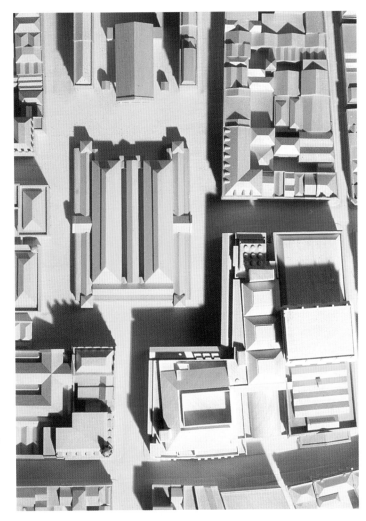

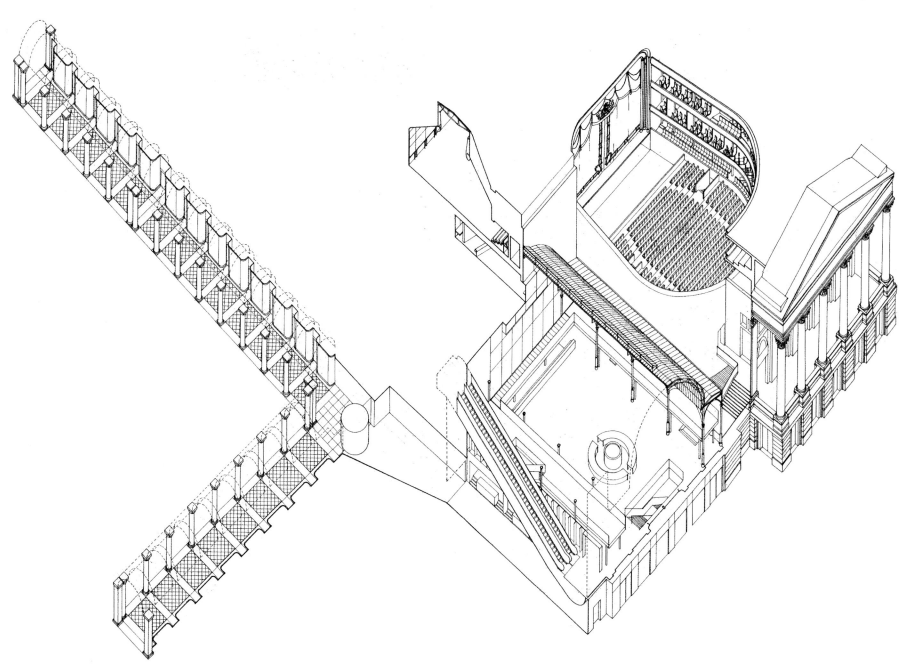

design therefore faced the dilemma of either copying the 'copy', replicating the original or, which was the chosen route, inventing a new version within the discipline of the type and the language of neoclassicism.

The urban design intentions and the appearance of the project are closely related. The conventional distinction between street and square relate the scheme to the historical order of the surrounding city – the square as regular and repetitive, and the streets as individual and informal. The project, occupying a whole city block, has adjacencies to both situations. Rather than looking for consistency the complex allows for various styles to develop simultaneously leading to an urban collage – neoclassical arcade on the piazza, modern street facades, and reconstruction of historic elements.

The facades of Barry's 1858 theatre are painted stucco. The new buildings use stone as the principle cladding material in two contrasting forms – in the piazza Portland stone is used as a three-dimensional carved material and, in the street elevations, Jura limestone provides a two-dimensional rainscreen. In this case the metalwork provides the three-dimensional modelling of the facade matching, in colour, the grey granite base.

Above Axonometric drawing showing the public areas and circulation.
Right Contrasting styles of the external and internal arcades.

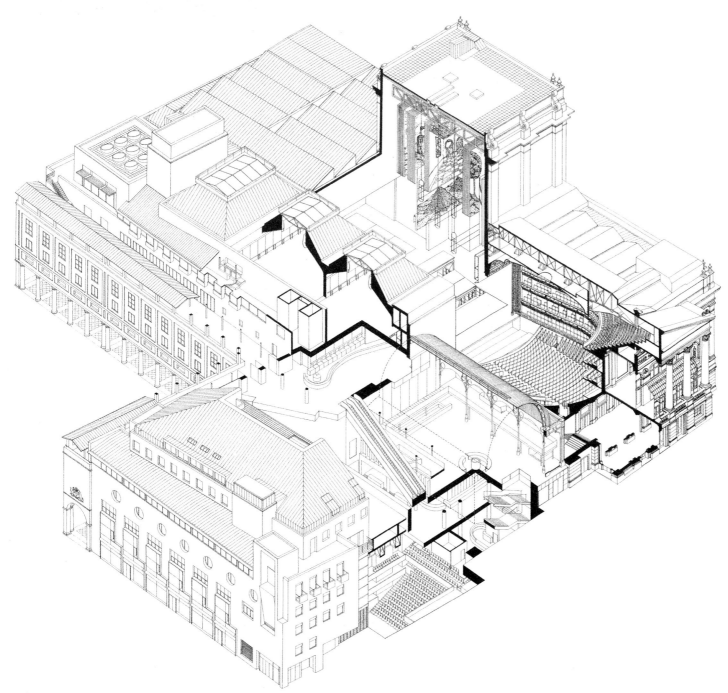

In place of the hierarchical public access of the old house – whereby the upper (ie cheaper) seats were reached from a separate side-entrance – all members of the audience can now enter through the main Bow Street portico. In addition there is a new public entrance from the north-east corner of Covent Garden square. Both entrances lead to the box office and cloakrooms directly below the Floral Hall. At each step along the route simple choices are presented. On arrival in the entrance foyer members of the audience can either proceed directly to the auditorium, via lifts to the amphitheatre or stairs to the stalls and balconies, or take a more leisurely promenade to their seats. The Grand Stair leads from the foyer up to the half-landing, where a doorway through the party wall leads to the principal foyer, the Floral Hall. Here one can remain for a drink or proceed through to a grand pair of escalators (visible

Traditionally the glamour associated with the foyers of an opera house is related to decorated and enclosed interiors. It was by no means obvious that a glass enclosure like the Floral Hall would create an appropriate atmosphere. What has turned out to be very successful is the way the Floral Hall responds to the changes in evening light that take place during a performance. Daylight produces a space with a high level of illumination where the structure of the Floral Hall is silhouetted dark against the light sky. In darkness the effect is reversed. The structure becomes white lines against a dark background. Similarly the mirror works in a straightforward way by day but produces a mysterious and almost disturbing effect by night. The window box to the amphitheatre foyer within the mirror looks, in dark reflections, precarious and isolated to the extent that I have heard members of the audience querying whether it is safe to go up there.

JD

Left Cutaway axonometric showing public areas.

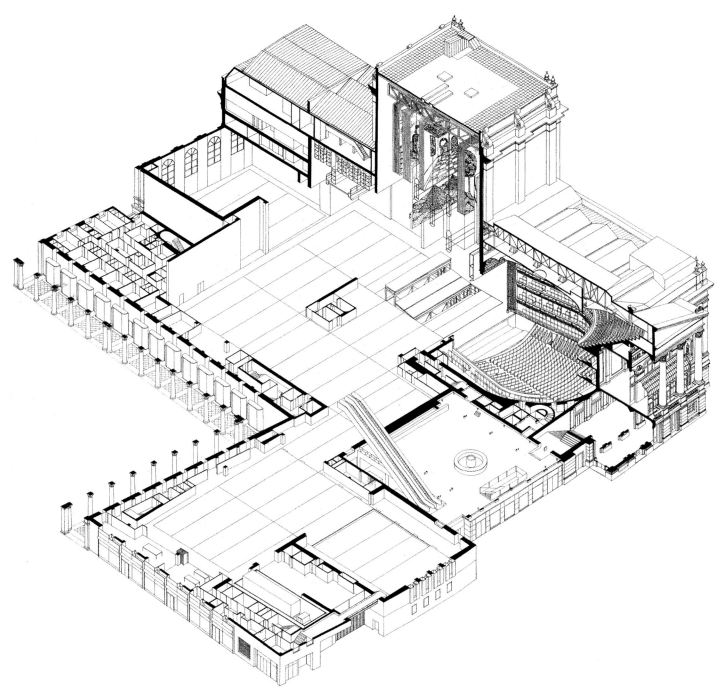

through the glass wall) to the amphitheatre bar above. Members of the audience ascending the escalator rise above the Floral Hall roof before emerging back in the building, looking into the vault of the Floral Hall itself. Here they either remain in the upper foyer or proceed further directly onto the open loggia overlooking Covent Garden piazza. In this sense the foyer serving the amphitheatre – with the cheapest seats in the house – enjoys amenities beyond even those of the main Floral Hall foyer. New stairs, lifts and toilets serve each level of the auditorium, accommodated between the inner horse-shoe and outer walls. Wheelchair users access each level except for the stalls. In contrast to the refurbished auditorium, the fly tower and stage is a new construction built as a steel frame behind the retained historical facade to Floral Street. The galleried fly tower – three times the height of the proscenium arch – accommodates flying sets and lighting bars. It is isolated from the side and rear stages by massive steel acoustic/fire doors, each weighing some 60 tonnes. To the rear and side of the stage, a single unobstructed three-storey volume extends from Russell Street to Floral Street, with the get-in for sets located on Bow Street. Within this space, sets for six productions can be erected, retained and moved on automatic stage wagons and compensating elevators, reducing the time-consuming and labour-intensive process of erecting and dismantling sets for individual productions.

Left Cutaway axonometric showing stage areas.
Right View into fly tower with the flying bars set at stage level for installation testing. Each bar is supported by seven wires, the sculptural effect of the reflections off 700 wires representing a unique moment in the process of completing the project.

Sections The two sections – one parallel to Bow Street through the Linbury studio theatre, Floral Hall and foyer, and the other perpendicular to this in the direction of the escalator – summarise the new circulation and public spaces. These are among the many beautiful drawings made for the office by David Naessens.

There is a simple typology to the traditional theatre as an isolated building. The axial nature of the relationship between the stage and the auditorium is extended to the rest of the building with symmetrical foyers, front entrance etc. There is a clear separation between front of house and back of house. This type is modified when a theatre has to fit into a particular urban site. Foyers become more organic in their relationship to the auditorium and the back of house makes the best of any circumstance that exists. The Royal Opera House is generically the second type but with an additional complication. Scenery is delivered at the south-east corner of the site near the junction of Bow Street and Russell Street. From here it moves diagonally through the plan to the north-west corner occupied by the stages. The public circulation takes place between the corner of Covent Garden square and the old main entrance to the building, a tendency from south west to north east that represents the opposite diagonal to that of the technical areas. This puts the back of house and the front of house into an unusual degree of overlap. There are definite advantages – everyone circulating in the building, both back of house and front of house, can use the loggia and there is a more subtle challenge to the theatre to look at creative ways of introducing aspects of the back of house to the public.

JD

To design in three or four manners simultaneously was a significant – even radical – experience of working on a project like the Royal Opera House. For some this would reflect a loss of nerve, schizophrenic even. This would appear to reverse one of the hallmarks of modern design, that of working in a unitary style with consistency. The facades facing Covent Garden square are in an historical style – close-jointed limestone with the impression of having been carved from the solid – in contrast to the modernity of the street elevations – open-jointed gridded limestone acting as a rainscreen; the conservation of the listed interiors versus the hybrid modern insertions in the Floral Hall and so on. The 'difficult whole' is represented here by architectural collage, a collage that reflects the necessary inclusiveness of reconstructing an entire urban block.

EJ

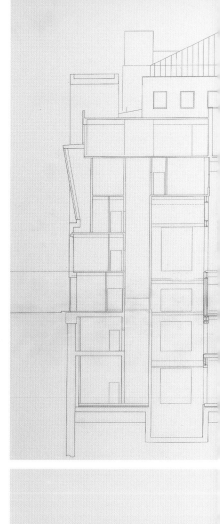

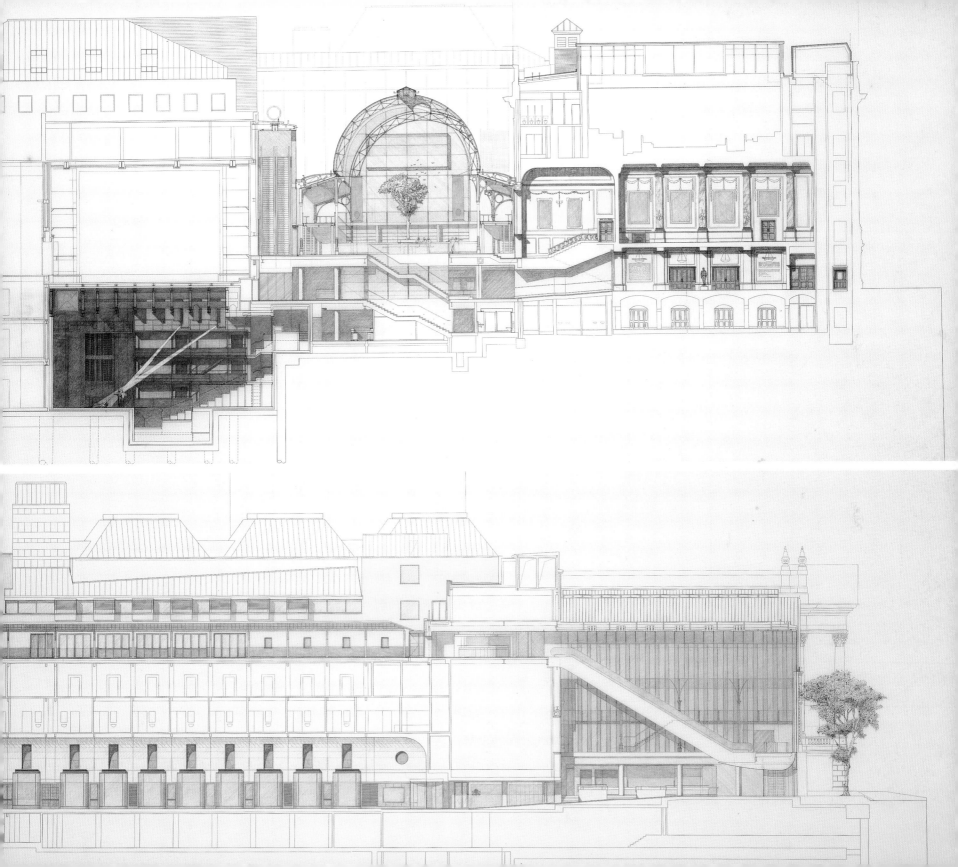

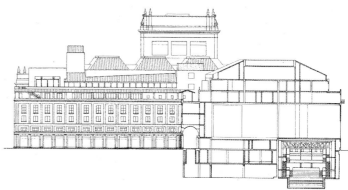

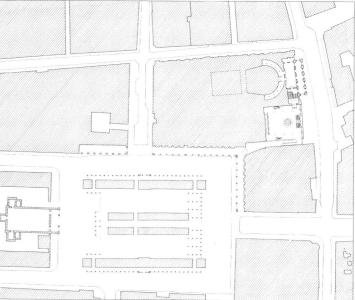

The project has taken 16 years and it would be strange if one's own opinions and taste had not developed during that period. The building programme has changed dramatically as have the personalities involved in every aspect of the project. At a certain stage it began to seem useful to allow parts of the project designed at one time to lie alongside parts designed at another time. Thus the scheme has accumulated its own archaeology. In this way the variety in the elevations is not only the consequence of the self-conscious changes of design made at a particular moment but is also an accumulation of changes over time that approximates to a compressed version of the natural development of a city.

JD

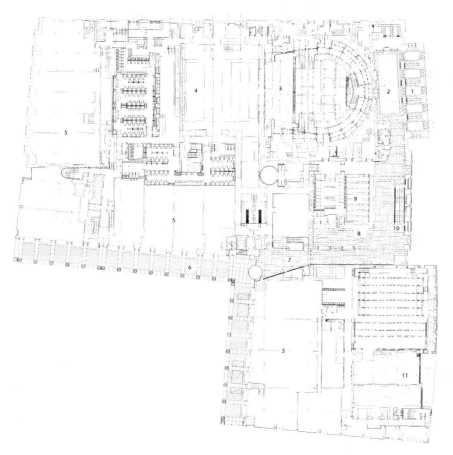

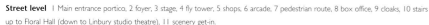

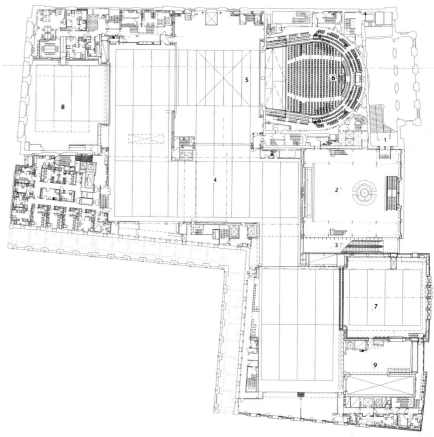

Street level 1 Main entrance portico, 2 foyer, 3 stage, 4 fly tower, 5 shops, 6 arcade, 7 pedestrian route, 8 box office, 9 cloaks, 10 stairs up to Floral Hall (down to Linbury studio theatre), 11 scenery get-in.

Stage/Floral Hall level 1 Grand stair, 2 Floral Hall, 3 escalators, 4 side/back stage, 5 stage with fly tower over, 6 existing auditorium, 7 new opera rehearsal room, 8 existing opera rehearsal room, 9 scenery get-in.

Plans

The main entrance to the opera house is from the existing classical portico. The entrance from the Covent Garden piazza is secondary and of a more informal nature. Between the two entrances and under the Floral Hall are the cloaks and toilets.

Previously the opera house was very short of foyer space – it had been built by a developer for a minimum cost. The Crush Bar was aptly named and it was impossible for the whole audience to gather in a single place. In the new project the renovated Floral Hall, which forms the main foyer, can hold a large proportion of the audience. The nineteenth-century iron-and-glass structure was dismantled and raised on a plinth, level with the half-landing of the Grand Stair. The hall is located on the south side of the auditorium, an unusual situation in that the foyer is asymmetrical to the axis of the auditorium. The Floral Hall thus becomes a building in its own right, separate from the theatre with its own independent life.

Vertical circulation plays an important part in the public circulation of the theatre. In the past the 800 seats of the amphitheatre were entirely separated from the rest of the auditorium with their own backstair access from Floral Street. Now the amphitheatre is linked dramatically to the rest of the foyer spaces. An escalator goes directly from the Floral Hall to amphitheatre level, where an amphitheatre bar looks back into the Floral Hall. At the same level an open loggia overlooks Covent Garden square, providing an additional attraction at the upper level of the foyers.

The aim is to encourage the audience to move up as well as down during intervals, reversing the sense of social hierarchy that existed within the old house. The studio theatre and its foyer are reached from the ground-floor circulation area under the Floral Hall. This means it can share the same cloaks and other facilities as the main theatre and also have access to the Floral Hall.

Public access is an important theme in the project. Vertical circulation by escalator and lifts, disabled access to almost all parts of this complex historic building, and access for the general public to parts of the foyers during the day are all vital to a more open opera house.

The roofscape, like the external elevations, is seen as a free composition of elements. When the structure rises to roof level over the stage areas, it is as if a new ground level has been created, marked by the loggia. On this are placed separately expressed elements such as the ballet studios, flytower, rooftop studio areas and core towers. It is as if there is a rooftop village of ROH activities and terraces.

112

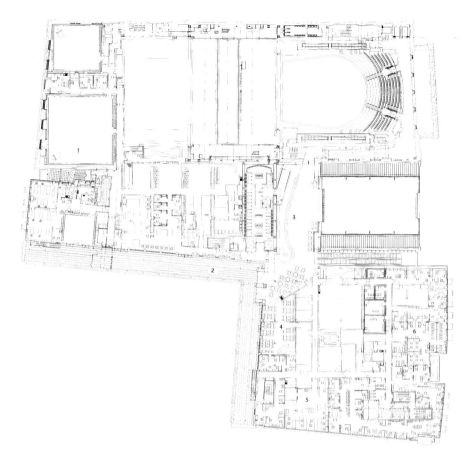

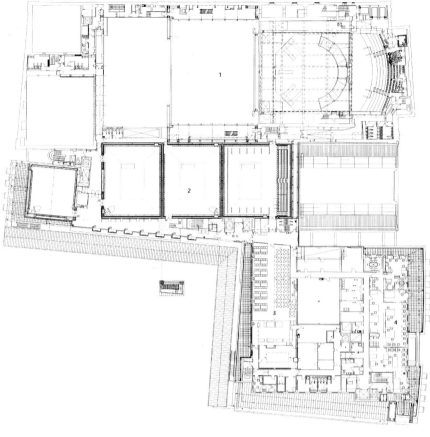

Loggia level | Ballet studio, 2 loggia, 3 amphitheatre bar, 4 restaurant, 5 workshops, 6 offices.

Attic level | Fly tower, 2 ballet studios, 3 staff canteen, 4 workshops.

Behind the scenes the building houses almost every conceivable form of employment, from people making and crafting things to engineering, stage assembly, finance, administration and management, alongside opera, dance and music activities – a miniature city within the city. This diversity is reflected in the way space has been provided. The ballet company has the roof level, so that ballet studios can be daylit and 'light' in every sense of the word. Jewellery, millinery, wigs and dyeing are located in interestingly shaped roof

spaces, with studio windows and views; costume-making and other crafts are one level below, with a long balcony overlooking Bow Street. The canteen is also located here, with its own terrace and views across Westminster. The canteen has a vital function in the ROH community of bringing together the various people who might not normally meet and is located in one of the most attractive places in the building.

The dressing rooms had to be no more than one level above or below stage (lift access for performers is

regarded as unacceptable). All the principal dressing rooms are located at first floor overlooking the square as part of the arcade building. Chorus dressing rooms are below stage to give easy access for quick changes of costume.

The arcade building, with its sense of being a principal frontage, houses a number of important rooms. On the first floor are the main dressing rooms and on the second are management areas. Corridors that give access to accommodation around the stage areas have windows overlooking the vast

stage spaces, giving a sense of location and allowing as many people as possible to see what is happening on stage.

The stage door on Floral Street leads to an extended staff and artists' foyer, with facilities for snacks and a small bar – a lot of waiting takes place around the stage door. The stage areas are served by the get-in on Bow Street, with the scenery assembly taking place in an area visible from the street. There is a new opera rehearsal room at stage level – the orchestra rehearses mainly in the pit but occasionally in the studio theatre.

This was a project involving a huge number of people and all kinds of contributions. By the time the building process started, Bill Jack had retired from the chairmanship of BDP and nominated Charles Broughton to become project director. The relationship between the two practices initiated by Bill Jack survived the many vicissitudes of the project remarkably well and Charles became a close colleague and lasting friend.

JD

Auditorium

EM Barry's 1858 grade 1 listed auditorium has been faithfully refurbished. Extensive interventions have improved sightlines, acoustics, comfort, access, audience facilities, seating capacity and theatrical lighting. Sightlines and seating are improved by re-raking the stalls and balconies, re-aligning the grand tier and balcony boxes and extending the amphitheatre. Extra seats are located at the back of the grand tier, balcony and amphitheatre. Absorbency is reduced and extraneous noise controlled by insulating the roof and structure and forming separation lobbies to foyers/staircases. The redecoration re-establishes the character of the auditorium, with 'ROH red' for the seat fabric, balcony fingerboards, wallpaper, carpets and soffits. The dome, balcony fronts and proscenium arch are selectively gilded, with extensive areas of light blue over the former and ivory over the latter. Unlike Garnier's Paris Opera, only highlights of the mouldings are gilded.

We were very lucky to have David Mlinaric advising on all aspects of the restoration of the existing building. He has a wonderful capacity for getting things absolutely right both in the process of restoration and in the tricky business of introducing new elements that, in his hands, can improve on the original.

JD

Linbury studio theatre

By 1995 the brief for the orchestra rehearsal space was extended to provide a public facility for 420 people catering for chamber, opera, dance and educational events. The space is experimental, informal and flexible, in direct contrast to the main house. Raked fixed seating is provided on the side galleries for dance and opera, with retractable seating providing a flat floor. A chamber orchestra pit was required for opera and a deep and wide stage for dance. Directly above is an opera rehearsal room. The theatre is entered from a foyer below street level, bringing the audience in at the top – the inverse of the main theatre.

Above View from the primary backstage corridor window across the stage area to the the auditorium.
Right The Queen and other members of the royal family attend the opening night; the Linbury theatre.

114

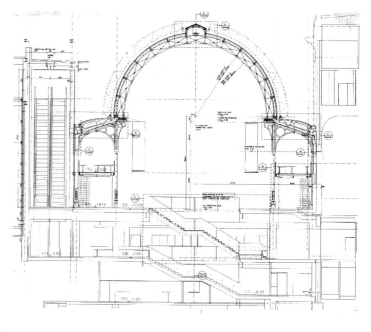

Floral Hall

The Vilar Floral Hall is the new centre and focus to the front-of-house, forming both a destination and a route. Four bays of the hall have been renovated, reinstating the barrel vault and fan elevation to Bow Street. A mirrored wall gives the illusion of the eight bays of the original structure, while making room for the new stage areas behind. The historic reconstruction is restricted to the cast iron structure and roof glazing – all new elements are explicitly modern. One side wall is the external enclosure to the historic auditorium while the other is the structural glass wall separating the hall from the escalator. Mezzanine structures along each side (for dining) are linked by a lit glass bridge that spans over the main bar at the end. Above this is the window to the amphitheatre bar overlooking the Floral Hall, appearing from below as a box floating within a mirror.

Left Bow Street facade detail.
Above Oblique views along the Bow Street frontage from the south and north.
Right Detail of Russell Street facade incorporating the south end of the new arcade; loggia outside the ballet studios.
Opposite The staff canteen terrace overlooks the piazza below.

119

Back-of-house

These areas (occupied by many of the 600 ROH staff) comprise the three-storey volume of rear and side stages, with plant- and store-rooms below and work-shops, offices and ballet studios above. Most dressing rooms are ranged around the stage, one level up or down. Four of the six ballet studios are within the roofscape. Three are large pyramidal forms which look particularly imposing from the square; internally they are airy roof-lit spaces full of natural light. The smaller fourth studio (above left) sits over the James Street corner building, with a picture window overlooking the square.

Left Dyeing room; large ballet studio; ballet rest area.
Right North-south section; amphitheatre bar.

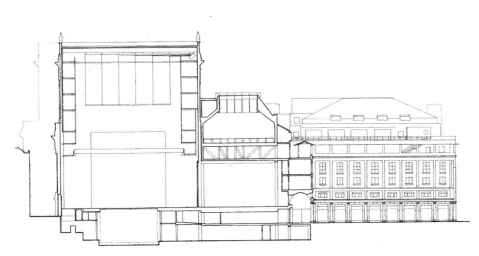

An architectural odyssey: renewing the Royal Opera House

Jeremy Isaacs

'Less aesthetics – more ethics' was the credo of the Seventh International Exhibition of Architecture at the Venice Biennale in the year 2000. 'Less ego – more use' one can envisage a British client echoing, counting pennies in a public cause. Not for everyone grand gestural architecture – a stand-alone gherkin or a reflector bowl. For some clients the building they commission must fulfil varied and precise functions, must attach itself to its neighbours and make itself at home in the existing cityscape. The architect, therefore, needs sensitivity to the needs of others, as well as his own imagination and invention, to succeed. Jeremy Dixon is such an architect. He looks to past and present for guidance in shaping possible futures. Edward Jones, co-author of an encyclopaedic guide to the architecture of London, is another. Here in London, I rejoice over their tactful intervention at Somerset House – the walkway onto the terrace from Waterloo Bridge; high-tech tentage for the outdoor restaurant; symphonic fountains in Chambers' great court. I enjoy, too, their deft additions to the National Portrait Gallery. In Venice, where they once designed a wondrous water-cooled circular bus station in Piazzale Roma, I thought of what might have been. They won the competition but the mayor could not secure the go-ahead to build. At Covent Garden, we worked together for a bumpy, hazardous, grindingly difficult decade. How they stuck it out, I could only wonder.

In 1974 the government recognised that the Royal Opera House, built in 1858, must redevelop or crumble. They gave the site to make redevelopment possible but gave no funds to pay for it. In 1984 the Royal Opera House board, unsure how to afford the cost but determined to proceed, chose by competition not a scheme but a collaboration between two individuals, Jeremy Dixon and Bill Jack of Building Design Partnership. It was not until July 1997 that the House closed so that building could start and December 1999 when it reopened. Along the way, in 1989, as revision succeeded revision, Edward Jones, who had gone to Canada having won the competition for Mississauga city hall, returned to rejoin his erstwhile partner, turning down a professorship at Princeton. Dixon and Jones worked together in harmonious and fruitful collaboration on every detail of the realised Opera House scheme. Closing my eyes, I see their faces now at meeting after meeting, calm, alert, thoughtful, unfazed by changes, crises, pressures, fits of temperament. Only one thing annoyed them – being left out of the loop ('let's meet without the architects'). At that, they put their foot down. It did not recur. Others came to the party and went away; the architects stayed on. On the long odyssey between concept and completion, more years passed than it took Ulysses to overcome the obstacles that Poseidon placed in his path before he found Ithaca and Penelope again. Calypso, Circe, the Cyclops, Scylla and Charybdis were as nothing compared to what lay in store for our latter-day heroes.

Their brief was simple. Preserve the auditorium, improving sight-lines and adding air-conditioning; modernise the technical facilities; add space and amenity for the public; house the ballet; and collect as many as possible of the House's multifarious craft departments under one roof. A further requirement, not simple, was to enhance the cityscape while creating property value realisable on site to help pay for the whole. At first, that was to be achieved by a massive office-block; later, happily, we did without. In any case when the Lottery came along, we were in the strong position of having a ready scheme, putting us at the head of the queue. We wanted to transform a cityscape blighted by void and vacuum since the Covent Garden fruit and vegetable market moved to Nine Elms. Westminster did not help by demanding an underground car-park, to be entered from Bow Street. In the end, under our stern gaze, this foolish tribute to the motor-car simply went away. Dixon's scheme, taking its cue from the Piazza degli Armi in Livorno, has completed the north east corner of Inigo Jones' plan for the Market Square. This is the enhancement to a living London that we sought.

The architects, heroically, remained constant throughout a decade. The same cannot be said of the client, though John Sainsbury – donor, leader and guide – was in at the start and at the end. Dixon and Jones, on their voyage, encountered more than one general director (I was there from 1988 to 1997); four-and-a-half chairmen of the board; at least half-a-dozen chairmen of the development board, several with experience in the property world; three project managers; and three ROH technical directors, the second of whom presciently stipulated a bigger and better stage facility than the first had requested. Every single cottage industry in the House – from construction to wigs, accounts to shoes, costumes to maintenance – made its needs known and each revised those upwards, if given half a chance. Quantity surveyors and property consultants were of the highest quality throughout; consulting engineers moved on; key advisers changed and their advice with them.

We tried to work with, and saw off, three prime ministers and several chancellors; more than half-a-dozen ministers for the arts, none crucially effective; three chairmen of the Arts Council; the Royal Fine Art Commission, in all its waffly assertiveness; English Heritage, both the London Committee and key officers, each adamant for good as he subjectively perceived it, each armed with virtually inexhaustible power to delay, prevent and obstruct (one long insisted that we should preserve the whole of the Floral Hall in situ, although that made quite impossible the improvement to the stage's functioning which was the rationale for the whole development). Their approval had to be obtained. In the end, it was. Great and good egos on the ROH board's committees and sub-committees spluttered and erupted as unpredictably as volcanoes. All were humoured. As regularly as the rising moon, Westminster city council appointed new enthusiasts to chair their crucial planning committee. Not all were enthusiasts for us. Unchanging in its agit-prop hostility was the quirky Covent Garden Community Association, which successfully went to law for a judicial review that, properly perhaps, held us up for two years. They fought every single move we made. Representatives of the disabled, fanatical in their excellent cause, stipulated the near-impossible; there can be no ideal provision for wheelchairs in a listed nineteenth-century auditorium. No less a talent than Sir Philip Dowson was brought in, at one point, to cast an acute eye over one aspect of the scheme. So was David Mlinaric. He advised, and amicably collaborated, on interior design, particularly of the auditorium and the Floral Hall. The Prince of Wales, patron of the Royal Opera, took an intermittent interest. He did not insist on a thatched roof but was keen on a matching pepper-pot at the corner of Bow Street and Russell Street.

All this, without temper or tantrum, the architects put up with. Whatever was suggested to them, I never saw Jeremy or Edward lose his cool. Jeremy had devised a spectacular double-helix

staircase at the back of the Floral Hall. It took up too much space and had to go. He never flinched; a mirror wall and an escalator did duty instead. Eager to pick out the individuality of disparate buildings, Dixon Jones proposed a brick frontage in James Street. Opera House boards prefer Portland stone. Their will was done. Committees and sub-committees inspected and approved each precise texture and colouring, from granite at the base to stucco at the summit. Dixon Jones kept calm. They never said 'never'. They never said 'certainly'. Their eloquent pens doodled. They nodded, pondered, went away and came back with their version of what we thought we wanted. They demonstrated a wonderful ingenuity in finding improvement through flexibility. Theirs was no mono-maniacal stubborn vision. Their creativity worked graciously in partnership and to a common end.

RA Butler, the cleverest Tory of the post-war years, used to remark sagely on 'the patience of politics'. Wait long enough, I think he meant, and the time to act will come. Jeremy Dixon and Edward Jones showed the patience of a saint. When the finished House finally re-opened, Jeremy Dixon had ruptured his Achilles tendon and was in plaster up to the hip. Immediately afterwards, Edward Jones went down with a debilitating complicated pleurisy. We could see then that the strain on each had been near intolerable. Yet they saw the job through. I hope they take pride, as we take pleasure, in the serendipities they found; the way that stone gradates to carpet as one enters at Bow Street; the passage through to Bow Street from the Market Square; the pristine sparkle on the auditorium's gilding; the glimpse of Nelson on his column at the top of the escalator; the fresh air delight of open-air walkways around the ballet studios; the entry from the grand staircase to the Floral Hall; the sinuous amphitheatre bar; the reflected view back down the escalator in the dark; the happiness of audiences moving through spaces they brought into being.

When the Royal Ballet dancers first jumped high in class and came down on the sprung floor of the handsome, airy and naturally lit studios that grace the roofscape, they clapped in gratitude. Applauding, they spoke for us all.

Sir Jeremy Isaacs was general director of the Royal Opera House from 1988 to 1997.

National Portrait Gallery
Ondaatje Wing
London

1994-2000

The Ondaatje Wing of the National Portrait Gallery creates a new heart to the gallery, increases the public and exhibition space by 50 per cent and significantly upgrades visitor facilities. It provides a dramatic central hall, lecture theatre, state-of-the-art IT gallery and two new exhibition spaces: the Balcony Gallery, accommodating the expanding twentieth-century collection; and the Tudor Gallery, where the Ditchley portrait of Elizabeth I and the collection of Holbein portraits – previously displayed on various staircase landings of the original building – can now be experienced as a group. Above, the rooftop restaurant gives new views out over Nelson's Column and Whitehall.

In 1994 the gallery decided it wanted to improve access to the collection and organised an open competition to select an architect. At that time only one in five visitors made their way to the seventeeth- and eighteenth-century galleries on the upper floors. Visitor facilities also needed to be upgraded and circulation improved within the L-shaped plan of the existing building.

We proposed that, to create the space for a new wing, there should be an exchange of property between the National Gallery and the NPG. By giving up those galleries running along

In the new entrance hall the daylight from the high level clerestory penetrates down to ground floor level by bouncing off a series of white surfaces. It is as if the daylight carves away the building in section. The structure, held up on a single column, spans the site lengthways at high level with the first floor supported by hangers. As a result there is less visible structure the lower down one is in the entrance hall space. Thus the 'carving' effect of the daylight and the reducing structure work together to dramatise the way the entrance hall hollows out the centre of the urban block.

JD

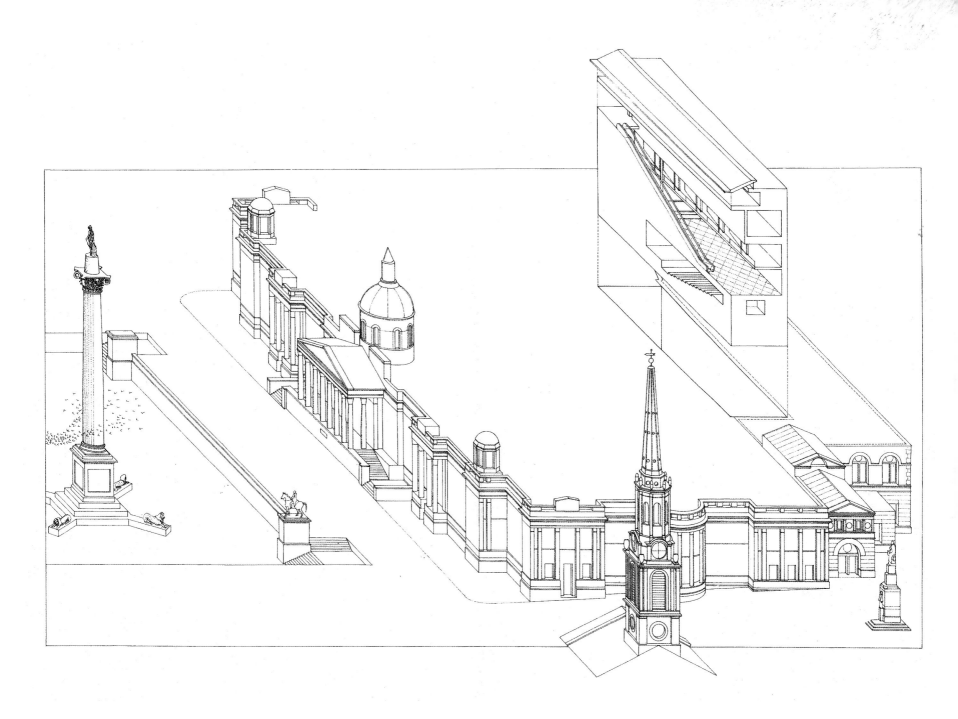

125

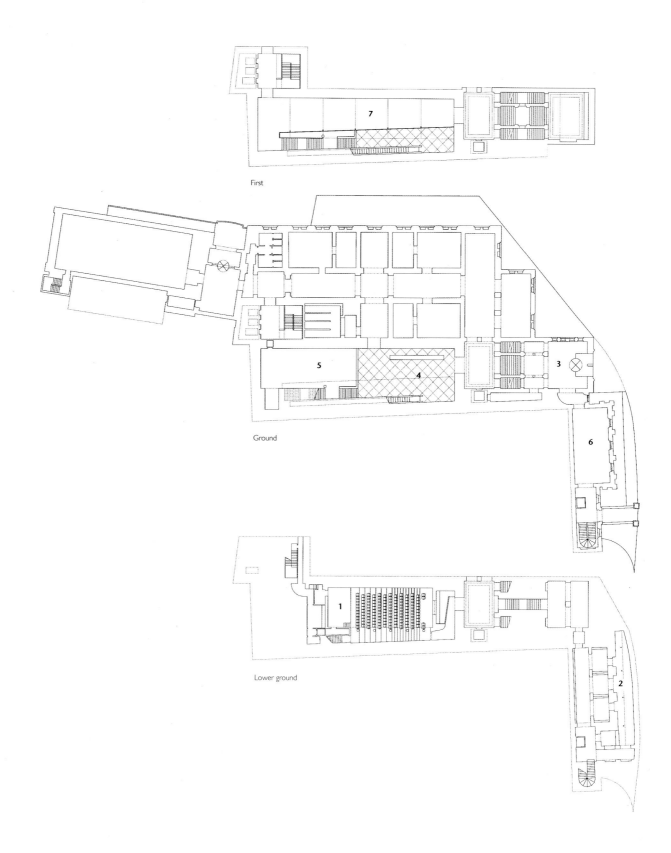

The genesis of the project involved a 'deal' between the National Portrait Gallery and the National Gallery. In our competition submission we noted that the east wing of the NPG was not frequently visited, and that the original architect Ewan Christian had been instructed to design the facade in the style of Wilkins' National Gallery, thereby establishing a lasting dilemma as to its identity. Further to this we noted that the rear courtyard separating the NPG from the National Gallery has inhibited, as a result of the rights of light, the possibility of development here. Our proposal was to exchange the east wing of the NPG for unencumbered development in this rear yard. To our surprise the 'deal' was struck between the two institutions, the windows to the National Gallery were bricked in and the generosity of the present scheme was realised. For the National Gallery the long east-west axis has now the possibility of terminating in Christian's bow window with its view to St Martins-in-the-Fields and the dilemma of its identity is at last resolved.

EJ

The flank walls of the Portrait Gallery and the National Gallery that define the space for the new project are slightly out of parallel. This irregularity is used to disturb the sense of perspective in the vertical space around the escalator. Different floor edges, walls and balustrades are variously aligned with either the Portrait Gallery or the National Gallery. What appears to be a simple rectangular arrangement consists in fact of lines and planes that are not parallel with the result that it is very difficult for the eye to sort out the precise relationships.

JD

Plans I lecture theatre, 2 cafe, 3 main entrance lobby, 4 new foyer, 5 IT gallery, 6 shop, 7 late- twentieth century gallery, 8 Tudor gallery, 9 miniatures room, 10 restaurant.

First

Ground

Lower ground

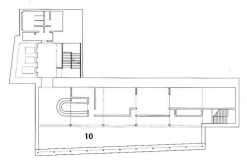

Third

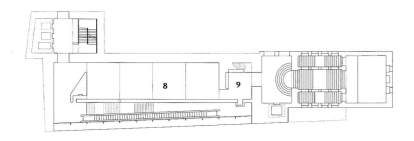

Second

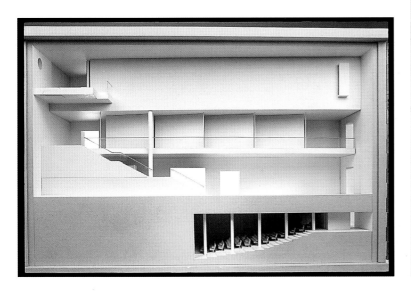

St Martin's Place to the National Gallery, in return for control of the once dingy service yard separating the two institutions, the NPG gained space for a triple-height hall that provides a new circulation and focal point to the museum. This 'deal' was struck in March 1995, allowing construction to begin in the autumn of 1998 and to be completed in the spring of 2000.

While virtually invisible on the outside, internally the new wing is a radical addition that creates a new sense of clarity for visitors to the collection. It eases circulation throughout the gallery while also encouraging visitors to start in the upper galleries, where the earliest paintings are displayed, and view the entire collection as they work their way down to the ground floor.

Entering through the original (1895) facade and passing through the restored entrance lobby, the public is drawn directly into the new, light-filled hall that serves to welcome and orientate visitors. Daylight is drawn deep into this triple-height space via south-facing clerestory glazing running its full length. The upper floors appear to rest on a single column, which supports a truss in the wall of the top gallery. From this central hall, visitors can either ascend the new stairs to the mezzanine IT gallery and first-floor Balcony Gallery or take the 23 metre-long escalator up to the second floor and the new Tudor Gallery. This is reminiscent of a Tudor long gallery, its deep grey walls creating a dramatic backdrop for the important collection of sixteenth-century portraits, with fibre optic lights in the ceiling spotlighting each painting. The Balcony Gallery below is suspended on cables from the Tudor Gallery and flanked by a walkway that overlooks the central hall. A series of four metre-high partitions, which are staggered to allow reflected natural light into the exhibition space,

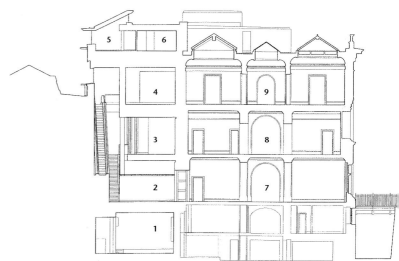

Cross section 1 Lecture theatre, 2 entrance foyer, 3 late twentieth-century gallery, 4 Tudor Gallery, 5 restaurant, 6 kitchen, 7 twentieth-century gallery, 8 Victorian gallery, 9 seventeenth/eighteenth century galleries.

The section of the rooftop restaurant is exactly the same as that of the sculpture gallery we proposed for Henry Moore at Perry Green. The situation is the same. The view is to the south and the window in that direction has to be 'closed down' to reduce brightness and solar penetration while at the same time giving a panoramic access to the view. The clerestory north light softens the contrast and distributes light through the section of the space. Sometimes an unbuilt scheme becomes built under unexpected circumstances.

JD

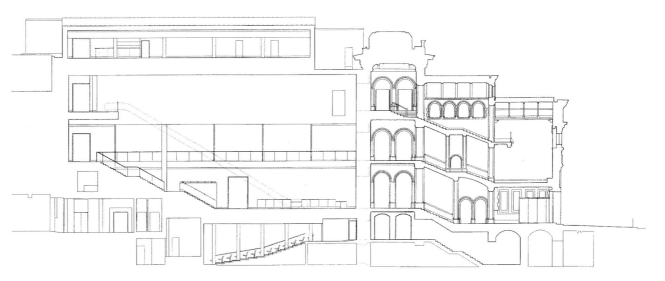

partially enclose the gallery.

Above, the 100-seat restaurant and bar reveal new panoramic views of Trafalgar Square, Nelson's Column and Whitehall. The restaurant has been designed as an implied loggia, with a sloping lead roof and a fully-glazed southern facade to maximise the breathtaking views.

The new lecture theatre on the lower-ground floor enables the gallery to further develop its education work, including lectures and performance. The theatre, which seats 150 people in a raked auditorium, includes the latest projection, sound and lighting systems and is acoustically engineered for music.

Significant restoration work has also been undertaken as part of the project. The original double-height staircase landing has been reinstated, removing a mezzanine inserted in the 70s, and the entrance lobby and upper galleries have been refurbished in keeping with the original scheme. By contrasting the architectural languages of the new and the original buildings, a conscious transition has been created in the journey through the gallery.

Phase one of the development was completed in 1998, with a new basement cafe and an extended gift/book-shop situated to the south of the entrance lobby. The cafe was inserted into a disused, open basement, revealing an intriguing vaulted brick space. A skylight covers half the cafe, bringing natural light into the seating area and providing views up to St Martin's Place.

The escalator leads, indeed, points towards the light. The entrance hall is entirely white. The various conditions of reflected daylight produce subtle variations of colour on the white walls. The destination of the escalator is the new Tudor Gallery where the dark walls match the backgrounds of the paintings – only the faces and lace ruffs stand out. The light of the entrance hall gives way to darkness, as if one is entering a new underworld that alludes to the sinister end of the lives of many of those portrayed.

JD

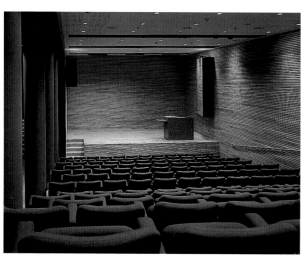

As a result of the somewhat ludicrous objections by the planners to the proposed restaurant roofscape, David Naessens was inspired to draw this cartoon in which the National Gallery and its various roofs are translated into an Italian hillside village. The new restaurant for the NPG sits comfortably as a terraced loggia and looks so natural that the objections were withdrawn.

JD

I remember Charles Jencks gently cricitising our rather discreet roof profile. Surely, he said, this is a public place and not a company boardroom or private penthouse. Surely, he said, as you benefit from the view of a varied and romantic roofline from your rooftop restaurant, should you not be making your own contribution? He is right of course. As it was, we conducted an extended debate with a particular planner at Westminster who was concerned that the roof might be just visible for someone travelling north up Whitehall on the top floor of a double-decker bus.

During the competition we requested to see the view from the roof – once seen, never forgotten! This panorama of 'Imperial London' (embracing institutions in which many of those commemorated in the NPG made their reputations) became a key idea. We entitled this re-presentation of a part of London (familiar from the ground), a National Portrait, framed in its singular long window.

EJ

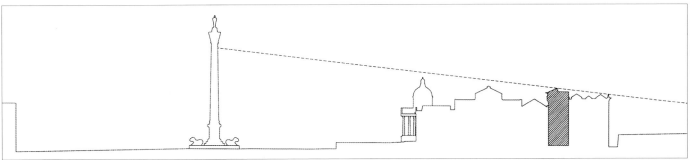

Access and authority: the Ondaatje Wing at the National Portrait Gallery

Charles Saumarez Smith

Above Dixon and Jones stand before John Lessore's painting of the two architects and their client Charles Saumarez Smith at the National Portrait Gallery.

The ideas which lie behind the National Portrait Gallery project go back to the period when I was appointed director in 1994. The NPG was enjoying a surge in visitor numbers owing to the atmosphere of much greater public accessibility and to the fact that much more of the contemporary collection was on display, including more photography. It seemed a good moment to stand back and consider its longer-term needs and plan how these might be accommodated not in a piecemeal fashion but more purposefully.

From discussions with staff it became clear that while the previous development project – based on the new ground-floor galleries by John Miller & Partners – had been extremely successful in providing new gallery space for the twentieth-century collection and new staff accommodation, it had done less in thinking about how visitors used and experienced the collection and the gallery as a whole. The front entrance lobby was too small and was not really equipped for the increased numbers of visitors coming to the gallery. The main staircase was set back behind the upper landing of the entrance lobby in such a way that many visitors were not aware that the great bulk of the collection was upstairs on the top two floors. The main staircase itself was long and oppressively monumental in a way that inhibited people from making the long trek up to the top floor. There was a pretty inadequate and rather claustrophobic lecture theatre. And there was absolutely no catering in the building.

The project derived therefore from a particular and quite tightly specified brief about how it might be possible to add three new things to an existing historic building: a new lecture theatre; some sort of cafe or restaurant; and an improvement, if possible, to the system of public circulation.

Having set out the brief, in 1994 we set about the task of selecting an architect. Stage one of the open competition consisted of the submission of outline ideas. The selection panel chaired by Sir Philip Dowson shortlisted five practices: Michael Hopkins & Partners, Jeremy Dixon and Edward Jones, MacCormac Jamieson Prichard, Ian Ritchie Architects and Eva Jiricna Architects. Each was given three weeks to come up with a set of four display boards demonstrating their approach to the solution of the problems.

Jeremy Dixon and Edward Jones were chosen for a variety of reasons. They showed that they were interested in working closely with the gallery and its staff in devising an intelligent and possibly adventurous building in the back yard between the NPG and the National Gallery. Rather than providing a single solution, they provided a set of three alternatives. Second, they are architects who have had a great deal of experience of working on sites where there is a need to have a strong sense of appropriate context and of history. This is evident, for example, in Jeremy Dixon's Darwin College study centre on the river at Cambridge, where he was faced with an extremely narrow site on one of the most sensitive places environmentally, lying between the city and the meadows which lead to Grantchester. Here he managed to design a building which is both responsive to the surrounding environment in its use of material, but also has a sense of puritanical authority, with beautiful, well worked out interior spaces, which are clearly geometric in a building which conspicuously has an odd ground-plan. It is also equally, but slightly differently, evident in Edward Jones's more astringent graduate hall of residence, also for Darwin College, which overlooks the playing fields at Newnham and which has qualities of a modern version of a boathouse, which is surely not accidental. Their architecture tends to be subtle, not readily identifiable as signature buildings (in other words, they provide different solutions to different problems, rather than having a unitary style); they are slightly low-tech in their use of traditional materials; and they have a sense of depth and strong architectural intelligence to them. I remember that one of the other architects who had entered the competition said afterwards that he had known that Jeremy Dixon and Edward Jones would be selected, because it was their sort of project. This was a post-rationalisation but it has a certain truth to it.

During the early spring of 1995, we worked on a cutback version of the project – called 'light angles' in the Dixon Jones competition entry – which respected the National Gallery's rights of light in the back yard. The National Gallery had a set of offices which overlooked the back yard; so although we owned the ground between the two buildings, we thought that we would be allowed to build only in the air space that we owned – essentially a triangle of space under a line drawn from the National Gallery's offices up to the top of our existing building.

This was just about acceptable at the bottom of the building

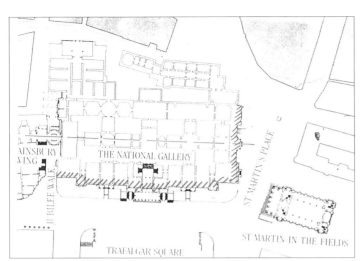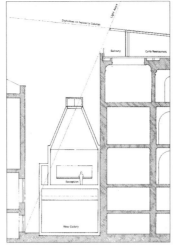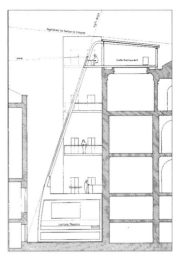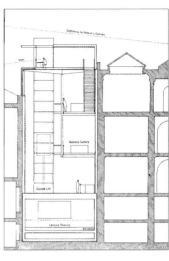

'Minimum' This largely single-storey insertion in the rear court protected the rights of light to the staff offices of the neighbouring National Gallery, as well as an escape route. A new reception space with a top-lit conical roof is set at a raised ground floor level and a new top-lit gallery is provided at basement level. The cafe/restaurant is built on top of the existing building, taking advantage of the spectacular view to the south.

'Light angles' The second option sought to maximise use of the courtyard while protecting the National Gallery's rights of light. This allows for the addition of a lecture theatre at basement level beneath a tapering and top-lit triple-height reception space. A new lift tower is added at the end of the space. The restaurant is built on top of the existing building, partially encroaching on the new structure.

'The Deal' The third option, largely as built, proposed ceding the east wing to the National Gallery in exchange for waiving its rights of light in the court. The five-storey structure provides a lecture theatre, triple-height hall, a balcony gallery and rooftop restaurant. In the event the lifts were placed elsewhere and (as at the Royal Opera House) an escalator was to form the main means of access.

where the architects had proposed a lecture theatre; it was fine at the level above, where it was suggested we should have a new front entrance; but it was much more problematic at the two upper levels where it would have produced a set of unsatisfactorily long, thin gallery spaces. It was most unsatisfactory of all at roof level, where it was suggested we should have a cafe on the roof of the existing building. English Heritage and Westminster City Council indicated that they would not be happy for us to block up the roof lights of the original building; rather they encouraged us to think of using the whole back yard, if possible.

We therefore returned to the most ambitious suggestion ('the deal') and the one that Dixon Jones strongly favoured. This involved a complex exchange of land rights between the NPG and the National Gallery, whereby we ceded ownership of our east wing while keeping the ground-floor shop and basement on a 100-year lease at a peppercorn rent. In exchange we got the right to build in the full back yard, thereby blocking up the windows of the offices which looked out onto the yard. It is testimony to the flexibility and supportiveness of Neil MacGregor, director of the National Gallery, and his trustees that this very complex exchange has happened entirely amicably, although not without a certain amount of tough negotiation.

The essential elements of the scheme as built are pretty much as proposed by Dixon Jones in their competition entry. In the course of detailed design there have been a myriad of minor, subtle and some more significant changes, some of which the architects may slightly regret, but which I hope represent a tightening-up of the scheme to our requirements, rather than a dilution of its original sense of purpose.

A key component in the project is the escalator which runs up nearly the full height of the building. This is the only part of the project that was modestly controversial when it went to the Royal Fine Arts Commission for approval and to the Heritage Lottery Fund for funding. There was a view vigorously expressed that escalators belonged to airports and shopping malls and not to a major national cultural institution. But the reality is that a one-way escalator beginning near the entrance and travelling upwards to where the collection begins is a fairly straightforward means of encouraging more people to visit the top floor, which was one of the main points of the project. And escalators are not without cultural resonances, as has been demonstrated by their use in the Louvre by IM Pei and Michel Macary, in the Museum of Modern Art in New York by Cesar Pelli and in the Museum of Contemporary Art in Tokyo by Takahiko Yanagisawa. All of these share some of the qualities intended by the escalator at the National Portrait Gallery – a smooth and quiet passageway from the everyday world up into the more contemplative environment of the top floor.

I view the project as a way of opening up the experience of the gallery to enhanced democratic access while at the same time retaining a sense of appropriate authority – in the sense that this is public, not private, space. It is not, and cannot be described as being, a high-tech revolution in the way that the NPG thinks about itself. Instead, I would like to think that it will provide a strong sense of organic development – systematic, incremental and purposeful. The language of the building is modern (stone, glass and touches of steel) but classical, cool and, I hope, intelligent and lucid, unflamboyant, enhancing the experience of the visitor but not at the expense of other parts of the gallery.

Charles Saumarez Smith has been director of the National Portrait Gallery since 1994.

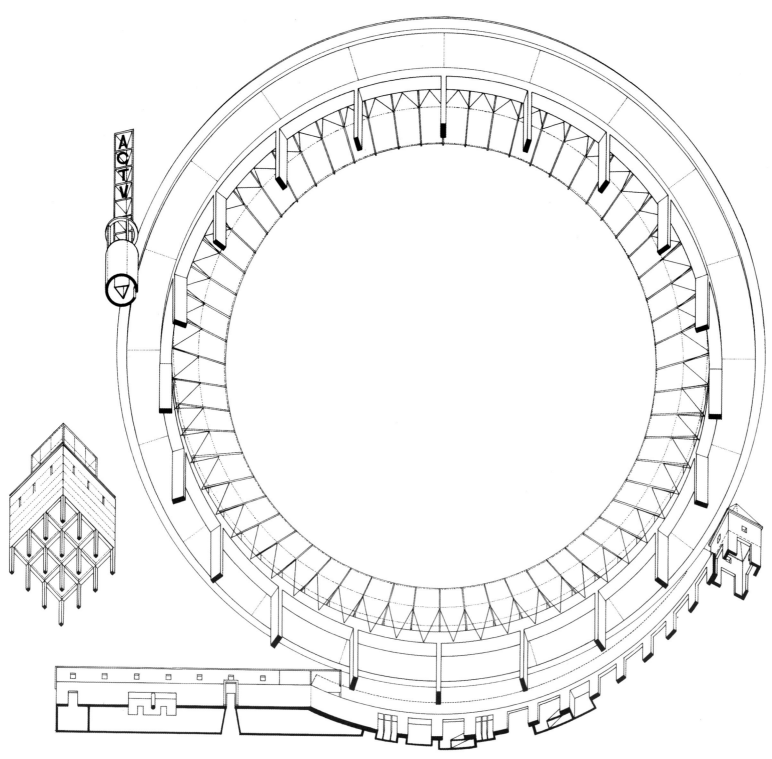

138

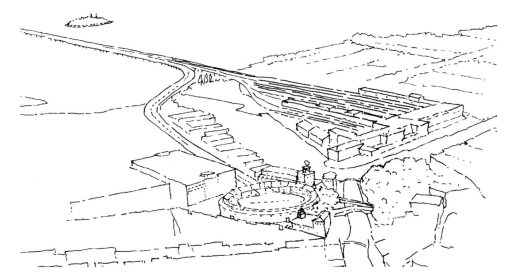

Venice bus station competition

1990

There is a particular drama to the moment of arrival in Venice. Modern transport systems – train, car, aeroplane, bus – have to be left behind, to be replaced by the gentle movement of boats and the pleasure of walking.

Whereas trains arrive and depart along a straight line, buses make a loop around a roundabout. The new bus station, which won first prize in the open international competition sponsored by the City and Biennale of Venice, organises movement in the form of a circus, a giant turn-around that expresses the cul de sac at the end of the causeway. The perimeter provides 20 platform spaces, the inner radial arrangement of buses allows space for 30 empty buses and coaches. In the centre is a cafe and rest-room for drivers.

The circular form arises as a mechanical solution to the organisation of the buses. At the same time it is a spatial idea, a new room in the city. But there is a distinction between this space, occupied more by buses than people, and the typical urban spaces in the rest of the city. People occupy only the perimeter and disperse radially into the surrounding city.

The bus station can be considered as three separate zones: a pedestrian area, an outer platform ring and an inner layover/rest area. Pedestrians, the running bus lane and the layover parking and manoeuvering zones are segregated for maximum safety. The saw-tooth arrangement allows buses easy access into each stance, driving counter-clockwise round the outer 12 metre wide perimeter lanes.

Right The Grand Canal, the bus station site and carnival views.
Left Train and bus movements and pattern of pedestrian routes.

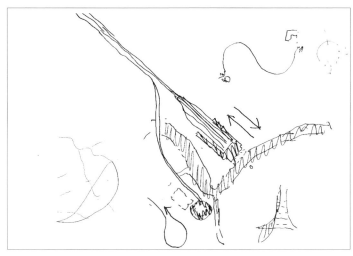

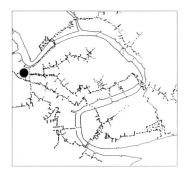

'There is nowhere in Venice that is not quicker to travel to on foot'.

Philip Tabor (occasional resident)

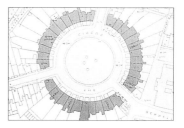

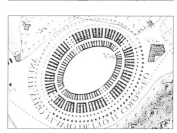

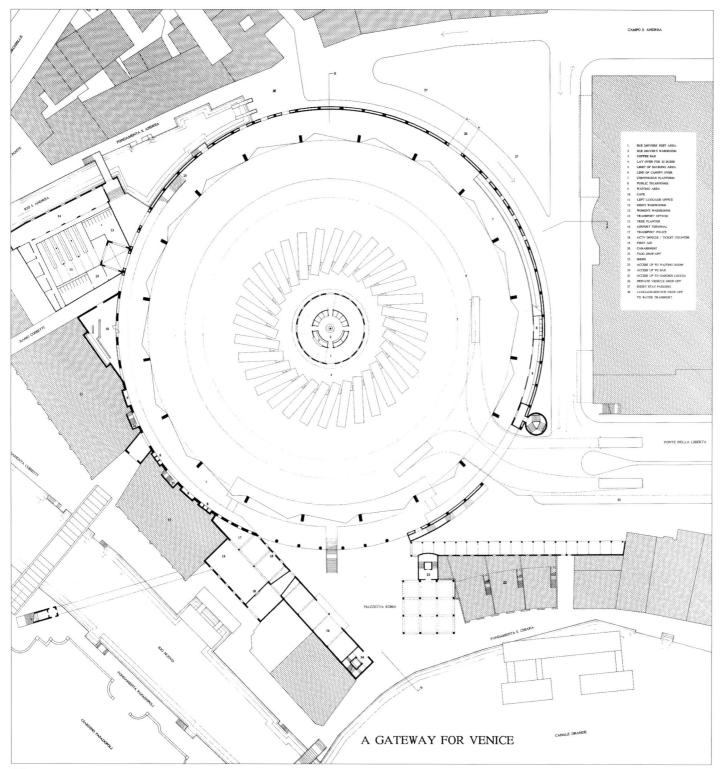

The legend in the plan (numbered list):

1. BUS DRIVERS' REST AREA
2. BUS DRIVER'S WASHROOM
3. COFFEE BAR
4. LAY OVER FOR 32 BUSES
5. LIMIT OF BACKING AREA
6. LINE OF CANOPY OVER
7. CONTINUOUS PLATFORM
8. PUBLIC TELEPHONES
9. WAITING AREA
10. CAFE
11. LEFT LUGGAGE OFFICE
12. MEN'S WASHROOMS
13. WOMEN'S WASHROOMS
14. TRANSPORT OFFICES
15. TREE PLANTER
16. AIRPORT TERMINAL
17. TRANSPORT POLICE
18. ACTV OFFICES / TICKET COUNTER
19. FIRST AID
20. CARABINIERI
21. TAXI DROP-OFF
22. SHOPS
23. ACCESS UP TO WAITING ROOM
24. ACCESS UP TO BAR
25. ACCESS UP TO GARDEN LOGGIA
26. PRIVATE VEHICLE DROP-OFF
27. SHORT STAY PARKING
28. LUGGAGE/SERVICE DROP-OFF
   TO WATER TRANSPORT

The circular form of the bus station is a composite –
it is part void and part solid, it is part 'carved' space
and part freestanding screen. We were interested to
note that its dimension (112 metres in diameter)
was similar both to the Royal Circus in Bath (top) as
an urban void and to the Colosseum in Rome
(above) as a freestanding object.

The importance of understanding the workings of
a bus station and the absence of a credible competition brief led us to invite the manager of Victoria
Coach Station in London to act as our surrogate
client. The circular form resulted from a combination
of factors: the circulation of the buses (functional);
the idea of a cul de sac turnaround; and the memorable urban form (compositional). Holding on to the
circle was then the challenge during the development of the scheme. Interestingly, in the 277 submissions to the competition, there were only two
essential diagrams – circles and stripes. Of the circles, ours was the only uncontaminated version –
competition juror Jim Stirling said we had done the
best tart!

EJ

A GATEWAY FOR VENICE

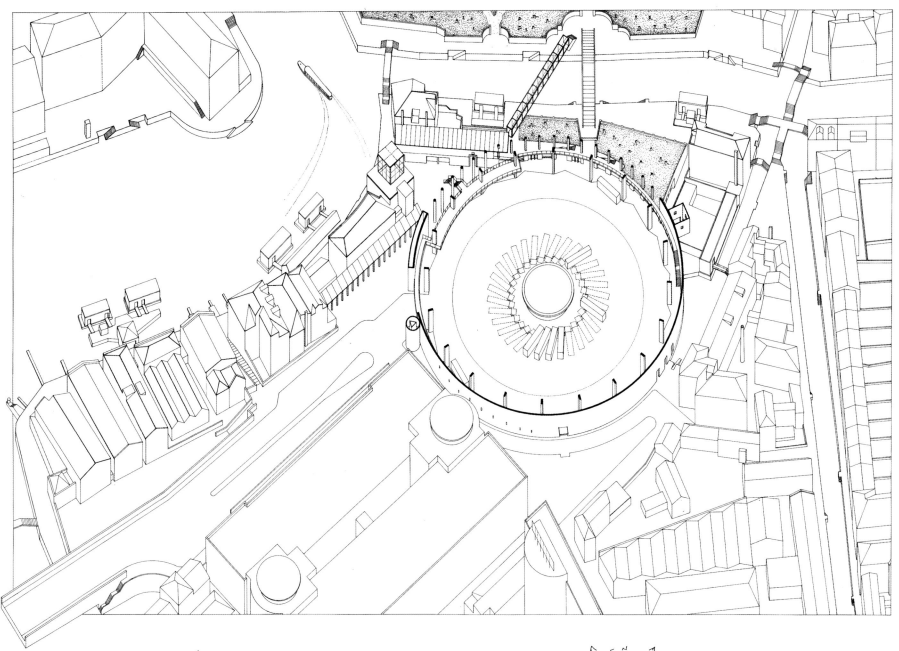

Although the work of the office is deliberately varied in style and approach, there are some preoccupations that recur. One such is an interest in pure forms and simple geometry, in particular the circle and the straight line. In the project for Northamptonshire county offices the circle appears in the form of a spiral – the geometry is a mecha-nism for organising and storing cars so that the 'obe-dience' of parked vehicles is used to form a conic spiral mound of cars, a sculpture on the scale of the surrounding landscape. The bus station in Venice has a circle similarly set up by the movement of traffic. Here a circle is carved out of a dense city fabric and the geometry is a product of the mechanism required to park and store buses at a terminal. The resultant space, a hidden place within the tight fabric of Venice, is not a pedestrian 'place' but a void full of traffic. The surrounding geometry is at pains to avoid re-stating the centre of the circle.

JD

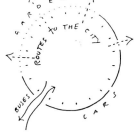

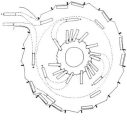

141

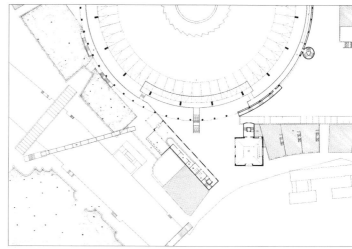

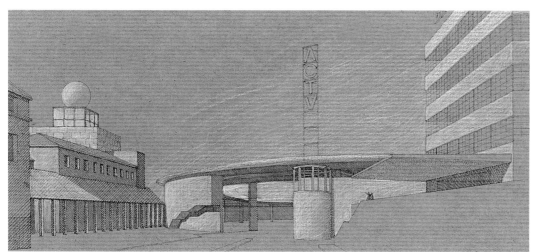

Above A trophy, designed by Massimo Scolari, was awarded to Dixon Jones for their first-placed competition entry; Dixon Jones meet Canova – exhibition posters vie for space on the walls of Venice.
Top left View of the Grand Canal, after Canaletto.

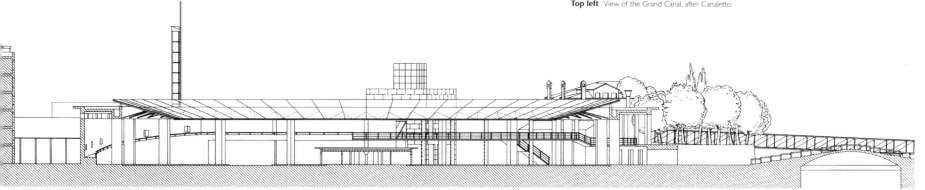

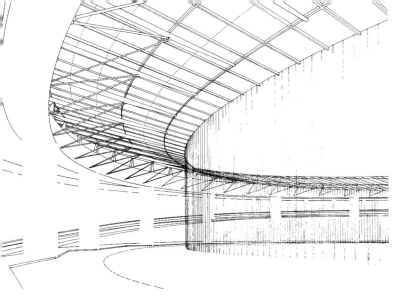

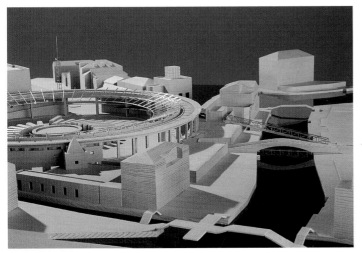

The new facility forms an interchange between buses, vaporetti and pedestrian routes. The new buildings fronting the Grand Canal, together with an existing building, form a free composition around a 'front door' to the bus station, facing the main axis of the canal. At ground level they house the ticketing facilities, while cafes and restaurants occupy the first floor, looking back at the Grand Canal. The bus station building is designed to accommodate the extremes of summer and winter weather in the city, as well as dissipating dangerous diesel fumes. It takes the form of a continuous open colonnade, made of concrete, which supports a rudimentary glass and steel cantilevered canopy that was inspired by the traditional Italian street parasol. Rain is allowed to fall from the inner edge of the canopy as a cylindrical wall of droplets, through which only the buses have to penetrate. On hot summer days this giant water sculpture can be turned on and the water curtain induces a downward movement of cool air towards waiting pedestrians – an oasis in the hot city.

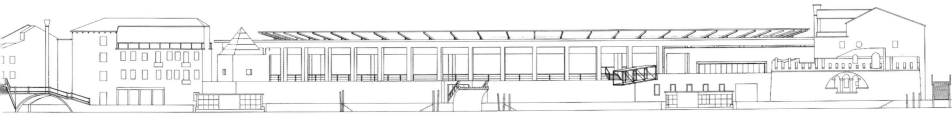

Practical means and poetic ends

Jeremy Dixon and Edward Jones

Above Jeremy Dixon, Edward Jones, Margot Jones and David Naessens at the Venice Biennale, photographed by Jim Stirling; Dixon and Jones with the mayor of Venice and interpreter at the bus station competition awards ceremony.

Jeremy Dixon We thought it might be interesting to look at a project we have worked on together, in a conversation that picks up some of the topics behind the ideas and the working process. The project we have chosen is the competition entry for Venice bus station or the Gateway to Venice. It is quite a loaded title.

Edward Jones It has a double reading – when you describe a bus station for Venice it has a utilitarian connotation, but as soon as it's described as a Gateway to Venice it conjures up all sorts of grand and symbolic meanings in the project.

JD Venice is a very difficult city to get one's hands on because it's not a typical European city. Its sensuousness and urban quality do not lend themselves immediately to the kind of typologies one normally looks at in relation to cities and urban spaces. So there are a number of topics in the competition that aroused our interest.

EJ Yes, the point of Venice not being a typical European city is evident clearly in that it doesn't have an obvious Roman origin – it doesn't have that classic cross that sets up the majority of cities in Europe. It is atypical in its origins and atypical in its fabric. So the act then of contemplating a motorised building, a building involving locomotion, is a very odd thing to be thinking about in Venice. It has a strange contradiction – buses in Venice.

JD It is actually a contradiction between modernity and history, because transport systems are essentially a product of the twentieth century. So how people arrive in Venice, how fast they arrive, and how quickly they would have to slow down to accommodate being on a water bus instead of being in an aeroplane is a telling moment of transition. So to do a building which is about how you arrive by modern transport and become involved in the historical and slower means of moving about Venice, either on foot or on a boat, has its own kind of poignancy. I think that actually became a central theme in the project.

EJ That moment of rest, or the moment of arrival and departure, started to give the project meanings other than pure utility.

JD If you look at the plan of Venice there is a very clear and memorable shape. On the one hand it is an island with a straight causeway and on the other hand the island is separated into two halves by the extended S-shape of the Grand Canal. The interesting thing

is that the bus station is located right at one end of the Grand Canal, the point at which the canal ceases to be a beautiful urban place and becomes a more utilitarian area to do with docklands. One of the counterpoints we looked at is between the bus station at one end and the Customs House, the arrival of shipping and the monitoring of shipping which takes place down at the other end of the Grand Canal.

EJ You could see this as a sort of front door and back door thing: in the eighteenth century the Customs House was the front door of the Grand Canal and the bus station site was a very minor player. So we are modifying that reading. And really it is difficult to examine the bus station without comparing it to the railway station. Both forms are, so to speak, alien to the history of the city. The buses and the trains share the causeway from Mestre to the island. But while the trains come and go in a piston-like fashion, the road to the bus station peels off and takes a freer pattern ending in Piazzale Roma, presently a very undistinguished space.

JD Arrival at the railway station is all about straightness. From the railway line, you come off a train onto a platform, again in a straight line, and you are projected out onto the square in front of the station and virtually tipped into a vaporetto waterbus. In contrast the road comes off as a curve and ends in a loop. This begins to generate the circle which is then the basis of the geometry of the project itself – a large roundabout – which allows buses to turn around and go back from whence they come.

EJ The circle could be said to be a cul de sac. In a most diagrammatic way the buses turn round.

JD If we are honest, this was immediately interesting because we are 'circle' people. There are projects in both our portfolios and indeed in our joint portfolio that seek to have circular shapes.

EJ I think the other powerful point that you were getting at was the sense that in the railway station the threshold is abrupt and dramatic in its relationship to the Grand Canal, whereas in the Piazzale Roma the space is buried. In our early considerations of the site, the most impressive building was the 1930s car park. The building dominates the Piazzale Roma and you have to take a point of view about it – I suppose what our project does is to establish an indifference to it in compositional terms.

JD The dilemma was that the scale of that building suggested that it might be part of the containing edge of the space of the Piazzale Roma. We didn't want that to happen. We tried to put the two objects close to each other so that there wasn't a conventional reading of a space created by edges. Rather, there's a left-over space between a rectangular object and a hollow circular machine.

EJ And the cars exist in a no-man's land between the two.

JD This relates to an aspect of the project that has been criticised – that it underplays the secondary spaces between the buildings.

EJ We should consider the ground-floor plan, where the circle is posited in the depth of the site and the relationship between the circle and the edge to the Grand Canal is intentionally accidental.

JD We should perhaps go back one step because the transport systems of Venice are not as simple as you might think. Most visitors want to get on a vaporetto and go in style down the Grand Canal looking at buildings, but a large number of those arriving are workers and residents. Where the railway station has visitors wanting to get onto the vaporetti, so at the bus station there are workers and schoolchildren who disperse radially into the city. Here again was a clue – it looked as if the circular form that is useful in organising buses has its radial counterpart in the way in which people disperse out into the city. Connected to this is the difficult issue of who the gateway is for. It's not so much a symbolic gateway for visitors as a quiet gateway for the workers and schoolchildren who come and go every day.

EJ Something that surprised us was the fact that the quickest way to get between two points in Venice is to walk – so the radial nature of the circle started to have an interest beyond being entirely an imploding and centering form. It starts to have readings other than the obvious. It works outwards and inwards – buses are drawn to the centre, pedestrians seek the edge and disperse.

JD I think if we're honest, one looks for useful bits of information to reinforce the form and it was very useful to find this distinction between pedestrian and waterborne traffic. One is looking for something that has several layers of credibility or interest, which allows you not only to sustain the shapes but to give them several

interpretations at once. Buses generate the circle and so do the people, and so does the idea of carving a circle into the city.

EJ This starts to raise the question of making a public place. If we say that the circle is a convenient form it also offers the possibility of seeing it as a large urban 'room'. It's not trying to to be a replica of St Mark's square – it's saying that buses are in the centre and the pedestrians are not so much promenading in the space as seeking the edge of it – and that maybe starts to give the project its contemporary nature. One is trying to find a form that is of the period but also contributes a memorable room or memorable urban space within the continuum of Venice.

JD The fact that it's more like a railway station than a piazza has allowed us to excuse what is really a Roman form in an essentially non-Roman city. That's a criticism we received but I think one has to argue that the form is generated not out of historical context but as a mechanism. Then you enjoy the space that's generated and you're very careful that its presence is handled so that it doesn't damage the surrounding more characteristic Venetian places. That led to a preoccupation of seeing the scheme primarily as an interior. The circle is seen only from outside in incidental views; the experience of the project is through a relatively informal set of paths, approaches and connections from which you get the surprise of entering this large circular room.

EJ It is large – at 112 metres in diameter it's the same dimension as the circus in Bath and the Colosseum in Rome at its narrowest point. We are dealing with something that is relatively big in plan but modest in section – an urban space that has the historically unprecedented height-to-width ratio – and as you say the external expression is very quiet but the interior would be a dramatic surprise. It has a Venetian counterpart – the spaces which you approach down minor paths and passages that then unexpectedly lead into an extraordinary void or volume – as at St Mark's square.

JD It might be appropriate to say just how the circle works. The outer perimeter has about 20 stopping points for the buses. We observed that buses stop for a short time to pick people up and put them down but, because this is a terminus, they also wait for about half an hour to give the drivers a rest. Up to 30 buses can wait in the centre of the circle in a sort of fan shape, allowing the drivers to get out and have a coffee in the little central circular building, with its handwash basin right at the central point.

EJ That introduces an interesting point about centring the circle. Here we avoid the aggrandising nineteenth-century effect of having a general on horseback in the middle; indeed the roof of our rest room has water on it that reflects the sky and dematerialises the centre. All the bridges and approaches, the supportive building programme for tickets etc are tangential to the circle – and indeed even the buses park in a turbine fashion – eschewing radial gestures towards the centre. It's the exact opposite of the railway station with its large terrace and steps with people sitting and the facade as a representation of the scale of the tracks and platforms behind. Our little cube is a condensation of quite a big thing into a very loaded small object. The dilemma is that the small object is rather diagrammatic yet has to carry its message persuasively.

JD We had a go at giving it a broader symbolic intention, adding a facsimile of the golden ball from the top of the Customs House. One of my favourite and most enduring images of Venice is the way the sun moves round and gives different reflections off the ball, topped by its silhouetted dancing figure.

EJ We then rubbed the ball out because it appeared too cute.

JD But when we exhibited the scheme we stuck it back in again.

EJ If we look at the organisation of the project, the sections are important in showing the opportunistic use of existing levels. The site has on its eastern edge a remarkable garden which is raised a metre or two above the level of Piazzale Roma so we established a second level, with a terrace looking over the Popodopoli gardens to the east, by lowering the site by about one metre. That then gave us a first-floor level that connected to the existing bridges and gave visitors and those waiting for buses a kind of theatrical view of the interior. And that's where we placed a cafe – we wanted to re-state the value of these gardens as a cool and pleasant place in summer to sit and view the spectacle of arrival and departure.

JD The problem with this project was not to do too much. Most of the other competition entries couldn't resist adding a huge tower to say 'gateway' or sticking a rhetorical object out in the water, whereas what was needed was restraint. The place is very delicate,

it can't take bullying. The projects we liked were understated, extracting something with minimal means out of the situation.

EJ This balance was very clear in the programme. What interested me in quite a particular way was the programme – just three or four lines of text saying they wanted 200 metres for tickets and left luggage and a cafe. In functional terms the programme was really very small but the impact of the new building was a transforming one. So I think Jeremy's absolutely right that the balance of doing too much or too little is central to the development of this project.

JD We have done a couple of projects in the past that looked at how transport systems can produce interesting geometries, transforming a banal use into something that has greater possibilities. The project for Northamptonshire county hall turned the car parking to advantage through the geometry of a spiral mound. The observation was that cars are obedient to any layout – if you tell a car where to go, on the whole it will do it, whereas if you try to tell people where to go, they won't. We were also able to develop the theme in the Sainsbury superstore in Plymouth, where we saw the business of arrival and parking as the main architectural possibility for a landscape idea, with the building being secondary.

EJ That's very true. I think the interest in the Venice project was that the supporting programme was part of a texture of building that already exists. The Plymouth project makes a great effort to establish the big store as something to do with a landscape idea – and to put a premium on the arcade and the drama of its car park. In Venice the drama of 50 buses all coming into one space at one time is like a ballet – a burlesque – an extraordinary theatrical thing that needs its containment. One aspect of our interior is that it is partly made by carving into a condition that exists. The edge makes a large screen so that the building, or the public place, is a little ambiguous about whether it's carving a space out of something that's already there or positing a new figure.

JD It is an attempt to make a circular urban space that's carved out of the city but on closer inspection it's partly made by wall – it's not quite as pure as it sets out to be in the first place and that means you're having to transform the edge of the circle to several different functions as you go round. I find that an extremely interesting topic – taking an elementary shape and undermining, stretching and pulling at it to the point that it's almost falling apart. It's a technique we use quite often but it has to be underpinned in the first move by something that's strong and obvious.

EJ And practical too. I think it would be a comment that Peter Cook might make about our work – we take ideas to the point of absurdum and then extract some poetry out of holding the line. In this case it was interesting that, while there are many circles among the 267 entries, the others tended to give up on the purity of the form. We kept faith with the circle and enjoyed, as Jeremy says, this extraordinary quality you get in an architectural project when you retain its essence. Around the circumference – about 400 metres long – the events change from a wall to canal to gardens to vendor stalls to taxi drop to the main entrance to the station itself, engaging ramps and stairs, so when you draw this as a flattened out elevation, you get an incredibly varied proposition.

JD There's a kind of (perhaps self-) criticism of banal neoclassical forms in our limited palate of pure forms, but we use those pure forms to generate a maximum secondary richness of incident which really is only supportable in relation to the pure form itself.

EJ Without the primary form you wouldn't have the original text and the design would be a series of episodic readings. I suppose this is true of the Northampton pyramid, the Royal Opera House, to some extent Mississauga city hall and this project – they exist within a conceptual frame which we might be trying to escape.

JD Maybe this is the last of them – maybe we've done it enough. I think we like to work by finding practical reasons for things which can be turned to poetic ends – the way buses move, the way pedestrians move – and we had a rather odd lateral line of thought about the climate of Venice and how we might handle that. Venice has the sort of climate that no building can really fit. In winter it's cold and you want protection – you want to be indoors. In summer it's hot, so you want a different kind of shelter. In between it's ideal and you want no shelter at all. So in the bus station we have a glass canopy cantilevered off a concrete circular ring structure which gives an interesting double-curve ribbon effect in perspective. The canopy tips downwards towards the centre, like the top of a volcano. Now as soon as you do that you realise the rain is going to fall towards the centre and you may need a heavy gutter or

something to deal with the inner line. It just became a radical possibility that you just let the water run off the edge. You have a thin glass edge to the circle and the drips define a drum shape. And as it's only buses that go through this curtain of water, maybe it could work. And then you start thinking about the climate and the possibility that this curtain of water could also generate a cooling downdraught in summer. So there's a possibly mad, possibly practical, idea for a giant circular drum fountain which derives from thinking about the climatic peculiarities of Venice.

EJ When people arrive in Venice water is very much on their minds, so the thought that the building might offer a theme to do with water in a very straightforward practical way seemed worth trying. The thought was triggered when we considered what the effect of adding a gutter to the edge of the glazed canopy would be – when one wanted it to virtually disappear. In a way the thought started from making drawings and looking. It didn't come from saying, 'let's do a fountain' – it came in a very untidy way – like most ideas in architecture it came from experiment and drawing it and seeing what the implications of water might be. A big cylinder of water would be a remarkable experience. If it was sufficiently remarkable to enjoy in winter, we thought then we might as well get it for the summer too, which starts to give the project a cooling device, like the fountains in traditional urban spaces.

JD When we finished the project we thought it was important to take it back and exhibit it in Venice to get a reaction from people. So with the help of the Foreign Office we hired a gallery overlooking the Grand Canal and, as a result, our announcement was fly-posted a thousand times around Venice – sometimes adjacent to a poster for an exhibition of Canova.

EJ When we were staying in Venice putting the exhibition up, the waiters in the hotel knew the project. The waiter charmingly said, 'Ah, the competition!' and then he said, 'Oh, you won it, you did the round scheme', which was very touching. So architecture in Italy has a sort of popular support and to be an architect in Italy for this short time was an experience one has never had in Britain.

JD To be a respected person.

EJ Architetto Dixon, Architetto Jones!

Above Posters for the exhibition of Jeremy Dixon and Edward Jones' prize-winning entry to the bus station competition were fly-posted throughout Venice.

The conversation is revised and edited from a recording made in 1992 by Pidgeon Audio Visual.

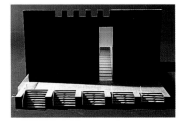

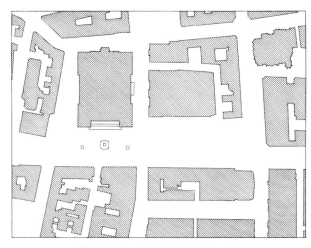

1903   Victoria Square centred on Town Hall

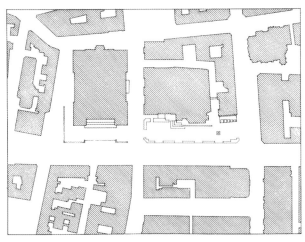

1933   Victoria Square enlarged by demolition of a city block

1993   New facades applied to exposed building flanks

Henry Moore Institute Leeds

1988-93

The Henry Moore Institute occupies three nineteenth-century wool merchants' offices at the end of Cookridge Street in the centre of the city. These buildings are domestic in character, with significant elevations to Cookridge Street and Alexander Street. The project had to strike a balance between the retention of existing structures and the particular needs of a sculpture institute.

The four-storey buildings divide naturally to give galleries on the upper ground floor, served by storage and plant rooms below. This leaves the first floor as a study centre and the second floor for administration. The only new building is the main gallery space created by filling in the three-sided courtyard to Alexander Street. A bridge at first floor level links the Institute with the adjacent City Art Gallery.

The sculpture galleries are simple white spaces with a minimum of detail. Their character comes from the quality of daylight and the contrasting scales of the spaces available within the existing structures. The study centre and administration floors are detailed in a different manner from the galleries, creating a relaxed working environment.

The design of the exterior is a response to the recent history of this part of the city. Now the main square in Leeds, the Headrow started as a much smaller public space in front of the Cuthbert Brodrick's town hall. The square was subsequently enlarged by removing a block of city buildings and by shortening Cookridge Street. This means that a number of public buildings now lining the square were never intended to face that direction. A new facade has been added to the City Art Gallery to relate it properly to the Headrow.

Before the creation of the new Institute, the exposed party wall of the

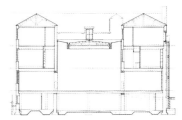

last merchants' building formed the facade to the Headrow. There was therefore a special responsibility to complete the series of new facades to the Headrow by making an appropriate main entrance to the Institute.

This new entrance takes the form of a minimalist sculptural idea, using the mechanical repetition of flights of steps generated as the ground falls across the frontage. The entrance doors are located in a stone wall placed against the end of the terrace so as to leave explicit the 'cut' made through Cookridge Street to create the enlarged Headrow. The whole entrance structure is made of granite used in its various natural forms. The vertical surfaces are polished and the horizontal surfaces are 'flamed' to give a contrasting rough texture. A tall eccentrically placed slot in the polished wall marks the entrance behind which is the shallow stepped passage that leads to the galleries.

Whereas the elevation to the Headrow expresses permanence, the

Below Sol Lewitt installation at the institute.

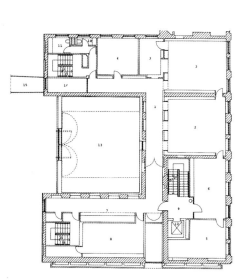

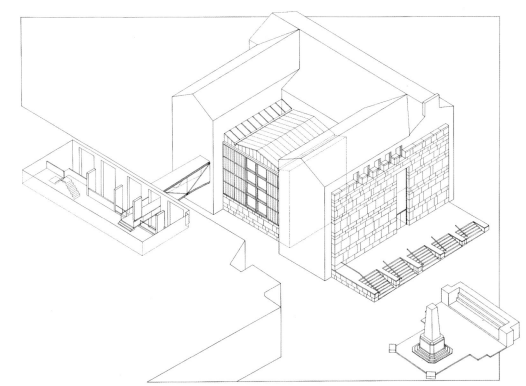

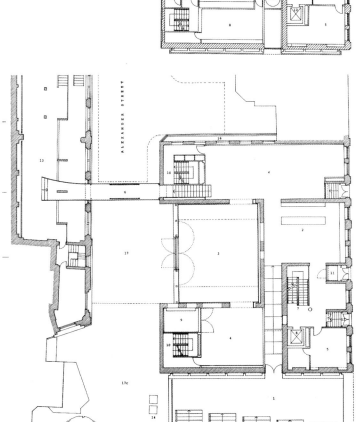

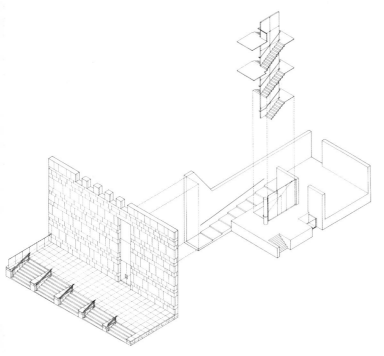

elevation to the new gallery that now occupies the courtyard is intended to look less permanent than the surrounding brick structure. It consists of a grid of bronze frames filled with natural oak and opaque glass, incorporating a pair of giant doors to give access for large sculptures.

In the design of a project one has to keep a look out for the useful accident; and perhaps there is a state of mind worth cultivating that allows the thought process to be deflected when an interesting accident appears. At the Henry Moore Institute the main entrance leads to the far end of the plan, before turning through a hairpin back on itself to enter the new day-lit main gallery. Progressing from the entrance deeper into the plan, the light level drops and the pupils of the eyes dilate. Turning 180 degrees to face the bright gallery hugely dramatises the shock of encountering raw daylight. For me this is the most unexpected moment in the building – even though the visual effect was completely unpredicted.

A chance visit to an exhibition of minimalist artists and sculptors at the Liverpool Tate in 1988 had a profound effect on the ideas for the institute. After many years of wrestling with the repair of cities and the visual complexities of the Royal Opera House project, the work of the minimalists came as a breath of cool fresh air. It jogged the memory that the reductive layouts of the Runcom and Milton Keynes housing projects had many of the identifying characteristics of minimalism. This was confirmed by a chance discovery of a series of 1972 Richard Serra sculptures identical to the simultaneous sculptural proposition for the Netherfield housing in Milton Keynes.

South facing steps are useful for sunbathing. One inspiration for the steps to the Institute was the discovery that half the population of Leeds, on a sunny day, sits out on the various steps along the Headrow.

JD

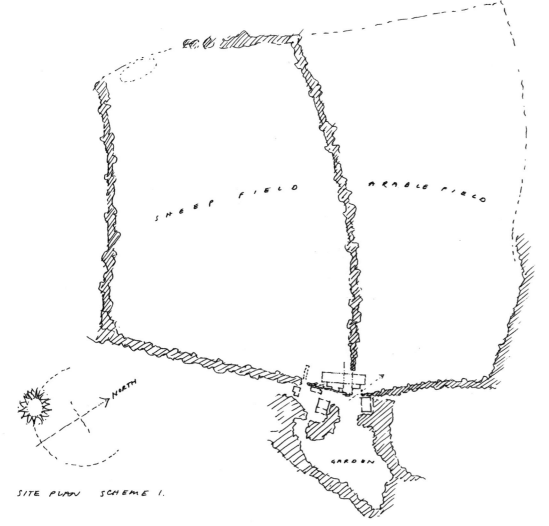

SITE PLAN SCHEME 1.

Henry Moore Foundation
Perry Green

1990

This project consists of three buildings and car parking located discreetly in an important rural landscape.

Henry Moore (1898-1986) lived and worked for the latter part of his life in Perry Green in Hertfordshire. During this time he acquired a substantial amount of property, including most of the buildings around the village green and extensive gardens and agricultural land to the rear of his house. The estate is now an important record of how Moore worked and lived, with a number of his studios and many of his sculptures set in the gardens and surrounding landscape.

As well as drawings and maquettes, Moore left a large number of sculptures which were unsuitable for outdoor display and which had not been accessible to the public. The new buildings were intended to store and display works on paper, provide a gallery for sculpture and provide a biographical gallery and reception area.

The three buildings are located in response to the sensitivity of the site.

As so often is the case, it was a first thought when visiting the site that stuck. The sculpture gallery space should span across the division between the two fields – Henry Moore's 'sheep field' and the arable field. The visitor goes through the hedge line at the bottom of the garden into a space that looks unexpectedly into the two contrasting fields. The sheep field stays the same all year round, the arable field changes colour with the seasons.

JD

154

Above The view from the sculpture gallery takes in two fields (left) – one used for grazing sheep and the other arable land, the colour of which changes with the seasons.

On reflection our proposal to demolish the hay barn and build the gallery in its place, although following good planning practice by replacing an existing building, was just the evidence the conservationists required in their case against the scheme. Why? The barn had been built by Henry Moore. Its retention was seen as essential to the visitor's authentic experience of Perry Green. In the ensuing debate, Deyan Sudjic wrote (Guardian 20 August 1992) that this mausoleum view of conservation might be further enhanced by 'Moore's corpse still sitting in his chair in his studio'.

EJ

155

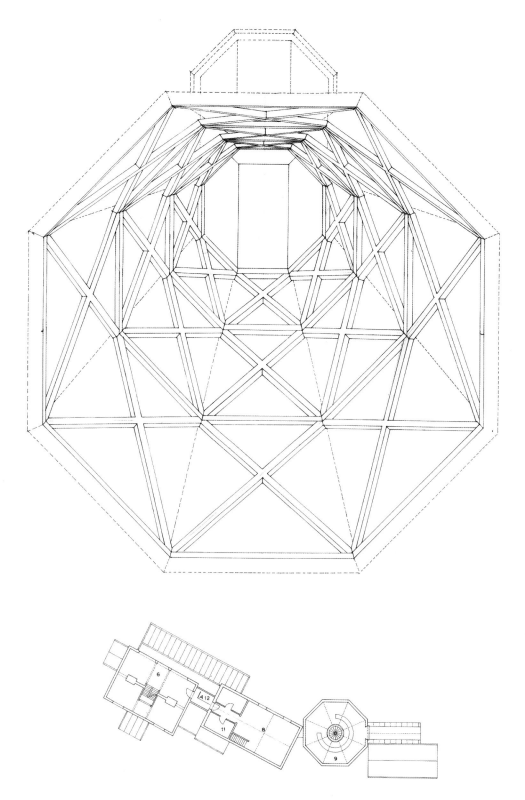

156

Right Part section, part elevation of the visitor reception building.

Left Site model; up-view showing the timber structure of the reception building.

The design of each building is characterised by a particular material – the sculpture gallery is made in steel, the study centre in brick and the reception building in timber.

The site as a whole had to be considered in relation to the discreet handling of an increased number of visitors so as to minimise interference with the unique atmosphere of the gardens and landscape.

The sculpture building stands outside the grounds on the threshold between garden and agricultural land. It also lies between two fields, each with a distinct character – one a green pasture for the sheep that Henry Moore would draw, the other arable land that changes colour with the seasons. The study centre extends the informal group of buildings started by Moore. It has an L-shaped plan enclosing a garden court. The main bulk of the building is lost amongst existing trees and bushes. The reception building, occupying the gap between two existing buildings, is a free-standing octagon with a lantern roof intended to aid visitor orientation.

The proposal to do three buildings in three different materials was, in part, a deliberate sentimental journey back in time to the AA second year programme. As students we were asked to study a village and add three buildings each constructed of a different material – timber, brick and steel. This was part of a teaching idea that spanned three years and introduced the topic of urban design by starting with a village and moving on to a small town and then to the city.

JD

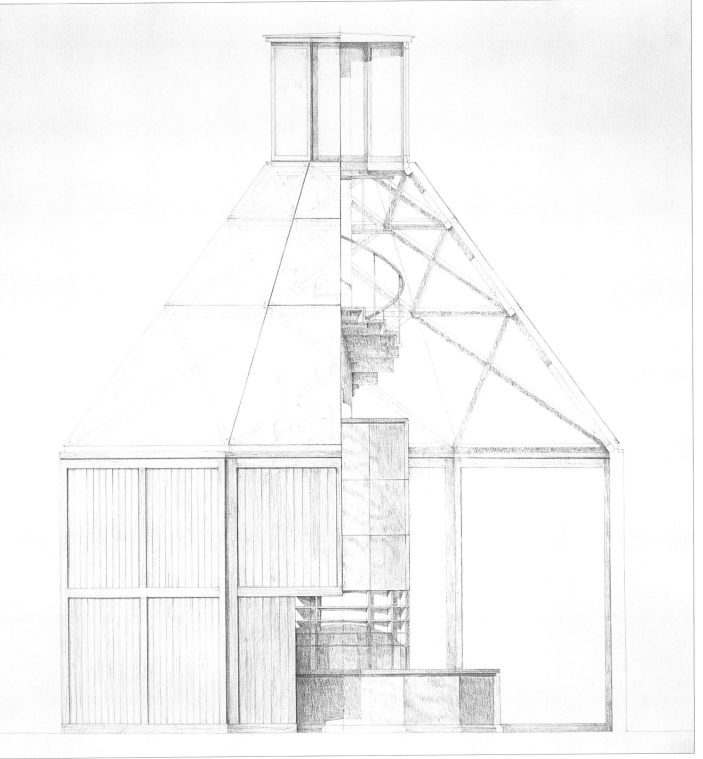

Darwin College
study centre
Cambridge

1989-94

The first concern of this project is to provide a good atmosphere within which to study. The building is designed to offer a choice of study environments for postgraduate students: overlooking the River Cam, sitting outside on the balcony or steps, looking towards Silver Street, sitting around a large table, choosing to be isolated under the lantern, relaxing on a sofa, or working in the computer rooms.

The site, a long narrow rectangle, lies between the curve of Silver Street and the Cam millpool. The college itself is linear in plan. Over time existing buildings were joined together by new connecting buildings. The site is therefore the linear end of a linear plan.

On the street side, the building is low and appears to emerge from the existing curved boundary wall. On the river side, there are two storeys of accommodation and within this section computer rooms are placed at ground level along the river front. The main reading room is a space that extends from ground floor to first floor and overlooks the water. This gives the opportunity to provide a variety of study spaces.

The interior of the building is like one large piece of furniture. Structure, cladding, windows, floors, bookcases and furniture are all made of oak. The timber has different characteristics varying from the dramatic texture of shakes and splits in the structure to the refinement of veneers in the furniture.

The dominant aspect of the interior space comes from the geometry of the roof. The straight line in the plan generated by the waterside and echoed by the clerestory is set against the curved wall to Silver Street. The inside of the curved wall is lined with books, while the rafters forming the roof reconcile the straight line to the curve and

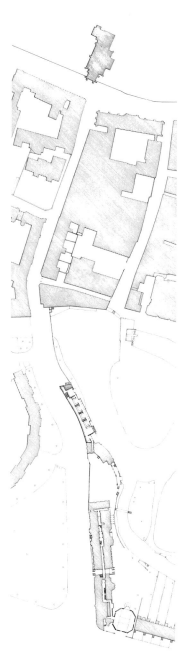

generate a gentle three dimensional curved plane when seen in perspective.

The building is made chiefly of brickwork and English oak. Soft lime mortar is used to avoid movement joints. The oak structure uses sections of a size that were only available 'green' (ie unseasoned). The timber was cut and dried for the project but moisture contents remain in the range of 25 to 60 per cent and the structure will continue to dry for several years. The timber joints which transfer load use a system of stainless steel fixings to allow the joints to be tightened as the timber dries. The oak rafters which form the surface act compositely with a double skin of plywood deck, providing lateral stability. The ground floor is natural stone and the roofs are natural slate and lead.

At the head of the plan are a seminar room, a small flat and a timber lantern. To avoid opening windows on the street side, the lantern opens and closes automatically providing cross ventilation in the reading areas.

Left The oval table, which is placed in a bay near the entrance to the study centre, was designed by Jeremy Dixon and realised by his brother, the furniture maker Joseph Dixon.

The extent to which inspiration is taken directly from different materials varies according to the project. For Darwin College study centre – in part in reaction to the prolonged involvement with the Royal Opera House – we proposed a rigorous idea of structure and materials. The building is a place to work in rather than a library and the principal concern was to provide an interior which had a pleasant atmosphere for study. The idea was to make the whole interior as if it was an extended piece of furniture all in the same material – English oak. The bookcase becomes the wall; the furniture becomes the frame and structure; the floor is the same as the facade. The (rough sawn) structure is made of green oak that splits dramatically over time. This contrasts with the planed oak used for secondary structures such as floors and in its most refined form for furniture and veneers.

JD

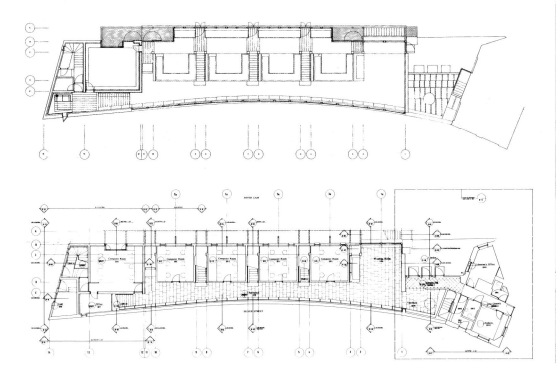

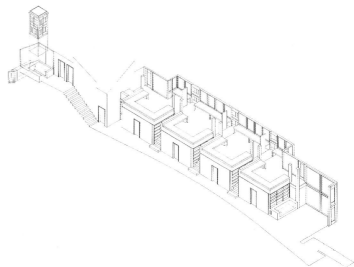

The study centre is a good example of the way in which the design of a project is influenced by many parallel preoccupations. Functionally the intention was to find an aesthetic that evolved from examining the question 'what makes a good environment in which to work?' Formally, the preoccupation is with the interaction of the curve of the street with the straight line created by the edge to the water and the possibility of creating a three-dimensional curved roof. In terms of experiencing the building there is another story. Darwin College is a string of existing new buildings linked by a corridor. The site for the study centre was at the far end of this linear plan. To get to the building you have to enter the main college entrance and walk through a series of corridors and garden areas to arrive at an anonymous door in an external wall. Through the door is the dramatic interior of the study centre overlooking the river. The pleasure is in the surprise and the unexpected nature of the entrance sequence. There is no relationship for the observer between the exterior of the building to the street and the experience of the interior. Thus the exterior to the street is deliberately very quiet and unexpressive, consisting mostly of a plain curved wall where there used to be a similar garden wall. The long curved wall of books set against the straight line of the river front relates back to the Weiss house, an early experiment in setting curves in section against straight lines in plan.

JD

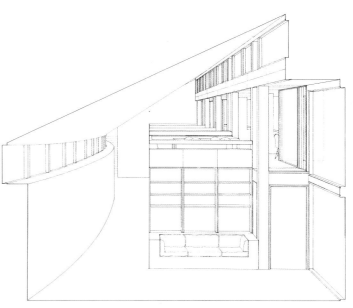

Ospedale Nuovo competition Milan

1991

This project is seen as a community of buildings set in a formal landscape. The manner of the composition of the buildings and landscape uses a free interpretation of grids and axes to give a combination of regularity and surprise. The Ospedale Nuovo is a large and complex community with in-patients and visitors, out-patients, nurses, doctors, support staff and consultants with their individual practices – a thousand people of all kinds of expertise and social and professional standing.

The hospital can therefore be seen like a small town with hierarchies and distinctions, important places and less important places, areas to work in and areas to live in, a distant relative perhaps of archetypal gridded towns such as Miletus in ancient Greece. The square, the court, the street, the arcade and the conservatory become the architectural elements. Some areas are permanent, such as wardrooms, administrative rooms and residential buildings, while others retain the flexibility needed by modern hospital departments.

The grid provides a way of handling the horizontally organised working areas in a manner that retains flexibility and allows for future expansion. The perimeter of the grid along the south and east contains the fixed elements of the brief and gives the opportunity for specific architectural places such as the square and courtyard.

The site, on the southern edge of Milan, is more countryside than city. The first impression is of a rather featureless landscape in the process of being compromised by new buildings. The site is asymmetrical with views to the south and west and less attractive aspects to the north and east. The traditional building type of the region, the courtyard farm, responds to the open flatness of the landscape by creating enclosed spaces, whereas more modern buildings appear as isolated objects.

The Ospedale Nuovo is a private hospital dependent on its reputation – so its perception in the city is important. The image should be of an efficient yet approachable facility that avoids the expression of a large-scale institution.

The building is experienced not as a whole but as a sequence of formal ideas and contrasting landscape and architectural spaces. The focus of the design is a square that brings together all the main entrances: in-patients, out-patients, consultants' patients and visitors. Two sides of the square are formed by hospital accommodation, the third by doctors' residences and the fourth opens to the landscape on the south. The approach is along an avenue bounded on one side by Lombardy poplars and on the other by a range of nurses' dwellings.

The entrances from the square are made specific to the different functions. The out-patient entrance leads directly to the out-patient waiting area. The in-patient and visitor entrances lead to the conservatory that links the wards. The entrance for consultants' patients leads to a generous hall with direct access to the consulting suites. The principle is to limit the experience of the different patients to the part of the building that they are to use, keeping the intimacies of the medical areas as far as possible in the background.

The courtyard elevations are relatively formal, with arcades and a variety of materials lending a civic presence. The wards are more functional, with areas of glass and pergola sunscreens that bring the landscape into contact with the building. The functioning areas comprise a simple grid of structure and services to give flexibility. The conservatory is a quiet meditative space in the middle of the building that extends the public entrance sequence to the wards.

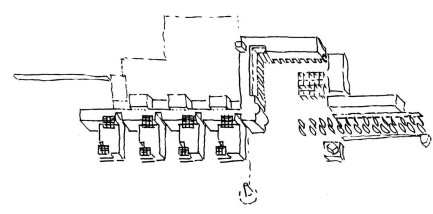

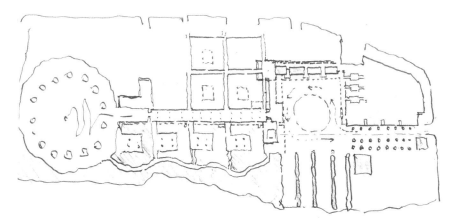

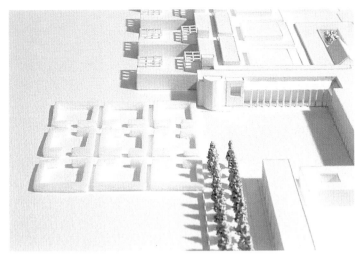

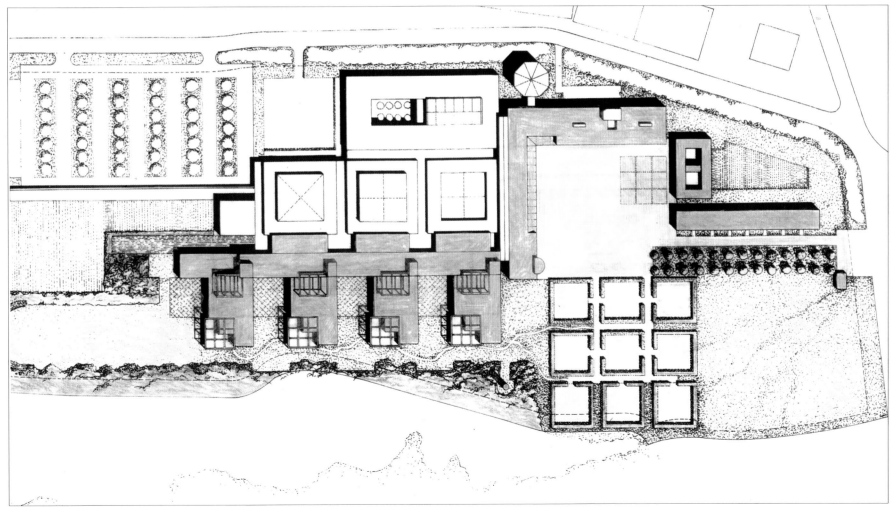

Sainsbury superstore
Plymouth

1991-94

Located at the head of the Plym estu-
ary, the site is visible from a distance as
the A38 comes over the brow of the hill
approaching Plymouth from the east.
The motorway is then elevated over the
existing roundabout adjacent to the
site, giving a second prominent view of
the building and the surrounding landscape. The south edge of the site is
bounded by the main railway line from
London to Plymouth. The unusual
prominence of the site thus offered the
opportunity to create a gateway to the
city of Plymouth.

The design centres on the idea that a
car park can form a romantic landscape, an 'outdoor room' with a strong
architectural identity. The form is a
grand semi-circle, lined on the curved
side by evergreen oak trees and on the
straight side by an arcaded walkway,
which is clad on one side in stainless
steel with dramatic overlapping sails.

This arcade canopy is the largest
object on the site and forms a special
element visible from the motorway. It is
made of semi-translucent fabric
stretched over an armature of fine
structural members, curved to evoke
the billowing sails associated with the
history of Plymouth. During the day the
white fabric is silhouetted against Efford
Fort Hill. At night the fabric glows, providing a powerful sculptural effect.

The superstore itself is treated as a
restrained and simple brick building.
The site is depressed into the ground
four metres below the approach road

Barbara Vine's novel The Chimney Sweeper's Boy
suggests that the building has become a landmark,
satisfying the client's initial brief: 'It was just after five
when Sue approached Plymouth. All lights were on
and Sainsbury's supermarket with its roof of sails,
gleamed like a fleet of white ships'.

EJ

We were given an ambitious brief by Sainsbury for
this prominent site, visible from up to 2.5 kilometres
away, and asked to provide a 'glamorous' building.
Our ideas centred around a number of themes: the
building as a sculptural object; the changing nature of
the building when seen from a speeding car; use of a
wide palette of materials; a necessary lack of consistency, with other architects working on the interior
of the supermarket; and the opportunity to collabo-
rate with the late Peter Rice of Ove Arup &
Partners on the design of the canopies.

EJ

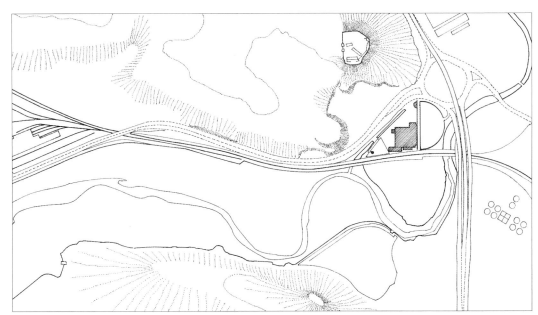

The canopy was an engineering experiment initiated by Peter Rice. His vision was of a stressed fabric structure where the material is stretched over a curved lattice of timber and steel. He wanted to find an organic structural progression between the fabric, the tertiary light timber frame, the secondary steel frame and the primary columns with their tree-like branches. Tragically Peter died before the fully refined version was complete. What has been built is a simplified version in which the fabric is stretched over a rigid steel frame. Tantalisingly, however, the original intention of expressing an extreme idea about materials remains unfulfilled. Working with Peter Rice was a reminder that it is possible to embark on a design idea without knowing what the final outcome will be. It involves taking a risk and it requires you to have the confidence that, in the end, you will always find a solution. If every journey simply reaches the destination first intended, life is pretty dull – just think of all the wonderful places discovered by straying off the obvious route.

JD

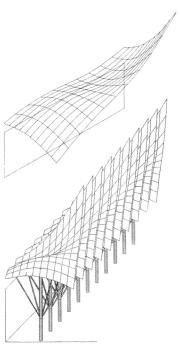

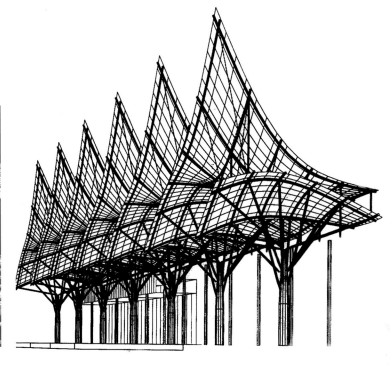

The patterns created by vehicles are used to generate a semi-circular car park. The logic is perhaps more to do with establishing an equidistance from vehicle to store entrance than an absolute road geometry. The straight line is the diameter of the semi-circle, which becomes the sculptural canopy. The stainless steel wall and the repeated sails simply stop at the end of the row without comment – no attempt is made to resolve the ends into a finite composition. The same reluctance to articulate the ends of a straight line recurs in the Netherfield and Runcorn housing plans. It is as if the straight line by itself is 'pure' and the tidying up of the ends into some more conventional composition would diminish its inherent power.

JD

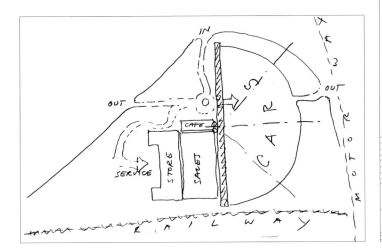

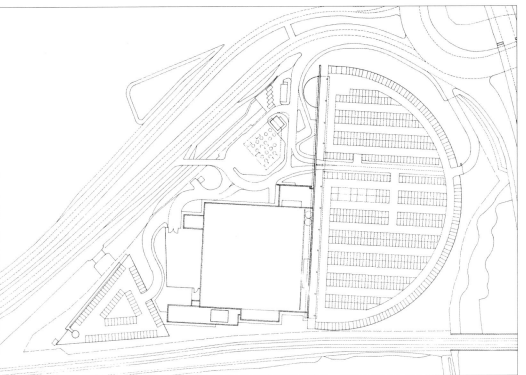

from Plymouth and the intention is to give the building itself as little prominence as possible, leaving the evocative shapes of the sails as the main expression. These are clearly visible over the superstore, the roof of which appears to be at eye level when approached by car from Plymouth. The curve of the trees and the strong shapes of the overlapping sails give the car park an immediate and interesting landscape character when seen from the roundabout. Finally the bulk of the building disappears behind these primary landscape features.

We wanted to use a palette of different materials to mark the relative importance of the different elements of the structure – and also to create an aesthetic of collage and overlay. While there is an urban sense of front and back, where the front is faced in stone and stainless steel laid over a brick box, the ensemble when viewed more randomly or obliquely, might equally be perceived as a free composition.

EJ

Left The bird hide.
Right Northamptonshire county hall (1972) and Venice bus station (1990).

There is a tendency to dismiss car parking as always a negative and regrettable feature. However, cars park where they are told to. Every car park has the possibility of being an interesting geometric pattern and the cars parked within become a sculptural idea. Cars are shiny, well-kept objects and their diversity of shape and colour registers as a random pattern within the regulated geometry.

JD

171

Stonehenge visitor centre competition

1992

The primitive symbolic nature of Stonehenge is trivialised by the existing visitor arrangements and this proposal sought to reinvest the visit with a sense of ritual and pilgrimage. The project is primarily about route and landscape and only secondarily about the provision of services and accommodation.

The proposal hides parked cars behind existing trees and provides visitor facilities within a landscaped terrace. Visitors arrive in the car park still unaware of the precise location of Stonehenge, which suddenly becomes visible on passing through the trees and onto the terrace.

The accommodation is arranged on two sides of a courtyard. The ticket and information offices are in a hall of columns that gives onto the courtyard. This arrangement presents the facilities in a direct and simple way. At the same time it ensures that those who want to proceed straight on to the walk and maintain their pilgrimage towards the monument can do so with the minimum of interference. The first priority of the project is the quality of the

unfolding landscape experiences in approaching Stonehenge.

The project treats the building as a series of landscape elements – a curved wall and embankment that continues the geometry of the existing tree belt, a grassed terrace with a 'ha-ha' detail to the curved wall and a timber trellised arcade forming the edge of the courtyard – all elements that could be read as evidence of a landscaped garden within the starker agricultural terrain.

The accommodation lies under the terrace with continuous glazed elevations to the two sides of the courtyard. All the facilities have access directly off the arcade. The structure of the building is a simple regular grid of concrete columns. The restaurant includes a glazed winter garden to give additional seating capacity. In general the building is a simple permanent structure with external surfaces of natural materials – oak, bronze, glass, stone and flint. The accommodation is independent of the structure, giving a long-term loose fit, and the weight and insulation created by carrying earth on the roof make a

low-energy envelope.

The terrace is an opportunity for a modern landscape. The plane of grass is dramatically incised to form the principal ramp. Structural glass slabs over the ramp and over rooflights to secondary accommodation appear like paving stones in the grass. The courtyard to the exhibition space is surrounded by a geometrical mound topped by a timber slatted walk. The boundary to the main courtyard, the timber arcade, becomes a raised timber boardwalk to edge the grass. The additional structural beams required to span the theatre form a cruciform of lines of stone paving, flush with the surface of the grass. The 'feel' of this part of the scheme is evoked by the landscape sculptures of Mary Miss.

When buildings are positioned in heroic or historically-loaded landscapes, the conventional architectural signs no longer apply. The architectural language becomes the sculptural manipulation of the groundplan and existing shelter-belts into a modern landscape, which here is complementary to the archaic setting of Stonehenge.

EJ

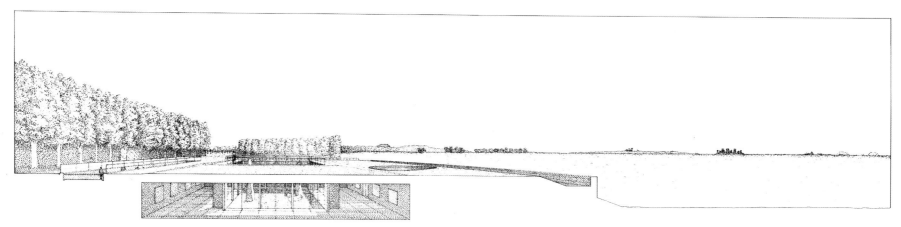

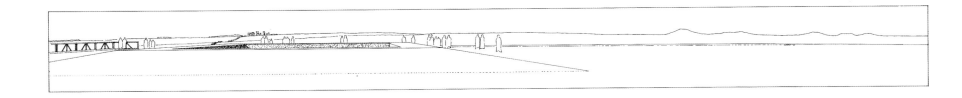

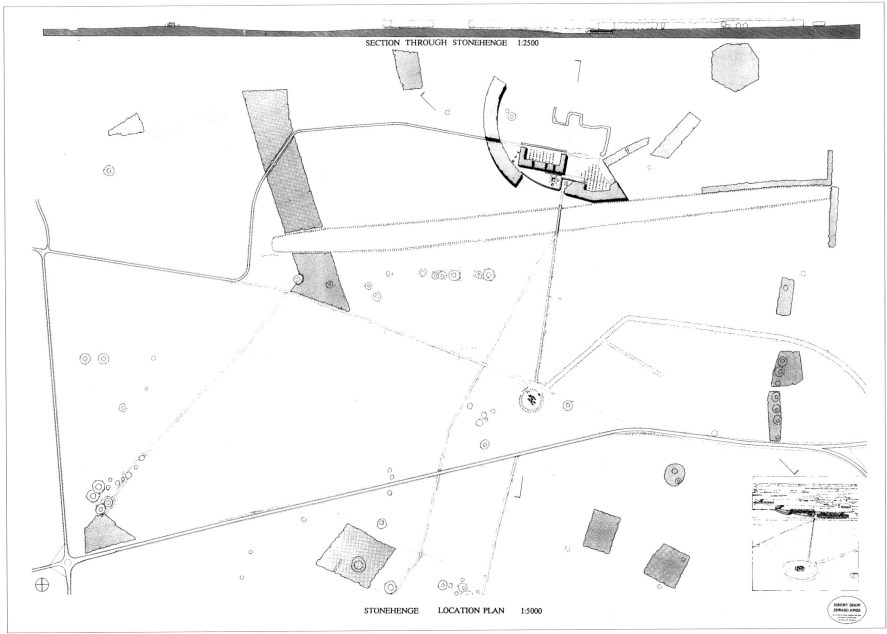

SECTION THROUGH STONEHENGE 1:2500

STONEHENGE   LOCATION PLAN   1:5000

JEREMY DIXON
EDWARD JONES

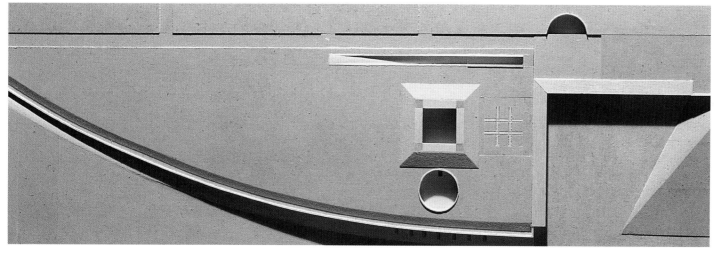

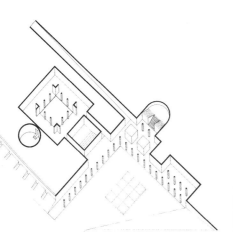

I have always made models. As a child I had the run of a workshop as well as making model aeroplanes. These lightweight structures that gain strength when covered with the stressed skin created by tissue paper and dope, are the best possible introduction to the principles of structure. I learnt how to make architectural models from Julian Thompson before he became the modelmaker at Arups. During most of my professional life there has been a workshop in the basement of our house, properly equipped with circular saw etc. This enables models to be made of hardwood with the consequent seductive precision and quality.

Models have a sculptural life of their own. In these illustrations the Plasticine model (made by the office) is a free interpretation of the relationship between the textures of landscape and the more precise building elements. The upper picture shows a hardwood and MDF model I made using the circular saw with special hollow ground blades that leave the cut material absolutely smooth. For me the act of making a model has often been the moment of fixing the design. In the modelmaking process it is possible to make fine adjustments of proportion and detail, working directly as with a piece of sculpture. In the example shown all irrelevant elements have been omitted in favour of sculptural clarity.

JD

SECTION DD

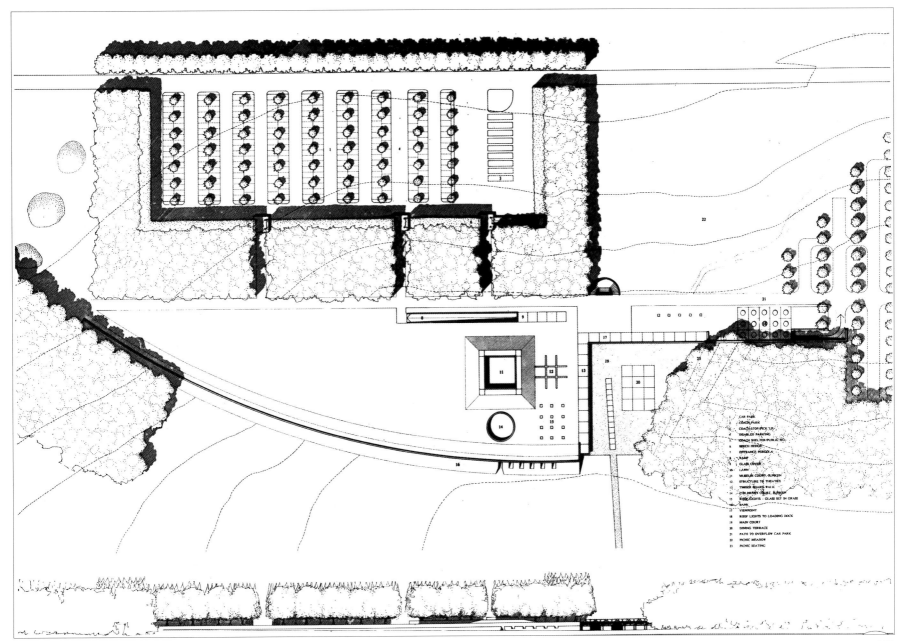

1 CAR PARK
2 COACH PARK
3 COACH STOP/PICK UP
4 DISABLED PARKING
5 COACH SHELTER/PUBLIC WC
6 BEECH HEDGE
7 ENTRANCE PERGOLA
8 RAMP
9 GLASS COVER
10 LAWN
11 MUSEUM COURT - SUNKEN
12 STRUCTURE TO THEATER
13 TIMBER BOARD WALK
14 CHILDREN'S COURT - SUNKEN
15 ROOF LIGHTS - GLASS SET IN GRASS
16 BANK
17 VIEWPOINT
18 ROOF LIGHTS TO LOADING DOCK
19 MAIN COURT
20 DINING TERRACE
21 PATH TO OVERFLOW CAR PARK
22 PICNIC MEADOW
23 PICNIC SEATING

Tower Houses
Robert Gordon University
Aberdeen

1992-93

These two new student residential buildings at Garthdee were the first stage in a programme of expansion at Aberdeen's Robert Gordon University. The siting and form of the buildings had therefore to fit into a larger idea for the campus, as well as standing on their own as individual designs.

In future the campus may have new faculty buildings in addition to those existing and these will have the characteristic large footprint of such building types. In broad terms the strategy will be to group these larger faculty buildings, so that wedges of the existing lawns and trees give a sense of continuity to the fine Deeside parkland. By contrast, the residential buildings can be limited in size and footprint, making the most of what is offered by the site.

The first two buildings are located at the top of the embankment overlooking the River Dee. They take the form of Scottish tower houses, using traditional forms and materials. The opportunity is taken to enhance the tree-lined ridge of the embankment by planning the buildings in a romantic and pictorial manner.

In one sense the towers are a study in isolation. How does an architect build on a beautiful wooded site without spoiling the qualities that are the inspiration in the first place? Delicate towers dotted among the trees make use of the landscape tradition associated with the great country houses, where objects are tastefully placed in the landscape. They also take inspiration from the Scottish tradition of the romantically isolated tower house. These are strong aesthetic considerations but they are not necessarily related to the aspirations of the students. Is it the right priority for students to have the experience of the 'beautiful place' at the expense of the richness and gutsy experiences associated with urban life?

JD

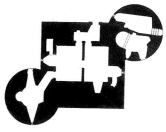

Above Traditional tower house plan.

The siting of the towers was determined by a field-party consisting of the client, the planners, an arboriculturist and the architects. We walked the site and collectively determined the locations. These were confirmed not by the abstract schema of the site plan but rather by how the buildings might actually be seen. At no time was there concern that the towers might threaten the landscape, as we might have expected in England where the invisibility of a project would be seen as an achievement. Here in Scotland, quite the opposite, the towers were regarded as a positive enhancement of the landscape by both client and planner. Our client, Dr Gavin Ross, had been a student of Louis Kahn's in Philadelphia (and coincidentally had introduced Kahn to the fortified tower houses of Scotland). The tower is not suggested here as a general solution. Rather it might be seen as part of a formal lexicon – should more student accommodation be required, it might take the form of a lodge building or the boundary to a walled garden etc.

EJ

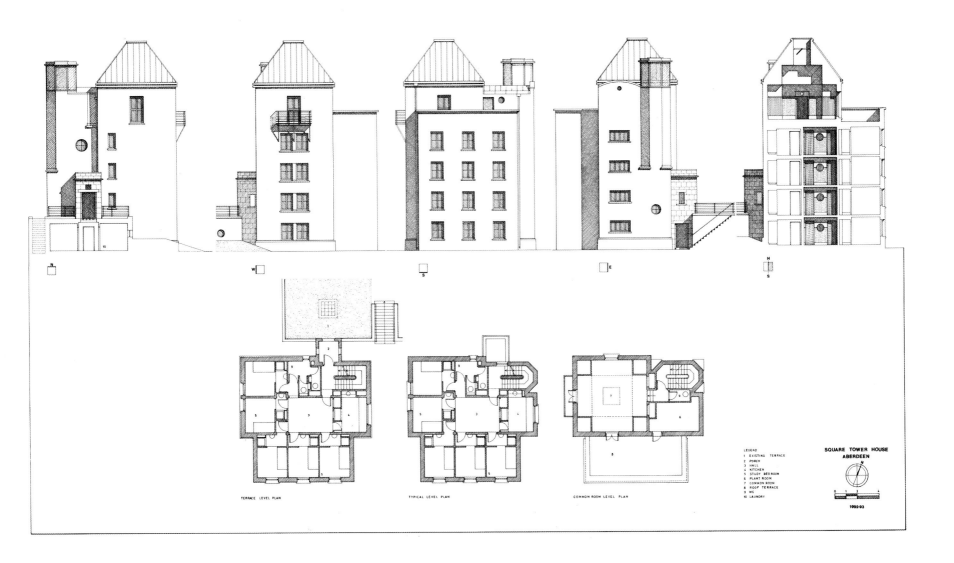

N

W
S

S

E

N
S

LEGEND
1 EXISTING TERRACE
2 PORCH
3 HALL
4 KITCHEN
5 STUDY BEDROOM
6 PLANT ROOM
7 COMMON ROOM
8 ROOF TERRACE
9 WC
10 LAUNDRY

SQUARE TOWER HOUSE
ABERDEEN

N

0 1 2   4

1992-93

TERRACE LEVEL PLAN

TYPICAL LEVEL PLAN

COMMON ROOM LEVEL PLAN

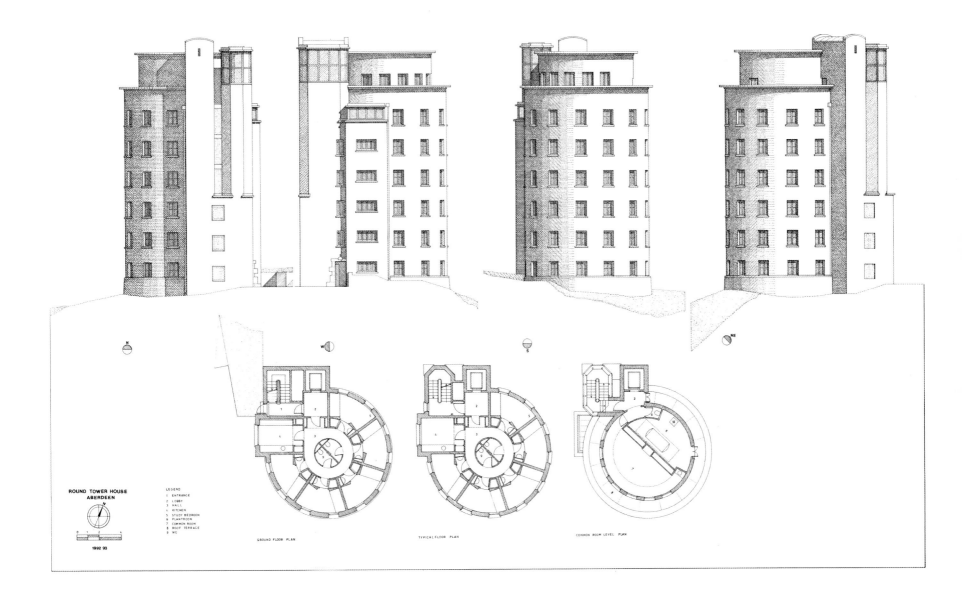

ROUND TOWER HOUSE
ABERDEEN

LEGEND
1 ENTRANCE
2 LOBBY
3 HALL
4 KITCHEN
5 STUDY BEDROOM
6 PLANTROOM
7 COMMON ROOM
8 ROOF TERRACE
9 WC

0 1 2   4

1992 93

GROUND FLOOR PLAN   TYPICAL FLOOR PLAN   COMMON ROOM LEVEL PLAN

The two buildings are placed adjacent to the Scott Sutherland School of Architecture and the School of Surveying. With the square building, the opportunity is taken to mask the unsightly precast concrete flank wall of the existing lecture theatre. The circular building is positioned to take full advantage of the dramatic relationship with the bend in the river. The circular form and the traditional pink harling colour – partly hidden amongst the trees – provide a memorable new element, both within the campus and when seen through the foliage across the valley.

An advantage of the tower house form is that the area taken up by the plan is minimised. The buildings are small in bulk compared with the dominating scale of the line of trees. The combination of groups of faculty buildings set further up the slope and discreet residential buildings of limited size gives the best opportunity of preserving the very special landscape character of this part of Deeside.

To build towers was a good idea, but only an idea. It still required imagination and a will to form on the part of the architects to turn the idea into a practical reality and not only not spoil, but positively improve, the campus: to deploy that in-between process that Louis Kahn characterised as the opportunity for design to correct intuition. From this process of meditation comes a whole series of crucial decisions: the decision to divide the accommodation into two; to have two towers of contrasting character; to site one romantically on the lip of the escarpment, the other more picturesquely attached to an existing building; to make use of the prime geometries of square and circle; to break the prime geometries into differentiated volumes that accentuate character and provide practical solutions; to subdivide the accommodation with only five study-bedrooms per floor; to offer the common room on the top floor as the ultimate definer of geometry; to study the planning on consecutive floors closely so that the tower geometry – square and round – does not constrain the layout, but emerges clearly only as the crowning shape; and so on.

Robert Maxwell, 1994

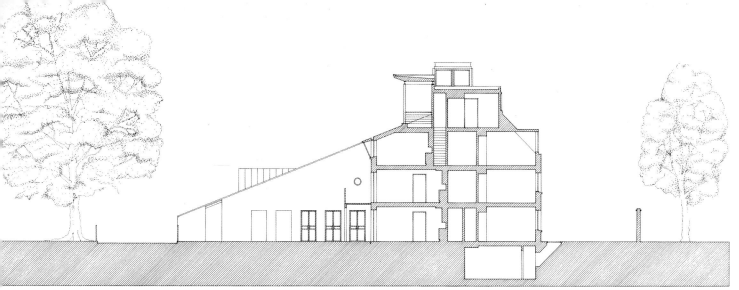

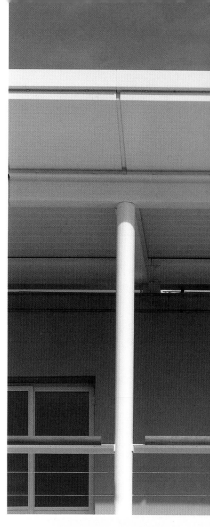

Darwin College housing Cambridge

1992-95

The site for these 28 student rooms has two opposing characteristics. The approach, from Wordsworth Grove to the north, is via a cul de sac of mixed residential buildings while to the south are the playing fields of Summerfield. In response to these conditions the project can be understood in two senses. From Wordsworth Grove it is seen as a large semi-detached house, consistent with the Edwardian semi-detached houses in the street, with two entrance courts set behind a 2.5 metre high garden wall and mature trees. On the other hand, facing Summerfield, the building transforms into the image of a single villa set in its own arcadian landscape, with its terrace, balcony and loggia forming a grandstand to the sporting life beyond.

The plan is a simple arrangement of two four-storey houses sharing a party wall, with two flats and one maisonette to each. Both houses have their own 'front' staircase accessed from an entrance court and a third common 'back' stair linking all the kitchens to the shared south-facing courtyard. Two

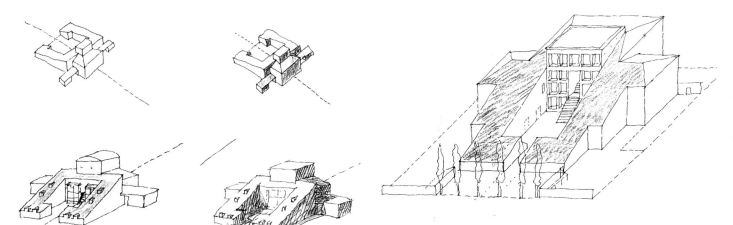

The building seems to rise out of the site, the long roof crowned by a tall heroic loggia flanked by giant lanterns. It is definitely unlike its neighbours: the terne-coated steel roof forms the base to a grand architectural skyline. Whereas Le Corbusier saw his rooftop compositional games as a 'jeu d'esprit', here the game is more controlled – less to do with the picturesque than with formality. The symmetrical steel-clad form that has materialised at the edge of a field has a strange dream-like quality – it still seems to be growing.

Brendan Woods, 1995

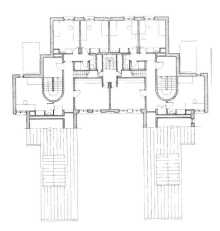

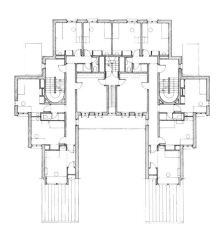

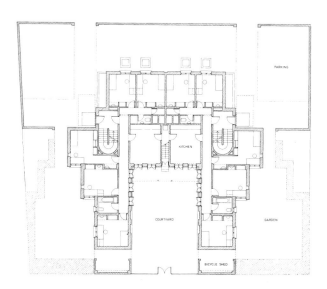

Conventional oppositions – between front and back, masonry and stucco, and the semi-detached versus the detached villa – are some of the ideas in the building. The plan is prototypical, the building volume is indebted distantly to the Tuscan vernacular and the nautical imagery is somehow accidental while the white loggia and roof lanterns attempt a conversation with Basil Champney's Widow's Walk for Newnham College next door.

The axonometric (right) shows the arrangement of front stairs/back stairs – the former expressing the semi-detached idea and the latter combining the two in the shared courtyard and the singular image of the villa.

EJ

Left Ground, first and third floor plans.

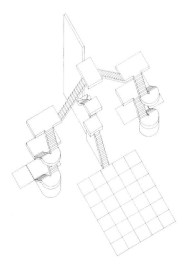

further connections give unity to the whole. At the fourth floor the two houses combine to share the loggia overlooking Summerfield and at basement level the two entrance stairs are connected by a crypto-porticus to share the laundry and trunk store.

The relationship between the form of

the building and its sub-division has resulted in much variety in the character and orientation of the study-bedrooms. In the attic these include crow's nest rooms, double-height and panoramic rooms under the long inclined roof and introspective rooms overlooking private gardens to the side.

The stepped plan avoids overlooking neighbouring properties and gives the majority of the study-bedrooms a south orientation and a view of Summerfield. In contrast to the variety of plans and volumes of the study bedrooms, the built-in furniture follows a consistent pattern with local modifications – white

185

lacquered fixed desks, wardrobes and bookshelves with adjustable shelves. The loose furniture is a collection of modern classics: Alvar Aalto stools, bentwood desk chairs, Lloyd Loom easy chairs and Best & Lloyd's desk and bed lamps.

The elevation to Wordsworth Grove and the side garden elevations are in brick. The courtyard elevation to Summerfield is white stucco with steel french windows and balcony. This elevation is topped by the loggia and two steel-framed lanterns to the staircases. The back wall to the loggia is stuccoed and painted blue. On fine days the blue dematerialises the wall, with the supporting columns standing free against a summer sky. At night the illuminated staircase lanterns act as beacons in the landscape.

The loggia (left) and the courtyard (right) overlooked by its balcony are shared external spaces. The former looks out over the rooftops of west Cambridge, the latter focuses on the fine oak tree positioned asymmetrically in the foreground and beyond to the sporting activities of Summerfield. In both cases, timber decking gives a 'floor' to the spaces, underwriting their intention as external 'rooms'.

EJ

Science Building
University of Portsmouth

1992-96

The planning brief for the new science building for the University of Portsmouth reflects its importance to both the city and the university. Firstly, the city planners required a building that would provide a suitable landmark to a prominent corner site in the city centre – the site is particularly visible from St Michael's Road. The building

was to anticipate the future development of the White Swan car park to the east, forming a transition between the adjacent six-storey university building and the future four-storey White Swan development.

Secondly, the building was one of the first elements in Colin Stansfield Smith's university masterplan, in which

the science departments were to be consolidated. To this end the new building forms an extension to the existing St Michael's building.

Unlike St Michael's and the free-standing King Henry building, the new science building almost totally fills its irregular site. Also, unlike the equivalent facades of these neighbouring

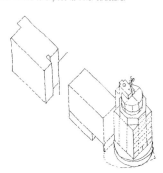

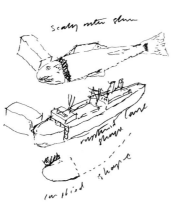

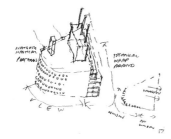

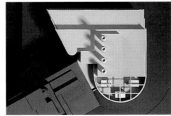

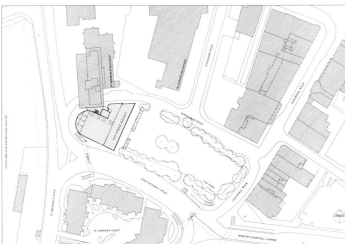

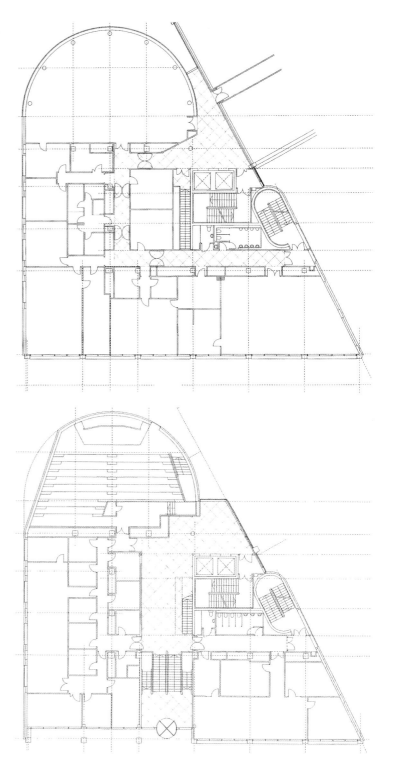

Plans Ground floor and typical laboratory level.

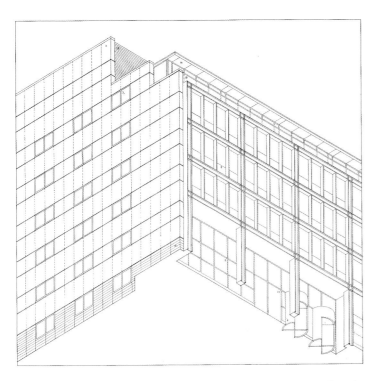

buildings, the science building provides distinct and different elevations. At the corner facing the intersection of St Michael's Road and King Richard I Street, the curved facade acts as a shield to the noise of traffic and the southerly exposure. The windows are set flush in the six-storey facade of silver aluminium panels, the semi-circular corner prow forming the landmark and concealing the exposed flank of the (incomplete) St Michael's building. At ground level a pedestrian pavement cuts into the corner forming a flat panel for the building sign.

The east elevation facing the city car park expresses the four-storey structural frame. It forms one side of a proposed pedestrian street which gives access to the main entrance serving both the new building and the St Michael's building. Turning the corner into White Swan Road, the facade is relatively neutral with windows to the escape stairs. Here are positioned the lift lobbies and connections to St Michael's, with natural light and views to the United Services

Although built on an arbitrarily shaped traffic island the plan is defined by three geometries: a semi-circular prow, a right angle corner, and a triangular acute corner. The diameter of the semicircle is half the dimension of the six bay facade facing the White Swan car park. The four exaggerated smoke stacks, which emit gases from the many fume cupboards, provide a nautical allusion.

EJ

The new science building reflects the moment at which a polytechnic, on becoming a university, wants a new and glamorous identity. The gloomy precast concrete post-war polytechnic buildings had the same gloom as mass housing of the period – somehow they read as second-best. The new building is a minor addition to one of several large concrete monsters and its brief was to add glamour and opti-

mism to the campus as a whole. Occupying a prominent corner site, it is located in one of those typical indeterminate urban areas where the continuous history of an older city has been fractured by the single-minded over-confidence of the road engineers. The natural system of pedestrian connections, streets and pavements are rudely interrupted, making a strange environment that might be called an

'edge city'. The area has the advantages of being close to city facilities, shops, restaurants, transport etc, but lacks the engaging qualities of traditional urban fabric.

JD

191

playing fields to the south west.

The building houses the pharmacy and physics undergraduate and research departments. Lecture theatres and large teaching laboratories are accommodated in the semi-circular corner, with the remaining accommodation planned in a less specific, more flexible manner.

Our clients firmly stipulated that the laboratories should be white with grey floors. No colour please. This prompted the thought that in contrast to this antiseptic world, colour should have a role in the general experience of the building. The red stair, the blue stair, the ochre stair and the Pompeian red to the lecture theatre are the result.

EJ

This architecture is very different from high tech, despite the high level of technology in the achievement of its finish and details. The smooth tin can is an enigmatic container for a series of highly specialised processes, suggesting this in its image and expression but not displaying its functions overtly. Instead of expressed services we have a game of opposites. The building is like a reversed shell, with encrustations on the inside and mother-of-pearl outside. The smooth abstraction of the outside is offset by the intensively figured and textured spaces inside, with colour playing a vital part in this contrast. Entering the almost monochromatic box you are met by walls of strong vibrant colours. The egg-yolk yellow of the long staircase wall with its red oxide handrails, the grid of flying saucer ceiling lights and the light white terrazzo of the floor and stair combine to make a beautiful space which retains a spare lightness of touch, despite the intensity of its design.

Sheila O'Donnell, 1996

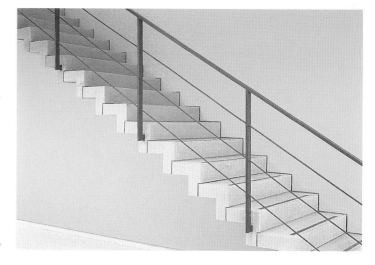

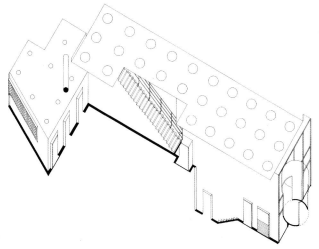

Croydon Initiative
community university

1992

Launched by the Architecture Foundation and the London Borough of Croydon, the Croydon Initiative was a series of urban regeneration studies addressing the poor self-image of this part of the capital. A number of architectural practices were invited to choose an aspect of Croydon to study. Our project developed the idea of a community university in the streets and backlands of the old town, as a means of giving a new identity to Croydon.

Towns and cities have personalities, and, like people, they can get depressed. The self-image of a town is the product of a continuous development through its history. It involves a balance of financial and cultural institutions that can be damaged by the sudden intervention of a new road system or new development that is out of scale. The moment at which a town turns itself around is not just a question of financial success or the nature of the buildings. It is also to do with the strength of its cultural base. It is difficult to identify which comes first: investment or the confidence to attract investment.

Croydon's natural development was upset by a dramatic office building boom and the introduction of urban motorways in the 60s and 70s. The old town was isolated by the new roads and the concentration of offices produced a commuter population whose main experience of the town was the journey between station and tower block. But there is still a clear diagram evident in a map of Croydon, centred on the axis of George Street, which links the main station to the old town. At right angles to the axis are bands of contrasting urban uses – first the tower blocks, then the High Street and market and finally the old town around Church Street.

Croydon has a college of further and higher education with 13,000 students. Its emphasis on part-time and vocational courses makes the college an interesting model for a community university serving all age groups. Its buildings include a 60s block (art and design) that is unfinished and overcrowded. These activities could be relocated to form the basis for a new cultural heart, bringing the status of a university town and

attracting professionals, artists and crafts people rather than losing its population every evening.

The previous generation of new universities tended to be built outside commercially valuable city centres but experience suggests that a city and its university have a complex, overlapping relationship. The old town is not a commercially valuable area but it is strategically close to Croydon's centre, so it has the potential to draw in all kinds of interesting creative functions. The dense matrix of streets and routes contrasts dramatically with the pattern of tower blocks in the newer districts. The streets have a mix of valued frontages and gaps leading to extensive backlands. This gives an opportunity to interpret the university departments as street frontages leading to backlands studios. Each department has a front with shop or gallery that takes its place among the other shops in the street. The department of catering would generate a restaurant and cafeteria. The life in the street and the life of the university would overlap. Studios located in the

backlands can be low-key single-storey rooflit flexible structures. Corridors become arcades, sometimes public and sometimes exclusive to departments. The adjacent terrace housing would be ideal for student accommodation.

The 'accidental' is important to the character of the project. The arbitrary factor is the pattern of existing buildings and routes. The latent energy that one feels in the graphics associated with the existing shops is an inspiration for an ad hoc architectural style that would be discovered in development of the project.

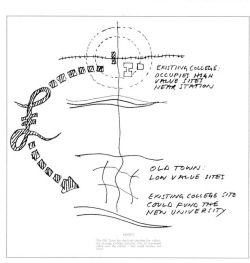

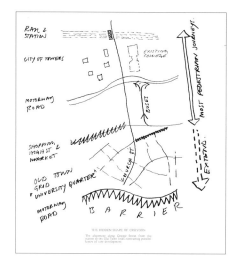

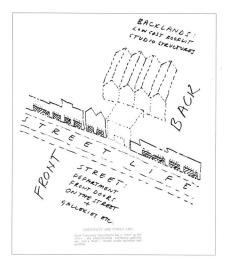

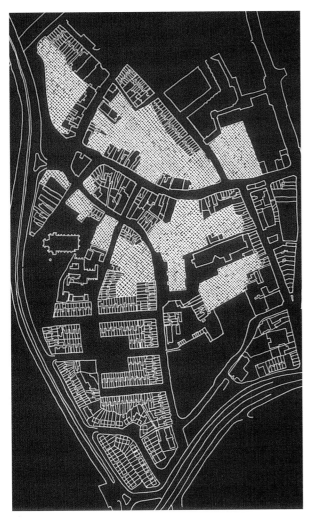

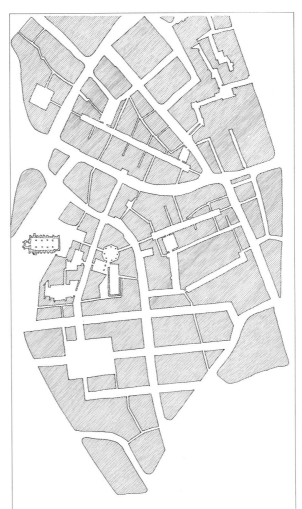

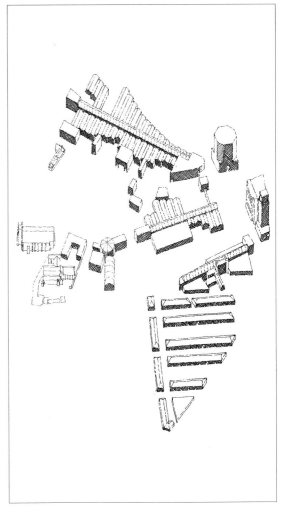

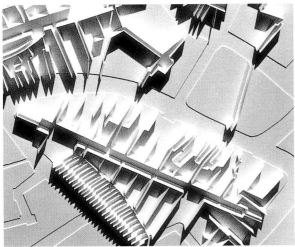

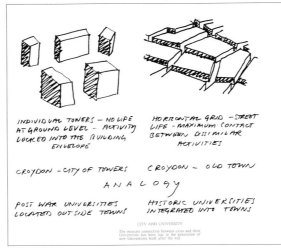

INDIVIDUAL TOWERS – NO LIFE
AT GROUND LEVEL – ACTIVITY
LOCKED INTO THE BUILDING
ENVELOPE

HORIZONTAL GRID – STREET
LIFE – MAXIMUM CONTACT
BETWEEN DISSIMILAR
ACTIVITIES

CROYDON – CITY OF TOWERS   CROYDON – OLD TOWN

A N A L O G Y

POST WAR UNIVERSITIES
LOCATED OUTSIDE TOWNS

HISTORIC UNIVERSITIES
INTEGRATED INTO TOWNS

CITY AND UNIVERSITY

The intimate connection between cities and their
Universities has been lost in the generation of
new Universities built after the war.

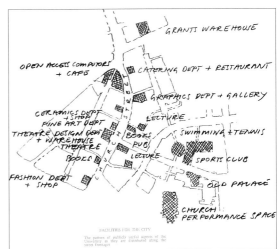

GRANTS WAREHOUSE

OPEN ACCESS COMPUTERS
+ CAFE

CATERING DEPT + RESTAURANT

GRAPHICS DEPT + GALLERY

CERAMICS DEPT
+ SHOP
FINE ART DEPT

LECTURE

THEATRE DESIGN DEPT
+ WAREHOUSE
THEATRE

BOOKS

PUB

SWIMMING + TENNIS

BOOKS

LECTURE

SPORTS CLUB

FASHION DEPT
+ SHOP

OLD PALACE

CHURCH
PERFORMANCE SPACE

FACILITIES FOR THE CITY

The pattern of publicly useful aspects of the
University as they are distributed along the
street frontages

195

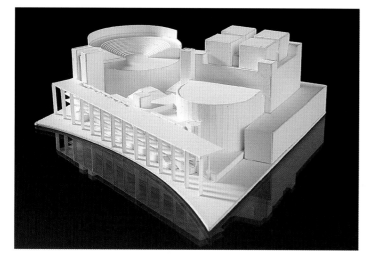

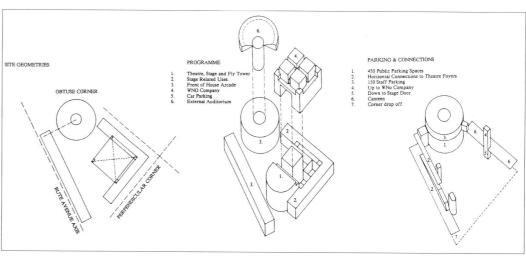

SITE GEOMETRIES

OBTUSE CORNER

BUTE AVENUE AXIS

PERPENDICULAR CORNER

PROGRAMME

1. Theatre, Stage and Fly Tower
2. Stage Related Uses
3. Front of House Arcade
4. WNO Company
5. Car Parking
6. External Auditorium

PARKING & CONNECTIONS

1. 450 Public Parking Spaces
2. Horizontal Connections to Theatre Foyers
3. 150 Staff Parking
4. Up to WNo Company
5. Down to Stage Door
6. Canteen
7. Corner drop off

Cardiff Opera House competition

1994

The Cardiff opera house competition had two motives. Firstly to provide a permanent home for the Welsh National Opera Company. Secondly to act as a catalyst for the regeneration of Cardiff in general and Cardiff Bay in particular. Here, since the disappearance of the coal trade, the waterfront has become neglected. The Barcelona firm of Martorell Bohigas Mackay was commissioned by the Cardiff Bay Development Corporation to draw up a plan to form connections between the docks and the rest of the city. The proposal resulted in a tree-lined boulevard (Bute Avenue) forming a direct connection between the city centre and the Oval Basin piazza on the waterfront. The site for the new opera house was to form part of this new piazza and in the promoters' minds it was also to act as a focus for new civic and cultural developments on the waterfront.

The brief for the building requested

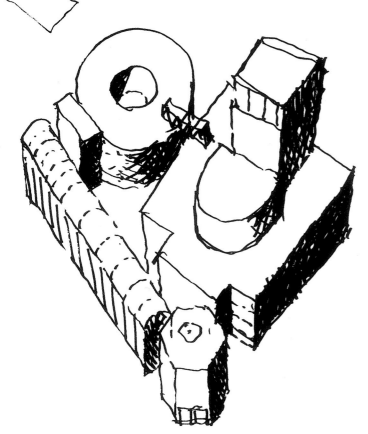

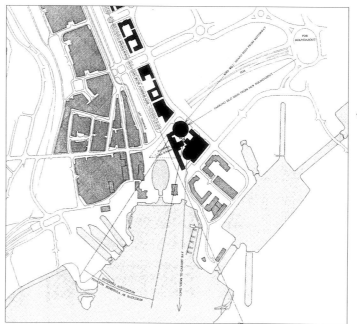

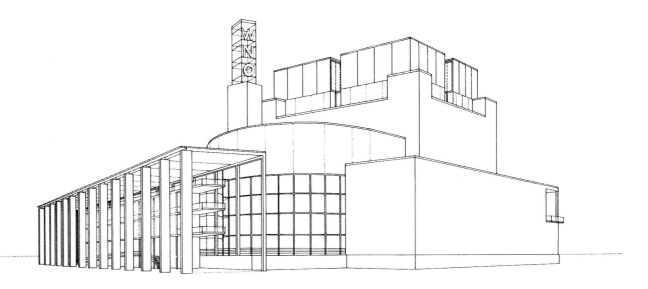

an auditorium with a minimum of 1750 seats. The character of the auditorium was to be intimate and dramatic. A horseshoe plan was strongly implied. A rehearsal studio capable of providing public performances was also requested. The building, its foyers, cafes and bars were to encourage use by the public even when the auditorium was not in use.

The opera house is to be a place of the people, with informal daytime activities as well as evening performances. The building needs to be both a formal 'house' for the presentation of opera and a meeting place – informal, modern and welcoming – for the other public activities generated within it.

It is possible to read the plan in two parts. The first is an orthogonal grouping of spaces around the stage, reflecting the practical issues of backstage planning. The second is the combination of circular car park and arcade that represents public arrival and identity. Between these two primary elements lies the informal zone of the foyers.

The building group is composed of six identifiable parts: the auditorium, its stage and flytower; a four-storey wall of stage-related uses; the front-of-house building which includes a protected external public concourse; the Welsh National Opera accommodation as a volume enclosing and extending the flytower as a landmark; a cylindrical multi-storey car park which acts as a giant billboard for the theatre; and an outdoor auditorium which caps the car park.

A high proportion of the audience will arrive by car. The vertical spiral drum of car parking gives points of arrival to the building at different levels. The roof of the 600 space car park can also be used as an outdoor amphitheatre for rock concerts or large-scale opera events, with a dramatic view across the bay and the peninsula.

The Cardiff opera house competition is now synonymous with a loss of nerve and opportunity and is in a sense the absolute opposite of Utzon's Sydney opera house forty years earlier, which created the benchmark for today's appetite for landmark buildings. We will never know Zaha's building. I think all those who entered this ill-fated competition felt keenly her loss and witnessed discredit to the competition system.

EJ

Plans Ground floor and balcony levels.

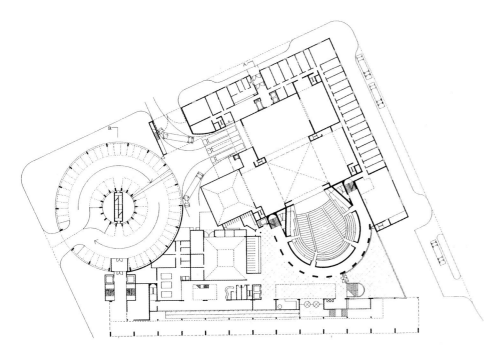

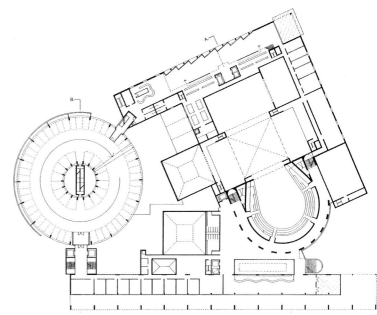

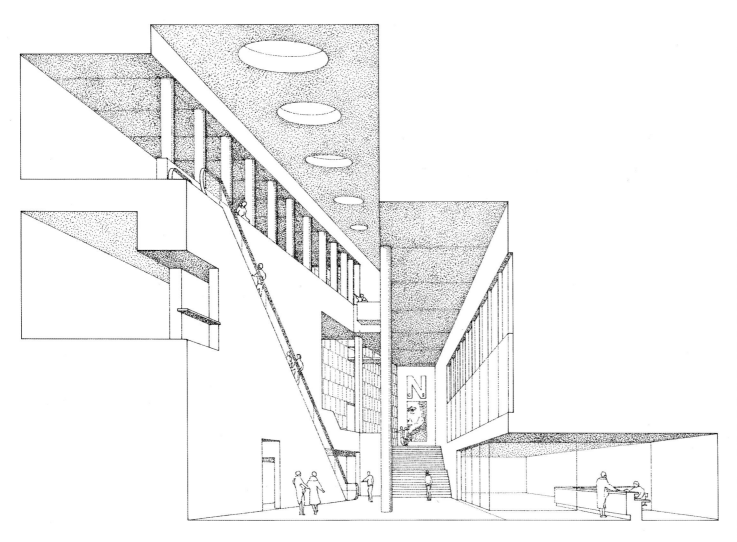

National Gallery of Ireland competition, Dublin

1996

This project, placed second in a limited competition, was intended to enhance the role and prominence of the National Gallery in the life of Dublin.

The interior organisation of the new building and its role in the extension of the existing gallery is based on overlapping ideas. The first is the strategic requirement for a connection between the two entrances from Clare Street and Merrion Square, thereby providing an internal public route for the gallery as a whole. The second is the characterisation of this route by a change in level across the site and its definition by a new wall. The wall extends from Clare Street to the rear of the original National Gallery building. The wall acts as a datum to the pivoting geometry of the west boundary of the site. From the new entrance, the wall and these two geometries are revealed and expressed by a triangular triple-height entrance hall.

Having passed through the wall, the visitor encounters a second place of orientation, a rectangular double-height inner hall which concludes the existing gallery sequences. The triangular entrance hall is identified with the travelling exhibition galleries and the rectangular inner hall with the permanent collection.

The shallow curve of the Clare Street elevation is designed to be seen in perspective. It does not act solely in a geometrical manner, blending Clare Street into Leinster Street South, but, significantly, on one side it steps forward emphasising its autonomy and relative importance when seen from the west. In contrast to the flat, brick and fenestrated neighbouring facades, the curved, stone-clad and mostly blind elevation set above its colonnaded ground floor is immediately distinguishable as belonging to a public institution, in the well-tried tradition of making clear distinctions between the city fabric and public buildings.

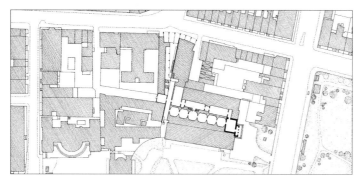

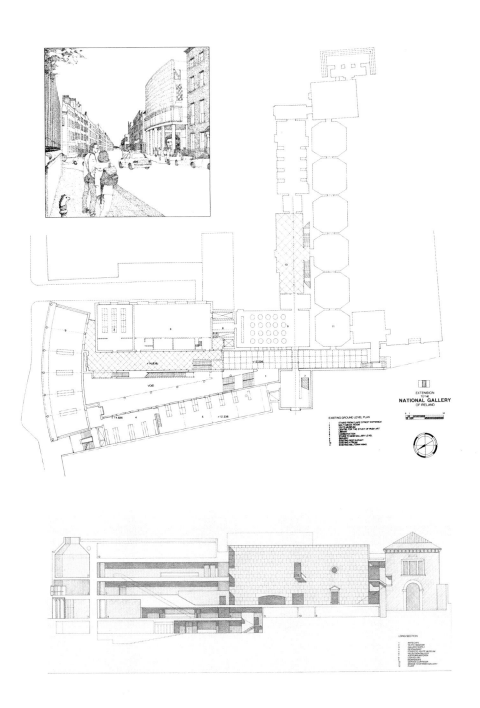

EXTENSION
TO THE
NATIONAL GALLERY
OF IRELAND

EXISTING GROUND LEVEL PLAN

LONG SECTION

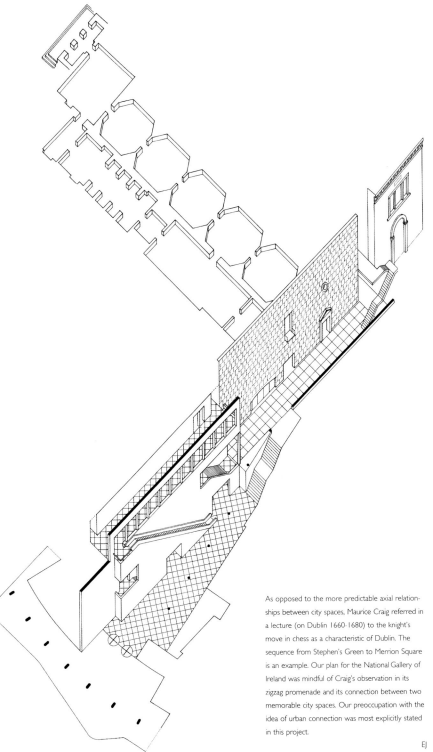

As opposed to the more predictable axial relationships between city spaces, Maurice Craig referred in a lecture (on Dublin 1660-1680) to the knight's move in chess as a characteristic of Dublin. The sequence from Stephen's Green to Merrion Square is an example. Our plan for the National Gallery of Ireland was mindful of Craig's observation in its zigzag promenade and its connection between two memorable city spaces. Our preoccupation with the idea of urban connection was most explicitly stated in this project.

EJ

199

Saïd Business School
Oxford

1997-2001

The commission for the eventual building, which is located near the main railway station, came about as a result of winning a limited competition involving a different site. The site, in Mansfield Road, had been given to the university by Merton College in 1963 on the understanding that it would not be built on in perpetuity. After the competition had taken place this became known and, at a particularly dramatic occasion at the Sheldonian Theatre, the project was thrown out by the university congregation. Much to his credit the benefactor, Wafic Saïd, was not disillusioned and he energetically pursued alternative sites. There were three principal reasons for the choice of the eventual site. First it was large enough to allow for future expansion; second it would help to revitalise the west end of the city; and third, and most important, its position opposite the railway station would place the school on the threshold between the outside world represented by the station and the introverted nature of the university. It might be noted that business schools, not unlike schools of architecture, have been accepted reluctantly into some of the older universities – Oxford University is still without a school of architecture.

The site allowed the school to create two new and important city spaces. Since the departure of the LMS station in the 1950s, the space opposite the railway station was used as a large surface car park and was certainly no celebration of arrival! The west facade of the school defines the station forecourt and clarifies it as a destination for those arriving by train. To the south the building forms a square for those arriving by car from the west along the Botley Road. This square might be understood as the equivalent of Magdalen Bridge to the east and St Giles to the north, as

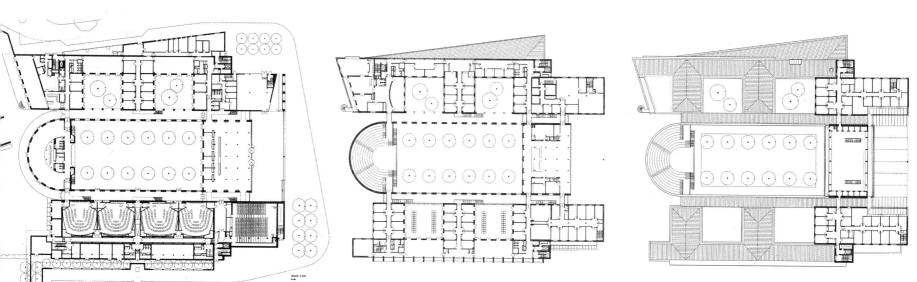

202

recognisable entrances to the university precinct. It is here the business school has its principal entrance. This is an urban site. The school builds to its boundaries and forms its own interior world, a modern equivalent of the traditional Oxford colleges.

Facing this new public square, the school presents an accessible and balanced composition. Two projecting wings and a fully glazed facade to the entrance hall and the library above form an entrance court. A horizontal brise-soleil adds to the sense of enclosure and protects the facade from its southern exposure. The hypostyle entrance hall leads to two double-height cloisters, one open, the other closed. The two cloisters define the central courtyard (30 by 60 metres) and

lead to the student common room and the walled garden beyond. This sequence, leading from the busy world of the Botley Road to the tranquility of the school's interior, form the essential, symmetrical and ideal armature of the school. Either side of this set-piece, the building responds more pragmatically to local conditions. To the west at ground floor a row of Harvard-style lecture rooms insulate the interior from the noise and distraction of the station forecourt. Above, single-storey courtyards are enclosed by professors' rooms. To the east, two-storey courtyards are enclosed by seminar rooms. Service rooms are accessed directly from Rewley Road. Forming the head of the composition is the vaulted reading room of the library, positioned above

the entrance hall. The central courtyard is closed by the amphitheatre which becomes part of the general circuit of circulation at first floor level.

Business schools have many small rooms and a few large common rooms and lecture theatres. The character of the school depends on how these various rooms are connected. The need for chance encounters between students when 'breaking out' from lectures and seminars suggests a peripatetic pattern; to this end circulation in its various forms – cloister/courtyard, staircase and hall – become an extension of teaching. The design of the building is therefore generous with horizontal and vertical movement. The net-to-gross ratio is deliberately high.

The building is built of brick with

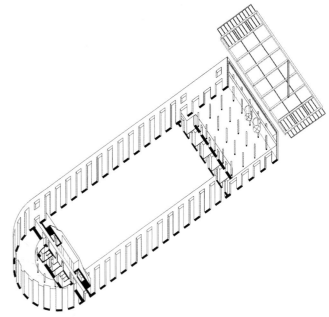

powder-coated grey aluminium doors and windows. Limestone is used sparingly to denote the relative importance of the elevations. The inclined roofs, concealed behind parapets, are clad in zinc. The exposed and inclined roof to the Rewley Road elevation, with its lean-to shed, emphasises its service role. The special and visible silhouettes of the tower and the vaulted library roof are clad in copper.

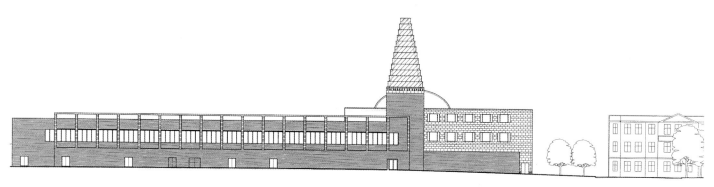

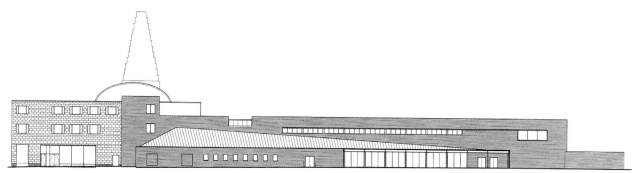

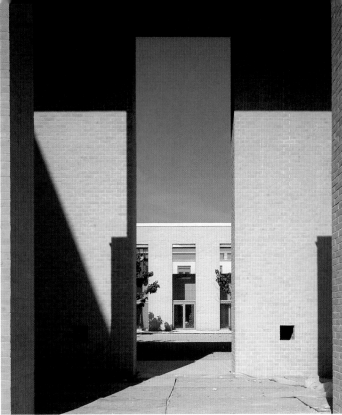

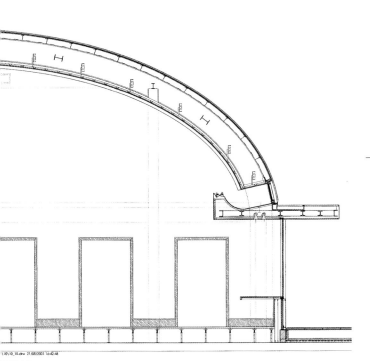

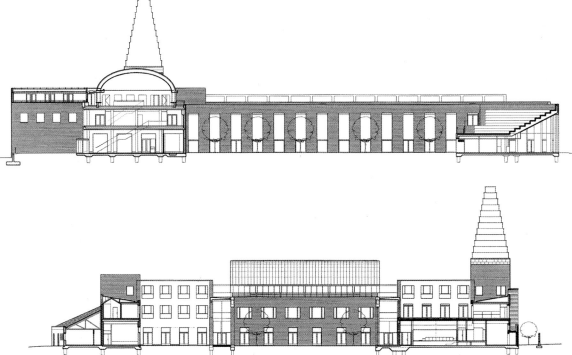

Academic arena

Alan Colquhoun

Spurred, no doubt, by the example of Cambridge, Oxford University has finally accepted that business management is a suitable subject to be taught in the hallowed groves of English academia. The Saïd Business School is the result of this change of heart.

The original site for the building was a field within the university precincts belonging to Merton College. But when it was discovered that the land was entailed and could never be built on, the university relocated the school to a larger site on the western boundary of the city next to the railway station.

The utterly different nature of the two sites – the smaller one within quiet university precincts, the larger one in a busy commercial quarter – largely explains the difference between the first and second projects. In the competition scheme, a few highly figural elements were informally and asymmetrically organised, so as to avoid overpowering the neighbouring buildings, to open the building up to its environment and preserve its semi-rural character. In the built scheme, the same set of elements reappears but these are now absorbed into a building with a high degree of unity and symmetry, setting it off from its surroundings.

At first sight this might seem like a perverse move – one whose ruling principle is one of contrast rather than integration. No question here of the new school of business responding with 'realism' to its undefined environment as, for instance, was the case with the Koolhaas congress centre at Lille – though such realism would of course have involved something much more indeterminate even than the first Oxford project. Nevertheless there is an impeccable logic behind Dixon and Jones' strategy. They have interpreted the encroachment of the university with the everyday commercial world as a chance to provide a model for future urban development. Instead of trying to make the building conform to a commercial Zeitgeist (a possible scenario if a school of business were taken as a symbol of free-market capitalism) they have set out to create an exemplary island of calm and order in the centre of an urban 'jungle'. The building creates an introverted world of its own, a microcosm or, even better, what Leibnitz would have termed a monad, with 'windows' onto the outside world in the two main facades.

The west facade facing the station forecourt has a slightly Italianate colonnade of piers with alternating brick and stone bands, intended to greet the visitor arriving by train. This colonnade cannot be mistaken for an entrance, since it springs from the first floor, which forms a high plinth.

The actual entry in the building occurs in the adjacent south facade, facing a main artery into the city. At this point the street begins to bifurcate and becomes so wide that it might seem like an urban square but for the fact that it is constantly traversed by fast traffic. The architects have compensated for this by setting the entrance well back behind symmetrical wings and creating a huge porte-cochere, covered with slatted brises-soleil, which protects the entrance hall from the sun. The hall itself is a deep hypostyle space, fully glazed in its outer face. By this clever move, the architects have created a public space within the curtilage of the building – a space that belongs ambiguously to both the city and the school. The actual boundary separating the public realm from the school as a private institution occurs at the back of

the entrance hall, where a thick service wall and a long reception desk conceal the school courtyard from public view.

This court acts as the social core of the building, voided yet full of associated meanings. Finished with light coloured gravel and occupied by a scattering of garden furniture, it exudes Mediterranean charm, recalling the architects' highly successful work in the court at Somerset House. The court is lined on both sides by two-storey high galleries, which constitute the major architectural promenades of the building. Visible beyond these galleries on either side of the court are a number of smaller courtyards wrapped on three sides by classrooms, faculty rooms and administration. On the west side these courts are raised to the first floor, above four lecture halls, which are designed,

according to the Harvard principle, as small amphitheatres to encourage student participation.

Access to the first floor is by open staircases within the galleries. Horizontal and vertical circulation is thus strategically placed in relation to both the central court and the classrooms. The galleries are structurally independent, with colonnades of brick piers which allow continuous views between the central court and its satellite courts. Everything is open and revealed in the most satisfying and exciting spatial interplay, although the massiveness of the piers gives them a rather depressing monumentality. Movement from one side of the central court to the other is possible at each end on both ground and first floors.

The entire arrangement gives

prominence to unallocated public space and casual encounters between seminars. It is also a way of avoiding what might have been a labyrinthine experience due to the access requirements of a large number of small classrooms. At the moment there are only a hundred or so students and the public spaces seem empty but this should change next year when the school realises its full complement of 400 students.

Two important spaces common to the whole school fill the ends of the court: the library, situated over the entrance hall, and the student common room, at garden level at the other end. Over the common room a Greek amphitheatre dominates the far end of the court. This element was also present, though in a different context, in the winning design for the initial site.

The form of the amphitheatre might certainly generate spontaneous collective uses but its purpose seems to be largely formal – or perhaps we should say 'typological' since Aldo Rossi's influence seems to be invoked here and in other places.

There is no doubt that the Oxford business school works admirably at a practical level and is often amazingly successful at an aesthetic level as well. This also appears to be the opinion of the users. The building must be accounted an unqualified success from practically every perspective.

The only reservation I have is a philosophical one and may seem remote from reality. The architects seem to believe that there are permanent and timeless architectural forms that somehow allow us to escape from our

finitude and our embeddedness in history. This position is arguable and difficult to dispute, since the ability to respond to all traditions is clearly one of the most characteristic attributes of modernity. Yet this ability surely comes at a price: the past is not available now as it was in the past; it cannot be reproduced 'naturally' but is inevitably clothed in irony, doubt and a certain melancholy (the work of Rossi is a prime example of this). This problem involves much more than a futile argument about style. Its roots lie in the relative philosophical claims of absolute as opposed to time-bound knowledge. Considering that, more than any of the other arts, architecture straddles the realms of truth (reason) and judgement (taste), there is curiously little debate today among architects on this matter.

National Gallery study London

1998-

It is one of the valued characteristics of the National Gallery that the whole collection is exhibited at one floor level. This gives an unusual sense of integration to the various schools of European painting. Below this 'piano nobile', at ground level, there is a whole floor of other accommodation. The gallery has taken the bold move to purchase an adjacent office building and to decant the activities presently occupying the ground floor, releasing it for public use. The gallery urgently needs to improve its facilities for visitors and would also like to develop other kinds of exhibition presentations. At the same time, the north side of Trafalgar Square is to be made pedestrian as part of the World Squares project. The ground floor entrances to the gallery will become much more significant and the development of the ground floor as a public area will have a strong relationship with the developing use of the square.

This study shows how the east and west ground floor doors can be linked to two of the courtyards to form a U-shaped armature of circulation. The rooflit courtyards provide for the important connection between ground and first floors. When Wilkins designed the front elevation he was constrained by the location of the street and had to restrict the depth of the entrance staircase. Now it would be possible to provide a grand flight of steps leading directly to the portico. This would emphasise the view across Trafalgar Square and down Whitehall and would form a natural meeting place.

At the main gallery level the axis is taken through to the bow-fronted bay that faces St Martin-in-the-Fields. This was made possible by the arrangements for the work at the adjacent National Portrait Gallery. The bow contains a stair linking the main axis of the first floor to that of the ground floor.

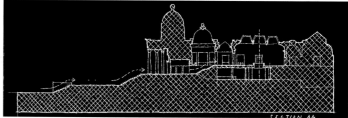

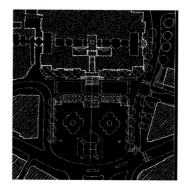

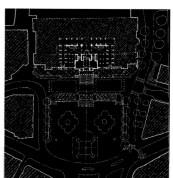

Cafe, bridge and fountains
Somerset House, London

1998-2000

The Somerset House Trust was formed in 1997 with the purpose in the short term of restoring the building fabric, of removing the car park from the courtyard and to initiate the longer term ambition of reintroducing Somerset House into the life of the city. As part of this process of reintegration, a competition was held in 1998 to investigate the possibility of providing a cafe on the south terrace. In our submission we became intrigued by the idea of connecting the south terrace to Waterloo Bridge. As a result a continuous promenade would be opened up from the South Bank, across the river, along the south terrace and by way of the East Street of King's College to the Strand

and beyond to the Inns of Court. The cafe terrace would be an event along this sequence. The connection to Waterloo Bridge is a simple ramped bridge which cuts through Gilbert Scott's stone abutments. It is made of steel clad in bronze, paved in York stone and with a glass balustrade, topped by an oversized oak leaning rail incorporating concealed lighting.

The cafe terrace is positioned on a raised timber platform 4.5 by 27 metres, distinguishing it from the large dimensions of the terrace. Six inverted umbrellas are positioned in series on the platform providing shelter and a sense of place. Glass screens provide further protection from the prevailing

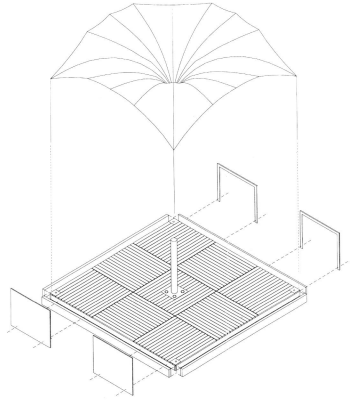

209

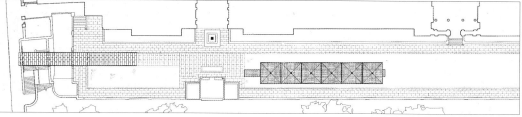

wind. The war memorial by Edwin Lutyens, relocated from the central courtyard, is placed on the axis of the West Street and forms part of this new composition. As the renovation of the courtyard was nearing completion we were invited to make recommendations as to how this large urban room might be furnished. Our principal reaction was that it should retain its open and flexible nature and that permanent structures and/or trees should be avoided. This would allow spontaneous and seasonal events to occur – for example open-air concerts and ice skating.

We observed however that with its new granite paving the courtyard would become inhospitably hot in the summer. As a result we proposed a fountain as a 'grove' of jets of water. Fifty-five stainless steel plates with a patinated finish are laid out on a grid 5 by 11.3 metres apart and set flush with the paving. The grid is generated by the geometry of the facades. When not in operation the plates are nearly invisible and events can take place above them. When in operation, 55 jets of water from one to six metres in height are released, controlled by a computer programme. At night, fibre optics concealed in the base plates illuminate the water. The fountains and floodlighting transform the courtyard from its previous use as a car park into one of London's most dramatic public rooms.

Sometimes life seems stranger than fiction. The fountains are dedicated to the memory of Edmond J Safra following a generous donation from his widow. The donation was made quite late in the project, when the fountains had already been designed and partially installed. At the dinner to celebrate the opening I found myself sitting next to one of the Safra family. She described how Edmond had always given generously to build projects and that part of his make-up was a somewhat superstitious preoccupation with numbers. His special number was 55 and, entirely independently, we had provided 11 rows of 5 fountains! There seems no rational explanation for this extraordinary coincidence.

JD

Right Somerset House has been transformed into a venue for skating, for concerts, for playing among fountains and even for London Fashion Week!

Project list

Built works are indicated by a span of dates and unbuilt works have a single date, unless otherwise stated. Works were carried out by Jeremy Dixon and Edward Jones as noted and/or under the auspices of: Cross Dixon Gold Jones Sansom Architects 1973-77; Edward Jones Architect 1977-82; Jeremy & Fenella Dixon 1977-84; Jones & Kirkland Architects 1982-87; Jeremy Dixon BDP 1984-90; Edward Jones Architect: 1987-89; Dixon Jones BDP 1990-; Jeremy Dixon Edward Jones, from 1989.

Photographic credits Jeremy Dixon: 25-29, 31, 35 (l), 38, 39, 40 (r), 41 (r), 42, 44 (r), 46 (tr), 47 (l), 49 (l), 50 (tl), 52-55, 101 (tr), 127 (bl), 129 (bl), 143 (r), 148, 152 (m), 154-156, 165, 174, 176 (r), 194, 195 (b), 208, 211 (l), 212 (South Bank, Tatlin), 213 (Weiss, Solar), 214 (Millbank, Sim), 215 (Compass, ROH), 216 (Cliveden, Estate), 217 (Darwin, Waterloo, Perry Green, Milan), 218 (Wilson, Stonehenge, Croydon), 220 (Nat Gallery); Anthea Sieveking: cover flap, 20 (b); Christopher Woodward: 30 (l); Fenella Dixon: 30 (m); Richard Davies: 32, 36, 213 (Northants); John Donat: 35 (m, r); Martin Charles: 40 (l), 4 (l), 43, 46 (b), 213 (St Marks, Tate); Jo Reid & John Peck: 44 (l), 45, 46 (t), 47 (r), 215 (Tate, Ashmill, Clifton); Richard Bryant: 56, 149, 150 (l), 151-153; Dennis Gilbert: 57, 100, 103, 105, 108, 110 (t), 111, 115-120, 121 (b), 124, 127 (r), 128-132, 134, 135, 158-163, 166, 168, 170 (t), 171, 182-187, 204 (b), 206, 207, 209, 210 (l, br), 211 (r), 217 (ROH), 218 (Darwin), 219 (NPG), 220 (Somerset); David Wild: 64 (br), 212 (Watford); Philippe Achache: 64 (tl); Michael Nicholson: 66; Margot Griffin: 67, 70 (t), 76 (m), 81, 91, 141, 210 (tr, mr), 217 (De Marco, Ainsley); Robert Burley: 73, 75, 76 (r), 77, 78 (l), 79, 90 (l), 92, 93, 215 (Miss); Twentieth Century Fox: 78 (r); Edward Jones: 90 (r); Realistic Photo Graphics: 101 (b); Rob Moore: 107, 114, 118 (bl), 121 (t); Chorley Handford: 110 (b), 168; Andrew Putler: 143 (l), 146 (m), 147 (l), 167, 169, 189 (m), 196, 200 (t, r), 202, 203, 204 (m) 216 (Molsen), 218 (Thamesmead, Bath), 219 (Brindleyplace); Jeremy Cockayne: 148 (b), 217 (Leeds); Susan Crowe: 150 (r); Pascal Madoc-Jones: 170 (l); Iain Rennie: 176 (l), 177, 180, 181; James Morris: 188-193, 218 (Portsmouth); Michael Murray: 200 (l), 204, 205, 220 (Oxford); Chris Honeywell: 201; Michael Gold: 213 (Pravda); Alex Blahova: 214 (Clarendon); Art James: 216 (Yolles).

Modelmakers Jeremy Dixon: 26, 31, 38, 41, 42, 46, 52 (t), 54, 55, 165 (r), 174 (t); JD with Gary Kugele: 49, 52 (b); Thurloe Models: 36; Dixon Jones office: 44, 148, 165 (l), 174 (m), 195, 196; Gary Kugele: 50, 101, 127, 154, 156, 208; Richard Armiger: 143, 147, 167, 169, 189.

Every effort has been made to acknowledge the source of photographs and illustrations; we apologise for any errors or omissions.

1959 Great Laxey Wheel, Isle of Man p24
Jeremy Dixon, Fenella Dixon, Christopher Woodward
Second year measured drawing, Architectural Association

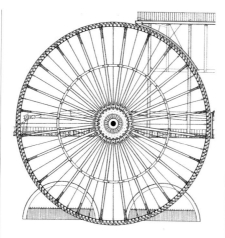

1962 South Bank housing, London p26
Jeremy Dixon, Fenella Dixon
Fourth year project, Architectural Association

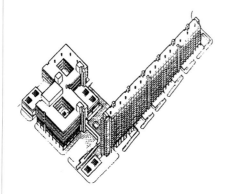

1963 Residential teacher training college, Swindon
Edward Jones, Paul Simpson
Fifth year thesis project, Architectural Association

1963-64 Offices, Watford
Douglas Stephen & Partners
David Wild, Edward Jones

1965 Portsdown housing, Portsmouth p62
Michael Brawne Architects
Edward Jones, Mike Gold
Competition entry

1966-71 Plough Way housing, Rotherhithe p27
Frederick MacManus & Partners
Jeremy Dixon

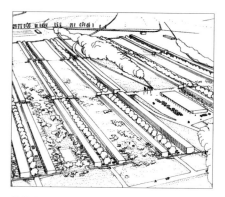

1966-71 Woolwich Polytechnic hostel
Frederick MacManus & Partners
Edward Jones, Christopher Cross, Brendan Woods

1968 Runcorn housing p28
Jeremy Dixon, Fenella Dixon, Christopher Cross, Adrian Sansom
Competition entry

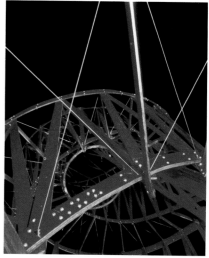

1971 Tatlin Tower reconstruction p30
Jeremy Dixon, Fenella Dixon, Christopher Cross, Christopher Woodward, Sven Rindl
Model for Art in Revolution exhibition, Hayward Gallery

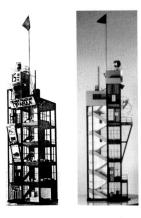

1971 Pravda Tower reconstruction
Edward Jones, Miike Gold, Chris Clark, Madhu Sarin, John Eger
Model for Art in Revolution exhibition, Hayward Gallery

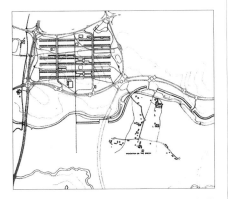

1971-73 Netherfield housing, Milton Keynes p29, 63
Milton Keynes Development Corporation
Christopher Cross, Jeremy Dixon, Mike Gold, Edward Jones

1973-76 Netherfield shopping, Milton Keynes
Milton Keynes Development Corporation
Jeremy Dixon, Edward Jones, Shay Cleary, Tony Murphy

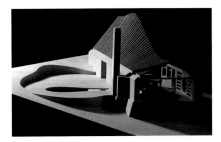

1973 Northamptonshire county hall p32
Stage one: Jeremy Dixon, Fenella Dixon
Stage two: Jeremy Dixon, Fenella Dixon, Edward Jones, Christopher Cross, Mike Gold, Adrian Sansom, Birkin Haward, Martin Francis, Sven Rindl (structure), Loren Butt (services)
Competition entry (first place), unbuilt

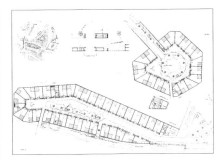

1973 Housing for the elderly, Haringey, London
Edward Jones, Mike Gold
Competition entry (second place)

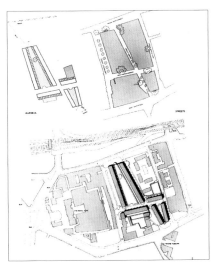

1974 Royal Mint Square housing, London
Edward Jones, Mike Gold
Competition entry

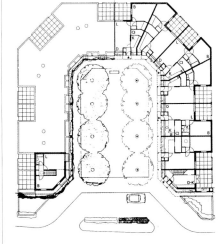

1974 Weiss house, Bucks p38
Jeremy Dixon, Fenella Dixon

1974-77 Cranford Lane housing for the elderly p67
Cross Dixon Gold Jones Sansom Architects
Edward Jones, Roger Huntley

1975 Rooftop housing, Covent Garden, London
Cross Dixon Gold Jones Sansom Architects
Edward Jones, Mike Gold

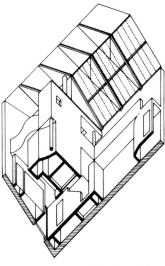

1975-77 Studio house, Glebe Place, Chelsea p64
Cross Dixon Gold Jones Sansom Architects
Edward Jones, Alexandra Blahova, Roger Huntley, Kiji Shirasaki, Michael Baumgarten (cabinet maker)

1975-79 St Mark's Road housing, Kensington p40
Cross Dixon Gold Jones Sansom Architects
Jeremy Dixon, Fenella Dixon, Steven Wright

1976 Solar Walk, High Wycombe, Bucks p39
Jeremy Dixon, Fenella Dixon
Competition entry

1977 Millbank housing, London p54
Jeremy Dixon, Fenella Dixon
Competition entry

1978 Natural History Museum garden
Jeremy Dixon
Competition entry

1979 Baltic Wharf housing, Bristol
Edward Jones, Margot Griffin, Edward Bowness
Competition entry

1981-83 Lanark Road housing, Maida Vale p43
Jeremy Dixon, Fenella Dixon, Robert Barnes, Dick
Knowles, Michael Taylor (developer/builder)
Competition, built

1977 Millbank housing, London
Edward Jones
Competition entry

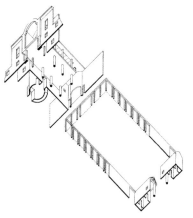

1978 Sim house, Essex
Jeremy Dixon, Fenella Dixon

1978 Schinkenchiku housing
Edward Jones, Donald Mackay, Roger Huntley
Competition entry

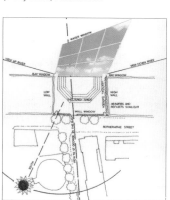

1979 Riverside Garden – Window Pond, Deptford
Jeremy Dixon, Fenella Dixon
Competition entry

1979 Taoiseach's house, Dublin p68
Edward Jones, Margot Griffin, Russell Bevington
Competition entry

1981 Schinkel Archives, Berlin p70
Edward Jones, Margot Griffin
Competition entry

1979-80 Clarendon Cross studio, London
Edward Jones, Alexandra Blahova

1981-83 Tate Gallery coffee shop p46
Jeremy Dixon, Fenella Dixon, Dick Knowles
Competition, built

1982 Vauxhall Cross, London
Edward Jones
Competition entry

1982-87 Mississauga City Hall, Canada p72
Jones & Kirkland Architects
Edward Jones, Michael Kirkland, Steve Teeple, Mark
Sterling, Kit Wallace, Maxim James, Mark Baraness, Chris
Rattigan, Gerry Lang, John Soules, Michael Griffin,
Margot Griffin, George Przybylski, Jeff Latto, Endel Eero,
Bernard Gillespie, Jack Shaw, Matt Poray, Dan McNeil,
Sarah Pearce, Pia Heine, Roly Bergman (structural engi-
neer), Bob Shute (mechanical engineer)
Competition, built

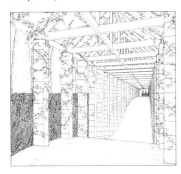

1983 Trinity Gardens, Toronto p80
Jones & Kirkland Architects
Edward Jones, Mark Sterling, Steve Teeple, Chris
Rattigan, Margot Griffin, Marc Baraness, Bob Hannah
(landscape)
Competition entry

1984 Tate Gallery restaurant p46
Jeremy Dixon, Fenella Dixon, Mark Pimlott

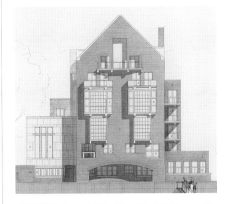

1985-87 St George's Wharf housing, London p54
Jeremy Dixon, Fenella Dixon, Mark Pimlott, Peter St John,
Carl Laubin, Steve Buck, Michael Taylor (developer/
builder)

1984 National Gallery extension, London p52
Jeremy Dixon, Fenella Dixon, Mark Pimlott, Ken Mackay,
Dick Knowles, Peter St John, Robert Barnes
Competition entry

1983-85 Ashmill Street housing, Maida Vale p45
Jeremy Dixon, Fenella Dixon, Dick Knowles, Michael
Taylor (developer/builder)

1984-85 Clifton Nurseries shop, Maida Vale p47
Jeremy Dixon, Fenella Dixon, Ken Mackay

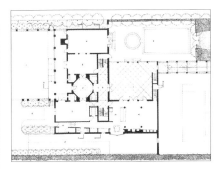

1984-86 Sherman residence, Toronto
Jones & Kirkland Architects
Edward Jones, Jeff Latto, Mark Sterling

1984-87 Compass Point, Isle of Dogs p44
Jeremy Dixon, Fenella Dixon, Dick Knowles, Ken Mackay,
Carl Laubin, Steven Buck, Suhas Shanbag, James Platts

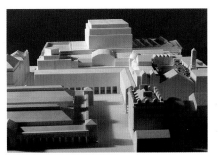

1984-89 Royal Opera House, Covent Garden p48
Dixon/BDP partnership (to first planning permission)
Bill Jack (BDP), Jeremy Dixon, Fenella Dixon, Martin
Ward, Ken Mackay, Dick Knowles, Peter St John, Mark
Pimlott, Annette LeCuyer, Robert Barnes, Carl Laubin,
Steve Buck, Alan Baxter (engineer)
Competition (first place); see also 1989-2000

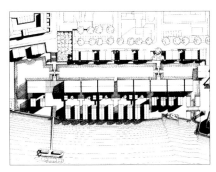

1985 Cherry Garden Pier, London p53
Jeremy Dixon, Fenella Dixon, Ken Mackay, Dick Knowles
Competition entry

215

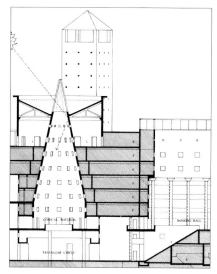

1985 Grand Buildings, London p88
Edward Jones, Kit Wallace, George Przybylski, Mark Sterling, Margot Griffin
Competition entry

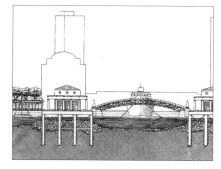

1985 Harbour Front masterplan, Toronto
Jones & Kirkland Architects
Edward Jones, Michael Kirkland
Unbuilt

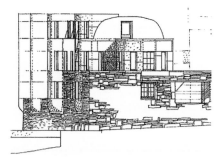

1986 Pembroke College residence, Oxford
Jeremy Dixon, Fenella Dixon, Mark Pimlott
Competition entry

1986 Minnesota State Capitol, USA
Jones & Kirkland Architects
Edward Jones, Mark Sterling, Gerry Lang, Kit Wallace
Competition entry

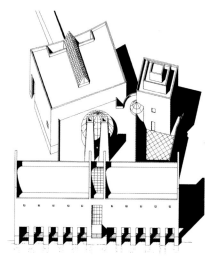

1986 Clay and Glass Museum, Ontario p86
Jones & Kirkland Architects
Edward Jones, Gerry Lang, Jeff Latto, Steve Teeple, Chris Rattigan
Competition entry

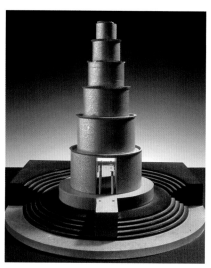

1986 Molsen Acqua sculpture, Toronto
Edward Jones
Competition entry

1986-91 Cliveden planned village, Bucks p55
Jeremy Dixon, Fenella Dixon, Peter St John, Steve Buck, Roger Goodliffe, Liam Hennessy, Robert Barnes, Annette LeCuyer, Celia Maxwell Scott
Unbuilt

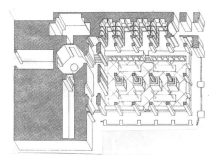

1987 Paul Stewart shop, New York
Edward Jones, Hamid Nouri

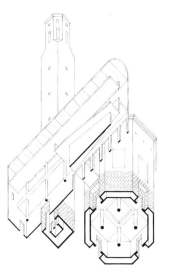

1987 West Hollywood civic centre, USA p82
Jones & Kirkland Architects
Edward Jones, David Weir, Steve Teeple, Suzanne Powadiuk, Jeff Latto
Competition entry (second place)

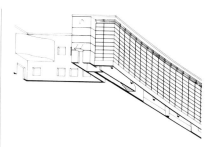

1987-89 SA Armstrong headquarters, Toronto p90
Edward Jones, Steve Teeple, Ralph Giannone, MS Yolles (structural engineer)

1987-89 Yolles building, Queen Street East, Toronto
Jones & Kirkland Architects
Edward Jones, Gerry Lang, Bernard Gillespie; MS Yolles (structural engineer)

1988 Cleto Munari silverware
Edward Jones

1988 Estate rehabilitation, Waltham Forest
Jeremy Dixon, Peter St John, Mark Pimlott

1988 Chateau Bordeaux
Jeremy Dixon, Fenella Dixon, Mark Pimlott, Carl Laubin (painting)
Proposal for exhibition

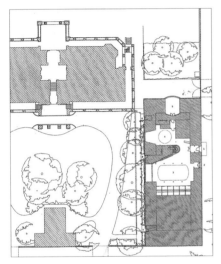

1988 British Embassy administrative offices, Cairo
Jeremy Dixon, Fenella Dixon, Roger Goodliffe
Unbuilt

1988-89 De Marco residence, Toronto
Edward Jones, Kit Wallace

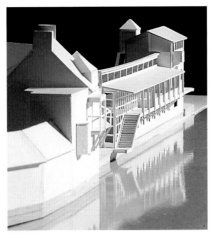

1988-89 Sandra Ainsley gallery, Toronto
Edward Jones, Kit Wallace

1988-93 Henry Moore Institute, Leeds p56, 148
Jeremy Dixon, Fenella Dixon, Edward Jones, John Moran, Roger Goodliffe

1989 Petershill offices, London
Edward Jones, Margot Griffin, Kit Wallace, Jeff Latto, Ralph Giannone, Mark Facer (Ove Arup & Partners)
Competition entry

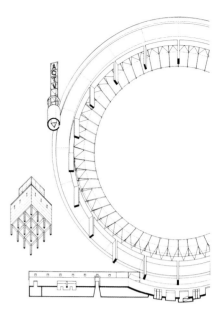

1989-94 Darwin College study centre, Cambridge p57, 158
Jeremy Dixon, Fenella Dixon, Edward Jones, John Moran, John Parker, Pascal Madoc-Jones, Aage Vellestad, Andrew Houlton, Mike Betts, Roger Hyde (structure)

1989-2000 Royal Opera House, Covent Garden p100
Dixon Jones BDP – joint office
Jeremy Dixon, Edward Jones, Charles Broughton, Nick Terry, Gordon Cousins, Ann Marsh, Tim Leach, Susan Mortimer, Anna Kosicka, Louise Cotter, Rebecca Granger, Will Stevens; Terry Barker, Robert Barnes, Charles Brett, Ingrid Brooke-Barnett, Mark Bunting, Christine Chabanne, Jeff Essen, Tim Gaymer, Jane Hymas, Peter Hull, Mark Janko, Justine Langford, David Lim, Pascal Madoc-Jones, Chris Milan, John Moran, David Naessens, Nina Noor, David Rhodes, Leonard Sequeira, Richard Thompson, Graham Vicary, Martin Ward, Adrian Westmacott, Anna Winstanley, Mlinaric Henry & Zervudachi

1990 Venice bus station p138
Jeremy Dixon, Edward Jones, David Naessens, John Moran, Kevin Hanvey, Kit Wallace, Mark Bunting, Anthony Hunt (structural engineer), Ninian Logan (transport engineer).
Competition entry (first place), unbuilt

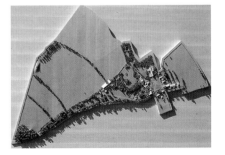

1990 London Dance Theatre, Waterloo
Jeremy Dixon, Edward Jones, Mark Bunting, John Moran

1990 Henry Moore Foundation, Perry Green p154
Jeremy Dixon, Edward Jones, Jeff Latto, John Moran

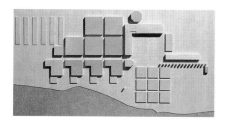

1991 Ospedale Nuovo, Milan p164
Jeremy Dixon, Edward Jones, Jeff Latto, David Naessens, Mark Bunting
Competition entry

1991 Regents Palace Hotel, London
Jeremy Dixon, Edward Jones, David Naessens, Jeff Latto

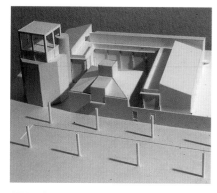

1991 Wilson building, Fitzwilliam College, Cambridge
Jeremy Dixon, Edward Jones, Mark Bunting
Competition entry

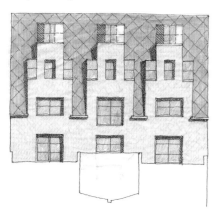

1991 Davies Street offices, London
Jeremy Dixon, Edward Jones, David Naessens

1991 Thamesmead housing
Jeremy Dixon, Edward Jones, David Naessens

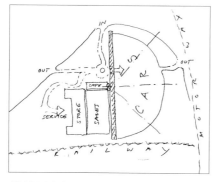

1991-94 Sainsbury superstore, Plymouth p166
Jeremy Dixon, Edward Jones, Peter Rice (engineer), Pascal Madoc-Jones, Gordon Cousins

1992 Stonehenge visitor centre p172
Jeremy Dixon, Edward Jones, John Moran, David Naessens, Martin Ward, Janet Jack (landscape)
Competition entry

1992 Croydon community university p194
Jeremy Dixon, Edward Jones, Mark Bunting

1992-93 Tower Houses, Aberdeen p176
Jeremy Dixon, Edward Jones, David Naessens, Louise Cotter, Gordon Cousins
Competition, built

1992-95 Darwin College housing, Cambridge p182
Jeremy Dixon, Edward Jones, David Naessens, Pascal Madoc-Jones, Margot Griffin

1992-96 Science building, Portsmouth University p188
Jeremy Dixon, Edward Jones, David Naessens, John Parker, Mark Bunting, Gordon Cousins, John Moran, Louise Cotter
Competition, built

1993 St Mary's Island housing, Chatham
Jeremy Dixon, Edward Jones, David Naessens, John Moran
Competition entry

1993 Sainsbury supermarket, Bath
Jeremy Dixon, Edward Jones, John Moran

1993 Brentford housing
Jeremy Dixon, Edward Jones, John Moran, John Parker

1993 Spitalfields office building, London
Jeremy Dixon, Edward Jones, David Naessens
Unbuilt

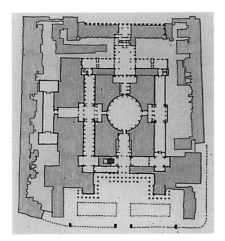

1994 British Museum courtyard, London
Jeremy Dixon, Edward Jones
Competition entry

1994 South Bank masterplan, London – 1
Jeremy Dixon, Edward Jones, John Moran, Jane Thompson
Competition entry

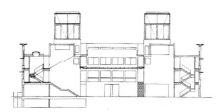

1994 UMIST business school, Manchester
Jeremy Dixon, Edward Jones, John Moran, David Naessens
Competition entry

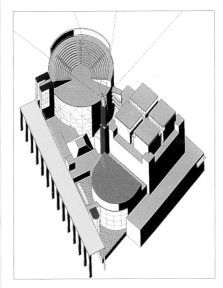

1994 Cardiff Opera House   p196
Jeremy Dixon, Edward Jones, John Moran, Jane Thompson
Competition entry

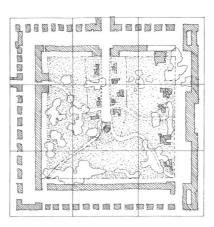

1994 New Delhi housing
Jeremy Dixon, Edward Jones, John Moran
Competition entry (first place)

1994-2000 National Portrait Gallery, London   p124
Jeremy Dixon, Edward Jones, John Moran, Nigel Bailey, Chris Milan, Jo da Silva (engineer)
Competition, built

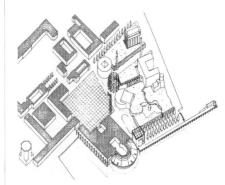

1995 Potsdam opera house, Germany
Jeremy Dixon, Edward Jones, John Moran
Competition entry

1995 Safeway, Wandsworth, London
Jeremy Dixon, Edward Jones, Tom Lacey, Sharni Howe

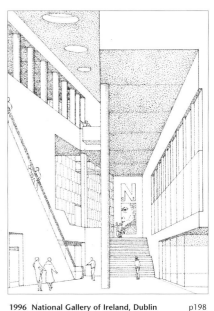

1996 National Gallery of Ireland, Dublin   p198
Jeremy Dixon, Edward Jones, David Naessens
Competition entry

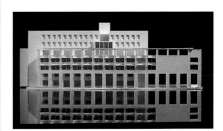

1996 Brindleyplace office, Birmingham
Jeremy Dixon, Edward Jones, Tom Lacey
Competition entry

1996 Guys Hospital new wing, London
Jeremy Dixon, Edward Jones, David Naessens
Competition entry

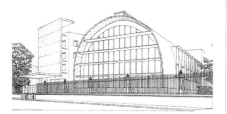

1997 Trinity College library, Dublin
Jeremy Dixon, Edward Jones, Anna Christiansen, Hal Ingberg
Competition entry

1997 University of North London
Jeremy Dixon, Edward Jones
Competition entry

1997 Said Business School, Oxford – 1   p200
Jeremy Dixon, Edward Jones, David Naessens, Robert Barnes, Peter Hull, Adrian Westmacott, Janet Jack (landscape)
Competition (first place), Mansfield Road site

1998 Queen's Gallery, Buckingham Palace, London
Jeremy Dixon, Edward Jones, Peter Hull, Alan Baxter (engineer)
Competition entry

1998-2001 Said Business School, Oxford – 2   p200
Jeremy Dixon, Edward Jones, Richard Thompson, Justine Langford, Adrian Westmacott, Rebecca Granger, John Moran, Gordon Cousins, Peter Hull
Station site, built

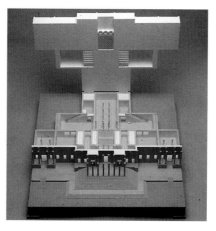

1998- National Gallery masterplan, London   p208
Jeremy Dixon, Edward Jones, Kathryn Firth, Nigel Bailey, Chris Milan, Peter Hull, Alan Baxter (engineer)
Competition entry (first place)

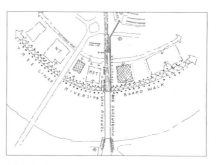

1999 South Bank masterplan, London – 2
Jeremy Dixon, Edward Jones, Kathryn Firth, Margot Griffin
Competition entry

2000 Cafe, bridge, fountains, Somerset House   p209
Jeremy Dixon, Edward Jones, David Cunningham, Philip Hastings, Kathryn Firth, Natalie Morton, Peter Hull, Michael Trigg, Tony Dyson (Donald Insall & Partners)
Competition (cafe and bridge), built

Jeremy Dixon was born in Bishops Stortford in 1939 and educated at Merchant Taylors School. He trained at the Architectural Association in London (1957-64) and registered as an architect in 1967. He studied with, and later married and worked with Fenella Clemens. They have a son and two daughters. The couple separated in 1989.

Dixon has taught at the Architectural Association (1971-80), the Bartlett at University College, London (1972-74) and the Royal College of Art, London. He has been an external examiner for the Royal Institute of British Architects and chaired regional RIBA award juries from 1994-99.

Dixon represented Britain at the Venice Biennale in 1980 and was a keynote speaker at the 'Annual Sessions and Forum' conference in Colombo, Sri Lanka, in 2001. He served as a member of the jury for the Royal Gold Medal for Architecture in 1992 and was a member of the competition juries for the Toronto Opera House and Walsall Art Gallery. He is also an architectural modelmaker and photographer.

Jeremy Dixon was knighted in the New Year honours list, 2000.

Edward Jones was born in St Albans in 1939 and educated at Haileybury. He studied at the Architectural Association in London (1958-63), qualifying as an architect in 1965. He has two daughters and one son from his first marriage. In 1978 he married Margot Griffin – they have one son and two daughters.

Jones has taught at the Regent Street Polytechnic, London (1968-71), University College, Dublin (1971-73), the Architectural Association, London (1971-73), and he was senior tutor at the Royal College of Art, London (1975-82). Since 1973 he has been a visiting critic at various North American universities including Cornell, Toronto, Waterloo, Penn, Harvard, Rice, Carlton, Princeton, Yale, Columbia, Syracuse and Kent State (Florence). He was a visiting professor at Cornell University (1973-76), Rice University (1982-94), Penn University (1983), Harvard University (1985) and Princeton University (1987-89), and he was professor of architecture at the University of Toronto (1983-89). Jones has also been an external examiner at the Architectural Association, Heriot-Watt, Kingston, Portsmouth, Cardiff and the Caribbean School of Architecture at Kingston, Jamaica.

Jones represented Britain at the Venice Biennale (1980) and the Santiago Biennale, Chile (1981). He was architect-in-residence at the American Academy in Rome (1987) and received the Governor General's Award for Mississauga City Hall. In 1992 he was an assessor for the RIBA President's Medals for architectural education, and was a member of the Royal Gold Medal jury in 1993 and 1994. He served on the AA Council (1995-99) and was chair of the assessors for the Laban Dance Centre competition. He was a member of the Diana, Princess of Wales, Memorial Fountain Committee, and in 2001 he was awarded an honorary doctorate by the University of Portsmouth and was made an honorary fellow by the University of Cardiff. Jones is co-author, with Christopher Woodward, of A Guide to the Architecture of London (1983, 1992 and 2000).

Bibliography

JEREMY DIXON and EDWARD JONES

• **Great Laxey Wheel, Isle of Man** – JD
AA Journal vol 75 no 842 (May 1960) pp210-225
AA Cahiers no 1 – 1946-71 (Architectural Association) p47

• **Housing project, South Bank** – JD
AA Cahiers no 1 – 1946-71 p55

• **Boiler House, St James, London** – JD
AA Cahiers no 1 – 1946-71 p55

• **Secondary school project** – JD
Arena vol 80 no 891 April 1965 p277-281

• **Residential teacher training college, Swindon** – EJ
Arena – AA Journal (Sept 1963)
AA Cahiers no 1 – 1946-71 p63
A+U no 10 (1977)

• **Portsdown housing, Portsmouth** – EJ
Arena – AA Journal vol 81 no 900 (March 1966) p236
Zodiac 18 (1968) p64 (ed Renzo Zovio)
Architectural Design vol 42 (June 1972) pp358-359
Another Chance for Housing (MoMA June 1973) p10
(Kenneth Frampton)

• **Plough Way housing, Rotherhithe** – JD
Architectural Design vol 42 (June 1972) pp63-66

• **Woolwich Polytechnic hostel** – EJ
Architectural Design vol 42 (June 1972) p355-358

• **Runcorn housing** – JD
Architectural Design vol 42 (June 1972) p61-62

• **Netherfield housing, Milton Keynes** – JD/EJ
Architectural Design vol 47 nos 9-10 (1977) p594, 658-659
Charles Jencks, 'The Language of Postmodern Architecture'
(Academy 1977)
Space Design (1978) pp32-33
Toshi Jutaku no 8010 (Oct 1980) p44

• **Netherfield shopping, Milton Keynes** – JD/EJ
Building Design (Nov 1976)
Architectural Design vol 47 nos 9-10 (1977) p646

• **Northamptonshire County Hall** – JD/EJ
Design no 301 (Jan 1974) pp56-61
Architects Journal centenary issue (9 March 1995) p151

• **Haringey housing for the elderly, London** – EJ
Architects Journal vol 157 no 7 (Feb 1973) p369
Architectural Design vol 47 no 9-10 (1977) p654
A+U no 10 (1977)
Architecture in Greece no 12 (1978) p45

• **Weiss house, Bucks** – JD
Architecture 1980 – Venice Biennale (Rizzoli), p146
Architectural Design vol 51 no 3/4 (1981) pp42-45

• **Cranford Lane housing for the elderly** – EJ
Architectural Design no 5 (1974) p295
Architectural Design 9-10 (1977) p648
Architecture in Greece no 12 (1978) p44

Architectural Review vol 165 no 984 (Feb 1979) p 105
Toshi Jutaku no 8010 (Oct 1980) p66
International Architect (5/1984) p17, 58 (Sibel Dostoglu)

• **Studio house, Glebe Place, London** – EJ
Architectural Design vol 47 no 9-10 (1977) pp594, 650-653
Domus 591 (Feb 1979) p28
Lotus 22 (1979) pp14-17
GA Houses 6 (1979) p148
House & Garden (Dec/Jan 1979-80) p122
Architecture 1980 – Venice Biennale (Rizzoli) p203
Archithese (Jan 1981) p650

• **St Mark's Road housing, Kensington** – JD
Charles Jencks, 'The Language of Post Modern Architecture'
(Academy 1977)
Building Design no 448 (1 June 1979) pp18-19
Architectural Design no 5/6 (1980) pp117-120
Architectural Review vol 168 no 1006 (Dec 1980) pp343-347
Architecture 1980 – Venice Biennale (Rizzoli) p146
A+U no 4 (April 1984) pp59-73
Cherry and Pevsner, Buildings of England: London NW,
pp530-531
Country Life vol 183 no 47 Nov 23 1989 p77

• **Millbank housing, London** – JD, EJ
Architectural Design (Aug 1977) pp531, 538
A+U 10 (1977)
Architecture in Greece no 12 (1978) p44
Architecture 1980 – Venice Biennale (Rizzoli) p146

• **Shinkenchiku housing** – EJ
Lotus 22 (1979) pp14-17
Architecture in Greece (1980)

• **Sim house, Bucks** – JD
Architecture 1980 – Venice Biennale (Rizzoli) p146
Architectural Design vol 51 no 3/4 (1981) pp42-45

• **Taoiseach's house, Dublin** – EJ
Architecture 1980 – Venice Biennale (Rizzoli) p204
International Architect no 4 vol 1 (1981) p6 (Margot Griffin)

• **Lanark Road housing, Maida Vale** – JD
Architects Journal vol 178 no 46 (16 Nov 1983) pp75-77
Building Design (15 April 1983) pp22-25
Architectural Review vol 174 no 1042 (Dec 1983) pp54-58
A+U no 4 (April 1984) pp59-73
Baumeister vol 83 no 10 (Dec 1986) pp44-45
Country Life vol 183 no 47 (23 Nov 1989) p76

• **Schinkel Archives, Berlin** – EJ
Architectural Design vol 52 no 5/6 (1982) p94
British Architecture/AD project awards (Academy, 1982) p117

• **Tate Gallery coffee shop** – JD
Building Design no 627 (4 Feb 1983) p10
Architectural Review vol 173 no 1032 (Feb 1983) pp50-53
Studio International vol 196 no 1001 (Aug 1983) pp50-52
A+U no 4 (April 1984) pp59-73
AA Files no 6 (1984) pp97-100

• **Mississauga City Hall, Canada** – EJ
Model Futures (ICA 1983) p169
Mississauga City Hall – A Canadian competition (Rizzoli 1984)
Architectural Design vol 54 (1984) p74
Progressive Architecture (Jan 1985) p101
Fifth Column vol 5 nos 3-4 (Dec 1985) p3
A Measure of Consensus – Canadian Architecture in Transition
(University of British Columbia 1986) pp19, 29, 39
Transactions 10 vol 5 no 2 (RIBA) p20
Progressive Architecture (Aug 1987) p69
Charles Jencks, 'The Language of Post Modern Architecture'
(Academy 1987) pp176-181
Post Modernism (Academy 1987) pp215, 252
Canadian Architect (June 1987) p20
A+U no 206 (Nov 1987) p19
Blueprint no 40 (1987) p48-52 (Janet Abrams)
Modern Classicism (Rizzoli 1988) pp57, 266
Architectural Design vol 58 no 1/2 (1988) pp11, 34
Architektur Canada (1988) p38
Fitzhenry & Whiteside, Contemporary Canadian Architecture
(1988) p202
Architecture and it's Image – Works from the Collection of the
Canadian Centre for Architecture (1989) p347
Tom Porter, 'Graphic Design Techniques for Architectural
Drawing' (1990) pp69, 83, 100
Sight Lines – Looking at Architecture in Canada (Toronto
University Press 1990) pp101, 155

• **Trinity Gardens, Toronto** – EJ
Architectural Design vol 54 (1984) p10
Section A vol 1 no 6 (Montreal 1984) p23
Princeton Journal no 2 (1985) pp188-193

• **Tate Gallery restaurant** – JD
Architectural Review vol 178 no 1063 (Sept 1985) pp78-79
Bauwelt (17 July 1987) pp1010-1011
Country Life vol 183 no 47 (1989) p78

• **St George's Wharf housing, London** – JD
Building Design no 874 (26 Feb 1988) pp22-23
CountryLife no 183 no 47 (1989) p77

• **National Gallery extension, London** – JD
Architects Journal vol 183 no 12 (19 March 1986) pp39-68
Architectural Design vol 56 no 1/2 (1986)

• **Ashmill Street housing, Maida Vale** – JD
Architects Journal vol 182 no 42 (2 Oct 1985) pp20-23

• **Clifton Nursery shop, Maida Vale** – JD
Building Design no 739 (17 May 1985) pp32-35
Architectural Review vol 178 no 1063 (Sept 1985) pp68-71
Country Life vol 183 no 47 (1989) p78

• **Royal Opera House, Covent Garden** – JD
Architects Journal vol 179 no 21 (23 May 1984) p35
Architects Journal vol 180 no 28 (11 July 1984) pp20-25
About the House 7 no 1 (1984) pp25-31
Architects Journal vol 184 no 40 (1 Oct 1986) pp47-62, 83-84
About the House vol 7 no 7 (1986) pp2-13

Architectural Design vol 57 no 1/2 (1987) pp9-24
Arquitectonica no 2 (Feb 1989) pp27-44
Country Life vol 183 no 47 (1989) p79
RSA Journal vol 141 no 5435 (Dec 1992) pp33-46

• **Grand Buildings, London** – EJ
Building Design (Sept 1985) pp30-31 (Ian Latham)
Tom Porter, 'Graphic Design Techniques for Architectural
Drawing' (1990) pp69, 83, 100

• **SA Armstrong headquarters, Toronto** – EJ
One hundred years of architecture in Ontario, Viewpoints
(1989) pp31, 60
Canadian Architect vol 34 no 7 (July 1989) p40
Progress Architecture 4 (1991)

JEREMY DIXON EDWARD JONES

• **Henry Moore Institute, Leeds**
Architecture Today no 39 (June 1993) p24 (Ian Latham)
Architectural Review (July 1993) (Patrick Nuttgens)
Baumeister no 8 (1993) (Dan Cruickshank)
Abitare no 325 (Jan 1994) p84 (Fulvio Irace)

• **Darwin College study centre, Cambridge**
Architecture Today no 49 (June 1994) pp24-29 (Peter Carolin)
Architectural Review no 1172 (Oct 1994) p50 (Peter Davey)
Arup Journal vol 31 no 1 (1996) pp16-18
Architecture Today no 100 (July 1999) p66
University Builders (Wiley 2001) p65

• **Royal Opera House, Covent Garden**
Prelude p4 (1999) (Peter Conrad, Rob Moore photographs)
Architects Journal (Dec 1999)
Architecture Today no 106 (March 2000) (Eric Parry, Peter St
John, Christopher Woodward)
Building vol 264 no 8082 (9 April 1999) pp44-51
Building Design (Nov 1999) p18
World Architecture no 85 (April 2000) pp70-93

ROH history as documented in national newspapers:
Colin Amery (Financial Times 5/7/86), John Grigsby (Daily
Telegraph 27/9/86), Colin Amery (FT 29/9/86), Martin Pawley
(Guardian 6/10/86), Gavin Stamp (DT 31/12/86), Laurence
Marks (Observer 8/2/87), Tom Pocock (Evening Standard
18/5/87), Kenneth Powell (DT 27/5/87), Colin Amery (FT
22/6/87), Stephen Games (Independent 24/6/87), Bryan
Appleyard (Times 26/6/87), Norman St John-Stevas (29/6/87),
Kenneth Powell (DT 30/6/87), Martin Pawley (G 2/7/87),
Laurence Marks (O 31/1/88), Gavin Stamp (ES 10/2/88), Dan
Cruikshank (ES 3/3/88), Fiona Maddocks (I 3/8/88), Kenneth
Powell (DT 8/8/88), Marcus Binney (ES 11/8/88), Siman
Jenkins (T 16/8/88), Andrew Billen (T 12/9/88), Malcolm
Grant (G 19/9/88), Colin Amery (FT 3/10/88), Law report
(I 20/10/88), Terence Shaw (DT 20/10/88), Kenneth Powell
(DT 20/10/88), David Hencke (G 7/2/89), David Hencke
(G 9/2/89), Paul Cheeseright (FT 11/2/89), Martin Bailey
(O 12/2/89), Gavin Stamp (I 15/2/89), Paul Cheeseright
(FT 6/3/89), Kenneth Powell (DT 18/4/89), Paul Cheeseright

Index